A Map of the Senses

a map of the senses

edited by rory runnells

with an introduction by doug arrell

A Map of the Senses: Twenty Years of Manitoba Plays
first published 2000 by
Scirocco Drama
An imprint of J. Gordon Shillingford Publishing Inc.
© 2000 the Authors

Cover design by Terry Gallagher/Doowah Design Inc.
Printed and bound in Canada

We acknowledge the financial support of the Manitoba Arts Council and The Canada
Council for the Arts for our publishing program.

The following previously published plays are reproduced with permission:

Thimblerig © Alf Silver (Turnstone Press, Winnipeg, 1981)
Footprints on the Moon © Maureen Hunter (Blizzard Publishing, Winnipeg, 1988)
Live With It © Elise Moore (Blizzard Publishing, Winnipeg, 1994)

Canadian Cataloguing in Publication Data

A map of the senses: twenty years of Manitoba plays

ISBN 1-896239-63-3

1. Canadian drama (English)—Manitoba. 2. Canadian
drama (English)—20th century. I. Runnells, Rory

PS8315.5.M35M36 2000   C812'.54'08'097127   C00-900171-9
PR9198.2.M272M36 2000

Table of Contents

Preface

When I edited a volume of Manitoba plays for Borealis Press in 1986, I had to scrounge around to find three plays worthy of publication. Borealis only wanted professionally-produced plays, and back then there were hardly any. I had to bend the rules a bit to include Bruce McManus's delightful *Caffé*, which had only been given a student production at the University of Winnipeg.

We've come a long way since then, as this volume abundantly demonstrates. It's wonderful to see such a richly interesting body of dramatic work from Manitoba, much of it printed here for the first time. It's especially gratifying to see some excellent plays that were originally viewed by tiny numbers of spectators at the Winnipeg Fringe Festival or one of our smaller theatres get a second chance to find their public. And this is only the tip of the iceberg. As Rory Runnells notes in his Introduction, there are many other plays and playwrights who really should have been included.

Of course, what Rory does not note is that this should really have been called "The Rory Runnells Collection of Manitoba Plays." Grumpy, acerbic, cynical, Rory's persona is not exactly that of Mr. Congeniality, but his gruff exterior hides a—well, let's just say that he is in many ways the heart and soul of the Manitoba playwriting community. Over 17 years, as coordinator of the Manitoba Association of Playwrights, scandalously underpaid, he has held the organization together through all the vicissitudes that voluntary groups are subject to and has negotiated the complex politics of the local arts scene with surprising diplomatic finesse. He has been persevering, resourceful, and adaptable in the face of ever-changing conditions. He has nurtured playwriting talent wherever he found it, and has always been especially welcoming to new writers. There is hardly a play in this collection that doesn't owe something to Rory, and whatever he says, this volume is a tribute to him.

Doug Arrell
Department of Theatre
University of Winnipeg

Twenty Years On: A Personal Introduction

How can I, as coordinator of MAP since 1983, four years after its founding on a hot August evening in 1979 at the Manitoba Theatre Workshop (soon to become Prairie Theatre Exchange), write an introduction to a collection, which, however representative it may wish to be of that 20 year stretch of playwriting activity, development and production, tells only a part of the Manitoba playwriting story? The facts of MAP and its subsequent history are simple enough; its impact is more difficult to assess. As coordinator can I put all the work done in the critical context it needs and which, I assure you, the playwrights of this community always desire? Well, no. Some indeed may even relate the history better, at least with a more bemused objectivity. I can, however, put down what I know, and lead to the plays in this volume. They are what is important; with MAP, let it be stated firmly, the work itself and the not the organization is what matters. No contradiction here. If we are not celebrating the churning continuum of a community's playwrights and their striving as artists no matter what the important input of its playwrights' centre, then there is little to celebrate.

As for what has taken place since that August night, who knew? Probably not the first group which came out of the Manitoba Playwright Search in 1979, and formed the original core of MAP. But, despite the hardy few, why wasn't there a body of playwrights in Winnipeg in the seventies? I wrote (fitfully) about the arts in Winnipeg in the seventies, and it baffled me. However, hindsight being a wonderful thing, especially someone else's, let me quote Doug Arrell writing in a recent issue of *Prairie Fire*. Speaking of the great so-called 'second wave' of theatrical nationalism which swept most of Canada during the seventies, he remarks of Winnipeg: "...we waited in vain for the trend to arrive. There were a number of theories current at the time as to why Winnipeg, almost alone among Canadian cities, did not develop its own alternative theatre during this period; among the factors usually mentioned were the MTC hegemony and the Winnipeg inferiority complex." The few local plays we did see from David King and the group Confidential Exchange, Brian Richardson, and Alf Silver (though mainly through young people's plays at the Manitoba Theatre Workshop), showed that there was no reason why a playwriting community shouldn't be here. It must be noted that the greatest activity was in French at the Le Cercle Molière, but the two solitudes persists even today, really, and what the bigger community could have taken from the energy of Le Cercle's home-grown playwriting never took place. If the problem was the seventies, then what seemed the solution was the eighties, and even the early nineties. Artistic sensibility and arts bureaucrat manoeuvring came together in the few years between 1979 and 1984 to settle a pattern of how and why new plays come to be done here, which lasts essentially until today—and will hindsight, again, probably not mine, tell us a new way might have produced greater results? Back to the story.

It's 1979 and Doug Arrell pins it exactly: "...we missed out on the wave of nationalist fervour and populist energy which transformed the theatre scene across the rest of the country." Instead we had the Playwrights Search, Alf Silver being produced at MTC, the establishment of Prairie Theatre Exchange, the arrival of Alan Williams, the flourishing of MAP's programs for playwrights development, and, let's not forget, Agassiz Theatre and then Theatre Projects, and, finally, the Winnipeg Fringe Festival. This brings us up to date, almost, and we did get our 'wave' in our own isolated, Winnipeg way.

The energy inducing Search came from the Manitoba Theatre Workshop's desire to actually produce a season of new plays, and to gauge what was 'out there'. It found the beginnings of a viable community; opportunity found its takers and they were on the move. Healthier theatrical climes had claimed a number of promising playwrights; now those who wanted to write yet stay could do both, however tentatively. MAP was formed, chiefly under the relentless drive of Alf Silver and William Horrocks, to assert the playwrights claim to attention, production, and development as a community. Then Alf Silver had three plays produced at the MTC Warehouse in as many years when Richard Ouzounian was artistic director. *Thimblerig* remains the most lively of the three, but along with *Clearances*, and *Climate of the Times*, Silver, without realizing it, came to define the three predominant thematic concerns that most of the plays which have come through MAP, and hence the theatres, have. Wide variations on these concerns have deepened the playwriting angle of Manitoba playwrights, with the growth, for example, of aboriginal and gay playwriting, but they remain persistent, even encased in what the community is about. Put briefly, they are the history revisited play (*Clearances*), the political-personal/social action play (*Climate of the Times*), and social urban realism play (*Thimblerig*), often called prairie realism. All their successors, or contemporaries, remain with this thematic base. Only the surreal world of younger playwrights like deco dawson which are not so text-based but infuse the world of film and new media into plays adds to the mix. But to continue.

The Manitoba Theatre Workshop became Prairie Theatre Exchange and in its second season produced Bill Horrocks's *St. Peter's Asylum*. When Kim McCaw arrived in 1984, PTE became, as Doug Arrell rightly puts it, "...the beginning of a collaboration between a group of theatre artists who saw the special value of locally written work and an audience who wanted to see it." Bruce McManus, Patrick Friesen, and above all Wendy Lill, with the breakthrough of *The Fighting Days*, became the PTE Manitoba writers; indeed the collaboration with Lill (though she was only a Winnipegger for part of the period she worked closely with McCaw) was one of the most important between theatre and playwright in the country. Since the move to a larger, some might say too large, space in the Portage Place mall, the commitment to what McCaw called in the heady days of 1985 the "sense of trust, sense of comfort" an audience felt in coming to see a new play which grew from them as a community, has been fitful at best. Michael Springate did produce several significant local plays: Ian Ross's *fareWel*, which won the Governor General's Award, Bill Harrar's controversial *InQuest*, which he later directed at Factory Theatre Lab, Margaret Sweatman's adaptation of her novel, *Fox*, two plays, most notably *Thirteen Hands*, by novelist Carol Shields and Nick Mitchell's *Tin Can Cathedral*, but though Michael had the commitment, I feel, somehow the PTE audience, in a transition which I never understood, didn't. In the McCaw years, *Inquest* would have caused a huge stir; under Springate, it was accepted as just another show in the season. Where is PTE now in relation to the Manitoba playwright? Springate's popular successor Allen MacInnis, like his predecessors, works with MAP in workshopping and encouraging playwrights, but to a limited extent so far. His enthusiasm for certain writers is high, and we have seen Brian Drader's light family comedy *The Norbals,* and Bruce McManus's excellent adaptation of *A Doll's House* (where Ibsen became the political-personal play meeting prairie realism set in the historically rich period of Winnipeg's boom years in the 'teens of the previous century!), and we will see more Ian Ross, and McManus. All to the good, but the audience which hankered after its own committed playwrights isn't in the seats every night at PTE as it used to be.

We're getting to MAP—in a sense, we haven't left it, of course—and to the plays in this collection, but we must continue the tale. Is it 14 years already since Alan Williams, whose definitions of his home town of Manchester could apply to Winnipeg, left after teaching at the University of Winnipeg? How can one judge his influence in encouraging playwriting here? I can't, really. His work with MAP in starting the Open Door program, a simple business of having a time and place for all playwrights, but mainly emerging ones, to come and be read, and wonderfully criticized by Williams in his full enthusiasm as a creator and lover of theatre, was immeasurable. We saw four of his plays in the 1985-86 season alone, though his one man monologues such as *The Cockroach That Ate Cincinnati* and *The White Dogs of Texas* remain his trademark as writer and performer. The young playwrights he met may have been devastated by him at times, but all knew they had been inspired.

A few words on MTC, and the "small" theatres, although a few won't suffice. MTC, vague about new plays except hit ones from London or New York, and sometimes Canadian ones for the Warehouse, took Maureen Hunter to its heart and deserves praise for consistently producing her work since *Beautiful Lake Winnipeg* in early 1990. This play, her last work so far to be set in Manitoba, or dealing with anything close to the community, was an effective thriller. Since then her work, *Transit of Venus* and *Atlantis,* has appeared on the Mainstage where it fits the big theatre's current aesthetic of 'international' hits. Will MTC take up anyone else? The question is rarely asked except by me since part of my job is to at least raise the possibilities of more Manitoba playwrights being produced at the biggest theatre in town. But for the moment I'll shut up about that and mention that, for better or for worse, and I'll state for the better, the MAP story is linked with the rise and fall, and continuing struggle, with the smaller theatres, which Doug Arrell calls a "third stage", offering mainly young, or newer playwrights productions of plays workshopped through MAP. At the start, it was the theatres seeking out what MAP had 'developed', and fitting it to the season; later, and this pattern seems set, it is the theatres which seek MAP as partner in developing the playwright's work aiming at production. Agassiz in the eighties, the Popular Theatre Alliance through the mid-nineties, now Theatre Projects, and not-to-be-ignored independent productions have offered the widest variety of playwrights and styles. If there was a community formed of playwrights in Manitoba, here was it, excepting what McCaw tried to do at PTE. Harry Rintoul (*Brave Hearts*), Elise Moore (*Live With It*), Yvette Nolan (*Job's Wife*), Brian Drader (*The Fruit Machine*), James Durham (*My Old Man*), Dale Lakevold (*Never Never Mind Kurt Kurt Cobain*), Dennis Trochim (*I Do, Do You?*), Ross McMillan (*Washing Spider Out*) and our two senior playwrights, if one can put it that way, Maureen Hunter, and Bruce McManus. Hunter started with Agassiz which produced her first three plays, as MTC has done the later ones. These include *Footprints on the Moon*, nominated for the Governor General's Award, an eminent representative of prairie realism. For McManus it was the Popular Theatre Alliance producing his greatest success *Selkirk Ave.* (1990), later produced by PTE, and also nominated for a Governor General's award, and his *Calenture* (1993), more bitter than many of his other plays, which, as he put it in the early eighties, sing the Winnipeg blues, but given its political and social insight into the collapse of the welfare state and the rise of the new right, accurate and layered. Only Theatre Projects, some independents, possibly Red Roots, remain, savaged by cutbacks, especially on the federal level, yet breathing and ready to rise again, their commitment to Manitoba playwriting strong and consistent. Here MAP's place is firm. And just what is that place? One more item and then I tell all. The final lynch in this theatrical pin is the Winnipeg Fringe Festival, for better or for worse.

At first it provided another place to be produced in a restricted production climate and was used as such by many writers, for example Bill Harrar, Harry Rintoul, Yvette Nolan, Rick Chafe, and Steve McIntyre. Bruce McManus found he could produce darker plays (pre-*Calenture*) there as his *Then Jesus Cut Me Up and Put the Pieces in the Freezer* showed. This aspect of the Fringe, a valuable opportunity and showcase, which was a hit from the start and grows every year, remains for newer writers from the nineties such as Dale Lakevold, Muriel Hogue, Michael Bell, Ted Wynne, Angus Kohm, and Dennis Trochim. Also, the Fringe has become the primary venue for first productions, or experiments, by young, emerging writers. Fine, but as a playwrights' centre like MAP can attest, and the writers themselves come to recognize, the Fringe style of an hour or so treatment of any topic, serious or comic, is ultimately limiting, not challenging. Maybe it's unfair to talk about playwrights "moving on" from the Fringe, as Chafe and Trochim have done, because this volume shows that a lot of strong, striking pieces came from it, but it remains a creative two edged sword for playwrights.

Does that cover the range? Does it lead to MAP? Has any of it led away?

When in 1982 the Manitoba Arts Council, farsightedly, created the Playwrights Development Program, and handed it to MAP, it became clear that whatever happened from the implications of the program—the developed would become the produced—this organization would be in the game for the long haul. That program has been a catch-all for our paradoxical efforts at helping a viable community grow: we have been consistent yet we improvise depending on what demand there is. We have attempted the boost of production, though at a workshop level, when we saw—OK, I saw—the necessity of offering a chance, or opening a door. Hence, the Women's Playwrights Project (1989), and Short Shots, a festival of short plays (though the experiment of making some longer has been tried) started in 1991 and taken over by Theatre Projects in 1996. Short Shots, in particular, has proven important. I've lost count of the number of playwrights, both experienced and emerging, who have been produced over the years. In some years, this was one of the few places to see new Manitoba work, however short, outside the Fringe. But they proved the impetus for longer plays, radio plays, short films, commissions, and many live on and on in production at high schools and community theatres due to their publication in two volumes from Blizzard Publishing. Whether Short Shots continues in some form remains to be seen, but it has already served the playwrights well, and they it. We have tried other things, all stemming from that initial Playwright Development Program entrusted to us by Council, aiming at two paths which must meet: development of the writer and production of Manitoba plays in our theatres. Other programs which have followed aimed at the commissioning of playwrights through Council, senior and emerging, or playwrights' colonies, or dramaturge development, with the list ever changing and rearranging, show that the theatrical culture (to use an overused word, but I prefer it to "ecology") of the city now has a fundamental shape: MAP as central resource, production gadfly, playwrights' home, theatres' inevitable assistant and annoyance. Nothing I wrote 17 years ago on MAP need be changed: that it is a vigorous attempt at making good Manitoba playwrights matter to themselves and the audience.

As for this volume, I hope the plays matter to the reader. Choices are essential in life, but often odious when putting together collections. Here are plays from 1982 to 1998, produced in the big and small theatres, and at the Fringe; here are plays which I think fit my critical bon mot about the three and one-half themes inherent in Manitoba drama; here are diverse plays representing the tensions, obsessions, and temperament of the times.

Take the five Fringe-written plays. Deborah O'Neil's *Columbia Ice Fields Tour* (1989, now titled *Worm Moon*), the earliest, is a bizarre play by a playwright who might be one of our "lost" writers (like Bill Horrocks from the early days, I think); that is, someone who has ceased to see playwriting as necessary any longer. Deborah's output, like Rick Chafe's, is small, but vital, and unusual in is surreal, quirky approach. Yet *Worm Moon* isn't unapproachable, being finally a family story though set in a forbidding future place of ice and death. Here was a play which needed the Fringe: what other theatre in Winnipeg then, or now, would have produced it? Rick Chafe's ambitious two-hander, *Zac and Speth*, attempts to seek compromise in the personal and the political as it careens through recent and even future Canadian history. Love wins out in a way in the play, which it does in Harry Rintoul's play within a play *Between Then and Now*, so different from his urban realism plays, and Dennis Trochim's *Better Looking Boys*, the latest of the Fringe pieces dating from 1997 (final version, 1998), which continues his look at urban gay life wittily. Yvette Nolan's *Blade* from 1991 is different, and closer to the stark politically charged world of McManus's *Calenture* (Popular Theatre Alliance, 1993), and Bill Harrar's *InQuest* (Prairie Theatre Exchange, 1994/Factory Theatre Lab, 1996), taking a topic from the Winnipeg headlines and urban social world and relating it in harsh terms. Her clear passion for justice, and the ambiguity of ever receiving it, seen in all her plays, starts with this deeply engaging Fringe piece. Harrar's *InQuest*, which shows the Winnipeg police disintegrating after the fatal shooting of aboriginal leader J.J. Harper, is more stringent and less impassioned, but quietly lays out the racism and police sloppiness which brought the tragedy on in character-filled detail. McManus's piece I've commented on; I'll only say that it remains underrated, and it is not out of date by any means. Ian Ross's second play, *Heart of a Distant Tribe* (Red Roots, 1996, and subsequently produced in Toronto), takes us into the urban world as well, away from his topsy-turvy reserve in *fareWel*. It is a gentler place, almost fable like, but not afraid to face the daily pressures aboriginals face in the city, while being filled with rich characters and ironic wit typical of his writing. *Live With It* by Elise Moore caused a stir when produced at Theatre Projects in 1994, and elsewhere, but the sensation of such a play about Joe Orton and his lover being written by a then 17-year-old shouldn't blind us to its qualities as a play. It remains daring, sophisticated, and vibrant. As is, I feel, Ross McMillan's *Washing*

Spider Out (Adhere and Deny/PTE Studio Series). Ross, I think, might be the first to suggest his writing in the early nineties didn't fit the local theatres' desires, but his independent productions of *Spider* and *Toby's Made Up Mind* proved they should have paid attention. Their dark look at identity, who we are and who we become, are fascinating and creepy.

We leave the oldest for last, but given the history related here, not the least. Alf Silver's *Thimblerig* (MTC, 1982) remains the starting point of the ongoing surge of Manitoba playwriting, and, I reiterate, in its urban story, the place from where a great many others are set. And *Footprints on the Moon* (Agassiz Theatre, 1986) is prairie realism, if we can define it at all; Hunter's poetic vision may have moved away from her native land, but *Footprints* reminds us her journey started here.

How I would like to have included so much more. Bill Horrocks's maddening *St. Peter's Asylum*, never quite finished; or Rick Chafe's later full length play *The Last Man and Woman on Earth* (Theatre Projects, 1999); Dale Lakevold's *Track Records* (New Play Centre, 1995), or his supple adaptation of Martha Ostenso's *Wild Geese*, originally commissioned by PTE but eventually performed at the University of Winnipeg, where it proved PTE was wrong to reject it; or Gary Jarvis's elegant and dark play about Lewis Carroll and the real Alice, *Looking Glass* (Playwrights Centre, Vancouver, 2000), or the parody musicals of Angus Kohm. Fortunately, more Manitoba plays are being published, and we wait for young energetic writers such as Leigh Anne Kehler, Bob Hume, and so many others to form the core of the next collection. No one volume can contain as complex, unruly and diverse body of work produced here over the past 20 years. In this one, we have tried. Meanwhile, the work proceeds.

Rory Runnells
March, 2000

Thimblerig

ALF SILVER

Production Information

Thimblerig, under its original title of *Dud Shuffle*, was performed as a work-in-progress at the Manitoba Theatre Workshop (now Prairie Theatre Exchange) in 1978. It was workshopped in 1979 with John Hirsch directing as part of the Manitoba Playwrights' Search at the Manitoba Theatre Workshop. In 1980 it was workshopped at Seattle Repertory Theatre with Dan Sullivan directing. It was first produced at the Manitoba Theatre Centre's Warehouse Theatre on January 11, 1982 with the following cast:

MAGGIE .... Michelle Fisk
LAURA .... Goldie Semple
BLACKJACK .... Lorne Kennedy
WILLY .... Kimble Hall
JOHN .... Jean-Pierre Fournier
BEN .... Peter Jordan

Directed by Louis W. Scheeder
Sets, Properties and Costumes design by Arthur Penson
Production Manager: Jack Timlock
Lighting design by Robert Thomson
Music Director/Arranger: Barry M. Dunford
Stage Manager: Tomas Montvila

Staging Notes

The play is structured in short scenes moving back and forth through four settings—three in each act. The restaurant setting is used only in the first act, the woodworking shop only in the second. One way to facilitate the quick changes necessary would be through a combination of area lighting and set pieces that revolve or track.

The band area is a constant, separated from the acting areas, with the band on and dimly visible between songs. The first production used a three-piece band: piano, bass and drums, with some doubling on guitar, percussion and wind instruments.

Setting

Winnipeg in the summer of 1972. All the characters except John Chapman are in their mid-twenties; he is slightly older.

Act One

Scene One

(Lights rise on WILLY with the band. Jubilantly, he sings to a marching band tune à la John Phillip Sousa.)

WILLY:
When we've eaten all the birds of land and fishes of the sea
When there's nothing left to feed on but your relatives and thee
Is there one among your neighbours and your friends and lovers, too
Who would not augment their diet with a healthy slice of you?
Is there anyone you might invite on over for a chat?
Who would not file down his canines if it ever came to that?

If you found you'd made a fortune which your good friends didn't share
Would you let yourself relax so they could catch you unawares?
Is there anyone among them wouldn't gladly catch you stoned
And let you throw it all away on them as if it was their own?

(A verse-long break is inserted of a Wild Cannibal Chorus, consisting of WILLY and the band adenoidally nyaahing over the music and blowing kazoos. The last verse is a cappella, with much gospel harmony.)

So be thankful for the simple meal between you on the ground
Be thankful for the almost empty pockets all around
'Cause if there wasn't quite enough to eat or too much on one end
We'd be nothing more than cannibals, and they make lousy friends.

(MAGGIE's apartment. A covered Salvation Army couch and chair, second-hand coffee table strewn with WILLY's scrapbooks and clippings and a couple of ornamental, carved boxes, the walls adorned with second-hand store framed prints and a couple of posters. A small desk and a board and brick bookcase stand on one wall. The room is tidy except for the mess around WILLY who's sitting on the floor by the coffee table. A doorway in one corner opens on a hallway leading to kitchen, bedroom, bathroom; the door to the back corridor is at the opposite end of the same wall. The wall is faced with dirty, ancient wallpaper. There is a large window in the middle of the wall. MAGGIE is sitting in an armchair drinking tea and working her abacus. She goes to the desk and takes a pad of paper from a drawer.)

WILLY: *(Paraphrasing clipping in his hand.)* 'A bus driver in Calgary stopped in the middle of rush hour traffic, announced to his passengers: "I've been driving a bus for 35 years and I've had it," put on his coat and left. The passengers all stood up and applauded as he walked out the door.' *(Laughs; she doesn't.)* Don't you find that amusing?

MAGGIE: How did they get home?

WILLY: Maybe they all had transfers.

MAGGIE: I don't know whether you've lost your sense of humour or I've just grown tired of it.

WILLY: Maybe you lost yours.

MAGGIE: Just when I need it most.

WILLY: *(Searching through one of the boxes on the table containing an assortment of drugs.)* Have you seen my Quaaludes?

MAGGIE: You ate them last night. *(Looking for a pen, finds one that doesn't work and carries on the search.)*

WILLY: Shit. I'm going to need some kind of downer to balance out my Ritalin.

MAGGIE: Try working out a grocery budget for two on a salary made for one. That's a fairly effective downer.

WILLY: Are you on that again? It just sticks in your throat that some people have better things to do than feed machines in some plastoid office block.

MAGGIE: If you really did something it wouldn't bother me. But you didn't tell me when you moved in here that you planned to spend the rest of your life pasting pictures in scrapbooks.

WILLY: You didn't tell me you were going to switch off your frontal lobes and become an efficient cog or gear or whatever your official title is. So we're both disappointed. Life's like that. Lice like that. Nice white hat. *(Western heavy.)* You funnin' me, bub?

MAGGIE: What happened to that black felt marker I had in here?

WILLY: Ask the file clerk.

    (MAGGIE spies the pen on the coffee table, reaches for it, WILLY snatches it away.)

MAGGIE: Give it to me.

WILLY: Where would you like it?

MAGGIE: *Give* me the *pen.*

WILLY: Fuck you. I'm using this to make notes.

MAGGIE: What, 'Cutting and pasting by Willy Teal, Age 4'? Give it to me.

WILLY: Find your own.

MAGGIE: That *is* mine.

WILLY: It's mine.

MAGGIE: It's *mine.*

(WILLY breaks the pen in two and tosses half to her.)

WILLY: There, now we've both got one.

(MAGGIE turns away from him and goes to rummage through the desk for a pen.)

Anyway, I carried your end when you needed support and I never bitched.

MAGGIE: Four months you worked in a foundry while I was finishing my courses. Four months out of two years. That's not much of an average.

WILLY: I didn't know anyone was keeping score.

MAGGIE: Look, can't you find another place to keep this stuff? I can't bring anyone home with pills all over the place...

WILLY: Who did you want to bring home?

MAGGIE: I don't know. Nobody right now. But I might actually end up making friends with somebody in the office someday...

WILLY: *(Singing.)* Send in the clones... Why should you?

MAGGIE: Right, why should I? Why should I ever want to talk to anybody except you? What if the police came in and found all this?

WILLY: *(Knocking on table.)* 'Good evening, this is the police doing our weekly door-to-door drug check.'

MAGGIE: How do I know they won't come and check you out for some reason? Then I end up charged with possession because it's my apartment, and they spread my name and address all over the papers? That's not the kind of publicity that Western Mortgage and Loan likes to seek in their systems analysts.

WILLY: Is that all you care about? Your little job at the android factory?

MAGGIE: I worked hard to get it. And I'm working hard to get a better one. I don't intend to lose it because of you.

WILLY: It doesn't mean anything.

MAGGIE: I can see how it pales to insignificance beside the collected scrapbooks of William Teal.

WILLY: You couldn't even begin to understand what's in here. *(Brandishing scrapbook.)* It can't be translated into punch cards. *(Puts book down and goes back to rummaging through drugs.)*

MAGGIE: I don't know if you've noticed, Willy, but there isn't much of a market for burnt-out acid gurus these days.

WILLY: *(Reading label on pill bottle.)* Placidyl. How can you argue with a name like that? This and the Ritalin should be like riding an underwater rocket sled in a lead suit. Two hundred milligrams. Best be cautious. I'll do six and see what happens.

(MAGGIE has picked up her pen and pad and started for the interior door.)

Where are you going?

MAGGIE: I thought I'd do something frivolous like figure out what we're

	going to eat for the next two weeks. Maybe when that gets too depressing I'll read a book.
WILLY:	You can't learn shit from books.
MAGGIE:	Whereas I can pick up a good quantity of it by listening to you.
WILLY:	Maybe if you tried listening for a—
MAGGIE:	I tried listening for two years. The first thing I learned was that you didn't *do* anything but talk. The second thing I learned was the only reason you said so many original things was because they were so obvious nobody else could be bothered to say them. The third thing I learned was that all I was hearing anymore was the sound of the marbles rattling around inside your head. I thought you told me you were going to strip this wallpaper off three weeks ago.
WILLY:	It's a spacey pattern. Geometric. If you want it stripped why don't you do it yourself?
MAGGIE:	Some of us have to work for a living.
WILLY:	Nobody has to do anything.
	(MAGGIE exits in disgust. WILLY's still pawing through his stash.)
	This is ridiculous. I'm going to have to hit another pharmacy soon.
MAGGIE:	*(Coming back on.)* What did you say?
WILLY:	I said I'm going to have to hit another pharmacy soon. Maybe your ears need re-wiring.
MAGGIE:	Maybe your brain needs re-wiring. Didn't I just finish telling you I can't afford to have the police come in here?
WILLY:	You think you're dealing with some fucking amateur? I don't get caught.
MAGGIE:	How did you end up in jail the last time?
WILLY:	Some kind-hearted citizen ratted on me. Or am I giving you ideas?
MAGGIE:	You belong in a cell. Or back in a psycho ward.
WILLY:	*(Parrotting.)* Psycho ward! Psycho ward! You say it like you know what it means. You know where they got the idea for shock treatments? Two psychologists were taking a tour of a slaughter-house and one of them noticed that the cows get very passive when they were hit over the head with a sledgehammer. 'Tink of how useful dat vould be, Rudolf, for violent patients.' 'But how to do it midout breaking bones?' 'Allectrrecity!' That's the kind of system you get up to work for every morning.
MAGGIE:	You better listen, Willy, if you go out to rob a drugstore don't bother coming back.
WILLY:	What are you scared of? I hit 'em in the night, bang bang, and I'm gone before the glass hits the floor.
MAGGIE:	You've got a record for breaking into drugstores. The police

could come around just to check you out. And look what's lying all around the apartment! *(Grabs and brandishes stash box.)*

WILLY: You keep your hands off that, it's mine.

MAGGIE: This is all you care about, isn't it?

WILLY: You'll find out if you don't put it down!

(Knock on the door. MAGGIE stands immobile with the box in her hand.)

Must be the Gestapo come to put your name up on billboards.

(Knock again. With a laugh at MAGGIE, WILLY starts to rise.)

MAGGIE: I'll get it.

(She puts the box down, goes to the door, opens it and finds BLACKJACK standing there. He's wearing a white suit, pale blue shirt. For a moment she just stands there saying nothing.)

BLACKJACK: Hello, Maggie.

MAGGIE: What are you doing here? I mean—I'm sorry, it's just that it's been a long time.

BLACKJACK: It has.

MAGGIE: *(Collecting herself.)* Won't you come in?

BLACKJACK: *(Doing so.)* Thanks. *(MAGGIE closes the door behind him.)* Hello, Willy. How's the apocalypse coming along?

WILLY: It talks. Amazing what they're doing with plastics these days.

MAGGIE: Well, sit down. Could I get you a drink? I've got some collins mix and gin...

WILLY: How chic. Have you been reading *Chatelaine* on your coffee breaks—or is that just part of the programming?

BLACKJACK: No. Thanks. Maybe later. You're looking good.

MAGGIE: You must be joking. So what brings you here?

BLACKJACK: I just thought it was time I came by to see how you're doing. So how are you doing?

MAGGIE: Oh... All right, I guess. How about you?

BLACKJACK: Could be better, could be worse.

MAGGIE: How's Laura?

BLACKJACK: Fine. Last I heard. Haven't seen her for a couple of weeks. We're separated.

MAGGIE: Oh. I haven't heard anything about you guys for so long...

WILLY: Nobody we know can afford to travel in Blackjack Thomas's circles anymore. Silk suits and cocaine and 'Out to de islands, mon, fo' de wintah'.

MAGGIE: I didn't even know you guys were still in the city.

BLACKJACK: I've been here most of the time. Running around trying to hustle a buck.

WILLY: How many throats did you cut in the process?

BLACKJACK: As many as I had to.

WILLY: Is that supposed to be a threat?

MAGGIE: Shut up.

WILLY: *(To MAGGIE.)* You think I don't know what you're up to? Sitting there sharpening your sickle?

MAGGIE: *(To BLACKJACK.)* So what are you doing these days?

BLACKJACK: Not much, actually. Doing a lot of thinking.

WILLY: Don't hurt yourself.

BLACKJACK: I won't.

WILLY: That makes one. You come in here with your white suit stinking of blood and expect old home week? You think you're running the machine—you're not. It's going to pick you up and crush you just like it does everybody else.

MAGGIE: If you don't have anything to say don't bother talking.

WILLY: Hey, Blackass Jerkoff.

    (BLACKJACK turns to him. WILLY holds up a plastic bottle of white glue and squirts it over the front of BLACKJACK's trousers.)

    (Laughing.) You would have done it yourself if you'd stared at her another minute.

    (BLACKJACK rises and dabs with a handkerchief at the glue.)

BLACKJACK: *(To MAGGIE.)* I'll call you another time.

    (MAGGIE just stares at WILLY. BLACKJACK walks at an even pace to the door and exits.)

WILLY: *(As door closes.)* Go on, get out of here. And don't come back.

MAGGIE: *(As soon as the door's closed behind BLACKJACK.)* Get your things together. If you're not out of here in half an hour I'm calling the police.

WILLY: What for?

MAGGIE: To tell them there's a dangerous psychopath in my living room whom I would like removed.

WILLY: You're throwing me out?

MAGGIE: You're catching on.

WILLY: That's hardly fair.

MAGGIE: I don't care if it's fair or not. This is my home and I don't want you in it anymore.

WILLY: All right. But first I'm going to strip that wallpaper off for you, just like I said I would. *(Going off through interior doorway.)* Don't say I never did anything for you.

MAGGIE: Don't bother.

WILLY: *(Coming back on carrying an axe.)* Oh, I owe you at least that much.

MAGGIE: What are you doing? Are you crazy?

WILLY: So they tell me. *(He chops at the wall, taking out a chunk of wallpaper and plaster.)*

MAGGIE: That's very cute, Willy, but if you swing that axe one more time I'm calling the police.

(WILLY continues to chop.)

(Going to the phone on an end table by the couch.) All right, if you want to be locked up again, that's your choice.

(She begins to dial. WILLY shifts sideways and swings the axe down on the table, severing the chord. He jerks the head loose and holds the axe laterally in front of him, grinning at MAGGIE.)

(With no assurance that he'll only chop inanimate objects.) I'm serious, Willy. They'll put you away.

(WILLY raises the axe over his head, suddenly swerves and brings the axe down on the back of the couch. MAGGIE slowly backs to the door and out as WILLY continues to chop.)

Scene Two

(At Ernie's: a coffee-shop-restaurant with slight European pretensions. A classical guitar plays softly on their stereo system. LAURA is sitting at a table drinking tea, pouring out the dregs of the pot. She's wearing a flamboyant skirt and blouse with a bright scarf. Most other women in such a costume would look over-dressed, but the clothing and make-up are subordinated to the woman just enough to keep her from looking like an animated magazine ad. JOHN CHAPMAN is sitting at another table, surreptitiously glancing at her appreciatively. JOHN is a largish individual, scruffy, about thirty, wearing a T-shirt and grungy jeans and jacket. BEN enters, carrying tea. He is a worn, comfortable-looking loose type with a grizzled beard. He dresses in a contemporary version of romantic academic: tweed and corduroy jackets, jeans, suede shoes. His speaking voice is very warm and reverberant, but not in a trained manner. He walks almost past LAURA. JOHN sees him and waves, BEN waves back and carries on toward him.)

LAURA: Hello, sailor.

BEN: *(Stopping.)* Oh. Hi. Anybody sitting here?

LAURA: Help yourself.

BEN: Thanks. *(Sits.)*

LAURA: What happened to you on Wednesday?

BEN: I was going to call you about that. I got my days mixed up. I was coming to see you on Thursday when I saw the date on a newspaper in one of those corner boxes. How did you know I'd be here?

LAURA: Actually, I came in here looking for Jack. My landlord's planning

	to raise my rent. He comes in here fairly often these days, doesn't he?
BEN:	Your landlord?
LAURA:	My husband.
BEN:	Yeah, you're right. Maybe I should go sit somewhere else.
LAURA:	Why? We're old friends. There's no law against us sitting in a restaurant together.
BEN:	Yeah, but if he comes in he's going to sit down here. I'm not very good at being Machiavellian.
LAURA:	You've got enough of a reputation for being scatterbrained to cover up any mistakes you make.
BEN:	I guess so. You're the one that doesn't want him to find out.
LAURA:	*(After pause.)* So how are you?
BEN:	Good. I got that gig I was talking about.
LAURA:	Great...
BEN:	Not that great. It's only for two weeks.
LAURA:	It's better than nothing.
BEN:	I got an offer to do a week in a bar, too. But I don't want to sit up there playing AM radio songs for drunks.
LAURA:	There's no reason why you should. Did you ever think of making an album? I read an article in a magazine a couple of days ago about people starting their own record companies.
BEN:	Which magazine?
LAURA:	I'm not sure. It's somewhere in the pile at home.
BEN:	I'd like to look at it.
LAURA:	What are you doing for dinner?
BEN:	*(Shrug.)* I don't know...
LAURA:	Why don't we go back to my place after you've finished your tea and I'll dig out the magazine for you and fix something for dinner.
BEN:	Sure.
LAURA:	Do you like zucchini?
BEN:	Sure.
LAURA:	I could make crepes... I'm glad you came in.
BEN:	*(Putting his hand on top of hers on the table.)* So am I.
LAURA:	*(Putting her other hand on top of his hand on top of hers.)* I don't know how I'd have got along without you over the last few weeks.
BEN:	Well, I... *(He reaches over his hand to complete the stack but knocks over his tea which spills across the table into LAURA's lap.)* Oh, I'm sorry, I...
LAURA:	*(Blotting it up with napkins.)* It's all right. I guess you've finished your tea.

(BLACKJACK and MAGGIE enter, BLACKJACK looking around for a table, MAGGIE seeming distracted. LAURA is busy blotting at her skirt and doesn't see them.)

BEN: Hi, Blackjack. Hi, Maggie.

(LAURA looks up quickly and tries to finish the wiping up unobtrusively. BLACKJACK nods curtly at BEN. MAGGIE looks around and starts for their table, BLACKJACK following in escort.)

LAURA: Hello. Hi, Maggie.

MAGGIE: *(Tight.)* Hi.

(She sits, BLACKJACK pushing her chair in.)

BEN: *(Overly innocent.)* Hi. What's happening?

BLACKJACK: Willy just spun out. Started re-decorating her apartment with an axe. She had to call the cops to take him away. *(To MAGGIE.)* Would you like some coffee or something? Or a glass of wine?

MAGGIE: Please. A glass of wine.

(BLACKJACK goes off.)

BEN: What happened?

MAGGIE: Like he said, Willy went crazy. I had to go down the street to call the police. It's lucky Jack was there. I haven't had much experience at talking to the police. I don't know what the apartment looks like.

LAURA: Jack was there when this guy went crazy?

MAGGIE: No, he'd left just before it got started. He was just starting to drive away when I came downstairs.

BEN: So is Willy in jail or what?

MAGGIE: I didn't press charges. They took him to the hospital.

LAURA: Was he hurt?

MAGGIE: They took him to the Psycho ward.

LAURA: Oh. Who was this guy?

BEN: Don't you remember Willy?

LAURA: Jack's friend, Willy?

BLACKJACK: *(Returning with a glass of wine and a large salad.)* That's stretching a point. *(Setting down salad and wine.)* Don't worry about the salad. I had to buy some food to get the wine.

MAGGIE: *(Lifting glass.)* Thanks.

LAURA: What happened to your suit?

BLACKJACK: What happened to your dress? *(Sitting.)*

LAURA: Oh, I spilled my tea.

BLACKJACK: So how are you?

LAURA: Fine. I came down here looking for you.

BLACKJACK: Oh?

LAURA: My landlord's planning to raise my rent.

> *(BEN starts nibbling on the salad.)*

BLACKJACK: How much?

LAURA: *(Although slightly reluctant to discuss money in public.)* Twenty-three dollars.

BLACKJACK: When?

LAURA: In two months.

BLACKJACK: Shouldn't be a problem.

BEN: I never thought Willy would blow it like that. I mean, you see somebody going on like that for years, you start to think they're invulnerable.

MAGGIE: So did he.

LAURA: *(To MAGGIE.)* What are you going to do now?

MAGGIE: Go back and clean up the mess, I guess.

LAURA: You can't go right back there.

MAGGIE: I'll have to eventually. I'm a little old for sleeping in the park.

LAURA: *(Suddenly.)* Come stay at my place tonight.

MAGGIE: *(Nonplussed.)* I have to work in the morning...

LAURA: I can lend you some clothes. I've got a day-nighter you can sleep on. We can order pizza and you can just sit and drink wine and watch TV all night if you want.

MAGGIE: I couldn't...

LAURA: It's no trouble.

MAGGIE: Are you sure?

LAURA: No problem.

> *(MAGGIE takes another healthy quaff of wine. Pause, BEN still nibbling at the salad.)*

BEN: I guess since he's an ex-mental patient he's really got no rights as far as that goes. They can throw him back in anytime.

BLACKJACK: *(To MAGGIE.)* If you want a hand with the cleaning up I could pick you up when you get off work tomorrow.

MAGGIE: Thanks. I dread to think what the place looks like. *(Finishes wine.)*

LAURA: Did you want to have another glass of wine or leave now?

MAGGIE: We might as well go. If you're ready...

LAURA: *(Rising.)* I'm ready...

BLACKJACK: I could give you a ride...

LAURA: It's not that far to walk. Or would you rather go in the car?

MAGGIE: Actually, I wouldn't mind a walk. *(To BLACKJACK.)* Thanks for being there for the police and all.

BLACKJACK: No problem.

BEN: See you.

LAURA: Bye.

MAGGIE: See you.

            (BLACKJACK waves. LAURA and MAGGIE exit. Pause.)

BEN: I feel sort of guilty about Willy. Everybody was always pushing him to go further. Like we all put our lunatic self destructive urges onto him and let him carry them. Almost like some kind of human sacrifice.

BLACKJACK: He could have quit anytime.

BEN: Once he got himself elected champeen loony he couldn't back down.

BLACKJACK: He could've if he didn't get off on the position. Even the village maniac has a certain amount of status.

            (JOHN finishes his coffee and starts out past their table.)

JOHN: Hi, Ben.

BEN: *(Not placing name.)* Hi, how're you doing, man?

JOHN: Hi, Blackjack.

BLACKJACK: Hi. *(Very short pause. Then, pointing at him.)* John.

JOHN: That's right. How you been?

BLACKJACK: Up and down. I'm trying to remember when I saw you last... Two years anyway.

JOHN: More than that. Before I got busted.

BLACKJACK: Yeah, I heard about that.

JOHN: *(Shrug.)* I been out for a while. Everybody gets caught eventually.

BLACKJACK: What are you doing now?

JOHN: Still carpentry, woodworking.

BLACKJACK: *(Remembering.)* Right. I should talk to you sometime. I was thinking of getting into some of that myself.

JOHN: You?

BLACKJACK: Well, somebody's got to do it. Do you have a phone?

JOHN: *(Digging in pocket.)* Here. Business card. Now all I need is some business. See you around.

BLACKJACK: Yeah. *(JOHN exits.)*

BEN: Uh, Blackjack, I was wondering—I've got this gig coming up next month, but right now...

BLACKJACK: How much do you need?

BEN: Well, twenty should get me by. *(BLACKJACK forks over.)* Thanks.

BLACKJACK: No problem.

BEN: Are you planning to be around for a while?

BLACKJACK: Another forty, fifty years, anyway. Why? You heard rumours to the contrary?

BEN: I mean am I going to be able to find you when I get paid? Or are you going to disappear off selling condominiums or whatever you've been doing?

BLACKJACK: No, me and the hustling business have come to a parting of the ways.

BEN: I had a feeling that would happen eventually. Regardless of what everybody else said, I always knew you weren't really like that. Not inside.

BLACKJACK: Like what?

BEN: You know, someone that could go around setting people up, and using them, like I heard you were doing.

BLACKJACK: If I hadn't been doing it to them they'd have been doing it to me.

BEN: You always talked a lot meaner than you are.

BLACKJACK: How's Laura doing, by the way? I didn't get a chance to ask her.

BEN: Oh, I just, uh, bumped into her by accident. I haven't seen her for a long time. *(Rising.)* I think I'll get some more hot water for my tea.

BLACKJACK: *(Standing.)* I have to find some dinner anyway. See you around.

BEN: Yeah. So long.

                (BLACKJACK goes out the front, BEN goes back for hot water.)

Scene Three

(LAURA's studio apartment in a fairly new block. We're looking at part of the living area, furnished in teak, brightly upholstered. A couple of Maxfield Parrish prints on the wall. Part of the wall is taken up with louvered closet doors. LAURA and MAGGIE, both flushed and stuffed, walk on from the kitchen.)

MAGGIE: ...so I told him, you know, 'You know Walter's going to be leaving in a few months. I'm as well qualified as anybody in the office. If you find somebody else to take his job I'm going to have to start thinking seriously about what kind of future prospects I've got here.'

LAURA: And what did he say?

MAGGIE: He said he'd think about it.

LAURA: What will you do if you don't get it?

MAGGIE: I guess I'll have to start looking around for another place to work. That's what I get for making threats. Are you still working at that ceramics shop?

LAURA: God no. That was years ago. I'm not working right now. I've looked around a little bit.

MAGGIE: How do you pay for this place?

LAURA: Jack pays for it... Well, he gives me money and I pay for it. After the divorce his lawyer will just send the money to my lawyer— You know, I worked out that on one of his schemes he made two hundred dollars an hour. Nobody *earns* two hundred dollars an hour.

MAGGIE: How did he do it?

LAURA: Well, that one, he found out from somebody that there were a hundred green leather jackets in the storeroom of one of the garment factories. They were an awful sort of lime green and nobody wanted them. So he talked the owner into selling them to him for four hundred dollars. Then he went down to the head office of a clothing store and said he'd just got hold of these great, outrageous jackets that were going to be the latest trend. The guy wouldn't believe him, I mean they were ugly jackets. But Jack talked him into taking five on consignment. In the meantime Jack had hired seven guys to go in over the next couple of days, five of them to buy jackets and two just to say they'd seen them and wanted them. So the guy got back to Jack and talked him into selling the whole lot for 16 dollars apiece. I figured out Jack spent five hours on it altogether and made a thousand dollars.

MAGGIE: What happened with you and Jack?

LAURA: Happened?

MAGGIE: Why are you getting divorced...? Look, if...

LAURA: No, it's fine— It's just, there isn't much to tell. It didn't work out so he left.

MAGGIE: He's got a habit of doing that.

LAURA: It wasn't his fault. He's just so used to moving from one thing to another. If something isn't exactly like he wants it he starts to feel trapped. I really hope something works out for him sometime. I do. Oh, I was going to lend you something to wear, wasn't I? *(Going off. MAGGIE follows.)* I don't think my suits would fit you, but I should have some dresses that would be right for the office.

Scene Four

(BLACKJACK with the band. He sings to an arrogantly lazy honky-tonk tune that changes character in mid-stream and then returns.)

I got a German-made sportscar that can turn and give change for a dime.
You know that table at Hy's, the one that's always reserved? Well it's mine.
And some spectacular honey
to help spend my money
Has never been too hard to find.
But what you bait your hook with is what determines what bites on your line.

I got a wife that would do any corporate executive proud.

I hang out with the best-dressed, most self-actuated of crowds.
Their second-hand jokes
and reciprocal strokes
Can envelope your brain in a cloud.
Their motto is: If you've got nothing to say say it loud.

   (Bridge)

You might've heard I wake up in a sweat every night
For fear of those I robbed with my lies.
The sad tale to tell is they all conned themselves
And I just went along for the ride.
You see the world is composed
of those who see it and those
who prefer to watch the stars in their eyes.
It's a simple place I settled in, it operates in twos
There's those who like to win and there are those who love to
      lose.
You can use what comes before you or become one of the used.
With those two roles to pick between can you guess which one I
      choose.
Still it seems there was a third choice once
And a half-forgotten face,
The last thing I recall before I came into this place.

My sound is state-of-the-art,
I got a high-rise apartment,
A wardrobe full of custom-made clothes.
I got a dream that recurs
Where I reach out for her
But she's gone before my fingers can close.
And those glittering types that thrilled my childhood
Follow me wherever I go.
They jump for joy when they see my toys,
They say: There goes that impossibly clever boy.

Scene Five

   *(MAGGIE's apartment, lit by daylight through the window. The
   hacked wallpaper has been replaced. WILLY's scrapbooks,
   magazines, pills, etc. are gone. There is a thumping and bumping
   offstage.)*

MAGGIE: *(Off.)* Careful, it's caught.

BLACKJACK: *(Off.)* Twist your end around.

MAGGIE: *(Off.)* OK.

   *(There is a bit more bumping, then the sound of something sliding
   across the corridor floor. A key rattles in the lock. MAGGIE opens the
   door and BLACKJACK drags in a new couch, tubular metalframe,
   smaller and much lighter than the old relic. MAGGIE is wearing new
   corduroy trousers, a new blouse and jacket; BLACKJACK has added*

a lightweight leather jacket to his clothes from the previous scene. As BLACKJACK drags the couch past her, MAGGIE grabs the end and closes the door.)

BLACKJACK: Where do you want it?

MAGGIE: Right there, where the old one is.

BLACKJACK: *(Pushing old couch back while manoeuvering the new one into place.)* Pretty adventurous interior decorator, aren't you?

MAGGIE: Why trifle with perfection?

BLACKJACK: Where does this *(Gesturing towards the old couch.)* have to go?

MAGGIE: By the garbage, in the lane. If you stick your head out the window you can see it right below.

BLACKJACK: *(Looking out window.)* You don't say. *(Checks hand measurements of window frame against the old couch.)*

MAGGIE: What are you doing?

BLACKJACK: Just checking out the shortest distance between two points. *(Dragging the old couch toward the window.)* Come on, grab an end.

MAGGIE: You're not serious.

BLACKJACK: Why not? Grab an end.

MAGGIE: *(Reluctantly complying.)* What if there's someone underneath?

BLACKJACK: Hard cheese on them. Don't worry, I'll shout. *(Shouting out window.)* 'Ware below! Dodge this, ya bastards! *(They dump it out, lean out the window and watch it fall. They lean back in, standing very close.)*

MAGGIE: You have this habit of making me take part in totally irrational acts.

BLACKJACK: I usually have to put a gun to your head, don't I?

(He puts his hands on her shoulders, kisses her and they embrace.)

I've been waiting to do that for a long time.

(They move a bit apart. BLACKJACK traces his fingertips along her cheek, staring into her face. She reaches up and takes his hand.)

MAGGIE: Come on. *(Leads him off.)*

Scene Six

(BEN on stage with the band.)

BEN: Good evening, ladies and gentlemen. My name's Ben Dudley and I'm going to be the entertainment here at Ernie's for the next two weeks. We're going to start off with a song I'm sure you're all familiar with.

(He launches into one song—the band starts another.)

No, not that one. We moved that to the end of the set, didn't we? Didn't I tell you?

Scene Seven

> (*MAGGIE's apartment. A very pale light, moonlight and streetlamps, glows outside the window. BLACKJACK comes on, wearing a sheet, bumps into the coffee table.*)

MAGGIE: (*Off.*) Ssh.

BLACKJACK: Why? (*Fumbles in his jacket draped on the couch, finds a fresh pack of cigarettes and matches.*)

MAGGIE: (*Off.*) I'm always afraid you're going to wake up my parents again.

BLACKJACK: *I'm* going to?

MAGGIE: (*Off*) Not fair!

> (*BLACKJACK lights a cigarette, carries a match over to a candle on the bookcase, lights the candle, brings it back to the coffee table and sits on the couch. MAGGIE comes on wearing a dressing gown, carrying two glasses of wine. She sits on the couch, leans against him, hands him glass.*)

BLACKJACK: (*Putting his arm around her.*) Thanks. (*Sips. Caresses her face.*)

MAGGIE: How do you do that so softly?

BLACKJACK: I don't have any choice. It's like there's no skin over the nerve endings in my fingertips. It's so intense it's almost painful.

MAGGIE: I've heard of overstimulation, but...

BLACKJACK: It's not just from tonight. (*She has leaned back against him, lounged across the couch.*) You know all that poetic drivel about hearts? Broken hearts and pains in hearts? Well one time a few months before Laura and I got married I saw you at a party at Jesse Bridge's place. You were there with Willy...

MAGGIE: Was that the night Willy tried to lead a revolution of the spiders in the basement?

BLACKJACK: I don't think so. I remember he was trying to start a campaign to give free lobotomies to all females over the age of twelve. He'd read in some psychology magazine that lobotomized women make great housewives, or housepets, I disremember. Anyway, his campaign slogan was going to be: "What have you got to lose?" I think he spraypainted that across Jesse's kitchen cupboards.

MAGGIE: Same night.

BLACKJACK: Anyway, I was watching you across the room, and this strange thing happened. It was like there was a hook, a barbed hook, fixed into my heart, and a tight line running out from it attached to you. Every time you moved I got this twitch of pain, just like the hook was twisting in my heart.

MAGGIE: I hate to disillusion you, but that wasn't a very romantic story.

BLACKJACK: It wasn't meant to be, it's just the truth.

MAGGIE: It doesn't sound like a very pleasant state to be in.

BLACKJACK: It wasn't, at the time.

MAGGIE: Then why didn't you just disconnect the emotion and forget about it?

BLACKJACK: Easy to say.

MAGGIE: I've done it, with a little concerted effort.

BLACKJACK: It couldn't have been something that meant very much to you.

MAGGIE: It felt like it did. I wandered around for a couple of months like I'd been hit by a truck. I never expected you'd leave me for some ballet dancer whose only recommendation was that she could move her body in three different directions at once. How long did that great romance last—three weeks? I felt like a slightly comic figure.

BLACKJACK: You've got a long memory.

MAGGIE: So do you.

BLACKJACK: Did I tell you I'm thinking of opening a woodworking shop?

MAGGIE: No.

BLACKJACK: I'm checking it out, anyway. I thought it might be kind of pleasant to build something for a change instead of flashing coloured lights in people's eyes and picking their pockets. Like every woman I've ever been with, except for you, it's always been a game, a challenge—trying to find out which buttons to push, the right angles to play, until she belongs to me. And then I've won and it's time to move on to another. I could never do that with you.

MAGGIE: I'd find it a lot easier to take in what you're saying if you weren't wearing a green flowered skirt.

(He grabs her in a headlock, pretends to knuckle the top of her head.)

Help!

BLACKJACK: Didn't anyone ever tell you about the fragility of the male ego?

MAGGIE: I've never seen a man it looked better on.

BLACKJACK: You look pretty good in red velvet. Not as good as you look out of it.

MAGGIE: I am out of it, believe me.

BLACKJACK: It's so simple. I mean, you find something you want to do and you do it, and you find somebody you love and you live with them. Why does it happen so rarely?

MAGGIE: *(Gently.)* It's late, and I have to work in the morning.

(She stands, picks up the candle, takes it back to the bookcase and blows it out. BLACKJACK gets up and follows her off.)

Scene Eight

(In a restaurant-coffee house, could be same table as Scene Two with

the band platform lit. LAURA is sitting at a table, wearing a print skirt, Danskin top, bright scarf, exotically made-up. BEN is onstage with the band, tuning his guitar.)

BEN: Well, it never fails, eh? Just when you've almost pulled it off. *(To harmonica player.)* Could you give me an E?

(MAGGIE and BLACKJACK enter, see LAURA, MAGGIE crosses to the table, BLACKJACK following her. LAURA composes herself as they approach.)

MAGGIE: Hi. *(Sitting.)* What did you do to your face?

LAURA: What?

MAGGIE: No, I mean it looks great. What's that green stuff?

(BLACKJACK sits.)

LAURA: Thank you, I think. I just mixed a couple of colours of eye-shadow together.

MAGGIE: Sorry I didn't call you this afternoon. It got crazy at work.

LAURA: I was out anyway.

BLACKJACK: I see Ben's doing his usual slick job.

LAURA: There are worse things than not being slick.

BLACKJACK: You're probably right. Now all you have to do is convince all the people that aren't here tonight.

BEN: *(Finally tuned.)* Uh, I'm going to finish off this set with a uh, song I haven't done for a while. It's a sort of an indictment, but not totally serious, of a, uh, trend in Western society over the last few hundred years. Or something along those lines.

(As soon as the music starts, BEN's hesitant manner fades away. With deadpan humour and a strong, unaffected, warm voice, he sings, to a minor key, flamboyant gypsy-fiddle tune:)

The lawn was dry and grey and dying
So we sprayed it green it just looked worse.
It took so much time to keep it thriving
That we tore it out and put in astroturf.

But the leaves and bird-droppings just lay there.
We replaced the trees with wrought-iron plinths,
Bought a flock of songbirds for the tape deck—
They don't exist unless we throw the switch.

(Chorus:)

But it's all right,
Living is so convenient now.
It's all right, we're in control.

My brother's girlfriend was a loudmouth
She would never let him have his way
So he bought a latex one from *Penthouse*
And inflates her anytime he wants to play.

(Chorus.)

(Bridge.)

And the time that we save
Between here and the grave
We can spend finding ways to replace
Every being that pursues
Some self-interest we can't use,
Every single living thing that isn't us.

Someday there'll be no will but ours left,
What a grand existence that will be.
No more confrontation, compromise or conflict—
We can sit around all day and watch TV

(Chorus.)

BEN: *(After polite applause.)* Thank you. I'll be back in a while.

(Lights fade on the band stage.)

MAGGIE: It sounds hard to believe, but all the time I've known Ben I don't think I've ever heard him play. Except for sitting around apartments and that sort of thing. Does he always sound that strong?

LAURA: It's a regular night. He lost a bit of momentum when he stopped to tune.

MAGGIE: *(Sniffing out territory.)* You and Ben seem to show up a lot of places together.

LAURA: Not really. I just seem to run into him every time I run into you guys.

BEN: *(Arriving at the table and sitting.)* Hi. Hi, Blackjack. What's happening?

MAGGIE: That was really good.

BEN: You like that song? So do I. Well, sometimes I don't like it for a while, but then I like it again.

(He takes a sip of LAURA's drink. She gets slightly uncomfortable at his proprietary display in front of BLACKJACK.)

MAGGIE: Do you play here a lot?

BEN: Not often. Once in a while. It's just about the only place left in the city to play. Hard to make a living out of one place.

MAGGIE: Isn't there lots of bars and places?

BEN: That's the problem. Ever since they changed the liquor laws all the music's been moving into the bars—you get your, uh, weepy country bars, and your rock-and-roll bars and your easy-listening bars. I don't fit in very well with any of the formulas.

LAURA: That's nothing you have to apologize for.

BEN: I'm not apologizing.

BLACKJACK: *(To MAGGIE.)* Do you want to eat here or just have something to drink? Like a guava milkshake...

MAGGIE: We might as well eat here.

BLACKJACK:	How fond are you of raw vegetables?
MAGGIE:	Maybe it'll be good for me.
LAURA:	*(Rising.)* I have to be going.
BEN:	I didn't know you had to leave.
LAURA:	I said I'd meet somebody.
MAGGIE:	Will you be home tomorrow night?
LAURA:	*(Stiffly.)* I might be. You can give me a call if you like. 'Bye.
MAGGIE:	Good night.
BEN:	See you. *(LAURA has exited.)*
BLACKJACK:	So are they paying you decently here?
BEN:	No, not even union scale. I'm going to get blacklisted again. That's about all the union ever does for me.
BLACKJACK:	It's a useful institution if you're playing second saxophone in a swing band.
BEN:	I don't get paid til the end of the week. I can pay you back then…
BLACKJACK:	Don't worry about it. Is it nap time for the waiters?
BEN:	Oh, they must be in the kitchen. I'll go see if I can find one.
	(He exits to the back.)
MAGGIE:	Do you think he's good at what he does?
BLACKJACK:	As far as the music goes, he's very good. But he's an agent's nightmare. He only plays what he likes and he couldn't tell a joke to save his soul.
MAGGIE:	You'd never think he had that much creative energy, I mean— just to talk to him casually. He seems to have thought a lot of things out very carefully.
BLACKJACK:	Yeah, everything except how to stay alive. *(Suddenly standing.)* Come on, I feel like a little chateaubriand and a nice dry red.
MAGGIE:	What about Ben?
BLACKJACK:	We can catch him another time. He's not going anywhere. Look, I know the thought of bernaise sauce turns your stomach, and armagnac and cherries flambé, but I've got this weird craving. Couldn't you indulge me?
MAGGIE:	*(Rising.)* All right. But not just this once.
	(They exit.)

Scene Nine

(MAGGIE's apartment, lit by daylight through the window. Knock on the door. Pause. Knock again. BEN stumbles on from interior doorway, wearing only jeans, fumbling with buttons, opens door. It's BLACKJACK, wearing a different shirt than previous scene. Pause while BEN focuses his eyes.)

BEN:	Oh, hi Blackjack. *(BLACKJACK just stares.)* Come on in...
BLACKJACK:	*(Not moving.)* What are you doing here?
BEN:	I asked myself the same question a few times last night. Then I stopped asking. Did you want to see Maggie? She's not quite awake yet. I could get her for you...
BLACKJACK:	No. It's all right. I was just cruising past. I'll see her another time.
BEN:	Oh. OK. See you around.
BLACKJACK:	*(Not moving.)* Yeah.
BEN:	*(Closing door.)* 'Bye.
MAGGIE:	*(Off.)* Who was that?
BEN:	*(Proceeding off.)* Blackjack.
MAGGIE:	*(Off.)* Oh. What did he want?
BEN:	Nothing special. *(Goes off.)*

Scene Ten

(LAURA's apartment. LAURA and MAGGIE come in. MAGGIE wearing office clothes, LAURA carrying a clothing-store box and grocery bag, checking through her mail. LAURA is slightly distracted and tense, but breezy on top.)

LAURA:	Just sit down for a minute, I'll get rid of these and we can go right out again. What time does it start?
MAGGIE:	Seven-thirty.
LAURA:	*(Opening bill.)* I won't bother to change, then. Oh hell, I thought I paid this last month. That's the problem when you've got nothing to do but spend money. I can't remember the last time I had to look at being in the city all summer. My sister asked me to come out to her place at Grand Beach but I don't think I could stand it. Three kids running around constantly and screaming and when she gets a minute to sit down she just stares out the window like she's got shell-shock. *(Going off with grocery bag.)* Twenty-nine years old and she's never been anywhere or done anything. She didn't have anything to say in the matter, it just happened to her.
MAGGIE:	She must have had some kind of choice in the matter.
LAURA:	*(Off.)* Not really. You didn't go around having babies in Silver Heights without getting married.
MAGGIE:	She could've had an abortion.
LAURA:	*(Off.)* Not in 1963. *(Coming back on.)* The worst part is that the kids are the most spiteful little demons I've ever seen. Always biting each other when nobody's looking. I guess if I had kids they'd be even worse.
MAGGIE:	I'd probably regiment kids to death. "It says in the book you're

supposed to get inquisitive at three months. Get on it, we've got a schedule to keep here."

LAURA: *(After a quick look in wall mirror.)* I guess I'm ready.

    (MAGGIE starts to rise. Door-bell rings.)

Probably the paper boy. *(To MAGGIE.)* Think of an excuse.

    (LAURA opens the door. It's BLACKJACK.)

BLACKJACK: Hi. I think I owe you a cheque.

LAURA: Oh, uh, come on in. We were just on our way out.

BLACKJACK: This'll just take a minute. Hello, Maggie.

MAGGIE: Hi.

BLACKJACK: How's the interior decorating biz?

MAGGIE: Well, the place is getting liveable.

BLACKJACK: *(Taking out chequebook.)* So, what will you need for June? Six hundred?

LAURA: I got this bill in the mail. From Holt's...

BLACKJACK: How much?

LAURA: A hundred and twenty-eight dollars.

BLACKJACK: OK. *(Starts writing up cheque.)*

LAURA: Look, Jack—I really have to talk to you sometime. About the divorce.

BLACKJACK: *(Bland.)* What about it?

LAURA: *(Would rather leave it to another time, but, unsure of when that might be.)* I really can't go on like this, living from month on whatever you decide to give me.

    (MAGGIE exits to the kitchen.)

BLACKJACK: *(Calm, eminently reasonable.)* Aren't I giving you enough?

LAURA: Sure— Well, I always feel like a beggar when I have to ask you for more. I'd feel a lot better about legally arranged payments, so I could plan ahead...

BLACKJACK: My lawyer's working on it. It's not easy to work out a no-fault divorce in this province.

LAURA: You're stalling.

BLACKJACK: Why would I be doing that?

LAURA: Maybe I didn't grow up in Brooklands where everybody had to scramble for a living, but I'm not stupid. You're up to something. You're trying to set it up so you can get the divorce without paying me anything.

BLACKJACK: How would I do that?

LAURA: Jack, I know you. You don't leave things dangling and give money away for nothing.

BLACKJACK: Everybody changes.

LAURA: Not that quickly.

BLACKJACK: Look, Laura, if you've got anything specific you want to accuse me of I'll be glad to talk to you about it. But right now we just seem to be going around in circles. Will this be enough for now?

LAURA: Sure.

BLACKJACK: Well, give me a call if anything else comes up.

LAURA: You're never home.

BLACKJACK: Well, I'll call you. See you. *(Exits.)*

LAURA: Bastard!

             (MAGGIE drifts back on, sipping glass of water.)

             If I could just get this divorce thing settled I could go somewhere else. I know he's up to something. I don't want much, but no, he's got to have it all.

MAGGIE: What do you think he's up to?

LAURA: Oh. I don't know. He's always got some kind of angle. I shouldn't—it isn't fair to blame him for it. He's always had to be like that, to survive.

MAGGIE: I don't think you're the one that should worry about being fair.

LAURA: Look, I don't really feel much like going out. Could we make it another night?

MAGGIE: Sure.

LAURA: I think I'll just make some tea and go to bed and read. Sorry…

MAGGIE: Don't worry about it. Why don't I call you tomorrow?

LAURA: Do. Thanks.

MAGGIE: No problem. Good night.

             (MAGGIE exits. LAURA immediately sits down and dials the phone.)

LAURA: Hi. How're you doing? Would you like to come over for a while? I'd appreciate it. No, not very good. Everything. Thanks. See you in a bit.

Scene Eleven

             (The coffeehouse BEN's been playing in, lit dimly. BEN is on, sitting at the table. A glass of juice is in front of him, another sitting on the table across from him. Background sounds of clean-up in kitchen. BLACKJACK comes on. He is somewhat withdrawn. He takes a mickey of vodka from inside his jacket, pours into both glasses of juice. BEN looks over his shoulder furtively.)

BLACKJACK: That should pick up the flavour considerably. *(Replaces bottle in jacket.)*

BEN: *(Picking up thread of interrupted conversation.)* You know you're right about the times changing. Three or four years ago I would have filled this place. And it's not just the liquor laws. Nobody's interested in songs that say anything anymore. I don't know what to do about it.

BLACKJACK: There's nothing you can do about it. You either adapt or you become a dinosaur.

BEN: You say the most comforting things. There's a really weird attitude going around these days, like that all the stuff that was going on a few years ago was some sort of con job.

BLACKJACK: It was, for a lot of people. Everybody was trying to break out of that old con game where you lose a third of your life doing something you don't want to do in order to get what somebody tells you you want to have. So a bunch of street punks with electric guitars got free of it, and the people that paid for it got some scratched up old records and a few colourful concert posters.

BEN: I don't think that's all there was to it...

BLACKJACK: It wasn't. Most of those poor damned fools that did make it didn't have any idea of what to do with it. They didn't have to punch a clock anymore, but all they could think of to do instead was drink and smoke and shoot up and fuck and read comic books. Some revolution.

BEN: I think the only revolutionary thing that was said back then was that everybody, everything, is alive. The same as you are, and has to be treated with respect. People use whatever hypocrisy went on back then as an excuse to forget that, because it's not an easy thing to live with.

BLACKJACK: Things have a habit of reminding you they're alive, even if you want to forget it.

BEN: It's amazing what people can ignore, even if it's going on right under their noses.

BLACKJACK: (Not airy, very slightly sinister.) You have to be able to tolerate things going off on their own directions from time to time, having their little flings.

BEN: (Unsure.) Yeah, I guess so.

BLACKJACK: But people have to realize that if they seriously get in someone else's way, they're liable to get hurt. Regardless of who they are.

BEN: It doesn't have to be like that.

BLACKJACK: There's only so much to go around. As long as that stays the same, people are going to keep running up against each other.

BEN: But people tend to assume it's life and death when it isn't...

BLACKJACK: When it isn't for somebody, maybe they should back off, because it might be for somebody else.

BEN: (Lightly.) You can get melodramatic at times.

BLACKJACK: The world can get melodramatic at times.

(Pause. The clean-up sounds have stopped. The kitchen lights *offstage go off, the stage gets darker.)*

BEN: I guess they want us to leave so they can go home. Do you want to go for coffee or anything?

BLACKJACK: I'm trying to get on an earlier schedule. See you around.

BEN: Yeah. Thanks for the drink.

(BLACKJACK has exited. BEN gets his guitar case from the stage and exits.)

Scene Twelve

(MAGGIE with the band. Acoustic guitar, mandolin and recorders play "Fairytales", a tinkly, music-box confection. She sings:)
I once believed the fairytales, the poetry and lies
That would send us off pursuing dreams, but then I realized
That what they'd have us think we needed never did exist
So I turned away from wishes to the concrete world I'd missed.
There is no work so worthwhile that doing it will bring me
    satisfaction
So I'll code machines and political schemes and build a profitable
    career. '
There are no enchanted crystal nights of human interaction,
So I've learned to ignore graceless social discords and take what
    joy is here.
There are no lifelong passions, no helpless attractions,
The best we can hope for is comfort and warmth.
I begin to feel there's one thing I need that I don't have,
A loving friend that I can trust to help me build a home.
A father to my children and a contracted companion
So I won't have to be afraid of growing old alone.

Scene Thirteen

(At Ernie's. BEN and BLACKJACK walk on, carrying coffees.)

BLACKJACK: So what did you want to talk to me about?

BEN: Well, actually Blackjack, I was, uh, wondering if you'd be my best man.

BLACKJACK: Your what?

BEN: My best man. Maggie and I are getting married.

BLACKJACK: You've got a great sense of humour, Ben.

BEN: Well, yeah, I guess it doesn't fit the Dudley image. Maybe it's time I changed the image. Anyway, I wondered if you'd uh, stand up with me.

(MAGGIE enters quickly.)

MAGGIE: Ben, Jesse Bridge saw Willy on the street. The hospital let him out

	on a day pass. He got a bunch of pills from Jesse and he's on his way to the apartment.
BEN:	Why?
BLACKJACK:	Because your fiancée had him committed and he wants to discuss it with her.
MAGGIE:	I'd just feel a lot better if you were there.
BEN:	Well, I'll come if you like...
BLACKJACK:	I don't think this is your kind of problem, Ben.
MAGGIE:	Look, if you want to play High Noon I passed a bunch of kids in a playground on the way here. I'm sure they'd be glad to have you.
BEN:	What's everybody getting so excited about? Willy might scream and shout and throw a few things around, but he'd never really hurt anybody.
MAGGIE:	Tell that to my furniture. He might be there already.
BLACKJACK:	I think you're setting yourselves up. *(To MAGGIE.)* As soon as Willy lays eyes on you he's going to spin right out. Somebody else might be able to calm him down, but not if you're there.
MAGGIE:	This isn't your problem.
BLACKJACK:	There might not *be* a problem if you're not there.
	(MAGGIE looks at BEN.)
BEN:	*(Shrug, rising.)* Sure. You stay here and I'll go wait for him...
BLACKJACK:	Maybe you and Willy can sit down and have a nice cup of herb tea, talk about old times. But if Willy isn't in a mood for conversation, what are you going to do?
MAGGIE:	We'll call the police now and tell them he's an escaped psycho...
BLACKJACK:	He hasn't done anything they can label him a psycho for. Yet. He's just a manic depressive that jumped a day pass. The police aren't going to stake out the block for that. Why don't you loan me your key and I'll go to your place and wait for him. I'll call you here when I've got rid of him.
MAGGIE:	What makes you think you could handle him any better than Ben could?
BLACKJACK:	I never said I could.
	(MAGGIE thinks it over, then hands BLACKJACK her key.)
	Thanks. It probably won't take long. Like you said, he might be there already. *(He exits.)*
BEN:	Are you sure we should have let him do that?
MAGGIE:	Don't worry. He can talk his way through anything. Almost.
BEN:	What if he can't?
MAGGIE:	Then that's his problem.

Scene Fourteen

(MAGGIE's apartment, lit only by exterior night lights. Key in the lock, door opens, BLACKJACK pokes his head in.)

BLACKJACK: I'm home dear. *(Enters, closing door behind him.)* Willy. *(He turns on a lamp by the couch.)* William. *(Proceeding into kitchen.)* Come out come out wherever you are. *(Off.)* Any loony around my base is It!

(The band has begun playing a sinister, creeping version of "Cannibals." Opening and closing of cupboard door off. BLACKJACK comes back on with a bottle of whiskey and a shot-glass.)

What do to while waiting for the psychopath?

(Pours a drink, sits on couch, takes a deck of cards from a box on the table, shuffles a bit, takes a drink while shuffling one-handed.)

Good evening friends and welcome to Blackjack's House of Cards, home of the dud shuffle where nobody wins. Tonight we're going to play a little one-on-one. *(Deals two blackjack hands.)* Queen of Diamonds showing, and the dealer has ten up. You'll stick with what you've got? And the dealer stands pat. Let's see what you're hiding. *(Turning over opponent's hole card.)* Two queens. Powerful combination, Mr. Dudley. But the dealer *(Flipping over ace of spades.)* has an ace in the hole. How's that? You suspect a little manipulation on the dealer's part? You're quite right. I may be rusty but I ain't dead. Playing by the rules is fine when the cards come your way, but when they don't there are no rules.

(He pours another drink, toys with the deck some more, then begins building a house of cards. Suddenly the door is kicked open. WILLY's standing silhouetted in the doorway.)

WILLY: I'm back from the dead, Green Man. I'm looking for the White Lady.

BLACKJACK: Then you've come to the right place, son. Come in, pull up a chair. Next time knock.

(End of Act One.)

Act Two

Scene One

(*Same as* Act One, Scene 14. *No time has elapsed.*)

WILLY: Where is she?

BLACKJACK: She's not here.

> (*WILLY stomps into the rear of the apartment. BLACKJACK continues building his card house, drinking. Off, the sound of drawers and cupboard doors yanked open. WILLY charges back on, begins yanking open desk drawers, dumping contents out. Throughout the scene, he will occasionally focus on a piece of furniture or picture that wasn't there before and stop in confusion for an instant.*)

BLACKJACK: I don't think she's hiding in there.

WILLY: Where are my scrapbooks?

BLACKJACK: Didn't she send them with your clothes and things to the hospital?

WILLY: No she didn't send them to the fucking hospital. Where are they?

BLACKJACK: I remember she threw out a bunch of your stuff.

> (*WILLY suddenly stops hunting, straightens up, stands a moment, then walks slowly over to BLACKJACK.*)

WILLY: (*Softly.*) Where is she?

BLACKJACK: She's not here.

> (*WILLY's face contorts in anger and his hand jerks out as to sweep the card house away—BLACKJACK puts out his hand to block him.*)

Hey, gimme a break. I think I can hit seven storeys tonight. I haven't done it since that night at Luther's. You remember that?

WILLY: (*Half-smile.*) Yeah, I remember. (*Suddenly sitting.*) Fuck, man. What am I gonna do?

BLACKJACK: Start over?

WILLY: I can't. That's five years of newspapers and magazines and books... I'll kill her.

BLACKJACK: (*Handing bottle to WILLY.*) And what'll that get you? They'll slap you back in Psycho for the rest of your life. Plug you into the wall socket every Saturday afternoon. Probably cause a blackout the first few times…

(WILLY smiles and nods, then suddenly focusses on BLACKJACK and shifts.)

WILLY: You're the one that took my place. I should start on you.

BLACKJACK: I didn't take anyone's place. She's going to marry Ben Dudley.

WILLY: *(Astounded.)* Dudley? She'll eat him alive.

BLACKJACK: No, I think she wants to keep this one.

WILLY: She threw them away?

BLACKJACK: I didn't see her doing it, or I'd have kept them myself…

WILLY: *(Not conned that easily.)* Don't give me that shit. *(Shifting to MAGGIE again, hands extending.)* I'll break her fucking neck.

BLACKJACK: You're too violent to ever do any real damage to anybody. If you really want to hurt someone, you have to be methodical. Find out what they build their lives on, in most cases it isn't much, and take it away from them.

WILLY: Cut out their heart.

BLACKJACK: Flamboyantly put, but that's the general idea. Just like she's done to you.

WILLY: If she's going to marry Dudley, what are you doing here?

BLACKJACK: She was afraid Ben might get hurt.

WILLY: *(Mystified.)* Who would do that?

BLACKJACK: You.

WILLY: *(Slightly offended.)* Me? Dudley's never done anything to me. Shit, I'm crazy, not rabid.

BLACKJACK: Some people can't tell the difference.

WILLY: Did I tell you I got laid in psycho? Poor little chick had been in for three months. Had the routine down pat. They figured they had me pacified with valium. *(Insulted.)* Valium! Shit. *(Shifting back to MAGGIE.)* You're trying to tell me that her heart is in this marriage with Dudley?

BLACKJACK: At this point in time, yeah.

WILLY: Dudley's idea of a long-term commitment is 'I'll meet you tomorrow for coffee.' The Amazing Mr. Vague.

BLACKJACK: *(Shrug.)* She can probably bulldoze him through doing his husbandly duty for the next forty years. They could both lead healthy and productive lives. As long as she remains ignorant of what he's doing on the side. He's still screwing Laura.

WILLY: Laura?

BLACKJACK: My wife. Ex.

WILLY: How do you know?

BLACKJACK: I've been gathering evidence so I can sue her for adultery.

WILLY: Sounds like you.

BLACKJACK: *(Placing last card.)* Seven.

WILLY: *(After counting storeys.)* Fucking right. Go for eight.

BLACKJACK: A man's reach should exceed his grasp or what's a heaven for? Marriage is a very powerful ritual. Maggie might be able to take it rationally if she found out a lover was screwing around on her. But the man who's going to be her husband? *(He pulls out the key card and the entire structure collapses.)*

WILLY: And you step in and pick up the pieces.

BLACKJACK: Maybe. What does it matter to you? You'll have got your retribution.

WILLY: That's *it!* That is what's fucking *it*, man.

                (Standing and moving with the power of his revelation. He suddenly sees himself as rewriting the most powerful and ancient of all myths.)

                Under the moon she scatters the king across the fields, but in the night the pieces come back together and this time it's not just the wind rattling the door.

                (He suddenly shifts to practicalities.)

                It'd be funny if Dudley got a dose.

BLACKJACK: That's not a bad idea. He could pick up a dose from Laura.

WILLY: *(Genuinely surprised.)* Your wife's got a dose?

BLACKJACK: Not yet. But there's no reason why some charming young man who'd gone out and got himself infected couldn't get in to her. By the time she'd found out and told Ben he'd have already passed it on to Maggie.

WILLY: If you think anyone's going to go out and get a dose on purpose you're crazy. You should be where I was.

BLACKJACK: A dose is nothing. You can clear it up with penicillin before it even starts to hurt. It's easy to get infected; there's an epidemic going on.

WILLY: *(Convinced.)* So do it.

BLACKJACK: My wife won't let me touch her. I think she's holding her body for ransom against the possibility of patching up our marriage. Laura doesn't screw around a lot, but she's a normal healthy female. If someone went at it persistently he'd eventually hit her on a night when she felt like being seduced.

WILLY: I never got into seducing. It's not the same thing as fucking. I'd be out of my element.

BLACKJACK: There's nothing to it. These days seduction consists of hanging around looking interesting and waiting for them to come on to you. I bet Ben wouldn't even have the jam to tell her. He'd probably just keep eating penicillin until they got the blood tests for the wedding. That'd be picturesque.

WILLY: It would.

BLACKJACK: I almost wish I could try it. Just to see if it would work.

WILLY: Try it, try it.

BLACKJACK: No. It's too complex. Too many moving parts.

WILLY: I like it.

BLACKJACK: Remember Crazy Schemes Incorporated. I look after the schemes, you look after the crazy.

WILLY: I'm holding up my end.

BLACKJACK: We need something simple and direct. The classic approach would be to get her to catch them in the act. If she really takes off the gloves and laces into him, Ben'll be gone so far and fast she'll never catch him. There's a few ways we could set it up so she'll walk in on them.

WILLY: I almost hope you manage to take Dudley's place. I couldn't think of a worse thing to do to her.

BLACKJACK: It should happen as close before the wedding as possible. I wish Dudley was a little more predictable. There's a couple of ways it could work.

WILLY: What's that got to do with me?

BLACKJACK: Somebody's got to watch them. Laura's apartment's on Roslyn Road. The first one up from Nassau. You could try to keep track of when Ben goes up there. *(Taking out some bills.)* You could probably use some money to live on.

> *(WILLY won't take it. BLACKJACK stuffs it in WILLY's shirt pocket.)*

WILLY: Don't think you can use me.

BLACKJACK: We're using each other, Willy. *(Dialing phone.)* There's nothing sordid about that. It's the basis of civilization.

> *(WILLY exits.)*

> Yes, I'm calling for Margaret Fenwick... Hello, Maggie? No, he wasn't hard to handle. I'll leave your key by the phone. No, I won't lock you out. Oh, and tell Ben I'd be happy to be his best man. Yeah, see you in church. 'Bye.

> *(Hangs up, switches off the light and exits.)*

Scene Two

> *(MAGGIE's apartment. MAGGIE and BEN enter.)*

MAGGIE: *(Looking at the room, dumped drawers, and the broken lock-housing.)* Looks like Willy made one of his grand entrances again.

BEN: *(Inspecting latch.)* I think I can fix it.

> *(MAGGIE goes off to the kitchen, BEN stands surveying the room.)*

> I guess he was looking for something.

(MAGGIE comes back on with the toolbox, hands it to BEN. He digs out a screwdriver and goes to work on the latch while she starts straightening general mess.)

MAGGIE: *(After pause.)* What are you going to do about that agent?

BEN: There's not much I can do about him. That college tour was like a carrot on a stick, to get me into his stable. As soon as he found out I wasn't prepared to be one of his boys, he took the carrot away.

MAGGIE: Why weren't you prepared to be one of his boys?

BEN: I don't want to be one of anybody's boys. It wouldn't have worked out. He wanted me to start wearing a tweed cap and smoking a pipe. If the college tour worked out he was talking about cutting an album, with a cover like me sitting on top of a hill smoking a pipe with a dog beside me—something like an English Sheepdog. He said he knew a place we could rent one. He figured it might sell. The cover, I mean—he didn't much care what was inside it, as long as it was bland enough not to offend anybody.

MAGGIE: It sounds like he was willing to invest a lot of time and money in you.

BEN: I don't want to turn what I do into a con job. I have to feel I've got some kind of respect for the people I'm playing to.

MAGGIE: Tightening up your act implies a certain amount of respect, doesn't it?

BEN: But what I do isn't an act. I mean, when I started, maybe it was just like a role I was playing. I made deadlines, like if it doesn't work out by my twenty-fourth birthday I'll go back to university. But the deadlines came and went and I kept on doing it. Because doing it is what I *am* now. I can't exploit that. If I try to turn it into a vending machine I'm liable to wake up one morning and find that all I've got left is some sort of pre-packaged process for making money.

MAGGIE: You could do worse.

BEN: There should be more to it than just something I do to make money.

MAGGIE: Why should there? I spend forty hours a week just doing something to make money. So does most of the rest of the world. Why should you be any different?

BEN: Maybe everybody else could be different if they wanted to be.

MAGGIE: As far as I'm concerned you can do whatever you want, as long as you can pay an equal share into the rent and the groceries and the savings account.

BEN: And if I can't?

MAGGIE: Then I'm going to have to start seriously re-thinking the idea of us getting married.

BEN: Is that all it is to you—a financial arrangement?

MAGGIE: It means a lot more to me than that. But I'm not going to spend the rest of my life supporting some hopeless dilettante.

BEN: Maybe that's all I'm allowed to be in this society.

MAGGIE: I hope not. Because if that's what you're going to be you'll have to do it without me. *(Pause.)* It's late, and I have to work in the morning.

BEN: I gotta think.

(Puts down the screwdriver and goes off. MAGGIE picks up the screwdriver and goes to work on the latch.)

Scene Three

(BEN with the band.)

BEN: Uh, I'm going to finish off the night with a, uh, song I wrote a couple of years ago. It's, uh, the song goes on as if it's about a woman, but it isn't. Not that I'm weird or anything, not that way anyway. It's sort of an allegory. You know what I mean. Or maybe you don't. Oh well. *(Music intro starts.)* I promised myself I'd never write songs about music. I only broke it once.

(He sings "H. G. Moan":)

We flirted discreetly in the days of my childhood
I courted you carelessly, you whispered to me
I forgot you a few times but I always came back to you
Lady of morning mists, voice of the sea.
You would come to me softly, with shadows to paint
And breathe your sweet secrets in the bones of my ears.
You wove your web well, I entangled myself
And I never fought totally clear.

(Chorus.)

I gave you my life, what did you ever give back
But a handful of shadows and a dance in the rain.
If I had my time back, knowing you like I do now,
Carnivorous lady, I'd do it again.

My friendships and love affairs, for you they all ended
You were always there waiting when the others had gone.
You brought me no comfort, but you helped me forget myself,
Lady of silences, kiss of the dawn
To those who don't know you, it seems like I've wasted
Every chance to be happy I've had
But their pity they can save till they dance on my grave
Though I may well be a fool and half mad.

(Chorus.)

Scene Four

(The woodworking shop. A workbench and a desk. A few steps at rear lead up to the back room. BLACKJACK and JOHN enter from the rear, BLACKJACK carrying an opened sales pamphlet on lathes.)

BLACKJACK: Five three by two foot six. We could put it right here.

JOHN: *(Checking floor space with tape measure.)* That's not going to leave a hell of a lot of working space.

BLACKJACK: How much do we need?

JOHN: Well you've gotta figure we're going to need a bit of open space for customers to come in.

BLACKJACK: I keep forgetting about them.

JOHN: They haven't been banging on the door to remind you. Maybe we should put it in the back room.

BLACKJACK: I was planning to put the overhead router in there.

JOHN: Shit. Where are you gonna put the crane and the front end loader?

BLACKJACK: There's no law against being prepared.

JOHN: It's your money. The wiring in that back room won't take a router and a lathe.

BLACKJACK: I was thinking of getting the place re-wired anyway. By the way, you know of anybody that wants to buy a car?

JOHN: Yours? Nobody I know's got that kind of money. That thing must be worth ten grand.

BLACKJACK: Twelve. But I'd settle for ten. It only cost me five. *(Amused.)* Seven hundred for a totalled SL at an Autopac auction, fifty for a receipt from a bankrupt auto shop in Calgary, forty-two hundred for a repainted hot SL from the coast and some loose change to get the serial numbers switched.

JOHN: I don't think I wanted to know that.

BLACKJACK: All right, you don't. Don't worry about the stuff in here. It's all legal. Almost retail, some of it.

JOHN: I didn't know you were that hard up that you have to sell your car.

BLACKJACK: I'm not. But most of my cash is busy being fruitful and multiplying. Never touch your capital, my old man used to say. I think at the time he owned two shares in a tool and die shop.

JOHN: *(Following Horatio Alger formula.)* What's he own now?

BLACKJACK: Two shares in a tool and die shop that folded in 1958.

(The front door opens, jingling a bell. WILLY comes in. He's extremely scruffy, unshaven, clothes looking like they're too well acquainted with his body.)

WILLY: Hail, intrepid carpenters.

BLACKJACK: Hello, Willy.

WILLY: *(Bopping about, checking out tools on bench.)* This place is great. Where do you keep the trees?

        (JOHN takes pamphlet from BLACKJACK and occupies himself taking measurements, trying to be politely interested in the conversation but not too much so, finding it difficult.)

        I've been scrambling up drainpipes, scurrying through the shadows. Me and Raymond Chandler. Gotta get a trenchcoat. Trailing them down the street at night. Dudley came up yesterday, day before. I wrote it down. *(Digging in his shoulder bag, coming up with a ring of keys.)* I found a little hidey-hole behind the boiler room in the university. Living like the king of basement rats. Look at these. *(Checking off keys.)* Lab door, swimming pool, infirmary...

BLACKJACK: Where'd you get the keys?

WILLY: I got 'em. I got some amyl nitrate, too. Wanna do a hit? Got a whole travelling infirmary right here in the bag.

        (JOHN looks askance at WILLY here and other places, in spite of his intentions.)

BLACKJACK: No thanks. When was Ben at Laura's?

WILLY: I got it written down. *(Digs out ratty notebook.)* Should be near the end. Right, the day after I cleaned out the tombs. Concrete rabbit-warren down by the bridge. Good place to sleep close. Wine and glue parties keeping me awake. So I cleared them out. Didn't sleep anyway. *(Finding entry.)* Wednesday afternoon. She started to wonder at me once during the day so I fade back, watch the place good. You got expensive taste in women. How much of other people's blood did she cost you?

BLACKJACK: Thanks, I think I can take it from here.

WILLY: Forget it. This is mine, too. Astarte and the women going 'Weep for Adonis, Poor Tammuz, Dionysus is dead' while they wash the blood off their hands. But this time, he remembers. No, I'm in this one and she's going to know it.

BLACKJACK: I have to close up the shop.

        (JOHN, figuring measurements on pad at desk, looks up surprised.)

WILLY: It's early.

BLACKJACK: I've got an appointment.

WILLY: Plots and counterplots. You never stop, do you? Maybe after I'm finished with her I'll start on you.

BLACKJACK: Come on, I've gotta close up.

WILLY: Hey, did I tell you I'm going to start a country and western band?

BLACKJACK: Oh?

WILLY: Yeah, I'm writing a song called 'I'm Going to Mend My Broken Heart with a Needle and No Thread.'

        (BLACKJACK hustles WILLY out, locks door, puts Closed sign up.

JOHN stares at him strangely, then pretends not to have stared or seen anything unusual.)

BLACKJACK: I guess we should measure out the back room, then.

(They go off.)

Scene Five

(LAURA's apartment. LAURA is on, wearing a dressing gown. BEN walks into the scene, buttoning his shirt.)

BEN: What am I doing? All my life I've been avoiding that kind of pressure and now I'm going to marry it.

LAURA: You're not going to marry *it*, you're going to marry Maggie.

BEN: It seems crazy. I mean I love Maggie—I've never found it all that difficult to fall in love. But there's been lots of women I've loved as much who didn't want me to change what I do. So why am I doing this?

LAURA: I don't think I'm the best person to ask that question.

BEN: It doesn't make any sense. If I'm going to marry anybody it should be you.

LAURA: That's very sweet of you, Ben, but just think about it for a minute.

BEN: But why marry Maggie instead?

LAURA: Why marry anybody?

BEN: I'm not twenty years old anymore.

LAURA: What kind of an answer is that?

BEN: It's an excellent answer. What time is it?

LAURA: Almost four o'clock.

BEN: *(Getting up quickly.)* Shit, I'm supposed to meet Maggie when she gets off work. *(Pecks her cheek and starts for the door.)* Are you going to be home tomorrow?

LAURA: Probably.

BEN: I'll give you a call. 'Bye.

(BEN hurries out the door. LAURA watches him go with a sort of distressed amusement; watches the door a moment after it's closed. She walks around the room, absently turns on the television. Sounds of The Roadrunner emanate from the tube. She looks at it a moment, picks up a magazine, glances, sets it down, goes off. Over the television mayhem, we hear the shower turned on.)

Scene Six

(Lights come up on the band. WILLY, wearing an ancient leather jacket, stumbles through the audience singing 'Needle Mama', an

aggressive bit of heavy metal based around a chord known as "E Demented":)

How you smile in my throat, chasing lullabies and dreams
Laughing in my eyelids like a Nautilus-burning Nemo.

(Chorus.)

I'm going to the river, mama, you know I won't be gone for long.
I'm going to the river, mama, I won't be gone for long.
You should know better than to ask me where I'm going, mama,
You won't even know I'm gone.

How madonna here on Calvary, cursing in the stands
With your hammer in the clouds punching holes into my hands.

(Chorus.)

Scene Seven

(LAURA's apartment, very dimly lit through the venetian blinds. The band plays softly in the background. LAURA is dimly discernible at one end of the couch, wearing a nightgown and a robe, a coverlet pulled over her legs. Her face and her right arm can only be seen as silhouettes. MAGGIE is sitting at the other end of the couch. MAGGIE fumbles a bit in her purse, then gets up and starts toward a lamp on the coffee table.)

LAURA: What are you doing?

MAGGIE: I can't find my matches in the dark.

LAURA: Don't turn the lamp on, just light the candle.

MAGGIE: Light the candle to look for my matches?

LAURA: Sure. There's a lighter by the candle. *(After a second they both start to laugh.)*

MAGGIE: Are you sure we should do any more of this stuff?

LAURA: What have we got to lose?

MAGGIE: *(Getting lighter by the end table next to LAURA.)* Actually, I wouldn't mind a bit of light...

LAURA: Set it over on the end of the coffee-table then, OK?

(MAGGIE moves candle to the end of the table furthest from LAURA, lights the candle and a tiny pipe. She and LAURA pass the pipe back and forth as they talk. Portions of LAURA's face are momentarily lit by the red glow of the pipe. Something seems amiss with her face, but it's impossible to tell exactly what.)

(Cough.) I'm out of practise; Jack doesn't smoke drugs...

MAGGIE: *(Angry.)* So what? You've been separated for five months—who cares what Jack does *(Pause.)* Sorry, I...

LAURA: No, you're right. I know it sounds ridiculous from the outside, but I can't just erase the last three years.

MAGGIE: That doesn't mean you have to spend the next twenty years waiting by the telephone. You can love him more than you're ever going to love anybody else, that doesn't change the fact that what he does to your life isn't healthy. You have to sit down and figure out what's best for you and then make that happen. It hurts for a while, but if you push it down long enough it fades away.

LAURA: That's awful. I mean...

MAGGIE: (Shrug.) You meant what you said. Maybe you're right. I just don't think it's as awful as letting your life be yanked in whatever direction he happens to be going in. (Knocking out pipe.) I guess that's it. I'll call you tomorrow on my coffee break. Do you need anything?

LAURA: No—I'm going to have to get some groceries sometime.

MAGGIE: Why don't you make up a list? I'll see if I can get Ben to come by and go to the store tomorrow.

LAURA: I wouldn't...

MAGGIE: No trouble. He doesn't do anything in the afternoons but wander around and go for coffee anyway. Get better, eh?

LAURA: I'm working on it.

MAGGIE: Do, I'll call you tomorrow.

           (MAGGIE exits. LAURA gets up and blows out the candle. The candle flame shows that her face is bruised and scratched. She sits back down.)

Scene Eight

           (A man wearing an ancient leather jacket and a ski mask and gloves runs across the stage into a spotlight. He takes off the mask and catches his breath. It's WILLY, grinning exuberantly. He fits the mask over his free hand like a puppet.)

WILLY: Good evening, sports fans. False-face and I would like to welcome you to tonight's Wild World of Retribution. (Sniffing his gloved hand.) Ether and other evidence. (Pulling glove off with his teeth.) You get a bath in the fire when we get home. (To mask.) Oh, didn't I tell you? The congregation to be cleansed with fire. We're in the heart of a strange breed, False Face, and we don't tie ourselves to the maws of their machines. Who would know? Quite true; only one and he's in no position to tell. Never send a man to do a boy's job. Still, we leave no tracks, we take no chances. That means you. (Snapping his fingers out through the eyeholes.) That made his eyes pop out, folks. (To mask.) What's a little ritual immolation to the privilege of contributing to a sacrificial dance older than the stones of Babylon? By the waters of Jerusalem I babble on. Beep beep. (Looking off.) You still there? Well if you're looking for a run, I'll give you one. (Runs off.)

Scene Nine

(*LAURA's apartment, a Wednesday afternoon, LAURA sitting as at end of Act II, Scene 7. The light through the tightly-slatted blinds is stronger; daylight. The theme from Coronation Street plays from the television—the screen's green light partly illuminates the room, although LAURA's face is still fully shadowed. Doorbell. LAURA sits for a moment, then gets up and turns off the television. Doorbell again.*)

LAURA: Who is it?

BLACKJACK: (*Off.*) It's Jack.

LAURA: Jack who?

BLACKJACK: Jack who? Jack your husband, remember me? We used to share a bank account.

LAURA: (*After thinking an instant.*) I can't come to the door.

BLACKJACK: What?

LAURA: Use your key, please.

(*Jingle of keys off. Rattle of lock. Door opens, casting light in from the corridor. LAURA has positioned herself so that the light won't fall on her arms or face. BLACKJACK enters, pausing in the doorway.*)

Hi.

BLACKJACK: Hi. (*Reaches for light switch on the wall.*)

LAURA: Don't! (*BLACKJACK lets his arm fall.*) Close the door, please.

BLACKJACK: (*Closing door.*) What's the matter? Why are you living in the dark...?

LAURA: I—have an infection in my eyes. The doctor said it would clear up in a few days but the light hurts them just now. What brings you here?

BLACKJACK: (*Slightly suspicious.*) I owe you a cheque for next month. I'm going to need some kind of light to write it out.

LAURA: Well, I could go in the kitchen and come back when you're done...

BLACKJACK: Or you could just close your eyes while the light's on.

LAURA: No, that wouldn't work...

BLACKJACK: What's wrong?

LAURA: Nothing. Just my eyes.

BLACKJACK: Like hell. (*Moves quickly and switches on the lamp by the couch. LAURA backs away with her arms thrown up in front of her face. One wrist has a tension bandage wrapped around it.*)

LAURA: (*Backing away.*) Don't Jack— It's not funny— Turn it off, please...

(*BLACKJACK takes hold of her arms and pulls them down from her face. She has a black eye, bruises, one cheek badly scraped.*)

BLACKJACK: (*After a moment, still holding her arms.*) What happened?

LAURA: I was attacked. No, that's not true. I was raped.

BLACKJACK: *(After pause.)* When?

LAURA: Sunday night. *(She does not intend to go on further, but the sentence seems to call for further explanation, the further explanation calls for another phrase and so on.)* I was coming across the bridge. It wasn't late. I thought I'd be safe.

BLACKJACK: *(After pause.)* Who was it?

LAURA: I never saw him. I never even heard his voice. He grabbed me from behind and held a rag over my face, with chloroform or something. When I woke up it was so dark, I couldn't see anything. He was behind me. He had me pressed down on some sort of concrete shelf. I tried to break away. He pulled me up and slammed me down on the concrete. I tried to shout, for help, but he hit me.

BLACKJACK: But how did he... Didn't anyone hear you?

LAURA: It was in that underground concrete thing, where they'd started to build that apartment block and then stopped—nobody could hear. I didn't know until he'd gone. I had to grope around in the dark to find a way out and then I saw where I was.

BLACKJACK: *(After pause; croak.)* I'm sorry

LAURA: What could you do about it? It's just one of the hazards of walking around alone. I'll have to get used to it.

BLACKJACK: I'm sorry...

            (LAURA looks at him strangely, then turns away, walks to the lamp and switches it off. She sits back down on the couch.)

Scene Ten

            (The shop. JOHN is working on a design at the bench. BLACKJACK comes in walking quickly, proceeds straight to the telephone.)

JOHN: Hi, Jack. Do you want to see that design I was talking about?

BLACKJACK: *(Dialing phone.)* Later. Yes, could I speak to George Morris, please. Jack Thomas. Tell him it won't wait. George? I want to cancel the divorce. Yeah, kill it. She's divorcing me. No, I don't want to fight it. I want you to figure out the quickest and simplest way to put it through. On her terms. I'll give you any grounds you need. Get back to me when you've got it figured out, all right? *(Hangs up and dials another number.)* Hello, Arthur? Blackjack. I want to talk to you about some business. I want ten cc's of pure liquid LSD. Can you get it? How long? Right, I need it in an ampule with a pharmaceutical label on it. What have you got for blank labels? University Infirmary is perfect. Can you type it up as Demerol? Ten percent solution. What'll it cost? Right. Call me as soon as it's ready. *(Hangs up.)*

JOHN: Uh, Jack, maybe it's none of my business, but if you're going to be dealing out of here I'd like to know. I've got a record...

BLACKJACK: I'm not dealing. This is just a one shot thing. I'm going to give it to somebody.

JOHN: That's some gift.

BLACKJACK: I owe him.

Scene Eleven

(MAGGIE's apartment. BEN comes in, wearing a bathrobe, carrying a vase of carnations, singing in music hall Irish tenor a tune that is a strange hybrid of 'A Little Bit of Heaven' and 'When You Were Sweet Sixteen':)

Come with me to the cowshed, Maud O'Connol
Though your father is an Orangemen it doesn't bother me.
Good Catholic girls are sweet to kiss and fondle,
But I don't wish to be bouncing any babies on my knee.

(As he's arranging the flowers on the coffee table, MAGGIE drags in through the front door.)

BEN: Hi. How was your day?

MAGGIE: *(Slumping down on couch.)* Generally awful. Office politics. I was going to stop in and see Laura, but I don't think I'd do a good job of cheering her up right now.

(BEN caresses her head, she pulls away.)

Don't.

BEN: I talked to Mel today.

MAGGIE: Mel?

BEN: Mel the agent. You remember. He's setting up a couple of out-of-town bookings for next month.

MAGGIE: That's great.

BEN: Well, it's not that great.

MAGGIE: *(Squeezing his leg.)* You know I don't want you to compromise your principles if it's going to make you unhappy.

BEN: It is going to make me a bit unhappy, I guess. But I wasn't cut out to be Vincent van Gogh. I think I'd be a lot more unhappy if I was. I have to try to find a bass player. And Mel wants me to work up some new material...

MAGGIE: I wish I had the energy to celebrate.

BEN: Why don't I run a hot bath and get you a glass of wine.

MAGGIE: You talked me into it.

BEN: Oh, I ran into Blackjack today. I went into Ernie's to get a cup of coffee and he was sitting in a corner drinking. He was glaring around like he wanted to kill someone. I sat down to talk to him and he just stood up and walked away. Weird. Oh, I was going to get you a glass of wine.

(*He goes off. MAGGIE's eyes drift around, light on the flowers.*)

MAGGIE: Nice flowers.

Scene Twelve

(*Inside the workshop at night. Light from the doorway of the back room where a table saw is running loudly. The locks on the front door turn, BLACKJACK enters, wearing a leather jacket over rumpled jeans. He locks the door behind him, goes to the desk and switches on the lamp. His left hand is bandaged. He takes an ampule of clear liquid from his pocket, looks at it in the light, unlocks a desk drawer, takes out a bottle and a glass. The saw stops. BLACKJACK puts the ampule in the drawer. JOHN comes out of the back room.*)

JOHN: What happened, they close the bars early?

(*BLACKJACK takes another glass from the drawer and pours two drinks. JOHN comes forward and takes one.*)

How's your hand?

BLACKJACK: All right.

JOHN: You wouldn't be so likely to jam yourself with chisels if your hands weren't shaking from the night before. Do you have any idea what blood does to white spruce?

BLACKJACK: The divorce settlement's going to cut down my consumption of alcohol anyway. By the time I finish paying the rent on my apartment and here I should have enough left each month to buy a carton of cigarettes. If we're going to eat this winter we're going to have to start making some money out of this place.

JOHN: If you're going to eat. I ain't paying no alimony.

BLACKJACK: You ain't making any money, either.

JOHN: This is a true fact.

(*Pause. JOHN sips his drink. BLACKJACK finishes his and pours another.*)

Maybe we should start doing instrument repairs.

BLACKJACK: That's fairly delicate work.

JOHN: (*Shrug.*) It's still wood. You just have to remember that you can't use nails.

(*Pause. They sit and sip.*)

What the hell are you doing trying to be a carpenter anyway? You keep this up much longer you're not going to have any fingers left.

BLACKJACK: I'm learning, aren't I?

JOHN: Yeah, if you don't bleed to death before you graduate.

BLACKJACK: (*After pause.*) What do you think of revenge?

JOHN: By me or on me?

BLACKJACK: For you. Say something had been done to you, something that really messed you up, and you couldn't do anything to the person who did it to you, but somebody else could.

JOHN: What kind of thing are you talking about?

BLACKJACK: You must have known guys that got raped in prison.

JOHN: Yeah.

BLACKJACK: That kind of thing.

JOHN: Well, in the slammer, if you let anybody push you around too much, it's like you're issuing a licence to everybody to walk all over you. But that's the way it is on the inside. I didn't like it in there.

BLACKJACK: But if somebody did something like that to you on the outside and got away with it, you might feel the same way—that you're a person who's supposed to get walked on. But if somebody cared enough about you to go out and bust up whoever did it to you, it'd be different.

JOHN: Why would anybody want to do that for me?

BLACKJACK: Because they want to try and make you feel better.

JOHN: You know, the few times I can think of when somebody said they were going to do something for me, what they really meant was they were going to do it for themselves only they wanted me to take the blame for it. Mind you, anybody that says revenge is beneath us enlightened twentieth-century types hasn't had much dealing with the law.

(BLACKJACK volunteers nothing further. JOHN finishes his drink.)

JOHN: Well, I'd better head home. *(Donning his jacket.)* You want to lock me out?

BLACKJACK: Sure. *(Goes to the door with JOHN.)* See you in the morning.

JOHN: Yeah, *(Nodding at the drink in BLACKJACK's hand.)* Maybe two or three of me.

(JOHN exits. BLACKJACK locks the door behind him. BLACKJACK goes to the desk again, re-fills his glass, puts the bottle back in the drawer, takes out the ampule again, shakes it up, looks at it in the light, puts it back, locks the drawer, dons his jacket, empties his glass and goes out.)

Scene Thirteen

(LAURA with the band. She sings:)

I was a decorative child,
Well it was easy to see that climbing up on a knee
And being sweet as could be was just the ticket for me
To get by.

I learned that kindness and smiles
And just a flicker of thigh would place what I wanted high
On the priority slides of people stronger and wiser than me.

>   *(Bridge.)*

I'm not talking about extortion or some shady come-on game.
I just heard if you pamper the ones you care for they're bound to
>   do the same.
Shirley Temple never lacked for influential friends,
Cute and classy, never brassy, loyal to the end,
But you can look on every movie screen for Shirley fully grown,
She won't be home.

Nobody warned me at all
That if you say you just look to be a human chinook
Without a string or a hook there is a chance you'll get took
At your word.

Scene Fourteen

>   *(Inside the woodshop, the only light a pale winter dawn through the window. The door is unlocked from outside and BLACKJACK comes in, bundled up for a long walk. He takes off his gloves, unzips his coat, switches a light on, starts the coffee machine and begins removing his coat and scarf. JOHN appears at the back stairs, sleep-rumpled, wearing a blanket and workboots, carrying a hammer. BLACKJACK's back is to him.)*

JOHN: If your name ain't Blackjack Thomas you better have a damn good reason for being here.

>   *(BLACKJACK turns to face him.)*

What the hell are you doing here?

BLACKJACK: I work here, remember?

JOHN: At seven o'clock in the morning?

BLACKJACK: Almost seven-thirty, don't exaggerate. I just love the way you've co-ordinated the hammer with the rest of the ensemble; accessories really are the key to a truly elegant look.

JOHN: Thank you. I thought someone was breaking in.

BLACKJACK: So you were going to come up here, drop your blanket, knock yourself on the head with the hammer and scare them away?

JOHN: Something like that.

BLACKJACK: Why don't you go back to sleep?

JOHN: *(Unaware of BLACKJACK's last.)* I think I'll go back to sleep. Here, you might as well take this hammer.

BLACKJACK: *(Paul Robeson.)* Should I take it to de captain an' tell him you'se gwine? What if he asks me was you runnin?

JOHN: *(Stumbling off.)* You can tell him I'se flyin', boy, you can tell him I'se flyin'.

(BLACKJACK puts the hammer on a rack above the workbench, checks the coffee's progress and then goes to work unenergetically pegging a drawer laid out on the bench. The door opens, jingling the bell, and MAGGIE enters hesitantly, lightly dusted with snow. They have not seen each other since the wedding in the fall.)

MAGGIE: Hello, Jack.

BLACKJACK: Hello, Maggie *(Going back to work.)* What are you doing out on the street at this ungodly hour?

MAGGIE: Going to work. I saw your light and thought I'd come in and get warm. *(She comes forward into the shop, looking things over.)* What are you doing open at this ungodly hour?

BLACKJACK: Mrs. Kowalchuk got into a fight with her husband when she woke him up this morning. I figured as long as I was awake I might as well come to work.

MAGGIE: This seems like a pleasant place to work. How's business?

BLACKJACK: Booming. My partner's sleeping in the basement on a roll-away cot because he can't afford to pay rent—and he gets fifty percent of the profits. If my alimony payments were any higher I'd be living down there with him.

MAGGIE: What are you doing?

BLACKJACK: Pegging a drawer together. If you set the pegs in snug enough you don't need glue or screws. It's a good system but nobody uses it anymore. It's almost a lost art.

MAGGIE: Are you going to revive it?

BLACKJACK: I doubt it. In my hands it becomes more of a game of chance. How are you?

MAGGIE: Oh, I'm fine. I'm running the data services department now, so there's enough to keep me busy.

BLACKJACK: Is Ben still on the road a lot?

MAGGIE: He's been home about four weeks out of the last three months.

BLACKJACK: I would have thought his manager wouldn't have too much trouble getting him bookings in town.

MAGGIE: I don't know if that's the case or if Ben's just embarrassed to play where people know him. Did you hear about Willy?

BLACKJACK: What about Willy?

MAGGIE: He's in Selkirk. He has been since the fall. The police found him sitting out in a park one day, just staring at nothing.

BLACKJACK: It was bound to happen eventually.

MAGGIE: Maybe. They don't know whether he just finally snapped completely or whether he took a huge overdose or something. I can't see him doing that. He liked dancing on the edge, but he'd never jump.

BLACKJACK: Accidents happen. *(Coffee percolator bings.)* Would you like a cup of coffee?

MAGGIE: I'd love one, but I have to get to work. Are you going to start opening this early all the time now?

BLACKJACK: Not if I can help it.

MAGGIE: That's too bad. I thought I might be able to stop in here sometime and sponge my morning coffee.

BLACKJACK: Well, we've got fairly irregular hours. If I wake up early I come down here. Chances are you'll catch us with the coffee on.

MAGGIE: I hope so. See you.

BLACKJACK: Yeah.

(MAGGIE exits. BLACKJACK pours himself a cup of coffee. JOHN comes on, still rumpled but dressed, and takes the cup from his hand.)

BLACKJACK: *(Pouring another.)* I thought you were going back to sleep.

JOHN: So did I. Can't sleep when there's somebody up here. Ridiculous hour to be awake. Sun's not even up yet.

BLACKJACK: You'd better get used to it.

JOHN: You're sick.

Scene Fifteen

(LAURA's apartment, slightly cluttered. Doorbell. LAURA comes on, partly made up, wearing dressing gown, and goes to the door.)

LAURA: Who is it?

BLACKJACK: *(Off.)* Jack. *(LAURA opens the door.)*

LAURA: Hi—I just… I wasn't exactly expecting you. Come on in.

(BLACKJACK does so, warily. He's wearing his winter garb, coat unzipped. He takes off his gloves but then keeps his hands in his pockets, his shoulders hunched.)

Would you like a cup of tea or something? As you can see, my housekeeping hasn't improved…

BLACKJACK: I just—stopped by for a minute. I can't stay. How are you?

LAURA: All right, I suppose. I've started back at university.

BLACKJACK: *(Stilted.)* Good. I'm glad.

LAURA: How are you?

(BLACKJACK shrugs.)

What did you want to see me about?

BLACKJACK: I just wanted to tell you… The man that… The guy that jumped you last summer. I know who he is. There isn't much left of him.

LAURA: *(After a long pause of staring at BLACKJACK, who avoids looking at her.)* Is that supposed to make me feel better?

BLACKJACK: I don't know. I just thought you should know. I guess I better go. Goodbye.

(He goes out quickly. LAURA stands looking at the door. Then she goes to it and slides the burglar chain home.)

Scene Sixteen

(The shop. MAGGIE is on, wearing her office clothes and winter boots, her coat on the coat tree. She's leaning against the bench, sipping a cup of coffee. An old acoustic guitar is sitting on the workbench. BLACKJACK enters from the back, brandishing a tuning fork.)

BLACKJACK: I knew it was in here somewhere. *(He sits on the bench, takes the guitar in hand and holds out the tuning fork to MAGGIE.)* How'd you like to give me a hand with this? Bang it on your knee and then press the point against the top of the guitar.

MAGGIE: I'd rather bang it on the table.

BLACKJACK: No, if it gets dented it'll go off pitch.

MAGGIE: I'm not going to bang it on my knee.

BLACKJACK: Bang it on my knee, then. Ow!

MAGGIE: Is that the note you wanted?

BLACKJACK: *(Gingerly flexing his leg.)* I think you broke my kneecap.

MAGGIE: Better yours then mine; I'm no fool.

BLACKJACK: *(Draping a rag over the edge of the bench.)* Here, hit it on that.

(She does so. He hits the appropriate harmonic.)

Damn close.

MAGGIE: It's flat.

BLACKJACK: It's close enough to tell that the bridge will hold.

MAGGIE: My mother always says "If a thing's worth doing at all it's worth doing right."

BLACKJACK: No wonder your father always looks so tired.

MAGGIE: You know, of all the people I might have thought would end up doing something like this, you would have been the last.

BLACKJACK: Watch that talk about 'ending up,' I'm not even thirty yet.

MAGGIE: You know what I mean. I know lots of people I'd expect to find making pottery and running health food stores

BLACKJACK: Gimme a break, eh? Do you see any copies of the *I Ching* lying around here?

MAGGIE: *Alice in Wonderland* is showing at the university next week. The animated version. Do you want to take me?

BLACKJACK: I don't know if I can. How much are they charging?

MAGGIE: I don't know. How about if I take you?

BLACKJACK: Sure.

MAGGIE: *(Donning her coat.)* I should get going. We're going out for dinner tonight with Ben's agent. I'm not sure of the dates for that movie. I'll stop by early next week. See you.

BLACKJACK: Yeah.

(MAGGIE exits. BLACKJACK finishes tuning. JOHN comes on from the back room, carrying a cup of coffee with a pencil in it.)

JOHN: Do you want to give me a hand setting some clamps?

BLACKJACK: Sure. Do you want this *(Tuning fork.)* back?

JOHN: No, I found a pencil.

BLACKJACK: *(Setting guitar down and taking up bill pad.)* How much do you want for trimming that bridge?

JOHN: Five bucks?

BLACKJACK: OK. *(Writing out bill.)* And I'll add five for taking the old one off and putting the new one on.

(The door opens and a man comes into the shop. He is freshly shaved and barbered, wearing new off-the-rack welfare clothes and ski jacket. He looks vaguely familiar, perhaps identifiable as the actor who played WILLY in another role. His eyes look watery and washed-out, his skin pale and soft.)

JOHN: Hello. Anything we can do for you?

WILLY: I'm not here on business. *(His voice is soft and halting. His face glows into an obsequious, nervous smile.)* Hi, Blackjack. Don't you remember me?

BLACKJACK: Hello, Willy.

WILLY: How are you today?

BLACKJACK: I'm all right. How about you?

WILLY: Oh fine. I'm fine. *(He smiles again. Pause. Then, as though suddenly remembering instructions, he strides over to JOHN with his hand held out.)* I don't believe we've met. My name is Willy Teal.

JOHN: *(Allowing his hand to be shook.)* John Chapman.

WILLY: I'm pleased to meet you. *(WILLY's words ring like under-rehearsed lines: patently false but striving for sincerity. Occasionally he stutters.)* Well I can't stay for long. I wonder if I could ask you to do a favour for me, Blackjack.

BLACKJACK: You can ask.

WILLY: It was arranged at the hospital that I could come out to see you— You did know I was in the hospital, didn't you?

BLACKJACK: Yeah.

WILLY: I still am. I was very sick but I'm getting better. Slowly. In order to help some of us adjust to—outside social behaviour, we're being sent out on day passes with special objectives. Like projects. For my first project—I was to pick a friend I used to know and drop in for a visit. I know that sounds like a simple thing to you, but believe me, it's not easy. *(A thin stream of saliva dribbles out the corner of his mouth. Embarassed, he furtively wipes it away, smiles apologetically.)* Excuse me. I think part of my medication is Stelazine. One of the side effects is overproduction of saliva. I told them at the hospital I would come to see you. They will be phoning you in a couple of days to talk to you about my visit. *(Pause.)* Well, I'm starting to get nervous and we haven't even had a conversation yet. I do like the smell of fresh-cut wood. How's business?

BLACKJACK: All right.

WILLY: How's your wife?

BLACKJACK: *(After staring sharply at WILLY a moment.)* She's fine.

WILLY: That's good. Well, I guess I have to be going now. It was nice talking to you. *(To JOHN.)* Nice to meet you.

JOHN: Yeah.

WILLY: Good-bye. See you. *(He exits.)*

JOHN: Is that the same Willy I heard you and Maggie talk about, that became a vegetable?

BLACKJACK: That's right. He studied hard, grew up and became a vegetable.

JOHN: I didn't know they could cure that.

BLACKJACK: You call that a cure? *(Starting off to the backroom.)* What are you trying to clamp?

JOHN: *(Following him off.)* That table leg, remember? The one that was cracking.

Scene Seventeen

(MAGGIE with the band. The music here is based around an acoustic guitar tuned to an open D, very rolling, with the melody striving to impose a feeling of placid control on top of it.)

You only pass an hour or so, politely entertained
Then continue on your way back home, it's perfectly mundane.
But long past the hour of midnight some intangible remains.
You passed this way so long ago, but the song remains the same.
Are you really slipping back into the undertow again?

The hands of fate played thimblerig, so you took your life in yours
By learning what you want and why and what that led towards.
But this comes from nowhere, goes nowhere and still won't be ignored.
After all this time of trying, when you're so close in to shore
Will you let yourself be pulled back in the undertow once more?

Scene Eighteen

(The shop. JOHN and BLACKJACK are on, examining a chair with a split woven back standing on the workbench. BLACKJACK studies it from one side, JOHN from the other. They move around the bench trading angles.)

JOHN: Maybe we should glue it.

BLACKJACK: Glue what to what?

JOHN: It was just a thought.

(They study it further.)

BLACKJACK: Maybe we should stitch it—sew the end of each broken strand to the next one…

JOHN: That's even stupider than gluing. Even if it held, which it wouldn't, the back would end up looking like a caesarean section.

BLACKJACK: Look, we're a woodworking shop, right? Not a caneworking shop or catgut shop or whatever this shit is. Call the old crock up and tell him he brought it to the wrong shop.

JOHN: Did I tell you how much that old crock will pay us to fix it?

BLACKJACK: Yeah, you told me.

JOHN: Two hundred dollars. It's part of a set. Two hundred dollars to fix one little chair.

BLACKJACK: If the goddamn thing's so precious to him why'd he let it get cut up in the first place?

JOHN: He couldn't help it. His grandson slashed it up with the new boy scout knife he gave him for Christmas.

BLACKJACK: Why don't we just cut it all out and re-weave the whole back?

JOHN: You'd never match the colour on the rest of the set. That stuff s been drinking sunlight for fifty years.

BLACKJACK: By the time we get it finished it'll match.

JOHN: What would you use to weave it?

BLACKJACK: Kid gut, the new wonder material. Tell the old fart to send his grandson down here.

(The front door opens and MAGGIE walks in, wearing a lighter coat than in Act Two, Scene 16. Her boots are spattered with slush. She walks a few paces into the shop, then stops.)

Well hello. I was beginning to worry about you. I thought maybe you'd fallen under a bus or forgot the address or something.

MAGGIE: I had to think something out. I just came by to tell you that I can't see you anymore.

JOHN: I think I hear my mother calling. *(He exits quickly to the back.)*

MAGGIE: Well, there, now I've told you. *(She turns to go.)*

BLACKJACK: Wait a minute. Do you mean you can't take me out to the occasional movie anymore, or you won't be coming in for your morning coffee on your way to work or your evening coffee on your way home, or what?

MAGGIE: Everything. I won't see you at all anymore.

BLACKJACK: Why? If you can't stand John's coffee we can start sending out. Or have I done something to offend you?

MAGGIE: No.

BLACKJACK: Then why?

MAGGIE: We're getting too close to each other.

BLACKJACK: What's that supposed to mean?

MAGGIE: Exactly what I said.

BLACKJACK: We're friends. What's wrong with that?

MAGGIE: More like lovers.

BLACKJACK: I never touched you.

MAGGIE: You didn't have to.

BLACKJACK: *(After assimilating that.)* Why do you want to throw that away?

MAGGIE: I don't want to. I have to. There are other people involved.

BLACKJACK: Ben?

MAGGIE: He doesn't have much to do with it.

BLACKJACK: Then who does? Besides you and me.

MAGGIE: Laura.

BLACKJACK: Laura? Why should she care what happens between us?

MAGGIE: She does. Or she would if she knew about it. Regardless of what she'd try to pretend, she'd resent it. She's my friend. That's too important to me to throw it away for a lover.

BLACKJACK: *(Quickly, angrily.)* Did you good friend Laura ever tell you what she does with her afternoons whenever...

(Suddenly he pulls up short. He turns away from MAGGIE and walks stiffly to the workbench.)

MAGGIE: What were you starting to tell me?

BLACKJACK: I was going to try and con you into believing that Laura isn't as good a friend as you think she is. Old habits die hard.

MAGGIE: I'm glad you didn't try.

BLACKJACK: It wouldn't have made any difference anyway. Laura's just an excuse.

MAGGIE: An excuse for what?

BLACKJACK: Come off it. You've got your safe little man that only comes out when you want to get your rocks off, and your safe job where you can play games without every laying too much on the line, and then you come in here a few times and something actually touches you and you can't put it in a box and control it so you're running scared.

MAGGIE: You're an expert on running scared. Sitting in here playing carpenter for the rest of your life.

BLACKJACK: *(After pause.)* If in the course of human events I happen to bump into you on the street, am I allowed to stop and inquire innocently after the state of your health?

MAGGIE: I'd be hurt if you didn't. This wasn't an easy decision for me to make, Jack. I didn't want to.

BLACKJACK: Then we still have something in common.

MAGGIE: Good-bye, Jack.

BLACKJACK: Yeah. Good-bye.

> *(MAGGIE turns and walks quickly out the door. BLACKJACK stands staring at the chair. Unseen by BLACKJACK, JOHN drifts into the entranceway from the back room. BLACKJACK suddenly swings the chair up over his head and starts to bring it down to smash it on the workbench. At the last instant he pulls up and sets it down gently. JOHN walks forward, pours himself a cup of coffee.)*

JOHN: What ever happened to that ounce of liquid LSD you bought in the ampule marked Demerol?

BLACKJACK: You've got a long memory.

JOHN: Some things stick in my mind. What did you do with it?

BLACKJACK: What difference does it make?

JOHN: A lot of difference. I was told a lot of things about you before I started working here. I just put it down to small town gossip and sour grapes. But I keep seeing a picture of somebody locked in a hospital room with the inside of his head all blown to hell. Did you give that acid to Willy?

BLACKJACK: What if I did?

JOHN: Then I'll go downstairs and pack my stuff and walk out the door.

BLACKJACK: I have no intention of passing judgement on you except on the work you do here and whether you deal honestly with the business of the shop. I expected the same sort of tolerance from you. I never asked you to approve of my existence, just to work with me.

JOHN: Did you give that acid to Willy?

BLACKJACK: No.

JOHN: You got any proof?

BLACKJACK: *(With brittle humour.)* Isn't my word good enough for you?

> *(JOHN slowly shakes his head. BLACKJACK unlocks the drawer, takes out the ampule and tosses it to JOHN.)*

JOHN: *(After studying the ampule.)* How do I know you didn't fake up another ampule just in case?

BLACKJACK: Well if you think that one's a fake why don't you just pop off the top and knock it back? Then you'll know for sure. Or if you don't want to try that you might try considering that if I had decided to do that to Willy I wouldn't worry about a seal of approval from you or anybody else that doesn't know fuck all about what kind of reasons I might have had.

JOHN: *(After pause.)* I don't owe you an apology.

BLACKJACK: And I don't owe you one.

JOHN: What were you going to do with it?

BLACKJACK: Give it to Willy. Just a question of slipping it in his bag.

JOHN: Why didn't you?

BLACKJACK: I couldn't find a good enough reason. Keep it. I've got no use for it.

> *(JOHN tosses the ampule contemplatively, then drops it on the floor and steps on it.)*

BLACKJACK: We're going to have a lot of weird mice. *(They both shift their attention to the broken chair as lights fade out.)*

Curtain

Footprints on the Moon

MAUREEN HUNTER

Production Information

Footprints on the Moon was first produced by Agassiz Theatre Company on January 21, 1988, at the Gas Station Theatre, Winnipeg, with the following cast:

JOANIE .... Pam MacDonald
DUNC CARR .... Wayne Nicklas
CAROL-ANN .... Natasha Klassen
BERYL .... Sharel McCulloch
BOONE .... Jonathan Barrett

Directed by Craig Walls
Set design by David Hewlett
Lighting design by Dennis Smith
Stage management by Charlene Wiest
Artistic Director: Craig Walls
Executive Producer: Julianne Krause

Footprints on the Moon was workshopped at the 1986 Playwrights Colony sponsored by the Manitoba Association of Playwrights. The playwright is grateful to George Toles for his insight, criticism and encouragement during the writing of this play.

This play is dedicated to the memory of my mother, Stella Horsman

Setting

Act One, Scenes One & Two: .... Rose Coulee, a prairie town, train station
Act One, Scenes Three to Six; Act Two: .... Joanie's kitchen and porch

Characters

JOANIE, 35
DUNC Carr, 40s
CAROL-ANN, 16
BERYL, 35
BOONE, 35-40

Act One

Scene One

(The train station. A hot Thursday afternoon in August. JOANIE enters carrying a paper bag and a vivid pink purse. She wears a sundress and high-heeled sandals; everything is a little too tight. She has just walked across town and is obviously hot and uncomfortable. She pulls the top of the sundress away from her body and fans her breast with the dress. She moves up centre and peers off left, shading her eyes, then glances off right, sighs, faces front, swats a mosquito. She removes one sandal, shakes something out of it, begins to put it back on but changes her mind and instead takes the other sandal off too. She moves to the station wall and leans against it. Realizing that the wall is cool, she presses one shoulder, then the other, against it. Then she slips to the ground and sits, her back against the wall, her legs straight out in front of her. She spreads her legs wide, raises the skirt of the dress and fans herself with it. Finally she pulls the dress back from her legs completely. She has just settled in when a truck is heard drawing closer, turning in. Brakes; the engine is turned off.)

JOANIE: Damn.

(A truck door slams. JOANIE stands reluctantly and is putting her sandals back on when DUNC enters, down right. He wears jeans, cowboy boots, a white shirt, a western-style hat and a wide leather belt with an ornate silver buckle. He's tanned, trim and very fit.

There's an awkward moment when they first see one another.)

Well, if it isn't.

DUNC: Joanie.

(DUNC moves up centre, peers left for a long moment, peers at the sky; he makes quite a show of checking things out.)

JOANIE: It's already been and gone.

DUNC: Sure it has.

JOANIE: It has.

DUNC: Then how come you're still here?

JOANIE: Maybe I enjoy the view.

DUNC: The view.

JOANIE: That one you are standing in front of.

(Their eyes meet, lock. JOANIE is the first to turn away. DUNC draws a package of cigarettes from his shirt pocket, lights one, looks her over.)

DUNC: Who're you waitin' for, anyhow? In them fancy new clothes.

JOANIE: Carol-Ann. *(Pointedly.)* My daughter.

DUNC: I remember who she is. *(Turns to stare off.)* Well, she's late.

JOANIE: *(Very sweet.)* We don't need to ask who you've come for.

DUNC: What's that supposed to mean?

JOANIE: Just—we don't need to ask.

> *(DUNC lets this pass. He takes off his hat, wipes an arm across his forehead.)*

DUNC: God, this heat. Ain't it hot out here? Nothin' to sit on, either. You'd think they could've left a goddamned bench. To even get the train to stop, you hafta call three days ahead. Whole town's goin' downhill.

JOANIE: No, it's not.

DUNC: Sure as hell is.

JOANIE: What are you trying to do, make me mad?

DUNC: I'm givin' it my best shot. *(He grins.)*

JOANIE: It's not going downhill. It's just kind of—plateau'd.

DUNC: Yeah? That what you wrote in that Prize Winnin' Essay?

JOANIE: Not exactly.

DUNC: What'd you write?

JOANIE: You'll see. They're printing it Friday, in *The News*. Maybe you'll remember to read it.

> *(JOANIE throws him a glance, then moves away, swinging her hips.)*

DUNC: Kinda nice to see you, all dolled up. A dress and everything. I like to see a woman in a dress. You don't wear 'em much, do you? You mostly wear those short-shorts the boys all let on they never notice.

JOANIE: What boys?

DUNC: Over at the Plains Inn.

JOANIE: The Plains Inn! Why don't you call that place what it is?

DUNC: What is it?

JOANIE: It's a dirty old machine shed, that's what.

DUNC: *(Shrugs.)* Sour grapes.

JOANIE: Huh! Think I want to hang around a place like that?

DUNC: I think you wanna be where you'd get a few laughs.

> *(He knows this will make her smile. It does, but she catches herself.)*

JOANIE: I don't see why it has to be "No Women Allowed."

DUNC: *(Very dry.)* Oh, there's a pretty good reason for that.

(*He grins broadly. JOANIE turns away.*)

So. Where's Carol-Ann been off to?

JOANIE: Ask me something you don't know.

(*A direct hit. DUNC shifts, drops his cigarette, grinds it out, stares off.*)

DUNC: Old Boone. Sure gotta give him credit.

JOANIE: Do you?

DUNC: Well, I mean, he sends for her every summer, don't he? Just like clockwork. Pays her way, too, or no?

JOANIE: A real hero.

DUNC: Lots do worse.

JOANIE: (*Abruptly.*) What goes on in there, anyhow?

DUNC: Where?

JOANIE: All of a sudden there's not a man to be seen anywhere, they're all hiding out in that dirty old machine shed. What goes on?

DUNC: Nothin'.

JOANIE: Nothin'!

DUNC: Honest to God, nothin' goes on. Don't know why you women are all so upset about it. It's just a bunch of guys sittin' around. Shootin' the breeze, playin' a little poker. Tossin' back a few...

JOANIE: Sounds awful dull to me.

DUNC: Dull's the one thing it ain't.

JOANIE: (*Leaning up against the station wall.*) You're a born bachelor, I guess. What a stroke of luck for your Mum.

DUNC: I'd make one lousy husband, that's for sure.

JOANIE: They all say that.

DUNC: Who?

JOANIE: Any man with sense. Any man I ever knew. What are you staring at?

DUNC: How come you're all dolled up, anyhow?

JOANIE: Orders.

DUNC: Who's givin' you orders?

(*He moves close to her, sets one hand against the station, leans in.*)

Nobody gives you orders.

JOANIE: (*Moving away.*) Carol-Ann, that's who. "Don't bother meeting me," she says, "or if you've got to come, dress decent!" That's how it is with kids. You start out by giving orders and end up taking them.

DUNC: I guess.

JOANIE: "Leave the short-shorts at home," she says. That's what she learns in The Big T.O. That kind of talk. I can already see her face—the look on it, when she steps off that train.

DUNC: She'll settle back in.

JOANIE: I bought her a present, to cheer her up.

          (She opens the paper bag, pulls out a woolen scarf and mitts.)

          Hand-knit mitts and a scarf to match! From the U.C. Tea and Bake Sale, last Saturday. I looked at blue, you know-sky blue? They would've matched her eyes perfect. But somehow or other I ended up with these. You haven't said yet how pretty they are.

DUNC: Well, they're pretty all right, but they're—wool aren't they?

JOANIE: *(Faltering.)* Well, sure. It was wool or aprons with matching pot holders—take your pick! *(Miserably.)* Oh maybe I shouldn't have got them, maybe I should save them for Christmas. *(Brightening.)* One thing about Carol-Ann, when you give her something she really cuts up. She's got what's called A Dramatic Personality, that's why. When she was little, she was always in front of the mirror—she's always in front of the mirror now. When she was little she...

          (Realizing she has lost his interest, she sticks the scarf and mitts back in the bag.)

          She'd cry her heart out over nothing, just to watch herself do it. *(By way of apology.)* I haven't seen her in three weeks.

DUNC: It's all right.

          (He draws a mickey from his pocket, uncaps it, offers it to her.)

JOANIE: I better not.

DUNC: Goes down real nice.

JOANIE: You know what happens when I drink it straight.

DUNC: *(Grins.)* Yeah—I do!

          (JOANIE gives him a look.)

          Just a swallow.

          (JOANIE takes a drink, makes a face, hands the bottle back.)

JOANIE: How's your Mum doing, anyways? Better?

DUNC: Aw...you know.

JOANIE: That's too bad.

DUNC: She's got this new specialist now. Best in the west—supposed to be. *(Indicating the track.)* That's where she's been all week. She seems to think he's helpin'. Me, I don't see it. I just hope one thing. *(Meaning "dies in her sleep:")* Hope she sleeps out.

JOANIE: I hope so too.

DUNC: Listen here, Joanie. How come you kept it so quiet? Carol-Ann bein' out of town. *(An obvious lie:)* I had no idea.

JOANIE: Well, how could you? Place the size of this.

DUNC: You should've advertised it. Raised a banner. Somethin'.

JOANIE: Anyone that mattered knew.

DUNC: Is that so?

JOANIE: Yes, it is.

          (DUNC grins, places one hand on the wall, and leans into her.)

DUNC: I don't think so.

JOANIE: You don't.

          (DUNC runs a finger along her arm.)

DUNC: I don't.

          (JOANIE throws off his hand.)

JOANIE: You never were no Rhode scholar. *(She moves away.)*

DUNC: Shit.

JOANIE: I didn't notice you letting it slip by last summer. Nor the summer before.

DUNC: All right, Joanie.

JOANIE: Every August like clockwork, you said it yourself.

DUNC: All right, have it your way! I knew, but I kept my distance. You wanna know why?

JOANIE: No! *(Pause.)* I know why.

          (DUNC is about to say more, thinks better of it. He moves upstage, stands with his back to her, staring off.)

          God, this weather. The air's so hot, it hums.

          (She paces, fanning herself.)

          I need to pee too. Where's a person supposed to pee, anyways? *(A smile grows.)* That Carol-Ann. When she was little she peed practically non-stop. Did I ever tell you that? She did. It wasn't her fault. She had this problem, something down there didn't work right, not 'till she was almost three. And one time— *(Laughs.)* One time Boone picked her up in her birthday suit and swung her across the table but not fast enough and she peed all over his Cream o' Wheat! She did. *(Pause.)* I notice you've still got that fender dent.

DUNC: Oh, that. Yeah.

JOANIE: How come?

DUNC: Haven't got around to fixin' it.

JOANIE: I thought maybe you'd kept it to remember me by.

DUNC: *(Facing her.)* I don't need no fender dent for that.

JOANIE: You're a devil, Dunc Carr, you know that? Lies just flow off your tongue like rain off a roof.

DUNC: I mean it, Joanie.

JOANIE: That fender dent. It's no wonder you got it. By the time you got to my place, you were half the time so pie-eyed you could hardly get through the door.

DUNC: Once I did, I managed fine.

JOANIE: You sure did! And now from what I hear you're managing fine over at Jamieson's.

> (*Dead silence.*)

From what I hear.

DUNC: You can't say I didn't warn you, Joanie.

JOANIE: Oh, well. You and half the town. (*Mimics.*) When a man comes calling at 2 a.m., it's for one thing only.

DUNC: Who'd say that?

JOANIE: Some of them were pals of yours.

DUNC: Jealous.

JOANIE: I wonder.

DUNC: I told you right at the start, I don't like to be counted on.

JOANIE: That'll be news to a few people around here. All the boys over at the Plains Inn—

DUNC: I don't like to be counted on by no woman!

JOANIE: I wonder if your Mum ever got that message?

DUNC: (*Flaring.*) Are you going to pick on her? Now? As things stand?

JOANIE: No. I'm not.

> (*She moves away, fanning herself.*)

I should've worn my shorts anyways. No matter what she said.

DUNC: (*Sulkily.*) It wasn't for one thing only!

JOANIE: She never used to talk like that, not Carol-Ann. She never used to order me around. He's done that, I guess—or Toronto. Or maybe I brought it on myself. I didn't always handle things so good, I know that. Starting right when she was three years old and crying, "Where is he, where'd he go, why-why-why!" I'd just always say the same thing. "Honey, all I know is this. He walked into the Drake Hotel one night and didn't bother coming out." What a mistake. She's never once gone by that damned hotel without staring at it like it was some kind of shrine! True. Enough to break your heart.

DUNC: You better come out of the sun, Joanie. Why don't you?

JOANIE: Dropped right out of sight for ten and a half years. But now he sends for her every summer, like you said. He's no make-believe hero now.

DUNC: C'mon over here where it's shady. I won't bite.

> (*JOANIE moves next to him, takes another drink.*)

That's better.

JOANIE: Even if you had come around, I wouldn't have let you in.

DUNC: You'd have let me in.

JOANIE: Unh-uh. I promised Carol-Ann.

DUNC: What? That you wouldn't see me?

JOANIE:	Swore it on my mother's grave. If she's got one.
DUNC:	Boy oh boy. And you stand there, doin' what? Workin' me over.
JOANIE:	Who's working you over? Not me.
DUNC:	Not much!
JOANIE:	All you had to do was come around! So I could tell you not to come around!

(Suddenly, JOANIE laughs. DUNC joins her. A silence.)

We had some good times, huh?

DUNC:	You bet we did.
JOANIE:	Yeah. We did.
DUNC:	Even if I do step around a bit—on principle. You're still my best girl. You know that.
JOANIE:	Do I.
DUNC:	Whole town knows it.
JOANIE:	I wonder.
DUNC:	Listen here, Joanie—what do you say. Next summer like clockwork, all right?

(JOANIE touches him lightly on the lips.)

JOANIE:	Shush, you.
DUNC:	Kinda answer is that?

(JOANIE shakes her head. He tries to kiss her. She backs away.)

Maybe you've found yourself another summertime man.

JOANIE:	Maybe I don't need one, now I'm a Valued Citizen.
DUNC:	You are?
JOANIE:	According to the mayor I am.

(She draws a letter from her purse and hands it to him.)

Here's the letter he says it in. Proof! They're printing that letter alongside my essay. Word for word. With pictures. And you'll be hearing me on the radio. If you happen to catch it.

DUNC:	*(Handing back the letter.)* That's real nice, Joanie. Carol-Ann's gonna be proud of you.
JOANIE:	Maybe. Anyways, she'll be surprised. I hate writing anything, she knows that—even a letter, even a grocery list. But I saw that contest advertised and I just said out loud to myself everything I felt—which I'm good at!—and then I wrote it all down, quick. And I won. *(Pause.)* You're looking good, Dunc Carr, you know that? You've kept your body real good.
DUNC:	I've stayed slim, anyhow.
JOANIE.	Slim and hard. Not like me. I've got whole sections of my body now, looking like the surface of the moon. Craters that deep!
DUNC:	You still got the best legs in town.

JOANIE: That's not saying much.

DUNC: You know it, too. *(Moving in.)* Don't you?

JOANIE: Maybe.

DUNC: Maybe!

               (He starts to caress her.)

JOANIE: Maybe that's one thing I've still got.

               (He kisses her. She tries to break away but he pulls her back. She begins to respond. The scene heats up.)

DUNC: Come on, Joanie.

JOANIE: No. I don't dare.

DUNC: My truck's right here.

               (He kisses her again, then leads her off, right. Lights fade slowly.)

Scene Two

               (Lights up on the station. CAROL-ANN stands up centre. There's a suitcase beside her. After a long moment, she sighs, picks up the suitcase and begins to move down centre. Suddenly JOANIE enters, down right, on the run.)

JOANIE: Carol-Ann!

CAROL-ANN: *(Big smile.)* Mum!

               (JOANIE runs to CAROL-ANN, hugs her, swings her.)

               What's the matter?

JOANIE: Nothing. I'm just so glad to have you back. You look so good, so...I think you've grown. Have you grown? You look just— beautiful!

               (JOANIE hugs CAROL-ANN again as DUNC enters, down right, carrying JOANIE's paper bag.)

DUNC: You, uh...you dropped this.

               (A very awkward moment. DUNC speaks to CAROL-ANN.)

               My mother's gettin' off, too—supposed to be. Maybe you seen her.

CAROL-ANN: *(Very chilly.)* Yes.

DUNC: Good.

               (He begins to move down left; he hesitates.)

               Uh—you folks want a ride?

JOANIE: No! Thanks.

DUNC: I could easy drop you but, uh...well.

               (He exits. Short silence. JOANIE tries to give CAROL-ANN a kiss on the cheek, but CAROL-ANN turns away.)

JOANIE: *(Gamely.)* You've cut your hair.

CAROL-ANN: You don't like it.

JOANIE: I like it, looks real pretty, only what's your Grandpa going to say? He's been cutting your hair since you were two years old.

CAROL-ANN: I knew you'd be mad.

JOANIE: I'm not mad, Carol-Ann. Look—I brought you a present. Open it, quick.

(CAROL-ANN refuses to accept the bag. JOANIE opens it and draws out the woolens.)

Hand-knit mitts and a scarf to match! Aren't they pretty? I looked at blue—the blue would've matched your eyes perfect. But somehow or other...

CAROL-ANN: Mitts. In this heat.

(JOANIE shoves the woolens back in the bag. CAROL-ANN starts to move off.)

JOANIE: Aren't you going to wait for me? Carol-Ann, you wait for me!

(CAROL-ANN stops, sets down the suitcase but doesn't turn around.)

I want you to understand.

CAROL-ANN: *(Bitterly.)* I understand.

JOANIE: No! It's not like it looks. This whole summer, that's the first I've seen of him. It is! It just happened we were meeting the same train. We got talking—

CAROL-ANN: Stop it.

JOANIE: There'll be no dirty talk, is what I'm saying.

CAROL-ANN: It doesn't matter.

JOANIE: It mattered last summer.

CAROL-ANN: Well, it doesn't matter now.

JOANIE: *(After a slight pause.)* Well! Then maybe you'll let me have that kiss. *(Pitifully.)* I really missed my little girl.

(CAROL-ANN submits to a kiss.)

Now then—tell me about your trip. Was it fun?

CAROL-ANN: Can't you wait? It's awful hot out here.

JOANIE: And how's your Dad?

CAROL-ANN: Fine.

JOANIE: That's all? Just—fine?

CAROL-ANN: Can we go now?

JOANIE: There, you see? It does matter. You say it doesn't, but it does.

CAROL-ANN: *(Turning on her.)* Why him, that's all. Why someone who doesn't give a damn about you?

JOANIE: He gives a damn.

CAROL-ANN: All he is is a sleazy old drunk. Ask anyone! Do you know what they say about him behind his back? Know what they say about you?

> (JOANIE slaps CAROL-ANN. This shocks them both. CAROL-ANN begins to cry.)

JOANIE: I told you, Carol-Ann. This whole summer, that's the first I've—

CAROL-ANN: He doesn't care about you! He's got half a dozen women on the line, don't you know that? All he cares about is himself, and his stupid old witch of a mother, and his stupid old horse, and his stupid buddies—

JOANIE: Aw, Carol-Ann...

CAROL-ANN: You promised! You broke your promise.

JOANIE: I did. I know I did. I'm sorry.

CAROL-ANN: I told you not to meet me. Didn't I tell you not to come and meet me? If you'd just stayed home!

JOANIE: I wore a dress, anyways, didn't I? At least I followed one order.

CAROL-ANN: Oh, Mum...

JOANIE: Sshh! Never mind.

> (She takes CAROL-ANN in her arms.)

I'm just so glad to have you home, you'll never know how glad. And you know what? I've been giving things a lot of thought and—listen. I'd like you to do me a favour. I'd like you to try real hard, now you're home, to not be thinking about Toronto and Rose Coulee and comparing the two—

CAROL-ANN: (Pulling away.) OK, Mum.

JOANIE: Either in your mind or out loud, because they really aren't the same, you know? Sometimes places look—the place you come from can look a little shabby, sometimes, when you first come back.

CAROL-ANN: How would you know?

JOANIE: You can't be stealing the spotlight on Awards Night, like you used to, if your mind's way off in Toronto. Can you?

CAROL-ANN: No.

JOANIE: So you'll do that for me?

CAROL-ANN: Can we go now?

JOANIE: First, promise.

CAROL-ANN: Now?

JOANIE: It only takes a second to say, "I promise."

CAROL-ANN: I can't.

JOANIE: Why not? Something's happened, I can feel it. What's happened!

CAROL-ANN: I wasn't going to tell you yet.

> (She moves away, takes a deep breath.)

I'm going back. I'm going to live with my Dad. He wants me to.

JOANIE: *(Very shaken.)* Well, sure he does. In a couple of years, when you're through school.

CAROL-ANN: Now. In a few weeks. I wasn't going to tell you right away, but you—

JOANIE: You're not going.

CAROL-ANN: You always have to start in with all that—business!

JOANIE: You're not going!

CAROL-ANN: I am.

JOANIE: No. You're not. It's too soon.

CAROL-ANN: For what?

JOANIE: For me! I want you here.

CAROL-ANN: There's nothing here.

JOANIE: I'm here! And your Grandpa, and all your friends. People who care about you—

CAROL-ANN: Dad cares about me!

JOANIE: *(Pause.)* I know he does, Carol-Ann. But you can't go yet. You've got to stay till you're through school, I told you that before.

CAROL-ANN: I can't.

JOANIE: If you're doing this because of Dunc Carr—

CAROL-ANN: No, Mum.

JOANIE: *(Turning away.)* I can't spend another minute in this dress!

CAROL-ANN: I'm going to live with my Dad. You can't stop me if I want to go. I'm 16 now—old enough to choose. He's already got me enrolled in a school there, it's—

JOANIE: Not one more word!

CAROL-ANN: I'm going. I only came back to pack.

> *(CAROL-ANN picks up the suitcase and exits, down right. JOANIE stares after her. After a moment, she notices the paper bag, opens it again and draws out the scarf.)*

JOANIE: She's right. A dumb present, in this heat. Even the blue would've been wrong.

> *(She shoves the scarf back in the bag and exits slowly, down right, as lights fade on the station. At blackout, JOANIE's voice is heard, obviously recorded, reading her essay. Alternatively, JOANIE can step into a spotlight and recite the essay live.)*

VOICE-OVER: "Why I love Rose Coulee by Joanie Birrell.

"I love Rose Coulee because no matter where you live or how much money you've got, you can see the sky and smell the rain when it comes.

"I like being able to pick up the phone and call someone and talk ten minutes for no reason at all. And if you happen to get a wrong number, you can still talk ten minutes. Try that in the city sometime!

"I like knowing I can walk across town and say "Hi" to everyone, and greet dogs and babies by name and teenagers I've known since they were just a secret hope in their mother's heart (or a secret ambition in their father's!)

"I like just about everybody in this town, and the older they get the more I seem to like them. Especially the ladies. I like the old old ladies who call you "Dearie" and slip their cool silky hand in yours, and ask you all about your life, and never complain about theirs but only laugh it off and walk away, and leave you staring at your empty hand, that never felt so full.

"I like ..."

(The recording is shut off.)

Scene Three

(JOANIE's house; the kitchen. It is Friday, supper-time. JOANIE and CAROL-ANN are at the table.)

JOANIE: Come on now, Carol-Ann. Eat up.

CAROL-ANN: I'm not hungry.

JOANIE: Eat up anyways.

CAROL-ANN: I hate stew. I hate everything on this plate.

JOANIE: Listen to you. You should be glad to have such a meal set in front of you. Look at all the things on that plate, that were once living but gave up their lives so you could have a nice wholesome—

(CAROL-ANN shoves her plate violently aside.)

It was a joke, Carol-Ann.

(She reaches out to brush CAROL-ANN's hair out of her face.)

I haven't seen you smile once since you got home. Did you know that? Haven't heard a word about your trip, either. Or your Dad. I notice you phoned him, though, last night. Talked 17 minutes—

CAROL-ANN: Collect.

JOANIE: More than you've talked to me all day. He's doing OK, then. Is he?

CAROL-ANN: Why?

JOANIE: I'm interested, why shouldn't I be? It's only natural. He must be interested in me, too, a little. He must sometimes ask about me.

(CAROL-ANN shrugs.)

See! What sort of things does he ask? I hope you don't make me sound too awful. I hope you don't tell him everything.

CAROL-ANN: What do you mean?

JOANIE: Like, you know, that I'm into a size 12.

CAROL-ANN: He doesn't give a damn what size you wear.

JOANIE: I'm only telling you one more time—eat up!

CAROL-ANN: I don't see why we have to have stew every single Friday night. In Toronto—

JOANIE: Eat!

(CAROL-ANN pulls her plate closer, picks up a fork, plays with her food.)

Stew's two-thirty-nine a pound, Carol-Ann.

CAROL-ANN: Aren't you ever going to learn metric? The whole world knows metric!

JOANIE: If you think that's true, you should spend a day with me behind the counter at Macleods. Hardly any of our customers have bothered to figure it out.

CAROL-ANN: Dad knows metric. So does Francesca.

JOANIE: Francesca?

CAROL-ANN: His girlfriend.

(JOANIE takes this like a fist in the stomach.)

What's the matter?

JOANIE: Francesca. Whoever heard of a name like that.

(She gets herself in hand.)

What's she like, I wonder, this—Francesca. Do you mind telling me?

CAROL-ANN: She's not like Dunc Carr, that's for sure.

JOANIE: I bet she's pretty. Is she?

CAROL-ANN: I suppose.

JOANIE: Blonde?

CAROL-ANN: Auburn.

JOANIE: Long? Or short?

CAROL-ANN: Long. What else do you want to know? Curly or straight? Curly! Natural or permed? Natural.

JOANIE: I'm getting real tired of this, Carol-Ann. Every summer it's worse. You step down off that train and prance around here like everything in the place smelled like bad meat. Me especially!

CAROL-ANN: I don't see why you want to know what she's like. You're just going to hate her, anyway.

JOANIE: Maybe I want to know what I'm hating!

(A silence.)

You're right, Carol-Ann. You're completely right.

CAROL-ANN: I'll tell you what she's like. She's got a closet a mile long full of clothes, that's one thing. I mean, a mile. And she never goes anywhere, not even to the Safeway, without perfume. *(Hamming it up.)* She wouldn't even walk the dog without perfume, without perfume she feels absolutely naked!

JOANIE: Oh.

CAROL-ANN: Yeah.

JOANIE: I bet she's skinny, too.

CAROL-ANN: She looks like a model. She was a model, once, but now when
                they call her up she almost always turns them down. She's a fibre
                artist now. She's all right.

JOANIE: Where does she live, I wonder?

                (The silence says it.)

                Oh.

CAROL-ANN: Since April. I doubt if he'll marry her, though. Mum?

JOANIE: Why should he? He's already got her, doesn't he. Now he wants
                you.

                (The phone rings.)

CAROL-ANN: He does.

JOANIE: *(Rising.)* He's going to be disappointed.

                (She picks up the phone.)

                Hello. Oh, yes! Well, thanks—thank you! I don't really see what's
                so good about it, but... Did you? Well, that's—well! I'm glad to
                hear that. I will, and thanks for calling!

                (She hangs up.)

                Phil Murray, Senior. *(Very proud.)* Just wanted to say how much
                he enjoyed my essay in *The News!* *(She sits at the table.)* And what
                about you, Carol-Ann? Did you enjoy it?

CAROL-ANN: Well, sure, yeah, it was good...

JOANIE: Only?

CAROL-ANN: Only I naturally don't agree with it.

JOANIE: What part? What part don't you agree with?

CAROL-ANN: Well, I don't agree with any of it. But, I mean, it's still good.

JOANIE: Not even the part about the Men's and Boys' Store? You don't
                agree with that? Or where I talk about the old old ladies, with
                their—

CAROL-ANN: I said it's good, didn't I? Just because I don't agree with it doesn't
                mean it isn't any good, does it?

JOANIE: I don't know.

CAROL-ANN: It doesn't.

JOANIE: Well, Mr. Murray liked it, anyways. He's already bought up six
                copies to send to all his relatives at the Coast!

CAROL-ANN: I'm glad you won, Mum. Honest. The pictures were nice.

JOANIE: I bet if your Dad had written that essay, you'd have liked it well
                enough.

CAROL-ANN: But he wouldn't have. He'd never have written any of those
                things.

JOANIE: He's not from here, that's why. He only moved here when he was 17, he's never really been considered—

CAROL-ANN: He likes Toronto! Where things happen.

(JOANIE rises abruptly and exits, with the plates. She returns immediately and sits.)

JOANIE: Listen, Carol-Ann. I was upstairs this afternoon—wandering around—and it suddenly hit me what we ought to do. We ought to knock out a wall! If we knocked out one wall, we could turn half the upstairs into one huge bedroom, all for you. Windows all around. And the other thing I decided was, it's time you had your own phone. If we're real careful, and count our pennies—

(CAROL-ANN turns abruptly away.)

A year ago you were begging for your own phone.

CAROL-ANN: I won't be here.

JOANIE: You'll be here.

CAROL-ANN: I won't.

JOANIE: You will. I can't let go of you, Carol-Ann, not yet. I'd like to be able to in a way, but—

(The phone begins to ring.)

I just can't. I'm going to hang onto you with my fingernails and teeth and toenails, if I have to.

CAROL-ANN: Like you did with Dad.

JOANIE: That was different.

CAROL-ANN: And look where that got you.

JOANIE: Answer it, for heaven's sake! Take a message.

(CAROL-ANN answers the phone.)

CAROL-ANN: Hello? No, this is Carol-Ann. Not right now. OK, I'll tell her.

(She hangs up.)

Mrs. Sawchuck. *(Mimics.)* That essay just says it all!

(CAROL-ANN moves towards the door.)

JOANIE: Where are you going? Carol-Ann. Come back here and sit down!

CAROL-ANN: Why?

JOANIE: I haven't excused you yet!

(CAROL-ANN slouches back to the table and sits.)

I could stand a round of crib, later on. You?

CAROL-ANN: I don't think so.

JOANIE: Maybe what you'd like is a nice hot bath. I've got some brand-new bath oil up there that Beryl gave me. Smells like a garden everything came up in! You know Beryl. I'd be glad to fill the tub for you

CAROL-ANN: I don't want a bath, OK?

JOANIE: I tell you what, Carol-Ann. From now on, I'm going to let you go to Toronto twice a year, instead of just once.

CAROL-ANN: *(Quietly, emphatically.)* I am going—to live with—my Dad.

JOANIE: You're not.

CAROL-ANN: If I was you, and you were me, you know what I'd do? I'd say, "Go!"

JOANIE: Oh no, you wouldn't.

CAROL-ANN: I'd know it was in your own best interests.

JOANIE: Don't talk to me about your best interests! Your best interests have been my first concern since you were two inches long!

CAROL-ANN: If that was true, you'd have made Dad happy.

JOANIE: That's an awful thing to say.

CAROL-ANN: You'd have given up that damn job at Macleods! You shouldn't have taken that job in the first place. Dad had a perfectly good job—

JOANIE: With the highways, part-time! And nowhere near enough money coming in. What good was it, talking about seeing the world, with no—

CAROL-ANN: That's not the reason.

JOANIE: What?

CAROL-ANN: I've heard that story a hundred times. Maybe you've told it so often you even believe it. It's twisted, you've got it all twisted up. I know the reason you hung onto that job.

JOANIE: What's the reason then, Miss Smarty-Pants?

CAROL-ANN: It was fear. You were scared to death if he ever got out into the big wide world, you'd lose him. What a joke on you!

JOANIE: Stop it, Carol-Ann.

CAROL-ANN: All you had to do was give up that job—

JOANIE: I did give it up!

CAROL-ANN: *(Faltering.)* That's not true.

JOANIE: I gave it up, and he left without me. He left without us, Carol-Ann.

> *(CAROL-ANN moves abruptly toward the door.)*

Where are you going? Don't you go running to your Grandpa with this, do you hear me? He's sick enough as it is!

CAROL-ANN: He'll have to find out sooner or later. I'm all packed.

> *(CAROL-ANN exits, slamming the door. JOANIE sits for a moment.)*

JOANIE: What good was it—talking about seeing the world! And one day, Mr. Walker at the Macleods store, he said to me, "Joanie, you ever need to make a dollar, you come see me." So I did, and he gave me a job.

(She turns toward the door.)

The hardest part was not seeing you eight hours a day. Your Grandpa had to keep you, at the Clip'n Curl. You were underfoot, I guess, but no one ever complained—you were so cute, you were the cutest little thing.

(She turns back.)

And then one night...oh, things weren't going too good between me and your Dad, and one night he said if I didn't quit my job, he'd leave me—just like that. So the very next morning I told Mr. Walker I had to quit. And that night when I told your Dad he said, "Good." Only, about an hour later he said, "I think I'll just slip over to the Drake for a beer," and he did, and he didn't come back. I was just lucky Mr. Walker let me have my job back. But I did quit—I did!

(Blackout.)

Scene Four

	(Immediately, BERYL's voice is heard in the blackout.)
BERYL:	So he says to me: Listen here, Beryl, I know you never liked me, always wondered why. And I says, well Dunc Carr, I'll tell you. You're a sycophant.

(BERYL explodes with laughter. Lights up on JOANIE's house; the back porch. It is Sunday morning. BERYL lolls across the steps.)

The look on his face! Doesn't have a clue what it means, right? And all his buddies—all his Plains Inn buddies—standing there, looking on. So finally one of them says, what's that mean, Dunc? What's a sycophant, anyways? And he says—listen, you know what he says? Joanie?

(JOANIE appears on the other side of the screen, wearing a dressing gown.)

Says, hell, it's obvious, ain't it. Means I'm a goddamn hunk. No kidding! That's Dunc for you. More guts than a slaughterhouse. What's the matter? This is your favourite subject I'm talking about.

JOANIE:	It's never been that.
BERYL:	*(Meaning high on the list.)* It's been up there.
JOANIE:	She's not talking to me now. At all. I feel like I'm living in an empty house...
BERYL:	Come out here, Joanie. Come on.

(JOANIE steps out onto the porch.)

| JOANIE: | I should've seen it coming, Beryl. Why didn't I? If I'd just used my head! I shouldn't have let her go off to Toronto the first time, let alone twice more. I don't know why I did. |

BERYL: Never mind that. Can't do a thing about it now.

JOANIE: I never thought he'd want her full-time. Not yet. I've tried everything I can think of to stop her. Threats. Pleading. Bribery. I keep telling her she can't go…

BERYL: And?

JOANIE: She just keeps packing!

            (The phone starts ringing.)

            And that damn phone, it hasn't stopped ringing.

BERYL: Well, what do you expect? You're a celebrity now. The genuine article. Pretty soon we'll all be saying We Knew Her When. Aren't you going to answer it? Joanie?

JOANIE: What?

            (The phone stops ringing.)

BERYL: Never mind.

JOANIE: I keep getting these—awful pictures in my head…can't sleep at all and when I do I keep having dreams… My mother! I keep seeing my mother and she never speaks, you know, she never says a word or smiles. Just stands there—big frown, cold—and before I know it turns and goes. That's all—just goes. You'd think she'd say something, wouldn't you, Beryl?

BERYL: You'd better sit down, Joanie. I mean it.

JOANIE: And also, of all things. I've been dreaming about those baby clothes—you remember all those clothes I knit for Carol-Ann, before she was born, how I kept making 'em and throwing 'em out, making 'em and throwing 'em out, it nearly drove Boone crazy.

BERYL: I'm only saying it one more time. Sit, or I'll sit on you!

            (JOANIE seems to notice BERYL for the first time.)

JOANIE: What are you doing here so early?

BERYL: Couldn't sleep. Tossed and turned all night long.

            (JOANIE gives her a look.)

            Well, I rolled around a bit. Good for me. Exercise. Not the kind of bedtime exercise I prefer, and require, and deserve—God, how I deserve it. But anyway.

JOANIE: *(Sitting.)* Oh, Beryl…

BERYL: You sounded awful on the phone last night. If I could have, I'd have come right over.

JOANIE: Were they mad I called?

BERYL: What if they were. Where are they going to find another cocktail hostess who can draw men to the place like flies, huh?

JOANIE: I had to talk to someone.

BERYL: Besides, it was a slow night.

JOANIE: Maybe she'll settle back in. I keep hoping…

(CAROL-ANN appears at the screen door.)

BERYL: Well! Here she is now. Miss Toronto.

CAROL-ANN: *(Entering.)* Hello, Beryl.

BERYL: Welcome home.

CAROL-ANN: I see you've painted your house.

BERYL: What do you think? Like it?

CAROL-ANN: If you want to know what I think—

JOANIE: She noticed it right away. *(A warning.)* Didn't you, Carol-Ann?

CAROL-ANN: I couldn't help it.

JOANIE: *(Sharp.)* Fetch us a coffee, Carol-Ann. And some of that chocolate cake I made.

CAROL-ANN: At nine in the morning?

(JOANIE and BERYL both turn to glare at CAROL-ANN. CAROL-ANN exits.)

BERYL: Doesn't like it, huh.

JOANIE: Sure she does.

(BERYL gives her a look.)

Well, what if she doesn't? You like it, and if you like it, Beryl, I like it.

(The phone rings, just once.)

BERYL: *(Proudly.)* It's a real smart shade of purple.

JOANIE: It stands out, all right.

CAROL-ANN: *(At the screen door.)* It's for you.

JOANIE: Say I'm out. Well, I am out!

(CAROL-ANN disappears again.)

To top it off, he's got a girlfriend now. Live-in. Francesca—that's her name. Seems to me a person with a name like that ought to be enough for one man, but no! Francesca. Spends half her life spraying herself with perfume. Skinny as a rake, too.

BERYL: Well, that's a stroke of luck. She won't last. Those skinny ones don't. Some little calamity comes along, they drop twenty pounds and blow away, like bits of paper in the wind. They do. I read that somewhere. Or if I didn't, I should have.

(CAROL-ANN enters with a tray, which she sets down. BERYL speaks to CAROL-ANN.)

Thanks, honey. I see you got your hair cut.

CAROL-ANN: Yes. Like it?

BERYL: I like it. Wonder if your Grandpa did?

JOANIE: Beryl.

BERYL: *(To CAROL-ANN.)* Did he?

CAROL-ANN: Who knows? He pretended he didn't see it. That's what people

	do around here. You can stick something right under their noses and they'll stare right through it, if they want to.
BERYL:	*(To JOANIE.)* Don't think she's in any danger of settling back in.
CAROL-ANN:	You're right about that.
BERYL:	*(To CAROL-ANN.)* Guess you know who you're hurting, huh.
JOANIE:	Never mind, Beryl.
BERYL:	Do you?
CAROL-ANN:	I'm not doing it to hurt her.
BERYL:	Then why?
CAROL-ANN:	To help myself.
BERYL:	You've got a lifetime for that.
CAROL-ANN:	I don't want to fight with you, Beryl.
	(CAROL-ANN begins to move off.)
JOANIE:	Where are you going?
BERYL:	*(Pointedly.)* Makes you look like an angel—that haircut.
JOANIE:	Carol-Ann, I asked you a question!
CAROL-ANN:	For a walk.
JOANIE:	Where to? Not that gloomy old graveyard.
CAROL-ANN:	I like the graveyard. *(Exits.)*
JOANIE:	If I told her to go there, it's the last place you'd find her!
BERYL:	Bet you're glad I came, huh. I bet you can't believe the influence I have on that child. Aw, don't worry, kid. You'll stop her.
JOANIE:	I couldn't stop Boone, could I?
BERYL:	This is a little different.
JOANIE:	Is it?
BERYL:	Sure it is. You've got rights. In fact, know what you should do? You should call a lawyer.
JOANIE:	A lawyer! Who's going to pay for that.
BERYL:	Maybe your father…
JOANIE:	With what, his life savings?
BERYL:	Then go to the bank.
JOANIE:	Even if I did, and fought him and won, what would I have at the end? A daughter who hates me, and blames me all her life. She would, I know it. She's just like him, Beryl, she's just exactly like him, she's even…she's got the exact same look in her eye, like she's already shut the door on me and left. How do you fight that, I'd like to know. What lawyer can fight that?
BERYL:	Well then, maybe you should help her pack. Don't look at me like that. She'd be going anyway, in a few years.
JOANIE:	I can't believe I'm hearing this.
BERYL:	Sometimes it's better, if they want to go, to just say—go.

JOANIE: Being a mother, you'd know this.

BERYL: OK, I'm not a mother.

JOANIE: That's right!

BERYL: But sometimes I think maybe you—

JOANIE: Beryl, just drop it! I'm not real anxious to be told all the things I've done wrong in my life. I already know them by heart.

BERYL: I wish you could hear yourself. You won't fight and you won't give in—

JOANIE: Maybe on the outside it looks simple. *(Beginning to lose control.)* Maybe to you. Maybe it looks like I ought to—give in gracefully. But Beryl, you know, I don't—

BERYL: Joanie—

JOANIE: —know how! *(Beginning to cry.)* Never did. Can't!

BERYL: I know, kid. Never mind. Here, come and sit.

> *(JOANIE sits next to BERYL, who throws an arm across her shoulders.)*

Don't pay any attention to me. Hardly anyone ever hung around me long enough to turn into a problem. Or maybe I was the problem—but what a problem, huh! Maybe I was their problem and they solved it. And, anyway, I let them. So who am I to talk? *(Big sigh.)* I guess under the circumstances there's only one thing to do.

> *(They look at one another, then at the cake. BERYL whoops and lunges for it. She speaks with a mouthful.)*

Good! See, this is the way I look at it. No matter how bad things get, there's always chocolate cake. Chocolate brownies. Chocolate chip cookies. And men. In that order. Hopefully.

> *(After a moment.)*

There's those cats again, peeing in your sandbox. You should get rid of that sandbox.

JOANIE: I know.

BERYL: You turned everything he ever touched into something sacred.

JOANIE: I did not, Beryl.

BERYL: Ha!

JOANIE: OK—it goes.

BERYL: When?

JOANIE: First thing this fall.

BERYL: Yeah. *(With a sigh.)* Well, I guess I can go home now. I guess now that I've made you as miserable as you can possibly be, I can go home.

> *(BERYL rises.)*

JOANIE: No, Beryl, I feel better. Calmer. If I can stay calm, maybe I can think of what to do.

BERYL:	Meanwhile, I'll get this gorgeous body back where it belongs. In bed. Unless you want to tell me what happened at the station Thursday.
JOANIE:	I already told you.
BERYL:	You roughed it in. It's the details I'm waiting for. I'm waiting to be forced to sit through all the sordid details.
JOANIE:	What happened shouldn't have, that's clear.
BERYL:	*(Pause.)* At the bar last night, they were all talking about you. Were your ears burning?
JOANIE:	Who was?
BERYL:	All the boys.
JOANIE:	They were?
BERYL:	They sure were. They were all talking about your essay.
JOANIE:	*(Pleased.)* Oh.
BERYL:	*(Laughs.)* She fell for it.

(She begins to move off.)

That essay's the last thing they think of when they think of you. Believe me, I know.

(BERYL exits. Lights fade on the porch.)

VOICE-OVER:	"I like the way people are good to one another. Like when a certain person kept telling that same joke about the plugged-up bull every single morning right up until the morning he died, nobody ever let on. And if another certain person got fed up being stuck in a wheelchair and started to run around town on her ride'm lawn mower, and scatter scraps for the birds, nobody minds. Instead what they do is, they start saving up scraps to give her.

"I like the names of places here—the Dew Drop Inn and the Clip'n Curl, and I like the smell of tobacco and wool that hits you when you open the door of the Men's and Boys' Store. And I think it's a shame the way businesses are fighting to stay alive. People should remember the dollars they spend at home come back to them but the dollars they spend away…"

(The recording is shut off.)

Scene Five

(Immediately, lights up on the kitchen. About a week later. There's music playing—"When a Man Loves a Woman," sung by Percy Sledge. JOANIE, still in the dressing gown, moves to the record player and turns up the volume. CAROL-ANN is at the table, reading. JOANIE sways to the music for a moment, then turns to CAROL-ANN.)

JOANIE: Dance with me, Carol-Ann. Come on. Didn't I teach you everything you know?

CAROL-ANN: You're not dressed. You hardly ever get dressed any more.

JOANIE: I get dressed for work.

CAROL-ANN: Half the time you don't even brush your hair.

JOANIE: Please?

> (CAROL-ANN rises reluctantly and dances with her mother.)

Isn't this better? Isn't it better if we try and get along?

CAROL-ANN: All these old records. Next thing you'll be playing Cohen.

JOANIE: Sshhh. (They dance quietly for a moment.)

CAROL-ANN: I guess when it comes down to it, I'm not a very nice person any more. Am I?

JOANIE: I think maybe you'll improve with age.

CAROL-ANN: I'm not like this in Toronto. I'm not! (Timidly.) You can't catch the wind in a bottle. Don't you know that? If you do, all you end up with is air.

JOANIE: Oh, that's real pretty. I know exactly who you got that from.

CAROL-ANN: (Pulling away.) See what I mean? It's hopeless.

> (CAROL-ANN moves to the record player and turns it off.)

JOANIE: I spent my whole life aching for the mother I never had, and you want to walk away from yours.

CAROL-ANN: It's not my fault this is happening. It's not. You shouldn't have hung around here after Dad left. I don't know why you did.

JOANIE: Where was I supposed to go?

CAROL-ANN: Anywhere!

JOANIE: Anywhere. With two mouths to feed.

CAROL-ANN: I'd have cleared out, that's for sure. I'd never let myself get stuck in a place with—purple houses, and people who look right through them.

JOANIE: Oh! Now it's Beryl's house.

CAROL-ANN: That house! The whole town knows how bad it looks but to her face what do they say? That's real nice, Beryl, that really stands out.

JOANIE: You don't think people should be kind?

CAROL-ANN: I bet there isn't a purple house in the whole of Toronto!

JOANIE: Well, that's one thing we've got that they haven't!

CAROL-ANN: Dad travelled all over the world after he left here. He was restless, that's why. And I'm the same—I take after him. I used to think there was something wrong with me, walking around here with a hole inside me bigger than an ocean...

> (CAROL-ANN trails off. In an attempt to make contact, JOANIE takes CAROL-ANN's hand.)

JOANIE: Is that what you do in that gloomy old graveyard? Dream about your Dad? It's a funny place to go for that.

CAROL-ANN: *(Pulling her hand away.)* At least in the graveyard, people aren't always saying this is the place to be!

                 (A train whistle sounds, off in the distance.)

JOANIE: Listen! When I was little—I probably told you this. Whenever I heard a train whistle, know what I thought it meant?

CAROL-ANN: Someone had died.

JOANIE: I thought some soul had just slipped free of a body and gone soaring up to heaven, and the train was singing that soul goodbye! I did. Now a train whistle is one sound I can hardly stand to hear.

CAROL-ANN: Now comes heaven.

JOANIE: When I was little...I couldn't wait to die. 'Cause I knew there was a heaven and I liked the way it looked. I knew when I got there I'd run right up to Jesus where he'd be sitting in his long white dress surrounded by all those kids. And if I looked past him, I'd see lambs and lions playing together by some stream and a whole field full of wild flowers and a sky that was always perfectly blue except for a rainbow off in the distance, blinking off and on like the neon sign on the Dew Drop Inn!

CAROL-ANN: Leave it, Mum.

JOANIE: You have different ideas, when you're little. All those ideas of mine, they didn't last too long. Went walking out the door one day when I was five—

                 (CAROL-ANN strides to JOANIE and grabs her by the shoulders.)

CAROL-ANN: Listen to me! You're wasting your time, do you understand? It won't do any good!

                 (She drops her hands; she is trying not to cry.)

                 You can sluff around here all you like in that dirty old dressing gown, and talk about all that stuff, but I'm still going. I'm going! There's two kinds of people in the world, don't you know that? Some leave, and some get left. And I know what I'm not going to be!

JOANIE: Carol-Ann—

                 (CAROL-ANN runs to the screen door and exits. JOANIE stares after her, frozen. The light fades gradually to a single spot, trained on the phone. Meanwhile, the recording is heard:)

VOICE-OVER: "I like knowing in advance how a day's going to shape up. Who you'll probably see and where and how they'll look. And if they've got a new dress or something, knowing it's new and being able to say how nice it is.

                 "I guess, when it comes down to it, I like Rose Coulee because it's where I come from. And when I'm too old to know where I am anymore, all I'll have to do is glance up at the P&H Elevator at the south end of Main Street and it'll still have Rose Coulee written across the top. That's if I can still see that far!"

(End of voice-over. JOANIE is on the phone.)

JOANIE: Hello...Francesca? This is Joanie calling, this is Carol-Ann's Mum? I need to talk to Boone. Oh...no! No, I can't, I really can't, I've got to talk to him now, tonight! Isn't there any way...? I see. I guess I better do that, I guess I have to. *(She takes a deep breath.)* See, the thing is, what I phoned to say is there's no point expecting Carol-Ann because she's not coming, she's not—coming, she's going to stay here with her Mum. Well sure, of her own free will, I can't lock her up, can I? She's had a change of heart, that's all. And the reason she hasn't told Boone is she's afraid to, afraid to hurt his feelings—thinks so much of her Dad! Now this part is real important. You've got to tell him if he really cares about his daughter, now's the time to show it. Tell him that exactly. Tell him he's to write her a letter, saying he's been thinking things over and he's decided she ought to stay here till she's through school. And he's not to mention this phone call at all, ever, period. Make sure you say that. Well, maybe so—I don't know about that, all I know is people can't always get their way, even Boone...even Boone can't always get his way. You can tell him that, too, if you want. I don't care what you tell him as long as he for once in his life does the one decent thing there is to do!

(JOANIE slams down the receiver. She's very upset. Blackout.)

Scene Six

(Moonlight on the porch, a week later. It is about 9:30 p.m. CAROL-ANN sits on the steps, brushing her hair. She wears a nightgown. JOANIE enters, in a shapeless polyester uniform. She sits wearily.)

JOANIE: Oh! Feels good just to sit.

CAROL-ANN: Busy tonight?

JOANIE: Busy! I don't know what it is about night shopping. Brings 'em all out.

(She takes off her shoes, leans back.)

You're all dressed for bed. How come? You're not sick?

(She feels CAROL-ANN's forehead.)

CAROL-ANN: I've been sitting here trying to remember something.

JOANIE: What?

CAROL-ANN: That song Dad used to sing me, when I was little. That one with the knight in it, and the beggar, and the bird...

JOANIE: Cohen. *(Dropping her hand.)* It would be Cohen—it was always Cohen! If it wasn't for me, you'd have ended up being called Suzanne for sure. Or Marianne. Instead of Carol-Ann. Which is much prettier! *(Pause.)* I bet he still likes Cohen.

CAROL-ANN: Guess again.

JOANIE: Go on, he must.

CAROL-ANN: He's progressed—you know?

JOANIE: Well, I haven't. I'm like that hot pink-and-lavender wallpaper in Beryl's downstairs bathroom. I got stuck back about 1969. *(Studying CAROL-ANN's face.)* Are you missing your Dad, Carol-Ann? If you are, you can phone him. I'll treat.

CAROL-ANN: It's all right.

JOANIE: *(Too casually.)* It's kind of funny you haven't heard from him. How long has it been?

CAROL-ANN: Only a few days. He called me.

JOANIE: What'd he have to say for himself?

CAROL-ANN: *(Avoiding her eyes.)* Not much.

JOANIE: Must've said something—

CAROL-ANN: *(Abruptly.)* Mum?

JOANIE: What, Carol-Ann.

CAROL-ANN: *(Thinking better of it.)* Want me to brush your hair?

JOANIE: Would you? I'd really like that.

    (CAROL-ANN kneels behind JOANIE and begins to brush.)

    Oh—feels so good! Your Dad used to do that for me. And, before that, I could sometimes get your Grandpa to, if I talked real nice. 'Course, at that time I had hair right down to my knees. It used to make your Grandpa awful nervous, all that hair. He used to sometimes catch me prancing past the Clip 'n Curl, and he'd call me in and say—

CAROL-ANN: Tame that goddamn mane!

JOANIE: *(Laughs.)* That's your Grandpa.

CAROL-ANN: And then?

JOANIE: What are you doing, Carol-Ann, humouring me?

CAROL-ANN: Go on.

JOANIE: Well—and then. He'd threaten to sit me down right there and give me a brush-cut. A lot of good it did. The minute he turned his back, I was gone, I was down at the Dew Drop Inn, sitting in a booth with Beryl. She was real pretty in those days, you'd be surprised. The two of us, what a pair. We lived—practically lived—at the Dew Drop Inn. After supper, especially, you'd always find us there, waiting. For the farm boys! Sometimes it'd be way past dark before they'd finally roll in. *(Happily.)* First they'd line up at the front counter—pretending not to see us—a dozen of them, sometimes, and every one of them brown from the sun and strong and...hair still wet from the shower. By the time their hair was dry, they'd have managed by some coincidence to find their way to our booth! Those boys. You could smell the fresh air on them, you actually could, it was as sweet as perfume. I remember this one time, Old Mr. Kee, that ran the place—I don't know why I'm telling you this—one time as he was setting down my Coke he said to me, "Drink it down slow, Joanie," only he didn't mean the Coke—I saw that right away. I saw, if I wasn't careful, those nights at the Dew Drop Inn, with those boys—fresh air boys!—would one day, when I looked back on them, seem to have been washed away in a minute, like a drink you gulped down too fast...so you stayed thirsty. Old Mr. Kee. He was right, too. 'Cause just after that I met your Dad, and those times—those boys—were all behind me. I didn't regret it then, not at first, but I sure did—after. Sometimes, even now, I...

CAROL-ANN: What?

JOANIE: That's enough, Carol-Ann. Let me have the brush.

(JOANIE begins to brush CAROL-ANN's hair.)

CAROL-ANN: You've never told that part before.

JOANIE: I don't know why I did now. Maybe to make you think. Appreciate!

CAROL-ANN: Tell about when you first met my Dad.

JOANIE: You don't want to hear that again.

CAROL-ANN: Sure I do.

JOANIE: It's not much of a story, anyways.

CAROL-ANN: I like it. I like to try and picture it.

JOANIE: I think maybe I've told it once too often.

CAROL-ANN: Go on.

JOANIE: I had my eye on this boy—a boy called Jamie. And he definitely had his eye on me! He'd started picking me up on Sunday afternoons in his Dad's half-ton and taking me out to look at the crops. At least, that's what we told your Grandpa! It was just fun, just—innocent. It was really Jamie I was waiting for, this one night, at the Dew Drop Inn. But I looked up, all of a sudden, and there he was—your Dad—staring at me. I turned away, I remember, and then I turned back. Couldn't help it. And all the prance I know went out of my step, and the saucy look your Grandpa always grumbled about dropped right off my face. He made me different, your Dad.

CAROL-ANN: Better.

JOANIE: Or worse. Not as brave. *(Pause.)* I don't know why he picked me, I really don't. But I know why I picked him. He was burning up inside. You could feel the heat in him, like a fire just below the skin. *(Catches herself.)* He always had a book in his pocket, and almost before he said hello he'd want to give you some idea out of that book—

CAROL-ANN: He's still like that.

JOANIE: Like it was a gift, like another boy might give you flowers. He'd drive right by a whole lane full of free lilacs and never think to pick one, but he'd hand you an idea like it was something just as pretty. It was, too, usually. I thought so, anyways, but what did I know? My favourite subject at school was noon hour! Not like you, Carol-Ann.

CAROL-ANN: Are you sorry?

JOANIE: For what?

CAROL-ANN: For marrying him.

JOANIE: How could I be? I got you, didn't I?

(JOANIE hugs CAROL-ANN. Then CAROL-ANN rises and moves to the screen door.)

Carol-Ann? It was nice of you to brush my hair. Just like old times.

CAROL-ANN: Mum? Do you think you'll ever go to Toronto?

JOANIE: Don't start on that, Carol-Ann. I've been on my feet since ten this morning. *(Pause.)* Why would I?

CAROL-ANN: I don't know. For a visit.

JOANIE: Who would I visit?

CAROL-ANN: Just to see it, even.

JOANIE: Shut the door, Carol-Ann, we'll be slapping mosquitoes all night long.

CAROL-ANN: Aren't you curious?

JOANIE: I guess not. I guess I just wasn't born curious.

CAROL-ANN: I'll never understand that.

JOANIE: Why is it, I'd like to know, I've got a whole collection of faults and vices, but somehow that one always ends up being the worst!

CAROL-ANN: *(After a moment.)* Goodnight, Mum.

JOANIE: 'Night, Carol-Ann.

(CAROL-ANN exits. JOANIE leans back, closes her eyes. Deepening moonlight denotes the passage of time, about an hour. JOANIE has been asleep but wakes with a start. There's music playing very softly, off.)

Mumma? Who's out there? Is someone out there?

(DUNC enters cautiously. JOANIE rises.)

I told you, never, never—

DUNC: I know.

JOANIE: This is the last place!

DUNC: I said I know!

(JOANIE is struck by something in his manner.)

JOANIE: What's wrong?

(DUNC tries to answer, can't.)

Hang on a bit.

(She opens the screen door, leans in, listens, calls softly.)

Carol-Ann?

(She closes the door.)

It'll be all right, I guess. Till the music stops.

DUNC:	Sure?

(JOANIE sits, pats the step.)

JOANIE:	Saved you my best chair.

(DUNC sits next to her.)

What time is it, anyways?

DUNC:	Eleven, almost.
JOANIE:	I must've dropped off. Admiring the man in the moon.
DUNC:	Well, now you can admire me instead.
JOANIE:	I don't know why I'd want to do that, Dunc Carr.
DUNC:	Aren't I better than some old shadow on the moon?
JOANIE:	That old shadow keeps his distance.

(DUNC seems about to rise to the challenge, then his face clouds. He looks away. JOANIE turns her face to the moon.)

There's more up there than shadows. Did you know that? There's footprints.

DUNC:	Sure there is. Whose?
JOANIE:	The astronauts'. They haven't gone away, and they're not going. Not for a thousand years. It's true. *(Abruptly.)* You look awful.
DUNC:	They put my mother back in hospital.
JOANIE:	Oh, no. When?
DUNC:	Last night. She won't be gettin' out this time.
JOANIE:	Sure she will.
DUNC:	No. They said not.
JOANIE:	What do they know.

(In the distance, a train whistle sounds. Both turn towards the sound.)

DUNC:	Eastbound.

(He checks his watch.)

On time. They've got her hooked up to so many machines, she don't even look human. Looks more like an octopus. Looks like if she had to sneeze, she'd snap in two.

JOANIE:	*(Taking his hand.)* She'll be OK.
DUNC:	Maybe.
JOANIE:	She will.
DUNC:	*(Not easily.)* When my Dad went down…I saw him go. It was like

somebody reached out and switched off a lamp. One minute he was there, then it turned dark. This is harder.

JOANIE: I know. (*After a moment.*) My mother went a different way—very different! Did I ever tell you how? Walked out the front door one morning when I was five. Left the kettle boiling on the stove and on the kitchen table a half-finished paperback with the page she'd got to marked by a Kleenex and three—three—safety pins twisted all out of shape. Twisted up and tossed in the ashtray. Didn't take a thing with her—not even a comb. Now here's a question for you. Ever thought how nice it'd be if you could freeze time?

DUNC: Nobody can do that.

JOANIE: Somebody did—up there. That old moon's got footprints frozen right smack across its face. I like thinking about that. I like thinking about the very second that astronaut put his foot down on the moon, and how that second is frozen there. For a thousand years! What's the matter?

DUNC: You're a funny one. Well, what's the point? You can't see those footprints, anyways.

JOANIE: Doesn't matter. They're there. And that means somebody—one person—found a way to freeze a little bit of time. You wouldn't want all of it, that's for sure. A minute here and there. Maybe you wouldn't even want to freeze it, exactly—maybe just stretch it out a bit. Like, for instance, there's that minute—that split second—my mother tossed down that last safety pin. If I could've grabbed that minute, and stretched it out, something tells me she'd have never got away. (*Pause.*) Listen to me, doing all the talking...

DUNC: It's all right. I like to hear you talk.

JOANIE: You do? You never told me that.

DUNC: Can't do everything at one time, can I?

> (*He grins, glances away. A pause.*)

I see Beryl's gone and painted her house.

JOANIE: She has.

DUNC: Stands out, don't it.

JOANIE: It does.

> (*They laugh. A train whistle sounds, far away.*)

The music's stopped.

> (*Both listen, briefly.*)

DUNC: You think I better go?

JOANIE: (*Uneasily.*) I don't know. She ought to be asleep by now.

DUNC: Then how come you're so jittery?

JOANIE: It's the weather, maybe. Maybe the weather's changing.

DUNC: Maybe it's me, givin' you the jitters.

JOANIE: It's awful quiet all of a sudden. Isn't it?

DUNC: Maybe I ought to slide on over one of these nights, and get you over those jitters.

JOANIE: I don't see why it's all of sudden so quiet. I'm just going to slip upstairs and check on her.

(She rises and opens the door.)

Don't you run away, Dunc Carr, I'm not through with you yet.

(JOANIE exits. DUNC stands, lights a a cigarette, takes a few drags, stares off, stares at the sky. Suddenly, a wail of anguish sounds from within.)

DUNC: Joanie?

(JOANIE throws open the screen door and runs down the steps, carrying a letter.)

Joanie!

JOANIE: *(Wild, disoriented.)* Take me to the station!

DUNC: Why?

JOANIE: I should've known! I should've known! Take me to the station!

DUNC: What's wrong?

JOANIE: Never mind—I'll go myself!

DUNC: All right, I'll take you. But the train's gone, Joanie. You heard it. She's already been 'n gone!

(Blackout.)

Act Two

Scene One

(Lights up on the porch. It is about six weeks later—a Sunday in early October. DUNC enters, wearing a jacket over his usual clothes. He climbs the steps, knocks on the screen door, waits, knocks again, very loud and insistent. A pause, then JOANIE, in a dressing gown, appears at the door.)

JOANIE: Well, if it isn't.

DUNC: You alone?

JOANIE: No.

DUNC: I thought maybe you'd have run the gamut.

JOANIE: I managed to find one more.

DUNC: Good for you.

(He sits and makes a show of getting comfortable.)

JOANIE: What do you think you're doing?

DUNC: Waitin'.

JOANIE: For what.

DUNC: To say what I come to say.

JOANIE: Honest to God, Dunc Carr, your timing's way off!

DUNC: Why? It's Sunday. Way past noon. A reasonable time for company.

JOANIE: I've got company.

DUNC: If I remember right, this house has two doors. Either you tell him which one to use, or I will.

JOANIE: You wouldn't dare.

(DUNC gives her a look.)

Never mind about him. Just talk. Make it snappy.

DUNC: You gonna come out here, or do I have to yell at you through the screen?

JOANIE: It's freezing out there.

DUNC: No, it's not, it's fine. Indian Summer.

(JOANIE enters, sulkily.)

Now sit down. Would you please sit?

(JOANIE sits next to him on the step.)

What I come to say is simple. This has got to stop.

JOANIE:	What?
DUNC:	Don't play dumb. You got the whole town talkin' about you—I guess you know that. I guess maybe you know and don't care. In six weeks only, you got yourself a reputation as bad as any I ever heard of.
JOANIE:	I've had some fun.
DUNC:	People looked the other way, at first. They felt bad for you, that's why, because of Carol-Ann. But now they're talkin'. Christ, it's a new story every morning.
JOANIE:	Who I come home with—or don't—is no business of yours.

(She rises abruptly, steps up onto the porch. He grabs one ankle.)

DUNC:	Half of them are married, Joanie.
JOANIE:	So?
DUNC:	What's got into you? You surely don't plan on keepin' this up? Lettin' yourself get used?
JOANIE:	You got it completely backwards. They're the ones getting used—by me!

(She pulls violently away from him.)

I spent my whole life, letting people tell me when they're coming and when they're going—mostly going! Not any more. I'm the one doing the telling now. I'm saying, "Hey you, take me home!" and in the morning I'm saying, "Now clear out." And you know what? They do it. And that's not all. It feels good! It feels so damn good, I'm starting to see why everyone's been doing it to me!

DUNC:	You're not includin' me, I hope.
JOANIE:	Why not?
DUNC:	You better not be includin' me!
JOANIE:	You checked in and out of here like you owned the place, two summers in a row.
DUNC:	You didn't complain too loud. Seems to me that arrangement suited you fine!
JOANIE:	But when Carol-Ann ran off—when I could have really used you—where were you? Nowhere to be found!
DUNC:	*(Flaring.)* I had a few problems, myself, remember? Nothin' major. A mother dyin' in hospital, is all. Lyin' in that goddamn hospital—
JOANIE:	All right!
DUNC:	I didn't see you beatin' a path across town to be with me. Not too often. Not even once! Maybe I could have used a little help—did you think of that? You didn't think of anyone but Joanie!

JOANIE:	Maybe if you had a daughter that ran off and left you—
DUNC:	She's alive, isn't she? At least she's alive! You can pick up the phone and call her, you can even see her if you want to, you could go down there and see her, and maybe bring her home. Why don't you? That's what everyone's sayin'. Why doesn't she just go and fetch Carol-Ann home, instead of throwin' herself at other women's men!
JOANIE:	If you've come here to pick a fight—
DUNC:	No. I haven't come for that. *(He takes a deep breath.)* I thought maybe I could help you out.
JOANIE:	I don't know why you'd want to do that, Dunc Carr. I might get to count on it. Then where would you be.
DUNC:	Oh, for Chrissakes, Joanie—cut the crap. For once just cut the crap! Don't you think I know what goes on in your head?
JOANIE:	You don't know!
DUNC:	I know. The boys, they couldn't ever figure you out. There goes Joanie, what a waste. That's as far as they got. But I sat down and I figured you out, and I figured right 'cause you let me in. I'm talkin' about before, when nobody got in. You let me in! Why'd you do that, Joanie? Huh? Do you even know? Now look. I want you to settle down and behave yourself.
JOANIE:	Why should I?
DUNC:	'Cause you're not doin' yourself any favours!
JOANIE:	Know what I think? I think now your mother's gone, you've got your eye out for a new cook.
DUNC:	I don't need a goddamn cook.
JOANIE:	A housemaid, then. Someone to wash your smelly socks.
DUNC:	I don't remember askin' you to move in. Did I ask you that?
JOANIE:	Well, what is it, then? Scared I'm going to finish up with the boys at the Drake and start in on your buddies over at the Plains Inn? Well, guess what? I am!
	(DUNC moves as if to strike her, stops himself. After a moment, JOANIE moves closer to him.)
	Give me a kiss.
DUNC:	Jesus!
JOANIE:	Come on.
DUNC:	I just about knocked you flat. You just about made me.
JOANIE:	*(Moving closer.)* Just a little one.
DUNC:	Oh, no you don't. I'm not fallin' for that.
JOANIE:	Come on.
DUNC:	What brings this on?
JOANIE:	Please!
DUNC:	Joanie, you know…

(He glances around, then kisses her quickly.)

JOANIE: Is that the best you can do?

DUNC: There's a time and a place.

JOANIE: You didn't use to care about that.

DUNC: You didn't use to pass it around!

(She begins to turn away. He grabs her, gives her a real kiss, draws away. She smiles.)

JOANIE: You're looking good, Dunc Carr.

DUNC: *(Pleased.)* Shit.

JOANIE: I mean it. How've you kept yourself so good?

DUNC: I don't know. Ridin'.

JOANIE: Riding! You like horses, don't you? I'm glad. I like a man who's good to animals.

(DUNC kisses her again, then starts to caress her. She responds briefly, then suddenly pulls back.)

Now. Dunc Carr, get off my property.

DUNC: What? You better be kiddin'! You're kickin' me off?

JOANIE: You got it.

DUNC: After what I done?

JOANIE: What have you done!

DUNC: Come over here, all set to help you out. I was even gonna forget all that talk I been hearin'—

JOANIE: Clear out!

DUNC: If I clear out of here now, I won't be back.

JOANIE: That'll break my heart.

(She opens the door. DUNC flies up the steps, slams the door shut and pins her against the wall.)

DUNC: You don't talk to me like that! You hear me? You never talk like that to me! You! I don't know what's got into you but I'll tell you somethin'. I hardly recognize you anymore. You know what you've turned into? Garbage. You're just a piece of rotten stinkin' garbage!

JOANIE: If that's what I am, what are you? Buzzing around!

DUNC: They warned me—I didn't believe it. I should've. If she's not garbage, where's her husband? That's what they said. Been sayin' it for years. How come people keep runnin' out on her, if she's not stinkin' garbage!

(He sees this has hit home. A silence.)

I don't know why I said that. That's a lie.

(JOANIE opens the screen door.)

Joanie? I thought we had somethin'—you and me.

JOANIE: I'll tell you what we had. A big fat nothin'.

(JOANIE exits, closing the inside door. DUNC stares after her briefly, then strides off. Lights rise on the kitchen. JOANIE stands for a while with her back against the door. She moves across the kitchen and speaks to an invisible man—calmly at first, then in a screech.)

Get out. Get out, get out, get out!

(She grabs something and throws it, off, as hard as she can.)

Get out!

(She faces downstage, covers her face with her hands. Lights fade on the porch and dim on the kitchen. The phone begins to ring. It seems to ring forever. Finally she answers it.)

Hello. Who is this? I don't remember you. I still don't remember. What do you want?

(A pause; she slams down the receiver and sinks into a chair. She seems very shaken. The phone rings again. She answers it on the second ring. There's a long pause.)

I tell you what. Maybe I'll consider it, on one condition. You've got to tell me who said to call. I'm curious, that's why, I like to know who's recommended me. I don't know anyone by that name. Well, I don't. Now, what I want you to do is listen real close. What's coming up is a message for him—whoever he is— and an answer for you. Are you listening?

(She slams down the receiver but doesn't move away. The phone begins to ring again. It rings half a dozen times. Finally she reaches out and picks up the receiver.)

Come.

(She hangs up. Blackout.)

Scene Two

(Immediately, lights rise on the kitchen. It is an afternoon in November. BERYL enters, wearing a winter coat and carrying a bag of groceries.)

BERYL: Joanie? Hey, Joanie! Brought you some food. Can you hear me? Bread, eggs, milk—all the boring stuff but listen to this, kid. Mocha fudge almond ice cream! Stacks of red licorice! *And*...I raided the Catholic church tea. Are you ready for this? Strawberry angel food cake! Chocolate fudge! Peanut butter crisps! Twelve thousand calories, minimum. You may want to share this, hint, hint. Joanie? Are you deaf or what? I've got your mail too.

(She reaches in a pocket and draws out letters.)

You won't believe the letters, must be half a dozen. Can you hear me? Letters from Carol-Ann! *(Waits.)* Damn it, Joanie, I'm not going to stand here all winter, you know. I'm going to stand here about two minutes more. Then too bad for you, you'll never find out what I did last night. With handcuffs! *(Waits.)* Aw, come on, Joanie. Think I don't know how bad you feel? Can't we talk about it? We could even talk through the door, if you want. Do you want to? *(Waits.)* All right, kid. Have it your way.

(BERYL begins to exit as JOANIE enters, in a dressing gown.)

My God. What a mess.

(JOANIE moves to the table, sits. She's dishevelled and unfocussed.)

Did you hear me? I said what a mess. It's you I'm talking about.

(The phone begins to ring. JOANIE ignores it. BERYL moves to answer it.)

JOANIE:	Don't.
BERYL:	For heaven's sake, you can't just—
JOANIE:	I've done everything wrong. Everything! All my life.
BERYL:	We all make mistakes—
JOANIE:	Listen! *(Timed to the rings.)* Dumb...dumb...dumb...

(BERYL strides to the phone, picks up the receiver, slams it down.)

Dumb.

BERYL:	Joanie, for pity's sake.

(JOANIE rises, begins to move. She's very agitated.)

JOANIE:	It rings. And rings...
BERYL:	Well, people are worried about you.

(JOANIE laughs.)

They are!

JOANIE:	Don't you know? My number. It's on the wall.
BERYL:	What wall. Huh?
JOANIE:	At the Drake. In the men's john. Under V.C.
BERYL:	What?
JOANIE:	V.C. Valued Citizen. Then Joanie. Then the number. Check it out.
BERYL:	Honest to God, this town.
JOANIE:	Doesn't matter. Brought it on myself.

(JOANIE suddenly sinks into a chair.)

I get a rush of energy and then all of a sudden... Can't sleep, that's why. Can—not—sleep...without dreaming.

(BERYL stares at JOANIE for a minute, then pulls a chair close to her, sits.)

BERYL:	Joanie, look at me. Look at me! Now listen. I may not be the brightest bulb on the porch—
JOANIE:	Don't, Beryl.

BERYL:	Don't what.
JOANIE:	Say it.

(BERYL leans back in her chair. She's very upset.)

BERYL:	Aw, Joanie…
JOANIE:	Sshh. Not a word.

(Pause. BERYL rises and moves to the door.)

To anyone.

(BERYL picks up the grocery bag, throws it down next to JOANIE.)

BERYL:	Do me a favour, huh. Don't let that food rot.

(BERYL exits. Blackout.)

Scene Three

(Immediately, a pounding is heard in the blackout.)

BOONE: *(Off.)* Joanie! Joanie, open up. It's Boone.

(Lights up fast on the kitchen. It is four days later. JOANIE is at the table, in her nightgown. Her feet are bare. There's a dressing gown tossed across the other chair. She has obviously heard BOONE's voice; it has frozen her in her seat.)

Joanie?

(He knocks again.)

Come on, open up. I want to talk to you.

(JOANIE rises and backs away from the door as lights rise on the porch. BOONE stands at the door. He is dressed casually, with a leather or suede jacket.)

JOANIE:	*(Too softly to be heard.)* Go away.
BOONE:	Joanie!

(He rattles the doorknob.)

JOANIE:	*(Still too softly.)* Go away, go away!
BOONE:	I've brought Carol-Ann back. That's what you want, isn't it? Can you hear me?

(At first JOANIE is too stunned to react. Then she moves fearfully to the door.)

JOANIE:	Where is she?
BOONE:	With her grandfather.
JOANIE:	She's all right?
BOONE:	She's fine. Come on now, let me in.
JOANIE:	*(Backing away.)* No.
BOONE:	Let me in.
JOANIE:	Just send Carol-Ann home and—go away!

BOONE: I can't do that. Now open up, or I swear to God I'll pack Carol-Ann up and take her straight back to Toronto.

JOANIE: If you come in here, I might just kill you.

BOONE: I'm going to count to ten. (*BOONE starts counting.*)

JOANIE: I don't know what you want but I know it's bad, it's got to be awful bad for me!

> (*BOONE goes on counting. When he gets to 10, there's silence. JOANIE flies to the door and throws it open. Then she steps back. BOONE enters and closes the door.*)

    Oh, you smell so good. I can smell the fresh air on you!

> (*This outburst embarrasses her. At the same time, she becomes aware of her appearance. She reaches for her dressing gown, puts it on.*)

    What are you staring at? Don't you know it's rude to stare.

BOONE: Sorry.

JOANIE: If you'd just phoned ahead, given me a little warning—

BOONE: I tried.

JOANIE: Look at this place, what a mess. Look at me. If I'd known you were coming, I'd have—

BOONE: It doesn't matter, Joanie. You look about the way I expected you to.

JOANIE: Oh! Do I?

BOONE: I didn't exactly mean that.

JOANIE: I don't know what you expect. You walk in here, out of the blue—

BOONE: All right!

> (*JOANIE moves farther away from him. An awkward silence. When she begins to speak again, the tempo of her speech is erratic, suggesting a struggle to pull herself back to reality.*)

JOANIE: You're sure she's OK?

BOONE: She's fine.

JOANIE: I can't believe she's here, can't believe you are! Maybe I'm dreaming. Don't look at me like that, it's no dream, I know that. So. She's here. That would be your idea. It wouldn't be Carol-Ann's.

BOONE: She's been worried sick about you. You didn't answer her letters—

JOANIE: I did! Some of them.

BOONE: You wouldn't even pick up the phone.

JOANIE: She's mad at me.

BOONE: I'd say she's resigned—

JOANIE: She's mad.

BOONE: A little. But she's here.

JOANIE:	I've got to see her.
BOONE:	Later.
JOANIE:	I'll call her.
	(They both move to the phone.)
BOONE:	First we have to talk.
	(BOONE takes the phone away.)
JOANIE:	Talk! About what.
BOONE:	Things. But not this way. Calmly, at the table—
JOANIE:	*(Starting to wind up.)* Things!
BOONE:	*(Sinking.)* Like adults…
JOANIE:	All of a sudden we have "Things" to talk about! Well, go ahead—talk.
	(She waits, but not long.)
	You don't know where to begin, do you? You're maybe better at endings than beginnings.
BOONE:	Oh, I definitely am.
	(He grins at her for the first time. For him it is a safety valve, but for JOANIE it is like striking a match.)
JOANIE:	I want you out of here, now.
BOONE:	Joanie, for God's sake—
JOANIE:	I don't know why you had to come!
BOONE:	It wasn't by choice, believe me.
JOANIE:	You're telling me that?!
BOONE:	*(A pause.)* I couldn't just send her back alone. I had to make sure you were going to be all right.
JOANIE:	Why wouldn't I be?
BOONE:	Come on, Joanie. I know what's been going on. You've had yourself locked up in here—
JOANIE:	You got in, didn't you? So everything's fine. I'm fine! Don't I look just fine?
BOONE:	You want me to tell you how you look?
	(JOANIE falters, turns away.)
	I know you've been laid off your job—
JOANIE:	Says who?
BOONE:	Beryl.
JOANIE:	*(Stunned.)* Beryl?
BOONE:	She thinks you can still get it back. If you play your cards right.
JOANIE:	What else did Beryl tell you?
BOONE:	Everything, I think. Now listen to me. I'm going to give you some time to sort yourself out. A few days, a week if you need it. If you

can pull things together I'll leave Carol-Ann here, but only until she's through school. I want that understood.

JOANIE: Did Beryl—did she say anything about…you know, after Carol-Ann left, there, for a while the house was so quiet I could hardly breathe and I started to…

BOONE: Pick up men.

JOANIE: You didn't tell Carol-Ann.

BOONE: Why would I do that?

JOANIE: I suppose you might as well've, she's going to hear all about it now. Oh…God—oh, I see what's coming, I see exactly what's coming now. She's going to hate me worse than ever.

BOONE: She doesn't hate you, Joanie.

JOANIE: Well, she doesn't like me an awful lot. Takes after her Dad.

(She falters, moves away.)

All this company, all of a sudden. I should get dressed. Wash my hair…

BOONE: It's all gone.

JOANIE: What?

BOONE: Your hair. You cut it all off.

(JOANIE quickly reaches up, touches her hair.)

JOANIE: For a minute there, I…

(She sees BOONE watching her.)

What did you come for, anyways?

BOONE: I just told you. I want an understanding, about Carol-Ann. When she's through school, she comes to live with me. And no fuss. Did you hear me?

JOANIE: Maybe you won't want her then.

BOONE: I'll want her.

JOANIE: Maybe she's just another passing interest.

BOONE: *(Trying to stay cool.)* I'm a little phobic about permanence, I guess I can't deny that. But with Carol-Ann…it's different.

JOANIE: Is it?

BOONE: For sure.

JOANIE: *(Deadly.)* I notice you brought her back fast enough.

BOONE: *(An explosion.)* You want me to fight you for her? I'll fight. Just give the word. But this time you better fight fair!

JOANIE: I don't know what you mean.

BOONE: You sure as hell do. Now listen. Either you agree to let Carol-Ann go—gracefully!—when she's ready, or I'll take her back to Toronto—now, tonight. And no amount of blackmail is going to make me bring her back.

JOANIE: Blackmail! Blackmail, he calls it.

BOONE: There's a better word?

JOANIE: It wasn't blackmail, don't say it was!

BOONE: Call it what you like. It worked, didn't it?

JOANIE: But I never planned it. I never—

BOONE: You don't want Carol-Ann back?

JOANIE: Sure I do, of course! *(An abrupt shift.)* Oh, I can see why you've come. To throw things in my face, see me at my worst—

BOONE: Don't be ridiculous. If she was coming I had to bring her, I couldn't just let her walk in here. God knows how she would have felt.

JOANIE: No. You didn't have to bring her—in person. After all this time. There were lots of other ways to do it. So what did you come for, really?

BOONE: Really? I came for my clothes.

            (He grins. It is dead quiet for a few seconds, then JOANIE tears into him with both fists flying.)

            OK, Joanie—

            (She hits him again. He gets a firm grip on her wrists. She struggles to break away.)

            Come on, cut it out.

            (Now she starts to kick him. She continues to struggle and manages to get one hand free. She goes for his face.)

            Cut it out!

            (She loses her balance and falls. He tries to help her up but she pulls away.)

JOANIE: Don't come near me! Ever! I mean it.

BOONE: *(Very shaken.)* I get the message.

JOANIE: You better.

BOONE: Loud and clear.

JOANIE: *(Rises.)* I said if I let you in I might just kill you and I might! Why shouldn't I? You come stomping in here, cold as ice—

BOONE: I was scared to death.

JOANIE: You weren't scared.

BOONE: You'd know.

JOANIE: You weren't scared, you were mad! I could feel how mad you were clear across the room. I can still feel it! What about me? I'm the one who should be mad. I've got reasons. I've got thirteen years of reasons!

BOONE: Does this mean I don't get my clothes?

            (JOANIE grabs the closest thing to hand and hurls it at him.)

            For Pete's sake, you used to have a sense of humour. Look, maybe I should walk out the door and turn around and come in all over again. Should I? Give you time to prepare yourself. Get dressed. Comb your hair. Hang the Welcome Home Banner. *(Grins.)* All right, I was mad. I had to get mad, to get through the door. I'm not mad now.

JOANIE: Just tell me honestly why you've come.

BOONE: Why don't you believe me?

JOANIE: I know there's more.

BOONE: Maybe it was time.

JOANIE: For what?

BOONE: *(With finality.)* It was time. Anyway. People always end up coming back to the spot where their life took on its colour. They can't seem to help themselves. That's Hawthorne. Maybe he's right. *(Pause.)* Can I take off my jacket now? Or will I still have to make a run for it?

> *(He grins; she turns away. He moves to the table, removes his jacket, drapes it over a chair, and turns to face her.)*

What else?

JOANIE: I'd like to know what you think you've got to be mad about.

BOONE: Would you?

JOANIE: Yes!

BOONIE: Then I'll tell you. You've manipulated us. Backed us into a corner. There were all kinds of sensible things that you could have done—

JOANIE: Sensible!

BOONE: And you didn't do any of them.

JOANIE: Such as?

BOONE: Such as picking up the phone and calling me.

JOANIE: When?

BOONE: In August. The minute she got home. Why didn't you? How am I supposed to know what you're feeling if you won't talk to me?

JOANIE: You should've known.

BOONE: *(Incredulously.)* What?

JOANIE: How I'd feel.

BOONE: Jesus, I'm not a mind reader.

JOANIE: You were once.

BOONE: *(Emphatically.)* That's not true. *(Pause.)* I'll tell you what I knew. Every summer Carol-Ann came down, and every summer she begged to stay. Cried her heart out when I put her on the train—

JOANIE: *(Moving away.)* I won't listen to this.

BOONE: Fine.

JOANIE: I should never have let her go down there, don't know why I did!

BOONE: It was the best thing anyone ever did for me. Joanie? I mean that.

(Pause.) I'd like to finish what I started to say. Will you let me do that? Every summer she came down and we—made plans. What we'd do when she came to live there, permanently. I wanted her to know…that I wanted her there. And then finally, last summer, I thought—she'll be coming anyway in a couple of years, why not now? I thought if you didn't like the idea, you'd let me know. That was a reasonable assumption, I thought. Apparently not. Anyway, that's my side of it. Enough said.

JOANIE: I did call. Talked to that—Francesca.

BOONE: You sure did.

JOANIE: And what did you do? Ignored every word.

BOONE: Not true.

JOANIE: Told my own daughter to just—run off!

BOONE: Not true! I told her we'd better reconsider, that's what I told her. I said maybe we should wait a while. And the next thing I knew, she was on my doorstep. I'll admit it made me mad, that phone call. That you'd try to pull that kind of stunt—

JOANIE: I hate it when you talk like that.

BOONE: Like what?

JOANIE: Like I was five years old.

BOONE: *(Pause.)* I realize now I misunderstood…what was happening around here. OK? Look, maybe we should have a drink or something. Want to do that? What have you got to drink?

JOANIE: Gin.

BOONE: Gin. I'll pass. You?

JOANIE: I hardly ever drink.

BOONE: I remember why. *(He grins. Pause.)* Listen…do you ever sit down?

> *(JOANIE makes a big show of obeying him. They stare at one another.)*

I can't believe you did that to your hair. You once promised me you'd never cut it.

JOANIE: Is that what we're going to talk about? Promises?

BOONE: Good point.

> *(A silence.)*

JOANIE: You don't look a day older.

BOONE: No?

JOANIE: Well, maybe a day.

BOONE: You've changed.

JOANIE: *(Defensively.)* I've gained some weight.

BOONE: *(Grins.)* You have.

JOANIE: Just have to glance at food and it winds up on my waistline. No matter how hard I watch it. Watching my waistline—it's like watching history unfold. That's supposed to be funny, that line. It's straight out of the *Reader's Digest*.

BOONE: The last time I saw you, you were skinny as a broomstick. Nothing in your face but eyes.

JOANIE: That's enough about that.

BOONE: You had on a pair of cut-off jeans and sandals. And a little red-and-white striped top—

JOANIE: I never in my life owned a red-striped top.

BOONE: You sure as hell did.

JOANIE: Never.

BOONE: OK, make it yellow. I was standing there, at the door, and you looked up and gave me this big smile...I don't suppose you ever smile, any more.

JOANIE: I don't like talk about my weight.

BOONE: I didn't say it didn't suit you, did I? All that weight. (*Quickly.*) All right! (*Pause.*) Tell me something. Do you think there's a chance in a million we're going to be able to talk to each other without fighting?

JOANIE: I don't know. I'm trying but I can't seem to...run things. Part of me's sitting here trying to be nice and part of me's standing over there, egging me on.

BOONE: That doesn't make sense.

JOANIE: Nothing makes sense. I don't make sense, even to myself. Especially to myself. I've been locked up in this house...how long? Listening. For what I don't know. Listening to the phone ring, and stop ringing. People banging at the door, going away. Listening for something that'll make sense out of Joanie! And my mother—you remember about my mother. She keeps coming to see me now, in my dreams. Stands there—big frown! Then turns and goes, walks out the door without a word. Or a backward glance. I keep thinking maybe it's her I'm listening for, maybe she's got an answer for me if I could just come up with the right question!

(*This outburst seems to exhaust her. She sinks back against the chair.*)

BOONE: What's happening to you?

JOANIE: (*Spontaneously, fearfully.*) I don't know!

BOONE: Maybe I'd better go.

JOANIE: No!

BOONE: You look exhausted.

JOANIE: I'm fine! I'll be fine. It's just—living, you know. I think living has nearly killed me.

(*Short silence. She smiles.*)

BOONE: *(Meaning the smile.)* There it is, finally.

         (He reaches out to touch her—playfully, like he might with CAROL-ANN. She grabs his hand.)

JOANIE: I always knew someday you'd come back!

BOONE: You knew more than I did, then.

         (He tries to pull away.)

JOANIE: I never stopped thinking about it! When, and how. What I'd be doing when you got here. Not this, though—never this! I saw myself—with fresh-washed hair, and a pink dress. Remember that pink dress I had before we were married, that you liked so much? Like that, but new. A new dress, and old music playing. Cohen, maybe.

         (He tries again to pull away.)

BOONE: Joanie—

JOANIE: And you'd stand at the door for the longest time, staring at me. Nobody would move. It would be—one of those moments when time freezes... And then you'd explain everything. And then you'd stay.

         (BOONE deliberately and with some force manages to get himself free. He leaves the table.)

         What's the matter? What did I say? I know you're not going to stay—don't worry. I do know that! I just wish one thing. Wish you didn't have to look so good!

BOONE: *(After a moment.)* Joanie, you know. When I came in that door, and saw you, I wanted to...wrap my arms around you and hold you—

JOANIE: Never mind!

BOONE: —into next week.

         (A silence.)

         You're supposed to hate me, don't you know that? You get hate and I get guilt, that's the way it works. Like two people who wind up in the same accident. Different injuries—both survive.

JOANIE: *(Not a question.)* How could I hate you.

BOONE: How.

JOANIE: That's what I said—how!

BOONE: Come on, Joanie. I walked.

JOANIE: I know what you did. I just wish you'd told me why.

BOONE: *(Pause.)* Jesus.

JOANIE: *(Winding up.)* I've been running all the reasons through my head ever since—all the possible reasons. But I still—in all this time I still don't know. I mean, I know...things weren't going so good. You hated it here. Wanted me to quit my job so I did—you asked me to, and I did. Though I notice for some reason you told Carol-Ann—

BOONE: You're not going to start this.

JOANIE: And that day, the day I quit, I took Carol-Ann and waited for you, outside. And the minute I saw you I said Boone, guess what, I quit my job. And you said Good. And gave me a big hug. And kissed Carol-Ann. And then we went inside, like nothing had happened. And after supper, you said—

BOONE: I know what I said.

JOANIE: And you never came back. That's all I know.

          (A silence.)

BOONE: Well. This is a kick in the face.

JOANIE: Sometimes...sometimes I wished you'd died. I did. Couldn't help it. Maybe one of those big machines you were driving at the time rolled and crushed you. That would have ended it, at least. I'd have known where to lay the blame! And then right away I'd hate myself for wishing that. I'd think maybe you couldn't help yourself, maybe you wanted to be content—here, with me—but you just couldn't. You had that curiosity about things, that Carol-Ann's got—that I sure don't have!—and it just...carried you away. *(Winding up again.)* You ought to be able to make people content, if you ask me. You ought to be able to—sit 'em down and give 'em a dose of contentment, like cough syrup. Or else, people that are content shouldn't have to get mixed up with people that aren't. But they do—look at me! Every time I turn around, I'm sitting down at the table with someone who doesn't want to be there. Why is that? How can you enjoy a meal, when nobody else is eating! *(She begins to wind down.)* And then sometimes I turn it all around again. I think maybe if I'd just known why you had to leave, I could've let you go, all right. But I suppose not, I suppose I wouldn't have been ready. I'm never ready! I feel as if my whole life I've been crying out the same two words. Not yet! And nobody ever listens. What's wrong with me? Something's got to be awful wrong with me. Why am I never enough for people?

          (A silence.)

BOONE: What a mess. I wish to God...

          (He moves abruptly to the table but doesn't sit.)

          Listen, there's something I want you to know. After Beryl phoned, and told us what was going on here, we sat down and discussed things—Carol-Ann and I. And then I left the decision to her. And she chose to come back. Did you hear me?

JOANIE: Chose.

BOONE: I thought you'd like to know that.

          (He picks up his jacket and puts it on.)

          I'll send her right over.

JOANIE: What are you doing?

BOONE: Good question. What am I doing? I don't know. I had some notion…crazy. I've had some crazy ideas, but this…

(He moves towards the door. JOANIE flies out of her chair and beats him to the door.)

Move, Joanie.

JOANIE: No!

BOONE: Move! Please.

JOANIE: Not yet. Not like this.

BOONE: We haven't done anything but fight since I came in the door.

JOANIE: No more. Promise.

BOONE: Might as well promise not to breathe.

(BOONE moves away from her.)

You want to dig it up? All that stuff?

JOANIE: Who buried it?

(A silence.)

BOONE: This is a hell of a lot to put a guy through for a box of old clothes.

JOANIE: Clothes!

BOONE: You must have kept them, you kept the sandbox. Why on earth did you keep that sandbox?

JOANIE: It goes—first thing next spring. She never used it, anyway.

BOONE: I'm not surprised. It was a lousy sandbox.

JOANIE: It was a beautiful sandbox!

(A silence.)

BOONE: *(Like a doomed man.)* You want to know why I left? I left to save myself.

JOANIE: From what? From me?

BOONE: Yes, all right, from you.

JOANIE: If you'd talked to me, if you'd just once—

BOONE: Joanie—

JOANIE: Talked to me! Instead you shut me out. Took the best part of yourself and locked it away. Then once in a while opened the door a crack and let me peek in. Why? What did I do that was so terrible?

BOONE: Joanie…you're as open as a book, you always were. It's one of the things I liked about you.

JOANIE: Liked!

BOONE: If you're going to quibble with every word—

JOANIE: I bet Francesca just opens that door and walks right in!

BOONE: She doesn't care if she does or not, that's the difference.

(JOANIE turns away.)

You brought her up. All right—I shut you out. I admit it.

JOANIE: Why?

BOONE: Had to.

JOANIE: Why!

BOONE: I had to have some part of me you couldn't leave teeth-marks on.

JOANIE: You make me sound like—a hyena.

BOONE: You wouldn't leave me alone. I'd go out of the room, you'd follow. Sit in the car, you'd come knocking on the window. I couldn't even take a shower without you poking your nose through the curtain.

JOANIE: Because you kept talking about leaving, that's why!

BOONE: If I was five minutes late, you'd be out on the street, pacing. Pacing! Right up until the very last night. That night, Jesus! Up and down, up and down, up and down. In your cut-off jeans and your red striped top. It was red, Joanie, it's burned into the back of my skull! I turned the corner and saw you and shrank back, and then I started to count. I got to a hundred and I was still shaking.

JOANIE: You've got a funny memory of things—

BOONE: Now you listen to me. Listen! Up until that moment, I really believed that if we could just get out of here, we could make it. But I watched you that night, pacing up and down, and I knew— here or anywhere, I couldn't live with you. With you I was finished. And a little later, after supper, you flashed me a smile— like sun on water. And I walked out the door and down to the station and it happened—it just happened there was a train pulling in. And the track, you know...the next morning when I woke up the train was just taking a curve and the sun glinted on the track and even though I hated myself to the soles of my feet I knew that was it, I'd done it. I'd done the worst thing I could imagine doing...and I was still alive. I'd survived! That's a kind of freedom, you know? After that, you can do anything you have to do.

JOANIE: Just like that. So easy.

BOONE: I didn't say it was easy. I said it taught me something— something ugly, that I needed to know. That I could do what I had to do to live. *(Pause.)* But, you know...I've just realized something. There's one thing worse than having to do the worst thing you can imagine doing, and that's—

JOANIE: Words!

BOONE: Are you interested in this?

JOANIE: You could always put words together to make things sound pretty. Even ugly things. The uglier the thing, the prettier the words!

BOONE: *(Very cool.)* Why don't you just tell me what you think I ought to say to you.

JOANIE: What do you mean?

BOONE: Tell me what to say and I'll say it.

JOANIE: What if it isn't true?

BOONE: Maybe I'll say it anyway.

JOANIE: I shouldn't have left. You could say that. Shouldn't have left, don't know why I did!

BOONE: I shouldn't have left.

JOANIE: Like you mean it!

BOONE: *(An explosion.)* Jesus, Joanie, you're a beggar for punishment! All right. You want it, you're going to get it. You say I should have talked to you. About what. Diapers? Dishes? How to make jelly out of goddamn rotten crabapples? What the neighbors were doing, or weren't doing, or would have done if it hadn't rained, snowed, stormed— *(Violently:)* Who cares! Even so, I tried. Hopeless. You wouldn't read a book, not even when I begged you to. An idea, you know—an idea, believe it or not, can be— fucking exciting, a thing of beauty, but you have to share it or it dries up. And you—

JOANIE: I tried. I did! But if I didn't catch on right away you'd turn so cold—

BOONE: That's right. Right again! I didn't have the patience. I couldn't wait, I couldn't sit still. Because the world—oh boy, the world. Is a remarkable place, you know? We were going to see it together, that was the deal—

JOANIE: Before Carol-Ann.

BOONE: Carol-Ann was just a better excuse.

JOANIE: No. I'd have left.

BOONE: You weren't going anywhere.

JOANIE: I quit my job.

BOONE: You weren't going anywhere, and neither was I—if you had to kill yourself to stop me.

JOANIE: *(Turning away.)* I was sleepwalking.

BOONE: Sure, sleepwalking. On the highway, in the middle of the night. In the traffic lane.

JOANIE: *(Softly.)* I couldn't stand the thought of losing you!

BOONE: I don't know what I was supposed to do. Drive a bulldozer the rest of my life. Go drinking with the boys at the Drake. Dig myself a hole you could pretty up with curtains and wallpaper... You wanted a cocoon. You wanted me to wrap myself around you like a second skin, you thought that would keep you safe, but it wouldn't have. Even if I'd stayed. I never had that kind of power. *(Pause.)* Is that enough? Or do you want more?

JOANIE: I guess you never loved me.

BOONE: Are you listening to me? Have you even heard a word I've said?

JOANIE:	Did you.
BOONE:	Maybe I didn't love you enough.
JOANIE:	You'd say that, you'd have to say that!
BOONE:	All right, I loved you too much. What do you want to hear?
JOANIE:	*(Vehemently.)* I want to hear there's something in the world—one thing only—that doesn't change!
BOONE:	Everything changes.
JOANIE:	On earth. Only on earth! I can see where I belong.
	(A silence.)
BOONE:	Christ, what am I doing? I didn't come here to do this. *(Pause.)* I don't know what you want. If it's answers, I'll give you answers. Have I been happy since I left here? Rarely. Sorry I left? Often. Would I come back? Never. *(Pause.)* Can I justify what I did? Sometimes. Forgive myself? No. But I'm trying. I think maybe if I can be a decent father to Carol-Ann…
	(His speech trails off. He turns to look at her; she seems lost in a world of her own. He moves to the door and opens it.)
JOANIE:	What about the fire? You used to say I was on fire, said we both were. Said it was a wonder the sheets didn't catch. What about that?
BOONE:	*(Without turning.)* I remember that.
JOANIE:	Well?
BOONE:	Fires go out.
	(He goes out, closes the door, strides down the steps. He hesitates, then exits, down left. Blackout.)

Scene Four

	(Music begins to play in the darkness. Lights up slow on the kitchen and porch. It is the next day. JOANIE sits in front of an old trunk, going through the contents. BERYL, in a coat, climbs the steps, crosses the porch and stops at the kitchen door.)
BERYL:	Joanie? It's me. Came to see you.
JOANIE:	Hello, Beryl.
	(BERYL enters the kitchen.)
BERYL:	What are you doing?
JOANIE:	Going through some old things.
BERYL:	You're not mad at me, I hope. Couldn't just sit by and do nothing, you know.
JOANIE:	I know.
	(BERYL takes off her coat, throws it across a chair.)
BERYL:	Whole town's buzzing—guess that won't surprise you. *(Mimics.)*

Is that Boone? My God, that's Boone. What's Boone doing here? (*In her normal voice.*) 'Course, nobody's asking him, or Carol-Ann. Or me, come to think of it. They just run around asking each other.

(*JOANIE pulls an infant's sweater from the trunk.*)

That's an opening I just gave you. You can pour it all out any time now.

(*JOANIE spreads the sweater across her knees.*)

JOANIE: Look, Beryl. How small.

BERYL: Aw. She was the cutest little thing.

JOANIE: She was, wasn't she?

(*BERYL starts to rummage in the trunk. JOANIE studies the sweater.*)

I think I might let her go, Beryl.

BERYL: Say that again.

JOANIE: Might let her go back with her Dad.

BERYL: Who put that idea in your head? Carol-Ann?

JOANIE: My mother. (*She laughs, a little self-consciously.*) It's true. You know all those dreams I've been having—I told you about them. Well, all of a sudden, it started to make sense. Her coming back, after all this time. When I needed her most. Why would she do that, Beryl?

BERYL: Beats me.

JOANIE: To show me they never pull free. That's what I think. If I'm dreaming about my mother now, when I haven't seen her in thirty years, don't even know if she's alive—it's because I can't let go of her. So how's Carol-Ann ever going to let go of me? She can't. Even if I send her away, I've got her. Only she doesn't know it yet. She'll be mad as hell when she figures it out.

(*BERYL pulls something outrageous from the trunk.*)

BERYL: Would you look at this? Oh my God.

(*BERYL puts it on.*)

JOANIE: People kept saying I was wrong, but I wasn't wrong. Some things do last. Anyways, one thing I know of does.

(*BERYL is pulling something else from the trunk.*)

BERYL: Ha! Get a load of this.

(*JOANIE puts the sweater back in the trunk, then pulls out a dress— the kind worn to high school graduations in the late 60s.*)

JOANIE: You remember this dress, don't you, Beryl?

BERYL: Could I forget?

JOANIE: This dress. I picked it out of the Simpson-Sears catalogue, sight unseen. Wore it one night only—to my high school grad dance. With a pink corsage that Boone gave me. A month after I wore it,

I was married. And a month after that, I was pregnant with Carol-Ann. And you know what, Beryl? I never liked it one bit— this dress. I really hated it, to tell the truth.

(*JOANIE begins to rip the dress apart.*)

BERYL: Stop that.

(*JOANIE goes on ripping.*)

Well, hell, if you feel that way…

(*BERYL begins to rip the dress, too. They start to laugh. When the dress is in pieces, scattered around the room, both suddenly fall silent. In the distance a train whistle sounds.*)

JOANIE: Listen! You ever been on a train, Beryl?

BERYL: Sure. Once.

JOANIE: I haven't. Or a plane, either. (*With a flash of the old style.*) I have sometimes gotten into a truck. Some people will tell you I've gotten into a few trucks I should've stayed out of.

BERYL: Amen to that.

JOANIE: (*Sinking into a chair.*) Oh, Beryl. What am I going to do?

BERYL: When?

JOANIE: For the rest of my life.

BERYL: (*After a moment.*) Well, kid, I tell you what. We'll do it together. I'll go down with you to the Macleods and we'll get you your job back. That's the first thing. Then we'll go to the Drake and celebrate. (*Quickly.*) No, we won't. We'll go on a diet, that's what we'll do.

JOANIE: Lose weight.

BERYL: Get in shape. Run two miles every morning. Stay out of bars.

JOANIE: Stay out of trucks.

BERYL: Stay out of trouble. Yeah. We'll be good girls. We did it once, we can do it again. (*Long pause.*) But can we stand it?

(*BERYL falls silent. JOANIE moves to the record player, turns up the music. It is Sam Cooke singing "Bring It On Home To Me."*)

JOANIE: Beryl? Dance with me?

(*BERYL turns to JOANIE and, with overdone formality, draws her onto "the floor." They dance briefly, then JOANIE spins away on her own. Lights down to a spotlight on JOANIE, dancing. Blackout.*)

The End

Calenture

A desire to seek your own destruction

BRUCE MCMANUS

Calenture: n. tropical delirium of sailors who think the sea is green fields. [F. f. Sp. calentura fever (calentar be hot f. Rom. * calentare f. L. calere be warm)]

Production Information

Calenture was first produced by the Popular Theatre Alliance of Manitoba at the Gas Station Theatre in Winnipeg, Manitoba, in January of 1992 with the following cast:

NEWS .... Mariam Bernstein
DAN .... Mark Hellman
SHELAGH .... Megan McArton
DENISE .... Lora Schroeder
PRINCE .... Gene Pyrz
DAVID .... David Warburton

Directed by Margo Charlton
Music by Cathy Nostady
Set Design by Rejean Labrie
Costume Design by Joan Murphy
Lighting Design by John Gilmore
Stage Manager: Katie R. East

About the Staging

The play is set in the present.

We begin the play at the end of our story with David offering his version of events that brought him to his current situation, incarcerated in a facility for the criminally insane perhaps, or out on the street and speaking from his favourite seat in a donut shop.

Subsequent scenes recall the past and David's understanding of the development of his malady.

Because of the rapid changes between events and the non-realistic nature of much of the stage action, all of the actors were on stage for the entire play, waiting to participate in David's journey and offering their own versions of events.

David sometimes speaks to the audience, and sometimes to the other characters. The News and the Prince sometimes speak to the audience, in the context of a newscast or political speech.

Dan, Denise and Shelagh sometimes speak as if they are conscious of the audience's evaluation of their behaviour.

A video screen is prominent and used where indicated.

The scenes are set in David and Shelagh's kitchen, a casino, a donut shop, an unspecified room in a government building, a park, and one scene in each of the couples' bedrooms.

A large table sits prominently on stage, with decks of cards on its surface.

About the Text

Dialogue in italics indicates a song.
Dialogue in small capital letters indicates video.

Act One

(The PRINCE, sometimes called MAITRE D', sits comfortably in the TV studio. The NEWS, sometimes playing the entertainer, or singer or trainer, hovers near the PRINCE. DENISE wears a hooded robe, SHELAGH wears a donut shop waitress uniform, and DAN a garish suit. DAVID wears a lab coat. It is Halloween. The characters might wear these costumes throughout the play, or add to or change these costumes as the play progresses. The couples are playing cards.)

DAVID: *(To the audience.)* The word mad means two things. In my case they mean the same thing, and that is sufficient to understand my story. *(DAVID stays in his area.)*

DAN: I don't understand David. For me there is sufficient life in every circumstance and situation I don't need to make change around me. In the air I'm a bird, in the seas a fish. I don't need to change and I hope you will understand this and get well. This is life. Goodbye.

    (DAN moves to the table and takes up the cards.)

DENISE: Get well if you choose. I'm amazed, astounded that you did anything. When and how did things make a logical chain that suggested action? Throw a coin in the air. Heads or tails you might think. It might never come down at all. It might rise forever until someone… Look. A new star. You see…goodbye David.

    (DENISE joins DAN.)

SHELAGH: Listen. Everyone who has had love will know the tenderness between us made our hearts soar. Everyone who has lost love knows it can disappear with no warning. But you let love slip and fall and walked away, too afraid to pick it up, too afraid to turn back and watch it wither. I don't hate you.

    (SHELAGH joins the others. DAN deals four hands of cards.)

DAVID: *(To the audience.)* I have a past. I have no future. I traded that for a present. Once upon a time we all felt good. Once upon a time we had a wonderful life.

NEWS: AND ON THE LIGHTER SIDE OF THE NEWS, ALAN STEVENS, 81, HAS RETURNED HIS PENSION TO THE GOVERNMENT. SAID MR. STEVENS, A VETERAN: "WE HAVE TO DO SOMETHING ABOUT THAT DAMN DEFICIT."

DAN:	Are we playing cards or not playing cards?
	(DAVID joins the others at the table.)
NEWS:	WE'RE VERY FORTUNATE TO HAVE WITH US TONIGHT THE PRIME MINISTER. IT'S GOOD TO SEE YOU AGAIN SIR.
PRINCE:	(NEWS is on video, PRINCE is not.) Thank you for being seen with me.
NEWS:	(Leaves the video and enters on stage.) Why do you say that sir?
PRINCE:	Hard things have to be done in this country. I'm doing them.
SHELAGH:	(Laying down a card.) I have to do this.
DAVID:	(DAVID takes the trick.) That's 13 hearts and the queen.
NEWS:	I want to ask you about the economy sir.
DAN:	How come you always win?
PRINCE:	I fear for my country.
NEWS:	Once upon a time there was a kingdom whose people were rich and happy.
DAVID:	Bio-pharmaceuticals?
PRINCE:	Was that enough?
DAN:	Electronics, miniaturization.
NEWS:	It was enough for most people, they were happy.
DENISE:	They make living organisms to cure living organisms.
DAN:	There's nothing sick about organisms.
NEWS:	No. some of the people wanted more and more.
PRINCE:	It was impossible to always have more.
DENISE:	In 15 years they won't make computers…they'll grow them.
NEWS:	The people did not know, and they did not want to know that the spell that made the kingdom happy and great also proscribed the limits of their wealth. They could not have more.
SHELAGH:	The only real investment is love.
PRINCE:	And there was the dragon of course. And the dragon which was kept from the kingdom by the magic spell that gave only some of the people more and more, lurked at the edge of the kingdom waiting, waiting hungrily, saliva dripping from its fangs… And when the people's greed for more and more broke down the magic spell protecting the kingdom…
DAN:	Listen to this shit.
	(The four turn and listen to the interview.)
PRINCE:	The dragon leapt into the opening, devouring the people in the sauce of their own greed, ignoring the cries of their own repentance, for dragons like money, have no conscience, until everyone was gone. Everyone. The satisfied, those who complained without forethought, and no one had enough. Of anything.

SHELAGH:	Everything has to be good versus evil.
DENISE:	Evil can't be measured.
DAN:	Evil is anything I don't like.
NEWS:	Thank you Mr. Prime Minister, we will return in a moment.
	(NEWS and PRINCE watch the others through the following.)
DENISE:	It's the only real growth in the stock market. Bio-pharmaceuticals and thievery. Plain old thievery is still booming.
SHELAGH:	Evil is a growth industry. Fundamentalist Christians rent themselves out in the third world as demon killers.
DAN:	Come on.
SHELAGH:	The kids I work with. They don't believe in mental illness...they believe in possession.
DAN:	Possession is eight points of the law. Right David?
DAVID:	It simplifies your life. Some bad thing happens to you...blame the devil.
DENISE:	I believe in evil.
DAVID:	I believe that for every drop of rain that falls...a babe is born.
DENISE:	*(Rising.)* Time to go.
SHELAGH:	*(Rising.)* They're singing.
DAVID:	*(Rising.)* I've got a big day tomorrow.
DAN:	Electronics. Miniaturization. I saw a tiny little stereo the other day, you wouldn't believe it...
DAVID:	I thought you were giving up gadgets.
DAN:	I want it. I'm going to buy it.
DENISE:	Save your money, Dan.
DAN:	You got the amplifier, a double tape player, the disc player and speakers and it's like this size. *(Showing the size with his hands.)*
SHELAGH:	Well you have to have it then.
DAN:	Exactly.
DENISE:	*(Stands in front of DAN, thrusting her breasts at him. By gestures she shows that DAN's hands are approximating the size and shape of breasts.)* So you understand why you want it Dan?
SHELAGH:	Men.
DAN:	Wow. That's marketing.
DAVID:	You're giving him ideas, Denise.
DAN:	Yes...yes you're giving me ideas. *(He embraces DENISE.)*
DAVID:	Who wants a drink?
DENISE:	Nope it's home for us.
SHELAGH:	I love your costume...
DAN:	And I love your costume, Dave. Dave...?

DAVID: All right I love your costume.

DAN: Boy you're slow . But... *(Hugging.)* Dave. But...you're my friend.

DENISE: Maudlin alert.

DAN: No really...we're so lucky...that we...

DENISE: ...have to go home.

DAN: ...no...that...

DAVID: That we didn't have one more drink.

DAN: No really...listen, we're really lucky and I've got to tell you...I mean I got to say... you know.

SHELAGH: Happy Halloween.

DAN: Right.

NEWS: I WON'T KEEP YOU SIR, BUT TELL US WHAT YOU THINK OF THAT WONDERFUL GESTURE BY MISTER STEVENS...THAT WONDERFUL GENTLEMAN WHO SURRENDERED HIS PENSION TO THE GOVERNMENT.

PRINCE: HE'S A WONDERFUL MAN WHO'S BET ON CANADA, A WONDERFUL MAN WHO UNDERSTANDS THE REALITIES OF THE GLOBAL ECONOMY...I'M GOING TO CALL HIM AND TELL HIM THAT HE IS THE KIND OF MAN WHO MADE CANADA WHAT IT IS TODAY.

NEWS: THANK YOU MR. PRIME MINISTER.

PRINCE: YOU'RE WELCOME, SANDRA.

NEWS: JUST REMEMBER NOW... *(On stage.)* ...when the going gets tough the tough get going. Now every Canadian is tough...don't you doubt it for a second. I'm Sandra and my job is to entertain you, make you feel the Happiness inside and let it loose. *(Sings.)*

How can you lose in a world like this
Our children walk with their heads held high
How can you lose in a world like this
A grandmother smiles as she takes a kiss
How can you lose in a world like this
How can you lose in a world like this
Every one of us free to talk
How can you lose in a world like this
Each time we choose, you know you can't miss
How can you lose in a world like this
I can't lose in a world like this
Don't poison me with your whining hiss
I don't need you're crying that you can't cope
I know you can't lose in a world like this
'Cause I've got grit and I've got hope
'Cause I can't lose in a world like this

    (The PRINCE smiles.)

DAN: Hurry up...we're going to miss it.

DAVID: Relax...

NEWS: They're at the post.

DAN: Here we go…

NEWS: And from the gate, it's Blue Moon moving to the inside…

DAN: Good start.

DAVID: That's our horse is it?

DAN: That's it.

NEWS: …Blue moon, Arkwright, Simple Steel, Gorgeous, and Time Bought bringing up the rear…

DAN: Still good…

NEWS: …at the turn, it's still Blue Moon, Simple Steel moving on the outside, then Arkwright, Gorgeous and Time Bought.

DAVID: He's OK.

DAN: Anything can happen…anything.

NEWS: Moving on the outside it's Arkwright, Gorgeous, Simple Steel and dropping behind…Time Bought.

DAN: I don't like that.

NEWS: Blue Moon by half a length, then Simple Steel, and Arkwright nose to nose.

DAN: Blue Moon….Blue Moon…

NEWS: And we're into the stretch, Blue Moon, then Arkwright head to head with… Simple Steel, now Simple Steel moving up…

DAN: I don't like it . I don't like it.

NEWS: …it's Simple Steel and Blue Moon side by side.

DAN: Come on Blue Moon.

NEWS: …and Arkwright moving up…

DAN: No.

NEWS: Blue Moon is fading, fading and at the wire…

DAN: No. Photo finish. What did you see, Dave? What do you think?

DAVID: I saw horses.

DAN: I think it was Blue Moon.

DAVID: OK. I'm sure it was…

NEWS: Ladies and gentlemen, the official results of the Harry Nelken Stakes. First…

DAN: Blue Moon…

NEWS: Arkwright.

            (DENISE and SHELAGH with lottery tickets in their hands. The newscaster is now the person watching those 6-49 balls drop into their slots.)

DAN: I could have run faster than that.

DAVID: That's what makes horse races.

NEWS: WELCOME TO WEDNESDAY'S DRAWING, AND WE'RE JUST ABOUT READY FOR OUR FIRST NUMBER.

DAN:	Betting makes horse races.
DAVID:	Don't tell me…
NEWS:	AND OUR FIRST NUMBER IS 44, 44.
DENISE:	Nope.
SHELAGH:	Nope.
DAN:	Five hundred dollars…down the tubes.
DAVID:	Ohh man.
NEWS:	AND OUR SECOND NUMBER IS 31, 31.
SHELAGH:	I was going to pick thirty-one.
DENISE:	Another great number I don't have.
DAN:	You have to have something down Dave, it makes your brain alive, it's the juice.
DAVID:	Barenaked entrepreneurialism.
NEWS:	AND OUR THIRD NUMBER IS 14, 14.
DAN:	Right.
SHELAGH:	I got my period at 14.
DENISE:	We shouldn't have missed that one.
DAVID:	But Jesus, five hundred dollars.
DAN:	Well…I might have been just as involved for 300 bucks…
DAVID:	You're a real hairy-chested, risk-taking…
NEWS:	OUR FOURTH NUMBER IS 26.
DAVID:	…world-class…
SHELAGH:	My best year…
DAVID:	Uhuhuhuhuhhhhh
DAN:	Competitive?
DAVID:	Right.
DAN:	I'm an asshole.
	(The men now "join" the women and listen in silence to the last two numbers drawn.)
NEWS:	OUR FIFTH NUMBER IS 39, 39. AND FINALLY…OUR LAST NUMBER IS 20, 20, 20.
DENISE:	She picked all the wrong numbers.
SHELAGH:	We're not rich. Again.
	(The four people are now conscious of each other. They are sitting at the table, DAN shuffling cards.)
SHELAGH:	You did the right thing.
	(DENISE looks appealingly to DAN.)
DAN:	*(After a moment.)* I guess you did.
SHELAGH:	Of course you did.

DENISE: I didn't mind some of the things. I joined up at a bad time. I was probably the only person in the world who willingly signed onto a sinking ship. The stock market was sinking and I was a trainee. The ship was going down and I was the cabin boy.

DAVID: Actually things are looking better.

DENISE: If you're a computer they're better. If you're a multinational they're better. Some days I wished I was a computer.

DAN: I don't get it.

DENISE: I've never been a good liar.

DAN: Everybody has to lie sometime.

DAVID: Leaving your answering machine on, monitoring calls.

DAN: The cheque is in the mail.

DENISE: Not like that. I...we...everybody there had to pretend we understood what was happening, that we could anticipate what would happen...that we could offer benefits to people based on what was going to happen but...

DAVID: Just don't blame computers, OK?

DENISE: Why not?

SHELAGH: Yeah, why not?

DAN: Stupid.

DAVID: They're only tools...

DENISE: No.

DAVID: Of course they are.

DENISE: They make decisions, David...

DAVID: Listen...

DENISE: No. They make decisions, sell, and they issue directives, buy, and they make decisions, sell...and we watch while they sell or buy.

DAVID: It's a good program.

DENISE: I'm not a program.

DAVID: *(Condescending.)* Well...

DENISE: It was a lie. If you have this much money *(Spreading her arms wide.)* you can benefit, if you have this much money *(Bringing her hands together.)* you can only lose...

SHELAGH: Then it's a good thing you quit.

DAVID: You have to believe in what you're doing.

DENISE: Belief isn't the problem. I'm at one end of a golden chain, one end is spiked into the universe of knowledge created by heartless little MBA's and the other end is my computer. In binary I hear, yes no yes no...I have an analog mind. I know justice. Yes no yes no...the system is created to interpret the knowledge that was created to serve the system, yes no yes no. When the stock market collapsed twice and we couldn't stop it, the second time even.

Well there is no difference between some Greek shepherd before Christ looking for signs of Greek gods and me, at one end of that golden chain.

SHELAGH: So it's not belief...

DENISE: I believe in my computer program, I have no faith.

DAN: *(Reaching in his pocket to take out his wallet.)* Well you know what?

DENISE: I'm sorry Dan. I had to quit.

DAN: We're a one-income family.

DENISE: What if I started believing in...revelation? Prediction, information, decisions...

DAN: We're a one-income family...you know what that means...

DAVID: *(Ignoring DAN.)* I'm sorry about this Denise, but you're getting carried away.

SHELAGH: You think so.

DAVID: It's time to downsize. It's time...

DAN: I said...you know what that means.

DAVID: We've been living beyond our means, and you're taking it personally. Computers aren't the problem...

DAN: Stop. We're a one-income family. For the first time since I was a kid, *(He takes out his credit cards and scissors and cuts them up.)* goodbye Visa, goodbye Mastercard... I'm afraid.

(DAN steps onto the chair and onto the table and screams.)

NEWS: *(Is now a busker in a park.)*

We got hard times
We sure have got the blues
All these bad signs mean
Hard times and the blues
If we got hard times
I want hard times with you

(SHELAGH and DAVID walk hand-in-hand in the park.)

SHELAGH: A great day, Dave. Thanks.

DAVID: You can't stay in that office all day, not on a day like this.

SHELAGH: There's so much work to do. I feel guilty.

DAVID: Shhh. The poor and the hopeless can get along without you for a while...

SHELAGH: There's so many more of them...

DAVID: You and I first. This time.

NEWS: *No rent is hard times*
Hard times and the blues
I see UIC long lines
While I got news for you
Hey baby,
Hard, hard times is what I want from you

DAVID: *(To the audience.)* In a sunny day, we swam as one, me, the sun and the brightest, Shelagh…three lights.

SHELAGH: I love you, you know.

DAVID: I know.

NEWS: *You give me hard times*
I'll give you the best
The very kill-the-blues best times
The best times, a rest time
From hard times
We all got the blues
So we got hard times
While I've got news baby those hard times
They're my times with you

SHELAGH: I love you.

(SHELAGH joins DENISE at the table. DAVID, alone, throws 10 dollars in front of the singer, sharing his happiness.)

NEWS: *(Near the end of the newscast.)* …THE PRIME MINISTER EMPHATICALLY DENIED THE CLC CLAIM THAT THE FREE TRADE AGREEMENT HAS COST CANADA FOUR HUNDRED THOUSAND JOBS THIS YEAR.

PRINCE: UHH, IT'S FAIR TO SAY THAT THIS REPORT IS, TO USE AN ECONOMIST'S TERM, A LOAD OF CRAP. DO YOU REALLY THINK I WOULD DO ANYTHING TO HURT THIS COUNTRY?

NEWS: AND ON THE LIGHTER SIDE, TEN YEAR OLD DAVID MILIGAN WAS ASKED WHAT WE ALL COULD DO TO SAVE THE ENVIRONMENT: HIS ANSWER: REDUCE THE DEFICIT. SMART BOY. AND THAT'S THE NEWS.

(DAN and DENISE and SHELAGH sit at the kitchen table playing cards.)

DAVID: *(To the audience.)* Have you stood outside at the beginning of a gentle rain, looking up at a barely grey sky and saying I am not wet, I am not wet. When you go inside at last, your shoes are full of water.

(DAVID joins the others.)

SHELAGH: It's getting bitter out there.

DAVID: It will be good for us in the long run.

SHELAGH: You really believe that?

DAVID: *(To DAN.)* Get a doctor.

DAN: Is her heart bleeding again?

SHELAGH: Very funny.

DAN: So…there's these two socialists eh?

DAVID: Did you hear the one about the socialist who won the lottery?

SHELAGH: I know this one…the punch line is…the Prime Minister is a prick?

DENISE: So…two socialists…?

DAN: *(Laughing.)* Two socialists. That's a good one, Denise.

DENISE:	You've got to get a sense of humour, Dan.
DAN:	No...I didn't hear about the socialist who won the lottery.
DAVID:	That's it. Nobody has heard of one...
SHELAGH:	I said, the Prime Minister is a prick. Well...I didn't say it was a really funny joke.
DAN:	All right. Let's concentrate. We're playing cards. Chicago, a fascinating game...
DENISE:	Aren't you a little bit worried?
DAVID:	There's not too many people in the country who can do what I do.
SHELAGH:	Computers. The future.
DAN:	Chicago.
DAVID:	And we'll always need social workers, Shelagh.
SHELAGH:	Especially now.
DAVID:	We're OK.
DAN:	All right then, Winnipeg low. A three card game with the lowest hand the winner...a terrific game for the old Peg.
DENISE:	Dan got laid off today.
DAN:	The way you play is, three cards, one draw and the loser wins.
DAVID:	I'm sorry.
DAN:	Ahhh, well.
SHELAGH:	What happened?
DAN:	They're sending everything to the States. Everything...concept to printing, processing, video transfer. The agency is just a post office. Don't worry about it. A salesman always has a job. *(DAN looks to the other three, all of whom are reluctant to speak.)* Come on you guys. It's no problem, I'm telling you. I've worked since I was 15. There's no problem. OK, no problem.
	(DAVID and SHELAGH move to the part of the stage that is their bedroom. Likewise DAN and DENISE. The PRINCE, who will become the MAITRE D', sets green felt on the table, turning it into a blackjack table. The NEWS addresses the audience.)
NEWS:	...AND SO THE RECESSION CONTINUES. AND ON THE LIGHTER SIDE, A SEVEN YEAR OLD HAS SENT HIS LIFE SAVINGS, 23 DOLLARS, TO THE PRIME MINISTER. SAID SEVEN-YEAR-OLD DAVID, "WE HAVE TO DO SOMETHING ABOUT THE DEFICIT. AND THAT'S THE NEWS.
	(The couples are in their respective bedrooms, dressing to go to the casino. The MAITRE D' stands ready at the card table.)
SHELAGH:	They need a good time.
DAVID:	I don't know Shelagh...it could be pretty depressing.
DAN:	We've planned it for months.
DENISE:	We planned it when we had money.

DAN: Don't worry about it.

SHELAGH: I think we should have bought them an anniversary present.

DAVID: I'll buy them a drink.

SHELAGH: David! They're our best friends.

DAVID: Well...not exactly.

DAN: All right. Let's forget everything tonight.

DENISE: Let's not spend too much.

SHELAGH: David...

DAVID: We haven't seen them in months.

SHELAGH: You don't want to see them. *(Pause.)* What happened to Dan isn't catching you know.

DAN: You have to spend money to make money. Let's win the rent.

                (The two couples are at the casino. The MAITRE D' stands ready.)

                Hi, guys.

SHELAGH: This is lovely.

DENISE: They spend money in here.

DAVID: They make money in here.

DAN: Let's get some of that money.

                (DAN heads to the table and sits. The others reluctantly follow. To the MAITRE D'.)

                Blackjack.

MAITRE D':   We have everything here sir. Closed circuit racing, table games and of course, cards.

DAN: Blackjack!

MAITRE D':   Of course. *(He deals.)* So the ladies and gentlemen wish to play?

DENISE: Maybe not.

SHELAGH: All right.

DAVID: I guess so.

                (The dealer lays out cards for SHELAGH and DAVID.)

MAITRE D':   Would this be a celebration tonight?

DENISE: Our wedding anniversary.

MAITRE D':   Our?

DENISE: *(Touching DAN.)* I'm with the good-looking one.

MAITRE D':   Lucky in love.

DAN: And cards. A card, please.

MAITRE D':   *(The MAITRE D' delivers.)* Sir?

DAN: Another card.

                (The MAITRE D' delivers.)

                Stay.

MAITRE D':   Eighteen showing. *(To SHELAGH.)* And you, Madame?
SHELAGH: Yes.

    (The MAITRE D' delivers. SHELAGH is over 21.)

    Whoops.

MAITRE D':   I'm sorry. And you, sir?
DAVID: OK.
MAITRE D':   *(Dealing another card to DAVID.)* We see 18 top. Another, sir?
DAVID: That's fine.
DAN: I'll take another card.
MAITRE D':   But…
DAN: I need another card…

    (The MAITRE D' delivers.)

DENISE: You bust, buddy.

    (The MAITRE D' picks up DAN's hand.)

DAN: It's up to you, David.
MAITRE D':   *(Dealing himself cards, the MAITRE D' breaks himself.)* The gentleman is a winner.
SHELAGH: I could come to like this a lot.
DAN: I could come to hate this a lot.
DENISE: All right, let's go take a look at this place.
DAN: Don't be ridiculous. Another hand, please.

    (MAITRE D' begins to deal.)

    Why don't you play, Denise?

DENISE: I'd rather stand in a field and rip up 20-dollar bills.
DAN: I'd like a card please. A good card.

    (MAITRE D' deals. DAN goes bust.)

    Shit…

    (The MAITRE D' deals to SHELAGH.)

SHELAGH: Oh…ummm. Let me think here.
DENISE: *(Looking at SHELAGH's hand.)* Your chances of drawing a card smaller than four or a four are about one in three. You have to take a card.
SHELAGH: All right…

    (The MAITRE D' deals. SHELAGH goes bust.)

DAN: It's you and me, Shelagh.
SHELAGH: I could just rip up 20-dollar bills.
DENISE: It would be faster.
MAITRE D':   *(To DAVID.)* And you, sir?
DAVID: I'm fine.

MAITRE D':   *(The MAITRE D' deals to himself.)* I have to take another card, sir. *(He does so and goes over.)* A winner.

DAN: I'm glad we're friends, buddy.

DENISE: Had enough?

DAN: One more, OK?

DENISE: Sure...we're rich.

SHELAGH: I'm out.

DAN: You got to keep playing, David. You're a winner.

DAVID: All right.

> *(The MAITRE D' deals and DAVID gets two cards the same allowing him to double.)*

DAN: Look at this. He can't lose. Go for it, Dave.

DAVID: All right.

> *(The MAITRE D' deals him another card and again DAVID can double.)*

DAN: This is impossible.

DAVID: Now what?

DAN: Go for it.

> *(DAVID nods to the MAITRE D' who again deals the same card.)*

DENISE: That happens about six hundred times in two and a half million.

SHELAGH: So what does it mean?

DENISE: It means the evening is on you.

DAN: We can pay our own way. *(To the MAITRE D'.)* Finish him off.

MAITRE D':   *(MAITRE D' deals to DAVID.)* (1st card) Blackjack. (2nd card) Blackjack. (3rd card) Blackjack. And... (4th card) Blackjack again. *(Paying off DAVID.)* Again, sir?

DAVID: You got to know when to fold 'em.

DAN: No...you got to play again.

DAVID: Forget it.

DAN: All right...play with me... Just one hand.

> *(An uncomfortable DAVID nods. To the MAITRE D'.)*

Cards...

> *(The MAITRE D' deals as DAN holds on to DAVID's arm.)*

Again. Again.

> *(DAN goes bust. Shaken.)*

OK.

> *(DAVID removes DAN's hand.)*

DENISE: *(Embracing DAN.)* Lucky at love.

DAN: I'm not a loser you know.

SHELAGH: Don't even think it.

DENISE:	It's time for a break there.
DAN:	Maybe.
MAITRE D':	You can't win if you don't play, sir.
	(Silence. The NEWS enters. The four turn to watch.)
NEWS:	*(As the entertainer.)* I'm just here to do a couple of songs for you right now...but I'll be back later tonight, when all you winners have your pockets full...but right now, I'm going to answer that age-old question... How do you tell the sheep from the goats: *(Up-tempo, happy.)*

How do you know a sheep from a goat
Throw them in the river
And the sheep won't float
He's gone and the goat goes on
How do you know a goat from a sheep
Put your hand in their pockets
And the sheep won't bleat
He's gone and the goat is gone
You can always tell a winner
With a wallet in his hands
The goat's got the money and the sheep's got the bill
How do you know a sheep from a goat
Throw them in the river
And the sheep won't float
He's gone and the goat is gone
How do you know...bad bad luck

	Thank you, and I'll see you all later. *(Exits.)*
DAN:	*(To the other three.)* I'm not going to take that personally.
SHELAGH:	Baaa.
DENISE:	Let's move on.
DAN:	Listen...I want to beat this table.
DENISE:	No.
DAN:	She has an intuition.
DENISE:	I know math.
DAN:	And you can't walk away, David. You're winning.
MAITRE D':	He's right. I've never seen such good luck, sir. It's immaterial to me whether you stay or go. I don't benefit, believe me. I've never seen such authority at a table before. It would be my pleasure to serve you.
DAVID:	Well... *(Looking at SHELAGH.)* What do you think?
SHELAGH:	I think I'm the only one that sleeps with you.
	(This remark has no effect on MAITRE D' who keeps smiling.)
DAVID:	I guess no.
DAN:	Well...look. why don't you guys head over to the bar and I'll join you, later.

DENISE: But not much later?

DAN: You know me.

            (DENISE, SHELAGH and DAVID all look at each other.)

TOGETHER: Hmmmm!

            (DAN turns to the MAITRE D' who deals him hand after hand. DAN always goes bust and the only dialogue through out is the MAITRE D' saying "no" as DAN loses.)

NEWS: ...THE MINISTER OF HEALTH ASSURED THE COMMITTEE THAT MEDICARE WAS SIMPLY NOT AT RISK.

            (DENISE watches the newscast.)

            ...AND IN FINANCIAL NEWS TODAY, THE CHIEF INVESTMENT OFFICER OF RICHARDSON/GREENSHIELD SAID TODAY WHEN ASKED ABOUT THE STOCK MARKET: PEOPLE MAKE MONEY BY...MAKING MONEY. IT'S SIMPLE.

            (DAVID and SHELAGH are in their bedroom area. The news turns to them.)

            ...AND ON THE BRIGHT SIDE, ROBERT BLACK, THE MAN WHO STOOD ON THE ROADSIDE HOLDING A SIGN SAYING "I WILL WORK FOR FOOD," HAS FOUND A JOB. MR. BLACK WILL BE WORKING AT A LOCAL FAST FOOD OUTLET. AND THAT'S THE NEWS. GOOD NIGHT.

SHELAGH: What do you call someone who works for food?

DAVID: Desperate?

SHELAGH: Think for a second.

DAVID: Dan. I think we could call him Dan.

SHELAGH: We should have got him out of there.

DAVID: He's an adult.

SHELAGH: A desperate adult. How much did you win tonight?

DAVID: How would you like to go to Mexico this Christmas?

SHELAGH: Let's give it to Dan and Denise.

DAVID: You're overreacting, Shelagh.

SHELAGH: They need it.

DAVID: If they get in trouble, and I don't think they're in trouble, they know where to come.

SHELAGH: Where?

DAVID: Lay off will you? I'm not a monster.

SHELAGH: What do you call someone who works for food?

DAVID: All right what do you call someone who works for food?

SHELAGH: A slave. *(Exits.)*

DAVID: Jesus Christ, Shelagh. Take a pill. It's not that bad. Shelagh...

DAN: *(Exhausted, asks the MAITRE D':)* Don't suppose I could cash a cheque here?

MAITRE D': Well sir, our general policy is, and I'm sure you'll understand, is that we only cash cheques from people who have money.

DAN:	It takes money to make money. Or cash a cheque.
MAITRE D':	Let me give you a tip… Pull up your socks, man.
DAN:	Every disaster is an opportunity.
MAITRE D':	Right.
DAN:	I believe that.

(DAVID stands alone. The MAITRE D' gathers the table cloth and gambling paraphernalia. He is apparently speaking to DAN.)

MAITRE D':	You better believe it.
DAVID:	*(Standing by himself, speaking to someone unseen.)* My wife just got laid off.
MAITRE D':	Listen buddy, what's the one thing you'll always have?
DAVID:	Look, isn't there something I can do here?
MAITRE D':	Yourself.
DAN:	Right.
MAITRE D':	That's what you have to sell.
DAN:	Myself.
DAVID:	Can I clean out my office?
MAITRE D':	You've had a bit of bad luck but you've still got yourself.
DAVID:	Do you have any idea when I might be called back?
DAN:	It's always been me against the world.
MAITRE D':	Life's a gamble.
DAN:	I got myself.
DAVID:	…You don't know when I might get called back.
SHELAGH:	David…over here.

(SHELAGH, DENISE and DAVID are in a doughnut shop, SHELAGH's new place of employment.)

I'm glad you came. *(She hands DAVID a paper.)* Everyone reads a paper in a doughnut shop. It's not so bad…cheer up. It's just like the office. You always said donut shops are the psychiatric service centres of our age. It's not going to kill me to do some honest work. I could get called back, you could find something. David…you have to pull yourself together.

DENISE:	You know of course that the unemployment rate is near 10 percent. There are 10 number cards in every suit. You naturally think first of the four other cards in each suit, starting with the face cards…this suggests 13 percent and of course there is the ace. That's significant.
SHELAGH:	I told you. It's just like work.

(Enter DAN/SALESMAN.)

DAVID:	What did she mean…the ace is significant?
SHELAGH:	Unemployment rate. January first.
DAN:	I sold the idea of death to young people.

SHELAGH: ...Insurance.

DAN: I sold pollution to asthmatics...

SHELAGH: Car sales.

DAN: I sold drugs to cops...

SHELAGH: Cigarettes.

DAN: By god, I sold doughnuts in intensive care, lifetime subscriptions to cancer patients, hope to the hopeless and the idea of wealth to the poor. I can sell you.

              (Enter JOB CREATION TRAINER/NEWS.)

SHELAGH: See...I'm still a social worker.

NEWS: Work...is not a right. It's a privilege. *(Pausing for effect.)* The marketplace does not owe you a living. *(Pause.)* In this time of global restructuring, the competitive nation has competitive workers. *(Significant pause.)* How do we become competitive? *(Pause.)* How do we become competitive?

DAN: *(Hesitantly.)* We sell ourselves.

NEWS: Yes, yes, yes, yes, now: You have no jobs. *(Waiting for a response.)* You have no jobs.

              (SHELAGH looks skeptical. The other three look hesitant.)

              Don't fight it. Don't flee into denial. You have no jobs.

THE THREE: We have no jobs.

NEWS: Good. You are here to learn how to get a job. You had jobs, and you lost them. Now...in some cases, some of you may have lost your job through no fault of your own.

DAN: ...through no fault of our own.

NEWS: *(Giving DAN a brief nod of approval.)* The economy is changing, and you didn't change with it. It's not necessarily your fault. But...the bottom line is...and we pay attention to the bottom line here... You have no jobs.

SHELAGH: This is ridiculous.

NEWS: *(With sympathy.)* Then you have a job?

SHELAGH: Yes.

NEWS: Tell me...tell me how lucky you are.

SHELAGH: I work in a doughnut shop.

NEWS: Darling, darling, really. Don't you want a real job, a real pay-your-own-way, hold-your-head-up, have-your-own-desk job?

SHELAGH: Well...of course.

NEWS: The kind of job you had and lost, through negligence perhaps, or maybe through no fault of your own?

              (SHELAGH nods.)

              Then pay attention! If you lost a job, you don't know everything do you? A job isn't a set of keys you know!

SHELAGH: *(Cowed.)* It just seems…ridiculous.

NEWS: We are going to do lots of things that will seem ridiculous. This isn't a perfect situation. I know some of you are required to attend these sessions in order to collect benefits or to qualify for programs that might get you a job. It's not the best situation to learn in, but it's our situation. Everything we do, we do for a reason. We start with confidence because when we lose our job, confidence goes with it. I've been where you are and believe me it's much better here. Now. How do we regain our competitiveness?

SHELAGH: We sell ourselves?

NEWS: Good! *(Exits.)*

               (The three look at each other repeating "we sell ourselves" as they gather around the table.)

DAN: *(Dealing cards to DAVID.)* You're looking a little glum there, buddy.

SHELAGH: Hey. *(Looking to DAVID.)* Hey. Smile. C'mon, smile.

DAVID: *(Tries a smile.)*

SHELAGH: Whoa. Don't smile.

DAN: Your shorts too tight?

DAVID: Deal.

DAN: I'm dealing and we're playing.

DENISE: Five card, one draw, nothing wild.

DAN: We've been married too long.

DENISE: That can change.

DAN: This game is a test of the soul.

DENISE: It's a test for fools.

DAN: Then it's a test I can always pass.

SHELAGH: No bickering.

DENISE: OK.

DAN: Shelagh?

SHELAGH: *(To DAVID.)* Would you lend me a quarter?

DAVID: Do I have to smile?

SHELAGH: You don't have to do anything you don't want to.

DAVID: Great. *(Throws SHELAGH a quarter ungraciously.)*

SHELAGH: You don't have to clean, or cook, or smile…

DAVID: …or listen…

SHELAGH: …or make love…

DAN: Are we going to fight? Are we? Because if we're going to fight, I just want to mention, Denise, you're putting on a lot of weight.

DENISE: Just trying to keep up with you, darling.

DAN:	So…are we going to fight?
SHELAGH:	*(To DAVID.)* I'm sorry.
DAVID:	Me too.
DAN:	No problemo, buddy. Cut some slack here… The first four weeks I didn't work, well…I could barely work, you know what I mean? It happens. So forget it.
DENISE:	Six weeks.
DAN:	Denise, stay with the peacemakers, OK.
DENISE:	You're doing it again, Dan.
DAN:	What?
DENISE:	Being half honest.
DAN:	I wasn't confessing for God's sake.
DENISE:	Well if you're going to be honest, be honest…
DAN:	And it wasn't six weeks.
DAVID:	Stop this.
DENISE:	…that's all I'm saying. Be honest.
DAVID:	We don't need to know each other's sex lives.
DAN:	Well, it sounds like you don't have one.
	(Silence for a second.)
	How many cards?
SHELAGH:	Two.
DAN:	Two. *(Dealing.)* Denise?
DENISE:	Five.
DAN:	You can't do that! You can't have a sure thing. That's why they call it gambling.
DENISE:	Five.
DAN:	You're out.
DENISE:	Dan.
DAN:	You're out. Dave?
DAVID:	One.
DAN:	Get this guy. One. You're drawing to a straight? OK… *(Dealing.)* and the winner takes two. *(Dealing.)* All right now. Shelagh, are you betting?
SHELAGH:	I'm out.
DAN:	It's just you and me, Dave. One to one.
DAVID:	A quarter.
DAN:	And I'll raise you 50.
DAVID:	All right…and a quarter.
DAN:	You don't have a straight and you know it. What are the odds, Denise?

DENISE: He's a lucky guy.

DAN: Never mind that. What are the odds?

DENISE: Be nice, Dan.

DAN: Five bucks. Five big ones.

DENISE: He's got about 10 thousand chances in two and one half million.

DAN: Let's see your balls, Dave.

DAVID: Five bucks? It used to be five hundred.

DAN: Ten. Let's make it 10. Limits off. Just you and me. We're just the same. I got the same job you got. None. Just the same.

DENISE: Dan...

DAN: No...the big man, you know how it was, you know how it's been. Well we're just the same now. 5Fifty. Let's pay the groceries. Fifty bucks.

DENISE: No way Dan.

DAVID: Fifty.

SHELAGH: Forget it.

DAN: We're just getting out of piker land here...a hundred bucks. Money talks, bullshit walks. A hundred.

SHELAGH: No. No way.

DENISE: Assholes.

DAN: You got a hundred bucks worth of belief in yourself? Dave, are you a loser, man?

            (After a moment DAVID nods.)

            My man, now we're playing, we're really playing.

DENISE: I want to talk to you.

DAN: No, this is the way it is, right Dave? The turn of the cards, the real thing...everything you are...on the turn of the card. This is fucking life. *(He turns over his cards.)* Full house.

            (Everyone looks at DAVID. After a moment he lays his hand down.)

            Yes. A winner.

            (DAVID leaves the others.)

DAN: Where you going? Dave...come back here. Dave...

            (Picks up and looks at DAVID's hand, he studies it perplexed.)

            Fuck. There's nothing here...nothing...not a pair, not an ace. Nothing. Nothing at all. Dave...

            (DAN follows DAVID out.)

DENISE: Dan.

            (The PRINCE and NEWS in the TV studio.)

PRINCE: Of course I'm going to be attacked and I hate it. I want to be loved and if I can't be loved I want to be respected. This is a very sick economy. I'm going to cure it. A surgeon has the better job. He

	cuts out cancer and the cancer doesn't complain. No one marches in support of cancer cells.
NEWS:	But people aren't cancer cells.
PRINCE:	Of course not. I'm saying I'm the surgeon and I'm making this country strong. It has to be done. I know people are hurt. I see it. I can feel it. If I could make this transition easier for them I would. I have too much courage to quit what has to be done, and too much doubt, too much feeling to take satisfaction. I'm a monster now. A hundred years from now I'll be a hero. You know what I've done for this country? Don't answer that. It's rhetorical. A bad habit, a politician's bad habit. I'll tell you what I've done. I've stopped people in this country from making jokes about people on welfare. You know why? *(Waving off the question.)* Everyone is so close to being on welfare. That's why! No. I'm not happy. I dream of warmer times, the sun shines and we are healed.

(DAVID sits alone, picks up the newspaper and calls offstage.)

DAVID:	The recession is over.
SHELAGH:	What?
DAVID:	"The Council of Canadian Business leaders announced today that the recession is over."
SHELAGH:	I can't hear you.
DAVID:	"There are no guarantees," said Richard MacConnel, executive Director of the Council, "but if I were a betting man, the odds show that the tide has turned." It's over.
SHELAGH:	*(Enters amorously, looking at DAVID.)* You could never take your eyes off me not so long ago. Did I dream that?
DAVID:	"The average wage of a Mexican worker is 69 cents an hour."
SHELAGH:	When you looked at me, something tight would loosen itself inside me.
DAVID:	"Bank profits are up 15 percent over last year."
SHELAGH:	You didn't even have to touch me.
DAVID:	"There are now 20 percent more millionaires in Canada than 20 years ago."
SHELAGH:	*(Touching herself in memory.)* You didn't even have to touch me.
DAVID:	"Personal bankruptcies are up 30 percent." That can't be.
SHELAGH:	*(Exits to the bedroom calling in a matter-of-fact voice.)* I left some money for you on the dresser.

(Enter DENISE and DAN wearing their Halloween costumes. They are moving to sit in the area reserved for the job creation seminars.)

DENISE:	*(Emphatically.)* The gods dispose.
DAN:	*(Quietly.)* Luck.

(DENISE glares at DAN for a moment then returns to waiting. SHELAGH enters from bedroom wearing her restaurant uniform.)

SHELAGH:	What were you mumbling?

DAVID: *(Confused for a second.)* The recession is over?

SHELAGH: Again?

DAVID: The third time this year.

SHELAGH: Don't be discouraged.

DAVID: No. *(Pause.)* Were you just here a moment ago? Talking about making love.

SHELAGH: *(Worried.)* It's just anxiety, you'll get it back. Think positively, OK?

> *(SHELAGH walks to DAVID and impulsively puts her arm around him.)*

OK?

DAVID: *(Uncomfortable, removes SHELAGH's arm.)* OK.

SHELAGH: *(Offended but understanding, steps back.)* I left some money for you on the dresser.

DAVID: You said that.

SHELAGH: Well...sorry to repeat myself.

DAVID: I didn't mean anything.

SHELAGH: *(After a moment accepting this.)* Positive, OK? Don't forget to buy a lottery ticket. *(Smiling broadly.)* Dave...? We'll get lucky again, and I mean that both ways, big guy.

> *(SHELAGH exits to sit with DAN and DENISE at the job creation seminar.)*

PRINCE: I think, I want to be cautious here, but I think the tide has turned.

> *(NEWS enters the job creation area.)*

...It's been hard. I know it's been hard, but Canadians must understand how lucky we are to live in a country that is a great country that will become even greater.

> *(The NEWS turns to the job seminar people and claps out a rhythm. When they catch on they all keep clapping, underscoring the following.)*

(Nearly chanting:) How will it become greater? We will improve our productivity. We will increase our international competitiveness. We will eliminate the deficit, we will reduce our debt. We will become the best, the most productive, the richest country in the world.

> *(The clapping becomes applause.)*

And every Canadian will have a job.

> *(The PRINCE enters and approaches DAVID.)*

Even you, David. *(Pause.)* My father, David. My father. Well, you know he worked in the mines. Everybody knows that. Not very many people know he was unemployed most of his life...the mines, eh? Resource-based economies have destroyed a lot of people in this country. Work is just sometimes. My father was one of the people who was a victim of the market prices of copper. A bystander, side-swiped by the economy. I loved that man. And he tested my love everyday. What do you do in a mining town when you're not working? Do you know, Dave? You sit in the bar and drink, and you become this blustery drunken stage Irishman, always with a quip and a joke and a winking eye, a smile that becomes a grimace and nodding and winking, pretending you know something...because you don't know anything at all...people with power know things, not unemployed Irishmen in mining town bars. No, you don't know anything. And after a while that man I loved couldn't work unless you call sitting in the bar from morning to night work. I used to like that stuff myself, you know. It wasn't the first drink, or the second drink...only the goddamn teetotalers believe that, right, David? No, it was the third, and the fourth...and the fifth...why not the sixth... *(With enthusiasm.)* ...ahh the sixth and the sliding down, down, deep in the warm moist consciousness of the barely conscious...but I don't do that anymore. I quit, you know. I guess you know. Everyone knows. My father. Well...I hated everything that made him a failure. I hated the rich, and the companies, and the companies that exploited the companies that exploited my father and made him a failure. *(Pause.)* You know what's wrong with that thinking, David? I'll tell you. Do you hate the sea? When you stand at the rail and look at the endlessness of the ocean, its infinite power...nothing is as powerful as the sea...there's nothing there but its power...no consciousness, no will. You know if you leap in you will die. The sea will not save you and it will not kill you. It is. It calls you, but it doesn't know your name. You cannot hate the sea. *(Standing.)* And you know in your heart, we all know in our hearts that our failure in life is our own failure. No one makes us a failure. We know that in our hearts.

NEWS: And Mr. Prime Minister, what do you do to relax?

PRINCE: *(The PRINCE picks up a fishing rod and turns smiling to the NEWS.)* I fish. *(He casts with the rod.)* I love to fish.

(He casts again and hooks DAVID. As he speaks he moves the rod as if playing with a fish. DAVID responds.)

The urge of a man to conquer. All human beings want to conquer...well... I find I am deeply satisfied by taking from the earth, from the sea in this case, the thing it does not want to surrender. Crack the crust of the earth for gold, scrape the crust of the earth for cellulose...take from the brooding will-less dangerous sea... It's life.

(The PRINCE pulls hard and the hook comes out of DAVID's mouth.)

You can lean over the rail then, you see, and look at the ocean, and when it calls to you... *(This is not what he wanted to say. He stops.)* Well I fish, Sandra. I'm a Canadian after all. *(Chuckling.)* Some people think that I'm not Canadian enough, but I fish.

NEWS: Thank you, Mr. Prime Minister.

PRINCE: And thank you, Sandra, and thank you, Canada, and thank you, David.

          (DAVID sits groggily.)

NEWS: And who has something to share with us today?

          (No one responds immediately. DAVID sits at the table, part of the group, but operating in two realities.)

          Come on people. You don't find a job by being timid.

          (SHELAGH, DAN and DENISE stare resentfully at NEWS. The PRINCE is amused. NEWS prompts the reluctant participants.)

          Henry David Littlejohn, born dirt poor to a family of 15, left home at the age of six. Despite a minimal education, he taught himself Greek and Latin. Dan...?

DAN: He yearned for a vocation as a teacher and a scholar, but the needs of his family, his sense of responsibility and the great economic adjustment of the thirties made it impossible.

PRINCE: That's the sad part. It always gets me.

NEWS: Lovely.

SHELAGH: Beatrice Turnbull was raised in a middle class home. Her upbringing, she said, in no way prepared her for the appalling poverty she found on most Northern reserves.

NEWS: Good for you, Shelagh.

PRINCE: All gamblers keep something back for the end of the night, David. The make-up bet.

NEWS: Denise?

DENISE: The basis of a truly rational society is founded on a market system that operates without prejudice on information freely circulated and uhhhhhhhhh... *(DENISE can't finish her part.)*

NEWS: That's all right dear, we'll get back to you.

PRINCE: *(To DAVID.)* Every gambler has something left. They think no one else knows that. Something left to redeem them. It's pathetic really.

SHELAGH: *(To DAN and DENISE as if they are alone at the kitchen table:)* Beatrice Turnbull. She was the most condescending biddy to ever hit the north. They hated her up there.

DAN: *(As if at the kitchen table:)* Littlejohn was the biggest thief since the CPR. The guy started out selling a cure for syphilis. It was cod liver oil.

DENISE: Information doesn't circulate freely. Air doesn't circulate freely.

PRINCE: *(To DAVID.)* This is called "keeping their integrity" I think. *(Laughs.)*

NEWS: *(As in a training session:)* Shelagh?

SHELAGH: *(In the session.)* Beatrice was devastated by the suffering she saw, and she returned to the cities of the south, begging money and foods, first from house to house, later from the corporate giants of Canada.

DAN: With diligence and native intelligence he carved out an empire unequalled in Canadian commercial history. He was famous for his philanthropy. *(Without pause to SHELAGH.)* The guy stashed his money in so-called philanthropic trusts, untaxable. His mother died impoverished in a nursing home.

SHELAGH: *(To DENISE and DAN.)* There are no children called Beatrice on any northern reserve, I can tell you that.

DENISE: *(To SHELAGH and DAN.)* You could be fired for freely circulating information.

NEWS: Denise, would you like to try again?

DENISE: *(Straight.)* Hickory, dicory, dock, the mouse ran up the clock.

NEWS: Close enough. Now!

(Everyone turns and looks at DAVID. It's his turn.)

PRINCE: You got to leave them that make-up bet, David. Integrity. *(He laughs.)*

SHELAGH: *(In the persona of BEATRICE, to DAVID.)* Well you can't just let them live like that.

DAN: *(In the persona of Littlejohn, to DAVID.)* I got where I am by plain hard work.

PRINCE: The truth is David, Dan doesn't want to look at his Mercedes and think, there are the broken bones of the poor. And it's a wonderful country when Shelagh can feel superior to someone every day and get paid for it.

DENISE: Information is nothing without a master.

SHELAGH: Compassion is nothing without power.

DAN: The strong survive , that's the way it is.

NEWS: Wonderful.

PRINCE: We want you with us, David.

DAN: Get well buddy, we're right behind you.

PRINCE: Lay down your burden.

SHELAGH: I have a new beginning, a new life.

PRINCE: Give up the fight.

DAN: I want you to look forward.

PRINCE: Feel the power.

DENISE: We'll come to visit you whenever we can.

PRINCE: Bathe in the light.

NEWS: *(Sings.) Lay down your burden*
Give up the fight
Feel the power
Bathe in the light

> *Of telling all fools*
> *Their end is in sight*
> *The word is calling*
> *It welcomes us all*
> *Those who have power will*
> *Welcome us all*
> *Lay down your burden*
> *Give up the fight*
> *Feel the power*
> *Bathe in the light*
> *Where the real is real*
> *And idealists fall*
> *The word is calling*
> *It welcomes us all*
> *Those who have power*
> *Will welcome us all*

> *(As the NEWS sings, DENISE, DAN and SHELAGH rise, singing along, and exit. NEWS thoughtfully walks the stage, humming to herself, then approaching DAVID from behind, hugs him.)*

NEWS: How are you, big guy?

DAVID: Oh...I guess I'm as good as I can be.

NEWS: Ahhh. *(Hugs him again.)* Hugs help don't they?

DAVID: I'd rather have a job.

NEWS: Look. It's hard. It's hard for everybody. But everybody else is making an effort.

DAVID: I try.

NEWS: You don't try.

DAVID: I'm trying.

NEWS: You're trying to piss people off is what you're doing.

DAVID: I'm good at what I do.

NEWS: Yes, you are. You're brilliant. You've got the most outstanding resume I've ever seen. But you got one thing wrong.

DAVID: What?

NEWS: You are the best at what you *used* to do.

DAVID: *(After a moment.)* You're right.

NEWS: You bet I'm right. *(Pause.)* How much do you want to bet I'm right. You want to bet a job? Because that's the stakes, David. A job.

DAVID: I want a job.

NEWS: David, you're a knowledge worker. Do you know what that means?

DAVID: I'm a knowledge worker.

NEWS: The future of Canada. That simple. *(Pause.)* The table is full. The cards are dealt, and dealt and dealt and one by one those who cannot compete fall away. Who is left? The person who believes. Who is that person? The future of Canada. You. You are the future of Canada. That's power, David. Now David. Show me your power face.

DAVID: I don't know what you mean.

NEWS: Get big. stand up...that's right, stand up. Right. Do you feel power? You should feel power because you are...?

DAVID: The future of Canada.

NEWS: Yes, the future of Canada. Show that in your face. Put on the face of power, show the mask that says this job is mine...you cannot refuse me this job. That's right, that's the bottom line face, I am power. Do you want to get bigger, David? Do you? Play with it, get up on that table, dominate, David. *(DAVID gets up on the table.)* Look down on those below you, who can no longer compete, who do not understand, who do not risk...all the little ones as they shrink and disappear. You're a winner David, a winner. *(Pause.)* You got it. That's it. *(Pause.)* Now who are you?

DAVID: I'm the future of Canada. I'm a winner.

(NEWS begins singing "O Canada." DAVID joins in. Enter SHELAGH in her donut shop costume carrying an artificial Christmas tree. She sees DAVID standing on the table singing O Canada. NEWS exits.)

SHELAGH: David? David?

DAVID: *(Finds himself standing on the table.)* No...I can't explain this.

SHELAGH: Don't bother. I'm getting used to you...how do you like it? *(Referring to the Christmas tree.)*

(As DAVID stands down, SHELAGH places the tree.)

DAVID: We always get a real one.

SHELAGH: It's cheap.

DAVID: It won't be much of a Christmas this year.

(SHELAGH deliberately ignores him.)

I like real ones.

SHELAGH: How was your day.

DAVID: It's like a call.

SHELAGH: What?

DAVID: Something's calling me...

SHELAGH: *(Touching DAVID tentatively.)* I know what you need.

DAVID: I need...power.

SHELAGH: We need to touch each other.

DAVID: Love is tenderness.

SHELAGH: *(Touching him.)* If you held me, you would see we're still the same.

DAVID: What? Make love before the deficit is reduced?

SHELAGH:	*(Laughs.)* What?
DAVID:	I mean it. Love is tenderness. What use is tenderness now? *(Laughs uncertainly.)*
SHELAGH:	We need it. We need it.
DAVID:	What is tenderness but empathy? I can't afford empathy. Eight o'clock news, 400 people laid off. Nine o'clock news, 600 people laid off. Ten o'clock news, 700 people laid off…
SHELAGH:	Don't listen to the news.
DAVID:	*(Desperate to explain himself, he speaks to SHELAGH and the audience.)* The woman came home. Her husband is sitting at the table. He's already been laid off. The kids are happy: Mom's home. There's no substitute for Mom.
SHELAGH:	We should have a child. When things get better.
DAVID:	He's made…Kraft Dinner. Kraft Dinner, it was on sale for 99 cents at Super Value and the kids will always eat it.
SHELAGH:	We always planned to have a child when things got better. They never seemed to get better.
DAVID:	So…Mom's home. An occasion to rejoice. Dad has sort of come to enjoy being with the kids…but they're small…they're demanding.
SHELAGH:	What did we mean by get better?
DAVID:	Listen. So Mom's home and it's happy time. Dad smiles wearily as he sets the youngest on the floor so they can both rush to Mom…
SHELAGH:	Why did we think things would get better?
DAVID:	…and they see her face. And they know. Children don't need information…I mean they don't exactly know what happened, but they know. And Dad knows. The mortgage is due, the car needs…the kids need…and you want me to feel again?
SHELAGH:	I want you to love me again.
DAVID:	Feeling will kill me. Love. I once knew how to love. Now I cannot even remember how I knew. There is so much fear inside me. I piss fear. *(He grabs her.)* I see Shelagh, my body wants to run, I touch Shelagh my body says flee.
SHELAGH:	You're hurting me.
	(SHELAGH pulls away. SHELAGH decorates the tree. The NEWS sings "Adeste Fideles." As the NEWS finishes the first verse, it tails off and SHELAGH hums the tune sadly.)
DAVID:	I can't even feel for myself. I'll see someone.
SHELAGH:	I think it's too late, David.
DAVID:	Don't say that.
SHELAGH:	Maybe we never loved each other.
DAVID:	I do love you.

SHELAGH: Did we love each other? Love. We drank from a single cup, a cup that neither of us can carry by ourselves. Now...I'm tired, David.

DAVID: If I could get a job...

(DAN and DENISE enter, costumed and physically transformed into bizarre manifestations of their personal journey, DAN as a clown, DENISE as a gypsy mystic.)

DAN: Well...I came over to see if I can help.

SHELAGH: Thanks Dan...but I don't think there's anything else to do.

DAVID: *(As if he is analyzing his own situation.)* I know that my fears, that my powerlessness to protect us, has manufactured an evil miasma that penetrates every action...but there's a core I can still feel that I know means I will never hurt you or us.

DAN: *(Ignoring DAVID.)* We can't pay the mortgage.

SHELAGH: Oh no.

DAN: Ahh, it's only a house.

DENISE: *(Enters.)* It's only a thing...but you two. *(She embraces SHELAGH.)* Have you really thought about this?

SHELAGH: Yes, I have. It's not a very merry Christmas.

DAN: You two belong together.

PRINCE: *(To NEWS.)* The core of our philosophy is the family. The family and family values. I'm particularly pleased to reaffirm this to Canadians at this holiday season, and to wish everyone a New Year of happiness and, uhhhh...

NEWS: *(Taking over responsibility.)* ...and of course prosperity.

PRINCE: *(Loses interest in the NEWS and watches the other four.)* Exactly, exactly. Just what you said.

NEWS: *(As if the PRINCE carried on.)* I know that my family represents to me the culmination of my dream of peace and prosperity.

PRINCE: Right, right.

DENISE: I dreamed of peaked roofs with wings. Do we all have a right to shelter? Only if we can secure it. But you two...we love you two.

DAVID: Please don't go Shelagh.

(DAN adds make-up. Making himself more clown like. DENISE makes herself more "mystical.")

NEWS: It's through my family that I can understand and appreciate the collective goals of the Canadian people as we set off together on our great adventure.

PRINCE: *(Prompting NEWS, he remains interested in the others.)* We will hurt a bit...but...

NEWS: It's through our sacrifices that we will find our place in a new industrial order.

PRINCE: Of course, of course.

SHELAGH: *(Gently.)* David...

DAN: Listen buddy...we've been friends a long time. You need help.

DENISE: *(To SHELAGH.)* I didn't know what you were dealing with, Shelagh.

DAVID: Look what's happened to us. Look.

SHELAGH: What's happened to us, David?

DAVID: Well...look at us.

> *(The other three look at each other with bewilderment. Everything appears perfectly normal to them.)*

We're changing.

SHELAGH: All right I'm not a high-paid, well moderately-paid professional, who works with people anymore. I'm a low-paid waitress who works with people. I can't honestly say I'm not doing society as much good in this job. Maybe I'm not doing as much harm. But I haven't given up.

DENISE: Don't leave each other, you guys.

SHELAGH: I think it's too late.

DAN: I think they should be alone, Denise.

DENISE: We are. We all are.

DAN: Well...we'll be in touch...

DENISE: But we didn't play hearts.

> *(Exit DAN and DENISE. SHELAGH looks at the Christmas tree.)*

SHELAGH: It's a good tree.

DAVID: Stay.

SHELAGH: Christmas was for me a celebration of our comfort and success, and then as things changed, it became a holiday of hope. The marking of not a very good year ended but the promise of better to come. And now...baubles and bangles...and bills...tawdry pretense in a commercial carnival. Buy, buy, buy to save your life. It was always that way and I didn't know it. I fooled myself...never again.

DAVID: It was never that way for us.

SHELAGH: Never again. The future might be hell but it's real.

> *(DAVID approachs SHELAGH.)*

Don't come near me.

DAVID: I love you.

SHELAGH: You won't let me love you. You amused me with your idea that humans could only fail other humans. So now we see it is true. You are right. You cannot go forward and I cannot bear your weight. I failed you. How happy you must be. *(Falsely gay.)* And no computer to comfort you. You miss the gentle touch of your plastic keyboard, don't you? You miss the hot plastic smell of plastic synapses inventing a world, don't you, dear? Your computer darling. All gone. All our human sweat and ideas that don't compute always made you queasy, like the proper gentleman who smells beer on a beggar.

(She throws the Christmas tree at him.)

Here, it's all plastic without sentiment or soul. Make yourself a world, David. I have to go to work. It's wonderful to say that since so many must say I have to find a job.

(Exit SHELAGH. DENISE and DAN stand on opposite sides of the stage.)

DAN: *(Laughing.)* I haven't lost my dignity. *(Laughing uncertainly.)* I haven't. Have I?

(DAVID bends down and sets the Christmas tree upright. As he does so he pulls a long brutal-looking sword from the branches.)

DENISE: I saw it all. It was so clear.

DAN: How many Poles does it take to screw in a light bulb?

DENISE: It's just dreams. *(Rhetorically.)* What do you think it means when a black man in Harlem has less chance to reach 40 than a man in Bangladesh? What do you think it means?

DAVID: I'm insane.

DENISE: No, no. I'm insane.

DAN: How many Poles? Stop, I'm a Pole. *(Laughing.)* That's a joke ...that's the joke.

DENISE: *(Laughing.)* It means things are getting better.

DAN: *(Laughing.)* I'll never be a black man.

DENISE: *(Laughing.)* I'm so glad I'm mad.

DAN: *(Laughing.)* Black men just don't win.

DENISE: Well, he's found it.

DAN: What Denise? What do you mean?

DENISE: They're just dreams.

DAN: We're going to make it honey, we really are.

DAVID: My life is empty but not at an end.

DENISE: All right, we can go for coffee now.

(DENISE and DAN walk to each other near DAVID who pays them no attention.)

DAVID: This is a goddamn sword.

DENISE: *(To DAN.)* I wouldn't know what to do with it either. I can see things. They're so obvious.

DAN: You're scaring me again.

DENISE: We're always given our own release.

DAN: Coffee, OK honey? We got hours before the job seminar.

DENISE: He's always had it.

DAN: I love the mall in the afternoon. The public square of our time. And cheap coffee.

DAVID: Believe in nothing, feel nothing and so I'm given something to feel with. *(He tests the blade. Brandishing the sword, to the audience.)* Like so many who cannot feel I cannot act. Insanity gave me a tool for both. Well, why not? I had a sword.

              (End of Act One.)

Act Two

(DAVID on stage with the sword, to the audience.)

DAVID: When I lost everything, I would sit every morning staring out the window at part of a church, older than I am, and one half of a sign that advertised fried chicken. I used to wonder, "What do I want?" without noticing, as time passed, and what I wanted was never discovered, or when it was discovered, was not possible, without my noticing I came to wonder, "What can I do?" "What can I do?" The chicken store was full of young and not so young doing what they could do. The church was never full. "What do I want? "What can I do?" The perfect diffusion of light in a solid gray sky, striking the church, the chicken sign day after day. "Let it end." "What do I want?" "What can I do?" "Let it end." The church has lost its parishioners but the funerals were regular. The frozen chickens come in the back door. "Let it end."

NEWS: *(Enters as the SINGER.)* I'm sorry to say it's true.
When it rains
It doesn't just rain on you
It's sad that you think
So, it makes me sad too
But when it rains, it doesn't
Just rain on you.

DAVID: I heard you sing once before, when I had love.

NEWS: Did you like it?

DAVID: Yes.

NEWS: Got a buck?

DAVID: Yes

NEWS: All right... *How do you know a sheep from a goat*
Throw them in a river

DAVID: No.

NEWS: *...and the sheep won't float. It's too bad, bad luck...*

DAVID: *(Agitated.)* Stop. Stop that.

NEWS: *(Stops.)* What's the matter with you.

DAVID: I'm insane.

NEWS: I'm only the singer.

DAVID: The other song... I want the other song.

NEWS: The Prime Minister said today the Free Trade agreement with Mexico would provide an unparalleled opportunity for Canadian businessmen and entrepreneurs...

DAVID: No...

NEWS: ...to maximize Canadian global competitiveness in international markets...

DAVID: Stop.

NEWS: ...in the international restructuring of the new economic order...

DAVID: I have a sword.

NEWS: *(Mocking.)* You have a sword.

DAVID: It's for me.

NEWS: That would be best.

DAVID: It would be best.

(NEWS shifts into her trainer persona. Everyone gathers round and sits.)

NEWS: *(Stops dramatically and looks at the four.)* Well, what a sorry looking bunch we have today. Watch that lower lip, Dan. You could trip on it. *(Assessing them for a second.)* All right. Everybody up. On your feet now. Come on.

(With groans of protest everyone gets to their feet.)

All right...stretch...stretch to the sky. *(Everyone stretches.)* Good... That's good... Higher, David, stretch it out... Now out to the sides and circle, circle, smaller circles Shelagh...make it hurt...all right, now jogging in place, here we go...one...two...three...four...remember you want to collect your pension...five six seven...eight, a healthy worker is a good worker... You need work on those thighs... *(NEWS stops jogging and counting cadence, from time to time inspects the four.)* You're getting fat, Dan... Most studies show that employers will not, simply not hire the obese. It's not just health... It's aesthetic...and speaking of which, Denise, you're going to have to do something with yourself... Look at Shelagh now...that should be your model. *(She stops at DAVID.)* David...you look all right...but there's an emptiness in your eyes that you must not ever let an employer see. All right. That's enough. *(The four thankfully sit.)*

(The NEWS starts enthusiastically clapping, she encourages the others to clap.)

Come on people. Let's hear it for a winner. Come on. Now...share the good news.

DAN: *(Holding a vacuum.)* I got lucky. *(He hoists the vacuum.)* It's not exactly what I wanted... Everyone has to learn to reduce their expectations. I have. I can sell anything. I didn't start out that way... I believed, well...

NEWS: Don't back off now. Go with that thought.

DAN: Well, I believed in art.

            (This is met with complete polite silence.)

            (Faltering.) Film. I believed in film...well movies, technically I guess...commercially speaking... I believed in the visual medium.

NEWS: That's all right.

DAN: I used to call it film. But...

NEWS: Film sounds like going bankrupt...

DAN: Exactly.

NEWS: ...it sounds like starving artists...

DAN: Yes.

NEWS: Like poverty, unintelligible and ultimately meaningless self-involved artistic masturbation.

DAN: Profitless...

NEWS: Film, it says no investors, no grants...

DAN: No profit...

NEWS: Adolescent...

DAN: ...poetic...

NEWS: ...hopeless...

DAN: I learned to call it product.

NEWS: Better.

DAN: Films run on money. I mean the product needs money.

NEWS: And you sold it.

DAN: I learned to sell it. Then...it all went to the States...

NEWS: Don't be negative now...

DAN: I mean our partners, south of here...our friends...who are much more productive than us, south of here...the product went there.

DAVID: *(Looking at the vacuum.)* I can't afford it.

DAN: You can't afford not to. Not at this price.

DAVID: I'm not working.

DAN: Don't be negative... *(He prepares his demonstration of the vacuum cleaner.)* You have credit. Now...this is the most recent advantage in smaller is better technology. See the size of this canister? Despite it's small size, it produces the vacuum equivalent of a unit many times it's size. Think of it as a very fine, small budget film.

DAVID: What?

DAN: It's very powerful, a tiny gem made by skilled Indonesian craftsmen, the kind of film that stays with you, a voice speaking directly to your experience...and cheap.

DAVID: I don't think...

DAN: This will make you think and feel. The budget itself is less than a tenth of those tax write-off turkeys made in Toronto by accountants and the muzzle velocity is not much less than an Uzi.

DAVID: An Uzi?

DAN: Now I want you to use your imagination. Can you do that?

DAVID: Do you mean like a machine gun?

DAN: I'll tell you why I want you to use your imagination. This machine does not actually work. *(Pause.)* There's a little flaw, fully covered by warranty, in this little demonstration model, but I wanted it to work you know? To show I was productive...?

DAVID: Competitive...

DAN: ...internationally competitive even...

DAVID: ...and productive.

DAN: Right. Now... There's a lyricism in its thrust that allows your imagination to participate in an experience that is at once personal and universal. It comes with a nine-slug clip, nine-millimetre ammunition.

DAVID: Like an Uzi?

DAN: Marketing is everything. Use your imagination. What is art but imagination? So...you see, imagine... *(Suits his action to words.)* I'm spreading dirt... see the dirt? See? Every kind of filth...cat hair, ashes, dead skin, socialists, negativists, old workers, immigrants, Sikhs, goddamn niggers... Now! Ready! *(DAN makes a noise like a vacuum cleaner.)* See...I'm cleaning it up, look at this little baby... There goes the cat hair...rmmmm, ashes...welfare cheats, immigrants, turban heads... *(DAN uses the vacuum hose like an Uzi. We hear a burst of gun fire. The gunfire ends.)* Everyone is going to want one of these babies.

SHELAGH: *(Standing.)* I was always a liberal.

DAN: I don't know what's happening, Dave.

SHELAGH: That's why I became a social worker.

DAN: I didn't know I was a failure. Now I've come to hate the poorest of the poor.

SHELAGH: There is one central liberal idea. Every human being has worth.

DAN: I spent years and years not knowing I was a failure.

SHELAGH: Every human being has intrinsic worth. It doesn't matter what they do, or what they look like, or where they are from...they have worth.

NEWS: Interesting.

SHELAGH: You can't do the work I do...you can't do the work I used to do...without believing in intrinsic worth.

DENISE: Gold, they believed had intrinsic worth, the medievalists, the alchemists. I believe gold is worth about $280 an ounce now.

SHELAGH: Then I had twice as many clients. Work harder. Work harder.

NEWS: Work will make you free.

DENISE: I believe in dreams.

NEWS: Do you dear?

SHELAGH: First the people disappeared, and they became paper...just stories, impossibly sad stories on paper.

DENISE: I dreamed about paper people.

SHELAGH: I started moving the paper from the left side of my desk to the right side of my desk. It exhausted me.

DAVID: You can't do everything,. Shelagh. You can't change the world.

SHELAGH: Moving the paper from the right side of my desk to the left side of my desk. I'm so tired.

DENISE: It's a matter of weight and mass. In space there is no weight but the mass remains.

NEWS: How interesting.

SHELAGH: Then I had no job. And when I left, the cost of administration and expenditure to each client was $1,120.43.

NEWS: Bravo.

SHELAGH: The value of a person... *(To DAVID, very brightly.)* ...let me get you some coffee, some warm reviving hot coffee...and a donut. Something to revive you...something to nourish you...to make you whole.

NEWS: Bravo, Shelagh. You lost your job and you went right out and...

SHELAGH: ...And?

NEWS: You got another job, right away, like that...and another job in the service industry. Bravo, Shelagh.

SHELAGH: I don't mind working. I'm a hard worker.

NEWS: You're a success, Shelagh.

SHELAGH: Yes...I have to get some...I have to...I should...

(NEWS expectantly turns to DENISE.)

NEWS: And you believe in dreams.

DENISE: *(Slyly.)* Not dangerous dreams. I don't live in dangerous dreams. No, I dreamed harmless dreams.

NEWS: What are dangerous dreams?

DENISE: Oh...let us say...dreams where everyone has a job...

NEWS: Ahhh.

DENISE: Children's dreams. Dreams for people...people who don't know about space weight and mass.

NEWS: *(Condescending.)* I don't understand.

DENISE: Weight is banned in space. Mass remains.

NEWS: A law of physics.

DENISE: *(Sly.)* Yes, think of it that way. Weight is banned in space by a law of physics... exactly... you see in space, you can lift anything...a small weak person like me can lift anything, but...if I come between an object that is massive and yet has no or insignificant weight and something like a wall...or a steel floor and the massive object...though it's so silly to imagine a steel floor in space... *(Laughing uncertainly, looking to DAVID.)*

DAVID: You were always hard to understand, Denise.

DENISE: ...Well looking all day at money on a computer and imagining trends...

NEWS: Surely not imagining...

DENISE: No, of course not. No...no... Weight is banned in space you see so... If I am caught between a steel floor and a massive object...in space, where weight is banned... I can be crushed. Crushed to death. Even though we have eliminated weight. I could be crushed to death but I could not say... That I was killed by a heavy weight. I especially could not say a heavy weight fell on me.

NEWS: You were crushed by a heavy mass.

DENISE: I think it's best not to name things.

NEWS: You were killed by a law of physics.

DENISE: Yes that's it. *(Turning away from the interrogation by NEWS, she shows DAVID cards.)* You see the spade. The ace is at the top and if we take that out and then we have the king at the top and we take that out and we have the queen and if we take that out we have the jack and if we take that out...well we only have numbers don't we. Their value is known you see and has a correspondence. Well the face cards don't. You see.

NEWS: I'm afraid you are one of our failures, dear.

DENISE: Yes.

NEWS: I think we're going to have to arrange some retraining for you.

DENISE: Oh.

NEWS: Training is the future of Canada.

DENISE: Yes.

NEWS: We are going to retrain everyone into the most productive, hardest working...

DENISE: ...best trained...

NEWS: ...best trained work force in the world.

DENISE: In the whole universe.

NEWS: Denise.

DENISE: *(Frightened that the NEWS has detected irony.)* Yes?

NEWS: Don't give up.

DENISE: No. I don't want to be a failure.

NEWS: And you won't be. Don't give up.

DENISE: I won't. I really won't.

NEWS: And you, David.

(Enter the PRINCE, shuffling cards.)

PRINCE: Let's play, David.

(The PRINCE deals and DAVID plays.)

DAVID: I have to be a winner.

PRINCE: I'll order up a wheelbarrow to carry your winnings.

NEWS: David... You look a little depressed. Doesn't he look depressed?

PRINCE: Financial?

DAVID: Yes.

PRINCE: And your love life, sir?

DAVID: I was offered love, I didn't recognize it.

(Throughout the PRINCE is dealing to DAVID and DAVID is busting.)

PRINCE: Too bad. No luck today. And do you hear the call?

DAVID: What?

PRINCE: You see, when you've sinned you must be punished. *(Referring to the cards.)* Ohhh, bad luck.

DAVID: When you've sinned?

PRINCE: Just an observation, Dave. You know it's often been said that gamblers don't gamble to win...

DAVID: I've heard that.

PRINCE: You are having bad luck aren't you? You know why they play to lose? They think they deserve it. If they win you see, they know they're not worthy... but when they lose, well, all of us know we don't deserve good things. So they bet to lose. They hear the call...

DAVID: I've been having trouble with reality.

PRINCE: Sin! *(To NEWS.)* We had to let daycare go. Yes we wanted it...it was our policy. But the people can't pay for it and if you can't pay for it you don't deserve it. It's a great personal disappointment to me. A bitter disappointment. I thought better of the people.

NEWS: And the deficit, Mr. Prime Minister.

PRINCE: Do you really believe the people deserve to be free of the deficit and the debt?

NEWS: Well...yes.

PRINCE: You've been listening to the idealists, the humanists, maybe even the socialists. It's not that easy. Yes, the crimes of the people can be prevented by taxation... all right, but the accumulated debt... Has God forgiven us original sin? You're not having much luck there, David.

NEWS: Mr. Prime Minister. Just what will get us out of the terrible situation we find ourselves in?

PRINCE: Fiscal responsibility, living within our means, increasing our productivity, reducing the debt, creating a business environment and above all... I'm tired of doing this all myself, goddamn doesn't anyone understand the times we live in but me? Above all...becoming more competitive. I sometimes feel I'm losing control. I see things so perfectly, I know what has to be done to save us all...but, David, do you care? It would mean so much to me if you cared.

DAVID: I...

PRINCE: *(Bitterly.)* Why should you be any different? *(Dealing.)* And one more... Oh dear. Bust again.

DAVID: These cards are all blank.

PRINCE: Are you all right sir?

NEWS: David, calm yourself.

DAVID: They're blank. There's nothing there.

NEWS: *(Singing.) He is our leader.*

PRINCE: Do you think I invented gambling? Do you?

NEWS: *He's guiding us by a light we cannot see...*

PRINCE: Do you think it's me that makes some people winners and others losers...

NEWS: *He holds our hand in adversity...*

PRINCE: Did I make the poor...

NEWS: *He leads us from poverty...*

PRINCE: Do you really believe that everything you have lost...your job, your wife...your sanity, is my fault?

DAVID: Yes.

PRINCE: There is a march of history that I lead. You can be a part of it, David. The green and the golden land, the fruit trees heavy with all that is best and the lowing of cows heavy with milk... come on...take a card.

NEWS: *Why can't we accept*
What we know to be true
Why don't we grab the knife
By the handle and not by the blade

PRINCE: Come now. Take a card! It's the nature of man to risk.

DAVID: I can't gamble anymore.

PRINCE: That's just it. There's always something more. When will you all understand that? To start again everything must be gone.

    (DAVID hesitantly takes a card, PRINCE and NEWS smile.)

DAN: Over here man... David, right here.

    (DAVID walks to sit in the coffee shop with DAN and DENISE.)

	Hey guy, glad to see you… it's been a while.
DENISE:	You're here for the 69-cent bottom line, aren't you.
	(DAVID looks inquiringly at DAN.)
DAN:	Forget it.
DAVID:	Have you got…
DAN:	Not now, OK… I didn't think you'd want to meet here…with Shelagh and all.
DAVID:	Any place is as good as any other place.
DENISE:	Now that's where you're wrong you see.
DAN:	We like it here. You get here early, there's lots of room. You get to see some people you know… It's good for business.
DENISE:	He wants to hear the 69-cent bottom line.
DAN:	Look, you're not in the market for a little… *(Puts his finger to his nose and sniffs.)* It's first-class stuff…?
DAVID:	Dan.
DAN:	It's all business man. And I'm making out like crazy…19 year olds…shit, 16 year olds. So what are you doing…
DAVID:	I'm going insane…
DENISE:	You can get provincial welfare if you're insane, but it isn't easy. The line ups are very long and there's always someone crazier than you.
DAN:	City welfare is just hopeless.
DENISE:	I was so surprised to find so many people crazier than the next person.
DAN:	So what have you got in the way of work?
DAVID:	I have a sword.
DAN:	I thought maybe, you know. Telephone solicitation but you know what? Those firms that do that, they're hiring guys in jail to do the telephoning. Yeah, the guys are perfect employees, always on time for work.
DENISE:	The 69-cent factor.
DAN:	They work for like nothing…it's the same old story…I wasn't qualified. I'm not in jail.
DENISE:	All the very young girls with babies come here in the afternoon to talk to each other you see. Now at one time the unit cost on an object was…oh let's say two dollars…
DAN:	I'm not prepared to go to jail to get a job yet.
DENISE:	The babies are beautiful. The mothers are beautiful.
DAN:	But I don't think that shows a lack of motivation.
DENISE:	Beautiful. And then they discovered that if they wanted a 30-cent profit on a unit, why people would work for less, or do the jobs of two people. So one person lost a job. Then they discovered in the

	States that people would work for less, and then they discovered in Mexico that people would work for a lot less…and lots of people here couldn't work at all. And they brought unit cost to 69 cents. That seems to be the bottom line. A plateau so to speak. We are waiting for a 69-cent breakthrough.
DAN:	I don't think this is defeatist do you? David? I mean everyone gets down sometimes.
DENISE:	All the beautiful young mothers who can't find jobs have beautiful 69-cent babies. What a beautiful 69-cent baby, I say. And you know the important thing…the amazing thing? The cheapest coffee in the mall is 69 cents.
DAN:	We're getting along, David. That's all I can tell you…getting along.
DENISE:	Have you come to court Shelagh?
DAVID:	No.
DAN:	Do you remember when we used to get together, the four of us, and…and…
DAVID:	I need something from you, Dan.
DAN:	I know it looks kind of…kind of different from what it was…but we're still in the game. We're still players.
	(SHELAGH enters wearing extreme make-up and prosthetic breasts.)
SHELAGH:	I love the mall. This is the best job I've ever had.
DENISE:	Are you on your break, sweetie?
DAN:	I mean…I still got my sense of humour. I mean my sense of humour is as bad as it ever was.
SHELAGH:	Everything has a price here. There's no guessing.
DAN:	Dave…look. It's not like things aren't going to get better.
SHELAGH:	Hello, David. Socks…89 cents to one dollar and 99 cents.
DAVID:	I love you.
SHELAGH:	Love. A blow job is about 25 to 50 bucks depending on who and where. The room is extra.
DAN:	*(Chuckling.)* You two still got the old spark.
DENISE:	The basic unit is 69 cents.
DAN:	Just like old times… *(He stands and pulls DAVID away from the others.)* Dave and I got a little business here… You guys just talk girl talk, OK?
DENISE:	Was he always like this?
SHELAGH:	I don't know.
DAN:	Are you shooting up or shooting down man?
DENISE:	Was I always like this?
SHELAGH:	I can't remember.

DAVID: I don't understand.

DAN: Are you going to take this thing to places where people have fire power or is it like 7-Elevens with scared young clerks?

DAVID: It's for me.

SHELAGH: I remember the way he used to touch me sometimes.

DAN: Yeah, yeah...I mean this is a pretty small item. You got to be close to do damage.

DAVID: I'll be close.

DENISE: Memory can become like something you learned in school. Like geometry.

DAN: When you say it's for you...you mean?

DAVID: It's for me.

SHELAGH: Like geometry. Something benign.

DENISE: And useful. It is useful isn't it?

DAN: Well... I guess somebody has to give up.

DAVID: I guess that's me.

DAN: Well. *(He pulls out a small pistol and hands it to DAVID.)* Put that away, OK, I got to work here. Listen Dave...? Buyer beware man, OK?

            (They return to SHELAGH and DENISE.)

DENISE: Geometry.

SHELAGH: Algebra.

DENISE: Bell curves, all statistics.

            (There is silence among the four for a second.)

DAN: Just like old times, eh?

            (The NEWS begins to call a horse race. The PRINCE continues talking, raising his voice to be heard as he speaks to DAVID.)

NEWS: They're at the post... And they're off...

            (DAN, DENISE and SHELAGH "become" horses, then they "run" the race.)

PRINCE: You know in that little mining town with my father, I had to take what models I could...

NEWS: In tight at the lead it's Gold Strike, Human Voice, Let it Rain...

PRINCE: That little town attracted a lot of American high-roller fisherman and hunters.

NEWS: On the inside, Let it Rain, Gold Strike, Human Voice...

PRINCE: The kind of people who made America great, and whatever you feel about the United States, it is a great country.

NEWS: And at the turn, we have Gold Strike, Human Voice and moving up the inside, Let it Rain...

PRINCE: And those people were great. Self-made men, who bucked the system...

NEWS:	Neck and neck, Gold Strike, Let it Rain and edging forward...Human Voice.
PRINCE:	They did it themselves, David. They did it themselves without help from anyone. Boot-strap men, visionaries...
NEWS:	Into the stretch, it's neck and neck...
PRINCE:	Diamonds in the rough, leaders...
NEWS:	Now Human Voice, now Let it Rain, now Gold Strike...
PRINCE:	Two fisted iron-jawed individuals...heroes, David, heroes.
NEWS:	...down the stretch, neck and neck, Gold Strike, Human Voice, Let it Rain...and at the wire...too close to call.
PRINCE:	Heroes aren't in fashion now I know, but they were giants in their time. Heroes. *(He walks to DAN and DENISE evaluating them.)* Not even sweating. They had hearts like bulls those men. They were men.

(*Reaching under DAN's jacket, with some effort PRINCE pulls out his liver. Turning to DENISE, the PRINCE draws from her body a cup of blood. He drinks deeply.*)

Wonderful, wonderful...

(*He offers the cup to DAVID.*)

David...refreshment.

NEWS:	*(Takes charge of DENISE and DAN as horses.)* All right Mr. Prime Minister...clearly we have lived beyond our means, clearly we had expectations and ideas that were unrealistic...
PRINCE:	More than that. Mad.
NEWS:	All right, mad...but is the cure worse than the disease?

(*NEWS begins to lead DENISE and DAN off as horses.*)

PRINCE:	Is the cure worse than the disease?
NEWS:	*(As if to a shying horse:)* Whoa.
PRINCE:	There will be a human cost.
DAVID:	Does it have to be that way?
PRINCE:	I don't want to be glib about this...people will hurt.
NEWS:	Whoa... It's for the best now. It's for the best.

(*NEWS leads DENISE and DAN off.*)

PRINCE:	How long can we fool ourselves? We are economic animals. We must eat. Do you think, David, that you are anything but alone? When you die will the world mourn?

(*SHELAGH nuzzles the PRINCE like a horse, he pets her.*)

No. Don't fool yourself. You will have what you can take. What you take you can keep only if you can keep it. And never doubt...never doubt that what you have will come from someone else. I know what you feel. I do. When I understood for the first time what I'm telling you, I wanted to flee. I said no.

But...you can't deny the sea. It's there. Accept. Don't live your whole life as a lie. Listen and accept it.

(SHELAGH becomes herself, no longer a horse, and gets a coffee pot. Enter DAN and DENISE. The NEWS enters the studio.)

SHELAGH: Coffee? Coffee anyone?

DAN: You bet I want coffee. Can't live without coffee.

SHELAGH: Why should I interfere with anyone who seeks their own destruction?

DENISE: I cannot exist without seeing. Does it matter who uses what I see?

DAN: God I love Halloween. Don't you love Halloween? I love it.

DAVID: I have a sword.

DAN: He told me he had a sword.

DENISE: I told him sidereal motion moves at acute angles to force.

DAN: I just love fucking Halloween.

DENISE: Or maybe oblique angles.

NEWS: Mr. Prime Minister.

DAN: It's the only time I feel like myself.

PRINCE: I know you feel it, David.

NEWS: You say, Mr. Prime Minister, that while the leading indicators are not positive, they are hopeful. When can we expect an improvement in our fortunes?

PRINCE: You've heard it, David. I know you have...the destination of the chosen, the perfect land where we do not live a lie, ordained by the true nature of man, the fittest rule.

NEWS: Let's assume that the people of this country can let go of their inherent complacency and work their way out of this global recession. What can we expect?

PRINCE: It's life, David, the most elemental life, without the turmoil of invented morality, the needs of our fellow man, the false caring.

NEWS: *(Turning to DAN.)* And what do you think, sir?

DAN: I think the coffee shop is the public square of our time, that this is a great country and hard things have to be done.

NEWS: That's wonderful. And what do you see in our future? *(Turning to DENISE.)*

DENISE: I see a legacy of flaking concrete falling to abandoned streets where men and women walk with their heads down cursing their own feet.

DAN: She means things are getting better. Really she does.

SHELAGH: Would you like some coffee?

DAVID: You appealed to our vanity. The successful man will triumph under a system that rewards prudence, hard work, foresight. Who sees himself as impulsive, lazy, stupid and unrealistic? Who sees himself as a loser?

PRINCE: Many must lose so that one can win. It's true.

NEWS: We are waiting for the P.M. at an ordinary coffee shop in an ordinary city somewhere in Canada.

DAVID: If we fail you say, then we must find the failure inside ourselves. It's the worst in us we know best.

(The PRINCE has turned and watches the coffee shop.)

NEWS: And here with me are three ordinary Canadians.

DAN: I'm so fucking ordinary you wouldn't believe it.

SHELAGH: If people can't feel anything anymore…well that's all right.

DENISE: Dead people are everywhere. They do a wonderful imitation of life…you can ask me anything.

DAVID: Do you know that the men and women you have created despise first themselves, and then everything. They have nothing left to lose.

(DAVID draws the sword.)

DAN: *(To NEWS.)* He was always talking about the call right? He heard a call, like? I said to him, "Hey buddy, is this like a collect call?" I don't take collect calls.

SHELAGH: I had to say to him…there is nothing we can do for you until you can accept the reality of the situation. Nothing.

DENISE: I told him to hide.

PRINCE: My people…

DAVID: Can I end this?

PRINCE: We are counting on it.

(DAVID looks at the sword.)

PRINCE: My people.

NEWS: *(Reporting to the audience.)* He was smiling at first, and I thought he was an aide to the minister. He had something in his hand.

SHELAGH: We tried to help.

DAN: David, if things change…get better…

SHELAGH: …pull yourself together…

DAN: You'll never find yourself alone man.

SHELAGH: I'll be the first one. If you need…something…

DAN: And I'll be right behind her…

DENISE: Don't know where I'll be.

NEWS: *(Reporting.)* The smile disarmed us all, and the minister turned, smiling in return, expecting I think a handshake.

SHELAGH: I couldn't love him anymore. He wouldn't let me.

DAN: I have to make it clear that we weren't really friends or anything. We weren't really close.

DENISE: I'm insane, truly insane, so it doesn't matter what I think…however…uhhh.

SHELAGH: I loved everyone.

DAN: I had so many things.

DENISE: Madness is madness. Most of the time.

NEWS: According to witnesses at the scene...still smiling, the man said, "Fuck the people."

DAVID: For the people...I said for the people

PRINCE: My beloved people, we contemplate the desert together, follow me to the other side.

SHELAGH: No one should be violent. Ever. It doesn't solve anything.

DAN: I guess we can all understand suicide but...

NEWS: Do you think this is the case of an embittered man frustrated by his inability to adjust to the paradise of the new world order?

DAN: Absolutely. Right on.

PRINCE: When you believe you are strong.

NEWS: I don't mean to keep you in your grief, but could this be a manifestation of personal guilt and ugly nationalism?

DENISE: Sure, sure.

PRINCE: When you are strong, we will go together. David...are you ready?

DAN: And what makes someone do this? I just can't imagine.

SHELAGH: We must forgive him. I forgive him.

DENISE: He forgives us, too. I know he does.

PRINCE: You see, David, they understand you. Come.

DAVID: (DAVID walks to the PRINCE.) Every time you speak, I am less. Every action you take kills.

      (DAN, DENISE and SHELAGH make the following statements on video, as if part of a newscast.)

DAN: I DON'T KNOW WHY YOU DID WHAT YOU DID, DAVID. YOU HAD EVERY CHANCE TO BE PART OF THE NEW ECONOMY. IT'S SAD MAN. REAL SAD.

DENISE: I'M AGAINST IT. (Uncertain.) COMPLETELY AGAINST IT. COMPLETELY. RIGHT?

SHELAGH: I CANNOT LOVE YOU AGAIN BUT I DON'T HATE YOU. FUNNY. THE ONLY ACTION YOU EVER TOOK WAS NOT FOR ME. I DON'T HATE YOU.

DAN: (Watching the screen.) I think that was all right.

SHELAGH: I hope he heard us. I hope he understood.

DENISE: Ahhhh. I forgot. I meant to say that the design shift from rear wheel to front wheel drive parallels our relationship to the state.

PRINCE: (To DAVID.) You won't be driven and you won't be led. Are you ready?

DAVID: I'm ready.

PRINCE: It was mad of you to personify the natural forces of the economy as alive and malignant.

DAVID: I do see.

PRINCE: Hard things must be done.

SHELAGH: He was a wonderful man, he really was.

DAN: He was something all right. Really made his mark, kind of.

DENISE: We had too many cats already when the red one had a litter. We put them in a plastic bag and threw them in the river... Oh...I mean, he was wonderful.

DAVID: (On video, interviewed by the NEWS.) I FELL INTO A STATE OF DESPAIR, I COULDN'T RECOGNIZE MYSELF AS A FAILURE, DIDN'T WANT TO SEE MYSELF AS A FAILURE. I COULDN'T RECOGNIZE THE ROLE I HAD PLAYED IN MY OWN DECLINE, SO I BLAMED EVERYONE ELSE. EVEN IN MOMENTS OF LUCIDITY, I SIMPLY COULDN'T ALLOW MYSELF TO SEE THE HARM I WAS DOING MYSELF, MY COUNTRY.

PRINCE: (Reproachfully.) David. Pick a card. Come on, be a winner for once in your life.

            (DAVID stabs the PRINCE. We hear a gun shot.)

DAVID: I LOVED MYSELF TOO MUCH AND TOO WRONGLY.

PRINCE: I called you.

DAVID: I answered.

NEWS: How did this happen?

DAVID: I JUST COULDN'T THINK.

            (On stage DAVID proceeds to stab the PRINCE many times and we hear gun shots. SHELAGH, DAN and DENISE scream at the stabs, partly out of horror but with an element of excited fascination. They scream with each stab, but control themselves when speaking.)

SHELAGH: You just couldn't feel. See...he doesn't feel anything.

DAN: We did what we could. Jesus. Look at that boy go.

DENISE: There's a lot of blood. There really is. And I'm against it.

NEWS: What do you mean you couldn't think?

DAVID: PROPERLY I MEAN...I MEAN...I THOUGHT I HAD A SWORD.

NEWS: But it all worked out for the best didn't it?

DENISE: (Watching DAVID on stage.) I love happy endings, but I'm against this. Completely.

DAVID: THE IMPORTANT THING IS...UHHH I MEAN I UNDERSTAND NOW...

NEWS: Hard things have to be done.

DAN: It's true.

SHELAGH: Things are changing.

DAVID: You bet.

DENISE: Doobie doobie doo.

DAVID: IT'S IMPORTANT I THINK THAT EVERYONE WHO HAS FELT LIKE ME RECOGNIZE THE CONSEQUENCES OF IGNORING THE FLIGHT FROM REALITY. I SUPPOSE YOU COULD SEE ME AS A WARNING... THIS ISN'T WANTON. THIS ISN'T EXCESS. THIS

IS THE MINIMUM NECESSARY FOR MY SURVIVAL. HARD THINGS HAVE TO BE DONE. I RECOGNIZE THAT NOW AND I'M SORRY.

NEWS: That's so wonderful... David? We have a surprise for you.

(The PRINCE comes on screen with DAVID. DAVID is frightened and uncertain. The PRINCE smiles, DAVID smiles in return.)

DAN: *(Shouting to the video screen.)* Dave...Dave? What's he really like?

SHELAGH: I tried to warn him. Didn't I? Or did I try to love him? I did one of those things. I'm sure I did. *(Hand to mouth sort of gesture.)* My God, it's really him.

DENISE: He'll always be there. *(More fervently, in case she is misunderstood.)* Our leader.

DAVID: IN TIMES LIKE THESE, EVERYONE MUST FIND HIS OR HER MINIMUM POSITION. I'M SORRY.

(PRINCE laughs and smiles. This image remains on the screen.)

(To the audience.) Our hatred of violence...I suppose it's simply a matter of never finding someone you must kill. I am not a man who takes pleasure in violence. Of course...every murderer says that. I am a murderer. Don't thank me.

NEWS: *How can you lose in a world like this...*

DAVID: I'm a murderer.

(Slowly DENISE, SHELAGH and DAN take up the song.)

ALL: *How can you lose in a world like this.*
Our children walk with heads held high
A grandmother smiles as she takes a kiss
How can we lose...

DAVID: I have lost hope, compassion, love...everyone I loved, who loved me. I have lost. There is no far-away horror anymore. It is right here in me. I've done the worst thing a human can imagine. Please, please don't blame yourself. You did nothing. Nothing at all. I am not the kind of madman who blames everything on others. I killed someone, perhaps, and it was only because I was mad you see, and I lost everything and I cannot , though I look and look, find it again. And I know you do not have what I lost and I am mad and you did nothing at all. Believe that. Something...possessed me. I cannot taste strawberries. The dancer's grace is not from the soul but from the machine. Let me tell you again, it is not your fault, you did nothing and I beg you, if you lose something, find it as soon as you can.

(All finish a chorus of "How Can We Lose in a World Like This.")

The End

Live With It

ELISE MOORE

CHASUBLE:	Your brother dead?
JACK:	Quite dead.
MISS PRISM:	What a lesson for him! I trust he will profit by it.

—Oscar Wilde, *The Importance of Being Earnest*

Production Information

Live With It was first produced by Theatre Projects, Winnipeg, Manitoba, on February 22, 1994, with the following cast:

KEN .... Richard Hurst
JOE .... Ross McMillan

Directed by Rick Skene
Assistant Director: Ardith Boxall
Set and Costume Design by Rick Skene
Lighting Design by John J. Gilmore
Stage Manager: Carolyn Kulchyera

An earlier version of *Live With It* was first workshopped by Manitoba Association of Playwrights (MAP). The director was Yvette Nolan and the actors were Gene Pyrz, Richard Hurst and Richard Hirschfield. A subsequent MAP workshop was held in December, 1993, featuring the director and cast of the première production.

Characters

JOE: Joe Orton, the playwright

KEN: Kenneth Halliwell, his lover

BOY: Played by the actor who plays Ken or by a third actor

Setting

London, England, August 9, 1967.

Prologue

(The present. KEN and JOE are handcuffed together in Hell, sitting side by side on a bed.)

JOE: I wish I knew where the loo was.

KEN: Why? Contemplating cottaging in Hell? It's obvious death hasn't changed you one bit.

JOE: What'd you think, killing me would teach me a lesson? "Why thank you, Kenneth, due to your bashing my brains out I've come to appreciate the spiritual aspects of life and will now mend my ways and embrace society."

KEN: You'd shove it up the collective arse of the Celestial Host if so propositioned in a public lavatory.

JOE: It's only polite to accomodate one's host.

KEN: You'd have a foursome with the Holy Trinity.

JOE: How could I refuse three such reputable phallocentrics?

KEN: You're going to alienate the audience as usual.

JOE: *(Blithely.)* Oh, they'll sit there looking progressive and open-minded whilst I commit necrocide with their liberal ideals and afterwards they'll go home and discuss whether it was art or pornography.

KEN: Would you kindly come down off your high horse a moment?

JOE: The way I feel right now I'd go down on my high horse. You could at least have informed me ahead of time—just a few crucial minutes—of the fate you had in store for me. Given me the option of a final fuck—to repay me for allowing you to share the residual glory of my fame and fortune.

KEN: The only residue I saw was the kind collected on the inside of your underpants as I was washing them out in the sink. The only glory I was aware of was when you'd drop names as I was picking your socks up off the floor. A sensation almost as gratifying as editing your ever-abundant redundancies.

JOE: Then let me take this opportunity to congratulate you on the fine job you did on my undergarments and manuscripts all those years. Except when you got them mixed up.

KEN: It was an honest mistake. They were both equally filthy.

JOE: And you, the man behind them both. Would you say you lived a full life, then, Ken? And you haven't even mentioned the occasional tug on my cock or Valium tablet you kindly supplied me with.

KEN: *(Sententiously.)* The times, like underwear, must change. But not you...you never change.

JOE: It's true I should've listened to my mum all those years ago: "Be sure to pack a sensible lunch and a change of underwear if you're going to be staying long in Hell."

KEN: I know there's no more pleasant way to pass an infernal eternity than insulting your audience's intelligence. Nevertheless, "liberal ideas" is an inexcusably archaic cliché.

JOE: A cliché, you say... Wish I could remember what that was. Wait, it's coming back to me. Rather like...bludgeoning?

KEN: *(Indicating the audience.)* They're desensitized to sex! Desensitized to you! *(Triumphantly.)* Now you finally know how I felt living with you all those years.

JOE: Cliché! Yes! Now it all comes back to me. *(To KEN.)* The world's smallest violin is playing just for you?

KEN: But to what avail? They're also desensitized to violins.

Elise Moore
February 1994

Act One

Scene One

(Spotlight on KEN's face in profile, bald-headed. He addresses the darkness in front of and just below him.)

KEN: Perpetual insomnia breeds strange nocturnal habits. *(Pause.)* A strange breed, we perpetual insomniacs. *(Pause. Musing.)* A self-perpetuating breed, we nocturnal strangers? *(Pause.)* Strangers in the night, exchanging venereal diseases... *(Laughs. Pause.)* Watching the *play* of shadows on your face—memorizing each *line*. Not a few of which I've been at least partially responsible for, as you'd be the first to admit. This is my time for reflections. Not the kind confronted in polished surfaces, but in heads...though in my case there's no need to make the distinction. I'd like to get inside your head and burrow in the breeding ground for polished wit and epigrams, a playground for the vernacular a verbatim, cheek at face value. Friends, Romans, countrymen...lend me your rears. If only I could be certain I'm already in your dreams, I wouldn't have to use...visual shock tactics. If only the sound of your breathing in the darkness wasn't the only thing arguing I'm not alone.

(Pause. A sound of applause in the darkness. KEN looks around in bewilderment.)

JOE: *(From the surrounding darkness.)* How do you take your comedy?

KEN: *(Startled and confused.)* I beg your—

JOE: *(Interrupting.)* You were supposed to respond, "Black."

KEN: *(Still confused.)* I'm sorry.

JOE: *(Chiding.)* It's too late for apologies now. You've gone and spoilt the mood. Though that's not out of character for you. Let's shed some light, shall we? Then you can feel free to spill your guts on your sleeve to your heart's content.

KEN: *(Confused but angry.)* No! No light. I'm warning you... *(Suddenly pleading.)* I'm begging you... *(Recovers a bit.)* Why can't you leave me to my memories? I'm not disturbing anyone, you least of all. My memories of us are the only thing I have left that's mine alone, and then only by default. Because you don't want them.

(Lights come on suddenly. Their bedroom: two single beds, a bureau of sorts for clothing, shelves overflowing with books, a couple of

> *chairs, also a telephone and record player There is a desk with a typewriter. Also on the desk is JOE's journal, on top of which rests KEN's suicide note, surrounded by pills and a can of juice. There are two doors, one leading outside, one to the kitchen. KEN sits on a chair facing JOE's bed on which there is a sleeping figure representing Orton. KEN wears a pair of pyjamas; there is a hammer in his lap. JOE is in jeans and a white T-shirt. The time is 1967.)*

JOE: *(With camp sarcasm.)* You vant to be left alone? What you want is teaching those lines flattering to wearers of false eyelashes are not equally suited to wearers of false hair. However immortal the line may be, it's all in the delivery.

KEN: *(Still disoriented from the sudden light.)* Not one of your choicer cuts.

JOE: Actually, it's one of yours. You told it me years ago, during our days as struggling thespians.

KEN: You shouldn't've paid my banal bravado any mind. I couldn't act my way out of a prophylactic.

JOE: Your emotionally manipulative melodramatics make you sound like something out of a '40s "women's picture" featuring some darling of the queens like Crawford or Davis.

KEN: I'd need a cigarette for that. In fact, I need a cigarette.

> *(He pulls out a pack of cigarettes; lights one.)*

JOE: *(Coughing and grimacing.)* I wish you wouldn't smoke those foul things in our flat.

> *(KEN takes a long drag and exhales as he speaks, à la Bette Davis.)*

KEN: I wish you wouldn't fuck strange men in theirs. It's a matter of tit for tat.

JOE: Kindly keep your tits out of the discourse.

> *(JOE catches sight of something in KEN's lap: the hammer. He clearly sees it and reacts to it but decides not to say anything for the moment. KEN goes back to studying the sleeping figure.)*

What do you find so captivating about watching me drool on my pillow? A wet-dream it's not. *(Peers over KEN's shoulder)* The lines aren't really that obvious, are they? The lighting could be kinder. But all in all—

KEN: I didn't say—

JOE: Not bad at all. I'm still a young man. Young, good-looking, healthy, talented, famous, tolerably well-off and unequivocally well-hung. There's nothing in that bed to give rise to your self-indulgent theatrics. *(Pause. Then, suddenly.)* Ken? What's that in your lap?

> *(KEN gives JOE a withering look, then glances down. He's surprised but tries not to show it.)*

KEN: It would appear to be a hammer.

JOE: *(A la Lady Bracknell.)* A handbag?!

(Beat.)

(Didactic.) All pauses should be natural pauses. None of your long significant shit. Pace, pace, pace! Building up to the inevitable outcome. Everything the characters say is true. The rest is violence. *(Pause. In his normal voice.)* Why are you cradling that tool in your lap? *(Aside.)* We're assuming the hammer is real and not another illegitimate offspring of his deranged brain.

KEN: *(Annoyed.)* Of course it's real! What would I be doing with an imaginary hammer?

JOE: Back up a minute. We're still attempting to figure out what you'd be doing with a real hammer.

KEN: I know what I'm doing.

JOE: Do you?

KEN: Yes.

JOE: Then what?

(KEN stares at the hammer.)

KEN: I don't remember.

JOE: So we've ascertained that you still retain the capacity to distinguish between reality and fantasy. *(Pause. Prodding.)* Well? Haven't we?

KEN: *(Confused.)* I suppose so.

JOE: Suppose?

KEN: *(Ashamed.)* I've already forgotten.

JOE: *(Chiding.)* Forgotten already?

KEN: *(Exploding.)* I really don't see why all this is necessary!

JOE: Bear with me. *(Takes the hammer from KEN and holds it up.)* Using myself as an example of fantasy, and this appliance as an example of reality, you can distinguish between us, can't you?

KEN: *(With certainty.)* Yes.

JOE: Are you absolutely sure?

KEN: *(Less certain.)* Yes.

JOE: Can you trust what your senses perceive?

KEN: *(Not at all certain.)* Yes.

JOE: Good. That's important. Being able to rely on the infallibility of one's sensual perception is essential to one's peace of mind. Or pieces, if one is going to them.

KEN: *(Impatiently.)* And where is it you think you're going with this?

JOE: Way ahead of you. I just had to be convinced of your sweeping preeminence in the realm of reality. Now you can tell me what exactly you were planning to do with that hammer.

KEN: *(Wearily insolent.)* I told you. I don't know. Hang a picture, maybe?

(JOE grabs him and shoves him to the floor.)

JOE:	Wrong answer.
KEN:	*(From the floor.)* I was acting under the assumption that the questions you've been posing are hypothetical, in which case there would be no right or wrong answers.
JOE:	*(In KEN's face.)* I'm hypothetical. This play is. My questions are not. Answer them accordingly. *(Helps KEN up.)* Get a grip on reality.

> *(JOE hands him the hammer; KEN flings it away violently.)*

KEN:	No!
JOE:	*(Calmly retrieving it.)* Shut up. You'll wake me. Then where will you be?

> *(JOE gently but firmly places the hammer in KEN's hand and holds it there.)*

Let's assume you know what you're doing.

KEN:	*(Warily.)* This is hypothetical?
JOE:	What do you think?
KEN:	You said assume. Therefore I'm assuming you meant to offer an hypothesis. Hypothetically, it could be that it's finally happened. I knew it was coming. I've experienced all the signs and symptoms.
JOE:	You realize you're babbling.
KEN:	*(With a kind of triumph.)* I've earned the right. I've lost my mind. Taken leave of my sense.
JOE:	*(Scornfully.)* You're stalling.
KEN:	I'm not—
JOE:	And you can shove your excuses up your assumptions. Words, Ken, just words. Go on—it's your moment! Plead insanity all you please. But my sympathy has already been exhausted on 16 years of trauma and trivia. All anticipating this. I like your suicidal style. My murder as accessory gives your pathetic end a touch of class. *(Picks up the note from the desk and reads.)* "If you read his diary all will be explained. K.H....P.S. Especially the latter part." *(Looks up at KEN.)* Very three-hanky. A hammer in hand, an ominous note and numerous Nembutals laid out meticulously on the desk.
KEN:	Don't forget the grapefruit juice.
JOE:	*(Sarcastically.)* And a can of grapefruit juice. Shall I also read the label?

> *(Pause.)*

(Exploding.) Pace, pace, pace! If you're going to do me in, do it now. It's what I'd do in your place.

KEN:	Whose side are you on?
JOE:	Ask yourself that.
KEN:	You think I haven't?

JOE:	What do I know about what you think?
KEN:	You know me.
JOE:	Is that what you think?
KEN:	Answer me!
JOE:	Tutu, Brutus?
KEN:	*(Enraged.)* Words, bleeding words!
JOE:	*(Without expression.)* Pace.
KEN:	I'm in pain!
JOE:	Pace.
KEN:	Pain!
JOE:	Pace.
	(Pause.)
KEN:	Pause.

(With a cry of rage KEN swings at JOE with the hammer. JOE catches KEN's arm and then, producing a pair of handcuffs, previously concealed, he handcuffs himself to KEN. JOE tries to force the hammer, which KEN is still clutching, down on the sleeping figure's head.)

No!

JOE:	Wrong answer.
KEN:	I can't—
JOE:	Haven't you heard? The queen is mightier than the sword.
KEN:	*(Pleading.)* Joe—?
JOE:	Everything the characters say is true.
KEN:	Please.
JOE:	And you say—
KEN:	Don't, Joe, please, I can't—
JOE:	Wrong answer. From the top. And you say—
KEN:	*(Quietly, desperately.)* Black.
JOE:	Again. Louder. And you say…
KEN:	Black!
	(KEN is losing the struggle; the hammer is going down.)
JOE:	And you say—
	(JOE abruptly loses interest and heads for his leather cap, resting on a chair; KEN, still handcuffed, is dragged after him.)
KEN:	Where are you going?
JOE:	For a walk.

(JOE puts on his cap; KEN drops the hammer. Lighting change. JOE drags KEN to an empty area of the stage. A spotlight follows them. Throughout the following JOE appears to be unaware of KEN's

presence. JOE eyes "The Boy, " who can be played by a third actor or by KEN speaking his lines. KEN addresses his next comments to the audience.)

KEN: This is Joe Orton on the prowl. Observe the strut: pelvis and lower lip out; obligatory rakish tilt to cap.

JOE and KEN: *(KEN mockingly.)* Smashing.

KEN: He'd pick himself up if he could.

(KEN looks in the direction JOE is peering in.)

The English urban fairy ogling a potential pick-up: the over-sexed in full pursuit of the under-aged. They eye each other up warily. "Not bad." But don't look too anxious. Is he or isn't he? Is he a cop?" Look around furtively. No one in sight. Fortune smiles on our trifles. How do I know all this? Do you imagine I partake in this sordid, squalid, socially-stigmatized ritual? No. But he returns following each foray with the bloody anecdote, still-dripping viscera, falling from his mouth as he stalks through the door. And I sit there looking blasé, trying to think up caustic comments which he'll include in his account of the encounter when he writes it up in his diary. The posteriors of every other anonymous queen in London, preserved for posterity. Including my own—in its supporting role.

JOE: Hey.

KEN: Here it comes.

BOY: Yes?

KEN: And here we go.

JOE: Got a name?

BOY: No.

JOE: My name's Kenneth.

KEN: Oh, lovely!

BOY: That's a nice name. Look, I have to—

KEN: But he won't.

BOY: I don't want to.

KEN: But he will.

JOE: Do you kiss?

BOY: No.

KEN: Yes—

JOE: Take it?

BOY: No!

KEN: Yes—

JOE: Got a place?

BOY: No.

KEN: Yes—

JOE:	See I'm handcuffed to someone at the moment which makes it awkward—
KEN:	*(In a rage.)* Yes, yes, yes!!!
JOE:	No one's about...
BOY:	No...
KEN:	*(To JOE.)* What am I then? An unsightly growth on your wrist? A figment of your depraved imagination?

> *(JOE mimes backing "the BOY" into a doorstep, glances around; KEN is dragged along.)*

Oh, lovely. A doorstep in broad daylight. This is really taking the concept of public sex a step too far.

JOE:	How old are you?
BOY:	Seventeen.
KEN:	Jailbait, Joe. Of course so were you when we started living together. Nevertheless I never took you in the open air in a public square like this.
JOE:	I like them about 14.
BOY:	Sorry.
JOE:	Don't apologize.
BOY:	Kenneth?
JOE and KEN:	Yes?
BOY:	What are you going to do with me?
JOE:	Well first I'm going to fuck you very quickly and thoroughly.
BOY:	No, please.
JOE:	Shut up. I'm going to fuck you now.
KEN:	*(To audience.)* Seen enough?

> *(JOE and the BOY freeze in their positions.)*

Now I finally have you where you can't get away or talk over me. Now I'm going to tell you what I think for once. I don't mind this. I mean, there's nothing I can do about it. What I mean is, I could live with this. Only, of course, I can't follow you about all the time and keep an eye on you—except in my mind's eye. Instead I sit with my thumb up my arse staring at the ceiling of our cozy claustrophobic closet, our exclusive cramped cell. Hugged and hemmed in by the four oppressive walls, held snugly in place, nursing kinks. But what did you expect? Pouring your poisonous repertoire in my ears at all hours... What do you expect? Do you keep me around as your conscience, or as your warden? Or as your prisoner? Who am I kidding? I'm just your glorified housemaid.

> *(Blackout.)*

Scene Two

(A kettle screams in the darkness. Lights up on the bedroom. JOE and KEN, free of handcuffs, sit on their separate beds. It is 1967.)

JOE: So all the while I fucked him up against the wall he kept shouting for me to stop. He was loud enough I was afraid someone would come running and discover us there. Some unsuspecting passing pedestrian. In fact a few individuals answering to that description did happen by and I had to pull out and pull up my jeans and give him my fist to suck on to keep him quiet. *(Grins at the memory.)* We must have looked a sight.

KEN: *(Getting up.)* I hear the kettle. *(As he goes towards the kitchen.)* He wasn't serious about wanting you to stop.

JOE: *(Calling to kitchen.)* Oh, no. I thought at first he might be, you see. But then I realized it was part of his obligatory kink. Afterwards he even thanked me for continuing. "How did you know exactly what I needed, Kenneth?'

(KEN re-enters with teapot, cups, etc., on a tray.)

KEN: "Kenneth"—?

JOE: I told him my name was Kenneth.

KEN: *(Pouring the tea.)* I wonder what my psychiatrist would say about that.

JOE: "What I really needed was a good fucking," he said. "Where did you learn to fuck like that? I haven't had such a good *(Mispronouncing.)* fuching—"

KEN: "Such a good *fucking.*" Sugar?

JOE: Thank you, and please. I haven't had such a fucking in ages." *(KEN hands JOE his tea; JOE takes a sip.)* I told him we must fuck again sometime.

KEN: So if anyone calls wanting to fuck with Kenneth, I'll know it's not for me.

JOE: *(Indicating the tea.)* It wants more sugar. I didn't give him our number.

KEN: I must've given you mine by mistake.

(They trade teacups, then sit sipping for a moment on their separate beds.)

Why don't you tell them your real name?

JOE: "Them"?

KEN: Your pick-ups.

JOE: I prefer my public and private lives not become gratuitously entangled. If they're relatively at ease, their dialogue is natural. Hence I get to observe the average working Joe in his natural habitat, and the sex is hotter into the bargain. Were they aware I'm a playwright of some repute, unnecessary complications could arise. The general public doesn't seem to understand that playwrights fuck and have shits and pick their noses. Just like you mere mortals.

KEN: I doubt any of them have heard of you anyway. You hardly pick and choose on the basis of cerebral endowments.

JOE: There's always the off-chance, now I've had my picture in the papers. Just the other day I had someone say to me on the bus, "Aren't you Joe Orton?" It's the first time I've been recognized.

KEN: Really? Just the other day I had someone on the bus say to me, "Get out of the way, arsehole, are you blind or just a moron?" *(Pause. Sips.)* How's your tea?

JOE: A little weak.

KEN: More sugar?

JOE: Have you any Valium?

KEN: Tea and Valium. How decadent.

> *(He fetches a bottle from a drawer of the desk. They both take a couple each.)*

JOE: *(Yawning.)* I ought to be getting to bed soon. Have to spend tomorrow typing. *(Pulling off his jeans.)* Wonder what the *Daily Telegraph* will say to this one?

KEN: "Orton Opens His Fly in the Face of Convention."

> *(They laugh. JOE moves to get ready for bed.)*

I don't suppose you feel like having sex.

JOE: Why? Did my tale excite your fancy?

KEN: *(Defensive.)* Nothing like that. It was merely a question.

JOE: In that case, not really.

KEN: Not really what?

JOE: I don't much feel like having it, no.

KEN: I see. Goodnight, then.

> *(KEN turns down the covers and prepares to climb into bed.)*

JOE: But if you want to I'm willing.

> *(Pause. KEN considers this. Then he sits on the bed beside JOE and allows JOE to undress him.)*

KEN: There's no point anyway. You'll just get me pleasantly aroused and then not be able to fuck me.

JOE: *(Pulling down KEN's bottoms.)* It's not some kind of elaborate plot on my part to make you feel even more inadequate than you already do.

KEN: So you constantly claim.

JOE: *(Half-jokingly.)* Perhaps I can never fuck you because I'm stopped by my reflection in your eyes. Did you ever think of that, Ken?

KEN: That's very poetic. I could always close them.

JOE: That wouldn't make any difference. I'd still be able to see myself

	reflected in your head.
KEN:	You epic-length prick.

(They make out on the bed. It should be equally passionate and comical. KEN struggles to keep his wig on.)

JOE:	This is amazing.
KEN:	Thank you.
JOE:	I meant the Valium.
KEN:	I know.

(Their passion increases and KEN's wig falls off. He sits up to retrieve it.)

(Replacing his wig.) You had to toss that in, didn't you?

JOE:	What?
KEN:	"I don't feel much like having sex."
JOE:	I've changed my mind. I'm being fickle and unpredictable. Just pretend my spontaneity arouses you.

(JOE tries to kiss KEN, who is angry and looking slightly ludicrous in his boxer shorts with his wig askew. KEN resists.)

KEN:	You're simply incapable of being in any way intimate with me without first making sure I realize you're doing me a favour.
JOE:	*(Also becoming angry.)* As I look at it, I am. I'm tired. I've had my sex for the evening. I wasn't interested in extending my library ticket.
KEN:	Pity.
JOE:	What is?
KEN:	You keep me around because you pity me. Don't you.
JOE:	You're right, Ken, all right? Your astounding ability to unravel the complexities of human nature has triumphed as usual. I've stayed with you these 16 years out of sheer pity just because I'm such a sensitive and caring human being.
KEN:	You make a mockery of everything!
JOE:	Don't fob your prefab paranoia off on me. I'm sorry it offends your fading Southern self-esteem that I can't fuck you. Perhaps your psychiatrist could explain it to you. I can't.
KEN:	This is not about sex! It's about your not touching me, or looking at me, or listening to me—
JOE:	I can't listen to this. I'm tired. I just want to go to bed. *(Pause.)* When I touch you lately you push me away or make excuses.
KEN:	Because I know you really don't want to.
JOE:	Silly me, I should've been more explicit. After all, I'm always forcing myself to do that which is repulsive to me. It has to do with the deep and intense guilt that plagues me concerning my homosexual activities.
KEN:	You go out and find some faceless boy to fuck!

JOE:	Exactly: faceless! Just a prick and some perfunctory dialogue. We wouldn't have to go through this again and again if you could somehow allow yourself to believe you might actually be more to me than—
KEN:	A glorified housemaid?
JOE:	*(After a disgusted pause.)* I hear Hell is nice this time of year. The social season is in full swing. Perhaps you'd care to peruse a brochure. As for me, I'm going to sleep.

(JOE reaches over and turns out the light.)

KEN:	*(In the darkness.)* I'm not going anywhere without you.

Scene Three

(Music: "She's Leaving Home." Lights fade up on the kitchen. KEN, in his wig, is sitting at the table, peering into a compact and applying some rouge. The door leading outside is heard opening and slamming shut. KEN pretends not to notice. JOE comes in wearing his jacket and cap, which he removes.)

JOE:	Trying for a more life-like appearance? Were I you I'd opt for professional help.
KEN:	A makeover? I don't think I've disintegrated to the decadent standards of Professor Aeschenbach during his dolorous last days, do you?
JOE:	I meant a mortician.

(Pause. JOE gets a bottle of milk from the fridge and a glass from the cupboard. He sits at the table and pours himself a glass. KEN puts away the compact. The music has faded completely away.)

KEN:	So where were you?
JOE:	Walking.
KEN:	Walking where?
JOE:	Walking around, up, down, in, out, about, through, by, under, over, all over. Walking. It's not one of my more insidious vices.

(He gulps the milk and pours himself another glass, which he sips at.)

KEN:	You're late.
JOE:	I was held up.
KEN:	How? By what? Or should I be asking by whom?
JOE:	Why do you care? I'm here, aren't I?
KEN:	You have no consideration. None. To a person with any consideration to speak of, the reason for my concern would be obvious. But as I'm talking to you I see I'll have to elaborate. You tell me you'll be home by a certain hour; I expect you home by a certain hour. When you don't show up, I get worried. Why do I care, indeed.

JOE: (*Casually.*) Yes, sorry. You wouldn't happened to've made dinner? I thought I smelled something when I came in.

KEN: (*Exploding.*) You're fucking right something smells! I made your dinner! I timed it to be ready twenty minutes ago! It's cold now! It's cold because you're twenty fucking minutes late!

JOE: (*Quietly, calmly.*) Thank you for making me dinner. I'm sorry it's cold but we could warm it up in the oven.

KEN: We wouldn't have to warm it up if you'd been on time in the first place!

JOE: I'll warm it up. Do you want me to warm it up?

KEN: What do you know about it?

JOE: I'm perfectly capable of preparing my own meals, Kenneth. I don't need you to cater to me like some glorified housemaid.

KEN: You'd be fucking nothing without me!

JOE: (*Shouting back now.*) What does that have to do with dinner? Nothing, that's what!

KEN: Everything! Everything. It has to do with respect. And the fact that I'm not—

         (*He catches himself and stops.*)

JOE: What? (*Mocking.*) "Getting any"?

KEN: (*Not backing down.*) That's exactly the sort of third-rate rot that would've kept you buried in obscurity were I not around to edit you.

JOE: (*Trying to regain control.*) How's this one then: Before this goes any further, why don't we eat our meal in peace like what I hesitantly call "normal people" do.

KEN: Fuck normal people!

         (*JOE rushes towards KEN, looking about to belt him. Instead he grabs his jacket from the table where he dumped it and heads for the door.*)

         Fine. Run away. That's all you're good for anymore. Run headlong into the wide-flung arms of your worshipful minions. You think it won't matter if you're a few minutes late. You actually expect me to compete for your attention with those slobbering, sycophantic court hermaphrodites who worship the ground you piss upon. (*Contemptuously.*) *John Kingsley Orton.* Does that name sound familiar to you? Why should it? No one's ever heard of it. No one who's anyone. You want some reminding of your humble beginnings?

         (*JOE collapses in a chair, exhausted.*)

JOE: I couldn't possibly forget. Not with you around.

KEN: (*Screaming.*) You're fucking right!

JOE: Stop screaming.

KEN: Does this sound like screaming to you?

JOE: Yes, actually.

KEN: Do you want to know why I'm screaming?

JOE: Actually—

KEN: *(Starting to cry.)* Because it's the only way I can get you to hear me. Joe, you've got to have some consideration for me.

JOE: *(Mumbling wearily, with his eyes closed.)* I'm sorry. I'll try harder next time.

KEN: But it hurts now.

JOE: I'm sorry.

KEN: Most of the time you don't act like you notice I'm here.

JOE: Sorry.

KEN: *(Screaming.)* You're not listening to me!

JOE: *(Opening his eyes and standing.)* I've got a fucking headache, OK? *(He goes to the cupboards and starts searching through them.)*

Where did you hide the Valium?

KEN: I ought to hide them, at the rate you're going through them.

(JOE finds the pills, takes a couple and offers the bottle to KEN, who shakes his head. KEN pulls out a cigarette and lights it.)

JOE: What'd I tell you about that?

KEN: You're using up all my Valium. You, the *raison d'être* for my dependency. I need something to soothe my nerves. *(Pause as KEN puffs.)* When's the last time we had sex?

JOE: What?

KEN: Sex, Joe. Fucking. We used to do that occasionally.

JOE: If you want to call it that.

KEN: Oh, pardon me. I realize your experience in the realm of *fucking* is far wider and more varied than my own. What's the word for what we used to do, and don't do anymore? Help me out. You're the playwright.

(JOE goes over to KEN, gently takes the cigarette from his fingers and sets it in an ashtray.)

You never touch me anymore.

(JOE touches KEN's shoulder)

JOE: *(Meaning it this time.)* I'm sorry.

KEN: You don't treat me like I'm alive.

JOE: *(Very softly.)* That's because you don't act like it.

KEN: *(Same.)* That's because you don't treat me like it.

JOE: That's because you don't act like it.

KEN: That's because…

(JOE kisses him on the lips and presses his body close. It's a very long kiss. JOE moves his hand to KEN's crotch; KEN abruptly shoves the

hand away and breaks away from the embrace. He resumes his cigarette.)

Your dinner's congealing.

JOE: *(Disgusted.)* I don't believe you.

KEN: I'm only thinking of you.

JOE: I'm going out.

KEN: Where?

JOE: For a walk.

KEN: For a walk *where?*

JOE: Don't wait up for me.

(He starts to go.)

KEN: Joe.

JOE: What?!

KEN: I'm sorry. Stay home tonight. For once. For me. I didn't mean to shove you away. It's just my nerves. And my health in general. I'm in a bad state. But I'm seeing a new doctor. Did I tell you? And I've an appointment with a new psychiatrist. I'm going to get better. *(Giggles nervously.)* My former psychiatrist said I feel guilty about my mother's death and that's the root of all my problems.

JOE: What on earth do you have to feel guilty about? There was nothing you could do.

KEN: I'm just telling you what he said. Are you staying? I'll make tea. We can...talk.

JOE: There's nothing left to talk about. Nothing left but to claw at the carcass of our former conversations. And I'm sick of it. I'm sick of death. I want to go for a walk.

KEN: Please, Joe.

JOE: *(Knowing he won't.)* You can come with me if you like.

KEN: You're going to pick someone up. Is that it?

JOE: *(Satirically.)* It'd give us something to chat about over tea.

KEN: *(Going into another rage.)* Well you're not to bring him back here. I'll not have you bringing rough trade up to the flat.

JOE: I don't pick up "rough trade," Kenneth. I've never had trouble with a boy in my life.

KEN: Well there's always a first time and I'll not have it happen here. I'll not have it, do you hear me? Anyway, who wants your trash cluttering up the room. And who wants you? You trash. I work at cleaning this place for you all day from top to fucking bottom and what do you do? You want to bring the garbage home and fuck it on the bed. *I'll not have it!*

(JOE has put on his jacket and cap and is heading for the door.) Joe? Don't you want some dinner before you go? It won't take me long to heat up. You can heat it up if you like.

JOE: *(Pausing by the doorway.)* No thanks. I'm not really hungry. *(Pause.)* You're sure you don't want to come.

KEN: No, thank you. No sense letting a good meal go to waste. I'll save you the leftovers. In a container in the refrigerator.

JOE: Thanks. I probably won't be in till late. I'll try not to wake you when I get in.

KEN: I'll probably be up. I don't sleep much lately.

    (Pause.)

JOE: I'm off then.

    (KEN doesn't respond. JOE turns to go, then pauses and turns back.)

    You've nothing to feel guilty about. Sleep on that.

    (Blackout. Pause. The outer door slams.)

Scene Four

    (The Royal Academy of Dramatic Art, 1951. An empty area of the stage. KEN enters dressed theatrically: a black pin-stripe suit, black tie, black beret—no wig—and a camel-hair overcoat with a sash belt. He walks a few steps, a spotlight following him, then suddenly stops and dramatically flings his coat into a corner. His expression is inscrutable. He begins to mime petting a cat, cuddling and stroking it lovingly. Suddenly his expression changes. He becomes enraged and violently strangles the imaginary animal. He holds the limp body for a moment, and then his expression once again becomes inscrutable. He takes his bows, then walks away. JOE enters and sits where KEN was last, cross-legged on the floor, reading a book. He wears nondescript trousers and a shirt. KEN re-enters, looks at JOE, looks around uncertainly.)

KEN: *(Calls to JOE.)* Excuse me.

    (JOE looks up in surprise, looks around.)

    Yes, you. Have you perchance seen a coat lying about here?

JOE: Coat?

    (JOE's responses are very nervous and faltering, his working class accent more noticeable here than in other scenes.)

KEN: It's difficult to miss. Genuine camel-hair, you know.

JOE: *(Glances around.)* Is that it over there?

    (KEN goes to fetch his coat.)

KEN: Thank God. I was afraid someone might've made off with it.

JOE: I was tempted. It looks very suptuous. *(Repeating the word in the hope that KEN won't notice he made a mistake the first time.)* That's exactly the word to describe it. Sumptuous.

KEN: *(Flinging the coat over his shoulder flamboyantly.)* Not really. Just one of my little affectations. I like to indulge myself occasionally.

JOE: That's a healthy attitude.

(Pause. JOE self-consciously goes back to reading his book. KEN pulls a handkerchief from the pocket of his overcoat, wipes his hands, dabs at his forehead, then strides towards JOE with a sense of purpose.)

KEN: What is it you're reading?

JOE: Shakespeare.

KEN: I see. *(Quoting dramatically.)* "My glass shall not persuade me I am old,/So long as youth and thou are of one date,/But when in thee Time's furrows I behold,/Then look I death my days should expiate. For all the beauty that doth cover thee/Is but a seemly raiment of my heart, Which in thy breast doth live, as thine in me./How can I then be elder than thou art?" *(Pause. He clears his throat.)* That's from the Sonnets. *(Pause.)*

JOE: That was very nice.

KEN: Which play are you reading? *(Quickly.)* Let me guess. *King Lear?*

JOE: *The Tempest.* I'm reading it for Ariel. It's my favourite part in all of Shakespeare.

KEN: So this isn't your first foray into the world of the immortal bard. Very impressive. Though I prefer Marlowe, myself. Given the choice, I'd rather have been a king's favourite than a queen. You?

JOE: *(Not having understood a word.)* I played Ariel once.

KEN: For a production, or for class? Either way, I regret to've missed it. You'd make an exceptional Ariel.

JOE: D'you think so?

KEN: Quite. Ariel must be interpreted by a male. There is no other way the part can be properly played. You know, of course, that all of Shakespeare's female roles were originally written for boy actors.

JOE: Of course. That's what I think, also. *(Hastily.)* But when I said I'd played Ariel, I'm afraid I only meant I read a speech for my elocution teacher, Madame Rothery. *(Trying desperately to appear sophisticated.)* Perhaps you've heard of her?

KEN: I don't believe so.

JOE: Well, it doesn't matter now, I got rid of the bitch as soon as I was accepted into the Academy. *(Bashfully.)* Sorry about the language.

KEN: What do you mean? A cunt by any other name would be as smelly a spectacle.

JOE: You're very different from my mum, you know.

KEN: I should hope so.

JOE: She can cuss like a sailor when something gets her dander up, but if she ever caught me following suit she'd threaten to wallop me one. She can do it, too.

KEN: What was your quarrel with this "Madame Rothery"?

JOE: She told me I sound gutter. That's why I was taking the lessons, see. To learn to sound more sophisticated, and refined. I didn't mind her saying so. Much. But the cunt *(Glances at KEN for approval.)* didn't think I could learn any better. Not that I've done much to prove her wrong. Yet.

KEN: I think your accent is charming. It sets you apart.

JOE: You think so?

KEN: That and your looks.

> *(Embarrassed pause.)*

What "gutter" is it you hail from?

JOE: *(With a grimace.)* Leicester. My dad's a gardener. He's almost blind.

KEN: And your blaspheming mother?

JOE: She doesn't work anymore. Her eyes are bad, too. Used to be she worked at a sewing machine—in a factory. It's what did her eyes in. Now she's a char. *(Pause.)* It wasn't a gutter so much as a well of boredom. Though Mum likes to pretend like we're lapping up luxury left and right. D'you know she once got herself up in gold lamé just to go around the corner? Even painted her shoes gold. The paint cracked when she walked and she left a trail of gold dust stretching from our front door on into the pub.

KEN: *(Laughing.)* No!

JOE: *(Same.)* Yes!

KEN: *(Slowly; making a pronouncement.)* I'll bet she hates fucking.

JOE: *(Eyes wide.)* What?

KEN: Sex. You know. Fucking.

JOE: D'you know you're right. That's what she's always saying. "How I ever got four children I'll never know. It were pure hell!" *(Pause.)* So what're your parents. Something real high-class and respected, I'll bet.

KEN: My parents are dead.

JOE: *(Taking this in stride.)* We should all be so blessed. Sorry if I sound in poor taste but I guess you start expecting these things to happen when you reach your age.

KEN: I'm 25.

JOE: *(Shocked.)* I thought you were a lot older than that. *(Catching himself.)* I mean you come off so much more distinguished than most of the other students. *(Pause.)* Most of them are afraid of you, Mr. Halliwell.

KEN: You may call me Kenneth. *(Suddenly realizing.)* How did you know my name?

JOE: *(Sheepishly.)* I noticed you in class. You're difficult to miss. I saw your mime in class this morning, with the cat.

KEN:	What did you think of it?
JOE:	*(Genuinely enthusiastic.)* Think of it? I loved it! *(Catches himself.)* That is, I thought it was…most effective. *(Pause.)* I'll bet you have no idea who I am.
KEN:	That's not true. You're Joe.
JOE:	John.
KEN:	Yes, of course.
JOE:	John Orton.
	(They shake hands awkwardly. Pause.)
KEN:	You said the other students are…"afraid" of me?
JOE:	Intimidated, I guess I mean.
KEN:	How do you know this?
JOE:	I know because they tell me. They treat me like I'm one of them. Because I make them laugh, I guess. I pretend to be friendly so they won't treat me badly on account of my accent. But I'm not. One of them. They can be so snobby and stand-offish, so…
KEN:	Pretentious?
JOE:	Yeah, exactly. Always pretending like they're fountains of knowledge, always spouting off…
KEN:	It's only to be expected, John. You know what happens when idle hands get hold of a little learning.
JOE:	Yeah. They're afraid of anyone who's different from average.
KEN:	Or better than the same.
JOE:	Like you.
KEN:	And like you.
JOE:	Yeah. *(Pause.)* I'm sorry.
KEN:	For?
JOE:	Your parents—what I said.
KEN:	That's all right. You didn't realize.
JOE:	That's no excuse. Anyway, I didn't mean it like it sounded.
KEN:	It's all right. My mother's been dead some time. And it wasn't difficult to adjust to my father's absence, as we never did make a habit of acknowledging each other's existence.
JOE:	What happened to them? Was it an accident?
KEN:	*(Sententiously.)* Dwelling on the morbid past is a mark of regression.
JOE:	Sorry.
KEN:	Don't apologize.
	(Pause.)
JOE:	I bet you don't find me so bleeding charming now.
KEN:	Certainly I do. In fact, I predict your charm will be a great asset to you in life. Lord knows I could use some.

JOE: But it's like I said, you're so distinguished, you don't need charm. *(Pause.)* That's not what I meant. *(Burning with embarrassment, he grabs his book and turns to go.)* I'd better be off.

KEN: John, wait.

        (Impulsively, he grasps JOE's shoulders and turns JOE to face him.)

JOE: *(Miserably.)* What do you want?

        (KEN takes the book from him and tosses it on the floor, then takes JOE's hands and looks straight at him.)

KEN: It's all right.

        (Pause. They look at each other. Then KEN nervously steps back, pulling out his handkerchief to wipe his hands.)

JOE: *(Remaining close to KEN.)* That really is a lovely coat. *(Pause.)* May I stroke your camel-fur?

KEN: *(Not looking at him.)* What? No!

        (Pause. KEN takes off the coat and hands it to JOE.)

        Here. You can have it.

JOE: *(Surprised and excited.)* I couldn't!

KEN: *(Almost angrily.)* Of course you can! Take it.

        (Pause. JOE is staring at KEN. He comes to a quick decision.)

JOE: *(Turning around and holding out his arms.)* Will you help me with it on?

KEN: *(Obliging grudgingly.)* I hardly think this is necessary. I'm sure you're capable of dressing yourself.

JOE: Four arms are better than two.

KEN: And foreskins are the most fun of all.

JOE: *(Turns to face KEN.)* What d'you think?

KEN: Sumptuous. Exactly the word to describe it.

JOE: So we're friends now.

KEN: That depends. Are you intimidated by me, John?

JOE: Never was. I thought you were mysterious and distinguished. Not dangerous.

KEN: Don't be so sure.

        (JOE struts across the stage, chin up, nose in the air.)

        Just what do you think you're doing?

JOE: *(Good-humouredly imitating KEN's didactic, prissy tone.)* I'm Kenneth Halliwell. I'm dangerous. *(Walks boldly up to KEN.)* To complete the effect.

        (He reaches to grab KEN's beret from his head.)

KEN: *(Sharply.)* John!

        (KEN reflexively slaps him. They are both shocked by the action. JOE stares at KEN a moment. Then he turns and hurriedly picks up his book.)

	(Blurts it out.) Let me buy you a drink.
JOE:	*(Astonished.)* Alcohol?
KEN:	Yes. *(With some of his former affectation.)* I'm of age.
JOE:	I don't drink.
KEN:	You could make an exception.
JOE:	Why should I?
KEN:	Because it's the least I can do.
	(Pause. JOE considers this.)
JOE:	That's true. *(Pause.)* You could buy me a Coke.
KEN:	*(Relieved.)* My pleasure.
JOE:	Then let's go.
	(JOE walks off, ignoring KEN, who hurries after him. Blackout.)

Scene Five

(Several months later. KEN's flat: a double-bed; books everywhere; a desk and a typewriter. KEN sits on the bed with JOE, who is reading, in his lap. KEN is stroking JOE's hair.)

KEN:	My pussycat.
JOE:	Piss off, Ken, I'm reading.
KEN:	I don't love you for your mind.
JOE:	I thought you were trying to educate it.
KEN:	There's more to life than books.
JOE:	*(Hands KEN a book.)* Here. Stimulate your intellect. Or wank yourself off with it for all I care. Only leave me read in peace. You're drooling all over the Symposium.

(KEN throws the book across the room. JOE ignores this and continues reading. KEN yanks the book out of JOE's hands and throws it after the other one. JOE sits perfectly still for a minute, then gets up to get it. KEN grabs him and spins him around.)

KEN:	I don't think you're even a proper homosexual.
JOE:	*(Shakes off KEN's hand.)* That's not worth a response. *(He sits back down with his book.)*
KEN:	I'll add that to my list of things you don't respond to. *(Pause.)* It's me, isn't it? Something I've done. Or something I could be doing I'm not.
JOE:	The area of my personal fetishes is a murky one. I'd advise you to keep out of it if you want to retain any respect for me as a fellow civilized human being.
KEN:	You've never pretended to be civilized. It's one of the things that attracted me to you in the first place.

(Pause.)

JOE: Sometimes… I don't appreciate the way you treat me.

KEN: What way is that.

JOE: Like I'm some kind of glorified…office-boy…geisha girl…

KEN: A titillating amalgam. Go on.

JOE: *(Becoming agitated.)* Like any time you want to use me for sex or to run your errands or endure another of your dramatic recitations I should automatically be ready as though I had nothing better to do than accommodate your least whim.

KEN: I'm working and looking towards the future. I'm thinking of you, too, you know. What're you contributing?

JOE: All I can! That's why I was sitting here reading a fucking book when I could be out pursuing more common, callow youthful activities. Like having fun.

KEN: And I'm no fun at all, am I?

JOE: You're bloody right you're not!

KEN: You're talking like a shop-assistant again.

JOE: *(Sulking.)* What do you care how I talk? You don't love me for my mind.

KEN: Don't be childish.

JOE: It's how you treat me. Carrying on half the time like we're destined for glory.

KEN: That's only on the rare occasion I can make myself heard over your bitching.

JOE: I wish on one such occasion you'd take advantage of the opportunity to explain how we're going to become famous actors playing walk-on parts in gloomy repertory theatres that no one ever attends because they're damp and cold and the plays are dead shitty. But there it is. What else can I do besides act—type?

KEN: *(Indicating his desk.)* Look in the second drawer on the far right.

    (JOE looks hesitant.)

Do it, John.

JOE: *(Retrieving a manuscript.)* What's this?

KEN: My novel.

JOE: *(In disbelief and awe.)* All this?

KEN: One day when I'm the published recipient of critical accolades, you'll be proud to've known Kenneth Halliwell.

JOE: *(Sits on KEN's knee.)* I already am. *(They kiss.)*

KEN: You could be of great help to me, you know.

JOE: *(Playfully.)* As your inspiration?

KEN: I meant you could put your skills, such as they are, to good use typing my manuscripts.

> *(KEN is unbuttoning JOE's shirt. He doesn't notice that JOE is no longer responding until JOE pushes him away, gets up and buttons his shirt.)*

JOE: I guess I'd better get started.

KEN: Started?

JOE: *(Sits at desk.)* On your manuscript.

KEN: Right now? You don't have to start right now.

JOE: Don't be modest. Thanks to you, Ken, I've finally found my calling in life. I'll be the world's only speed-typing male whore. Six inches and 100 words per minute. Gives head and takes shorthand, too.

KEN: I hope you don't think you're impressing anyone. Sulking is counter-productive.

JOE: If the sight of my idolatry offends you so deeply you could pass me that manuscript. Or you could leave.

KEN: "Idolatry" means "to worship." I don't think that's the word you were looking for.

JOE: You're right. The word I'm looking for is bugger off.

KEN: This is my flat, I'll thank you to remember. My inheritance is the only thing between you and the streets.

JOE: You begged me to come live with you.

KEN: I hardly begged. I took pity on you when you had nowhere else to go. I didn't have to invite you to stay here.

JOE: Forgive me, I forgot the hoards of eager young men coming to blows in the streets over who's to share a flat with Ken Halliwell. It's a privilege all right, having one's cock sucked by a bobbing boiled egg !

KEN: The only way I want to see your six inches is six feet under! *(Silence. Then they start giggling, trying hard not to.)*

JOE: *(Sobering.)* You never act like you're happy with me.

KEN: *(Astonished.)* Don't I? *(Pause.)* Perhaps it's because I don't have much experience being happy. Sometimes it's hard for me to believe I am. But I am. I'm happy.

> *(Pause. Then JOE impulsively removes his pants while KEN looks on expectantly. Pants off, JOE bounds onto the bed and strikes a pose designed to entice. KEN, dignified and sedate, sits with him. JOE stretches out with his head in KEN's lap. KEN pushes JOE away.)*

Back to your book. Stop pestering me. Kids.

> *(They sit side by side on the bed for a few moments, reading. JOE leans back and rests his feet in KEN's lap.)*

What's this?

JOE: Come across something of interest?

KEN: Nothing you'd know of.

(They continue reading. JOE strokes KEN's face with one foot and plays in his lap with the other.)

This is a new development.

JOE: Care to share it with me?

KEN: It's over your head.

(Pause. JOE tosses his book away.)

JOE: Ken...tell me some more about the Greek gods and goddesses.

KEN: *(Sighs heavily.)* We've been all through that.

JOE: Tell me again.

KEN: I don't know why I put up with you.

(He puts his book aside after carefully marking his place.)

Have I told you the story of Pygmalion and Galatea?

JOE: Tell me again.

KEN: *(Removes JOE's sock.)* Pygmalion was a young, handsome brilliant sculptor, famous throughout Cyprus. Only he despised women.

JOE: Sounds like a real catch.

KEN: *(Kissing JOE's toes.)* He had sworn never to marry. His art, he told himself, sufficed to fulfill him. *(Kisses JOE's heel.)* Nevertheless, he devoted his creative genius to sculpting a magnificent statue of a woman, a woman more beautiful than your wildest imaginings. *(Kisses JOE's calf.)* And she grew ever more beautiful the more he worked on her. There had never been woman nor statue in existence lovely as she. Until one day he had to admit to himself *(Kisses JOE's knee.)* that he'd fallen in love with her. His glorious creation. This hopeless love tormented him.

JOE: Poor bloke.

KEN: He kissed the cold, hard, lifeless body all over, caressing the limbs his own had moulded.

(He kisses JOE's thigh. Blackout.)

JOE: What happened next?

Scene Six

(Years later: 1962. Their new flat: the bedroom, as in Scene One, but without the telephone. KEN is sitting on his bed, cutting pictures out of a large art book. Pictures and scraps cover the bed and surrounding floor. JOE is at the desk, typing on the flap of a book's dust-jacket. On his bed is the book with its plastic cover removed, beside it. JOE wears the top of a pair of pyjamas and briefs, KEN the bottoms with no shirt. After a few moments, JOE stops typing and takes out the jacket, reading it over.)

KEN: Did you ever hear back from that publisher?

JOE: *(Goes to his bed with the jacket.)* Yes.

KEN: *(Surprised.)* And?

JOE: *(Replacing the jacket and cover on the book.)* Lots of encouraging notes scribbled on the manuscript. But the verdict was it's too "rarefied" for publication. And you?

KEN: I'm expecting word any day. Though I doubt they'll find it commercially viable.

JOE: *(Examines the book.)* A novel called *Priapus In The Shrubbery* that's not commercially viable? It's unthinkable. *(Holds up the book to KEN.)* There. Can you tell it's been interfered with?

KEN: Give it here.

        (JOE throws it to him. KEN examines the book.)

        It appears absolutely innocuous. You can't tell anyone's tampered with it until you lay it open.

JOE: *(Grinning.)* Like me.

        (KEN tosses it back. JOE places it on a shelf with a pile of others.)

        I'm bored, Ken.

KEN: Make up another dirty blurb.

JOE: I've filled the flaps of every volume we nicked. All that's left is to sneak them back in.

KEN: The library's closed now.

JOE: I know. I meant tomorrow. And this time we're waiting around until some unsuspecting undiscriminating member of the reading public picks one up and has the shit shocked out of him. It's no fun being subversive when nobody's paying attention.

KEN: I've been doing some thinking. About where our careers are going.

JOE: What's to think about?

KEN: That's it exactly. Perhaps we were too hasty in deciding to abort our collaborative efforts after *Last Days of Sodom* was rejected.

JOE: It doesn't seem to've injured our anonymity in any way. Besides, I've just started on a new play. When I'm through I want to send it in to the BBC. See what comes of it.

KEN: A play? *(Pause.)* What about?

JOE: Us.

KEN: I'd advise you to abandon that topic in favour of something with a broader commercial appeal—like being strung up by the short hairs.

JOE: Not us as is. *(Pause.)* I took the plot of *The Boy Hairdresser* and converted it into a radio play.

KEN: Isn't that a bit presumptuous? Making use of our manuscripts without first consulting me.

JOE: Rejected manuscripts, Ken. We are as yet prominent members of

The Great Unpublished. You should be grateful one at least is being put to some use other than keeping the dust mites company under your bed.

KEN: You're one to expect gratitude, after all I've done for you.

JOE: I thought your intention was for me to gain independence. I wasn't aware that you still wanted *(Searches for an appropriate term.)* ...the Delphic oracle.

KEN: *(Impressed in spite of himself.)* Now *you're* putting words in *my* mouth.

(JOE walks over to KEN and sits in his lap.)

JOE: It's big enough for both of us.

KEN: All the better to accommodate you.

(JOE swings around so he's straddling KEN.)

JOE: Why don't we read to each other? That's always fun. *The Decline and Fall of the Roman Empire.* Why wasn't there one written about "The Rise"?

KEN: *(Setting aside his scissors.)* Too rarefied for publication, no doubt.

(There is a loud knocking on the door.)

Are you expecting someone? *(JOE shakes his head.)* This is odd. We never have unexpected visitors.

JOE: We never have expected visitors. *(He climbs off KEN and moves towards the kitchen door.)* It'll be Mrs. Corden from across the hall. She threatened to come by to tell us all about her holiday seaside.

(More knocking. KEN notices JOE is about to leave the room.)

KEN: Don't leave her on my hands.

(JOE hurriedly grabs a shirt and pants off the floor and goes through the kitchen door, disappearing from sight.)

JOE: *(Off.)* I'm not decent. I have to make myself presentable.

KEN: *(Calling after.)* You'll never get anywhere in life with that attitude.

(Male voices from beyond the door call "Mr. Halliwell? Mr Orton?" Hearing this KEN looks startled.)

John? *(Pause.)* Shit.

(He goes through the door into the darkness beyond, pulling on a bathrobe. His voice can be heard, off. Also abrasive masculine voices, their words indistinct.)

Oh, dear. Yes, I see. Would you wait here a moment? I'd like a chance to inform my roommate. Mr. Orton, yes.

(KEN comes back into the light looking dazed and frightened. He sees the books, scraps and scissors. In a panic, he gets on his hands and knees and tries to stuff them under the bed. Stops and sits on the bed, near tears.)

(Calling.) John!

JOE: Is it safe to come out?

KEN: I have to speak to you. Now. *(JOE comes in, tucking in his shirt.)*

JOE: You look traumatized. What happened? Did she assail you with pictures of herself and Mr. Corden frolicking in their swimming costumes?

KEN: *(In a low hiss.)* There are two police officers at the door. They have a warrant to search the flat.

JOE: Better hide the Vaseline.

KEN: John, I'm serious!

JOE: *(Realizing it's true.)* Calm down, Ken. Maybe it's a mistake. Did they say what this is about?

KEN: Yes.

              (Voice calling, "Mr. Halliwell, we're coming in now.")

              The books.

JOE: *(Collapses in a chair.)* Oh, shit.

              (Lighting shift. In the following KEN acts the part of the prison psychiatrist, interrogating JOE, who squirms beneath a spotlight.)

PSYCHIATRIST: Mr. Orton, I suppose you know why you're here.

JOE: Damaging public property, I'm told.

PSYCHIATRIST: More than simply damaging, Mr. Orton. What fascinates and disturbs me is the time and energy you expended on the ruination of library books.

JOE: We've no circumstances, no means. No money. We wanted those books but couldn't afford them. It made us mad.

PSYCHIATRIST: That doesn't account for the care you put into creating such deranged images. A monkey's face peering from a rose? Dame Sybil Thorndike confronted with a Greco-Roman phallus? Or the so called "blurbs" you typed in the flaps, deliberately dreadfully misleading the reader as to the books' contents. *(Sounding truly bewildered.)* I simply cannot fathom your reasoning. Why did you do it? Do you even know yourself?

JOE: It's like I said. *(Sheepishly.)* I guess we let our anger get out of hand.

PSYCHIATRIST: You seem a nice, decent young man, Mr. Orton. If you don't mind my saying so, you remind me a bit of my own son. In character alone, you understand. He's been known to get into a few scrapes of his own, I don't mind telling you. But he's basically a good sort.

JOE: That's very flattering, sir.

PSYCHIATRIST: Therefore I regret to ask you this. *(Clears his throat.)* What is the nature of your relationship with Mr. Halliwell?

JOE: He's my mate.

              (Spotlight shifts to KEN, seated. Now JOE takes over as the psychiatrist.)

KEN: We're lovers.

PSYCHIATRIST: *(Shocked.)* Could you be more specific, Mr. Halliwell?

KEN: You don't want me to get much more specific than that. We live together. Share a flat. We collaborate on a literary basis. We have sex.

PSYCHIATRIST: Do you mean you want to…be intimate with Mr. Orton?

KEN: *(Confused.)* Right now?

           (Pause.)

PSYCHIATRIST: I won't pretend to understand exactly what you're experiencing, Mr. Halliwell. But I imagine it must entail a great deal of frustration, this…unhealthy idolatry for your young friend. Especially considering he's a family man.

KEN: John? Married? *(Pause.)* Are you delusional, doctor?

PSYCHIATRIST: In fact, he claims you're the one introduced him to his wife.

           (Pause. KEN is dumbfounded.)

           Well, Mr. Halliwell, I suppose I have all the answers I need from you. All but one. What have you learned from your prison experience?

           (Pause during which JOE-as-psychiatrist blurs back into JOE-as-himself. He pulls out the handcuffs and attaches himself to KEN.)

JOE: Chin up, Kenneth. It can't get any worse.

KEN: It's not going to get any better, is it?

           (Tableau. Blackout.)

Act Two

Scene One

(1961: the kitchen. The radio is playing a very early and relentlessly upbeat Beatles tune. The table is set for two. In the middle of the table is a pathetic assortment of wilted flowers in a cheap vase. KEN is bustling around making breakfast. He's dressed in his pyjamas. JOE enters from the bedroom in his briefs and a T-shirt. He turns off the radio.)

KEN: *(Turning to JOE.)* John! I thought you'd never get up. Sit down, I'll get your tea.

JOE: *(Half-awake.)* What's got you so excited first thing in the morning? Did you have special success wanking off your wake-up hard-on?

KEN: *(Sets tea on the table.)* Life. Life has me excited, John.

(He takes JOE by the shoulders and sits him down at the table.)

Drink your tea. I'm fixing breakfast.

JOE: We never have breakfast.

KEN: Well this morning we're having fried eggs, bacon, toast and marmalade.

JOE: How'd you manage that?

KEN: It's all compliments of Miss Boynes from the flat below. I met her as I was picking up the mail. When I mentioned we'd been making do on the dole since *(Allowing himself a moment's irony.)* *Reading Gaol*, she promptly buried me alive in her benevolence. Although I insisted we're perfectly happy in our picturesque poverty. We don't need much to be content—just each other and a typewriter. Though it would be nice to be able to indulge oneself once in a while. Even with only marmalade.

(Pause. KEN looks sad, distant. Then he forces himself to brighten.)

Aren't the flowers lovely, John? She gave them me fresh from her window-box.

JOE: She certainly seems fond of you, Kenneth. Always having you for tea.

KEN: *(As he cooks.)* She's just a lonely old lady.

JOE: An especially unsavoury variety of cunt. She ought to be symbolically immolated.

KEN: She doesn't seem to have any friends. I suppose they've all passed on. Now all she has are her budgerigars, and they keep dying on her too. *(Shrugs.)* She's harmless enough. And the flowers are lovely, John. Just smell them.

JOE: *(Leaning over them warily.)* They're crawling with insects. *(He plucks a spider from a petal, examines it.)* Women should die upon spawning, like spiders, a far nobler species. I can admire spiders.

    (He crushes the spider between his fingers.)

KEN: I think they're pretty. Cheery. We need something to liven up this sepulchral atmosphere... *(Puts eggs on their plates.)* Here's your eggs. The toast is coming.

JOE: *(Stares suspiciously at the eggs.)* Was there anything of consequence in the post? A letter from a publisher, perhaps?

KEN: Nothing like that. That's one of the reasons I feel so strangely optimistic this morning. I sent my latest manuscript to yet another publisher only yesterday, so there's no chance I could be receiving a letter of rejection so soon. There is a rather mysterious piece of mail addressed to you.

JOE: *(As KEN puts bacon on their plates.)* Mysterious? Then it can't be for me.

KEN: I put it on the desk. Mind the toast.

    (KEN goes into the bedroom. The toast immediately pops up, burnt. He returns with the letter.)

JOE: The toast is burnt.

KEN: Shit.

    (He hands the letter to JOE, takes the toast and begins scraping off the black part with a knife.)

JOE: *(Reading the envelope.)* Who's "Margaret Ramsey"?

KEN: If you don't know I certainly don't.

    (JOE opens up the letter and reads.)

    Really, John, now you've decided to take up with women, at least make an arrangement with your lovers so they don't send their correspondence to our mutual address. The neighbours will talk. *(Sets toast on plates.)* It's the best I can do.

    (JOE leaps up, jolting the table and upsetting the vase, which shatters on the floor. Flowers and water spill everywhere. KEN's food is soaked.)

    John! Honestly.

    (He gets up and starts to clean up the mess.)

JOE: *(Sits back down in a daze.)* Margaret Ramsey is a play agent. Listen to this: "I was very pleased to receive *Entertaining Mr. Sloane*, which I think is extremely fresh and interesting—"

KEN: *(Interrupting.)* You sent her a copy of *Sloane* and didn't bother telling me?

JOE: *(Gets up and starts pacing.)* I forgot all about it. The BBC producer sent her my radio play when he was through with it. I didn't think anything'd come of it.

KEN: Sit down and eat. Stop leaping about. It's spoiling my appetite.

(JOE takes a swipe at the marmalade, sucking a gob off his finger.)

Does she explicitly state she's wanting to have it produced?

JOE: *(Sits and reads.)* "I'm not absolutely sure it will hold a whole evening but I think it might." *(Looks up.)* That's encouraging, isn't it?

KEN: Eat up. And give me that. *(Takes letter from JOE.)* You're getting it all sticky with marmalade. *(Reads.)* She wants to meet with you.

(JOE leaps up and lunges for the fridge.)

JOE: I know. *(He takes out a bottle of milk.)* You'll come with me, won't you?

(Swigs.)

KEN: Don't drink milk from the bottle. *(He pours a glass of milk for JOE.)* Are you certain Miss Ramsey would appreciate my presence?

JOE: If she doesn't she can fuck her extremely fresh and interesting self.

(KEN is reasonably satisfied by this answer, but continues to fuss.)

KEN: Who's going to clean up this mess?

JOE: I made the mess, I'll clean it up.

(JOE takes a dish rag and starts wiping up the table with a dramatic flourish.)

Look, I'm Kenneth Halliwell.

KEN: *(Scowling.)* That's not the way you do it. You're spilling crumbs all over my *(With self-conscious irony.)* nice clean floor.

(Takes the rag from JOE.)

Your problem, John, is that you do everything for dramatic effect, at the cost of practical results. Now, watch. *(Demonstrating.)* Take the rag and wipe the crumbs into the palm of your hand, cupped and placed like so.

(JOE comes up behind KEN and seizes KEN's crotch.)

JOE: Cupped and placed—like so?

KEN: You never cease to amaze yourself.

JOE: *(Grabs the letter from KEN.)* I'm so overcome I think I'll have a piss to celebrate. *(He heads for the lavatory with the letter.)* I knew it had to happen eventually. I knew. Didn't you?

(Pause. KEN doesn't respond.)

Ken? Didn't you always know?

(JOE disappears from sight. KEN takes out the broom and dustpan, starts sweeping up the shattered vase.)

KEN: *(Not at all certain.)* Of course I knew.

(Lights fade.)

Scene Two

(1966. JOE sits on his bed, talking. He looks, and sounds, completely exhausted. KEN moves around in the background, unpacking JOE's suitcase. JOE is in his jeans and T-shirt; KEN wears his pyjamas.)

JOE: ...the lead actress becoming hysterical and having to be led off-stage, taken home and sedated. Irate old bitches tearing their programs to bits in the aisles. Conversations overheard in the lobby during intermission: "It's about Jesus, d'you see, being a queer." Christ! It was a farce all right but no one was laughing. Me least of all. The director took me out to dinner one night towards the end. Ostensibly to discuss his new technique of having the actors speak in time with a metronome. To "emphasize style." I suppose in the hope that the content might be politely overlooked. "You can't communicate, Joe," he said to me. "It's your one great flaw as an artist and as a human being," he said. I told him to manoeuver his metronome up his middle-class ass and asked if I'd communicated my meaning to his satisfaction. Well no, I didn't but I wish I had. Perhaps he's right. I've rewritten the play beyond recognition or redemption. When I try to sleep I dream I'm still rewriting in some nondescript hotel room, each one as hostile to compulsory inspiration as the one previous, at that fucking portable typewriter, the only consistent element. It kept me from bouncing off the nondescript walls. Along with your letters. Why didn't you ring me, Ken? I know it must have been lonely here. But you know all I could think of was getting home. *(Looks up at KEN whose expression is inscrutable.)* To your welcoming arms and your comforting words, I think it was. *(Pause. No response.)* Or your welcoming words and your comforting arms. *(Pause.)* All right, if you're not going to comfort me you could at least pity me. Out loud, if you please.

(JOE lies back on the bed. KEN stands over him and looks down.)

KEN: Moan moan moan. That's all it ever is from you. This room isn't big enough for two Lady Macbeths.

JOE: I could always clasp an asp to my bosom.

KEN: Asps are so passé. Besides, the poor creature would probably die of boredom. It would be far more practical if you'd settle for gouging out your eyes with a butter knife. Only you'll have to hold off on the gouging-out bit till I get around to doing the dishes. Can't have you committing suicide with soiled silver-ware.

JOE: I've already told Peggy I shan't continue like this. I can't work under these circumstances.

KEN: Remember when we had no circumstances? You didn't go around swooning and moaning then.

JOE: I'm beginning to take myself too seriously, in your opinion.

KEN: In my opinion, yes. But perhaps I've caught you just in time. In the act, as it were. What we both need is a change of scenery. To be specific: a holiday.

JOE: *(Dazed.)* A holiday...

KEN: Away from the miserable, typical, fog-and-pissing-rain weather as well as the misty memories, I can recover from the blow Peggy Ramsey dealt me.

JOE: You were attacked by my agent?

KEN: The wounds are figurative only. *(Pause.)* She rejected my play.

JOE: Ken, I'm sorry. I know how hard you worked. *(Pause.)* Did she have anything positive to say?

KEN: She did mention it was unique in one respect.

JOE: There you go.

KEN: She said it was so unbearably boring she couldn't force herself to read the whole thing. The rejection was based upon the first scene. She suggested I enter into a profession better suited to my literary abilities—like dentistry.

JOE: She didn't.

KEN: Shall I produce her commentary?

JOE: *(Almost amused in spite of himself.)* I'll have to have a talk with her.

KEN: I don't need you to defend my honour. I'd rather confront the truth of what people think of me.

JOE: Peggy thinks a great deal of you. You mustn't let her wording put you off. When she first read *Sloane* she told me she found it derivative.

KEN: Perhaps she had that in mind when she called my play "drivel."

JOE: You can't let this—

KEN: *(Shrieking.)* Shut up! Just shut up, would you? And don't expect me to be sympathetic and comforting when you start going on about "renouncing the theatre." *You* have a choice.

JOE: You have real talent—

KEN: *(Near tears.)* And don't say that! I don't want to hear that anymore, do you understand me? You *knew*, didn't you. *(Pause. JOE avoids looking at him.)* You knew the play was shit. You just wanted to watch me humiliate myself.

JOE: You know that isn't true. You know I want you to succeed.

KEN: *(Gaining momentum.)* Why? Because you think you owe me? Because you want to unburden yourself of your misguided guilt?

JOE: Try because I *love* you.

KEN: *(Out of control.)* There *is* a God! *(Pause.)*

JOE: I don't know what more you want.

KEN: A church wedding.

JOE: I just told you I loved you. Out loud. To your face. With my clothes on. What is it you want? Me to prove it to you? Because I will. Because I do owe you, Ken, and I want to help you.

KEN: What can you do? Unless it's true the rumour you parted the Red Sea with your prick.

JOE: There's still your collages. Whenever we've anyone in it's the first thing they remark upon. That reporter who was here the other day, he was so busy admiring them and going on about how "professional" they look I had to remind him of his reason for coming.

KEN: *(Sulking.)* How would I know that? You exile me from the flat whenever you're being interviewed.

JOE: That's why I'm telling you. I have influence now; connections, you know. *(Remembering.)* That's if I've a reputation left after this apocalyptic production. I still think *Loot* can be a success. I think it's the best thing I've written. You thought so too, remember? If it's ever given a proper production— *(He notices KEN's expression and stops. Defensively.)* Well after all, the play's the thing. D'you like that? I just made it up. *(Pause.)* Ken. Let me arrange a showing for you.

KEN: I've failed at everything else I've undertaken. Why should this be any different?

JOE: *(Bluntly.)* I don't know.

KEN: Thank you for admitting that.

JOE: Would you rather I patronize you?

KEN: I'm not asking to be patronized. I'd be content with an outdated display of conjugal support.

JOE: *(With disdain.)* "Conjugal support" —it sounds like a type of brassiere.

KEN: Of course I know what intense distaste such terms inspire in you. I know how necessary it is for you to believe everything in your life is disposable. Temporary. Transitory. It's just a stage.

JOE: The whole world's a stage. *(Pause.)* Where would we go? If we had our holiday.

KEN: *(Suddenly excited.)* I've already thought of that. I made some inquiries while you were in Cambridge. Tangier's the answer. Everyone who's been raves like mad about it. Think of it—

scantily clad Moroccan boys swarming the beaches. And all available!

JOE: I think we've found your calling, Ken. Ever consider becoming a travel agent?

KEN: I'm told in confidence the boys'll do anything for a scant few dirhams. They *all* take it, or so I hear.

JOE: But you don't ask them to do anything. *(Over KEN's protests.)* Mutual masturbation and other dormitory schoolboy antics.

KEN: I didn't mention me specifically. I was making the point that they'll do anything for *your* benefit. And for your knowledge I've been fucked without a qualm by various other parties. It's *you* who has the sexual block.

JOE: Only with you.

KEN: And for a second it slipped my mind I'm living with the connoisseur of London's low-life. A connoisseur of sewage.

JOE: Save the rest of it for a time when I can appreciate it. Or throw it back. *(Starts to remove his jeans.)* I'm so tired right now I don't even know what I'm saying. I don't want to talk about sex.

KEN: Now I believe you're tired. *(KEN starts helping JOE off with his jeans.)*

JOE: *(Moans.)* Ken, I just *said*—

KEN: Oh give your whining a rest. I'm not partial to necrophilia.

> *(He folds the jeans and socks neatly and drapes them over the back of a chair. Takes the blanket from his own bed and gently tucks it around JOE, who's lying on top of the covers. He sits on a chair by the bed, watching JOE.)*

JOE: *(Without opening his eyes.)* Ken?

KEN: Go to sleep.

JOE: We have to get you a wig.

KEN: *(Feels his bald head.)* A wig?

JOE: So that when we get to Morocco, the boys won't mistakenly think they're wanking off the King and I instead of an old queen.

> *(KEN gets up and turns out the lights. Lighting change. He sits back down.)*

KEN: John? *(No answer. He forces himself to use the new name.)* Joe. Doesn't it ever frighten you? The futility of it. Anonymous sex with indifferent strangers. *(Quickly.)* I just want to know. *(Pause.)* I need to know. *(Pause.)* You owe me that.

JOE: *(Sits up a little and stares at KEN.)* What is it you think you'll get out of me, Confessor 'Iggins? Come back and see me on my deathbed. Maybe then you'll get what you want. But only maybe.

KEN: Everyone's afraid. You can't tell me you're not.

JOE: What if I told you there's no room in me to be frightened—

	nothing left of me to be scared. I'm too fucking angry.
KEN:	I know you are. I am too.
JOE:	Not like I am.
KEN:	I know. Why are you so angry?
JOE:	*(Sitting up fully.)* Why *aren't* you? What are you so frightened of, Ken? What is it about what I do that scares you so much you can't even be as angry as you should be? It's not the danger, the risks involved. Not that alone. And it's not the fear that I'll form an emotional attachment in the space of a few hours spent sweating and moaning, because we both know that won't happen.
KEN:	That's it. It's your attitude. You're so cold. Hard. *You* frighten me. When did it happen? When did you change? *(Pause.)* Did I do this?
JOE:	*(Mocking.)* Don't torment yourself.
KEN:	I'm scared. It's true. But so are you—I know you are. *(Pause. A realization.)* You're afraid of *real intimacy.*
JOE:	*(With intensity, but without emotion.)* And you're a fucking elitist snob. Men forced to seek each other out to suck each other off in shadows, dark corners, and derelict houses, always wary, ever alert, always predatory. However much you whine and bitch you're always willing to listen to my grim fairy tales so long as there's a punch line. Then you can afford to be amused, reassured of the fact that you're "above" that sort of behaviour. That *is* what you think, isn't it?
KEN:	*(With dignity.)* Yes. It is.
JOE:	And I'm the heartless bastard. Do you understand what it is to be forced into a position that offers no options, no alternatives, no *choice?*
KEN:	*(Turns to JOE and takes his hand.)* But John, you do have another choice.
JOE:	*(Yanks his hand away.)* So I do.
	(He turns over to face the wall. KEN continues to sit staring.)

Scene Three

	(Lighting change. Same set as above; same positions.)
KEN:	My mother died when I was eleven.
JOE:	*(Rising from the bed.)* Oh Christ, here it comes. Run for cover.
KEN:	Shut up. I'm trying to ellicit some sympathy here.
	(JOE pulls out the handcuffs, and clasps himself to KEN. They sit side by side, JOE on the bed, KEN on a chair, facing the audience.)
JOE:	It's "Pity Ken" time. If you let him go on he'll never stop.
KEN:	*(Ignoring him.)* My mother died of a wasp sting. It bit her in the

mouth. She was dead in a matter of minutes. I know because I was there. I watched her suffocate. There was nothing I could do. I was 11. *(To JOE.)* There, I think I handled that with a reasonable amount of dignity. Nothing maudlin in my delivery.

JOE:	I wasn't listening. Get to your father, did you?
KEN:	No, I was saving that.
JOE:	Allow me. His father stuck his head in an oven 12 years later.
KEN:	I found him when I came down for breakfast.
JOE:	He didn't bother with a note.
KEN:	We never communicated much.
JOE:	So he turned off the gas—
KEN:	Safety first.
JOE:	Put on the kettle—
KEN:	For my morning tea.
JOE:	Shaved—
KEN:	And called the police. *(Pause. To JOE.)* Do they look sympathetic to you?
JOE:	It might've been more diplomatic to omit the parts about the shaving and tea-drinking.
KEN:	Oh well. It was an honest effort.
JOE:	I learnt diplomacy from my mum.
KEN:	She was the Perfect Wife and Mother.
JOE:	At least when she had an audience. We kids were essential to her performance.
KEN:	The props she put on display.
JOE:	When the curtain came down we ceased to exist.
KEN:	In theory.
JOE:	In reality we cramped her style, always underfoot, always doing something embarrassing like forgetting our lines.
KEN:	Or straying from the script.
JOE:	If the curtain ever came down around her ears she wouldn't've noticed.
KEN:	She would've pretended it was part of the act.
JOE:	I learnt to improvise from my mum, too. If life hands you a pile of shit you make lemonade.
KEN:	And smile whilst you're drinking it, too.
JOE:	*(Becoming agitated.)* My father fit right in as he only existed in theory to begin with.
KEN:	He behaved like an inanimate object and that's how she treated him.
JOE:	*(Gaining momentum.)* We kids had no choice, you see, but he

allowed her to carry on the way she did. I wish once he would've belted her.

KEN: She was wanting it.

JOE: *(Out of control.)* Just once he should've hit her hard enough she'd realize he was alive! He should've—

KEN: Bashed her brains out in her bed?

(Blackout.)

Scene Four

(1966. KEN is in his chair, JOE asleep in bed. The handcuffs are gone. KEN is reading JOE's journal. The phone rings. JOE sits bolt upright in bed. He sees KEN; sees the diary. They stare at each other a moment. Then JOE gets out of bed and answers the phone.)

JOE: Hello. It's Joe. Yes. I understand. *(Hangs up. Pause.)* That was George.

KEN: *(Setting the journal on the desk.)* Your sister's husband. Why'd he pick this hour to suddenly start extending familial courtesies?

JOE: My mum's dead.

KEN: Joe.

JOE: Bugger didn't say when the funeral's to be. I'll have to telegram for details.

KEN: I remember what it was like when my mother died.

JOE: Oh no. We're not getting into that. This is my problem, these are my feelings. Go tell yours to your analyst. I'm going back to sleep.

KEN: Do you want to talk?

JOE: *(Suddenly vulnerable, on the verge of tears.)* I just wish…I wish we'd had an…opportunity to overcome our…past differences and…come to understand each other's circumstances as…rational, adult human beings.

KEN: *(Moves to comfort him.)* Joe, don't—

(JOE shoves KEN away. His voice is cold. The tears were fake.)

JOE: Only I don't write that way, Kenneth. I don't feel that way. All this means to my life is I'm going to have to spend a couple of days bidding farewell to the corpse of a woman I never knew and avoiding sobbing relatives who did and didn't give a shit while she was alive. Not everybody can play the martyr as definitively as you.

KEN: I'm not—

JOE: And you're not going to. I won't let you. You're jealous of everything in my life, including the death of my blessed mum, may she roast in peace. I'm not letting you have this. It's mine; I'll deal with it my way.

KEN: You're in pain—

JOE: I'm indifferent. Your mother sprang this mortal coil thirty years ago. It's time you got over it. I'm already over mine.

(JOE turns to face the wall again.

Blackout.)

Scene Five

(The bedroom. KEN is once again unpacking for JOE, who's playing with a pair of dentures.)

KEN: Did you reach out and extract them from the jaws of death whilst everyone else kept occupied reflecting on life's tragic transience? Or did she bequeath them to you in her will, as her legacy?

JOE: Found them in a drawer, to tell the prosaic truth.

KEN: A little token to remember her by. It's your sentimental side making itself apparent.

JOE: I'm going to show them to the cast. Give them a taste of the real thing. They need to be shocked out of their smug complacency.

KEN: Why? It doesn't seem to've done us much good. *(Pause.)* How was the funeral?

JOE: It was a moan. The floral arrangements and eulogy alike displayed a depressing lack of creativity. If I hadn't happened upon these teeth the whole weekend would've been a loss. I did have some good sex though.

KEN: With whom? A precocious choirboy, was it, or a carnally inclined vicar?

JOE: Vicarious fucking is more your area, isn't it? I got mine in on the way to and from. *(Pause.)* Did you see that clipping that came in the post this morning? It said I'd written the best play of 1966, called "Loo." *(Pause.)* Don't look so amused, Kenneth. Wouldn't want anyone to suspect such mundane, inept humdrummery actually tickled you.

KEN: I'm supposed to find it amusing that the papers can't even spell the names of your plays correctly? The only fucking thing I visibly contribute to that fucking play and they have to go fucking it up.

JOE: It's shocking, all right! You ought to write a letter of complaint. It's a tradition amongst bored housewives with nothing better to do.

KEN: I have plenty of things better to do. For instance, I could sit here graciously tolerating your prattle all day.

(The phone rings.)

JOE: Or you could answer the phone.

KEN: You know very well there hasn't been a single phone call for me since you installed that instrument of torture.

JOE: Come now, Ken. You know the only reason I had it installed was the same reason that purblind reporter made his sadistic spelling error: to torment you. In fact, that's the only reason anything happens around here. It's the reason the world keeps turning. You mustn't disappoint your many fans.

> *(Pause. JOE is nonchalant, KEN agitated. Finally KEN jumps up and answers the phone.)*

KEN: *(With exaggerated gaiety.)* Joe Orton's residence! *(Pause.)* Hello, Peggy. Yes, it's me. Joe hasn't bothered to acquire an anatomically accurate housemaid yet. Joe has very low personal standards of living.

JOE: *(To the teeth.)* Look what I live with.

KEN: *(Into phone.)* Yes, he's right here. Me? Why even ask? You know I'm always happy, fulfilled and thrilled with the state of my life. Joe's enthusiastic nature rubs off on me. And so does he occasionally. *(Pause.)* Hold on, I'll ask. *(To JOE.)* Peggy wants to know if we're still dedicated to going through with our "little Moroccan adventure."

JOE: Tell Peggy we're leaving as soon as we can find somewhere reasonable to stay far from the omnipresent glare of Moroccan law enforcement.

KEN: *(Into phone.)* Joe says yes. *(Pause. To JOE.)* Peggy says I'll have to look out for you. "Don't want anything unforeseen befalling my number-one commodity," she says. "One hears of such dreadful goings-on in these free-living foreign countries," Peggy says.

JOE: Fuck "Peggy says."

KEN: *(Into phone.)* Joe thanks you for your concern. All right. One second. *(To JOE.)* Peggy says she has some exciting news for you.

> *(JOE yawns, stretches, rises reluctantly and saunters languidly across the room to take the phone.)*

JOE: She wasn't so concerned the last time we pissed off to Tangier. Now *Loot's* been remounted a success suddenly she's afraid to let me go to the lavatory by myself. *(Takes phone.)* Hi, Peggy, how are you? Ken is fine. He's just experiencing an allergic reaction to all those laurel leaves gracing his brow. *(Pause.)* Yes. Yes, I know. Yes, Peggy. Peggy—yes. It's not like we're venturing into volatile enemy territory. We returned from our last visit unscathed, aside from the obligatory sunburns and venereal diseases, both of which I bore with pride. *No*, I will *not* be working on the play. I intend this holiday to be dedicated to sun, boys, and hashish. The only reason I'm taking the typewriter along is so I can put the trip down as a tax write-off, "gathering information for a play," that sort of thing. Yes. That's a good idea. *(To KEN, who has his back to JOE.)* Peggy says I should use you as a tax write-off, too. Put you down as my "personal assistant."

(*JOE holds out the receiver expectantly.*)

KEN: (*Mimicking.*) Fuck "Peggy says."

(*He turns in time to see what JOE has done.*)

JOE: (*Into phone.*) Right. (*To KEN, chiding.*) She heard that.

KEN: Tell Peggy I'm just being a queen. My crown's a size too small.

JOE: It's the size of your sceptre I'd be worried about. (*Into phone.*) Ken's apologies. What's the big news? (*Pause as JOE listens.*) Yes. Well that is exciting then. Right. Happy? I'm fucking on air! (*He suddenly notices that KEN has become curious. Forcing himself to be casual.*) Yes, we've heard. Yes well I suppose it would, Peggy, only I prefer to fuck 14-year-olds. (*Pause.*) Ring me as soon as you know then. (*Hangs up phone. To KEN, casually.*) Peggy congratulates us on the new over-twenty-one law. (*Pause.*) Dinner ready?

(*KEN glares at him, then gets up and heads for the kitchen. Blurts it out.*)

Loot has won the *Evening Standard* Drama Award for best play of the year.

KEN: (*Truly impressed.*) Joe, that's…My God.

JOE: (*Allowing himself to become excited.*) You do realize what this will mean at the box office? It's precisely the boost we needed. The stalls'll be packed tighter than the Pope's arsehole once word of the award gets out. I'm to appear on the television for the attending ceremony. You'll have to help me with the acceptance speech.

KEN: (*Considering.*) The occasion requires something that'll sound spontaneously witty and gracious but not too humble.

JOE: I'm not very good at that.

KEN: Which, sounding gracious or being humble?

JOE: Both. That's what I need you for. What shall I wear? We've nothing suitable for the telly. You'll have to help me pick something out. Something loud. Ken—*we've done it.*

(*Pause.*)

KEN: (*In a hollow voice.*) Will it say that on the trophy?

JOE: What do you mean?

KEN: I'm asking if the trophy will bear the names "Joe Orton and Kenneth Halliwell."

JOE: Of course not.

KEN: Then whence this "we"?

JOE: Both of us know I couldn't've written it without you.

KEN: Two people in the entire world who know that. And I'm not absolutely convinced I'm not a figment of your imagination.

JOE: I've always acknowledged how much you help me.

KEN: To *me* you've acknowledged it. You're preaching to your sole convert. What would please me would be if you got up on that platform in front of God, the television cameras, your precious peers and everyone, "*We'd* like to thank all the little people out there without whom none of this would be possible..." Instead you include me in that category.

JOE: You'll always be a big pain in the arse to me, Kenneth. *(Pause.)* Come with me to the ceremony. I'm required to bring a guest. Peggy said.

KEN: *(Stiffly.)* Ask Peggy. I'm sure she'll be enchanted. As for me, nothing on earth could entice me to attend such a funereal affair.

JOE: I seem to sense we're having some domestic problems.

KEN: Oedipus had domestic problems. We're dead fucked. *(He starts rummaging through the desk drawers.)* Have you seen my pills? I need my pills.

     (JOE goes into the kitchen. KEN finds the jar of pills: different shapes and colours mixed together. He also takes out his compact. He swallows a few pills. Opens up the compact and peers into it. He addresses his reflection while dabbing some rouge on his face.)

     How do you do? I'm Kenneth Halliwell. No, you won't have heard of me. I'm Joe Orton's personal assistant. But you can just call me his bitter half. Joe's accepting the award for play of the year. Yes, he's the one wrote *Loot*. Only the title is mine. Did you know? No, you wouldn't have. All the titles are mine, all the trophies are his. Also, he's wearing my suit. I don't mind. He wears it well.

     (He stares hard at himself for a moment. Then he snaps the compact shut and lets it drop on the floor. He crushes it beneath his foot, as if extinguishing a cigarette.)

     Smashing.

     (He picks up the jar of pills. Looks around to make sure JOE isn't in sight, and starts over.)

     Hello, how do you do? Kenneth Halliwell. The pleasure's all mine. You won't have heard of me. I'm accepting the award on Joe Orton's behalf. Best play of the year, yes. I'm so glad you like it. Joe would be too, only he's dead. Unfortunate accident. His typewriter tripped—and fell on his head! Splat. Dreadful machines. Ought to bear a warning label.

JOE: *(Off.)* Ken? Are you saying something?

     (KEN starts, dropping the jar. The pills spill all over the floor. He gets down on his hands and knees, grabs them in handfuls and dumps them on the bed.)

     (Entering.) They're not in the kitchen. *(He sees KEN.)* What're you doing? I wouldn't go committing suicide were I you. You'll have nothing left to hold over my head.

KEN:	I'll do it one of these days and then where will you be?
JOE:	Fuck you. You're not ruining this for me. *(He puts on his jacket.)* I'm going out. I can't listen to this again.
KEN:	You'd leave me when I'm like this?
JOE:	I'm doing us both a fucking lot of good by staying, is that it?
KEN:	Go, then! But don't be surprised if I'm gone when you get back.
JOE:	I'll make it a point not to be.
KEN:	*(Wailing.)* Look what you're doing to me!
JOE:	I don't want to look. I can't look. I'm going out.
KEN:	Who wants you here?
JOE:	That's what I'd like to know.
KEN:	Don't come back!
JOE:	*(Mimicking.)* One of these days I won't and then where will you be?
KEN:	You know the answer to that!
	(JOE start to go.)
	Joe!
	(He pauses in the doorway.)
	You are coming back, aren't you?
JOE:	After 15 years you still don't know the answer?
	(KEN has no response. JOE puts on his cap and leaves. Blackout.)

Scene Six

(KEN is at the typewriter. He's wearing his wig. JOE comes in wearing his jacket and carrying a record album.)

JOE:	What're you doing at the typewriter?
KEN:	I didn't realize I needed a specific reason to use my own typewriter.
JOE:	I was making conversation. I didn't realize I needed special permission to inquire after your activities.
KEN:	As it happens, I'm composing a letter to Peggy—about my artwork. Since she seemed so intrigued by the little she's seen. How is Peggy?
JOE:	Same old. I told her I've started a diary. She was most pleased, going on as she does. *(He puts the record on the turntable.)* "The publishers will simply eat it up, dear. Eat it up!" *(Pause. The music begins: "Sgt. Pepper.")* She wants to know if you're keeping a journal as well. As she suggested.
KEN:	*(Quoting Miss Prism.)* "Memory is the diary we all carry around with us." I have a hard enough time remembering everything I

	want to forget without writing it down. *(Irritably.)* What's that?
JOE:	The Beatles' new one. *(He hands KEN the sleeve.)* I thought you might find the cover of interest. It's a collage.
KEN:	*(Studies it.)* Look! There's Oscar Wilde.
JOE:	Where?
KEN:	*(Points.)* Behind John.
JOE:	Dirty old bastard. *(Pause.)* Who d'you imagine's the more famous?
KEN:	Now or in the long run? Oscar met with a premature end. That's always a boon to fame. Or infamy. *(Innocently.)* Where are you?
JOE:	*(As he heads for the kitchen.)* Oh ye of little phallus. I'll get there yet.

(JOE disappears into the kitchen.)

KEN:	*(Calling to JOE.)* Perhaps Peggy can be of some assistance. God knows that so-called "show" you arranged for me wasn't. Stuck in a smelly basement up the arse-end of the King's Road.
JOE:	*(From the kitchen.)* I tried, Ken. I'm still trying. The other day I received an invitation to view some modern art at some gallery or other.
KEN:	Why would they want a playwright to look at their artwork?
JOE:	It's my name they're after. Well I hope it's not my money. They can't expect I'll purchase any of their abstract rubbish. I'm only going because it might help you.
KEN:	Poor Joe. The weight of the world in your pants.

(Sounds of the fridge door being slammed and JOE angrily banging around.)

Don't take it out on the household appliances. It's always the innocents that suffer.

JOE:	*(Sticking his head through the doorway.)* There's nothing to eat.
KEN:	So go to the shops. Unless your status as an established playwright has impaired your ability to shop for food.
JOE:	*(Sauntering back into the room.)* Paul McCartney says John has forgotten how to use the phone he's had others doing it for him so long.
KEN:	Did he tell you that in person?
JOE:	No. I read it somewhere.
KEN:	Myself I read in some magazine that one can tell a great deal about a person by having them name their favourite Beatle. I told this to my psychiatrist and he said, "Very well, Kenneth. Who is your favourite Beatle?"
JOE:	And you said?
KEN:	And I said, "I have no opinion about them, actually. But Joe says Paul McCartney's a delightful chap."
JOE:	You should've told him I said he was a delightful fuck.

KEN: Joe! *(Curious.)* He's not that way, is he?

JOE: *(In mock-horror)* Heavens no! What're you thinking of? The Beatles—fairies? You're talking about the disfigured heads of a cultural revolution.

KEN: You're still sore because they rejected your film script.

JOE: My dignity was injured, it's true. But who needs dignity who has a senile producer offering to buy a rejected screenplay for a ridiculous sum.

KEN: Doris has sold her flat. The Cordens will be next. Everyone's moving on but us.

JOE: Why not us?

KEN: I was just thinking the same thing. In fact, I've already begun perusing properties in the paper.

JOE: I could keep this flat to work in, and purchase a house to live in properly.

KEN: *(Suddenly and viciously.)* I haven't shit in two days! What do you think it means?

          (JOE involuntarily clutches at his temples. He goes to the turntable and takes the needle off the record.)

JOE: What did you expect? You haven't eaten anything in a week. You just keep sucking milk through a straw. It's creepy.

KEN: My digestion isn't functioning properly. I can't eat solid food.

JOE: I'm sick of discussing your digestion.

KEN: *(Stuffily.)* I'm sorry if the subject of my health isn't one best-suited to hold your interest, but it is a source of great concern to me.

JOE: I'll start being concerned when there's something wrong with you you're not doing to yourself.

KEN: I suppose you're wanting dinner.

JOE: I told you there's nothing to eat. Anyway I'm going out tonight, remember? To the Lord Mayor of London's banquet.

KEN: Is that tonight? *(Pause.)* Look in the cupboard for a can of sardines. There might be one left. It's not likely you'll find anything edible at your rubbishy dinner.

JOE: Oh, I don't know. It's rumoured they serve an excellent turtle soup.

KEN: You must bring me some home in a doggy bag.

JOE: *(Pauses in the doorway, holding out a sardine.)* Want one?

KEN: *(Shudders.)* No. *(Pause.)* You're not wearing that.

JOE: *(Coming back into the room.)* I'll wear my good shirt. And my old suit. Unless you'd—

KEN: No.

JOE: Why not? You never wear them. They just rot in the closet.

KEN: That's not the point. They're still mine. I bought them with my own money.

(*Pause.*)

JOE: I have to get a new suit. Several new suits.

KEN: And new shirts. (*Pause.*) And socks. All your socks have holes in them. If you can afford a new house you can afford a new pair of socks to go to the Lord Mayor's banquet.

JOE: Too late now.

(*He wiggles his toes, which stick out of the holes in his socks.*)

I'm fond of my socks.

KEN: They're disgusting. Old, torn and worn.

JOE: Dirty socks are kinky, like dirty underwear. Dirty socks, dirty sex. (*Pause.*) I remember a time when my holes weren't so distasteful to you.

KEN: I remember indulging you because of your youth. You no longer have that as an excuse.

(*JOE looks through the closet. Takes out a shirt and holds it up.*)

JOE: There's a hole in my shirt. (*Sticks his hand through.*) My best shirt. And my only clean good shirt. How did this happen?

KEN: I can't imagine. Are you certain you didn't tear it during one of your flirtations with the forbidden and forgot about it in the heat of the moment? Try to think back. Perhaps it would refresh your memory if I were to flush the toilet a few times.

JOE: I wouldn't wear my good shirt out cottaging. For one thing it'd make me look poncy.

KEN: (*Suddenly accommodating.*) I'll have it mended, Joe. In the meantime borrow one of mine.

JOE: Why would you want to have it mended?

KEN: Because it's torn.

JOE: I mean, *I* could have it mended.

KEN: Suit yourself.

JOE: Is there any special reason you'd want to have my shirt mended?

KEN: I don't need a special reason to have a torn shirt mended!

(*Pause.*)

I know what this is about.

JOE: Just lend me one of your shirts and shut up.

KEN: Don't think for a moment you're fooling me.

JOE: Lend me a shirt.

KEN: You think I tore your shirt.

JOE: (*Warning.*) Ken.

KEN: You honestly think I've nothing better to do than sit in this room tearing holes in your clothing for entertainment.

JOE:	I don't want to fight with you over a fucking shirt.
KEN:	We're not fighting—yet. But if we were—just supposing—we'd be fighting over the fact that *you think I tore your shirt!*
JOE:	I didn't say that.
KEN:	You didn't have to.
JOE:	*(Lying.)* I didn't think that.
KEN:	Now you're lying.
JOE:	Now we're fighting.
KEN:	*(Shouting.)* No we are not!
	(Pause.)
JOE:	I can't say I wasn't expecting this. The relative peace we've known since our return had an ominous tinge to it. I knew it couldn't last. *(Pause.)* You were happy in Tangier. I like seeing you happy.
KEN:	That was then and there. This is here and now. Life only makes sense in terms of the here and now. And sometimes not even then.
JOE:	It's still the same us.
KEN:	It's different.
JOE:	What can I do—
KEN:	There's nothing you can do! Just accept what is.
JOE:	I won't live like this.
KEN:	Not much longer.
JOE:	I can't.
KEN:	You don't have to.
JOE:	I don't want to feel the way you do.
KEN:	Do you think I do?
JOE:	But I want to understand the way you feel.
KEN:	You think I don't?
JOE:	Do you?
KEN:	The honeymoon's over. The holiday's over. Everything's back to normal. We just have to adjust.
JOE:	Fuck our normal! I want out.
KEN:	What about me?
JOE:	You'll adjust.
KEN:	*(Out of control.)* You're *committed*...you...stupid...*cunt! We're* committed.
	(Pause.)
JOE:	*(Frigidly.)* One of us should be. And if bets were being placed—
KEN:	They'd be on me like flies on feces?

JOE: Just lend me a shirt.

KEN: First admit it.

JOE: Admit what?

KEN: What you were thinking.

JOE: Give me a shirt.

KEN: First admit it.

JOE: Admit what? *What am I guilty of?*

KEN: Admit that you think I tore your shirt.

JOE: First *give me a shirt.*

> (*Pause. They glare at each other. KEN, in a rage, grabs several shirts from the closet and throws them at JOE.*)

KEN: (*Screaming.*) I hate you!

JOE: (*Going through the shirts.*) Thank you. (*He picks one out and puts it on.*) The thought had crossed my mind.

KEN: What thought.

JOE: That you tore my shirt. It's human nature. I have to go now. Peggy's picking me up.

> (*He moves to go. KEN clutches at his sleeve.*)

KEN: Give me my shirt back.

JOE: (*Jerking away.*) What's the matter with you?

KEN: With me?

JOE: There's nothing wrong with me but you.

KEN: That's not true.

JOE: It is.

KEN: Well I did.

JOE: Did what?

KEN: Tear your shirt.

JOE: I know. Why?

KEN: You know why.

JOE: Second-best?

KEN: While we're being honest.

JOE: Go on!

KEN: Just tell me.

JOE: Tell you what.

KEN: Do you love me or not?

JOE: It's not that simple.

KEN: Grow up, Joe! It *is* that simple.

> (*Long pause.*)

Oh. Oh, my God.

JOE:	It's not what you think.
KEN:	*(Searching frantically.)* My pills.
JOE:	I'm trying to… I'm trying—
KEN:	Shut up. I don't want to hear it. Do you understand?
JOE:	I won't leave you.
KEN:	It's up to you, John.
JOE:	Joe.
KEN:	Who?
JOE:	Me.
KEN:	What?
JOE:	It's my name. Joe. You said "John."
KEN:	*(Dazed.)* Did I?
JOE:	It's been three years now. It's not as though I changed something of great import, like my sex.
KEN:	If you'd had a sex change I'd have no trouble keeping it straight. As it is, I forget. *(With sarcastic emphasis.)* Joe.
JOE:	*(Pleasantly.)* Yes, Kenneth?
KEN:	You wanted to know what all this is about. I'm telling you. It's all about names.
JOE:	How is it about names?
KEN:	I'm coming to that. I'll tell you, but first you have to do something for me.
JOE:	Name it.
KEN:	Take off that shirt.
JOE:	Ken.
KEN:	I'm not letting you borrow it. I've changed my mind. I'm being fickle. Pretend my spontaneity amuses you. I'm the spice in your life. Or the fly in your K-Y. Take it off.
JOE:	I don't have time for this shit.
KEN:	Take off that fucking shirt or I'll tear it from you.

(JOE removes the shirt in a fury, ripping it in the process. Buttons fly; KEN cringes. JOE puts on the torn shirt and a suit jacket over that.)

(As JOE is changing.) Now I'll tell you about names. Witness my signature.

(He shows JOE the paper he was typing on.)

JOE:	*(Reads.)* "Kenneth Halliwell, Secretary to Joe Orton." So?
KEN:	I've never signed myself as your secretary before. There's something wrong with that signature and we both of us know what it is. That's not your name, *John*. And I'm not your secretary.

JOE:	Yes you are. And yes, *I am.* Joe Orton. That's who I am. Live with it.
KEN:	I won't…I won't accept that…
JOE:	It's up to you. In the meantime I'm going out to dinner. Smile and pretend you're happy for me and maybe I'll come back.

(KEN glares at him.)

Come on, Ken. Smile and pretend.

KEN:	*(Turning his back to JOE, with dignity.)* I dislike pretense intensely.
JOE:	Oh do you.

(Pause. Then JOE comes up behind KEN and yanks his wig from his head.)

KEN:	Joe!
JOE:	It's John, remember? John! No more pretense between old friends. This is *real intimacy.*

(KEN chases JOE, who is laughing, around the room.)

KEN:	Joe! John, please. *(Becoming increasingly hysterical.)* Give it back!

(With a cry of rage he leaps on JOE, knocking him to the floor and pinning him there. He tries to pry the wig from JOE's hands.)

You're going to tear it, you're going to tear it!

(JOE throws the wig and KEN scrambles after it. Kneeling, he puts it on, gasping and trembling.)

JOE:	*(Watching him with disgust.)* Look at yourself. You're pathetic. Pathetic. What am I doing here with you?

(JOE leaves. KEN wrenches the wig from his head and throws it across the room.)

Scene Seven

(Lighting shift. Maybe the same night or maybe a few weeks later. 1967. KEN, in his pyjamas, is sitting on his bed reading the journal. On JOE's bed is a suitcase. JOE enters from outside.)

JOE:	I told you not to wait up for me. What're you reading?
KEN:	Your diary.

(JOE goes over to KEN and take it from him; reads a bit; laughs.)

JOE:	Look, there you are.
KEN:	I know. *(Pause.)* Kenneth H.
JOE:	What?
KEN:	My name. *(Pause.)* I finished packing for you. Look.

(He takes some socks from JOE's suitcase and holds them up.)

JOE:	New socks.
KEN:	I also went to see Dr. Ismay. I didn't have an appointment but he

agreed to see me anyway. He prescribed some medication. Which I went immediately to purchase. And took some. I'm just beginning to feel the effects. It's...quite miraculous. I feel incredibly calm. At peace, almost.

JOE: Only a few months more. Then we'll be back in Tangier.

KEN: I can't wait.

JOE: Meanwhile there are signs of life beyond this hell-hole-in-the-wall. I'll find you a new home. Lots of room to roam around in. Lots of...space.

KEN: And where will you be while I'm roaming round and round my spacious new accommodations?

(*JOE begins to undress.*)

JOE: I don't know yet. Not here. *(Pause.)* I'll stop by every weekend to see you.

KEN: So it's gone from "I'll never leave you" to "I'll stop by on weekends."

JOE: *(Simply.)* I'm not responsible for you.

KEN: *(Quietly.)* You're right.

JOE: *(Caught off guard.)* I know I am.

KEN: *(Slowly.)* And I understand that.

JOE: Do you?

KEN: Yes, now.

JOE: Then I'm glad.

KEN: Don't pretend you care.

JOE: But I do care.

KEN: I'm going to prove to you, Joe, that I can be responsible for myself.

JOE: I hope you do.

(*He removes his underwear and sits naked on the bed. KEN turns to him. Pause.*)

Ken—

KEN: What?

JOE: *(After a pause.)* Never mind.

KEN: What is it?

JOE: *(Climbing under the covers.)* Nothing. Just turn out the light when you're ready to go to sleep. *(Pause.)* Leicester tomorrow. The prodigal son returns in triumph. I've become a cliché.

KEN: *(A whisper.)* How does it feel?

(*Pause as JOE considers.*)

JOE: Good.

KEN: Why?

JOE: Revenge. *(Pause.)*

KEN:	Revenge?
JOE:	I know you understand. *(Pause.)* You're invited, you know. To Leicester—with me. D'you want to come?
KEN:	*(Surprised.)* No.
JOE:	You don't want to see *Sloane* with me one more time?
KEN:	I've never visited your sister and her family before. They wouldn't know what to make of me, I'm sure.
JOE:	You'd be with me. They wouldn't have to make anything of you. *(Pause.)* You'll be all right on your own, then?
KEN:	I told you, Joe. I'm responsible for myself now.
JOE:	Right. Thought I should ask.
KEN:	No, you go. Enjoy your revenge.
JOE:	I will.

(KEN reaches over to turn off the light. Blackout.)

Scene Eight

(Spotlight on KEN, who sits in the chair by JOE's bed, gripping the hammer. JOE steps from the shadows and takes the hammer from him. He goes over to his bed where he is again obscured by shadows. There is the sound of a hammer penetrating flesh and skull. Nine blows. The gore flies, hitting the walls, hitting KEN. When it's over JOE drops the hammer at KEN's feet. KEN rises and addresses the audience.)

KEN:	*(As if resuming a rudely interrupted conversation.)* You see, I've envisioned all the ways it could be undertaken, this...ending we're having. And I decided it would have to end in comedy.

(JOE steps out of the shadows, his body glistening with blood. KEN begins to undress.)

JOE:	Comedy?
KEN:	Yes. *Black* comedy. I have evolved, somewhat, somehow, through pain. Once I would've thought tragedy the only fitting conclusion to our grim fairy tale. But now—and don't think I expect *you* to understand this—I've been...humbled.
JOE:	*(Staring contemplatively at his bed.)* Life does that to one. Death, too.
KEN:	*(With palpable relief)* You do understand.
JOE:	I do.

(JOE comes up behind KEN, who is now stripped naked. JOE takes KEN's pyjamas, folds them neatly, and drapes them over the desk chair)

KEN:	I have been humbled, wrenched from my high horse and trampled in the dirt beneath its hoofs... *hooves?* See? I haven't

even mastered syntax and now I'm going to have to... What was
I—?

JOE: You were being humbled.

KEN: Yes. I no longer feel superior to your...primitive methods of
         obtaining...physical release. I'm having such difficulty—!

JOE: Fucking?

KEN: Hhmmrn?

JOE: Is that what you meant by "physical release"?

KEN: More than mere "fucking," J— Well. I mean desire! Passion! The
         fact that precedes all else. It doesn't matter what the object of that
         desire is: animal, vegetable, mineral...

JOE: Visceral.

KEN: Desire's the fact. And we must use whatever methods are at our
         disposal, our humble human disposal, to...fulfill, to...reach, a
         point of...completion...consummation...where nothing is
         showing seams...

         *(They are sitting on the floor. JOE, behind KEN, feeds him the pills
         and juice, one by one, sip by sip. When they're gone:)*

JOE: I suppose there's nothing left to ask you, except... What do you
         miss most about being alive?

KEN: *(After a long pause.)* Cleaning. *(Pause.)* Why hasn't there ever been
         any comfort for me? *(Pause.)* Am I wrong to ask that? Is this what
         it's like for everyone? *(Pause.)* It can't be true. It must just be me.
         (Pause. With some irony.) That's a comforting thought.

JOE: You want to know what I think? I think this is all a nightmare. It's
         all obviously a horrible dream.

KEN: *(Staring at his wrists.)* J— ...Look! *(A flash of joy.)* We're free. No
         more handcuffs or handbags hanging between us... *(Followed by
         horror.)* I'm free! *(Shudders.)* Hold me!

         *(KEN closes his eyes and lays his head in JOE's lap. JOE reflexively
         clutches at KEN.)*

JOE: Only I can't be dreaming it because I'm dead. And whenever
         whoever is dreaming it wakes up I'll be gone. I want to live.

         *(Looks at KEN for the first time during the scene and addresses the
         still, silent figure.)*

         Don't wake up.

         (Tableau. Lights fade.)

         The End

Inquest

WILLIAM HARRAR

Production Information

Inquest was first produced by Prairie Theatre Exchange, Winnipeg, on November 17, 1994 with the following cast:

CHIEF .... Frank Adamson
INSPECTOR .... Richard Hirst
SERGEANT .... Cheryl Swarts
CONSTABLE .... Arne MacPherson

Directed by Nancy Drake
Set and Costume design by John Dinning
Lighting design by Aisling Sampson
Original music by Peter Hannan
Stage Manager: Maureen Shelley

Characters

CONSTABLE, about 30
SERGEANT, female, about 35
INSPECTOR, about 45
CHIEF, about 55

The following characters are voices only and may be pre-recorded:
EDITOR, FIRST OFFICER, SECOND OFFICER, THIRD OFFICER, DISPATCH

Setting

Winnipeg, 1988

Part One

Scene One

(Night, a city street and park bench in a residential area, late winter, lit by streetlights high among leafless elm branches.

Sound: pre-recorded copy of police radio transmissions, characterized by static, delays, timing beeps, and an editor's voice intoning the time.)

EDITOR: The time is now 2:37:17.

FIRST
OFFICER: I got him right here, guys, he's coming out to you right now. Got him going down, down

DISPATCH: What is your location?

SECOND
OFFICER: ...03...

DISPATCH: You're breaking up. Try again. Your location...

SECOND
OFFICER: He's chasing him, ah, we're on Electa or something. Yeah, Electa.

THIRD
OFFICER: He's going up on the dike, grey jacket, native.

DISPATCH: All units, he's on the dike, grey jacket and pants.

THIRD
OFFICER: I got him.

DISPATCH: Received.

SECOND
OFFICER: They say they got him?

DISPATCH: I believe one of them said thay got him on the dike.

THIRD
OFFICER: We got him at the, ah, south side of the dike in the house there.

DISPATCH: Just a confirmation, do you have him in custody or just spotted in that area?

November 203, do you have this male in custody or just in sight at that area?

THIRD
OFFICER: We have him in custody.

DISPATCH: Received.

(A figure, his shadow cast on the backdrop, enters upstage and crosses to downstage and off.)

EDITOR: The time is 2:40:37.

(From offstage, a gunshot is heard, accompanied by a blue flash. After a few seconds the CONSTABLE staggers in. He wears a police uniform and a waistlength jacket. There is blood on the right cuff and below the right pocket of the jacket. There is also blood below the right knee of the pants as well as on his left boot. Snow and mud are evident on his back and on the seat of his pants. His cap is off and his hair is mussed and dirty. He is breathing heavily. He looks around to get his bearings. He holds his gun in his right hand. With his left, he takes his portable phone from his service belt.)

CONSTABLE: *(After several seconds.)* Portable November 202.

DISPATCH: November 202.

CONSTABLE: November 202, I'm just west of Winks. I need my partner here and I also need an ambulance.

DISPATCH: Is that west of Winks or near Alexander then?

CONSTABLE: That's west of Winks on, ah, I believe I'm on Logan.

DISPATCH: Received. Is this person conscious?

CONSTABLE: That's negative.

(Sound: very still. Only occasional distant traffic on wet streets punctuate the groans and gurgles of an unseen male offstage. The CONSTABLE scans the audience as if looking for a familiar face.

Shock cut...an explosion of flashing blue and red lights, loud traffic, radio transmissions, music, a low voice repeating 'I don't have to show you nuttin'. Heartbeats—sensory overload. A car door slams.)

CONSTABLE: *(Pointing to the wounded man offstage and addressing the offstage police officers.)* He went for my gun and I shot him.

SERGEANT: *(Offstage.)* Take it easy, fella. We're trying to help. *(Pause.)* You call an ambulance?

CONSTABLE: Yes. *(The SERGEANT enters, dressed like the CONSTABLE.)*

SERGEANT: He's a strong mother. Native? ...Hey, are you all right? Hello? Did you get hit? Say something.

CONSTABLE: No.

SERGEANT: Well, look at you. What the hell is the situation? *(She brushes snow and dirt off his back and shoulders.)*

CONSTABLE: I happened to reach for my gun, I happened to pull the trigger.

SERGEANT: Steady, steady. Go sit down.

(She runs off and returns with a roll of yellow barrier tape marked "Police Line Do Not Cross".)

(On the phone.) Rush that ambulance. Is the duty inspector coming out?

DISPATCH: On his way.

SERGEANT: Where's your partner? *(She does not wait for a reply and rushes offstage for a moment.)*

Jesus, we got a bleeder. Must have hit an artery.

(Entering, she calls back over her shoulder.)

There are bandages in my van.

SERGEANT: *(To the CONSTABLE.)* I have to take your gun.

CONSTABLE: They're going to investigate?

SERGEANT: Better believe it.

(She puts her own gun in a pocket, carefully takes the CONSTABLE's by the butt with thumb and forefinger, and places it in her own holster.)

CONSTABLE: He jumped me. I was on my back on the ground and he went for my gun.

SERGEANT: Hey, I'm not questioning you. But if you're lucky, that fucker dies. Cuz, for sure, he's gonna have a different story.

(Sound another police car arrives.)

SERGEANT: *(Pointing offstage.)* There's your partner. Why don't you go sit down? Relax.

CONSTABLE: He went for my gun

SERGEANT: It was an accident. Just say it was an accident. Okay?

CONSTABLE: Okay.

SERGEANT: *(Looking offstage.)* Just say it that way. Who's that little fat kid in the back seat?

CONSTABLE: Passenger in the stolen car. We were chasing it

SERGEANT: We'll have to put him in another car.

(The INSPECTOR enters, writing in a notebook.

Sound arriving ambulance.)

INSPECTOR: So much shit the fan won't turn?

SERGEANT: Sir?

INSPECTOR: I want to see some barrier tape around the scene. There down to there, back along there, over there. Here, I'll help you. Get the Identification Unit out here. Show them what's what. Then do a canvass of those houses across the street. Maybe we got a witness.

SERGEANT: Yes, sir.

INSPECTOR: Then go back to the station and wait in my office. Did you seize the gun?

SERGEANT: Yes, sir. *(She shows him her holster.)*

INSPECTOR: How many rounds were fired?

SERGEANT: *(Drawing the gun and examining the cylinder.)* One.

INSPECTOR: *(Referring to the gun.)* Careful. Is that him?

SERGEANT: Yes.

              (Sound departing ambulance.)

INSPECTOR: Don't clean him up. I'm going to the hospital to get a statement. *(He scribbles in his notebook and exits.)*

SERGEANT: *(Exiting.)* Get that kid out of your car. C'mon, you're going in another car. You little thief, if you hadn't stolen that vehicle, none of this would have happened. *(Fading to inaudibility.)*

              (Sudden silence. The CONSTABLE is left alone. A loud blast on a car horn startles him.)

Scene Two

              (A corridor and room in police headquarters. The Inspector's spartan office is suggested by an inexpensive desk, chairs, a filing cabinet, and a coat rack. It is still an hour before sunrise.)

SERGEANT: Come on inside. Hurry up. I'm freezing my nuts off.

CONSTABLE: *(Entering.)* What am I supposed to do? Should I call a lawyer?

SERGEANT: Nah. Maybe talk to somebody from the union. You're allowed one phone call. Ha ha. Hey, maybe you better call home.

CONSTABLE: What would I say? Like how would I...

SERGEANT: I don't know. In here. This is the detective's room. Now don't worry. I'll be around to help out. I'm this close to making Sergeant Two and I don't want to get shot in the ass.

CONSTABLE: You can make just as much money with overtime.

SERGEANT: No, I'm going to show those pricks. Okay, take off your uniform. The stuff with the blood. Jacket, pants, boots...

CONSTABLE: Now?

SERGEANT: Yes. It's evidence. Anyway, you'll look nice and pathetic.

CONSTABLE: You want me in my gotch?

SERGEANT: Definitely. And don't let him think you're ignorant. I'll be the stupid one. You gotta be the angel. Cuz if you're clear, I'm clear.

CONSTABLE: You see the blood?

SERGEANT: Where?

CONSTABLE: On my ankle.

SERGEANT: It's running upside down.

CONSTABLE: That's because he was on top of me. I was holding him off with my foot. Slam. Stuff spurts out.

SERGEANT: Okay, we'll wait in the office.

CONSTABLE: What's going to happen now?

SERGEANT: Well, a detective will take your statement.

CONSTABLE: What about the duty Inspector?

SERGEANT: Well, he said he wants to see you when he gets back. You know him?

CONSTABLE: No.

SERGEANT: Your tough luck, he's acting Inspector for the Crime division. He's a goddamn head hunter. A hot shot that wants to be a big shot. He did the internal on that cop who killed who was it? A brother-in-law?

CONSTABLE: I didn't kill anybody.

SERGEANT: Yeah, yeah, but he's got a left brain problem. He likes words. Reports. Notes. Eyewitness notes. So you better make some while you're waiting.

(She begins making notes.)

The guy you shot was native, right?

CONSTABLE: I didn't shoot him.

SERGEANT: The guy who shot himself with your gun—he was native, wasn't he?

CONSTABLE: Yeah.

SERGEANT: Well, don't say nothing about natives.

CONSTABLE: What do you mean?

SERGEANT: Just don't say nothing. Must have been some homeless guy, eh?

CONSTABLE: Homeless guy?

SERGEANT: Yeah, just some homeless guy, wasn't he? Did he ask you for money?

CONSTABLE: No. I don't carry no change, anyway.

SERGEANT: Yeah. Sorry, buddy, I spent all my money on Lysol.

CONSTABLE: "I'm just a Indian. You won't give me any money cuz I'm just a Indian." —They always say that.

SERGEANT: Yeah, typical.

CONSTABLE: Trying to make you feel guilty.

SERGEANT: They do a good job. *(She whispers.)* Whoa, he's back already.

INSPECTOR: *(Brisk, chipper.)* G'morning. Rock and roll time, ladies and gentlemen.

SERGEANT: Sorry to get you out so early.

INSPECTOR: Don't worry. I love it.

SERGEANT: This here is the Constable In Question.

CONSTABLE: *(Mumbling.)* It was an accident.

INSPECTOR: Is the area secure?

SERGEANT: Yes, sir.

INSPECTOR: Identification Unit?

SERGEANT: IDENT is at the scene.

INSPECTOR: Witnesses?

SERGEANT: No. I checked the houses across the street. Nothing.

INSPECTOR: I need reports from all the officers on the scene. And Supplementaries on the discharge of the firearm.

SERGEANT: Yes, sir.

INSPECTOR: That would include you.

SERGEANT: Right. *(She exits.)*

INSPECTOR: So you're the fuck-up? *(He smiles.)*

CONSTABLE: I guess.

INSPECTOR: Well? Tell me about it.

CONSTABLE: I come out on Logan. I look across the street. This guy's walking along, so I go over and ask him for ID. We get into a fight. Before I know it, he's on top of me. *Blam!!* Jesus.

INSPECTOR: Let's take it slow and easy.

CONSTABLE: We'd been chasing a couple of kids—they stole a car. I grabbed one. Then I heard on the radio that they had the other one across the park. So I went up to see.

SERGEANT: Coffee, sir?

INSPECTOR: Hey, why not?

SERGEANT: You?

CONSTABLE: Okay.

SERGEANT: Donut?

INSPECTOR: We don't do donuts on my shift.

SERGEANT: *(Her mouth full.)* Hm-m-m?

INSPECTOR: We do coffee, we do cigarettes. We don't do donuts.

SERGEANT: *(Her mouth full.)* You're kidding.

INSPECTOR: Yeah, I'm kidding. *(He's not.)*

SERGEANT: You see that blood on his leg? It's running upside down. Proves the guy was on top of him.

INSPECTOR: Sergeant

SERGEANT: Yes, sir, I'll get a camera.

INSPECTOR: No. You do your job. IDENT will do theirs. How about getting me the communications log for this incident, Number 88-245-419.

SERGEANT: Yes, sir. *(She exits.)*

INSPECTOR: You've been on the Force since—

CONSTABLE: Four years.

INSPECTOR: So you know better than to pick fights when you're all by yourself.

CONSTABLE: I didn't start it. I just stopped him. I wanted to check his ID.

INSPECTOR: What is this—South Africa? What was he doing?

CONSTABLE: Walking down the sidewalk. I go up to him. Before I know it — *Blam!!*

INSPECTOR: We'll nail this thing down if you go slow. I want to get the big picture. And don't mess my head around. I don't appreciate it. I've been on this job eighteen years and I've seen every trick in the book. Just give it to me straight and you'll save yourself a lot of heartache.

SERGEANT: *(Entering.)* Excuse me, sir. Here's the printout.

INSPECTOR: Thanks. Can I see your notes on this?

SERGEANT: I got 'em right here.

INSPECTOR: Have you made notes on this?

CONSTABLE: Um…

INSPECTOR: Don't forget. *(He peruses the SERGEANTs notebook and compares it to the printout.)* A couple of mistakes here. Check this address. Was the guy wearing a black jacket or a grey jacket?

SERGEANT: Which guy—the thief or the one in the hospital?

INSPECTOR: You tell me. Just get it right. How come you wrote leather jacket?

SERGEANT: Um… *(To the CONSTABLE.)* Didn't you…I don't know.

INSPECTOR: You were there. Didn't you have your eyes open? It was a cloth jacket. And things are supposed to be in chronological order.

SERGEANT: Oh, right.

INSPECTOR: Are you going to get him some clothes?

SERGEANT: Oh, right. *(She exits.)*

INSPECTOR: Was the guy you shot one of the car thieves?

CONSTABLE: Well, I don't know. He pushed me.

INSPECTOR: He pushed you and you fell down?

CONSTABLE: Yeah.

INSPECTOR: On your back?

CONSTABLE: Yeah.

INSPECTOR: I thought he was trying to take your gun.

CONSTABLE: When I fell down, I he leaned over. I was trying to push him off with my foot and he was trying to grab my gun.

INSPECTOR: You had your gun drawn already?

CONSTABLE: When?

INSPECTOR: When he pushed you.

CONSTABLE: Ah…

INSPECTOR: He pushed you so you shot him.

CONSTABLE: No. He tried to yank the gun out of my holster.

INSPECTOR: How did he ever…

SERGEANT: *(Entering.)* Here's some pants. I got some…

INSPECTOR: Excuse me.

SERGEANT:	I brought his personal…
INSPECTOR:	Excuse me. Every police officer should be able to handle an unarmed pedestrian, no matter what he does, without shooting him.
SERGEANT:	It was life or death, sir.
INSPECTOR:	Did you see it?
SERGEANT:	Almost.
INSPECTOR:	You didn't see shit. What's all this?
SERGEANT:	His personal effects. They just brought them over.

(The CONSTABLE stands up, alarmed.)

INSPECTOR:	His wallet's a bloody filing cabinet. For crissakes, this guy's an executive director.
SERGEANT:	No way.
INSPECTOR:	"Executive Director…Tribal Council." Oh, he's native. *(Pause.)* He's native?
CONSTABLE:	Well…yeah.
INSPECTOR:	When you stopped him, did you know he was native?
CONSTABLE:	Well, I figured, maybe…
INSPECTOR:	We don't do racial discrimination on my shift, either.
CONSTABLE:	No, sir.

(The SERGEANT has begun reading a letter found among the contents.)

INSPECTOR:	*(Taking the letter from the SERGEANT.)* From his wife, I guess. "Every time you drink…" Was he drunk?
SERGEANT:	Hospital said he was point two two.
INSPECTOR:	*(Whistling.)* He was loaded. Okay. He was loaded. You didn't tell me that.

(The CONSTABLE shrugs.)

SERGEANT:	They called it at twenty after three. They said it was loss of blood. He was more or less DOA.
CONSTABLE:	Oh, Jesus. I called the ambulance first thing.
SERGEANT:	He was a strong son of a bitch. I thought he'd make it.
INSPECTOR:	Sergeant, you are going to find out about his drinking problem.
SERGEANT:	Sir, I'm off work in half an hour.

(The INSPECTOR just smiles. The SERGEANT exits.)

INSPECTOR:	*(Gently.)* Get dressed. I'll find somebody to take your statement.
CONSTABLE:	I can't give a statement. I can't remember what happened.
INSPECTOR:	Sure you can. We'll go through it one step at a time.
CONSTABLE:	We were chasing a stolen vehicle. It hit a snow bank. Two males out of the car. The driver runs straight down the lane. The short one—I catch him. I bring him back to the car.

INSPECTOR: You're doing good.

CONSTABLE: Some other guys say they caught the driver. On the radio. I go up to Logan to see. Along comes this native. Big, smells like a brewery.

INSPECTOR: So he wasn't the other car thief.

CONSTABLE: No. Well, he could have been.

INSPECTOR: Did he match the description?

CONSTABLE: Uh, let's see…

INSPECTOR: (Reading from the communications log.) "Male, native, dark clothes." He matched, didnt he?

CONSTABLE: Yeah.

INSPECTOR: You asked him for ID?

CONSTABLE: Yeah. He wouldn't show me. I said I was looking for a car thief. Knocked me down. I wasn't ready for that. I should have been.

INSPECTOR: No argument here.

CONSTABLE: Then he's going for my gun. He's grabbing, I'm grabbing. It went off. It was an accident. At first, I wasn't sure if it was him or me who got hit.

INSPECTOR: Two forty-one you call for help.

CONSTABLE: It was awful.

INSPECTOR: It's okay now. Get dressed.

CONSTABLE: These pants don't fit.

INSPECTOR: Oh don't worry, you look great. (Pause.) Essentially, you called this executive type a car thief. He took it personally. He was drunk. I know how it is out there. He probably hates us. Next time, take it easy. You understand? Cool it. Okay, get the paperwork done and you can go home. We'll get you some time off. C'mon, let's see you smile.

CONSTABLE: Hey, everybody, I'm home. A guy got shot right on top of me.

               (He gives a quick exaggerated grin meant to protest the INSPECTOR's command. The INSPECTOR smiles himself and as he exits, he runs into the returning SERGEANT who carries a paper bag.)

INSPECTOR: Have they finished at the scene?

SERGEANT: I don't know.

INSPECTOR: When they do, they should call the Fire Department and get a water truck. Wash it all down.

SERGEANT: Yes, sir. There was a lot of blood.

INSPECTOR: Not more donuts, I hope.

SERGEANT: It's the gun. What do I do with it?

INSPECTOR: Has IDENT finished with it?

SERGEANT: They don't want it.

INSPECTOR: Did they check it for prints?

SERGEANT: Not yet. It's still wet. It must have fallen in the snow.

INSPECTOR: What's that?

SERGEANT: What?

INSPECTOR: Right there.

SERGEANT: Looks like blood.

INSPECTOR: I guess he must have been at close range.

SERGEANT: Fingerprints?

INSPECTOR: Well?

SERGEANT: They wouldn't prove anything.

INSPECTOR: What?

SERGEANT: Fingerprints won't say who started the fight. Or what the motive was for grabbing the gun.

INSPECTOR: According to regulations, it goes to the Firearms Officer. But I could order that the gun be printed.

SERGEANT: What if there's nothing there?

INSPECTOR: We know there won't be anything there. Too wet, probably.

SERGEANT: It wouldn't be fair if they couldn't find one.

INSPECTOR: Fair?

SERGEANT: I mean, people don't understand that there's hardly ever any good prints when it's outside. Still, if you want to go through the motions

INSPECTOR: *(After staring at the CONSTABLE for a moment.)* Firearms Officer. Let him do the ballistics. The results will mean something. *(Exiting with the SERGEANT.)* You know where he is? I'll be happy to show you.

CONSTABLE: *(To himself, rehearsing in a whisper.)* Linda? I'm home. I know I'm late. I had some trouble. An Indian. Tried to kill me.

Scene Three

(A locker room.)

SERGEANT: *(Storming in and flinging down her jacket.)* How do you wink at an Indian?

CONSTABLE: What?

(The SERGEANT mimes lifting a rifle to her shoulder and sighting a target by closing one eye.)

What's that supposed to mean?

SERGEANT: I don't know. I heard it upstairs. It's a joke. Like this job. How come you're still here?

CONSTABLE: Paperwork.

SERGEANT: Tell me about it.

CONSTABLE: What took you so long?

SERGEANT: Had the wrong address. Didn't find his house until nine o'clock.

CONSTABLE: So? What happened?

SERGEANT: Nothing.

CONSTABLE: Come on.

SERGEANT: I go up on the porch. I knock. Police.Would you open the door, please. I have to speak to you. It's your husband. Last night. He got shot. He passed away.

CONSTABLE: What did she say? Did she want to know who shot him?

SERGEANT: Yeah. I told her. A police officer. Accident.

CONSTABLE: Did she buy that?

SERGEANT: You kidding?

CONSTABLE: What did she say?

SERGEANT: She said she already sent the kids to school and they don't know and they're going to find out the hard way.

CONSTABLE: All she has to do is...

SERGEANT: I told her. Call the school. Get them excused. I tell her that his remains are at Health Sciences. I give her a number to call. Gave her the personal possessions I had. Everything of her husband's in a little plastic bag. God...

CONSTABLE: She start crying?

SERGEANT: Yes. I'm a good cop, so I ignore that. I tell her I have to ask her this. Ma'am, does your husband... Did your husband have a drinking problem? Did he get violent?

CONSTABLE: Bet your ass

SERGEANT: I say it again. Ma'am, he'd been drinking. He jumped the officer. Tried to take his gun. We have this letter you wrote to him last year. Said you didn't feel safe when he was drinking. Would you spell that out for me?

CONSTABLE: She say anything?

SERGEANT: Just "I try not to, but I hate the police." Told her I'm sorry you feel that way.

CONSTABLE: I guess it runs in the family.

SERGEANT: I get this feeling, you know, this feeling that I'm getting nowhere, that I've overstayed my welcome.You know, like Christ I don't get paid enough to do this kind of crap. Then I hear her talking—she's still crying—talking to somebody else in the house. She says, "Where are his glasses." You know. His eyeglasses. He wore glasses?

CONSTABLE: Uh, yeah, he did.

SERGEANT: So where the hell are they?

Scene Four

> *(The CHIEF's office, with blue carpeting, a potted plant, and a large window covered by drawn blinds.*
>
> *Sound: distant Aboriginal drums.*
>
> *The CHIEF smokes a pipe and peers through the blinds.)*

CHIEF: *(To an offstage secretary.)* Book the press room for four-thirty. I want the Superintendant here at five. I'll send a copy of the press release to the Mayor's office. They should have it by five, five-thirty. If he wants to talk to me, tell him any time tomorrow morning. Who? Oh, yes, send him in.

> *(He returns to the window as the INSPECTOR enters.)*

Indians wear glasses. Not every Indian. But many do. I think optical care is a treaty obligation.

INSPECTOR: Sir?

CHIEF: Are we prejudiced against Indians?

INSPECTOR: No.

CHIEF: The Assembly of Manitoba Chiefs think so. They say we do sloppy work when a native is the victim. We don't care.

INSPECTOR: That's not true.

CHIEF: A reporter from the *Sun* found his glasses.

INSPECTOR: Whose? The native guy's?

CHIEF: A reporter found his glasses not ten feet from where he was shot.

INSPECTOR: My fault. I should have preserved the scene until daylight.

CHIEF: That I find out at one-thirty. At two-thirty that hippy yuppy from the *Free Press* comes waltzing in here to tell me he's been to the scene and that none of the nearby residents have been contacted by the police. And if the dead man had been a stockbroker, wouldn't you have had cops out there like the vermin they are combing the street for witnesses?

INSPECTOR: I'll get right on that, sir.

CHIEF: And then I get a call from the Attorney General's office. Sorry, but any death involving a police officer requires a Provincial Inquest—one that is open to the public, where lawyers for the family will have standing—and they are scheduling one in three weeks.

INSPECTOR: Good. That gives us time to put together a half-decent forensics package. We'll do a complete investigation. We'll make sure all the facts are in.

CHIEF: *(Interrupting.)* And then the City wants to know if we need legal counsel.

INSPECTOR: What for?

CHIEF: Just a friendly reminder that they better not be the target of any lawsuit for negligence. They won't be, will they?

INSPECTOR: No.

CHIEF: Then that bunch down there shows up for a demonstration. Drums and all. *(He imitates a native speaker.)* "Nothing will ever convince us that our brother did not try his best to avoid violence the night he was murdered by the Winnipeg Police." We have good relations with the native community. Didn't I go to a symposium just last month? They must have got themselves a lawyer.

INSPECTOR: Maybe so.

CHIEF: For sure. I wish it *had* been a stockbroker. I wish it had been *my* stockbroker. I'm a student of history. Did you know that? I'm a student of history. "He who is ignorant of the past is condemned to repeat it." Did you know that?

INSPECTOR: Yes, sir, we had an in-service. The actual quote is...

CHIEF: What am I reading here?

INSPECTOR: *The Prince.*

CHIEF: Do you know who the Prince is?

INSPECTOR: Yes, sir. The Prince is a French aviator who flew to the moon.

CHIEF: Nope. The Prince is me. I know you fellows think we do nothing at our conventions but sip pina coladas and watch girlie shows.

INSPECTOR: I know better.

CHIEF: We also attend seminars. We expose ourselves to great ideas. Listen to this. "Cruelties should be committed all at once, as in that way each separate one is felt less. Benefits, on the other hand, should be conferred one at a time, for in that way, they will be more appreciated."

INSPECTOR: Sound advice.

CHIEF: The wisdom of the ages. Now, if I tell the media that there is no juicy anti-police story here, is that a cruelty or a benefit?

INSPECTOR: Obviously, it's a... ah...

CHIEF: Well, I figure it's a cruelty. Therefore, do it all at once. The Crown has agreed not to lay charges. So, I'm shutting this thing down.

INSPECTOR: Yes, sir.

CHIEF: I've called a press conference a half hour from now. You know, when I became Chief Constable, the media found out that I went to work via limousine service. "You can't do that. You haven't been to university. Even the mayor doesn't have a limousine." They took it away. Oh, I don't mind driving. I like to drive. But it was a slap in the face. Every officer on the Force felt it. The same officers that stand between those fat cat media bank accounts and the rest of the world.What it all boils down to is—I get nothing but abuse from the media, but I protect the media from criminals. Do I need analysis or what?

INSPECTOR: Yes, sir. No, sir.

CHIEF:	Okay, the press release. I want to say, "As the officer attempted to push the perpetrator back, he reached down and grabbed the butt of the officer's revolver. In the ensuing struggle, the revolver came free from the holster. The officer managed to hold the butt while the deceased pulled on the barrel of the weapon." See? Right from his statement. You haven't read this?
INSPECTOR:	I debriefed him, but... Yes, I've seen it.
CHIEF:	What I want to do is talk about forensics. Like fingerprints.
INSPECTOR:	Fingerprints?
CHIEF:	If the Indian grabbed the gun, we ought to find some prints.
INSPECTOR:	I don't believe we printed the gun.
CHIEF:	What?
INSPECTOR:	I mean, I haven't seen a report.
CHIEF:	Nothing on the gun?
INSPECTOR:	Ballistics. We did ballistics instead. The gun was working properly.
CHIEF:	No kidding.
INSPECTOR:	And it was fired from point blank range. No way the officer took a pot shot at the guy. If you want forensics, you could mention that the guy's alcohol was point two two.
CHIEF:	I'm staying away from that one. They'll say I'm prejudiced. I'll wait for a question. I sure hope somebody will tell me what happened to the fingerprints. How about the holster?
INSPECTOR:	What do you mean?
CHIEF:	Officer says the guy grabbed his holster. Did you print the holster?
INSPECTOR:	I'll check.
CHIEF:	Okay, now I got "the Police Department's Firearms Board of Inquiry blah blab blab found no negligence on the part of the officer—
INSPECTOR:	The investigation is continuing—
CHIEF:	*(Cutting him off.)* —and I have concurred with their findings."
INSPECTOR:	Yes, sir.
CHIEF:	No negligence.
INSPECTOR:	Well...
CHIEF:	Except for the investigation.
INSPECTOR:	I'll straighten that out. We'll canvass all the houses. I'll review the forensics on the body and clothing.
CHIEF:	If the evidence is lost, it's lost. What I want you to do is make sure that we present the evidence we do have clearly, forcefully, and sincerely.
INSPECTOR:	I'll get right on it.
CHIEF:	Don't look so down. Everybody makes mistakes. That's how we

learn. Show me a guy who's never made a mistake, and I'll show you a... I'll show you... You know what I mean.

INSPECTOR: Yes, sir. *(He exits.)*

Scene Five

(The INSPECTOR's office. The INSPECTOR is at his desk.)

INSPECTOR: *(Beckoning.)* Don't he shy.

(The SERGEANT approaches his desk with the CONSTABLE, whom she wordlessly urges to do something.)

What is it?

CONSTABLE: I'm sorry about last night.

INSPECTOR: Last night? It was two weeks ago.

CONSTABLE: I mean about the speeders.

INSPECTOR: What speeders?

CONSTABLE: I thought you got a report. *(To the SERGEANT.)* I told you.

INSPECTOR: I haven't read it yet, so you can tell me now yourself.

CONSTABLE: Just...you know... I, ah, well I pulled over a car last night. Big old Buick rust bucket. Doing ninety in a fifty-klick zone. I couldn't... I just couldn't get out and talk to them. A car full of natives. I guess I lost my nerve. My partner, too. We just sat there for ten minutes. They must have been thinking weird, fucking cops. Finally I floored it. Took off.

INSPECTOR: Okay, sit down. You're probably feeling a bit of stress. You almost got killed and it's hard to get that out of your mind. Have you seen a counsellor?

CONSTABLE: Like a lawyer?

INSPECTOR: No. A peer counsellor. Like a psychiatrist, sort of.

CONSTABLE: They sent me guy. All he knew was alcoholism. Listen, I'm not crazy. I can handle it.

INSPECTOR: Maybe it will help you to know that a lot of guys—me included— have had times like that. Losing your nerve. Can't do the job they want you to. Just can't talk to the public. It will pass. As soon as the inquest is over. Here is your statement. I want you to study it. Diligently. Meanwhile, the Sergeant and I are going to review her evidence.

SERGEANT: Acting Sergeant. As soon as some guys get back from vacation, I'm back to constable.

INSPECTOR: Well, speaking of acting, I take it you been in court before, ha ha?

SERGEANT: Sure.

INSPECTOR: This is no different, and I probably don't need to rehearse you, but there will be a lot of lawyers and reporters, and they'll all be looking for chinks in your armor.

CONSTABLE: Chinks.

INSPECTOR: I want everything to go off like clockwork. You'll come in and sit down at the witness table. Microphone—get it adjusted. They will swear you in. State your name. Talk loud. Sit up straight. Don't fidget. If you don't know what to do with your hands, get them out of sight. In your lap. Don't hug yourself. It's supposed to be a sign of defensiveness. Everybody will be looking at you, sizing you up.

SERGEANT: Geez, what do you think about eye shadow?

INSPECTOR: No no no, you look fine. Don't chew gum.

SERGEANT: My mouth will be dry.

INSPECTOR: There will he some water on the table. Just don't spill it. I mean, if your hands are shaking, don't touch it. Pour some water first thing.

CONSTABLE: Don't gargle.

INSPECTOR: Right. Be sure to look at the judge as much as possible. You're giving evidence for him, not those little nobody lawyers. The Crown is going to ask you about your first impressions when you got to the scene. What exactly was this guy (*Meaning the CONSTABLE.*) doing? What did he say? Go ahead.

SERGEANT: Well, I... ah...

INSPECTOR: Try not to say "well" and try not to look like you have to think up an answer. Go right into it.

SERGEANT: When I arrived...

INSPECTOR: Good.

SERGEANT: ...there were two officers attending to the male on the sidewalk. They seemed to have things...

INSPECTOR: "Appeared." Talk their language if you can.

SERGEANT: They appeared to have things under control—they were administering first aid—so I approached the Constable. He was... well, I mean, he had dirt and snow on his back and on his hair. His cap had been knocked off. I brushed off some of the snow...I'm sorry, I did that, sir.

INSPECTOR: You're not sorry.You never say that on the stand. Never apologize.You understand? That's not your department. You don't want to give them an opening. Only the Chief apologizes. Now go on. The Constable...

SERGEANT: The Constable was standing with his arms at his side. He had his service revolver in one hand—his right hand—and his portable phone in the other. I looked into his eyes and they... I've attended many traffic accidents in my career, and I know the look of someone just before they die in your arms. The Constable's eyes had that same look. Glassy. Far away. I asked him, "Have you been shot?" He said—I remember exactly what he said. I'll never forget the words. "He jumped me. I was on my back on the ground and he went for my gun."... Then I seized the weapon...

INSPECTOR: That's good, you'll do fine. I want to focus on a couple of other topics that you'll be asked about. First, why weren't fingerprints taken from his revolver?

SERGEANT: I guess we screwed up.

INSPECTOR: No, somebody higher up will say that, if necessary.

SERGEANT: We didn't print the gun because it wouldn't have given us any useful information. It wouldn't have proved who started the fight or why the male was grabbing the gun... (*The INSPECTOR drums on the desktop with the pencil.*)

Ballistics? The process of fingerprinting the gun can contaminate the barrel of the gun, so that when you do a range check and check for fibers of clothing going back in the barrel, your results are invalidated? We chose instead to do the ballistic tests?

INSPECTOR: Okay. Okay. The canvass. Why weren't all the houses on that block of Logan Avenue—in fact, all the houses that command a view of the shooting—why were they not canvassed immediately for witnesses?

SERGEANT: Three houses closest to the scene were canvassed right away. There were no witnesses. The remainder had to wait until until they could find...until sufficient personnel were available. A lot of fellows were doing a stake-out that day—some bank robbers, I think.

INSPECTOR: The glasses.

SERGEANT: The scene was washed down carefully. The glasses were not found because they had landed in some snow over ten feet away.

INSPECTOR: (*Just curious.*) How did they get there?

SERGEANT: Um...

CONSTABLE: I knocked them off. They went flying.

INSPECTOR: Oh. Continue.

SERGEANT: Later in the day the snow melted and a reporter found them. We did send an officer back in daylight to doublecheck the scene. We had to wash the scene down because we didn't want children walking to school to see all the blood.

INSPECTOR: ...Okay. Good. It's not good that we made those mistakes. But I think you'll do good. Do you have your notes from that night?

SERGEANT: Yes.

INSPECTOR: They are very important. Go over them carefully.

SERGEANT: Yes, sir. May I go now? I'm working tonight and I have baseball practice in a few minutes.

INSPECTOR: Baseball?

SERGEANT: First practice of the season.

INSPECTOR: Does the Department have a team?

SERGEANT: This is fastpitch. Girls. Women.

INSPECTOR: Civilians?

SERGEANT: Yes.

INSPECTOR: Do they know you're a cop?

SERGEANT: Some of them are beginning to suspect.

INSPECTOR: I guess you can't work twenty-four hours a day. When can you do your homework?

SERGEANT: Tomorrow morning.

INSPECTOR: Take off.

SERGEANT: Yes, sir.

INSPECTOR: You ready?

CONSTABLE: Yup.

INSPECTOR: The Crown will lead you through your evidence. He'll let you do as much talking as you want. The only problem will be the ambulance chasers that the family hired. If you say something that doesn't agree with your statement, no matter how picky, they'll jump all over you. That's why you should know your statement cold.

CONSTABLE: I do.

INSPECTOR: Let's hear you talk about when you met the fellow.

CONSTABLE: *(Reciting his somewhat stilted statement.)* I approached him by angling northwest across Logan Avenue intercepting him on the north sidewalk of Logan between Winks and Blame Street. I stopped him and asked him, "Sir, can you show me some identification." He replied, No, I don't have to show you any." *(Conversationally.)* Well, excuuuse me. I mean like what's with this guy.

INSPECTOR: "At this time…"

CONSTABLE: At this time I could smell liquor on his breath and he seemed belligerent, so I advised him, "You match the description of a suspect I am looking for, for the theft of an auto, and I would like to see some identification." He stated, "I don't have to show you nothing," and started walking east on the sidewalk. To be honest I can't quite remember the sequence of events. But I think I must have…

INSPECTOR: You've got your notes.

CONSTABLE: But the whole thing was over in fifteen seconds.

INSPECTOR: Well, say that. You had quite a shock. One of the signs of that is partial memory loss. You can be honest about that.

CONSTABLE: Yeah like when I say he was grabbing for the gun and I was grabbing and he had the barrel…it's really hard to remember what happened when.

INSPECTOR: Do the best you can. We have someone to testify on how easy it is to pull a gun out of these new holsters from the front.

CHIEF: *(Entering.)* The old ones were better.

INSPECTOR: Hello, sir.

CHIEF: How is it going?

INSPECTOR: Fine.

CHIEF: Good. I'm counting on you to get us through Death Valley. We've been getting a lot of letters.

INSPECTOR: Oh?

CHIEF: Supporting us.

INSPECTOR: Great.

CHIEF: Uh uh. When the kooks start thinking you need help, you're in trouble. Ready for the inquest?

INSPECTOR: We're getting there.

CHIEF: Any surprises?

INSPECTOR: What do you mean?

CHIEF: Are there going to be any surprises?

INSPECTOR: I'm not planning on any.

CHIEF: How's forensics?

INSPECTOR: Pretty good package. Range test-point blank, confirms the Constable's story.

CHIEF: Powder burns on the Indian?

INSPECTOR: Blood washed a lot away.

CHIEF: He was grabbing the gun. On his hands?

INSPECTOR: They didn't check that. Said they didn't have the equipment. There was blood on the officer's left leg. Flowing upwards-consistent with an arterial gush wound. You know, the guy being on top of him. And there was something, maybe powder, blow by, on the Constable's right palm, like he was holding on to the cylinder when the gun went off.

CHIEF: Great! let's see.

INSPECTOR: *(Pulling out a document.)* This statement by the detective who...

CHIEF: A statement? I mean a picture.

INSPECTOR: Didn't take a picture.

CHIEF: Geez. Some days it's hard to radiate confidence. Is the officer ready to testify?

INSPECTOR: We've just been reviewing...

CHIEF: Oh, hello there. Boy, you sure stirred up a hornet's nest. They're really on the warpath.

CONSTABLE: Sorry. I...

CHIEF: You have nothing to apologize for.

CONSTABLE: Yes, sir.

CHIEF: Can you defend yourself? That's the number one question. Can you defend yourself?

CONSTABLE: Yes, sir.

CHIEF: Because, if you can't, the public loses respect for us. Next thing you know, people are taking pot shots at us. Our lives in danger. I killed a man once. Him and his buddy were robbing a bank. I yelled at him—Hold it. Police! He turned around. I saw something metallic nickel-plated—in his hand. You better believe I got off a shot. Bullet went right in here. *(He touches a spot near the INSPECTOR's right ear.)* Turned out all he had was a screwdriver. Oh, they had a big inquest, just like you. *(Pause.)* These judges and lawyers have days and weeks to second-guess you. But you only have a split-second to decide. If you can't do it, you shouldn't be a police officer.

I got a gold medal for that. Of course, your case isn't quite the same. But it should be. Well, I better be going. Good luck, tomorrow. I've got a plane to catch. *(Exiting.)* I wish.

Scene Six

(A hallway in the Law Courts Building. The CONSTABLE paces and studies some notes.)

SERGEANT: *(Entering from a courtroom.)* Ps-s-st.

CONSTABLE: What?

SERGEANT: *(Beckoning him downstage and talking in hushed tones.)* You know what's going on in there? They had this native girl saying she was driving down Logan that night and she saw a cop with his gun out.

CONSTABLE: Yeah, I heard.

SERGEANT: Well?

CONSTABLE: It wasn't me. So it doesn't matter.

SERGEANT: Yeah, but you know what people think. If one cop does it, they all do it.

CONSTABLE: You think they'll believe her?

SERGEANT: No, she's kind of soft-spoken. Takes a while to say anything. But then there's the kid, the one in the back seat.

CONSTABLE: The passenger in the stolen car?

SERGEANT: Yeah. He says he's been having nightmares. He says an officer blamed the whole shooting on him. "If you hadn't stolen the car, none of this would have happened."

CONSTABLE: So?

SERGEANT: He heard racist remarks.

CONSTABLE: Not from me.

SERGEANT: He heard someone tell you to say it was an accident. *(Pause.)*

CONSTABLE: It was.

SERGEANT: It doesn't sound so good. Look, they are going to recess any minute. You better get out of here.

INSPECTOR: *(Entering from where the SERGEANT entered.)* Sergeant? My office.

CHIEF: *(Almost offstage.)* Inspector, my office, please. *(The INSPECTOR motions to the SERGEANT to accompany him.)*

Scene Seven

(The CHIEF's office)

CHIEF: "That's right, bleed the sucker dry."

SERGEANT: There was no talking at the scene.

CHIEF: Nobody said, "That's right, bleed him dry?"

SERGEANT: No.

CHIEF: There were no racist remarks?

SERGEANT: No.

CHIEF: "Blue-eyed fucking Indian"?

SERGEANT: No.

CHIEF: The little kid said that somebody—and it seems to be you—called him a blue-eyed fucking Indian.

SERGEANT: I never use that term. And even if I might, it was too dark to see what colour anybody's eyes were. I believe he's mixed it up with some other occasion. He's got a prior.

CHIEF: Police officers had their guns out? Did the Constable have his gun out?

SERGEANT: With all due respect, sir, we don't chase unarmed teenagers with our guns out.

CHIEF: Of course not. By god, in my day, you were a sissy if you drew your gun. *(To the INSPECTOR.)* We've got a public relations problem here. As usual. You know what they say, don't you?

INSPECTOR: Yes, sir.

SERGEANT: No, sir.

CHIEF: The best defence is a good offence. I don't have that right, do I?

SERGEANT: No, sir.

INSPECTOR: Yes, sir.

CHIEF: Well, then, what do we have on the perpetrator, other than the fact that he once helped an RCMP officer out of a ditch?

INSPECTOR: The evidence of the Chief Medical Examiner. He talked about the gunshot wound.

CHIEF: No, no, no.

INSPECTOR: His blood alcohol level.

CHIEF: Yes, yes.

INSPECTOR: It was point two two. Almost three times the legal limit for driving.

SERGEANT: Good thing he didn't try to drive home.

INSPECTOR: The Examiner talked about how alcohol lowers inhibitions in some people. Increases belligerence. But he also said that a habitual drinker can put away a whole lot and not show it.

CHIEF: This habitual drinker attacked our man.

INSPECTOR: We have the C-PIC record on the guy. We haven't introduced it, yet.

CHIEF: Let's hear it.

INSPECTOR: He's been detained twice under the Intoxicated Persons Act and taken to the drunk tank—the Main Street Project—to sleep it off. On one of these occasions he was disruptive and uncooperative towards both the police and the staff, and so was placed in a security cell for his own safety as well as for the safety of everyone else.

CHIEF: When was this?

INSPECTOR: Almost two years ago. Christmas Day, to be exact.

CHIEF: Hm. A little out of date, but it sure ought to be in the public interest. Anything else? Wasn't there a letter?

INSPECTOR: The letter we found on his person. From his wife.

CHIEF: Yes. Didn't it say...

INSPECTOR: She (*Meaning the SERGEANT.*) asked the wife about it, but...

CHIEF: You verified that she wrote it?

SERGEANT: Yes. I mean, she didn't deny it.

CHIEF: Would you read it?

SERGEANT: I have.

CHIEF: Out loud. Like you were in court.

SERGEANT: "We can't go on like this. I need a home where I feel safe. I can't seem to find it with you. You said the other night I wish I could make it easier on you. I don't know what you were referring to, but each time you drink, it drives us further apart and makes it seem easier to leave."

CHIEF: Continue.

SERGEANT: "But I've got to leave. I can't spend the rest of my life like this." (*Pause.*) It's personal.

INSPECTOR: It's probably not admissible.

CHIEF: Well, give it a try, man. It only has to make it in to the newspapers. Look, I can appreciate the disappointment of a people when one of their leaders, a man they are putting their hopes on, turns out to be just a...the kind of person who picks fights with policemen at two-thirty in the morning. But a fellow officer's career is on the line. We are in the middle of a judicial inquest, a legal proceeding where, you know...a cathedral, a temple of justice where we are gathered together to discover the truth. We are obliged to tell all we know, especially when the other side is finding people who'll say anything under oath. The truth is this man, the deceased, when intoxicated, was capable of violence. The judge will see that.

INSPECTOR: Yes, sir.

CHIEF: Damn it, society has given the police a tough job, a dirty job. We're not perfect, but we do we best we can with my funding level. We're on the front lines of a war. A war we didn't start, but a war where we pay the price for what our ancestors did or didn't do. We've made some careless mistakes in this case, but I don't think the judge will condemn a man because of the colour of his uniform. He will exonerate the Constable, no?

INSPECTO R: Yes, sir.

SERGEANT: Yes, sir.

Scene Eight

> *(A locker room. The SERGEANT is dressing.*
>
> *The CONSTABLE enters quietly and mysteriously circles her. Suddenly he lets out a whoop of joy, embraces her, and runs around the stage shouting out I THEREFORE EXONERATE THE CONSTABLE, ALL RIGHTs, WAY-TO-G0s, and YAHOOs. He exits, still shouting.*
>
> *The SERGEANT shrugs.)*

Scene Nine

> *(A bar. The CHIEF and the INSPECTOR share a table.)*

CHIEF: May I propose a toast?

INSPECTOR: You may.

CHIEF: To the judge.

INSPECTOR: To the judge.

CHIEF: "It appears to me that death resulted, in whole or in part, from the unlawful act or culpable negligence of the following person: No one."

> *(He drinks.)*

"Once the shooting had occurred, by and large proper investigation followed."

> *(He drinks.)*

Good forensics.

INSPECTOR: It was piss poor. I'm sorry I made such a mess.

CHIEF: Hey, you got me out of a mess. You went in there, rolled up your sleeves and went to work. Nobody had to tell you what to do. You are the unsung hero. You are my good Minister, and I intend to bestow riches upon you. How would you like to go south?

INSPECTOR: The weather hasn't been that bad last few weeks.

CHIEF: No, no, no.

INSPECTOR: District Six? You want to transfer me to District Six? Please...

CHIEF: Quantico, Virginia. FBI school. There's a slot available for the fall term and I'm thinking of forwarding your name.

INSPECTOR: That's a...that's a big honour. I'm only acting Inspector, A Staff Sergeant.

CHIEF: This can sure speed your promotion.

INSPECTOR: But there's guys ahead of me.

CHIEF: Are you questioning my judgement?

INSPECTOR: No. But isn't there a committee or something?

CHIEF: Are you fishing for compliments?

INSPECTOR: No. I simply don't deserve it.

CHIEF: Look, I know a good man when I see one. You'll get notification next week. Besides, there has been a Staff Sergeant who's gone to FBI school.

INSPECTOR: Who?

CHIEF: The Chief Constable. Moi.

INSPECTOR: Well...thanks.

CHIEF: You act like the verdict went against us.

INSPECTOR: He said "certain shortcomings"...

CHIEF: What he said was, "In conclusion, despite certain shortcomings in the area of police investigation, it is my view that the shooting occurred as a result of the deceased pushing down the officer and then attempting to take his revolver. I therefore exonerate the Constable." Cheers.

INSPECTOR: Cheers.

CHIEF: You know why the investigation was screwed up? We don't have the manpower. Maybe the politicians will get the message now. Anyway you'll get another chance.

INSPECTOR: What do you mean?

CHIEF: If that whatchamacallit, that...

INSPECTOR: Aboriginal Justice Inquiry.

CHIEF: If that goes through, if we can't convince them it's a waste of time and taxpayer money, they are going to look at all this again. But, meanwhile... Relax. You know, once you make Inspector, you are going to have time on your hands. When five o'clock comes, you go home. You'll have time for your hobbies. Don't you work on old cars or something?

INSPECTOR: No.

CHIEF: What do you do?

INSPECTOR: I don't know. I work.

CHIEF: On your days off, I mean.

INSPECTOR: Days off? There's always another case. I like digging for the truth.

CHIEF: Have you tried gardening?

INSPECTOR: No. I grew up on a farm. It wasn't a fun thing.

CHIEF: Bagpipes.

INSPECTOR: What?

CHIEF: That's what I want to do. On a deserted tropical beach somewhere. *(He sighs.)* ...Can you draw?

INSPECTOR: In here?

CHIEF: Not your gun. Pictures. Paintings. I figured out why all the society people like Indians so much. They are all making a killing on native art. If they had a nice little bull market in law enforcement art, we wouldn't get all the flak we do from the media. We'd finally get some respect. Don't we have any artists on the Force?

INSPECTOR: There's the guy who sketches the suspects.

CHIEF: That's a start. It seems to me, with the kinds of things we put up with, day in and day out, that we kind of represent modern life, and whatever pictures we draw make a statement about um... Well, think about it. look, I gotta go. I have to show up for an interview at dawn tomorrow.

CONSTABLE: *(Entering, preceded by his shouts and trailed by the SERGEANT.)* Great news, eh?

CHIEF: Congratulations. You were solid up there.

CONSTABLE: Well, who would believe those kids? Is there a party?

CHIEF: Go ahead. I have to get my beauty rest. I have a TV interview tomorrow. Me and some native chief.

SERGEANT: Two chiefs on the same show. Ha ha.

CHIEF: Yes. I heard him today, saying that the verdict means an open season on natives. He said if I think that relations with natives are good, I must be living in a dream world. So I'm going to set the record straight tomorrow morning. If I don't sleep in. Ha ha.

CONSTABLE: You can tell them that the guy was the author of his own demise. The natives drink and they get in trouble. Blaming the police for their troubles is like an alcoholic blaming the liquor store for being open late.

SERGEANT: I think what he'll try to do is calm things down.

CHIEF: Absolutely. Good night, all. *(He exits.)*

CONSTABLE: Sir, I'd like to thank you for everything you did.

INSPECTOR: I didn't do bugger all.

SERGEANT: Sure, you did. The judge said it was an accident.

CONSTABLE: "The death resulted from the culpable negligence of...no one!"

INSPECTOR: *(Suddenly snatching the SERGEANT's gun from her holster.)* The gun went off by accident?

CONSTABLE: We were fighting...

INSPECTOR: Look, I can play catch with this gun, I can do cowboy tricks with it, I can hit my head with it, I can throw it on the floor. I just can't seem to make it go off by accident. Somebody has to squeeze the trigger.

CONSTABLE: If somebody goes for my gun, I have to figure he's trying to kill me. If my life or anybody else's life is threatened, I am authorized to use deadly force.

SERGEANT: Let's settle down. *(He pushes the CONSTABLE away.)* Maybe you guys have had too much to drink.

INSPECTOR: I haven't had enough. *(He exits.)*

CONSTABLE: What a great party.

(Intermission.)

Part Two
The Inquiry

Scene One

(The CHIEF's office. The INSPECTOR, now in a white shirt, is not visible at first, and we think the CHIEF speaks to us.)

CHIEF: I'm at a convention—Law Enforcement in the Twenty-First Century or some such thing and we've all been sent to the beach to get a suntan, because a suntan on my face will raise the morale of the troops when we return home—they'll see that thirty years of public service will allow any officer to live the life of the ruling classes. There I am, hot sun, pounding surf, screaming seagulls...I've collected a pile of beautiful seashells and put them around what is clearly the best sand castle I've ever made. Then a cloud crosses the sun. I look up and I see three ships, black sails, coming closer. Boom. Artillery? This is supposed to be a resort. They come ashore—a group of monkeys, I think, wearing lots of coloured cloth to hide their tails. They have a big green and yellow flag on a pole and they take it and stab my beach. All of a sudden I'm naked and they're coming after me with their swords. Boy, that fellow Sigmund Freud would have a field day with me.

INSPECTOR: It's Columbus.

CHIEF: I know. Columbus, 1492. The question is, why would I be dreaming that? I'm a soldier, not an explorer.

INSPECTOR: Dreams are the brain's attempt to make sense out of random electrical discharges from the brain stem.

CHIEF: I know. But...that dream was meant for somebody else, and I got it. Why? Am I on the verge of a great discovery?

INSPECTOR: Don't know.

CHIEF: A great discovery... Well, that's when the phone call woke me up. The Court of Appeals has ruled that the Aboriginal Justice Inquiry Commissioners may make findings of fact and name the names of persons whose conduct they consider should be called into question. They may also order production by City of Winnipeg police officers of photocopies of relevant portions of their notebooks.

INSPECTOR: You want to put me in charge, then, eh?

CHIEF: Actually, I want you to testify.

INSPECTOR: You want to put me on the stand?

CHIEF: Just to talk about the changes we made to that manual...uh, what's it called?

INSPECTOR: Evidence gathering in police shootings.

CHIEF: Yes. You're to show them we can learn from our mistakes. They're going to have a bunch of four hundred dollar-a-day lawyers going over every police report with an electron microscope. They're going to have the RCMP double-check all the physical evidence—you can help co-ordinate that—and you can be sure those horsemen will keep checking until they find something racial. With all the public money they're spending, they'll find something racial, whether it's there or not. We're the Yahoos in this story. Have I got this right? The government gives money to Indians so they can sue the government for more money?... You have time to do this, don't you? You're up in Communications?

INSPECTOR: Oh yeah. The place practically runs itself. I'd like to get back in the thick of things.

CHIEF: Too bad it has to be this.

INSPECTOR: I'll go organize the data.

CHIEF: *(To himself shaking his head.)* Tierra! Tierra! Gracias a Dios! Boom!

Scene Two

(The INSPECTOR enters his office with a stack of files, sits at his desk, and begins to examine them. He picks up the phone.)

INSPECTOR: Hi, Sweetie, is Mom home?...Oh, that's right. Well, tell her I'm going to be real late. *(Pause.)* I don't know when. There's some leftover meatloaf. *(Pause.)* How about your homework? ...None? Geez, you can have some of mine. Okay, so long. *(Pause.)* Bye.

(He hangs up. He loosens his tie, rolls up his sleeves, and begins reading and making notes.

The lights on the INSPECTOR fade and come up across stage on the SERGEANT. She is at her locker. She pulls a small notebook out from a jacket pocket. She flips through it. She ponders. She puts it back. She takes it out again. She makes her way to the INSPECTOR's office.)

SERGEANT: Excuse me? Inspector?

(The INSPECTOR is now seen to be fast asleep, head on the desk, one hand on the desk gripping his service revolver by its barrel.

The SERGEANT approaches the INSPECTOR with fear, nudges him to see if he's dead.)

INSPECTOR: *(Awakening.)* Oh.

(He takes several seconds fully rouse himself. As he does so, a dark cloud seems to enter his psyche. He knocks some folders off his desk.)

Garbage.

SERGEANT: It's 0800 hours.

INSPECTOR: Good morning.

SERGEANT: Were you here all night?

INSPECTOR: No. I just came in early to finish up some work. I heard you passed your sergeant's exam.

SERGEANT: Yeah, the written part. I can write good.

INSPECTOR: Where are you now?

SERGEANT: Division twenty-four. Stolen cars.

INSPECTOR: How's it going?

SERGEANT: No shortage of work. You? *(Indicating his white shirt.)* I see you made Inspector. What...? *(Referring to the gun on the desk.)*

INSPECTOR: *(Examining his hand.)* It leaves a mark. See? If you grab the barrel of a gun, the sight *(Pointing to it at the tip of the barrel.)* digs into your hand. It leaves a mark.

SERGEANT: Oh. God, I didn't know what to think. I saw you there, head on your desk, the gun...

INSPECTOR: Funny thing is, there were no marks like this on that fellow's hands.

SERGEANT: *(Shrugging.)* ...Actually, that's sort of what I have to talk to you about. I want to ask you what I should do. I found this in my locker. It's the notebook from last year. The shooting.

INSPECTOR: No, I have yours in here. We had to xerox them for the subpoena.

SERGEANT: Right. That's the good copy.

INSPECTOR: What do you mean?

SERGEANT: This one that I found is the original. It's a mess. You have the good one.

INSPECTOR: What do you mean "good"?

SERGEANT: When I made these original notes, I never dreamed there would be such a kerfuffle over what happened that night. But when there was, I copied them over. I guess. I don't remember doing it, but I must have.

INSPECTOR: The whole notebook?

SERGEANT: Yes.

INSPECTOR: By hand?

SERGEANT: Yes. Everything's in chronological order.

INSPECTOR: You copied over the whole notebook, not just that one night.

SERGEANT: There were some mistakes, some clerical errors...

INSPECTOR: Let me see your original. *(He reads and compares.)*

SERGEANT: I remember I had an address wrong. I had to correct it when I saw the Communications log.

INSPECTOR: You changed the colour of the car thief's jacket from grey to black. What colour jacket was the Indian wearing?

SERGEANT: Um...

INSPECTOR: Black. It might look to somebody that you changed the colour so that he matched the description of the car thief more closely.

SERGEANT: All I changed—and I didn't change, I corrected—was the description put out by the dispatcher. I wrote that the dispatcher said grey, when actually she said black.

INSPECTOR: You weren't covering for the Constable?

SERGEANT: No.

INSPECTOR: You and he were partners a few years ago. Only natural that you'd do something to help him.

SERGEANT: I didn't.

INSPECTOR: But you put a lot of time and effort into making it look like this corrected notebook was an original.

SERGEANT: I just didn't want everyone to see how disorganized...

INSPECTOR: I have to send the original to the Commissioners.

SERGEANT: Fine.

INSPECTOR: Do other officers copy over their notes?

SERGEANT: I doubt it.

INSPECTOR: Your original has signed statements by witnesses to crimes.

SERGEANT: I paraphrased them.

INSPECTOR: That's not acceptable. You'll get a reprimand in your file.

SERGEANT: Jesus.

CONSTABLE: *(Entering.)* Here I am.

INSPECTOR: Just wait a second. No, come in. *(To the SERGEANT.)* I'll let you know what happens.

(The SERGEANT starts to leave.)

No, wait. I want you to hear this.

(He points to a chair and she sits.)

Constable.

CONSTABLE: Good morning, sir.

INSPECTOR: Good morning. Before I give evidence at the Inquiry, it is very important to me that I have a clear picture of what happened that night.

SERGEANT: We're going to be on TV.

CONSTABLE: You're kidding.

SERGEANT: The public's right to know.

INSPECTOR: I have been reviewing the case and a few inconsistencies have surfaced. Which means I read this stuff over and over and it never adds up.

CONSTABLE: Shit happens, eh?

INSPECTOR: Not in my division. I'm reading your statement. "Sir, can you show me some identification." He replied, No, I don't have to show you any." At this time I could smell liquor on his breath, and he seemed belligerent, so I advised him, "You match the description of a suspect I'm looking for in the theft of an auto and I would like to see some identification."

CONSTABLE: It's hard to remember exactly what I said.

INSPECTOR: Matched the description? You stopped him because he matched the description?

CONSTABLE: Of the car thief. You know.

INSPECTOR: But you had seen the car thief already.

CONSTABLE: I don't get your meaning.

INSPECTOR: Sorry. I'll try to make it clear. You and your partner are out there on Logan. It's after midnight.

CONSTABLE: Yes.

INSPECTOR: You set up radar.

CONSTABLE: Uh huh.

INSPECTOR: Stop anybody?

CONSTABLE: Yes, we booked one.

INSPECTOR: Then?

CONSTABLE: It's about two o'clock. Time for our lunch break. It's also closing time for the bars. We've already heard the stolen car report so we figure we'll swing by the Westbrook and see if anyone is driving away with it.

INSPECTOR: (With a touch of sarcasm.) Good idea.

CONSTABLE: Just doing my job.

INSPECTOR: Sure.

CONSTABLE: Just trying to catch the bad guys.

INSPECTOR: And you did.

CONSTABLE: I caught a lot of flak.

INSPECTOR: Comes with the territory, eh? You spot the car, you give chase down Alexander.

CONSTABLE: He blows three or four stop signs, a traffic light, north onto Winks, into a snowbank.

INSPECTOR: Was it icy?

CONSTABLE: Here and there. Driver gets out, beetles down the back lane between Alexander and Logan.

INSPECTOR: Did you see him?

CONSTABLE: Not real good. Half a block away.

INSPECTOR: On the radio, your partner said dark clothing.

CONSTABLE: Yeah.

INSPECTOR: There are streetlights on that lane. Did you chase him?

CONSTABLE: The kid was down the lane. Running away. I'm not going to catch him.

INSPECTOR: Okay, the passenger.

CONSTABLE: He gets out the driver's side, throws off this big leather jacket, cuts south between two houses.

INSPECTOR: You're chasing him.

CONSTABLE: Yeah.

INSPECTOR: Why did you draw your revolver?

CONSTABLE: What are you doing to me?

INSPECTOR: Kid said you went for your gun. "Freeze or I'll shoot."

CONSTABLE: He was crouching by the fence. He couldn't climb over it. I saw him. Then I slipped. I put my hands out to break my fall. Maybe he thought I was going for my gun. I didn't say "freeze." Just "stop"... "give it up" "you're caught" —stuff like that.

INSPECTOR: You took him back to your car. Then what?

CONSTABLE: We asked him for a description of the driver.

INSPECTOR: Black jacket, blue jeans.

CONSTABLE: Something like that.

INSPECTOR: Age?

CONSTABLE: Kid didn't seem to know. Say one thing. Say another. Twenties.

INSPECTOR: The kid states that he didn't know what the driver was wearing. That he never told you nothing except that the age was nineteen or seventeen. But you broadcast a description of black jacket, blue jeans, twenty-two years old, so you must have seen the driver yourself. You said he was native. You must have seen his hair.

CONSTABLE: You believe that kid?

INSPECTOR: Too scared to make stuff up. Wouldn't you think?

CONSTABLE: He should have been interviewed that night. Why did they let him go home and cook up a story?

INSPECTOR: You deny the kid's story?

CONSTABLE: Of course. How can he be objective? He hates us.

INSPECTOR: You leave the kid in the car with your partner. You walk down the lane. Then up between some houses to Logan. Why?

CONSTABLE: On the radio. Says he's across Logan.

INSPECTOR: The driver of the stolen vehicle?

CONSTABLE: Yes. Some of the guys are chasing him across the park.

INSPECTOR: Why don't you go back to your car?

CONSTABLE: I want to go and see what's happening. Maybe he's going to double back.

INSPECTOR: You getting hungry?

CONSTABLE: No, I tried to eat something a little while ago.

INSPECTOR: Were you hungry at two-thirty in the morning?

CONSTABLE: No.

INSPECTOR: Were you tired?

CONSTABLE: No.

INSPECTOR: Two-thirty in the morning. Four days on, four days off. Rotating shifts.You're never used to it.

CONSTABLE: I can do my job same as anybody else.

INSPECTOR: Not quite the same. At two-thirty another officer sees the Indian—another officer who is chasing the suspect—he sees the Indian walking along Logan, west of where you are, and he runs right by him. Nothing suspicious.

CONSTABLE: He matched the description.

INSPECTOR: Help me on this, Constable.You'd seen the suspect, early twenties, if not younger, male, native, dark clothes, no glasses, running to beat the band, and now comes along this thirty seven-year-old one hundred eighty-five pounder, six feet tall, glasses, walking along not out of breath, walking toward the stolen vehicle…what, you figured the guy was a master of disguise?

CONSTABLE: I never got a good look at the driver.

INSPECTOR: You'd just heard that they'd caught the suspect up on Gallagher.

CONSTABLE: The one they got on radio doesn't match the description. They say sweater jacket.

INSPECTOR: Grey jacket. The arresting officer said grey jacket. It's as clear as a bell.

CONSTABLE: Not on my portable. Static, words cut off. I thought he said sweater jacket. Then I see a guy walking on the other side of Logan. Tall, black jacket. Blue jeans.

INSPECTOR: Native?

CONSTABLE: Maybe native.

INSPECTOR: (To himself.) Leave him alone.

CONSTABLE: Leave him alone. See something wrong—never mind. Go get a donut.

INSPECTOR: You giving me a lecture?

CONSTABLE: No, sir. But I don't think I need one either.

INSPECTOR: (Laughing at his chutzpah.) When you got close, you must have seen his hair was short and he wasn't any twenty-two years old.

CONSTABLE: I can't tell age like that. The juvenile says this, says that, maybe this, maybe that, he don't remember, he's not sure, he might be protecting the driver, so you don't take what he says to be a sure thing.

INSPECTOR: Does this one hundred eighty-five pound guy look like a kid who can jump out of a car and haul ass down a back lane?

CONSTABLE: You never know.

INSPECTOR: Did you stop him because he was native?

CONSTABLE: No.

INSPECTOR: Did you stop him because you were high?

CONSTABLE: No.

INSPECTOR: You don't want to level with me, do you?

CONSTABLE: Yes, I do.

INSPECTOR: Well, I'm not getting the answers. You had evidence—very strong evidence—that the suspect was apprehended moments before you saw a middle-aged pedestrian plodding along towards the stolen vehicle, hands in his pocket, not out of breath, not suspicious in any way...

CONSTABLE: ...the suspect...they did get the right one...but...

INSPECTOR: You knew that, didn't you?

CONSTABLE: I thought they might have the wrong person.

INSPECTOR: You thought? That's what I'm wondering about. Were you thinking? Or were you so hyper from chasing those pesky redskins that you would have stopped a stray cat?

CONSTABLE: I wasn't hyper.

INSPECTOR: What do you think, Sergeant? Would you believe this story?

SERGEANT: Well, sure...

INSPECTOR: If this was a question on your Sergeants Exam, what would you say? Eh? I think you'd cheek the box that said, "This is a crock." So. You stop this guy. You ask him for ID. He says he don't have to show you nothing. Which is true. But most people stop for us. Natives stop. Intoxicated males stop. What happened?

CONSTABLE: I was respectful.

INSPECTOR: He pissed you off so you grabbed him. You assaulted him.

CONSTABLE: He knocked me down. Now you're saying that I assaulted him?

INSPECTOR: You grabbed the guy. You weren't going to arrest him. Then you're telling me you ended up on your back with him leaning over you because he pushed you. There's no corroborating evidence that he pushed you.

CONSTABLE: He...

INSPECTOR: Maybe you just slipped on the ice.

CONSTABLE: ...pushed me.

INSPECTOR: Maybe he was reaching down to help you up.

CONSTABLE: ...What do you mean "grab the guy"?

INSPECTOR: (Reading from the CONSTABLE's statement.) "He had only made a step or two when I reached out and took hold of his upper right arm with my right hand and he turned to face me. So I reached out with my left hand, taking his right wrist." You did all this without intending to arrest him?

CONSTABLE: He was drunk. I had to reason with him.

INSPECTOR: In fact, you didn't grab him with your right hand because you had drawn your gun.

CONSTABLE: No way.

INSPECTOR: I have witnesses saying police had their guns drawn that night. You're a cop. You follow procedure.

CONSTABLE: That isn't procedure.

INSPECTOR: It's common practice. Come on. The witnesses are very sincere. One of them is even white.

CONSTABLE: It's all in their minds. There they are, driving down a empty street, two o'clock in the morning, suddenly—they're not expecting it—they catch a glimpse of a cop. His arm's in the air. Their brain supplies a gun. I'm fighting Hollywood.

INSPECTOR: Or living it. Show me. You guys show me. Let's see how it happened. If it could happen. You seem to be the only one who knows what that guy did to you. So you be him. I'll be you. You walk along the sidewalk. Hands in your back pocket. It's a couple of degrees below zero. There was a little rain earlier that day. There's snow and frozen slush and ice. You're walking... *(To the SERGEANT.)* What do we know about his mental state?

SERGEANT: Drunk.

INSPECTOR: Drunk. But he's functioning.

SERGEANT: Wanted to go home in a taxi with his ex-girlfriend; she says thanks but no thanks; he walks.

INSPECTOR: *(To the CONSTABLE.)* Okay, what are you thinking about?

CONSTABLE: I hate cops.

INSPECTOR: You're thinking...it's late. You're an executive director of a tribal council. You're thinking about the work you have to do tomorrow.

CONSTABLE: I'm thinking about old times with my girlfriend and I'm pissed off she said no.

INSPECTOR: Actually, we don't know what you're thinking. You belong to a different culture.

SERGEANT: Think about spirits.

INSPECTOR: Think whatever you want. I'm only interested in the laws of physics. *(To the SERGEANT.)* Take him over there, tell him you're not going to sleep with him, and...

SERGEANT: He don't need to be told that.

INSPECTOR: ... and send him this way.

SERGEANT: *(Drawing the CONSTABLE to one side of the stage.)* Go home by yourself, turkey.

INSPECTOR: Excuse me, I'd like to see some ID.

CONSTABLE: Jesus, I don't know where it is.

INSPECTOR: *(With his hand on the CONSTABLE's shoulder.)* You match the description of a car thief. Let me see some ID.

CONSTABLE: What?

INSPECTOR: Push me. Give me a good shove.

SERGEANT: You can't recreate the exact situation.

INSPECTOR: You do it. You know what I want.

> *(The SERGEANT walks across the stage, hands in her back pockets, humming the Atlanta Braves baseball team war chant. The INSPECTOR intercepts her.)*

I'd like to see some ID.

SERGEANT: I don't have to show you nuttin'. *(She keeps walking.)*

> *(The INSPECTOR puts his hand on her upper arm and spins her around. The SERGEANT pushes his shoulders but he doesn't lose his balance.)*

INSPECTOR: Is that the best you can do?

SERGEANT: *(Pushing him again without effect.)* Well, shit, he was six feet tall, a hundred and eighty something, a big fucking hockey player. He pushes people every time he's on the ice.

INSPECTOR: If you're on the Force, you're supposed to be able to handle a guy like that. Push me like this.

> *(He shoves her shoulders. She staggers back, trips over something and falls. He offers to help her up. The SERGEANT refuses the offer. When she gets to her feet, she suddenly gives the INSPECTOR a shove. The INSPECTOR almost loses his balance. The CONSTABLE grins broadly.)*

Pretty good. If the sidewalk was icy, maybe I would have gone down. Maybe. If this intoxicated guy had given me a really strong push, quick, unexpected—even though I feel he's belligerent—a sudden hard push with both hands, even though I was hanging on to one of them already, maybe I go down. That's the easy part. But now I fall and bring you with me. How did that happen?

CONSTABLE: When I started to fall, I tried to grab onto whatever I could to stop my fall. I got a hold of his arms—you know, the sleeves of his jacket? So when I go down, he comes with me.

INSPECTOR: I don't see how you knocked his glasses off.

CONSTABLE: My arms are going like this. *(A windmill.)* I caught the corner of his glasses and sent them flying.

INSPECTOR: *(Though looking at the SERGEANT.)* Do you really remember this, or did somebody ask you to put this in your statement in order to hide the fact that maybe somebody stepped on his glasses and kicked them into the snow.

CONSTABLE: My mind is a complete blank.

SERGEANT: He gave his statement before they found the glasses.

INSPECTOR: I guess I can check that out. But right now I have to believe this story that says you received a strong, totally unexpected push from a guy you considered excessively belligerent, that you waved your arms and knocked off his glasses and then you grabbed his arms and then you fell backwards and pulled him down. It's an action we can't seem to duplicate here, but, you know, one can't recreate the exact situation, and, after all, police don't tell lies under oath since that would be against everything they stand for, so I'm going to accept this story of the big push. *(To the SERGEANT.)* When I pushed you and you hit the ground, your arm went like this. *(He bends his right elbow.)*

SERGEANT: Did it?

INSPECTOR: Looked like you wanted to go for your gun.

CONSTABLE: He grabbed my gun.

INSPECTOR: The man is drunk—practically three times the legal driving limit. You knocked his glasses off. How can he even see your gun?

CONSTABLE: I fall, I pull him down with me. His feet are still planted on the ground, but he's leaning over me. His face is about a foot from my service belt. I don't know what he's thinking, but I bet he sees the gun and it gives him some ideas. He starts yanking and I start hanging on for dear life. The damn thing comes out. Holy mother, this Indian's going to shoot me.

INSPECTOR: You panic.

CONSTABLE: I panic.

INSPECTOR: Let's try it.

CONSTABLE: I don't have to.

SERGEANT: Come on.

CONSTABLE: No.

(The SERGEANT gets on her back and puts up a foot. The INSPECTOR approaches as if to enact the role of the victim, but the CONSTABLE pushes him aside and bends over the SERGEANT. He struggles to reach her holster.)

There was tugging at my holster. The gun came out.

INSPECTOR: Are you telling me that he undid the holster strap?

CONSTABLE: I don't know what happened. All I know is blam. He looks at me.

INSPECTOR: He stands up. You said he stands up. You got something backwards.

CONSTABLE: No. That's what happened.

INSPECTOR: You're on your back. He's leaning over you. The only way he can reach for your holster with both hands is if he's bent way over you, his one hundred eighty-five pounds on your foot, which is planted in the middle of his chest. Your leg is so compressed that you can't push him off, right?

CONSTABLE: Right.

INSPECTOR: His weight is not on his feet. It's on you. You shoot this tired intoxicated man, close range, bullet expands on impact, hurts like hell, and he stands up?

SERGEANT: ...It doesn't hurt at first. *(She pushes the CONSTABLE upright.)*

INSPECTOR: What?

SERGEANT: The bullet. It doesn't hurt at first.

(Pause.)

CONSTABLE: I still can't stop the feeling from coming back. I pick up one of my kids. I want to give them a hug. But...he's on top of me, breathing on me, pulling my holster. Why? Why does he want to kill me? I didn't do anything.

INSPECTOR: You hassled him.

CONSTABLE: *(Getting to his feet.)* I gave him a chance. He wouldn't stop. It's not my fault he's in a bad mood. It wasn't me spending the evening getting plastered, dancing with my old girlfriend, getting turned down, walking home pissed off, it wasn't me who went for the gun.

INSPECTOR: You stopped the guy for no reason at all.

CONSTABLE: He matched the description. They're so poor. They got nothing. He says it's my fault. I took everything he had and I don't have any way to give it back. He hates my guts. Thinks he owns the place walking two-thirty in the morning telling me to kiss off. Why isn't he home? In some nice warm home? Why are they always hanging around outside looking at us?

INSPECTOR: You pathetic bigot.

SERGEANT: Everybody is a racist. But it doesn't mean we hate them. You can't help it. You meet a stranger and you have to know what he's going to do, what he's capable of. So you make an educated...

CONSTABLE: Educated?

SERGEANT: ...educated from your own experience and you base your guess on his appearance. Especially if you're a police officer. You don't wait for him to give you his resume. That's the way your brains work.

INSPECTOR: I don't ignore facts because the guy looks like he's native.

SERGEANT: Never? Well, me, I got it down to three seconds. I see an Indian that I don't know, and naturally my brain says, "There goes somebody who don't belong to my tribe, a primitive, watch out." But—three seconds and my other brain kicks in with, "Wait a minute. He's a person like you. Give him a break." If I could get it down to two seconds, I bet I could make Staff Sergeant. Down to zero and...nah, I'd have to turn my brain off. But then I could make Inspector.

INSPECTOR: Maybe you could. But you know what I am? Fuck this white shirt. You know what I am? I'm a detective. An investigator. I get to the bottom of things. That's what I'm good at. That's what I'm paid for. If I didn't do that, I'd be a pencil pusher, and we don't need any more of those around here. What is the truth. That is the number one question. There's no justice if there's no truth. It's just garbage in, garbage out.

SERGEANT: You're going to hurt some people around here.

INSPECTOR: It must have been you who told him to say it was an accident.

SERGEANT: No.

INSPECTOR: No. Okay, no. I shouldn't accept the word of those native witnesses, should I. They don't talk very loud, do they? Sometimes they mumble. Their answers are so short. They don't volunteer anything. They don't know where to look. And of course, they are out to get us.

SERGEANT: If I said to say it was an accident, I would just be using that word to sum things up. There were so many details he couldn't remember.

INSPECTOR: But he didn't follow your advice, did he. He never did say it was an accident. He said it was self-defence. He was being attacked by a drunken Indian. *(Pause.)* We had to shoot the guy twice. First him. Then his reputation.

What did he *(Meaning the CONSTABLE.)* say to you before I got there? No shit. What did he say?

SERGEANT: *(Quietly.)* He jumped me. I was on my back on the ground and he went for my gun.

INSPECTOR: I've been suckered, haven't I? Get out.

(The SERGEANT and the CONSTABLE exit.)

Why didn't I see it?

(The SERGEANT returns and reminds him of the dialogue at the end Part One, Scene 2.)

SERGEANT: The gun. What should I do with it? IDENT doesn't want it. Should we check it for prints? Would they prove anything? Would it be fair to the constable if nothing was found?

INSPECTOR: It was a judgement call.

SERGEANT: Prejudgement.

INSPECTOR: You mishandled the gun.

SERGEANT: What?

INSPECTOR: You should have put it in a cardboard box.

SERGEANT: I didn't have a cardboard box. So what I did was I held it by the butt, *(She indicates the method with her thumb and forefinger.)* I put it in my holster...

INSPECTOR: ...which would have wiped off any prints.

SERGEANT: The holster doesn't rub the barrel. It's not that tight. Be easy to check. Grab the barrel, holster the gun, then check it for prints. Oh. You want me to take the bullet on this one. First Time Acting Sergeant Messes Up Police Investigation. I get it. Sorry I'm so slow. *(She exits.)*

Scene Three

(The bar: The INSPECTOR sits alone.)

INSPECTOR: *(Muttering to himself, he mimics a prosecutor.)* Inspector, tell the world why you failed to fingerprint the gun or the holster, both of which were supposedly handled by the deceased.

(As himself.) It wouldn't have proved who started the fight. *(He shakes his head no.)*

…Uncontaminated ballistic tests were deemed more important. *(Shakes his head no.)*

…At that time the regulations for police shootings said to turn the weapon over to the Firearms Officer. I correctly followed stupid regulations. *(Shakes his head no.)*

…It wouldn't have been fair. I knew that no fingerprints would he found. No, not because the fellow never grabbed the gun. Because, first it was a damp, cool night. Prints don't get left when there is high humidity. Second, they were struggling for the gun. Any prints would have been smudged. Third, the gun was mishandled by the duty officer. She put the gun in her own holster. Probably erased any prints that might have been available. *(Shakes his head no.)*

Gentlemen, I inadvertently mishandled the weapon…

No, damm it, I did my best, I've spent a lifetime on this case and all you're doing is trying to make as much money as you can. Well, I resign. Sorry, boys, you won't get your chance to humiliate me. Goddamn lawyers, goddamn Indians, you fucking Indians…

(He looks around the bar self-consciously.)

Scene Four

(The CHIEF's office. A spotlight is on the SERGEANT—with noticeable eye make-up at a witness table.)

SERGEANT: I am not a liar. Grey was incorrect. I should have written black. The one we caught was actually wearing a grey jacket. But when we were chasing him, the description broadcast was black. Except the first one said dark. I got confused.

(Sound: laughter. The SERGEANT pours herself a splash of water into a trembling glass and takes a sip.)

I want to apologize *(Her voice breaking.)* for any embarrassment to the Department and to my family and to the people I serve.

(She freezes.

The CHIEF presses a remote, "rewinds," and "plays" the SERGEANT's testimony again.)

…I just got confused.

(Sound: laughter. The SERGEANT pours herself a splash of water into a trembling glass and takes a sip.)

I want to apologize *(Her voice breaking.)* for any embarrassment to the Department and to my family and to the people I serve. *(She freezes.)*

CHIEF: Geez. Bad news. She looks like a mud puddle. *(He turns off the SERGEANT.)* What kind of men are we getting on the Force these days? *(Mimicking the SERGEANT's testimony.)* "I want to apologize..." Can you believe it—breaking down on the stand? A police officer. A veteran police officer.

INSPECTOR: I'm sure she did the best she could. She put in a lot of hours. She shouldn't have to go through that TV stuff. She was inexperienced. She should have had more help from senior officers.

CHIEF: She should know enough not to change her notebook. Too bad she has to be demoted.

INSPECTOR: Morale isn't too good right now.

CHIEF: You're telling me?

(He examines his face with a mirror he's found in the desk.)

"A Prince, therefore, should not mind..." How does it go? *(He pulls out his book.)* ...should not mind the ill-repute of cruelty, when he can thereby keep his subjects united and loyal; for a few displays of severity will really he more merciful than to allow, by an excess of clemency, disorders to occur, which are apt to result in plunder and murder."

INSPECTOR: She only copied over a notebook.

CHIEF: It's plunder and murder to the media. Believe me, giving them the satisfaction hurts me more than it's going to hurt the Sergeant. But the media are not going to quit until they get their pound of flesh, until they can blame all the native problems on a few neanderthals in blue.

Do you have any information on the Constable? Like where is he?

INSPECTOR: No.

CHIEF: He's scheduled to appear at the inquiry in six days. Rumour has him in hospital.

INSPECTOR: Why?

CHIEF: I was hoping you'd know.

INSPECTOR: I'll find out.

CHIEF: Hard to believe, isn't it? Policemen crying. The Constable going and cracking up. Put in a bloody psycho ward.

INSPECTOR: Psycho?

CHIEF: Rumour.

INSPECTOR: He shot a man. Stress.

CHIEF:	Stress—just another phantom of the opera. One of these days they are going to prove that it doesn't exist. And then all those shrinks will have to find another scam. Either you can do the job or you can't.
INSPECTOR:	I can't.
CHIEF:	Say that again.
INSPECTOR:	I'm resigning.
CHIEF:	Uh uh.
INSPECTOR:	I prejudiced the case.
CHIEF:	Nobody leaves the stockade.
INSPECTOR:	If I'd done a better job, if I'd just fingerprinted the gun, none of this would have happened.
CHIEF:	That's something we have to live with now. You've been pretty busy, haven't you?
INSPECTOR:	Well, I got the Miller case in court.
CHIEF:	How's it going?
INSPECTOR:	The little puke. He's trying to get temporary insanity.
CHIEF:	But he assaulted three different girls. Three different months.
INSPECTOR:	Chronic temporary insanity.
CHIEF:	Yeah, I know the feeling. I guess you do, too. *(He puts a hand on the INSPECTOR's shoulder.)* I'm tired. All I'm trying to do now is stay in the ring. Go the distance.
	I'm taking you off the case—I mean as far as co-ordinating our presentation to the Inquiry. I want you to concentrate full time on your testimony. What did we ask you for?
INSPECTOR:	The changes we've made since the incident regarding the regulations manual on police shootings—evidence gathering.
CHIEF:	Right. You're the expert on the case. All those lawyers know you. They know you don't have a racial bone in your body. I want you to talk about the changes we have made to procedure, like we can learn from our mistakes. But that's not enough, any more. Things haven't been going well for us. We need a rebuttal witness for a whole list of alleged improprieties. Who knows what the Constable's going to say, and after the crybaby... We need somebody up there who speaks the same language as those yuppies...
INSPECTOR:	I'm not a yuppy. _
CHIEF:	I'm not calling you a yuppy. But you're educated, up-beat. You can make them think someone's minding the store, for crissakes. We got to get our story out there.
INSPECTOR:	Well, the facts of the case don't add up.
CHIEF:	You know as well as I do that there are no facts. It's who screams the loudest. Now come on. You can do it. I know you can. I've seen you. Hell, I was your first Sergeant, wasn't I? You've been

on the Force must be twenty years. Do you want to give that all up?

INSPECTOR: I can't do the job.

CHIEF: I didn't send you to FBI school to take a course on leisure time activities. You are a full Inspector now. You're management. You got responsibilites.

INSPECTOR: I know. That's why I want to...

CHIEF: A guy could go see the Constable. A guy could tell him to stay in bed, to rest his vocal cords. Eh? You're not going to let me down.

Are you?

(He presses the remote and the SERGEANT lights up.)

SERGEANT: ...and to the people I serve.

VOICE: Do you wish to take a recess?

SERGEANT: No.

VOICE: Constable, who was your superior officer?

SERGEANT: Um, I don't remember. I can look it up.

VOICE: Well, then, who read your reports?

SERGEANT: A staff sergeant, I guess. I also wrote a Supplementary that's supposed to go to the Chief, but I couldn't tell you who actually reads it.

VOICE: Who was in charge of investigating this incident?

SERGEANT: At what point in time?

VOICE: Who was in charge of the investigation into this shooting?

SERGEANT: It's hard to say.

VOICE: Were you ordered by a superior officer to copy over your notebook?

SERGEANT: No.

VOICE: That's all. That's all.You may step down.

(Lights fade on the SERGEANT.)

Scene Five

(A hospital bed and privacy curtains.)

INSPECTOR: *(Opening the curtains.)* They got orders not to let any cops in here.What's going on? I had to say I was visiting my sick mother. Here, mom.

(He puts flowers on the bed.)

What's the matter with you?

CONSTABLE: Go away.

INSPECTOR: This is a psychiatric ward for crissakes. At least you two got a room to yourselves. That's a joke.

CONSTABLE: Wanna hear something really funny?

INSPECTOR: You bet.

CONSTABLE: I checked in here voluntarily. I asked for a private room. 'Cause my shrink, she says I need environmental relief. So what do I get? This room. Already occupied. I tell the nurse that there's an Indian in here and she says, "Don't complain. He was here first."

   And I say, "He's dead, and if he's dead, you're supposed to take him out and change the sheets."

INSPECTOR: I'll get him out of here.

CONSTABLE: Sure.

INSPECTOR: I'll take him with me when I go.

CONSTABLE: What I don't get is if he's got a big goverment job,why is he out drinking until two a.m. on a week night?

INSPECTOR: Gee, nobody I know ever does that. They have a rough time coming down here from the north, trying to fit in.

CONSTABLE: He didn't do so well.

INSPECTOR: His fault?

CONSTABLE: So why is it my fault? I gotta pay for the last five hundred years?

INSPECTOR: He paid, too.

CONSTABLE: Did you see what they did to her?

INSPECTOR: The Sergeant?

CONSTABLE: They asked her if she ever ran with her gun out. She said no. It's dangerous. Then they show a news video of her downtown running with her gun out. Jesus.

INSPECTOR: You don't have to testify. We don't expect you to. The Inquiry already had your evidence from the inquest. You can stay in bed.

CONSTABLE: It's in all the newspapers. I had to take a leave of absence. Some cop I am, eh? Is it tomorrow? I'm supposed to go up there tomorrow?

INSPECTOR: Just stay in bed. Get better. Get your strength back.

CONSTABLE: They just had my shrink on TV. What did she say? Insomnia. Hyper-something. Emotional something. Memory loss, weight loss, dizzy spells, diarrhea. Is that how you want me to be remembered? The cop who couldn't testify because he crapped his pants? If I don't go up there, I'm dead meat.

INSPECTOR: You'll get reinstated. The union will make sure of that.

CONSTABLE: So now everyone wants me to kill myself.

INSPECTOR: Won't solve anything.

CONSTABLE: It would solve everything. Wouldn't it? Everything. They come in here and ask you these questions: "Agree or disagree—I'm just no good."

INSPECTOR: What?

CONSTABLE: "Agree or disagree—nobody cares about me." That's what they ask you. Things are never going to get better for me. My family would be better off without me." They would, wouldn't they?

INSPECTOR: No. Disagree.

CONSTABLE: A gun is no good. You can blow the side of your head off and still be alive. I got a call to a house where a guy had run a hose from the exhaust pipe into his car. It worked, but he had puked all over the front seat.

INSPECTOR: If you killed yourself, people would say you had a guilty conscience. You had something to hide.

CONSTABLE: I probably wouldn't care much what they said.

INSPECTOR: But your family. The guys who supported you.

CONSTABLE: Leave a note.

INSPECTOR: A note?

CONSTABLE: A note. Explain things. To whom it may concern.

INSPECTOR: Yeah...

CONSTABLE: "I can't take it any more." No. "Sorry, you won't get your chance to humiliate me."

INSPECTOR: "...Everyday they put another officer on the stand and make him look like a stupid jerk."

CONSTABLE: Yeah. With taxpayers' money.

INSPECTOR: The media just eats it up.

CONSTABLE: They won't stop 'til they get their pound of flesh.

INSPECTOR: So I'll be the sacrifice.

CONSTABLE: Hey, let me write this stuff down.

INSPECTOR: Forget it.

CONSTABLE: Jesus, they must have given me another pill. I think it's starting to kick in.

INSPECTOR: You wanna rest?

CONSTABLE: No, no. Stay. We can chew the rag a little.

INSPECTOR: Sure.

CONSTABLE: I never sleep anyway.

INSPECTOR: Not telling the truth is what's making you sick.

CONSTABLE: What truth?

INSPECTOR: You're sorry, you made a mistake, you stopped a native, he said piss off, you grabbed, he pushed, you fell, you panicked, you drew your gun, he tried to grab it, you had to shoot...

CONSTABLE: (Beginning during the above.) "I explained to him that he matched the description of a suspect I was looking for in the theft of an auto, and that I would like to see some identification." See? I haven't forgotten. I don't have a memory loss.

INSPECTOR: Tell the truth. You'll live longer.

CONSTABLE: Who cares. Being a police officer, being on the Force—that's my life. I just want things to be like they were. Before. Like I remember when we called a patrol car from District Eleven and told them to come out to Polo Park because somebody was throwing water balloons at cars. They went through the underpass and we really bombed them. They got out and we tried to throw more balloons but we were laughing too hard.

INSPECTOR: I love the Force.

CONSTABLE: I love the Force. *(Pause.)* You got tears in your eyes. You do. I'm going to tell. *(They both laugh.)*

INSPECTOR: Man, we got ourselves in a real mess.

CONSTABLE: Back before the Inquest, his father, the guy's father, said he wanted to talk to me, to find out what I had done, and if I was innocent—or if I just didn't mean to do it he'd forgive me. Maybe I'd have to do something for the family, but he'd say, "Go in peace" or something, "You have my blessing…" But I don't think he spoke English, so how was that going to happen? Anyway the Department would never have let me go see him.

INSPECTOR: So I should tell them you're going to testify.

CONSTABLE: Yes.

INSPECTOR: I hope you do okay.

CONSTABLE: Thanks. I need some support from you guys.

INSPECTOR: *(Smiling.)* Well, I'm still mad at you for what you did.

CONSTABLE: I'm still mad at you.

INSPECTOR: Yeah. I guess you should be.

CONSTABLE: Where are you going?

(INSPECTOR indicates "out of here".)

You said you'd take the Indian with you.

INSPECTOR: I will.

CONSTABLE: *(Laughing.)* She said she was only jogging. They said she was running with her gun out, but she said she was only jogging.

Scene Six

(The front porch of the SERGEANT's bungalow at twilight. Sound: crickets.)

INSPECTOR: *(Uncharacterisically disordered in dress.)* Police. Would you open the door, please.

(The porch light goes on.)

SERGEANT: *(Off.)* What do you want?

INSPECTOR: Ma'am we're looking for witnesses to a shooting that took place near your house. Were you home last Tuesday night?

SERGEANT: *(Entering, wearing a bathrobe.)* It's you. I thought I was having one of my nightmares.

INSPECTOR: I just wanted to stop by to...

SERGEANT: Come in, if you want.

INSPECTOR: Who's...

SERGEANT: My kids. We're watching a movie. A dumb cop movie.

INSPECTOR: It's late.

SERGEANT: Only chance I get. We could talk out here. It's a warm night and I think the bugs have gone. Sit down. I'll go turn out the light in case I'm wrong about the bugs.

INSPECTOR: Oh, hey, I brought some fancy ice cream. Would your kids like some?

SERGEANT: No question about it. How about you?

INSPECTOR: No, thanks.

SERGEANT: What's this? *(The bag with the ice cream contains a second package.)*

INSPECTOR: That's something for the Chief. I was going to mail it but it's too late now. Can you get it to him sometime?

SERGEANT: What is it?

INSPECTOR: Just some evidence.

SERGEANT: Okay

(She exits. The light goes off.

The INSPECTOR stands alone, ill at ease, listening to distant traffic noises. He suddenly makes a break for the street just as the SERGEANT returns.)

Are you leaving?

INSPECTOR: Oh. No. I...

SERGEANT: I had a dream about that native kid in the car.

INSPECTOR: Big Mouth.

SERGEANT: I dreamed I bought him some fancy ice cream.

INSPECTOR: Did you really call him a...

SERGEANT: I read an article about those guys who twitch and swear all the time. Can't help it. What's it called? Tourette's Syndrome? There was a sweet little old lady who got it probably never been out of her stately mansion, probably never heard an angry word in her life. They said she swore every damn word in the book. It just comes out of somewhere. Like you're born with it.

INSPECTOR: Like it's in the air.

SERGEANT: You don't even know it until the words come out.

INSPECTOR: Right.

SERGEANT: There's medication you can take for Tourette's. To suppress the symptoms.

INSPECTOR: ...I have to tell you... It's hard to say this.

SERGEANT: You want a beer?

INSPECTOR: No. They're taking you off the detective assignment. You're going back to Uniform. Foot Patrol, I think.

SERGEANT: I heard already. More or less.

INSPECTOR: I'm sorry. I thought I should be the one to tell you. I should have protected you.

SERGEANT: Let me take care of myself. It builds character.

INSPECTOR: It's really just a reassignment. In six months you'll be back on track.

SERGEANT: We'll see.

INSPECTOR: I went to visit his grave just now.

SERGEANT: I thought they buried him up north. Island Lake.

INSPECTOR: No, I mean my old work buddy. Did you know him? Vic. Victor Boyko? I bring him flowers now and then.

SERGEANT: Is he dead or something?

INSPECTOR: Yeah. Gone but not forgotten. I usually go visit him at this time of year. When it's warm. When the days are still long. Him and me. You put in a twelve-hour day, you leave the station, and it's still light outside. Dusty. Warm. People friendly. Even the drunks on Main Street. "Hi, officer." "Evening, officer."

              Me and Vic go have a cool one and we don't have to think which bar we can go in and not get hassled. He had a heart attack one day. Just like that. When the sun is low and orange and red, the light makes me miss him.

SERGEANT: I don't remember the guy.

INSPECTOR: He was a good partner. Everything had to be perfect. Took full responsibilty for every case he worked on. Never complained about the hours he put in, never said no to management. A new joke every day. Did you bear this one?

SERGEANT: I'm not sure.

INSPECTOR: It seems that Goldilocks was sitting down with her mama and papa to breakfast porridge, of course, but it was too hot, so they take a walk in the woods while it cools off. Guess who shows up?

SERGEANT: The police?

INSPECTOR: No. A bear. He's got a machine gun. He wolfs down all the porridge, if you'll pardon the expression. Then he takes his gun and shoots up the place—the windows, the dishes—bullets everywhere. Then he waddles off, as mysteriously as he came. Goldilocks and her mama and her papa come back from their walk. Holy moley, says Goldilocks, my porridge is all gone. Never mind that, says papa, the windows are all shot to pieces. Pieces? says mama, you want pieces, take a look at my Royal Dalton. What kind of a bear would do this to us?

SERGEANT: A cop?

(Pause.)

INSPECTOR: *(With difficulty.)* What kind of a bear would do this to us? Well, Goldilocks whips over to her Encyclopedia Britannica. Here, she says, it must have been a koala bear. A koala bear? says papa. A koala bear? says mama. Yes, says Goldilocks. It says right here. A koala bear eats shoots and leaves.

    (He laughs.)

    You didn't like it.

SERGEANT: No, it was good. I'm just tired.

INSPECTOR: You want me to go, eh?

SERGEANT: Well, you got a big day tomorrow.

INSPECTOR: No problem. I've got my testimony all written out. I just have to sign it. I'd stay here all night if I wasn't... If I didn't...

SERGEANT: If you weren't dreaming. I'll give you a ride if you want.

INSPECTOR: You're going to be home tomorrow morning, aren't you?

SERGEANT: I guess so.

INSPECTOR: Are you sure?

SERGEANT: I'm working from two to twelve. You want me to come watch you testify?

INSPECTOR: No no. It's nothing. You're the only one who understands me.

SERGEANT: Me?

INSPECTOR: I might have something to show you.

SERGEANT: Are you sure you don't want a ride?

INSPECTOR: I want to walk. I don't have far to go.

SERGEANT: Okay.

INSPECTOR: You're going to be home tomorrow, aren't you?

SERGEANT: Yes.

INSPECTOR: Be seeing ya.

SERGEANT: G'night.

INSPECTOR: You know, where Vic is now, it would make a nice drawing. Really nice. The bill, the stones, the river, and across the river a field, stubble and summer fallow, barb wire fencing, black trees at the edge, the sky, the big sky. Late in the day, it all turns red. Somebody ought to tell the Chief.

    (He steps off the porch to begin his walk home. The SERGEANT watches him leave, and remains on the porch, listening to the night.

    Sound: crickets, urban traffic, police radio transmissions, drums, footsteps, a man humming an Aboriginal melody.

    The INSPECTOR pauses near the spot where the Indian was shot. The humming stops in mid-phrase. The CONSTABLE sits up suddenly in his hospital bed, panting, sweating.

    The INSPECTOR exits. Lights fade on the CONSTABLE)

Scene Seven

> (The CHIEF's office. There is little light; the blinds are drawn. The CHIEF sits slumped at his desk, his head in his hands.)

SERGEANT: He called the next morning. A quarter after nine. He had something to show me. It could not wait. I offered to meet him downtown at the bearings because I knew he was scheduled to testify. He said no, couldn't I come to his house right away. He tried to joke about it, and I joked back, but he was serious. He said, "Please, please, would you come now."

I got there by ten. I knocked on the side door. Nobody answered. The door as open. I thought he'd be at the kitchen table with a pile of paperwork. Like I figured he'd found something, you know, something about the investigation. He wasn't in the kitchen. Where was he? I heard somebody talking downstairs. In the den. On a desk there's a television. One of our guys at the scene is getting cross-examined. There are no lights on. Just the television. Where is he?

There's a room off the hall, an exercise room. I see his briefcase on a bench. It's open. A few pieces of paper, legal pad, big handwriting, they're taped to the top of the case. Where is he? (She cannot continue for a moment.)

He had to lie there all night pretending to sleep, listening to his wife sleep, waiting for morning, thinking about what he was going to do.

CHIEF: Tell me.

SERGEANT: Over on the floor, he's lying twisted on the floor, his shoulders up against the the wall, his head flopped forward, a line of blood runs along the side of his face from above his ear down to the corner of his mouth. There's a glass of, you know, a drink under his...he's fallen on it. I check. There's no pulse.

> (The phone rings. The CHIEF makes no move. Finally the SERGEANT answers.)

SERGEANT: Yeah?... (To the CHIEF.) It's for you. Somebody from the newspaper.

CHIEF: Ask him how it feels to be a murderer.

SERGEANT: (On the phone.) He can't speak right now. (She hangs up.) ...It's my fault.

CHIEF: The guys involved in the investigation did the best they could and it's not their fault.

SERGEANT: We didn't do the best we could.

CHIEF: I failed to provide the leadership and direction. I just didn't make the right decisions. I was the one in charge and I was responsible.

SERGEANT: Don't punish yourself, sir. Oh, that's what he wrote?

CHIEF: I'm going to punish someone. (Pause.) You coming?

SERGEANT: Where?

CHIEF: To the service.

SERGEANT: No. I'm going on duty now. The streets of St. Boniface.

CHIEF: Who's your commanding officer? I can get you compassionate.

SERGEANT: No. I don't think he'd want me...

CHIEF: I'll talk to him.

SERGEANT: I mean the Inspector. I think he'd prefer it if I spent this day on the job. I better go. Oh, here, this is for you. He gave it to me before... Said he didn't have time to mail it.

(While the CHIEF examines the package as if it was a letter bomb, she surveys and even rearranges the office, as if one day it would be hers, finally opening the window blinds.) I'm not going to spend the day cooped up in the dark at a funeral. What he did was stupid, right, and, really, it's like he shot his gun at each of us for not helping him; he did something very cruel to his family and to his friends, and he should have faced the music and gotten it over with, but I don't care. I'm happy, I feel twenty pounds lighter, ten years younger, I'm floating again, I'm floating like when I first got this job, I was going to make a difference, but the job weighs a ton, the job is paperwork, it's promotions, it's bitching at your boss, taking it out on the asshole civilians, and every day I got to be a robot, and if one more kid gets smartass with me, I'm going to blow up. So when the Inspector says it matters what you do, it really matters that you get things right, that you help people nobody else will touch with a ten-foot pole, that good police work is to die for...well *(She laughs.)* I got to be on my way.

(The CHIEF opens the package.)

What is it?

CHIEF: His gold badge.

SERGEANT: God, it's beautiful. You keep it all nice and polished—it's beautiful. I guess you'll return it to his wife.

CHIEF: If she'll accept it.

(He empties out the package. A pair of eyeglasses, broken into four pieces, lands on his desk.)

His eyeglasses. They got broken.

SERGEANT: I think they're the ones that, you know, they belong to...

CONSTABLE: The Indian.

SERGEANT: Yeah.

CHIEF: Call somebody in Legal. Contact their lawyer. *(He exits.)*

SERGEANT: No, I'll just take them back to the family, myself. I never told them that we were sorry.

The End

Washing Spider Out

Ross McMillan

Production Information

Washing Spider Out received a week-long workshop through the Manitoba Association of Playwrights in April, 1994, with the following cast:

SANDY .... Ellen Peterson
MURIEL .... Linda Huffman
ROBBIE .... Arne MacPherson
MARGARET .... Sharon Bajer
ROY .... Grahah Ashmore

Directed by George Toles
Stage Manager: Maureen Shelley

The play was first produced in Prairie Theatre Exchange's studio series (co-produced by Adhere and Deny) with the following cast:

SANDY .... Sarah Neville
MURIEL .... Nancy Drake
ROBBIE .... Ross McMillan
MARGARET .... Tamara Walsh
ROY .... Graham Ashmore

Directed by George Toles
Designed by Grant Guy
Sound Design by George Toles
Stage Manager: Maureen Shelley

The playwright wishes to thank Rory Runnells, who fostered the play's development, all the actors who contributed so much, and George Toles, whose ideas have often found their way into this version.

Setting

The main settings are a sculptor's live-in studio and a prison cell. Each has a roughly 8 x 8 ft wall, probably upstage. The prison cell wall is unremarkable; the studio wall is a large metal sculpture made of panels. It is incomplete. The studio has a small table with chairs. Tools. The prison cell has a bed and a toilet. Offstage voices are done by the actor playing Roy.

Act One

Scene One

SANDY:

(*SANDY alone.*)

Sometimes, when I want to close my eyes, but in the dark my mind races, images come to me. I don't know where they come from and they don't seem to have any connection. They flash up, flash up, always always different. Spiky feathers. Sharp flames. Streaky sky. Black stars. Wiggling fingers. Curling petals. They don't come even long enough to concentrate on them, and that makes it feel like they're not coming from inside me. It scares me. I have to open my eyes. But I want to close them. Close my eyes, and have one image, any one, which can stay, and I can look at it, turn it around in my mind.

Scene Two

(*ROBBIE's cell. ROBBIE is looking away as MURIEL cleans his toilet.*)

MURIEL: What do you mean you don't want the parole?

ROBBIE: I have to admit guilt. To show I take seriously what I did, to show remorse. Otherwise I don't get the parole.

MURIEL: I know. I know. You've spent 15 years saying you didn't do it. That's enough. If you stay in here another 15 years they still won't believe you, it's just a game. You say you did it, they get to feel justified, you know you're just saying some words, you get out. They're finally going to let you out.

ROBBIE: I didn't do it.

MURIEL: I know, we know that. So what difference does it make? Say the words.

ROBBIE: I didn't do it.

MURIEL: What? What's the big deal? This one little moment of lying would hurt so much? Do you remember any of the last 15 years? What you've been through? Would saying those words hurt

	more than, than… Christ! Than any of the torment you've been through? Or what I've suffered? Do the things I've suffered mean less than biting down on a few words to the parole board?
ROBBIE:	Mom, don't say that.
MURIEL:	I could pick any one of a hundred times I've died watching you in here. And that means nothing?
ROBBIE:	*(Stands.)* Those times, Mom…
MURIEL:	You don't know how I've suffered.
ROBBIE:	I can't say those words. It would be wrong.
MURIEL:	Say, "The cow jumped over the moon." Say it. The cow jumped over the moon.
ROBBIE:	The cow…cow?…jumped…but it didn't! The cow didn't jump over the moon!
MURIEL:	It's just a noise coming out of your mouth. You don't have to even think there's any meaning to it. Say it as though it doesn't mean anything. Say it as though it's a foreign language.
ROBBIE:	*(Slow, like a child.)* The cow.
MURIEL:	There. That's a start.

Scene Three

	(ROY's studio.)
MARGARET:	I hate women.
ROY	You said that before.
MARGARET:	They're fucking stupid sheep and cattle, all, you know, "Hello".
ROY:	You have nice hairy legs.
MARGARET:	I have maybe the loveliest breasts in the world too, but I'm not all giggly about it.
ROY:	Why are you telling me that?
MARGARET:	It's just a fact. I'm just telling you.
ROY:	You like my work?
MARGARET:	I think it's great.
ROY:	Uh-huh. Look. *(He fingers an area on the wall.)*
MARGARET:	I wish I had your sensitivity.
ROY:	Maybe yours comes out in different ways.
MARGARET:	*(Feeling the wall.)* You think so?
	(ROY gestures to a gaudy figurine on the table.)
ROY:	Like when we were shopping. I didn't notice half the bargains you do.
MARGARET:	*(Their fingers touch.)* What?

ROY: Is something happening here?

MARGARET: I hope so. Do you think I'm too young for you?

ROY: Well, um...how did that come up?

MARGARET: It just did.

ROY: It seems kinda jolly that we can talk like this. That we can be together. I mean it's unlikely, and there's something jolly about that.

MARGARET: Jolly?

ROY: Don't you think?

MARGARET: *(Sings.)* "Itsy bitsy spider, climbing up the spout. Along came the rain and washed the spider out. Along comes the sun and dries up all the rain..." *(She kisses him deeply.)*

ROY: That's quite the cavity you've got in there. You should get some metal in it.

> *(MARGARET looks confused.)*

I could help you with it. Would you let me do that? Pay for a filling? It would be like there's a little piece of me in you.

MARGARET: That's not funny. Don't do that.

ROY: Come on.

MARGARET: No! That doesn't fit, that doesn't feel right.

ROY: OK. OK. Let's start over.

MARGARET: Be more gushy. Be more confused.

ROY: Alright. Go.

MARGARET: I hate women.

ROY: You said that before.

MARGARET: I've never had this much fun with anybody. You are such fun.

ROY: You're like a little bird. I want you to trust me. I can help you. You can trust me.

MARGARET: *(Indicating the figurine she bought.)* Isn't it great?

> *(ROY grimaces.)*

Scene Four

> *(ROBBIE's cell. MURIEL has come to visit, and as they speak, ROBBIE rummages through her purse, examining each object in turn, seemingly without recognizing them, discarding each on the floor. He's partly a boy again, but he's pumped up, hyper. He seems cunning, in a way we'd like to share. MURIEL has a calm which seems inappropriate, as though talking to a baby.)*

ROBBIE: What are you doing here? What do you want?

MURIEL: It's me. Mum.

ROBBIE:	No, no. You're not my mum.
MURIEL:	What do you mean, Robbie?
ROBBIE:	My mum can't come in here.
MURIEL:	Please look at me.
ROBBIE:	*(Not looking at her.)* I'm looking.
MURIEL:	But you don't see me.
ROBBIE:	So, you're not there, so, go away.
MURIEL:	I came out from the city to see you.
ROBBIE:	No you didn't.
MURIEL:	Don't you recognize me?
ROBBIE:	*(Patiently explaining.)* You're not here. You're from inside my head. *(He finds an object in his hand and throws it away.)* Ugh!
MURIEL:	Now, that game is a silly one. If that's true, then whose purse is that? What are you looking for in there?
	(She struggles for the purse and pulls it from his hands.)
ROBBIE:	Well. We'll know that when we find it, won't we?
MURIEL:	At least it's nice and quiet in here.
	(Loud scream from offstage.)

Scene Five

(ROY's studio.)

ROY:	Are you OK? Really, are you OK?
MARGARET:	I think so. Calling me "Ma'am".
ROY:	It's only Safeway.
MARGARET:	To me, it's terrifying.
ROY:	I know. I'm sorry. There's nothing so strange about that, really.
MARGARET:	There isn't?
ROY:	Well, in degree, but not in type. Just take it easy. Did you get milk?
	(MARGARET tenses up, shivers.)
	Never mind, we don't need it.
MARGARET:	Are you going to dump me?
ROY:	Honey, Margaret, don't be silly. I like you very much. Very much.
MARGARET:	I'm not worth it, really I'm not.
ROY:	I love you. It doesn't make any sense. It's wonderful.
MARGARET:	You don't know me, you don't know how bad I am.
ROY:	I want more.

MARGARET: Can I stay here?

ROY: Of course you can. Do you want to move in? *(Quietly:)* Oh fuck oh fuck what did I just say?

MARGARET: Do I ever have to leave? Ever?

ROY: Well, sometimes of course.

(She starts to freak out.)

Hey, come on, I just meant, as a matter of fact.

(Worse freakout, whimpering.)

Margaret, what is it? I don't know what to do when you do this, please!

(She curls up in a corner, whimpers.)

OK, it's OK. I'll sit down. Can I...? Is there...? Oh Christ.

(ROY has stupidly picked up one of the spilled items from Safeway and, in a reflex, offered it to MARGARET on his last line. Now he holds it and gazes at it.)

MARGARET: What are you looking at?

ROY: This label.

MARGARET: What is it?

ROY: It's an image.

MARGARET: What do you mean by that? You always say that, like it means something that I don't get.

ROY: Image. I-ma-go. Logos. Understanding. Seeing. The world flickers, like an old movie. Each flicker...images are very small. But very big also. Huge. But tiny. Each one that you have is different, because your eyes are never in exactly the same place twice. Every image is unique. When you see, that's what you're always seeing. Uniqueness. Novelty. Except, with some kind of content. And that's all we see. The content. When you can relax enough to ignore the content of everything that you see, then everything is interesting.

MARGARET: Everything?

(ROY nods.)

Is everything like that for you?

(ROY nods.)

But am I more interesting than...a car?

ROY: *(Pause.)* Oh yes.

MARGARET: A bird?

(He starts to come toward her.)

A restaurant? A lottery ticket?

(His hand reaches toward her.)

Scene Six

(ROBBIE's cell. ROBBIE is sitting and whistling "Swingin' Down the Lane." We hear a voice from behind the wall.)

VOICE: HEY! Hey you!

ROBBIE: Yeah?

VOICE: You stop that fuckin' whistling.

ROBBIE: Sorry.

VOICE: What? Did you say "Sorry"? (Hysterical laugh.) Hey kid, what're you in for?

ROBBIE: Nothing! I didn't do it, it's a mistake!

VOICE: What?

ROBBIE: I didn't do it!

VOICE: You just got here, right?

ROBBIE: Yeah!

VOICE: Guess what? I didn't do it either!

ROBBIE: No way!

VOICE: You callin' me a liar?

ROBBIE: No, no way, man!

VOICE: (Hysterical laugh.)

ROBBIE: What?

VOICE: Every guy in this place is gonna tell you he didn't do it.

ROBBIE: But I didn't do it!

VOICE: Hey, shut up! I'm trying to sleep!

ROBBIE: But it's not the same!

VOICE: How come?

ROBBIE: Really! I don't belong in here!

VOICE: Hey!

ROBBIE: What?

VOICE: You think anybody fuckin' belongs in here? The day you understand that nobody belongs in here, then you'll understand that you do belong in here. Anybody who's in here belongs in here. So don't you fuckin' whistle. You don't see me whistlin'. Hey!

ROBBIE: What?

VOICE: How come you're whistlin' Sinatra, you sound a little young.

ROBBIE: I didn't know it's Sinatra. This cop who arrested me, God, he was so lazy, he stopped off at his house for dinner on the way to the police station. Handcuffed me to a chair in his rec room and when he came out from his dinner, he made me listen to him playing along with this song on his trombone. I can't get it out of my head, you know?

VOICE:	Tough break.
ROBBIE:	No kidding.
VOICE:	Hey! What's this crime that you didn't do?
ROBBIE:	Oh, this girl got raped and strangled. Hey! HEY! Hey!

Scene Seven

(ROY's studio. MARGARET is freaking a little. ROY is trying to conceal excitement about another matter.)

ROY: Now, take it easy, OK, it's nothing to get worked up about.

MARGARET: Who says?

ROY: Look! We've been through enough shit lately, I think we can handle this!

MARGARET: What's to handle? Your old girlfriend's coming to stay.

ROY: Oh come on. She's not my old girlfriend, I haven't seen her in 15 years. Listen, we were 15 years old, we saw this guy strangling a girl in the back lane, we saw his face. Now it seems like maybe the wrong guy was put in prison for it, he's been in there for years, for much of your life as a matter of fact, so let's just be a little cool about it.

MARGARET: So?

ROY: So, Sandy, she's coming here, she found out that this guy in prison came up for parole, and he turned it down. He turned it down, he said no, because he refuses to say that he did it. So maybe he didn't. Maybe he's innocent. And we never said a fucking thing about it, because we would have got in great shit for what WE were doing there, and now she's scared that he's the wrong guy, so she got in touch with the guy's mother and she's coming here and we're going to see his face and see if it's him, OK?

MARGARET: What were you doing in this alley that was so fucking important?

ROY: Nothing. We were smooching.

(Pause.)

MARGARET: Were you...

ROY: What?

MARGARET: You know.

ROY: No. Well, we almost did, but she changed her mind at the last minute. But her parents didn't like me and they would have been crushed and they wouldn't have believed we weren't having sex, and she really loved her parents, so it just didn't seem worth it, saying anything.

MARGARET: So she was a nice girl.

ROY: Hey, leave that alone, that's none of your...that's like a spring that you're one end of, and she's coiled way back far away. Um, that's no…alright? Come on.

MARGARET: Is she gonna be a dink?

ROY: I don't know her!

MARGARET: Do you think I'm fat?

ROY: I think you're lovely.

MARGARET: I went out for a walk.

ROY: That's good.

MARGARET: I kept thinking about how you tie your bathrobe.

ROY: Is that good?

MARGARET: No. I don't like the way you do it.

ROY: I'm sorry about that.

MARGARET: If he is the wrong guy, the two of you screwed up pretty bad.

ROY: Yes, that's true! So it's important…

(*MARGARET tenses up, stares.*)

It's OK, look…

(*She quivers, looks terrified.*)

Hey, hey…

(*She whimpers, shakes.*)

But you can see, what I said is true?

Scene Eight

(*SANDY alone.*)

SANDY: Sometimes, after a long day of worrying, I want to close my eyes. But I get one image appearing, and it won't go away. It doesn't seem to matter what it is, just that it's there. I try to think of other things, but the image sits there like a face that's so beautiful I can't tear my eyes away, except it's not beautiful, it's just an image, and it's simple, it has no parts, no details. Any part of it I look at, I see the whole thing. And I want it to go away, but I know that when it does, another one will appear, another one that just sits there, stupidly signifying something. What I want, is an image of nothing. (*She touches her thumb and forefinger together.*) I touch my fingers together, and it feels like there's a planet between them. Or a grain of sand, it could be. A planet. And I'm moving turning it slowly in my fingertips, and I feel calm, always calm. And faintly, I hear this noise. It's me, grinding the axis of this planet. Like a mill.

Scene Nine

(ROY's studio. SANDY, MARGARET and ROY are sitting round a small table.)

MARGARET: So how come the two of you were in this back lane and you were about to do it, then you didn't. How come?

ROY: It's nice to see you again after all this time, Sandy.

SANDY: No, that's OK, it's just a question. Perhaps we'll get to that, Margaret.

ROY: Honey?

MARGARET: No, go ahead, I'm dying to hear.

ROY: What, ah, what do you do now?

SANDY: I'm a poet.

MARGARET: Can we hear some?

ROY: Margaret.

SANDY: Ahm, nothing's coming to me right now. I think...we should get straight about something. Margaret, you seem to feel threatened by my being here.

MARGARET: Oh sure.

SANDY: Roy and I were little kiddie-lovers. Not like you. All that is so long ago...it would be like me asking you if you still wear diapers, or throw tantrums.

ROY: So, yeah. We should talk about this business. Yeah? What's...how is this going to happen?

SANDY: I got in touch with the mother, Muriel, and she's coming over here this evening. She wants us to go and look at her son's face and see if it's the same face of course, but she wants us to wait until after we've talked to her, so there's nothing to worry about till then.

MARGARET: This guy's been in jail for 15 years, and you say there's nothing to worry about? What if it's not him? Have you thought about that?

ROY: Honey, take it easy.

MARGARET: Don't shush me, are you shushing me?

SANDY: Would you rather I leave?

ROY: No.

SANDY: Margaret, we weren't to know. The cops picked someone up the very next day, and when they say they've got the guy, you believe them.

MARGARET: You should've gone anyway.

SANDY: Well, maybe, but we were just glad it was over.

MARGARET: So? What was such a big deal? What was happening?

SANDY: Margaret, Roy and I were...what?

ROY: Childhood friends.

SANDY: No, Roy, if Margaret wants to hear about it, I don't mind. It's only memories, it's not like it's got anything to do with who we are now.

ROY: Right.

MARGARET: So?

SANDY: You know, we were like sweethearts, I mean that's part of the story, that won't make you uncomfortable, will it?

MARGARET: No! I'd like to hear all about it, unless that makes you uncomfortable.

SANDY: Not at all. OK, the night in question, we were 15. I had just called Roy, we were both all shy, like it wasn't a big deal, and told him my family was moving away in a few weeks. Neither of us did anything about it till about a week before we left. I called him up and we went out walking and talking till really late. We were near my house and we couldn't say goodbye. I led him to the back of the house, where my mother had a large cat-breeding operation, and inside the little house of the prize Persian, just big enough for us, heated, plexiglass window, the cat was upset but I calmed him, we were fooling around in there, and a faint noise made us both look out the window onto the back lane. We saw a man raping and strangling a woman. We froze. We went home and never talked again until now.

MARGARET: Tell me about how you were fooling around.

ROY: Margaret.

MARGARET: Be realistic! This guy's mother is going to ask you way tougher questions than that!

SANDY: She's right. I'll just tell the memories as they appear. We kissed silently. My long deep-green dress, my eyes, my red hair. We talked for the first time about the strange way we'd had with each other when we were kids. You'd always liked my red hair. You said I was like a girl from ancient times who had spent her life discovering iron in the ground. Digging with my fingers until the iron had travelled up the nerves into my hair. Our bodies were bared by unseen hands that suddenly seemed to have a perfect knowledge of how to take off clothes, having waited all their lives. Perhaps I embroider. We wept and we touched each other, then we were cradled so that there was only one small movement before you would enter me, and I changed my mind, I said no. We were both very still for a moment, then we heard this noise.

MARGARET: Is this upsetting you, Roy?

ROY: No no.

MARGARET: Are you sure?

ROY: I'd forgotten...some details.

MARGARET: Tell me about when you were kids. Do you mind?

SANDY: Margaret, they're just memories, there's no reason for any of us to take them personally. Almost from when I could first speak, there was this boy, Roy. We always looked at each other, even as small children, like we were two prisoners, like even the things closest to us, our families, were a kind of suffering compared to the freedom we could offer each other. We barely dared to glance at each other, this secret was so precious. We had an unspoken pact never to speak to each other. We both knew that the other knew. We knew that words would poison us. Everything fell short of our secret love, even both of us did, so we had no right to talk to each other.

MARGARET: *(Sighs loudly.)*

ROY: It was! It was like that! It was perfect! *(Pause.)* I mean, for kids.

MARGARET: Is she married?

SANDY: No, I'm not married. Are you living here together?

MARGARET: Yes.

SANDY: Do you wish you were happier?

MARGARET: What? What was that?

SANDY: You didn't have to answer if you didn't want.

MARGARET: Don't get stuck-up with me!

SANDY: Hey, for you to respond to my question like that has nothing to do with my question. Just because somebody asks you a question, doesn't mean you have to answer it.

MARGARET: What are you talking about?

SANDY: I hope you won't see me as someone who wants something from Roy.

MARGARET: What? Do you believe this?

ROY: What's wrong with that? She's just saying…

MARGARET: You… *(She tenses and shakes.)*

ROY: Margaret, it's OK.

   (MARGARET opens her mouth and twitches.)

SANDY: I think Margaret feels I'm a threat to your relationship.

ROY: Honey, it's really OK, please, please, let me hold you. Margaret gets attacks of terror.

SANDY: Attacks of terror.

ROY: Please!

   (MARGARET cowers.)

SANDY: Is that what you say, Margaret? Are you having an attack of terror?

   (MARGARET stops shaking, looks at her.)

SANDY: That's up to you. That's your way.

MARGARET: Give me the car keys!

ROY: Honey…

MARGARET: Give them to me!

        (ROY gives her the keys, she storms out.)

SANDY: Poor thing. What do you see in her?

ROY: Huh?

SANDY: I don't mean it in a judging way, it's just a question.

ROY: What happened to you?

SANDY: Do I seem so different?

ROY: You keep saying all this about not taking anything personally. *(SANDY picks up an envelope.)*

SANDY: What's this?

ROY: It's a pledge form from the lung association.

SANDY: What are you going to do with it?

ROY: Send them some money.

SANDY: Really? You know what I do? I tell them to send me the form, just to get them off the phone, then when it comes I throw it in the garbage. And I don't give it another thought.

ROY: How come?

SANDY: Have you ever done that?

ROY: *(Pause.)* Yeah.

SANDY: Just because somebody sends you a letter doesn't mean you have to open it. People bully each other so much, it's such a waste of time. I'd like to let go of all that. It really is what makes people unhappy, wanting things from each other.

ROY: Margaret's had a pretty tough life. I feel very tenderly about her.

SANDY: Do you feel in love with her?

ROY: I suppose so. Sometimes. Sometimes very much.

SANDY: You feel guilty about not being in love with her.

ROY: You sound pretty sure about that.

SANDY: When you don't want anything from people, you can see them much more clearly.

ROY: If you have anything else to tell me about it, I'll listen, I won't necessarily agree with you.

SANDY: *(Pause.)* You tell yourself that you feel sorry for her, but really she's a cardboard cutout that you colour in with your own pain. You use her to feel sorry for yourself.

ROY: *(Pause.)* Maybe you're right.

SANDY: This is like a really simple children's game for me.

Scene Ten

        (ROBBIE's cell. ROBBIE sits on his toilet, chanting his name.)

ROBBIE:	Robbie Chalmers Robbie Chalmers Robbie Chalmers Robbie Chalmers Robbie Chalmers Robbie Chalmers Robbie...
	(MARGARET enters.)
MARGARET:	Hello. Are you Robbie?
ROBBIE:	Robbie Chalmers.
MARGARET:	My name's Margaret. I'm a reporter. I work for a newspaper, and I believe you're innocent. I heard that you turned down your parole. I'd like to talk with you, you know, give you some publicity. Do an interview. I'd love to try and understand how you've been able to stay in your right mind in here.
ROBBIE:	*(Singing.)* Wooooo. Woooooooooooo. *(MARGARET tenses up. ROBBIE stands and works his body like a restless horse.)* I never read anything like that, newspapers, magazines. There's something creepy about them. They make it look like they're speaking to YOU, and you read it, and you think "they're speaking to you" and they're not. People think the words are written TO THEM, personally. It's like they don't understand anything unless it's meant specially for them. I see words in a newspaper, and I think there's something creepy about them. They're just out there.
MARGARET:	What about TV?
ROBBIE:	Now those people who take out a whole billboard saying, "I love you", or "Marry me", they're asking the whole fucking world to marry them. 'Scuse me.
MARGARET:	That's OK.
ROBBIE:	No, 'scuse me, I forgot, I forget how to talk to girls. Oh shit! I didn't want to say that!
MARGARET:	That's OK, it'll come back to you.
ROBBIE:	Nooo! I didn't want to say it!
MARGARET:	Everybody does that sometimes, it's...
ROBBIE:	I'm not *every*body!
MARGARET:	OK.
ROBBIE:	I'm sorry. Did I scare you?
MARGARET:	Yes, a little.
ROBBIE:	I won't do it again.
MARGARET:	Alright.
ROBBIE:	I do know how to talk to girls.
MARGARET:	Alright.
ROBBIE:	I'll tell you, if you like, how come I didn't go out of my mind. There's one thing in particular...no. Never mind.
MARGARET:	What?

ROBBIE: I can't tell you. You'd think I was crazy. Don't write that, OK?
           There's several things that are important, uh, I can only think of
           one of them right now, you know, it's like they're difficult to
           think of, so you only remember them when you really need to
           use them. Number one, is this. There's lots of guys in here want
           to get in your face, right? Muscle up to you, shove you around,
           push you around, but I was lucky, right? I saw, BOOM! that you
           can give up your physical space, act like it's hurting you to give
           it up, but it isn't. You can still have all the space you need, inside
           your head. They can think they're scaring you, and you can let
           them think that. See? But *you* know, that what they think is what
           you want them to think. It's *you* who's pulling *their* strings. And
           that helped me a lot. Sorry, are you OK?

MARGARET: Yeah, fine.

ROBBIE: What did you want to ask me about?

MARGARET: This place, I came in here and there's a guard literally rattling the
           bars of one of the cells. And they're walking up and down and
           saying horrible things to the prisoners, and the prisoners are
           threatening to kill them. They really seem to hate each other.

ROBBIE: No kidding.

MARGARET: Is it like that all the time?

ROBBIE: Course it is.

MARGARET: Is it about something?

ROBBIE: *All* the cons hate *all* the screws and vice versa. When a new guy
           comes in here, or a new screw, they gotta do like everybody else
           does. See, this place only makes sense if we all hate each other. If
           we didn't hate each other, they'd have to close this place down.

MARGARET: That's very insightful.

ROBBIE: Ahh, it was my mum, she said that, she thought of that. Maybe
           you have to be on the outside to figure that out.

MARGARET: Well, what happened? How come you ended up in here, do you
           think?

ROBBIE: There's only one thing that could have happened. The guy who
           did it, he got away with it, but that was 15 years ago. He must
           have done it again and again, why would he not? If he liked it. He
           would've done it again and again, and he got caught and put
           away, and he's in prison somewhere, just like me, except he
           knows my name and I don't know his.

MARGARET: Do you get...sad?

ROBBIE: I get depressed sometimes, they have to give me medication for
           it. Yeah, so if I seem a little...I'm a little bit on medication right
           now, if I seem, you know, acting strangely or anything, it's not
           really me, it's just, you know.

MARGARET: (Nods.) Sometimes I have to take medication, for depression.

ROBBIE: Really? But you're young and beautiful...and smart, you got a
           good job, why would you get depressed?

MARGARET: Can I get a picture?!

(*She produces a Polaroid camera.*)

ROBBIE: They don't use cameras like that, do they?

MARGARET: Not for the paper, just for me. The two of us together. Can I?

(*She puts one arm around him and snaps a picture with her other hand, holding the camera at arm's length. The upstage wall is in the background. ROBBIE is upset about this. She waits for the picture to develop.*)

Look, it's coming. Don't you want to look at it?

ROBBIE: No.

MARGARET: Why not?

ROBBIE: I can't tell you.

MARGARET: Please. This picture is just for me, to keep. Please.

ROBBIE: You won't tell anybody?

MARGARET: No.

ROBBIE   The wall is in the picture, the wall behind us. I've been in this cell for 15 years, and I've never looked at that wall. I trained myself to block out my peripheral vision when I look at the other walls. This is my secret, how I didn't go crazy. It's like I have this whole part of the world, a quarter of the world, that I'm saving, that's fresh, and nobody would ever suspect it. Bizarre, eh? One day, when I feel like it, I'll look at it. It'll be new.

MARGARET: I think that's beautiful.

ROBBIE   Is the picture done yet?

MARGARET: Not yet. Robbie, I want to tell you something. I believe in you, that you're innocent, but I'm not a reporter, I just said that so's I could get in here. I'm sorry.

ROBBIE: DON'T LIE TO ME! OK?

MARGARET: Never again. Ever.

Scene Eleven

(*ROY's studio. MARGARET and SANDY stalk into the room.*)

MARGARET: Are you going to get off this?

SANDY: It's not me who's on it, Margaret.

MARGARET: You're on my ass.

SANDY: It's nothing to do with me, forget it, forget about it.

MARGARET: So get off it.

SANDY: Why don't you look at the violence of what you did?

MARGARET: We couldn't get across the goddamn street!

SANDY: You don't break through a funeral procession, that's just common decency.

MARGARET: If we'd waited for all of them to go by, we'd have been there all fucking day!

SANDY: You don't give them the finger, and you don't yell *that* at a funeral procession!

MARGARET: I didn't mean "Get a life," I meant "Get a life and stop being so pompous. The guy's dead, he doesn't care." Or woman or whatever. Look, I apologize. Anyway, I thought nothing gets to you.

SANDY: Everything gets to me, I just don't take it personally.

MARGARET: Except this, except when it's me making an honest mistake.

SANDY: I didn't mean to pick on you.

MARGARET: You don't like me very much, well that's OK.

SANDY: Don't think that. I hardly like or dislike anyone. I love people, I try to. No, I don't try to, I often just…do.

MARGARET: What did you and Roy talk about after I was gone?

SANDY: About Robbie, about our memories of each other.

MARGARET: Do you still love him?

SANDY: No.

MARGARET: What about him?

SANDY: He…loves you.

MARGARET: How do you feel about him?

SANDY: It's an awful long time ago. It's like moving through a cloud of sound, for me, thinking about that.

MARGARET: What do you mean?

SANDY: I don't know.

MARGARET: No offense, but it's kind of like you're not here half the time.

SANDY: I know. I sit and watch myself talking to you as though I was watching someone else.

MARGARET: And how do you get through to people?

 (*SANDY gazes at MARGARET.*)

 Why are you looking at me like that?

SANDY: Like what?

MARGARET: Are you saying there's some way you get through to people?

SANDY: No.

MARGARET: By staring at them?

SANDY: I'm sorry if I'm staring at you, I find you so beautiful.

MARGARET: Would you mind not looking at me.

SANDY: How can my looking at you…

 (*MARGARET starts to stare and quiver.*)

 OK! (*Averting her eyes.*)

 What am I thinking of?

(*MARGARET quivers more.*)

You know, that looks really...stagey, kind of...fakey. Are you OK? You know...shall I tell you what I'm seeing? You...yeah, you got scared, but then you made it look fakey, why? And then the fact that you'd done *that* terrified you and you got really scared again, and then you had to make fun of *that* fear, like you don't even deserve to feel bad emotions, never mind good ones, so you make fun of yourself, and dare us not to take you seriously. You impersonate yourself.

MARGARET: Bullshit.

SANDY: Whatever. I don't want to fight.

MARGARET: Bullshit.

SANDY: Why can't we just talk to each other?

MARGARET: Don't you fucking analyse me, you fuck, you girl.

SANDY: Margaret, I'm dying. I have cancer.

MARGARET: Oh God. Oh God.

SANDY: I don't want Roy to know, he's so...he would treat me differently. This thing, it was special between us, it was, we were children, we were innocent. I need to know if that memory has any relevance. I hope it doesn't.

MARGARET: I won't say anything.

SANDY: Thanks.

Scene Twelve

(*ROY's studio. ROY is working on his sculpture. SANDY enters with grocery bags.*)

ROY: Oh, you didn't need to do that.

SANDY: I wanted to. And I'm so glad I did.

ROY: Are you OK?

SANDY: I just had a remarkable experience. In the Safeway.

ROY: What happened?

SANDY: There were two express checkouts, but only one of them was open, and a huge lineup. I thought, wait a minute, they usually open the other one up when it's like this, so I'll have a little leap of faith and go and stand at the other checkout, but I stood there and stood there and no-one came, and of course people are looking at me. See, what people expected was for me to feel foolish and get back in line, and I suddenly became so interested in that, looking at these people, knowing I was expected to feel a certain way, them being so sure of that, that they felt quite OK about staring at me. But I didn't feel embarrassed. I kept standing there just because it was so fascinating to stare back at these people. I was staring at them, and trying to say with my face, "Look, can't you see that you're staring at me?" And one lady offered to let me back in the line, ahead of her, and I told her, how can you offer that on behalf of all the people behind you? And she was all offended, isn't that silly?

(Knock at the door. It's MURIEL.)

ROY: Mrs. Chalmers? Hello, please come in. I'm Roy.

MURIEL: How do you do.

ROY: This is Sandy.

MURIEL: Ah.

SANDY: Oh! We met at Safeway! You know, it was kind of you to offer me your place in line, you must think I'm a strange person.

MURIEL: If I'd been you, I'd have accepted the offer.

SANDY: But I thought it was wrong of you, really, to offer me your space. To really do that, you should have offered me your own space and left the line yourself. Do you see what I mean?

MURIEL: Let's just drop it, shall we?

SANDY: Muriel, may I call you Muriel? I understand that you felt you were being polite, and I'm grateful for that. When I say that about your offer, I'm talking as though it was two other people. I honestly don't mean anything personally. If my way of speaking sounds a little funny, it's just that I naturally say the things I really think. To be untruthful makes me feel physically ill.

MURIEL: Well, you'll be good in court then. We should get down to business. Two things I have to find out, first is this. Do you remember the face you saw?

SANDY: Yes.

ROY: Uh-huh.

MURIEL: It's 15 years ago.

ROY: *(Just coming out of his mouth.)* Oh you don't forget something like that. I remember the turning of the head, the eyes...

SANDY: I remember all my memories of the face, how they always agree perfectly with each other.

ROY: That's right! You always know you're remembering correctly, with something like that.

SANDY: That poor girl has floated over my life as though I was the one who was supposed to save her, by looking up sooner or crying out, and she's still waiting for me to do it.

MURIEL: Excuse me! Do you remember the face?

SANDY & ROY: Yes.

MURIEL: The second thing I have to know is...what kind of people are you? That's what the lawyer would be getting at, you see, if

	there's a new trial. If they find anything, you know, unusual about you, then they don't have to believe you.
ROY:	Uh-huh.
MURIEL:	Roy. You're unemployed?
ROY:	Well, I'm a sculptor, I make things, but it's not like a steady job, no.
MURIEL:	I see. Any police record?
ROY:	No.
MURIEL:	Substance abuse?
ROY:	Oh, not to speak of, you know, once in a while…
MURIEL:	Have you ever smoked pot? Many people have.
	(ROY studies her.)
ROY:	No.
MURIEL:	Good! Good. Always answer yes or no in court, that's what they'll tell you, yes or no, yes or no. Those are the two things they can't twist around, and then it's more difficult for them because they have to think up trickier questions.
SANDY:	Roy, surely you've smoked pot some time in your life?
MURIEL:	Do you think the police always tell the truth? And the lawyers? The truth is whether or not they should treat you like trustworthy people. We want the real truth. Sandy. Any history of mental illness in your family?
SANDY:	Nothing out of the ordinary. I think almost everyone is mentally ill.
MURIEL:	That's not a good answer.
SANDY:	Sorry. No.
MURIEL:	Do you feel up to this?
SANDY:	Yes.
MURIEL:	Good. It's important to me that we all go together, to see Robbie. I think we should give it a few days, if that's OK, he's not feeling very good at the moment.
	(MARGARET enters.)
ROY:	Hi. Mrs. Chalmers, Muriel, this is Margaret.
MURIEL:	Hello dear. Oh, yes, I see, there's a real family resemblance, you're Daddy's little girl.
MARGARET:	What?
ROY:	Margaret isn't my daughter, Muriel, we're a couple.
MURIEL:	Oh. Excuse me. How old are you dear?
	(MARGARET stares at her.)
SANDY:	Muriel, what did you mean about Robbie? What's wrong with him?
MURIEL:	Nothing's *wrong* with him.

MARGARET: He's depressed, he's almost wacko.

MURIEL: I beg your pardon, I think we can get along without your speculations about my son's mental state.

MARGARET: How come he's on medication?

MURIEL: I beg your pardon? Who told you that?

MARGARET: He did. I went to see him.

ROY: You what?

MARGARET: He's innocent, he didn't do it. You put the wrong guy away.

ROY: We'll know that when we see his face.

MARGARET: Well here, take a look.

(She produces the Polaroid of her and ROBBIE. ROY and SANDY turn their faces away from it.)

ROY: A picture's no good. We have to see his face.

MARGARET: Take a look! Why don't you look at it! Both of you. If your memories are so good, you'll know right here and now.

MURIEL: You will not visit my son again. You can't just walk in there and understand him. I don't see any reason for this person to visit him at the present time.

MARGARET: Person? What gives you the right to call me that?

MURIEL: You will not visit my son again.

MARGARET: Why not? He likes me. Does that bother you?

ROY: Margaret, just cool it, OK?

(MURIEL grabs the Polaroid and rips it up.)

MARGARET: Oh sure! I've only met him once, and I know how to *prove* he's innocent.

SANDY: How?

MARGARET: If he did it, you know what would show it better than anything? If you made him re-create the crime. I mean, we go there to the prison and her and Roy in the positions they were in, and I could play the murdered girl, he could be murdering me, then they turn around just like before, and we'd know by his face if he did it, and you'd know if they were remembering right or not.

(Silence.)

MURIEL: What do you two think of that?

Scene Thirteen

(ROBBIE's visiting room. ROY, SANDY, MARGARET, and MURIEL, who is positioning ROY and SANDY downsatge, facing away from the door.)

MURIEL: Now if anyone saw us there'd be awful trouble, so we have to get this right first time. Don't look round 'til you hear Margaret make the whimpering noise, you showed her how to do it?

(*MARGARET makes a whimpering noise.*)

SANDY: That's it exactly.

MURIEL: Don't look round.

SANDY: Are you OK Margaret?

MARGARET: I'm...OK, yes, it's not like he's going to hurt me.

MURIEL: That's right. Now. You two, without looking in the corner over here, you have to lie down with each other, like you were back then, do that now. Is that right?

SANDY: That looks good.

(*SANDY and ROY have awkwardly lain down, he on top of her.*)

MURIEL: Whatever you do, don't look over here. I think I hear Robbie coming, he knows what to do. I'll just get out of the way back here, so you won't feel too self-conscious.

MARGARET: Roy, Sandy has cancer. She's dying, ask her.

(*SANDY clutches ROY hard. ROBBIE enters, goes to MARGARET. He pretends to strangle her. MARGARET does not freak out. She whimpers. SANDY and ROY don't respond. They are totally involved with each other. ROBBIE is panicking. MARGARET whimpers again. No response. MARGARET starts to freak out as ROBBIE's hands remain around her throat. One of his hands goes over her mouth as she starts to freak out.*)

End of Act One

Act Two

Scene Fourteen

(ROY's studio.)

SANDY: Do you find it a good age to be, thirty?

ROY: You're old enough to forgive yourself some things. I sometimes feel my life is like a big wool coat, and all the things I used to demand of myself have slid into warm, silk-lined pockets, because they want quiet and darkness. I pass my hand over the pockets and the things inside wake up just enough to say, "Yes, we're happy in here, we just want to sleep."

SANDY: And what do your hands want to do, now that they're free?

ROY: Take hold of somebody, just take hold of them.

SANDY: What do you think Margaret wants from you?

ROY: There have been moments when we loved each other.

SANDY: You think that's love?

(ROY hugs her.)

ROY: Yes I think it's love.

(She disengages.)

Is there nothing that can be done?

SANDY: No they found it too late. Roy, don't treat me like I'm dying.

ROY: I won't. I won't.

SANDY: Death is nothing to be afraid of. It's part of life, it's fine. And life, even a little moment of life that's lived without fear, with no fear of anything, is worth a whole life. That's what I've wanted to believe, to see, to know. But I was fooling myself, like some mad woman. I was wasting my time. Wasting my time.

ROY: You're taking it so smoothly.

SANDY: I had this moment, like a flash, where all of that was true. I came out of the hospital one day and I was walking down the street with a full understanding that I was going to die. Suddenly I had this moment of indescribable peace. I wasn't separate from the street, I wasn't walking down the street. The air in front of me was opening up, taking on my shape as the space I'd just occupied went back to it's old shape. The air was passing my shape along.

ROY: That's beautiful.

SANDY: It lasted for four days. Then one morning the phone rang…it was gone. The feeling went away.

ROY: You can stay here as long as you like.

SANDY: I wish that was true.

            (MARGARET enters.)

SANDY: Margaret, before you say anything, I want to apologize. I've said foolish things. Forgive me, please, will you?

MARGARET: I'm sorry I blurted that out like that, at the prison.

SANDY: You did me a big favour. I think I was avoiding things. I was being a bit of a pain in the ass.

MARGARET: It's OK, I wasn't bothered.

ROY: I'm sorry we ran off like that. Sandy had to get out of there.

MARGARET: I understand. Now. Well. Well? Was it him?

ROY: I can say definitely, it wasn't the same face I saw in that back lane.

MARGARET: Oh! Yes! That is so cool! Sandy?

SANDY: I don't know.

MARGARET: What do you mean?

SANDY: I don't know. I just couldn't say. It maybe wasn't, but I don't know. I guess I thought I remembered the face, but not well enough.

MARGARET: Think about it now, think about the face.

SANDY: I just see Robbie's face now, it's confused, I'm sorry.

MARGARET: Well think!

ROY: Hey, uh, maybe we just need some more time.

MARGARET: *You* were sure about it, isn't that enough?

ROY: I don't know.

SANDY: Maybe tomorrow I'll remember.

MARGARET: I'm sure he'll be thrilled to hear that. Why don't you just say it wasn't him? That wouldn't cost you anything.

SANDY: Lie in court?

MARGARET: The guy refused his parole, he didn't do it! Anyway, even if he was guilty, which he isn't, he's done all his time now anyway. What's the difference?

SANDY: But lie in court. They would know. I might not be able to do it. I might give it away.

MARGARET: Well maybe you should just grow up a little. Roy, would you rub my neck? I'm really tense. I am.

            (ROY doesn't move.)

Scene Fifteen

> (SANDY is outside, distractedly hurrying along the street. She stops abruptly when she sees MURIEL.)

MURIEL: I know it was hard for you. Do you think you…

SANDY: Madam. If you want me to treat your son's case impartially, I must tell you it's best that you don't approach me.

MURIEL: You don't remember then. He stays in jail.

SANDY: How old is your body?

MURIEL: What?

SANDY   I meant your son.

> (MURIEL's hand flutters involuntarily around her throat.)

MURIEL: He's 33. I understand you're…not going to be with us.

SANDY: I'm not for you or against you.

MURIEL: I meant with us in the land of the living.

SANDY: Oh. Long enough. I, ah, they were telling me I should just say it wasn't him. Because he's innocent.

MURIEL: Well that's right, he is. You don't remember. I can't hold that against you, I suppose. You were a different person then. Just a child, really. You don't remember. But I was a mother even then. I was the same as I am now.

SANDY: What do you want?

MURIEL: Hmm?

SANDY: You were waiting here for me.

MURIEL: I just want you to know I'm a human being, even if our places in life are different.

SANDY: I'm not trying to be difficult.

MURIEL: I know dear. You can trust me. You have to trust me.

SANDY: I don't want to die.

MURIEL: I know.

SANDY: I don't want to die.

MURIEL: Well tell me. Is it like a block? Or is it just impossible for you to remember?

SANDY: I think it's impossible.

MURIEL: Don't be upset. I can understand that. I can.

SANDY: Do you think it's normal?

MURIEL: Uh-huh. And I think Robbie is going to be a better person when he gets up in front of that parole board and says, "I did it, and I'm sorry." It's a lesson about life that you and I have had to learn the hard way, that you're not free unless you're free to tell a lie freely, or to make a mistake.

SANDY: I have to go now. I've got my own, you know, things to think about.

MURIEL: But we've talked.

SANDY: I don't know, for now. *(Exits.)*

MURIEL: Hey!

Scene Sixteen

(ROBBIE's cell.)

MURIEL: Son, believe me, it's not going to work, it's got a bad smell. The woman is unstable. And the other one, the young one, is completely unpredictable. We cannot rely on these people.

ROBBIE: Maybe she's gonna remember.

MURIEL: And maybe she isn't. There's an easier way.

(We hear demented shouts and wails from another cell.)

ROBBIE: I'm not going to stand up there and say I did it. The guy remembered, he knew it wasn't me.

MURIEL: It's only a few words.

ROBBIE: I DIDN'T DO IT!

MURIEL: I know that.

ROBBIE: I'm sorry.

(MURIEL leans against the upstage wall.)

MURIEL: I only want what's best for you.

ROBBIE: Why are you standing there? Are you crying?

MURIEL: I'll be fine.

(More demented wails.)

ROBBIE: Mum?

MURIEL: Yes, dear?

ROBBIE: Did you never think of making a reward, for information?

MURIEL: What do you mean?

ROBBIE: Well, Margaret was saying to me. Someone coulda done that years ago, you know, if you'd thought of doing that, we could have found these people years ago, when it was still fresh in their heads.

MURIEL: What did she say to you?

ROBBIE: How come? How come you never thought of doing that, do you think?

(Silence.)

Mum?

MURIEL: I did think of doing that. I didn't think it would work, for one thing. And I've never had a lot of money to throw around. That's one thing you haven't had to think about. What else did I forget to do?

ROBBIE:	Nothing.
MUIRIEL	What else did she say?
ROBBIE:	Nothing. We were just talking. She's nice.
	(Howls from behind the wall.)
MURIEL:	She does what she's told. I asked her to be nice to you, she's just doing what I asked her. Don't you start imagining things.
ROBBIE:	She likes me though.
MURIEL:	She's nice to you, that doesn't mean she likes you.
ROBBIE:	She believes me. She believes I didn't do it. I know she does.
	(Silence.)

Scene Seventeen

(ROY's studio. ROY is working on his sculpture, from behind. We see the eerie irridescence of the welding torch, punctuated with super-bright flashes that look like photo flashes. He is installing a face. MARGARET enters. She has adopted a new strategy—she is playing the "good girl.")

ROY:	Oh!
MARGARET:	What's that?
ROY:	It's a face.
MARGARET:	Is it you?
ROY:	No. It's the face I remember, from the murder. I started working on it weeks ago, puttering. I didn't understand what it was, but I think that's what it is.
MARGARET:	The murderer looked like that?
ROY:	Well, no. It's an image. An image. Maybe that's how I see myself when I remember the face, I don't know. But it's an image, you know.
MARGARET:	It's ugly.
ROY:	Don't you like it?
MARGARET:	Oh no, it's great. Roy, why am I so bad?
ROY:	You're only bad sometimes.
MARGARET:	It was just seeing the two of you together.
ROY:	Don't think that.
MARGARET:	Do you forgive me?
ROY:	Of course I do. Don't even think about it.
MARGARET:	I guess I was jealous.
ROY:	Margaret, I care about you.
MARGARET:	I don't mind what happens between you now, it all seems so small. All I care about is getting this thing to work out for

everybody. Even Sandy. Especially Sandy. I don't feel bad towards her at all.

ROY: That's really wonderful.

MARGARET: Even though, of course, she's only saying she doesn't remember to get back at me. Oh, it's true, and I understand it completely. We just have to find a way around it. Make her say it's the wrong guy. You have to. You know it wasn't him.

ROY: I'll talk to her. I'll talk to her.

MARGARET: You'll tell her?

(SANDY enters, depressed.)

SANDY: Hi.

MARGARET: Good evening. How are things?

SANDY: Alright. I think I'm going to bed.

MARGARET: Don't go yet. Look! Roy put up this new piece, have a look.

(MARGARET takes ROY by the hand and goes to the sculpture wall. SANDY turns her face away.)

SANDY: It's good work.

MARGARET: It's dedicated to me, isn't it?

ROY: Ah, it sure is.

(MARGARET kisses him.)

MARGARET: Guess what it is.

SANDY: I don't know.

MARGARET: Do you think it looks like Robbie?

SANDY: Not really.

MARGARET: That's because it's the face of the murderer and Robbie isn't the murderer.

SANDY: Oh.

ROY: We were talking. About what to do.

MARGARET: I don't blame you, Sandy. All the same, it's weird how you remember stuff about Roy so clearly, but not this other thing.

SANDY: If you say so.

MARGARET: I'm just trying to be honest. Like, if you loved each other so much, why did you wait until he was about to "enter" you, then say no?

ROY: OK, that's enough.

MARGARET: Fine. It was the moment right before you saw the face. It was her moment, not yours. It's the one thing we haven't tried, that's all. Forget it.

SANDY: *(Pause.)* Suddenly I saw him about to enter me, and I saw myself separate, and imagined that I was there alone. And all of a sudden I couldn't stand him looking at me and I just wanted him out of my sight, so I said no, and turned my head away. And we both just lay there like that, and he was trying to get me to look at him, and he lay down beside me, all disappointed like a child, and he put his hand on my arm.

MARGARET: That's good. And then?

SANDY: And then…her voice crying, looking through the window, seeing…

MARGARET: Seeing what?

SANDY: Seeing…a man…it could have been Robbie.

ROY: I think you should do it. I think you should just say it wasn't him.

   (MARGARET exits.)

SANDY: Are you scared of her?

ROY: No.

SANDY: Do you really think I should?

ROY: I think you should do what feels right.

SANDY: Would you…hold me?

   (They embrace. ROY's hand finds a lump, he recoils. SANDY's hand covers the spot.)

   It's just a tumour. It won't bite you.

Scene Eighteen

   (ROBBIE's cell. ROBBIE is asleep as MARGARET enters and whispers to him.)

MARGARET: Hi.

ROBBIE: Wake up, wake up. Ah! What are you doing here?

MARGARET: I came to see you.

ROBBIE: Oh. Did you want to ask me some more questions?

MARGARET: What do you mean?

ROBBIE: For the newspaper.

   (We hear a taunting voice from behind the wall.)

VOICE: Chalmers! Hey Chalmers you fuckin'—

ROBBIE: SHUT UP!

VOICE: FUCKIN' ASSHOLE!

MARGARET: I told you, I don't really work at a newspaper.

ROBBIE: Oh that's right! I must be some kind of real idiot or something!

MARGARET: Are they giving you a rough time?

ROBBIE: What would you know about it?

   (They both start to whisper.)

MARGARET: What's the matter?

ROBBIE: What do you want? What did you come here for?

MARGARET: I wanted to tell you. I'm getting Roy to work on Sandy, you know? To get her to say it wasn't you, and I'm sure, I just know it's gonna work, I know it is.

ROBBIE: Oh, that's great. OK.

MARGARET: Yeah.

ROBBIE: And you're doing that for me.

MARGARET: I think she's just doing it because she's mad at me, because she's jealous of me. That's why I had to get him to do it. But it's really like it's me that's doing it.

ROBBIE: So she thinks it's him that's doing it but it's really you that's doing it.

MARGARET: Well, yeah.

ROBBIE: *(Ending the whispers.)* You need a good slap.

MARGARET: Robbie, what's the matter with you? What did I do?

> *(ROBBIE slaps her. She kneels.)*

VOICE: Ro-bieeee!

ROBBIE: SHUT UP!

VOICE: Oo-oooo!

> *(MARGARET shakes and gasps, her hands fluttering around her face. ROBBIE does not look at her.)*

ROBBIE She told me all about it, so you don't need to pretend. You're only "nice" to me because she asked you to do that. She told me. So I'm sorry for slapping you but from now on you just tell me what you have to say and then you go, OK?

MARGARET: Your mother? What did she say? She didn't say anything like that! That's a lie! I swear!

ROBBIE: Why don't you shut up.

MARGARET: I can't believe that, that she would say that! That is so typical! Look at me! Look at me!

> *(ROBBIE doesn't look around.)*

ROBBIE: You saying my mother's...a liar?

MARGARET: Yes I'm saying your mother's a liar.

VOICE: Chalmers! Hey...

MARGARET: SHUT UP!

> *(Silence.)*

ROBBIE: Why would she do that?

MARGARET: She doesn't like me, for one thing.

ROBBIE: How? How come?

MARGARET: I dunno. Maybe she's jealous. Maybe she thinks I'll make you all confused.

ROBBIE: Maybe.

MARGARET: I believe in you so much. I would die for you. You have to believe me.

ROBBIE: I'm sorry.

MARGARET: Well look at me then. You just called me a liar.

(He goes to turn toward her, but she's against the forbidden wall, and he can't.)

ROBBIE: I can't do that. Come round this side.

MARGARET: I do like you.

ROBBIE: Yeah I like you too and all that.

MARGARET: You're going to get out pretty soon anyway, you don't have to save this wall up any more. Couldn't it be me standing here when you look at it? Why can't you look at me?

(ROBBIE doesn't move. She takes her shirt off and throws it at his feet. He picks it up, smells it, throws it behind him.)

ROBBIE: Put that back on before somebody sees.

(MARGARET takes off her bra and throws it at his feet. This is strangely non-sexual. She is exposing herself in a different way which is not easy for her.)

MARGARET: My eyes are closed. I won't know if you look or not.

ROBBIE: You go now. Just… You. Go.

Scene Nineteen

(ROY's studio. ROY comes in to SANDY.)

ROY: Can I get you anything?

SANDY: No.

ROY: Can we talk?

SANDY: Sure.

ROY: Have you…thought about it?

SANDY: You know, it doesn't seem to make that much difference. He stays in jail, he gets out. What's the difference? He'll be just like me. I've forgotten that I'm dying. I can't remember. I keep forgetting and wondering what's on TV. What good would it do him to get out?

ROY: It would make a big difference to him.

SANDY: How do you know that?

ROY: That's just common sense.

SANDY: Do you think it would make a big difference to you if you had to go to jail? It wouldn't, you know. You'd just do what you always do. You'd have your feelings. You'd feel scared or angry or sad or lonely, and you'd feel comfortable, because those feelings are so comfortable.

ROY: It's me you're talking to, you know.

SANDY: If you could see how pathetic you are, I wonder if you'd stand the shock.

ROY: Why would you want to hurt my feelings like that?

SANDY: Your feelings are so important aren't they.

ROY: Maybe it's OK to have feelings.

SANDY: Or maybe they're a dirty stupid trick that's been played on us. Maybe they're bad—all of them. Maybe they blind us.

ROY: Blind us to what?

SANDY: I don't know. To happiness.

ROY: Happiness is a feeling.

SANDY: How would you know? *(Pause.)* I didn't think so.

ROY: Remember when we were about seven or eight. Sitting in Miss Yellow's class, glancing at each other. Do you remember that? I wonder if it's the same day we're remembering? It was like looking up and seeing myself sitting across the room, except I was a girl, and I wanted to stare, but I couldn't. It was like the voice of the teacher, the other kids—I remember listening and thinking, "babble" —it was all just a fog that I wanted to drift through to look at you.

SANDY: I was always so quiet, because any time I answered a question, any time I spoke, I was speaking to you, and I knew that you could tell that. You were the boy. That's what you were. The boy.

ROY: I always made sure you were ahead of me when we left the room, because I liked to watch you walk through the door.

SANDY: I always wanted you to be watching me, and I always knew you were, without even glancing backwards. The way I walked was for you. You were inside me, walking me through the door. My little eight-year-old walk.

    (He takes her hand.)

ROY: What do you think God is like?

    (She kisses his hand. MARGARET enters.)

MARGARET: Oh weeeell! That's nice, that's a nice picture!

ROY: We were just reminiscing.

MARGARET: Who gives a shit! *(To SANDY.)* You! What are you going to do? I want to know, now!

SANDY: I don't know.

MARGARET: That's not good enough!

ROY: Calm down.

MARGARET: He's not guilty. You are. You are guilty.

ROY: What's the matter?

MARGARET: Do you know what his mother said? She told him I was only being nice to him because she told me to. THAT BITCH!

ROY: It's OK. We'll talk to her about it.

SANDY: Why did she say that?

MARGARET: Because she's a worm, like you.

SANDY: I don't deserve that from you.

MARGARET: Oh I'm sorry. I'll make it up to you. Is there anything special you'd like us to do, by way of when we have your funeral? Something personal.

(SANDY runs out of the room, ROY goes after her.)

MARGARET: You come back here! Come back here! COME BACK HERE! I am really angry with you Roy! I am angry! VERY! Grr. Grr. Oh. I am so pissed. I AM FUCKING ANGRY! Yes, I'm angry, are you angry, children? YOU BASTARD!

(In a fury, picks up welding torch and attacks the new face sculpture from behind. The lights dim and come up on ROBBIE'S cell. He is being taunted by a voice. He contorts himself. The sculpture face begins to glow.)

VOICE: Chalmers! Chalmers! I know why you turned down your parole. You want me to tell you? Sure you do. It's because the one thing you could never take is for your mom to think you're guilty. That's why you can't say you did it. Am I right? Chalmers! Chalmers!

Scene Twenty

(SANDY runs on to extreme downstage. ROY runs on. SANDY whirls on him.)

SANDY: Haughty! Haughty! Proud and haughty! I don't want you feeling sorry. I don't deserve it and I don't need it! I tell you, that girl stimulates me more than you do. Yes. I feel wonderfully awful. Awful! And are you going to make me feel comfortable? More than I feel now?

ROY: Can I tell you the truth? I love you. I'm melting.

SANDY: *(Explosive.)* Your tongue! You have the tongue of a fish! My tongue is a sword! Shut up! Maybe you'll find one small thing to say that's not to get what you want and not to protect you and say it and hear that it's a true thing and then feel the truth come out of your mouth like a sword. Feel it glide and slice and comfort me. You'll know, because a sword feels like it has no natural home inside your mouth.

(ROY grabs her and kisses her, sticking his tongue down her throat, it seems.)

SANDY: Now you're going to live my life for me. Show me. Lead me, boy.

Scene Twenty-One

(ROBBIE's cell. MARGARET storms in, Polaroid camera in hand. ROBBIE is against the wall. She faces him, back to the audience, and begins to take off her shirt and bra. This time she's out to degrade herself.)

MARGARET: Don't you dare look! Close your eyes!

ROBBIE: What are you doing?

(ROBBIE closes his eyes and looks away, MARGARET, bare-breasted, goes and stands beside him with her back to the wall. ROBBIE moves downstage and opens his eyes.)

ROBBIE: I'm not going to look at you if you stand there.

MARGARET: What a gentleman.

ROBBIE: You better go.

MARGARET: I'm going.

(She takes a Polaroid of herself against the wall.)

Give me my clothes.

(She snatches the clothes from him and puts them on as the picture develops. She sticks the picture to the wall.)

Here. Here's a picture for you. A pretty well-developed picture, I'd say. You can look at a picture, can't you? You won't be breaking any rules. If you want to take a look at it you can, and you can let me know if you like it.

(MARGARET leaves. ROBBIE backs up to the wall and feels for the picture. He retrieves it and holds it against his chest. He struggles mightily. He brings the picture slowly to his eyes.)

Scene Twenty-Two

(In the prison waiting room. MURIEL hurries in, MARGARET is sitting with one leg crossed over the other, bouncing the top leg in agitation.)

MURIEL: Oh my God I can't believe you're doing that. OK, let's, yes, let's just forget everything for a moment and just be aware of what's going on around us, here in this room. *(Shaking her head.)* Let's start from scratch. Are you comfortable? Nothing against you personally. You're a very pretty girl. You're making him confused, you're not helping him, you're taking his attention away, do you see? You're making him weak. Do you understand what I'm talking about?

MARGARET: Why do you keep looking at my leg?

MURIEL: Look at you. Do you think I don't know what you're doing? Rubbing your legs together like that? Sitting there playing with yourself, masturbating yourself and it's so second nature, you don't even know you're doing it.

MARGARET: Bullshit.

MURIEL: You think I'm an old...cake that nobody would...I know things. Do you think I don't? I've lived. I know. You do that too much and...first it'll get so that a real man doesn't do anything for you, next thing you'll have to get yourself off on the side of a door before you feel anything. It's what keeps you from growing up. In terms of connecting with other people. You've got to believe me. I know it sounds old-fashioned. The *only* reason I'm talking about this is that it's something self-destructive that can be cleared up easily, just by pointing it out.

MARGARET: Are you telling me that you...?

MURIEL: Yes! I know what I'm talking about!

MARGARET: Wow!

MURIEL: Yes. You're making him weak.

MARGARET: Because he's playing with himself.

MURIEL: Yes. It puts you out of touch with other people.

MARGARET: Playing with himself and thinking about...me! Why shouldn't he? I would! He's probably doing it right now. Know what he told me? That you used to touch him all the time, when he was a kid. Naughty.

MURIEL: *(Pause.)* No he didn't.

MARGARET: *(Exiting.)* Oh, he did.

MURIEL: I can see you're not interested in continuing.

Scene Twenty-Three

> *(ROBBIE's cell. MURIEL enters. ROBBIE stuffs the Polaroid in his pocket.)*

MURIEL: What did you just put into your pocket?

ROBBIE: It's private. Private correspondence.

MURIEL: What the hell is going on?

ROBBIE: Nothing.

MURIEL: Stand up.

ROBBIE: No. Don't feel like it.

MURIEL: *(Pause.)* I see. Shall I leave? I can go away and never bother you again, if that's what you'd like. Your girlfriend can get you out. With all her wisdom, all her experience. Or who cares? If you stay in here forever, she can come and visit you. Every day. With all her...youth. And sparkle. Until one day when she doesn't show up. You try to contact her, she's disappeared. Found someone else. With nicer hair, maybe. And didn't even tell you. And you sit here. *(Pause.)* I can walk out of here and get on with my life, but I promise you something, I will never think of you again. I will protect myself. Never allow it to enter my head.

ROBBIE: Stop. She's not coming back. She's mad at me.

MURIEL: Why?

ROBBIE: She wanted me to look at her, naked, and I wouldn't.

MURIEL: *(Embracing him.)* Oh God my son has sense. I knew you did. I'm so proud of you. Do you know that?

ROBBIE: Don't. I'm feeling…itchy.

MURIEL: You mean the world to me.

> *(ROBBIE bellows and throws his body around in total frustration. He does the next bit spooky, not raging.)*

ROBBIE: That story you told me about what the Japs did.

MURIEL: What?

ROBBIE: The Japs.

MURIEL: What story?

ROBBIE: In the war.

MURIEL: What war?

ROBBIE: The Second World War.

MURIEL: What they did to who?

ROBBIE: To our boys.

MURIEL: I don't know what you're talking about.

ROBBIE: You told me this story, in the bath.

MURIEL: I don't remember.

ROBBIE: You *know*. They made them get…excited, they brought in naked women to the prison camp and made them look at them.

MURIEL: Well why would they do that?

ROBBIE: So they'd get a fucking hard-on! And they cut a slit around the foreskin and stick a glass test-tube down between the penis and the skin and then break it with a little hammer.

> *(Silence.)*

MURIEL: Oh that. Yes. That was common knowledge.

ROBBIE: *(Agitated.)* I always accepted that, but, you know, where do they get, in a prison camp, naked women… OK maybe they could find them, but glass test tubes? And little hammers? *(Pause.)* Who told you about it?

MURIEL: I don't know.

ROBBIE: What the fuck did you *do* that for? Wasn't true. Little hammers!?

MURIEL: For God's sake, I'm sorry.

ROBBIE: I'm all fucked up.

MURIEL: Robbie, *I didn't know.* I didn't. We were told such lies. We had no idea. I must have believed the story at the time, and it just popped out. I didn't make it up, in order to *do* something to you. I would never do that. For God's sake, Robbie, you *know* me. You *know* me.

Scene Twenty-Four

(ROY is defending himself to MARGARET, who will not look at him.)

ROY: Margaret? Margaret? *(Pause.)* Say something. *(Pause.)* I did try. Surely you can understand that she...at this time in her life...has to...it was you that freaked her out. I'm sorry. I tried. *(Pause.)* You have to understand. I have to make her comfortable, help her. I can't help it.

MARGARET: It's not like you and me had been together very long anyway.

ROY: Well...yeah.

MARGARET: *(Looking at him.)* You have betrayed me. I trusted you. You have made me into a Jew and stuck me in an oven.

ROY: I didn't mean to.

(Pause. SANDY enters.)

MARGARET: He is innocent. He is innocent, you can see that if you look at him and how he insists he does not belong in there. One wall of his cell, he has never looked at, ever, as simple as that. That kind of...imagination...comes from innocence. He has never looked at it, so that he'll remember his cell has really nothing to do with him, is not the place he belongs. I believe this, I know this so clearly, I would stake my life on it. I would die for him, if it would help. I would die for him.

SANDY: Roy, when I die, it will be for you.

ROY: Oh my God.

SANDY: And of course that's nonsense.

ROY: *(Pause.)* Yeah.

SANDY: Games that he plays with his cell aren't imagination, they aren't any kind of grace, any kind of innocence. They're delusions. Let's speak plainly. And you saying you would die for him, that's nonsense. Let me pick my words carefully. First, you don't know what you're offering, you don't know anything about dying. Second, Margaret, you imagine that death, death the "big thing", you would *really feel* something for once. Especially if it was a death for some good cause, so you pick on Robbie and you have to project this noble innocence on him so he'll be worthy of the great fantasy project of your death. The fact is, your death would be just as unreal to you as your life.

MARGARET: I would die for him.

(Silence.)

SANDY: Life is a banquet. Why are we all starving to death?

(MURIEL and ROBBIE enter unannounced.)

ROY: Ah, hello.

MURIEL: I think we've all met, but not really properly. This is my son, Robbie, a human being, not a convict, not a murderer. Robbie, this is Roy, who's unemployed, and Margaret, who you've met. Robbie has got a day pass, the first one he's ever had. They're trying to tempt him with a little freedom. We have been shopping and we have been relaxing in a bar, a treat for Robbie.

ROBBIE: Mom?

MURIEL: Robbie would like to use your washroom.

ROY: It's through there.

ROBBIE: Can I have the key?

ROY: (Beat.) It doesn't need a key.

ROBBIE: (Beat.) Oh, yeah. (ROBBIE exits.)

MURIEL: (To SANDY.) I thought it would be a good idea for you to see my son's face again, when we're all a little more relaxed.

SANDY: Muriel, I've decided not to testify. I can't do it, my mouth wouldn't open. I wouldn't be able to do it. There's nothing more to be said.

MURIEL: Wait a goddamn minute! You will do me the courtesy of taking a long, true look at Robbie's face, and then say that to him. I think you owe us that much.

SANDY: Alright.

               (ROBBIE re-enters. He goes to the sculpture that MARGARET bought.)

ROBBIE: (To ROY.) Wow! That's beautiful. You're talented, man. The bathroom smells really nice an' that.

MARGARET: That's me, I put stuff in there.

ROBBIE: (Pause.) The towels are really nice. Not like in the joint. The towels! Woh! They are not perfect, let me tell you. They're other people's, basically. They're old. Other people have used them, you can tell, lots and lots of times. Guys who are dead now have used those those towels. Oh yeah, the laundry cleans the dirt off them, I know, and they steam all the germs out of them, I believe in that, but you never know who's wiped their bum on it, or...whatever. (Giggles.) I'm just saying, I'd rather have my own dirty towels than someone else's clean towels.

SANDY: Robbie, what colour is the wall in the bathroom?

ROBBIE: Uh, I don't know, I didn't notice.

               (SANDY approaches him, staring at his face.)

SANDY: I don't know if it was you. I can't lie to a judge about it. I'm sorry if this will upset you.

MURIEL: You are a destructive person.

ROBBIE: Wait! Look at me! It wasn't me!

SANDY: Robbie, it doesn't matter what the parole board thinks. It doesn't matter what anyone thinks of you. Them, me. Margaret, even your mother.

MURIEL:	Oh you are so pompous.
MARGARET:	Roy?
SANDY:	*(To ROY.)* You may *not* lie.
MARGARET:	I believe in you, Robbie.
MURIEL:	And you too, you're just as bad, you little tramp.
ROY:	Hey...
MARGARET:	*(To MURIEL.)* You fucking liar! You told him I was nice to him because you asked me to be!

(MURIEL produces a Polaroid.)

MURIEL:	Nice to him?
ROBBIE:	Oh God Mom, no.
MURIEL:	Quiet! Smutting up his head with this trash! Let's see what our boyfriend thinks of it.

(She gives the picture to ROY. MARGARET panics.)

Trash. Boobs hanging out. And stop that bullshit, look at you!

(ROBBIE gentles MARGARET.)

You've had your head twisted around enough by this little tart.

ROBBIE:	It's just because she asked how come you never thought of other things to help get me out.
MURIEL:	It's not up to me if something crosses my mind! You can't make an idea come into your head if you don't know what it is!
ROBBIE:	Don't get upset.
MURIEL:	We are going now. We don't need these people. You are going to tell that board you did it. Say it now.
MARGARET:	Don't say it, Robbie. Don't ever say that.
ROBBIE:	*(To SANDY, but with one hand on MARGARET's head, trying to contain her.)* First you. You tell them it wasn't me. It wasn't me you saw.
MURIEL:	*(To SANDY.)* Well? Go on. For God's sake! Just say it here and now.
SANDY:	I'll say it, if you'll say something first.
MURIEL:	What little words must I say?
SANDY:	Say, "I've never really believed my son was innocent."

(Silence.)

MURIEL:	Well that's just ridiculous. I'm not going to say that!

(Everyone stares at MURIEL, except ROBBIE, who cannot look at her. MARGARET snatches up an electric drill and holds it to her own head.)

MARGARET:	You say it, or I'm gonna stick this in my head.
ROY:	Margaret this is no time for fucking around.
MARGARET:	I'll do it.

SANDY: Margaret that could be dangerous.

MARGARET: I mean it, I'll…

ROBBIE: SHUT UP!

MARGARET: Robbie?

                (ROBBIE slowly turns to his mother.)

ROBBIE: I did it. I killed the girl.

MURIEL: Just you wait til your father gets home.

                (MARGARET drills herself in the head, collapses with her eyes closed. SANDY screams.)

                Oh my God!

ROBBIE: Margaret! Margaret!

MURIEL: Get it out! Get it out!

ROY: How?

SANDY: Try it!

ROY: It won't move, it won't move!

MURIEL: Reverse the drill and drill it out.

SANDY: No leave it.

ROY: It has to come out.

                (ROY drills it out. ROBBIE supports her. She opens her eyes.)

MARGARET: I was sleeping. I dreamed that all my fillings fell out. But they weren't in my teeth, they were in my eyes, in the white part. There were all these holes, and I was trying to hide from people, I was turning my eyes all around in my head so people wouldn't see. Everyone thought I was crazy. Are my eyes OK?

ROBBIE: Yes, they're lovely. Lovely eyes.

Scene Twenty-Five

                (ROY and SANDY. They have just tried to have sex but ROY couldn't do it. He is awkwardly zipping up her dress.)

SANDY   I don't blame you.

ROY: I could…we could try again.

SANDY: No. It's not the same body you remember.

                (ROY has got part of SANDY's zipper caught in his sweater. He tugs to free it, damaging her zipper.)

ROY: Oh shit. Can it be fixed?

SANDY: It was just never meant to happen between us.

ROY: We could just lie together, and talk, and touch. I've never forgotten you.

SANDY: Oh thank you, but I have to go.

ROY: Can I write to you?

SANDY: Do you want to?

ROY: No.

SANDY: I'm alone. It was just an accident that we ever met.

ROY: No. It wasn't.

SANDY: I'm on my own. I know I'll forget that I'm alone. I'll get all scared
            again, and that's why this feels so good. I know it's real because
            I know it's going to go away.

            *(MARGARET wanders slowly onstage, her head bandaged. She is
            humming "Itsy Bitsy Spider". She approaches SANDY and they
            stare at each other. SANDY exits. MARGARET surveys the room.)*

MARGARET: I remember this place.

            The End

Worm Moon

Deborah O'Neil

Production Information

Worm Moon (originally titled *The Columbia Ice Fields Tour*) was produced at the Winnipeg Fringe Festival, 1990. The cast was as follows:

ABACUS .... Karin Randoja
BONIFACE .... Rona Risman

Directed by Nancy Drake

The play was subsequently workshopped in December, 1990 at the Minneapolis Playwrights' Centre where the third character was added.

Characters

ABACUS: the fisherwoman, 20
BONIFACE: the seamstress and designated Mother, 40
HANNAH: the headwasher and box builder, 30

Act One

(Winter in the future; a riverbank and a quarantined camp of 10 icefishing skids or huts on runners. HANNAH and BONIFACE wear fluorescent coveralls, HANNAH green, BONIFACE yellow. ABACUS wears street clothes. All wear medical face masks at various times. Strong smell of liniment.

As play opens, ABACUS and HANNAH are in the skid. ABACUS is restrained in a lawn chair, wearing a large plastic cape around her neck and shoulders. HANNAH is standing behind, holding a container of shampoo powder over her.

ABACUS pushes the powder away.)

ABACUS: And I tell you I'm not sick! Look! Just look at my arms. And my legs. You can see for yourself. There's not a lesion on me.

HANNAH: You *are* a specimen. I am impressed.

ABACUS: There's no boils. My hair's not falling out is it? I told the church, just check my nostrils. You'll see.

HANNAH: What'd you expect? They only do souls, not nostrils.

ABACUS: But I don't belong on the river. I'm clean.

HANNAH: Blah, blah, blah. So, where's your writ?

ABACUS: It's in my bag.

HANNAH: And stamped?

ABACUS: Do I have a choice?

HANNAH: Stamped what?

ABACUS: *(Pause.)* It's stamped "infected." OK? Infected!

HANNAH: So, girl. Welcome to Tour Duty.

ABACUS: Some tour. They herded me into the back of some fruit truck like I was church property or something.

HANNAH: You are! Who the hell else wants us?

ABACUS: It's like I don't exist anymore.

HANNAH: The less they have to think about us down here, the better. Am I right?

ABACUS: It's crazy up there! People running naked through the streets.

334 /A Map of the Senses

	Kids riding on these wild little machines, shooting pigeons off statues. Neighbours patrolling the river banks. It doesn't stop. But we've got supporters. It's only a matter of time.
HANNAH:	Before what? The doctors and gravediggers form a new union? No. You look after number one, kid.
ABACUS:	I'm just a student.
HANNAH:	So, what's left to study? Tell me.
ABACUS:	They made a mistake.
HANNAH:	The mistake, Abacus, was sticking around...
ABACUS:	Don't call me that.
HANNAH:	The mistake was letting the Waste Board catch up with you in the first place. Didn't you see the postings? Didn't you hear the goings on?
ABACUS:	It doesn't matter. Those monks up there turn their backs for a second and I'm out of here.
HANNAH:	You're never going to see no monks. They're too damn busy praying for our souls and wasted bodies. Too damn busy collecting donations of three day old bread and worn out apples.
ABACUS:	I'm gone, first chance I get. Up that riverbank and over the fence. *(Pause.)*
HANNAH:	I'd kill for fresh fruit.
ABACUS:	I can get you anything you want! Tangarine? Kiwi?
HANNAH:	I hate kiwi.
ABACUS:	We could find something. We could do it together.
HANNAH:	You got me tasting it already, girl.
ABACUS:	Is it a go then?
HANNAH:	The fence idea won't work.
ABACUS:	Says who? *(Pause.)* Stop! *(She pushes HANNAH away.)* Stop with the powder! Just leave it there. I'll do it myself.
HANNAH:	Yeah, right, bosses and bitches. We need another one of both around here.

(HANNAH yanks back on ABACUS' hair to hold her.)

Listen up. And good. There's only one person in charge of shampoo around here. Learn that. I don't *leave* it for nobody.

(Lets go of ABACUS' hair. Pause.)

Besides, you don't think they've added a few zaps to that fence? It saves them having to check on us. The fence idea's stupid. It's been stopped, dropped and rolled to death. Believe me, it's not a pretty sight. You got a better chance waiting for breakup and surfing the ice floes out of here.

ABACUS:	Then *you've* heard too?
HANNAH:	There's talk. We're even taking bets on when the river's going to break. You want in?

ABACUS:	They won't go through with it.
HANNAH:	Men are sleeping with their daughters! They won't think twice about dumping the likes of us to the bottom of this river.
ABACUS:	Well, I'm not waiting for thaw.
	(Pause. HANNAH closes her eyes.)
HANNAH:	I mean, what better way of getting rid of this whole, stinking mess and not blaming God for his deliverance. No. This way Mother Nature can be the bitch.
ABACUS:	You got another idea, don't you?
HANNAH:	You think I plan on washing scalps for the rest of my life?
ABACUS:	Well, I'm not fishing either.
HANNAH:	Everybody does their job. While you're here, you just do your job. *(Pause.)* Of course, I heard that you could have had the Soupmaker's.
ABACUS:	There's only one thing I hate more than fishing.
HANNAH:	First pick over the food donations. I would have grabbed it like that.
ABACUS:	Well, I didn't. That's my business.
HANNAH:	No. That's everybody's business. News travels faster than speed through these fish huts. Besides, we all knew the job was up for grabs. We haven't had soup for a week.
ABACUS:	Well, I'd quit too if I had the likes of you looking over my shoulder all the time.
HANNAH:	What's the matter, Abacus? You don't like my company? *(Rubs gently.)*
ABACUS:	I've got a Mother, you know.
HANNAH:	Mothers! A dime a dozen around here. No, it's friends you need. *(Pause.)* Wanda was my friend. *(Rubs vigourously.)* Besides, nobody quits nothing around here. Earl hauled her out of here in a crate.
ABACUS:	She's dead?
HANNAH:	I sure hope she was dead 'cause there wasn't much leg room inside that little box.
ABACUS:	You saw it?
	(ABACUS struggles to release cape. HANNAH holds her.)
HANNAH:	Hell, I built it myself! You didn't even need handles, it was so portable. I call it my lap top model. Could have slid it under my arm, right here, and carried it away like a regular businesswoman.
ABACUS:	I don't want to hear this.
HANNAH:	Suit yourself. *(Pause.)* My money's riding on Worm Moon 16. What do you think, girl? A good time for spring thaw?
ABACUS:	I'm not a girl! I haven't been a girl for a long time.

HANNAH: Touchy. Very touchy.

    (Pause. HANNAH releases hold on ABACUS and straightens cape.)

    Woman, then. *(Pause.)*

ABACUS: So who's this Earl guy anyway? Is he a monk?

HANNAH: *(Laughs.)* A monk? Monks don't get their hands dirty. No, they get the Earls of this world to do their shit for them. All *he* gets is enough moonshine to forget the smell. *(Pause.)* What's the matter? Somebody's got to be doing the digging and burying. I mean. Can you see the robes knee high in dirt? They should be calling *him* saint. Yeah, I like that. Saint Earl.

ABACUS: Were they friends?

    (HANNAH massages ABACUS' hair gently. ABACUS relaxes.)

HANNAH: Sure. Wanda made soup. He ate it. She'd spoon it out and Earl would jazz out a chant and the three of us would sit for hours just...anyways. You could have had the job but you opened your big mouth and told them your talents.

ABACUS: What talents? I told them the first thing that came into my head.

HANNAH: So now you get to fish.

ABACUS: I can't fish. I mean, I used to fish when the river flowed. When I was a kid. But it was just for fun. It was never for food!

HANNAH: So now it is. No big deal. You fish your quota, ration it out and we all get to eat for another day.

ABACUS: I like to watch them, not eat them.

HANNAH: *(Laughs.)* Watch the fish! We lose the best soupmaker around and we get a dreamer instead.

ABACUS: There's nothing wrong with having dreams. You still have them, I bet. Even here.

HANNAH: I feed off them down here. But I can't eat them. I can't fill up my belly on them.

ABACUS: I didn't think you'd understand. Anybody who builds boxes wouldn't. Six sides, that's all you know about.

HANNAH: Who said anything about six sides?

ABACUS: There's got to be a lid!

HANNAH: You're saying it can't be a box without a lid? Is that what you're saying?

ABACUS: Yeah, it needs a cover. You know...to keep everything together...inside.

HANNAH: Some dreamer you are! Where's all that imagination, all those big plans. You talk about escaping.

HANNAH: You talk about getting the hell out of here. And then you slam a damn lid on it? You're just like the rest of them around here. Bunch of laylows!

ABACUS: You're talking about the dead, about Wanda.

HANNAH: No, you are. I'm talking about those of us still alive and trying to dig our way out of here. *(Pause.)* And it's no matter about the dead now. They're packed in those peat grounds so tight, nobody's going anywheres. I made sure of that.

ABACUS: Then let's do away with the bottom too. *(Pause.)*

HANNAH: I'm just saying, you really got me thinking now. I mean, about this art of containment.

ABACUS: Leave me out of this.

HANNAH: Hell, I couldn't squeeze you in if I tried. The place is full up. Sorry.

ABACUS: I wasn't asking.

HANNAH: Well plenty do. What do I tell them? *(Pause.)* I wonder just how many sides I can really get away with.

ABACUS: Why not just nail them to a plank and be done with it.

HANNAH: That's what I love about newcomers. Always full of ideas.

ABACUS: You're crazy!

(HANNAH stops shampooing to think.)

HANNAH: Yeah, I told you. Comes with the territory. Yeah. Me and Earl'll have to do some real visioning on this one. In the meantime, remember. You got to catch the fish, not watch them. Rule number one.

ABACUS: There's more?

HANNAH: There's a new rule every time you flick your butt in a new direction. Rules for washing, rules for levies, rules for the church and standing and sitting and rules for facing and cleansing, breathing and dying. Hallelujah!

ABACUS: So I should fish. Is that what you're saying?

HANNAH: You're a smart girl. A pretty one, too.

(Caresses ABACUS's face. ABACUS is uncomfortable. She points at HANNAH's sores. Pause.)

ABACUS: So, do the sores hurt?

HANNAH: No, they're environmentally friendly.

ABACUS: Nothing's friendly here.

HANNAH: We're friends. Earl could be your friend.

ABACUS: So who says I want him. *(Pause.)* I asked you if they hurt?

HANNAH: Only when I pull them off. Wanna see?

ABACUS: I'm tired. It's been a long day.

HANNAH: You ask stupid questions you know. Of course they hurt!

ABACUS: I needed to know. OK?

HANNAH: Is the grass green?

ABACUS: Where do I sleep?

HANNAH: Does anybody really sleep? That's the question. Is the sky still blue? Does water still freeze? Well, does it?

(ABACUS ignores her and drags her duffel bag over to a cot.)

The question is, how fast do people?

(HANNAH presses her body against ABACUS.)

Or do we all of us just lose feeling?

(HANNAH laughs and walks away from ABACUS.)

ABACUS: How much time do you figure?

HANNAH: I don't figure. *(She twirls around.)* It's not my job, remember? I just do what I do when I do it.

ABACUS: Well, do people go quickly? Did Wanda?

(HANNAH starts to pace and rub powder into her own scalp, frenzied. ABACUS grabs her hands and stops her.)

HANNAH: Now *she* knows sleep!

ABACUS: You must have thought about it. When you build the boxes?

HANNAH: I'm a master crafter. That's me. I can build them with my eyes closed. I don't even look inside anymore.

ABACUS: You looked at the Soupmaker, didn't you.

HANNAH: No! I just pushed at her until she fit. Until all her parts were inside. She didn't feel a damn thing. *(Pause.)* They don't give me a lot of wood, you know. I make do. We all have to make do out here.

(Lights up on BONIFACE at back of stage facing fence, her back to audience. Stands on a wooden box making hand gestures and turning from side to side. Appears to be talking.)

ABACUS: Do you think about your own box?

HANNAH: No!

ABACUS: What will it look like? What kind of wood will you use?

HANNAH: There's only Jesus planks. Nothing else.

ABACUS: Planks of what? Will it have leg room? An inscription? Will it tell who you really are?

HANNAH: I don't plan on building me a box for one thing.

ABACUS: Yours will have a lid, though, won't it?

HANNAH: Earl's my friend. There won't be a box if I tell him. No damn box and no damn peat. See, no problem. I'll tell him I want...sand. Yeah, that's it. I want a sandy beach instead.

ABACUS: And where's he going to find one of those?

HANNAH: I'll leave that to him. He's in charge of navigation.

ABACUS: He's got a map?

HANNAH: Damned right! Right here.

(HANNAH points to head. BONIFACE points to her head as well. Then she steps down from box and lifts a bushel basket up onto her hip and walks towards ABACUS and HANNAH.)

	And there's a beach. There's one…by the coast. *(Pause.)*
ABACUS:	There's nothing left by the coast anymore.
HANNAH:	Hearsay. It's just hidden, that's all. Where the water's blue.
ABACUS:	When I was growing up, the water was already green.

(BONIFACE stops, lowers basket to ground.)

HANNAH:	I hate green.

(HANNAH rubs at her fluorescent coveralls. BONIFACE starts taking big breaths.)

It makes me puke.

BONIFACE:	And don't you 'Mother' me. Nothing's healthy out here. A woman needs to keep her space. That's all I'm saying.

(Lights off BONIFACE.)

HANNAH:	No. Blue water. White sand. That's the picture I'm getting. You like it?
ABACUS:	Sure, I liked the beach.
HANNAH:	And I'll tell Earl we want straw hats too 'cause the sun's going to be blazing all the time.
ABACUS:	Sounds fancy to me.
HANNAH:	We can be gals again. It'll be our gig. A gal gig.
ABACUS:	OK. Then make mine a sombrero. The bigger, the better. I have delicate skin, you know. And plenty of cigarillos! Those skinny, wine-soaked ones the tourists all smoke.
HANNAH:	No!

(HANNAH starts to breathe heavily, alternately with BONIFACE. Their breathing forms a frantic rhythm.)

ABACUS:	And music. We'll need music too. I've got this chapter blaster that really belts out a number. Speakers this big and it doesn't weigh more than a hand.

(ABACUS reaches out for HANNAH's hand. BONIFACE stops her heavy breathing suddenly.)

When do we leave?

(BONIFACE turns suddenly towards ABACUS.)

BONIFACE:	Wanda?

(HANNAH hyperventilates.)

ABACUS:	You have to let me come, Hannah!

(BONIFACE wipes her eyes, picks up basket and makes her way towards the two women.)

HANNAH:	Stinking, foul smoke. We still got peat fires burning since freeze up. Nobody could keep them down. Everybody thought it was my job.
ABACUS:	OK, Hannah. Slow down.

(ABACUS sets HANNAH down in the lawn chair. ABACUS starts

340 / A Map of the Senses

to massage HANNAH's shoulders.)

HANNAH: But they just keep burning under the snow. You can't see a thing. *(She closes her eyes.)* But your eyes scorch and your lungs gag for air.

ABACUS: Take a breath. Think of the coast. Just sun and sombreros and sand and blue water. We might even be lucky and see a reflection. *(Still massaging.)* And maybe some fish for me to watch.

(HANNAH jumps up from chair.)

HANNAH: Yeah, you'll fish alright. And you'll learn to fillet fast and eat anything you haul out of that fish hole. No matter what size. No matter what shape or colour. Or age. You'll clean them if they're soft and full of maggots and you'll eat them if they're hard and tough as knots. You'll eat them and then you'll keep your bloody mouth shut. You don't talk to nobody about this.

ABACUS: I won't. *(She sits.)*

(HANNAH pulls a brush from a nearby bushel basket. Stoops to smell ABACUS' hair. Starts to brush ABACUS' hair.)

HANNAH: You're right. There is no coast. There's nothing. And Earl is a figment of my imagination, you hear?

ABACUS: Whatever you say, Hannah.

HANNAH: Just stick to the rules. That fish hole is your life.

ABACUS: Then what?

HANNAH: *(Handing the brush to ABACUS.)* One hundred and one strokes. *(Pause.)* We'll get back to you. We're betting on you, Earl and me.

(Pushes ABACUS' head down between her legs.)

Now bend over. Let's get this done before I puke.

(ABACUS starts to brush. HANNAH exits to stage left where we see her "visioning" about the planks and construction of boxes.

Next day. BONIFACE enters and sets down her basket. BONIFACE removes packages of dried foods from basket. ABACUS looks up from brushing.)

ABACUS: So what'd we get today?

BONIFACE: You always bother asking. Why do you do that?

ABACUS: Hannah says mangoes.

BONIFACE: And only an idiot would say mangoes.

ABACUS: Tomatoes? Lentils, then?

BONIFACE: You've been here long enough.

ABACUS: Somebody might. You never know. *(She takes bread from the bushel.)* How about stale bread? And how can I forget the beets?

	(Holds them up.) I'm still trying to get the stain off my hands from last time. *(Shows stains.)*
BONIFACE:	You'll get used to it. It could be worse.
ABACUS:	And how do you see that?
BONIFACE:	We could be eating eggplant! I hate eggplant!

(ABACUS looks through basket. BONIFACE starts to assemble pieces of cloth on the floor.)

ABACUS:	*(Throws a beet.)* You make me sick with your taking of everything they dish out.
BONIFACE:	That's right. Because anything they give is better than the nothing we could be getting.
ABACUS:	*(Holds up stale bread.)* This is what they think of you! And what does eggplant have to do with my life? I don't even know what day it is anymore.
BONIFACE:	It doesn't matter. All you have to worry about is keeping yourself busy.
ABACUS:	Then everything's under control. Just like you.
BONIFACE:	I just like to know what's going on, that's all. What I'll be doing. I need to know that when I go out to that fence again today that there'll be people waiting to ask me everything they can about this place.

(ABACUS notices pieces of cloth.)

ABACUS:	What's all this crap? What are you up to?

(BONIFACE continues to pin pieces together. ABACUS grabs BONIFACE's wrists.)

What the hell are you up, Boniface?

BONIFACE:	Piece it together yourself. You're so smart.
ABACUS:	You're the seamstress!
BONIFACE:	Yes. With all the emphasis on *stress.* Are *all* daughters like you?
ABACUS:	Look, the joke's over.
BONIFACE:	So you're not the perfect daughter. We have lots of…
ABACUS:	Rules? *(Pause.)* The rules say Monday you cut sleeves. Tuesday, fronts. Backs on Wednesday. Backs! The calendar's right there. Wednesday you cut out bloody backs. Look at it! *(Pause. BONIFACE looks at her.)*
BONIFACE:	I don't need to look at it. You don't think that calendar is etched into my brain? Every day of the week. Every hour of every day?
ABACUS:	Well, give the woman a beet. Remember, control, Mother.
BONIFACE:	I know when the sun's the highest, when the shadows are the shortest and when the next moon will appear. I can even count on you nagging me without fail.
ABACUS:	Those are not backs.

BONIFACE: The schedule's been change. Pockets are now on Wednesdays.

ABACUS: Pockets aren't allowed!

BONIFACE: Just because we share this skid doesn't mean I tell you everything that runs through my head.

ABACUS: And when did the Waste Board put you in charge?

BONIFACE: You look. I'm the designated Mother around here. I get to ask the questions. Not you.

ABACUS: Designated to what? Getting us both thrown out of here? Do you know how long we'd last upland? You don't go looking for trouble.

BONIFACE: I don't have to go anywhere. I got you.

(ABACUS *ignores her.*)

There are still good people around. They don't care what I cut on Wednesday.

ABACUS: That's right. They don't give a damn about you or this place.

BONIFACE: It's just hard for them to show it.

ABACUS: They come to gawk!

BONIFACE: They're trying to make sense of all this too.

ABACUS: They come to see how many more sores you have this week than you did last week. You think you're the only one counting? It makes them feel better. It has nothing to do with you or me anymore.

BONIFACE: Those people are family. They're friends.

ABACUS: Don't start with that family and friends crap again. I'm sick of hearing how much I'm still loved and wanted. I don't see anybody with open arms.

BONIFACE: Give them a chance. Tour days like this keep us talking. Help them understand us.

ABACUS: OK, then ask them for an exchange. I'm ready anytime. (*Grabs rattle at her waist.*) Maybe if I held my rattle real tight, I might get as far as the Heights before they caught up with me.

And you, Mother. They'd have you pitted front down, body flexed and facing east before you could say *grave goods*. You wouldn't make it to the Buffer Zone. (*Pause.*) The Buffer. Has this soft, deadening ring to it, doesn't it? Kind of like wet mittens. Or sand on the streets. Your legs wouldn't even carry you off this river, let alone upland. The idea is to have a plan if you want to be a fugitive.

BONIFACE: But, I'm not going anywhere. We can't all run. Somebody has to make a stand.

ABACUS: You're not going to be standing anywhere come Worm Moon. You're going to be flushed down this toilet of a river!

BONIFACE: You newcomers. Always talking about plans.

ABACUS: You're damned right! When I go, I'm going to be ready.

BONIFACE: Always planning what you're going to be doing when you're better. Planning where you're going to live when you get out of here. Forget the past. You don't live in that country anymore. You live in quarantine! Make the best of it.

ABACUS: Well I want more.

BONIFACE: You want to know my plan? It's Wednesday. This is the day I make pockets and talk some sense into those tourists up there.

ABACUS: Pockets. Who would have thought the master plan could be so simple.

BONIFACE: One day at a time. That's all. Tomorrow's Thursday. Cuffs and collar day. Simple.

ABACUS: They wouldn't even know what to do with pockets.

BONIFACE: It hasn't been that long. We could show them. We could do it together. Just you and me. I want every woman on this river to have a pocket.

ABACUS: So what's to save! Soup bones? Would a pocket have saved Wanda?

BONIFACE: You leave Wanda out of this!

ABACUS: Maybe I could fill mine with fish spines. *(Pause.)* Ice?

BONIFACE: We could make it fun. Like a game. We could make it anything we want.

ABACUS: We have baskets.

BONIFACE: You need arms and hands to carry them. That's all. You see, Abacus, it's already too complicated.

ABACUS: At least you get to live.

BONIFACE: And that's how you want to live?

ABACUS: Yes, until I know what's going on. Rule #12. Bare hands must be seen and cupped in front at all times. With pockets, you're dead before you hit the floorboards.

BONIFACE: No. Just numbed to all of this until they have a change of heart.

ABACUS: Dead. One way or another.

BONIFACE: We're all in this mess together. We can't keep putting up fences and ice and rivers between us thinking that that's going to keep everybody's neighbourhood safe. Keep your lesions there and mine here. My skin here, theirs someplace else.

ABACUS: We're dropping like fish flies. Nothing's going to stop that.

BONIFACE: Maybe not today or tomorrow. But it'll come soon.

ABACUS: In what year? 'Cause I don't have time to wait it out.

BONIFACE: We just have to stick together. Things are going to change. They always do.

ABACUS: Yeah, I used to be able to drink the water. I used to be able to touch the dirt with my bare hands. Skin used to hold to my bones.

BONIFACE:	You know what I mean. Why are you making this so difficult? Changes for the better always take more…
ABACUS:	More what? Time? Or do you mean more stale bread? More fences? More fish huts? Or maybe thinner ice would solve everything.
BONIFACE:	I can't tell you how to fish.
ABACUS:	Oh, is that what they're called.
BONIFACE:	Remember the greenbacks? Now *they* were fish. They'd cruise by your hook, so sleek and bossy like. Like they had a better appointment somewhere else. Just back and forth they'd go. And you'd wait.
ABACUS:	I knew they'd grab!
BONIFACE:	You were both so patient.
ABACUS:	No fish is going to get the better of me!
BONIFACE:	You'd wait each other out. Then when his curiosity got the better of him, he'd go for it. And still you let him think he'd gotten away with something.
ABACUS:	Then, just when he'd pulled out enough to hang himself, I'd snap it hard. That's when the fun would really start.
BONIFACE:	It'll be fun again, Abacus. I know it. *(Pause.)*
ABACUS:	Earl says that upriver…
BONIFACE:	Oh. So, we're back to Earl again. That's all I hear. So you saw him this time?
ABACUS:	Hannah says.
BONIFACE:	Oh, well, then, if Hannah says, then it must be so.
ABACUS:	Earl says that upriver, maybe five klicks, between the locks and the mouth of the river, goldeye are jumping out of fish holes. Just jumping out of their fish holes onto their backs.
BONIFACE:	That should make your job easier.
ABACUS:	Don't you see?
BONIFACE:	Yes! I do.
ABACUS:	Time's running out. Even the fish know it.
BONIFACE:	What is it about you? You trust a man you've never seen. I've never seen. But you don't trust your own family?
ABACUS:	Family? What the hell's that? The family's gone in case you haven't noticed.
	(BONIFACE approaches ABACUS.)
BONIFACE:	No! I'm here. I'm standing right in front of you.
ABACUS:	Don't come any closer.
BONIFACE:	Why can't you touch me, Abacus? *This* is flesh and blood. This is your family.
ABACUS:	No! Family's just a leftover in the dictionary alongside fish huts

and fumigate. It used to mean something. *(ABACUS points to river ice and fish below.)* And the only things left down there are bottom feeders. Nothing more than mouth. I hate fish. I hate everything about them. The slime. Their fins. Scales all over the floorboards.

BONIFACE: You take away those fish and you're nothing. That's who you are. You're the fisherwoman. Remember that.

ABACUS: Woman? That's a laugh. They've even managed to take that away from us. It's bad enough they have to look at these wrecks of bodies, they don't want us bleeding as well.

BONIFACE: They can never take that away from us.

ABACUS: Yeah, well I stopped counting moons and cycles long ago.

BONIFACE: So what are you counting now?

ABACUS: I'm counting nothing.

BONIFACE: Every last woman in this place is counting something.

ABACUS: There's nothing! Look around.

BONIFACE: Come on. Think of something dammit.

ABACUS: Like what? Scars? Scabs?

BONIFACE: If need be.

ABACUS: Head lice? Cracks in the ice?

BONIFACE: Anything!

ABACUS: Then what about all the bodies carried off this river in boxes so small, you wonder how that could be.

BONIFACE: Count the living, girl. You're alive. It doesn't matter what you look like or how much of you is left. You're still a fine, young woman. Be thankful for that. Be thankful for small things. But most important now. You're the fisher. You stick to your fish. Keep the goldeye and the greenbacks and any other memory in this pocket. *(She points to her head.)* And let me worry about everything else. *(BONIFACE pulls overalls from bushel basket.)* Here. Put these on. *(Holds up orange fluorescent overalls.)*

ABACUS: There's no way. *(Throws them back. She adjusts dried fish hanging at back of skid.)* They're ugly. How can you sew those things? I'd go blind. *(Laughs.)* I'll scare the fish away.

BONIFACE: All you need to worry about is staying warm.

ABACUS: So who says I'm cold?

BONIFACE: Then freeze your ass off if that's what you want 'cause if the wind-chill doesn't get you, the affliction will.

ABACUS: I don't wear orange. Doesn't go with my complexion.

BONIFACE: Fine. But in a couple weeks, you'll have a complexion and a half and we can all stand around and watch it peel away.

ABACUS: I want green.

(Pause.)

BONIFACE:	You can't have green.
ABACUS:	Hannah's got green.
BONIFACE:	And she deserves it.

(Pause. ABACUS approaches BONIFACE.)

They warned her.

ABACUS:	Hannah's been outside? When?
HANNAH:	You can't really call one day out a vacation.
ABACUS:	How? How far did she get? Did she make it past the Buffer?
BONIFACE:	She's wearing green! That should tell you right there how far she got. She's got no chances left!
ABACUS:	I've heard if you make it as far as the Exchange, you're pretty well home free.
BONIFACE:	You just don't get it, do you? This is home! This is it! And out there are just a lot of scared people. You got a bed. You got a roof and a job. And, like it or not, you got me. This is as good as it gets if you just do what you're told. *(Pause. BONIFACE walks over again with overalls for ABACUS.)*
BONIFACE:	Do you want help?

(ABACUS takes overalls.)

ABACUS:	What's your real name?

(BONIFACE turns away.)

BONIFACE:	Weren't you studying to be smart? I mean, you look the part.
ABACUS:	I want you to call me by my other name.
BONIFACE:	No, I don't want to know it!
ABACUS:	It's Liddy. Short for Lydia.
BONIFACE:	No, it's short for stupid. I said I don't care.
ABACUS:	They didn't have to change our names.
BONIFACE:	But they have. It's done with.
ABACUS:	Somebody has to know who I am? Where I came from? I don't belong here. I'm not sick. I don't know how to fish! What am I supposed to do! What do I do first!

(BONIFACE stops ABACUS.)

BONIFACE:	You relax. Breathe in. That's first. Good. Then we warm you up. *(Helping ABACUS into overalls.)* Stop worrying. You'll get along. Everybody gets along. I'm here to help. OK?
ABACUS:	And I suppose yellow's for 40-year-olds who sew ugly clothes and always stand on the leeward?
BONIFACE:	That's something Wanda would've said.

(BONIFACE zips up overalls and hugs ABACUS around shoulders briefly.)

You're right. About the leeward side. The hideous part is still in dispute.

ABACUS: Tell me about her.

BONIFACE: I don't have that much time.

ABACUS: Anything.

             (Pause.)

BONIFACE: Yellow's for designated Mothers.

ABACUS: No, it's not! You just made that up.

BONIFACE: It's the one rule I can live with.

ABACUS: Yeah, just one, happy family. That's us.

BONIFACE: It's a beginning. We can work from there.

ABACUS: Well, don't do me any favours because you wouldn't even know where to start.

BONIFACE: I thought we already had.

ABACUS: With pockets? Yeah, right, Mother. You really know how to start a revolution.

BONIFACE: You just tell that box-building, grave-smoothing, scalp-smelling friend of yours to stay away until she's due. Tell her I'm watching. I'm always watching.

             (Look at each other. Freeze.)

             (Next scene. Same positions. ABACUS is looking at some of the books given to BONIFACE as donations.)

ABACUS: Yeah, maybe you'll luck out soon and they'll make you Wisewoman, you're so smart. Hey, you wouldn't have to sew anymore.

             (BONIFACE takes book. Places it into her basket.)

BONIFACE: I'll take that as a compliment.

ABACUS: I mean, look at these books. *Harvesting the Northern Wilds?*

             (Starts to rummage quickly through basket and then stops.)

BONIFACE: Yes. I can make vitamins or tea…even convolutions from a single cattail. How about that? *(She looks at ABACUS.)* What kinds of things do the others get?

ABACUS: I don't know. Frisbees? *(She laughs.)* Maybe foot massagers. Plasticene?

BONIFACE: They never say?

ABACUS: They don't tell me. Have you read all this stuff?

BONIFACE: Every page I can get my hands on. And what do you say?

ABACUS: About what? Books? My life as a whole?

             (Pause.)

BONIFACE: My pockets. The rest of my pockets are gone.

ABACUS: How the hell am I supposed to know where they are?

BONIFACE:	They were right here in my basket.
ABACUS:	Maybe they fell down a fish hole or something. I don't know. Maybe when you were cleaning up.
BONIFACE:	You're saying it was an accident?
ABACUS:	I'm saying I don't know anything about it.
	(Pause.)
BONIFACE:	Then Hannah took them.
ABACUS:	Hannah? How can you just say, Hannah took them? Maybe it's your counting.
BONIFACE:	That I didn't have as much as I thought? You're kidding, right?
ABACUS:	You can't just accuse people.
BONIFACE:	She was just here.
ABACUS:	She's always here.
BONIFACE:	Exactly. What was she doing dropping off wood? That's not her job.
ABACUS:	She works hard.
BONIFACE:	At what? She's been nosing around again.
ABACUS:	What would she want with your old pockets?
BONIFACE:	You tell me. I want to hear it from you.
ABACUS:	Maybe you sewed them all on. Probably every woman on this river is walking around with a pocket today and you can't even remember doing it.
	(Lights up on HANNAH who can be seen sewing squares of cloth together by hand. She sits outside by her planks and box. ABACUS now starts to talk to both women simultaneously in this scene.)
HANNAH:	You know she preaches there in the same spot every day. Her and her little wooden box. If they asked her to jump through friggin' hoops she would.
ABACUS:	Maybe we have to tell her. Ask her to come with us.
HANNAH:	And leave her job. She loves being Tour Guide! She gets to cry her heart out every day.
BONIFACE:	You know what those pockets mean to me. I'd remember sewing them on.
ABACUS:	*(To HANNAH.)* There'll be more.
HANNAH:	There better be.
BONIFACE:	There has to be.
ABACUS:	*(To BONIFACE.)* It was only a matter of time. You think the Waste Board wasn't onto you and your pockets.
HANNAH:	We'll never be ready if you keep this up.
ABACUS:	*(To HANNAH.)* You'll get them. It's just got to be gradual.
HANNAH:	The river's not going to be breaking gradual, is it? It's sure as hell

	not going to wait for the likes of you! When it goes, I go. You understand?
ABACUS:	*(To HANNAH.)* It's just too risky.
BONIFACE:	For who? You and Hannah?
ABACUS:	All of us. You still have your overalls.
BONIFACE:	The overalls. I almost forgot. Hideous, isn't that what you called them.
ABACUS:	That wasn't my word.
BONIFACE:	Well, they are. I know they're outrageous. I feel like the Amazon Queen on some pinball machine who lights up every time she's struck.
HANNAH:	You're getting scared!
ABACUS:	I'm not.
HANNAH:	Then you're getting sweet on her.
ABACUS:	I hate her!
BONIFACE:	You know, I always wanted to embroider. All these different designs, fancy threads.
HANNAH:	Admit it, Liddy. You're getting used to having her around.
BONIFACE:	All designer originals.
ABACUS:	I'm just trying to cover all the bases, that's all. *(ABACUS looks towards HANNAH.)*
HANNAH:	And I'm not working on the Motherhood angle. I'm working on getting us out of here. What are you doing?
BONIFACE:	I miss the faces…the rhythmic flare of nostrils on a laughing face. Those small creases that used to dance at the corner of mouths. I want them back. *(BONIFACE touches and holds ABACUS' face.)*
HANNAH:	Pronto! Do you hear? Pronto!
ABACUS:	*(To HANNAH and BONIFACE.)* Don't treat me like a kid!
	(Lights start to fade on HANNAH.)
HANNAH:	Then stop looking for a Mother.
	(ABACUS pushes BONIFACE's hands away.)
BONIFACE:	Why do I have to make the last clothes they'll wear?
ABACUS:	Who else can do the job? You're the seamstress.
BONIFACE:	It's strange; all I wanted was for you to like me. I thought we could be family. I think we got close a few times. But family or not, no one is going to stop me from making those pockets. Not Hannah, not you.
ABACUS:	I'll tell you what's strange. Not Hannah and not even you and your damn pockets. But walking on fish. All that separates you and me from the moving mouths down there is this half-meter slab of ice. And that scares me to death.
BONIFACE:	You think I'm not scared?

ABACUS: Even there on the bank, I can feel the gills moving under my feet. You must have felt it.

BONIFACE: Of course, I can feel it.

ABACUS: Those floorboards are going to be floating. Soon you'll be standing on your mattress trying to keep dry. A lot of good your pockets will be to you when you get yanked into this river.

BONIFACE: You took them! It wasn't Hannah at all.

ABACUS: Yes! And I'm not waiting around to fill them up with fish either!

BONIFACE: You had no right. You could have at least asked. I'm still your designated Mother, if nothing else.

ABACUS: I needed a friend!

BONIFACE: You never gave me a chance. You spent more time huddled over those fish holes with that Headwasher than you ever did around here.

ABACUS: Her name is Hannah! It's important that you call her by her name!

BONIFACE: You can't trust her! She'd skim ice from your fish holes in the morning and be spreading peat over your bones later the same day. She wouldn't give it a second thought.

ABACUS: There's no time for second thoughts. This river is just going to give one, big burp. And you, the beds, your pockets...everything is going to be floating down river. You're going to be fighting the fishes for air. Oh, it'll be Worm Moon for the rest of the world, alright. They'll all be here. Still on their side of the fence, rubbing shoulders with the worms for a spot along the riverbank to watch the breakup.

(Pause.)

BONIFACE: I suppose *she* calls you Liddy.

ABACUS: You never did.

(Pause.)

BONIFACE: So what do you two talk about?

ABACUS: We talk about the water. *(Very quietly.)* Hannah says the water's black.

BONIFACE: But what do you say?

ABACUS: I say, they wouldn't put us on a healthy piece of river, that's for sure.

BONIFACE: And besides the water and fish stories? They must all be told by now. *(She shrugs.)*

ABACUS: *(Pause.)* We talk about the boat.

BONIFACE: So it's a boat this time. The woman wears green! She's had her three strikes and there's no such thing as honour out here.

ABACUS: You asked me and I told you. Do you want to be my Mother or not?

BONIFACE:	You've seen this boat?
ABACUS:	Earl's hiding it...
BONIFACE:	Earl!
ABACUS:	...in the peat grounds where the four parishes meet. It's supposed to be good luck.
BONIFACE:	Luck? Not if Hannah's in charge.
ABACUS:	We're sailing the first wind out of here.
BONIFACE:	Well, then, there you go. I can see my pockets slapping the wind already.
ABACUS:	We had no choice.
BONIFACE:	And neither do you, 'cause Hannah and her imagination are going to have to sail it alone.
ABACUS:	You don't believe me.
BONIFACE:	You said it yourself. You wouldn't last a day out there. And even less with Hannah. They'd have you tracked in no time. What kind of a friend would I be sending you out there? What kind of Mother?
ABACUS:	I didn't ask for help.
BONIFACE:	No, you never did. You just stole it.
ABACUS:	OK... Then I'm asking now.
BONIFACE:	You already have my pockets. What more do you want?
ABACUS:	I want you to come with me.

(Lights out. End of Act One.)

Act Two

(ABACUS sits on box sewing the cloth pieces together. HANNAH is examining the rest of the sail which is hanging at this point.)

HANNAH: No, it's Earl's counting on you, Liddy.

ABACUS: Earl, Earl. That's all I get from you. I need to meet him. I need to see his work.

HANNAH: Everything's A-OK.

ABACUS: I need to see the boat.

HANNAH: Kind of late to be thinking about that now, isn't it?

ABACUS: Is he a carpenter?

HANNAH: You've been talking to your Mother again, haven't you? She's the one getting you all spooked like this.

ABACUS: He *is* a carpenter, right? Is that what he did before?

HANNAH: There is no before. Only *after* this hell hole.

ABACUS: I mean before he was brought here.

HANNAH: He helps out around the place.

ABACUS: Meaning? He comes when he wants?

HANNAH: He volunteered.

ABACUS: Who in their right mind would volunteer?

HANNAH: I told you Earl was a figment of my imagination, didn't I?

ABACUS: Boniface says there is no Earl.

HANNAH: You got a mind of your own. Do you or don't you? *(Pause.)* Then start using it 'cause we're not going to be needing half-wits on board.

ABACUS: Where's he come from?

(ABACUS scurries around on her hands and knees grabbing up all the pockets. She holds them away from HANNAH.)

HANNAH: You need to be treading lightly on peat. Do you know that, Abacus? *(Pause.)* OK. *(She gets up.)* So he comes from the Pit. So what? Who else do you see taking any risks around here.

ABACUS: The pit? He's monatti!

HANNAH: Ankle bells and all!

ABACUS:	What's he in for? No, no. Forget it! I don't want to know.
HANNAH:	What's the matter? You run out of stupid questions?
ABACUS:	It doesn't matter. Convict, headwasher, fisher, gravedigger. It doesn't matter anymore.
HANNAH:	Right! It doesn't matter. It's all the same boat, Liddy.
ABACUS:	You're right. What's the big difference? Carpenter, backstabber.
HANNAH:	Well, he *does* like to be called a builder.
ABACUS:	I can see why. Jailbird just doesn't have the same ring to it.
HANNAH:	I mean, he doesn't think of himself as a carpenter. He says there's an ocean of difference. It's a matter of options, he says. Extremes.
ABACUS:	Extremes?
HANNAH:	Says it's a measure of sufficiencies.
ABACUS:	Yeah, well, I've had enough too. I want to see the boat.
HANNAH:	Just picture it! You, trimming the sail. Me at the tiller…
ABACUS:	Who made you captain? I'm the one who knows the bloody river. I'm the fisherwoman. I know the currents. The pattern of the fish. The movement of the river.
HANNAH:	You're just a kid.
ABACUS:	But I'm stronger. It just makes sense.
HANNAH:	A captain needs to know her boat.
ABACUS:	Then Earl. Who better?
HANNAH:	Well, then, Earl's already promised me, you see. Says I'd make a damn fine captain.
ABACUS:	But these are my pockets.
	(HANNAH looks at her.)
	My contribution. A captain has to know her sails…what it takes to get the most out of the wind. I can do that!
HANNAH:	And it was my smarts got us all these extra planks. I had the vision first. I still got it. Liddy. *(Pause.)* I'll make you first mate.
ABACUS:	No! No way. You're not going to cut me out now. I've been with you on this from the start.
HANNAH:	The hell you have! It's always been just me and Earl. And you, girl, arrived just in time to lean yourself up against the lifelines.
ABACUS:	Lifelines? This boat's getting bigger every time I talk to you. We don't need lifelines. We don't have time. Next thing you'll be talking about a cabin and a deck and a four kilo anchor.
HANNAH:	So Earl changed his mind. He's apt to do that with the load he carries. Who am I to argue? Remember, he's got the map? I do what I'm told, like you do. Get it?
	(ABACUS allows HANNAH to take back the rest of the pockets. HANNAH sees BONIFACE. Lights up on other side of stage. BONIFACE is in peat grounds on her hands and knees, chanting and

354 /A Map of the Senses

holding the mandible of a bear and jabbing the jawbone into the darkness.)

And there's the problem with working with fluorescence too long.

(ABACUS starts for other side of the stage. Two settings become one as they talk.)

I'm afraid she's lost it for good this time.

ABACUS: *(To BONIFACE.)* And you complain about my little fish spines? What are you doing?

BONIFACE: The timing couldn't have been better. Thank you, Hannah. I knew you'd keep your word.

ABACUS: What word? *(Looks to HANNAH.)*

HANNAH: She hasn't been herself since the Soupmaker.

BONIFACE: No, this is the spot. I can feel it alright. Light. Dry. Slip-through-your-fingers kind of peat.

ABACUS: This isn't a spot.

BONIFACE: Hannah's been saving it.

ABACUS: You said there were no spots.

HANNAH: She's lying. Just like she's lying about being your Mother. Being Wanda's mother. She was never designated. She designates herself.

BONIFACE: No, no mistake. I got my planks today. That only means one thing.

HANNAH: The hell you did! *(She throws the pieces down and approaches ABACUS and BONIFACE.)*

ABACUS: You said, no more burials, no more grave goods protecting us from unwanted demons, no flowers, no kind words. Those were your words, Hannah.

HANNAH: The place is jam-packed. You're lying. You got no planks!

ABACUS: But you're in charge.

HANNAH: You're damn right. Who else would do my job?

ABACUS: Boniface, there's no spot. That's why we're leaving.

HANNAH: There's no way anybody else would be laying out my planks. No way!

BONIFACE: Not laying. Standing. I'm to be buried standing by the looks of it.

HANNAH: I don't just throw these boxes into the ground like 52 pick-up. There's a pattern here, you know.

BONIFACE: It doesn't matter to me. One way or other. As long as I'm in.

HANNAH: No! Nobody gets buried standing if I have anything to say about it.

BONIFACE: I hope you didn't get re-assigned.

ABACUS: That would explain it. There's been a mix-up.

HANNAH: Nobody else is taking this job!

BONIFACE: Feet down. My head'll be pointing to heaven. I'll be half-way there. I can't think of a better way to go.

HANNAH: There's no way I'd waste five planks.

BONIFACE: You mean, on me?

(She starts to arrange grave goods on the peat.)

HANNAH: Nobody just jumps themselves into these spots.

BONIFACE: How many exactly, Hannah?

HANNAH: That's your problem, old lady. You always have to be counting something. Counting on some miracle to put this hellhole into some kind of order. Feet down, heads up like human time bombs. Would that do it for you? Would that make sense of it all for you?

BONIFACE: You're on your honour. You know what that means.

HANNAH: It means I don't sit back and waste nothing.

ABACUS: It'll be different this time. Everything's planned to the last detail.

HANNAH: No! She wants to wait around for a miracle. I'll give her one. There it is. *(She points to peat.)* Number 17. I'll slip you in personally.

ABACUS: No, Hannah.

HANNAH: Take it or leave it.

ABACUS: There's nothing here!

BONIFACE: I knew there were spots. I knew I'd have one.

ABACUS: She doesn't want it, Hannah. She's coming with us.

HANNAH: She wants it. Don't you want it, old girl?

ABACUS: Don't do this!

(BONIFACE is silent.)

HANNAH: Maybe you just want to get yourself pickled instead.

ABACUS: Stop it.

HANNAH: Start a new fad, here. I'd be more than happy to oblige you since you're so bent on staying.

ABACUS: You're talking stupid.

HANNAH: No, I'm talking big. This big jar of brine. I could set you down in the southwest corner of the common room. Tourists could come by and see what a martyr you are.

BONIFACE: That's what you think I'm trying to be? A martyr?

HANNAH: That's what the plaque will say. Here lies pickled a rare human specimen.

BONIFACE: No, Hannah, that was my Wanda. She's the one who trusted you.

HANNAH: Is this the place where I start apologizing?

BONIFACE: No, not to me you don't. I learn by my mistakes. And Wanda...well, she didn't even feel the voltage that hit her. Thank God.

HANNAH: You're still thanking God for all of this? This is His doing?

BONIFACE: I thank God she went as quickly as she did. That I didn't have to stand and hear her fry on that fence a second longer.

ABACUS: She was electrocuted?

HANNAH: It wasn't my fault, Liddy.

BONIFACE: We needed you to be there.

HANNAH: I was there.

BONIFACE: Just like Earl was there? You see, Abacus, you can't count on either of them.

(Pause.)

HANNAH: Yeah, this big jar of brine. It's perfect. You'd make a great performance piece. Toxin art.

BONIFACE: And what about Abacus? What are you doing with her?

HANNAH: Do you want this ground or don't you? I got plenty of callers, you know.

BONIFACE: What plans do you have for her?

ABACUS: I can make my own plans.

HANNAH: Liddy and I are together on this.

BONIFACE: Together in what? Some half-baked escape by boat? Some wild rescue by the ever invisible Earl? And don't forget my patchwork of sails that will lie dead to the wind just when you need them.

ABACUS: Where's Earl, Hannah?

HANNAH: Earl?

ABACUS: Yeah, remember, Earl, the convict-cum-builder?

(HANNAH runs to the sail. ABACUS follows.)

HANNAH: Well, while, you're at the bow hanking on the sheets, Earl'll be plotting our course to freedom.

ABACUS: I mean now! Where's Earl now?

(HANNAH rolls her body along the length of the sail, up one side and down the other.)

HANNAH: And just as he lays out the charts, this gust of wind grabs hold of us.

(HANNAH grabs ABACUS through the sail and holds her as she spins her around, enveloping her within the sail.)

ABACUS: Stop! Stop it. Let me out.

HANNAH: Too late! 'cause the ginny fills with wind and we pass under the shadows of the trees.

ABACUS: Hannah, I'm getting sick.

(HANNAH starts to pull and push ABACUS back and forth, still inside the sail. ABACUS hollers.)

HANNAH: Sea sick? Not a good sign.

ABACUS: Stop it!

HANNAH: *Be ready to tack! Load 'er up!* I get to yell 'cause I'm the captain.

              (ABACUS struggles to free herself from the sail. They fall and wrestle in the sail.)

ABACUS: Never. You'll never be captain.

HANNAH: Decided! It's damn well decided.

ABACUS: No! Not 'til I see Earl.

HANNAH: And then the boat swerves to the right just in time and we're heading for open waters.

              (ABACUS frees herself from sail. Throws it at HANNAH.)

ABACUS: Hannah, I want to see that boat.

HANNAH: I want. I want. You're starting to sound just like *her*. *(Pause.)* Does she have you calling her Mom yet?

ABACUS: Hannah! Don't do this!

              (HANNAH moves to peat and BONIFACE.)

HANNAH: I think you had better get down on your hands and knees again. Listen to the peat real good this time.

BONIFACE: Now the *peat* is talking to you, Hannah?

ABACUS: Stop it! Both of you!

HANNAH: It's alive, you know.

BONIFACE: First Earl, now the peat. What next? The boat? The sail?

HANNAH: Alive as you and me.

              If you listen real quiet at night, you can almost hear the peat heaving up and down with incomplete thoughts; unanswered questions of everybody who already gave up.

              There's no peace here. Nobody's resting. *(She puts her ear to ground.)* Can't you hear it? There's flesh stacked here, one on top of another.

BONIFACE: Well, I say it's far from full. If you didn't leave the planks then the church did.

              (HANNAH jumps up. Paces.)

HANNAH: No! I'm the only one who knows the count.

ABACUS: Maybe there's more than you figured.

HANNAH: No.

BONIFACE: Then it was Earl.

ABACUS: Maybe it *was* Earl, Hannah. He left the planks.

HANNAH: Earl wouldn't do that.

BONIFACE: There's room. He'll tell you.

              (HANNAH paces.)

ABACUS: Sure. He can tell you.

HANNAH: He didn't leave nothing!

ABACUS:	Who else?
HANNAH:	There's nobody else.
BONIFACE:	There's your answer, Abacus.
ABACUS:	Hannah? *(She stops HANNAH.)*
HANNAH:	You've never liked Earl. You never have. Even after all the plans he made for you.
BONIFACE:	Call him, Hannah. *(BONIFACE yells out across peat.)* Earl! Where are you, Earl? *(She pushes HANNAH.)* Call him!
ABACUS:	Maybe he just forgot to tell you, Hannah. Maybe with him being busy finishing the boat and all.
HANNAH:	Earl never forgets a thing.
BONIFACE:	He wasn't at the fence when we needed him to be there! And he's not here now!
HANNAH:	He was there! I know. That's the way it works.
ABACUS:	What works, Hannah?
HANNAH:	He tells me everything. We're partners.
BONIFACE:	Just go ask him. That's easy enough.
ABACUS:	Call him, Hannah. *(She pushes HANNAH.)*
HANNAH:	I can't ask him.
ABACUS:	Why?
BONIFACE:	Why not? You two are such good friends.
HANNAH:	Of course we're friends. *(Pause.)*
ABACUS:	Hannah, call him for me.
HANNAH:	But I haven't seen him for a while.
BONIFACE:	Since when?
ABACUS:	You were just talking to him. That's what you said. *(Pause.)* Where is he? How long's it been?
BONIFACE:	He's nowhere.
ABACUS:	Let her talk. Hannah? When?
HANNAH:	A week.
ABACUS:	A week ago? Since Friday?
HANNAH:	Yeah, maybe a week. Maybe less. I can't remember exactly. Things have been busy, you know.
ABACUS:	It couldn't have been Friday.
BONIFACE:	Well, just think about it. Who's been stacking wood outside our door? And who's been scraping the ice from the fish holes? And flattening the paths before you wake up?
ABACUS:	You're saying you're doing his chores? His job? You?
HANNAH:	I'm only doing it till he comes back. Only for a while.
	(HANNAH starts to sort out the sail and straighten it. Busy-work.)
ABACUS:	We can't take that risk now.

BONIFACE: That's right, Hannah. You're just asking for trouble. They'll find you out.

HANNAH: He'll be back soon enough. I'm not worried about that.

ABACUS: But maybe they've taken him away! Have you thought about that?

HANNAH: No one has taken him away!

ABACUS: Maybe he's working on his own. Maybe he got tired of waiting for the sail. Hannah?

HANNAH: No! I said no! (*Starts to collect the sail again into a ball.*)

BONIFACE: Then he's been sent to map out new peat grounds.

HANNAH: No! (*She holds the ball of sail in her lap.*)

ABACUS: But if it's full?

HANNAH: Maybe it's not. Maybe I did miss a few.

ABACUS: But you can't be certain.

HANNAH: I know damned sure how many! *I'm* in charge of the peat. I've always been the only one. I'm the one out here digging with my bare hands. Pacing out for the next spot. Packing them in. The hell you got planks today! The hell you did!

BONIFACE: How many? How many are left?

HANNAH: You can't build your own box! They can't just give my job to anybody!

BONIFACE: Tell her Hannah. Tell Abacus how many.

(*HANNAH starts to count on her fingers.*)

HANNAH: One.

ABACUS: All along I believed you.

BONIFACE: How many, Hannah?

ABACUS: She said they were full.

HANNAH: Stop talking. Now. I can't count.

BONIFACE: How many in the south parish?

ABACUS: Hannah. Maybe Earl's been re-assigned to body inspections.

BONIFACE: How many, Hannah?

HANNAH: Everybody's always talking so much.

ABACUS: He's just been re-assigned. That's all.

HANNAH: Earl could never inspect the bodies. He couldn't look at them. He just couldn't do it anymore. I'm the one who has to push the parts inside.

ABACUS: Then he just chickened out. He couldn't go through with it.

HANNAH: It doesn't bother me.

BONIFACE: How many left, Hannah?

HANNAH: He just left me...without a word!

(*BONIFACE grabs HANNAH by the shoulders.*)

BONIFACE: Then you don't need him anymore.

HANNAH: I need to talk to him.

ABACUS: Hannah! Boniface is right. Who needs him anyways.

(HANNAH moves to boxes.)

HANNAH: I need him. He tells me what to do. What to do next. Cut the plank. Now hammer it to the crossbeam. Hammer hard. Harder. Make sure it's on. It's good.

It's good, Hannah, he says. You're a damn fine builder. We'll get you out of here. Damned good. He told me that. Just the other week.

(BONIFACE holds HANNAH as she rocks back and forth.)

BONIFACE: You did a fine job. Nobody could have done better.

ABACUS: Right. We'll do it without him. We'll just finish the job ourselves. Just the three of us. Who needs him anyways.

HANNAH: No! I can't go without Earl. Not without Earl. He'd never forgive me. There's still time. I'm not worried about that.

ABACUS: I'm still here, Hannah.

BONIFACE: You still can't be thinking…

ABACUS: What? That Earl was going to put a clamp on things?

BONIFACE: There never was an Earl!

ABACUS: We've got enough sail. And there's still a boat out there, right, Hannah? Where'd you leave the boat?

BONIFACE: There is no boat, dammit. Get it through your head.

ABACUS: Hannah knows where it is. She helped build the damn thing. She saved planks. She just has to remember where it is, that's all. We can do it. Come on, Hannah. Where'd you put the boat? Think hard now. *(She shakes HANNAH.)*

BONIFACE: She's not going anywhere.

ABACUS: She's going. If I have to carry her myself, she's going. And what you have to decide, and now, is whether you want to end up in this river, floating by with your beloved pockets filled with more than just bad memories, or whether we do this together.

BONIFACE: There's nowhere to go.

(ABACUS runs over to sail to scoop it up in her arms.)

ABACUS: We're going to the coast. Hannah says the water's blue.

BONIFACE: Nowhere, Liddy.

ABACUS: It's too late for name calling.

(Lights down.)

The End

Blade

Yvette Nolan

Production Information

Blade was first performed at the 1990 Winnipeg Fringe Festival with the following cast:

ANGELA .... Maria Lamont
JACK/KYLE .... Gene Pyrz
CONNIE .... Charlene Wiest
MRS. ERHART .... Margaret Anne MacLeod

Directed by Yvette Nolan
Dramaturgy by Laurie Lam
Costume Design by Alana Shewchuk
Stage Managed by Margaret Brook

(The set is minimal, lighting by areas. CS there is a child's car seat. The time is the present.

Pool of light up DSR on girl. She is young, early 20s, dressed in a jeanskirt and a sweatshirt, flat shoes and dark stockings.)

ANGELA: I knew that hookers were being killed—everyone in the country knew it and we here knew it better than anyone because it was splashed all over the front page—with pictures usually. I knew better than most, 'cause I actually knew one of the girls who had been killed. Well, not really knew her but she was in my intro History class at university. Cindy Bear, her name was—you know, like Yogi Bear's girlfriend. She was native, and very quiet, but I think she did quite well in that class because I saw her get back a test once with an 88% on it. I only got about 75 on that test. It was about colonialism in South Africa and I just couldn't get interested. So anyway, when Cindy Bear—no one ever called her just Cindy, it was always Cindy Bear—when Cindy Bear got killed by the hooker-killer, some people at school said "Oh, I never knew she was a prostitute—I never would have guessed" and others said "I always thought she was a whore—where else would she get the money to go to school? They usually are, you know." I thought it was a little funny that Cindy Bear should be a hooker because I knew she was going to school through some special program, and she was always prepared for class, so when did she have time?

Anyway, Cindy Bear got herself killed in the usual way. *(Shivers.)* Oh it was ugly, I guess the photographers got there a lot faster than they normally do because there was a gruesome picture on the front page of the paper, in colour. The body was all covered up and everything, but still it was really disturbing. Beside the covered up body were these dots, that looked like someone had spilled a box of smarties around Cindy Bear, except bigger, you know, like Loonies. Those dots really bothered me, you know, and I looked at them and looked at them until I finally realized that they weren't dots, they were drops, drops of blood, Cindy Bear's blood. And at one corner of the blanket, if you looked really, really hard, you could see a piece of body poking out…at least I think it was a finger. And I looked so hard at that finger that I could imagine her hand under there all curled up…

The cops were desperate to catch the guy, and they were on the news every other day saying how hard they were working to catch the killer. They sure cared a lot more about those girls when they were dead than when they were alive, that's for sure. I mean, most of the girls who had been killed were young native girls, 14, 15, runaways, mostly, and…well, I don't know if you're from around here, but natives are sort of the low guys on the totem pole in Winnipeg. *(She gets it, and laughs a little embarrassed.)*

So I knew all that, when I was walking home across the Disraeli Street bridge, but I wasn't really thinking about it, you know? Like I just wasn't paying attention…I mean I had just had a fight with Kyle and I left his place in a fury. Not a serious fight, I mean it was then but in retrospect it wasn't anything really…the usual…if you loved me you'd tell me you cared, you wouldn't act so damn indifferent all the time, you'd be more demonstrative, you don't love me as much as I love you…well, he didn't, but then, what couple ever loves each other equally.

So I wasn't paying attention, and I was feeling a little low, and I was running over the fight in my head. Just not paying attention. Now, of course, looking back, I see all the warning signals, all the things I should've noticed, and would've, normally, except I wasn't paying attention.

That's right, he started beeping at me before I even came off the bridge… Are you from here? The Disraeli bridge is actually two bridges—one over the river and one over the Higgins area. Well, I was coming off the second bridge, and I guess he was down a coupla blocks on Higgins, and he musta been looking real hard for someone that day, because he started beeping at me from way down on Higgins. But I was distracted, and I didn't really notice the beeping, or didn't think it was intended for me cause the guy was so far away. But as I came down off the bridge I saw that he had circled around to cut me off on Henry, right where it meets the freeway.

(Lights come up CS on JACK in the car.)

JACK: You wanna ride?

ANGELA: What? *(She walks over to the car and leans into the window.)*

JACK: I said, do you wanna ride.

          (ANGELA pauses, looks at the baby seat.)

ANGELA: Where you headed?

JACK: River Heights. But I'll take you where you wanna go.

ANGELA: I guess so. Thanks. *(She gets in, puts on seatbelt.)*

          (He begins to drive.)

ANGELA: Cold.

JACK: Umm.

          (She discovers a soother she has been sitting on, pulls it out from under her.)

ANGELA: You've got kids.

JACK:	Uh huh.
ANGELA:	Boys? Girls? How many?
JACK:	One. A boy. *(Pause.)* Where you coming from?
ANGELA:	Huh? Oh, from my boyfriend's place.
JACK:	*(Sardonic.)* Boyfriend, eh? Huh. What are you doing, walking the streets this part of town?
ANGELA:	Nothing, I was just walking home.
JACK:	Shouldn't be walking around this area. Why didn't you take a cab?
ANGELA:	*(Laughing.)* Well, I'm a student. Traditionally, we don't have much money to throw away on cabs.
JACK:	Not much money, eh? No jobs, eh?
ANGELA:	Yeah, I got a job. But you don't make a hell of a lot as a waitress.
JACK:	*(Laughing.)* Is that what they call it these days? How come your boyfriend kicked you out? Holding out on him?
ANGELA:	Look, mister, maybe this isn't such a good idea. *(She undoes seatbelt.)* Why don't you just let me out here...a bus should be along in a minute.
JACK:	I bet you got a lot of boyfriends, young good-looking girl like you. I could be one of your boyfriends...
ANGELA:	*(Amazed.)* What?
JACK:	I got money, I could be one of your boyfriends, couldn't I? How much would it take? Twenty, forty bucks?
ANGELA:	*(Finally realizing.)* A hooker? You thought I was a hooker? Oh look, mister, you've got me all wrong, I'm sorry, I didn't realize you thought...Oh geez, you picked me up because you thought I was a prostitute *(Laughs.)* Sorry to disappoint you. Look, just let me...
JACK:	*(Suddenly menacing.)* Why are you laughing? Couldn't I be one of your boyfriends?
ANGELA:	Look. Mister. I'm sorry I'm not the girl you thought I was. I thought you were just offering me a ride. I only took it because you seemed OK, I mean, you have a baby seat in the back. I'm sorry, why don't you just pull over here and I'll get out.
JACK:	Why do you do this?
ANGELA:	Do what?! Look, fella, I'm sorry but... *(Suddenly angry.)* Jesus, what kind of a jerk are you anyway? You have a wife and a baby at home waiting for you and you're out looking for a prostitute? Unbelievable. Look, just let me out OK? Hey, where you going? Stop the car.
JACK:	I'll just drive you down here and drop you off.
ANGELA:	Look, I don't know what you think you're doing...just stop the car, OK? Stop the CAR! STOP THE CAR! STOP THE CAR!!

(The car stops. ANGELA reaches for the handle. JACK grabs her

head with one hand. He mounts her, back to the audience, grabs the knife from where it is stuck in his pants at the back, stabs her.)

Let me go, let me out, look, I... *(Screams.)*

(Finally, he sits back. ANGELA slumps forward and over towards the car door. JACK reaches over her, opens her door. JACK pushes ANGELA out of the car. She tumbles to the floor SR of the car. JACK reaches into the back seat and pulls out a baby blanket, with which he wipes the knife carefully. When it is obviously clean enough, he places it under the seat. He looks at himself in the rear-view mirror, half heartedly tries to wipe off some blood from his face, then from his hands. He tucks the blanket under the passenger side seat, then leans further and pulls the car door shut. He turns on the ignition. Blackout.

JACK exits in black. The lights restore and ANGELA stirs. She gets up, dusts herself off. She crosses to the DS spot again.)

ANGELA: *(She sort of nods, shrugs apologetically.)* Yeah...I'm not really here. I'm actually just sort of an after-image, you know? Like when you turn off your TV, and you can still see the picture there for a split second. Well, this is a split-second, for me. Like, the powers that be are letting me hang around for a little bit, just to... *(She cringes a little, eyes up.)* All right. *(To the audience.)* This may be a little harder than I thought. *(She composes herself for a moment.)*

The papers said RIPPER CLAIMS FOURTH VICTIM. And of course, they made me out to be a prostitute. The media coverage was full of denials. The police said there was no evidence that I was a prostitute, classmates they interviewed said they had no idea I was hooking for a living, my boss at work flat-out denied that I could possibly be a prostitute but... Well nothing works like denial, does it?

(She looks down at her sweatshirt, "sees" that it is covered in blood, looks at her bloody hands. She removes the sweatshirt, wipes her hands on the inside of it, drops it. Underneath she is wearing a camisole.)

They hauled in Kyle, my boyfriend, who was already so distraught because the last thing we had done together was argue...

(KYLE is sitting on the car seat with his head in his hands, elbows on knees.)

KYLE: We had a fight, OK? People have arguments, even lovers have arguments—especially lovers have arguments. Christ, whaddaya want from me? *(He looks blankly at his questioner.)* I dunno, the usual. I didn't love her as much as she loved me, I wasn't committed to her, I drove her crazy because I—well, I'm not a real affectionate guy, you know, I don't show my emotions all that well. But that doesn't mean I don't love her! *(Pause.)*

Didn't. *(Pause.)* Christ.

What? No, of course I never hit her, Jesus. I never hit anybody. It was an argument, you know, argument? We exchanged words, we had a heated discussion, she yelled at me, and I…well, I sort of just waited it out. I think that's what made her so goddamned mad, I just sort of stared at her patiently, I wouldn't be dragged into a yelling match. What's the point? And it always ends the same, with her packing up all her stuff she's got laying around my place and stalking out. She usually takes the bus home, though. I guess it wasn't coming fast enough for her cause it was Sunday schedule, and she didn't have much stuff to carry, just a toothbrush and a sweatshirt or two. Or maybe she just wanted to cool off. Sometimes, just the trip home will calm her down enough and she'll phone me when she gets to her place and ask me to come and get her. And I always do. *(Pause.)* Did.

(Furious.) None of your fucking business! *(Pause while he listens to his questioner.)* No, it was me. We had sex first thing in the morning when we woke up. Yes, we had sex and then we fought. I dunno, that's just the way it happened. Jesus, if I'd known she was gonna get killed on her way home from my place, you think I would've fought with her, you think I would've let her go? *(Bows his head.)*

You want me to what? Into a jar? Why? How the hell am I supposed to do that? I can't come on command! *(He turns his head SR, infuriated, embarrassed. ANGELA is standing there.)*

ANGELA: *(Amused, gently.)* Want some help?

KYLE: *(Turning back.)* Gimme that thing.

ANGELA: *(She is reading a paper.)* Oo, yeah. "An autopsy discovered traces of semen, indicating that she had engaged in intercourse in the three or four hours preceding her death." That was pretty damning, alright. No mention of poor Kyle until days later, no mention of any boyfriend at all until days later…hmm, no mention of a lot of things… "traces of semen"…no mention of a vagina, or any sort of repository for these traces…

You know what really gets me? It's that if I was a hooker, then it was almost OK that I got myself killed, you know? Like I've given up the right to life, like I've given up some basic rights by choosing to make my living with my body? Suffering Jesus, what makes me any less valuable than an accountant, or an actress, or a waitress?

And my mother. My death almost killed her, anyway, and on top of that she is trying to deal with people's questions and insinuations and pity. Like, not pity that she's lost a daughter, pity that her daughter was a hooker and she didn't even know it.

My best friend, Connie, couldn't stand it, that everyone thought I was working for a living. It drove her nuts, she became obsessed with clearing my name—that's what she called it— clearing Angela's name. As if it mattered.

She knocked on doors, she badgered reporters… Finally, she went to the one man she figured held the balance of power…

(Lights come up CS. CONNIE enters from USC.)

CONNIE: Mr. Sinclair? My name is Connie Lamont… It's about my girlfriend Angela who was killed…see the papers are calling her a hooker, and I know she wasn't…well, I thought you could help me clear her name…

(During this, ANGELA crosses to CS and drapes herself over the car seat.)

ANGELA: Don't bother Connie. I don't care what they think.

CONNIE: *(Laughing.)* It's funny, me trying to clear her name…she wouldn't care what people thought…never really did. Besides, she didn't really think there was anything wrong with being a prostitute—called them working girls—she even talked about trying it once, just to see what it felt like to do it for money. She always said …

ANGELA
& CONNIE: Once makes you a philosopher, twice makes you a pervert.

(They laugh, pause. ANGELA starts.)

ANGELA: But I would never do it!

CONNIE: *(Starts.)* But she would never do it. No, no. I think it was just some kind of a statement. She was always turning things into some kind of statement.

ANGELA: Life is political, Connie.

CONNIE: Life is political, Connie, she'd always be saying. We've been friends—we had been friends—for 10 years. I was just a kid when I met her, I know her. She taught me a lot of things, I know her.

She was always broke, you know. And we were very loose about money, when we lived together. Well, we still are…or were, oh…like, she got student aid one year and I didn't, so she paid the rent. And then I had a job and she was broke so I paid everything, you know, and gave her an allowance for coffee and lunch and stuff. But even when we were both flat broke, we never worried about money, because Angela always believed that things would work out.

So this one Boxing Day we were broke, just busted, 50 bucks between the two of us, nothing in the house and the rent for January not paid, no bus passes to get back to school in the new year, and we're depressed because—well, Christmas can be sort of depressing. So Angela says, let's have a party.

ANGELA: Fifty bucks wasn't going to pay the rent anyway!

CONNIE: Fifty bucks wasn't going to pay the rent anyway. And Angela said something would turn up. So I said what the heck. We went out and spent the 50 bucks, every cent of it, on fixings for party food and mix, and called people, and spent the afternoon cooking and threw the best party. And you know what? Two days later, she goes out to pick up the mail, and there's a scholarship cheque in the mailbox for her—for 500 bucks. Two days before the end of the month! So she paid the rent and bought bus passes for us both. That's when I really started to believe in her, you know, to believe that things would turn out, that there were reasons for everything.

ANGELA: You never told me that.

CONNIE: Once—once when she was really really broke and wouldn't ask for allowance, I forced her to take money, and you know what she did? She wrote me a poem and sent in to me in the mail. A sonnet! She wrote a sonnet for me. I couldn't write a sonnet to save my life.

(Answering a question.) What was she like? Optimistic. Like, she believed that things happened for a reason, that everything would work out. Independent—and proud. I guess that's why she and Kyle fought so much. Neither of them would ever admit they were wrong.

ANGELA: *(Surprised.)* Is that why we fought so much?

CONNIE: Uh uh, no way. I know they pulled Kyle and questioned him, he's getting a bum rap in the papers, on TV... Poor Kyle. No, Kyle was the best thing that ever happened to her. All the boyfriends she'd ever had, correction—all the other men she'd ever been involved with—they always thought they wanted one thing, but as soon as they were "involved", that one thing was what they tried to stamp out of her. Like, they were attracted to her independence, but two weeks into the relationship, they'd be sulking because she was so independent. Or they'd talk about her sense of humour and a month later they'd be calling her silly. Only Kyle really knew what he was getting into... And he's a good man, no matter what the papers say about him. Very fair, very unbiased, like not an "ist" or any sort, you know. Racist, sexist, age-ist, none of those...

ANGELA: What?

CONNIE: What? Oh—well—no, "all the other men" is just an expression, really. There weren't that many. I mean, over the years, there's been a few, but I've known her for years...

How many over the years? *(Controlled anger.)* Why? What difference does it make? *(She stares him down.)* She was strong, in every way, and many men don't like strong women. I don't know much about the results of the autopsy, I can't get Mrs. Erhart to talk about it, but I would bet you anything in the world that she fought him, whoever he was, fought him hard.

(Answering.) I don't know why she got in the car, I just don't know. Unless he forced her. Or she knew him. Maybe she knew him?

ANGELA: I didn't know him. He didn't force me.

CONNIE: I dunno. It baffles me. But she wasn't hooking, I can tell you that, not because it was wrong, or bad or anything like that, just because she didn't take dumb chances, I mean, she knew you could never predict how a situation was gonna turn out, what the consequences of your actions were gonna be.

She always says that things happen for a reason. There are reasons for everything, she says. But no matter how I look at this, no matter how hard I try, I can't see the reason for this, can you?

ANGELA: Is that it? Is that it?

(At the door CONNIE stops, turns around.)

CONNIE: You know what else she was optimistic about? The press, the media, isn't that a laugh? She thought that only the media ensured some kind of justice.

ANGELA: I still believe it, Connie.

CONNIE: She believed in the media and now look what the media's done to her. Maybe she wouldn't care, but I care!

ANGELA: I do care!

CONNIE: I care!

ANGELA: Constance.

(CONNIE sees her, reaches out to her, stops. Obviously is spoken to. Turns back to SINCLAIR.)

CONNIE: What? No I'm OK. Yeah.

(Glances back to where ANGELA was, but she is gone. Blackout.

Lights up on ANGELA's DSR pool, where she is sitting, taking off her boots and socks as she talks.)

ANGELA: So my reputation, or what was left of it, was almost saved by the champion of the Relax page. Almost. And it would have done the trick too, boy, it was a moving article about my tarnished virtue. In another time and reality, it would have moved me to tears but... But no one saw the article.

See, the day Connie was talking to Sinclair, some new evidence surfaced in the Harper case, an eyewitness, and white, no less, and so Sinclair was on the phone to McNicholl, and the now disbanded Inquiry, trying to get a comment, and the next day the column about me was axed, and Sinclair wrote about the Inquiry and the investigation and the murder of JJ. And then the night before the column would have been rescheduled, the "Hooker-Killer" was turned in by his wife.

(Lights up on JACK on the car seat. His manner is easy, charming, initially, but becoming more bewildered throughout the monologue.)

JACK: I met my wife, Helen, in college. She was so beautiful to me, fresh, you know. She's still a beautiful woman, but she's older now and since Jason's birth she has a different kind of look, you know? Older, more worldly. I guess that comes with having a child. But I look at her now—Helen—and I still see her exactly the way she looked the very first time I laid eyes on her. Long blonde hair, those big innocent eyes, the little bounce in her step... She carried her books like a schoolgirl, hugging them up against her chest, she looked like she couldn't have been more than 15 years old.

We have a son, did I tell you? Jason, he's only a baby, newborn, really. We weren't really planning to have a child, not yet at least, but well, things happen, don't they? And Helen, she came from a big family, and I guess she really wanted kids...

I remember, I watched her for a long time before I ever asked her out, but I knew she really kind of looked up to me. And then, when I finally asked her out, she stood there, looking up at me with those eyes, and I could see she was really sort of shy, and kind of—well—awed.

I was with her in the delivery room, during the birth of the baby...she really wanted me there, although I'm sort of old-fashioned and I would have been just as happy to pace in the waiting-room, and had a doctor in sterile whites come out and say "Congratulations, it's a boy!" Still, it wasn't as bad as I thought it might be, but still I was surprised by the amount of blood... I never thought that having a baby was a really bloody operation, well, I guess I never really thought about it at all before...

You wanna see a picture of Helen? She's— *(He reaches for his wallet, doesn't find it.)* Oh right, they took my wallet. My wedding ring, too. *(Holds up his hand.)* Well, people say she looks sort of like Uma Thurman, but I don't really think so...

I have a son, did I tell you? Jason, his name is...

(Lights restore on ANGELA who is facing US in her pool. She is putting on big earrings.)

ANGELA: He was absolutely looney tunes, you know. I mean, they kept sending him into different psychiatric evaluations with different shrinks just to try and establish if he was sane enough to stand trial. Then, before he could go to trial, he managed to get ahold of enough rope to hang himself, sealing my fate and Cindy Bear's forever.

(She finishes speaking. Undoes her skirt, pulls it off. Underneath, the rest of her "hooker dress", stockings with the garter belt showing. Looks at the audience, a bit blankly, crosses US of the carseat. Stands there.

MRS. ERHART enters to DSR pool of light, kind of blinking, nervous but firm. She picks up ANGELA's skirt. She waits, as if waiting for quiet to happen. When it does, she clears her throat and begins. During this, ANGELA stands behind the car seat, then moves to sit on the car seat, not demurely, to put on her makeup. She has put on high high heels and she puts up her hair.)

MRS. ERHART: I know there's no reason for you people to believe me, I know there's no way you will, but I have to say what I have to say, so maybe I can sleep nights again. My daughter Angela—she was a good girl. She didn't do drugs and she didn't drink, and though I know none of you will believe me, she didn't prostitute herself either. Why are you so willing to believe the worst? What if it were your daughter?

I have been trying to pray, I have been trying to find some comfort in prayer, but I just can't seem to keep my mind on it, and I just can't seem to believe that I am getting through to God. And all the time I am trying to pray, this thought keeps pushing its way into my brain...*why wasn't she a son?* And no matter how hard I try to push that thought out again, no matter how guilty I feel about it, I just can't shake it... At least if she were a son, maybe it would be a little easier to accept, maybe then I could make my peace with God.

I know you're all so willing to believe that my daughter was a whore, that she was taking money for sex, makes a better story I know, and I've been guilty of it too, but now, the police are saying it looks like this last girl was not a prostitute either... So I've been thinking about this, very early mornings when I wake up and realize my daughter is gone, and I'm beginning to think that maybe if the police had been looking for a man who was killing women, instead of a man who was killing whores, maybe he'd have been stopped a lot sooner. I don't know. And now that man who did this, that crazy man with the knife, he's hanged himself, so there will be no trial, no verdict, no... May God have mercy on his soul...and grant my daughter peace...

(She bows her head. ANGELA, transformation complete, gets up off the car seat, walks to the DSL pool as if looking in a mirror, checking out her appearance. JACK enters, sits in the car seat, CONNIE enters, stands with MRS. ERHART, watches ANGELA. JACK leans out of the car window.)

JACK: Wanna ride?

(Long pause. ANGELA registers, comprehends, turns and blackout.)

The End

Zac and Speth

Rick Chafe

Production Information

Zac and Speth was first produced in a slightly different form at the 1992 Winnipeg Fringe Festival with the following cast:

ZAC .... Ross McMillan
SPETH .... Sharon Bajer

Directed by Chris Sigurdson
Stage Manager: Tamara Mauthe

The author gratefully acknowledges the financial assistance of the Manitoba Arts Council and the Manitoba Association of Playwrights, and the advice and contributions of Sharon Bajer, Ross McMillan, Chris Sigurdson, and dramaturge Bruce McManus, in the development of this play.

Staging

The play is set on the front steps of the Manitoba Legislature, a July 4 of some near future, and jumps back and forth over the preceding ten years, mainly between Winnipeg, Vancouver and Toronto.

Although reference is made to the characters handling many different objects, there should be no actual props used other than Zac's chain and guitar; any objects referred to should be either mimed or implied by the action. The various time, location and character switches should also be created entirely by the actors, very simply and without light changes or pauses except as indicated.

(*The set consists of two or three stone steps with a stone column or flag pole at the top step. ZAC sits leaning against the column or pole; he's chained to it, although that may not be obvious yet. One end of the chain is padlocked around his waist, the other end padlocked to the pole, leaving a good six to eight foot length to allow him limited movement around the stage.*

He has an acoustic guitar. He's bored; he picks repeatedly at a single string—it's an annoying sound, a habit of irritation. Suddenly he breaks into a twanging, banging version of "Heartbreak Hotel.")

ZAC:	*Ever since my baby left me,* *I found a new place to dwell* *It's down at the end of Lonely Street* *At—* *(He pulls a string hard.)* Ow! *(As he sticks his finger in his mouth, he sees SPETH enter. Pause.)* Hi. *(Beat.)* Fingernail.
SPETH:	War is hell. *(Beat.)* Sorry.
ZAC:	Heard you were in town. Thanks for coming.
SPETH:	How's it going?
ZAC:	Would have thought there'd be five or ten thousand people in Winnipeg with something to say about this. No real crowd control problems though. Guess I won't have to worry about pepper spray—
SPETH:	I meant in general.
ZAC:	Ah. *(Offering an open padlock.)* Well, lots of chain.
SPETH:	I came for the fireworks.
ZAC:	Nice view from here anyway.
SPETH:	Guess I wanted company.
ZAC:	Yeah?
SPETH:	*(Sitting.)* I keep going over and over it. Always seems like everything changed overnight. There must have been something we could have done.
ZAC:	I guess we both saw it coming.
SPETH:	I meant the campaign.

ZAC:	Oh.
SPETH:	*(Beat.)* Yeah. We saw it coming.
ZAC:	You did what you could, the people spoke.
SPETH:	No, I meant us.
ZAC:	*(Pause.)* You know, I think about you a lot. All the time. I wasn't really hoping for ten thousand people. Just hoping you might come by so I could say something. Like, marry me, Elspeth.
SPETH:	*(Chuckling.)* As if.
ZAC:	Which on the surface may seem a little ridiculous…
SPETH:	*Oh* yeah…
ZAC:	But if you'll allow me to say one thing…
SPETH:	Zac, there is *nothing* you could say—
ZAC:	Two minutes. Just give me two minutes.
	(Pause. SPETH shrugs.)
	The first time I met you—
SPETH:	Really bad place to start.
ZAC:	Not the *first* first time. The second first time. The first time we had an actual conversation…you were spectacular. And you continued to be spectacular until I fell madly, completely and forever in love with you.
SPETH:	You were already in love with me from the first first time.
ZAC:	Don't flatter yourself. I was highly interested. But I wasn't in love.
SPETH:	And you're gonna tell me what did it for you?
ZAC:	In the Albert, on the dance floor, completely alone, singing. Remember?
SPETH:	Nope.
ZAC:	*(Singing Vilolent Femmes' "Add It Up".)*
	Why can't I get, *Just one kiss?* *Why can't I get* *Just one kiss?*
	Dancing your guts out, drunk to beat the band.
	Maybe it's something that I wouldn't miss *But I waited my life for just one—*
	You knocked over a table and broke three draft glasses and kept right on dancing—you seriously don't remember this?
SPETH:	I wasn't drunk, I was freaked out. That was the day I found out I was pregnant.
ZAC:	You're kidding? That was the day…? That's why you were so…?
SPETH:	You were going to say something about falling in love?
ZAC:	I just—oh my God, I'm seeing the whole thing differently…

(Wanting to get on with it, SPETH takes over, dancing as a 17-year-old.)

SPETH: *Day…After Day*
I get angry! And I will say
That the day, is in my sights—

ZAC: *(As a 17-year-old.)* Speth!

SPETH: *What.*

ZAC: Welcome home.

SPETH: Some home.

ZAC: The Albert reeks of homeliness. It's my home. I live here now.

SPETH: In the hotel?

ZAC: Second floor, it's great. Like, in a really, really bad way. Smelly old men, you gotta share the toilet and everything, not nice really, but great, you know?

SPETH: Why would anyone live here?

ZAC: I'm probably going out to Vancouver pretty soon anyway.

SPETH: Really?

ZAC: I mean, I got kicked out of home, right? So, it's not bad with my mom or anything, it's just, you know, menopause and stuff. I understand.

SPETH: What, your mom?

ZAC: Oh yeah. Serious change of life, hormones and everything. I mean, she's 40, 45 or something, I accept it. It's hard on her, kids and everything. But I visit her, you know, support what she's doing.

SPETH: OK, whatever.

ZAC: How 'bout you, school good? Hummin' along?

SPETH: I quit today.

ZAC: Oh well, lots of time for school later.

SPETH: I gotta go, I'll see ya.

ZAC: No, listen. I know, I'm getting the impression, you aren't exactly comfortable with me right now, and I can understand that—

SPETH: Just don't even—

ZAC: —and I know, that, look: you used to be at the Albert five times a week, minimum, and then suddenly you're not here at all, and…I am. I can work that out, but, that night—

SPETH: First, I was on major rebound from Andy, second I was majorly *drunk*, which means third, no way ever again. Understand?

ZAC: OK, right, and that's exactly what I'm saying, it's OK, I don't feel used or anything. I mean, it was *great*…

SPETH: It wasn't great …

ZAC: No, not great. OK, sort of shitty…

SPETH: I didn't say it was shitty ...

ZAC: Sort of, so-so, mediocre, middle-of-the-road. But great too, for me; I mean that. And definitely could get better.

SPETH: No. It couldn't.

ZAC: Which is my whole point. I'm saying I get it. Space—there it is. OK? Truce? Friends until at least you're finished this beer?

           (He offers his hand. Beat.)

SPETH: *(Accepting the handshake.)* OK. *(Beat.)* Life sucks.

ZAC: Life is the greatest thing ever invented.

SPETH: Yeah, right.

ZAC: Well sure, things suck big time. But you have fun while you can.

SPETH: Yeah, and then what? Get a job and get married and have kids and die?

ZAC: Sure, but you can buy it or you don't.

SPETH: Everybody I know buys it. That's what bugs me. Everybody just swallows the whole thing.

ZAC: But there's a million options. Just stick your head out and start looking. If you don't like the world then change it.

SPETH: You do that?

ZAC: Totally. You gotta have a little bit of hope. Just because it's a shitty world doesn't mean you can't do something beautiful.

SPETH: You really going to Vancouver?

ZAC: Oh yeah! I'll get a few buddies together; I've got friends there I can stay with, party a little, get some stuff happening.

SPETH: My mom took me out there one time.

ZAC: Vancouver's the greatest. It's the only real city we've got in this country.

SPETH: There's some actually really cool people there.

ZAC: They're living in a city where you can look up and see a mountain. How can you not be more in touch? More laid back?

SPETH: I met a guy in Robson Square. I was only like, 14, and he was 19, so this is sort of scary, right? He pulls out one of his earrings and just gives it to me.

ZAC: Yeah, *exactly.*

SPETH: And I know his whole life in five minutes. He never even *tried* to hit on me.

ZAC: That's the coast.

SPETH: This is my own hometown but I felt way more home there.

ZAC: Oh yeah! You can walk down Granville and there's 200 people dressed weirder than we are. You can be a freak in Vancouver.

SPETH: And don't feel like a freak.

ZAC: Man, we should just check out what a bus costs.

SPETH: A hundred and 48.

ZAC: Really?

SPETH: You can't tell anyone.

ZAC: What.

SPETH: I've almost got six hundred saved.

ZAC: Right on!

SPETH: I'm going this summer. Or, fuck. Maybe I'm not going this summer.

ZAC: Are you kidding? Let's go now!

SPETH: Oh fuck...

ZAC: You just quit school, you're completely free...

SPETH: No...everything's screwed up right now.

ZAC: Come on, we can go straight to the bus station!

SPETH: Oh shit shit shit...

ZAC: I can get money, we can stay with my friends, they're cool, they've got a huge house...

SPETH: Really?

ZAC: Yes! Right now! We're going to the bus station!

SPETH: You're sure we can stay with them?

ZAC: Bob and Zingo are the coolest people alive. Life is an adventure; you've gotta do this.

SPETH: This is just...I mean, we're travelling partners and that's it, right? You understand that?

ZAC: Absolutely!

           (SPETH, age 27, breaks from the memory with a derisive snort.)

ZAC: *(Age 27.)* And...you said yes.

SPETH: And you fell in love.

ZAC: Not yet.

SPETH: You're way over two minutes.

ZAC: Then we should change the subject?

           (Beat. SPETH doesn't move, continuing to look at him as noncommittally as possible. He smiles.)

ZAC: *(On the phone, 17.)* Hi Mom! I'm at the bus station. Yeah, the bus station—Winnipeg. No no, I'm not coming back, I'm going! Vancouver! Yes I'm serious... Well Christ, at least I called first!... I thought it would make you happy—I'm kidding!

           (SPETH as a 27-year-old has been sitting back watching ZAC play this out, now she gets up as a 17-year-old and tugs at his sleeve to hurry.)

           Look, bus is going, Mom, I used your bank card, but it's OK, I dropped it in the overnight chute, they'll mail it back, I only took two hundred. But get your credit limit upped. Gotta go Mom, I love you. Oh shut up, I do so. Bye!

(They sit, profiles to the audience, creating the bus. ZAC sits several feet back from SPETH.)

A bus trip! I was going to have her beside me for 38 hours to talk, share stories, sing dopey songs, play tic-tac-toe and battleships, snuggle and watch the scenery go by and find out everything about each others' lives. Instead there's only two seats left—she sits beside a woman with a yellow mohair blanket and a spare pillow, and I sit at the back, beside the washroom door right over the bus engine on the bench seat that doesn't tilt back, beside a large, hairy, nasty-looking biker-type who smells very bad, until the mohair blanket lady finally reaches her destination. Which is Kelowna.

(He takes the seat beside SPETH, who is trying to find a sleeping position.)

Hi, we've been riding this bus for 28 hours and it's sort of occurred to me that we really don't know each other that well, so I thought I'd introduce myself. Hi, I'm Zac—that's Zachary—Halliwell, I'm a Libra, I smoke Player's Light, and I wonder if you'd like to share any deep dark secrets with me?

(SPETH, who has been peering at him groggily, now turns completely away.)

I know we must have a lot in common, right? We both like hanging around the Albert, and we both like draft beer and the Screaming Zombie Messiahs, but neither one of us are wild about Jesus Mouse or the Cadillacs of the Living Dead, is that fair to say?

SPETH: I'm really tired, OK?

ZAC: Really? When I don't sleep I just get wired. But this is just surface stuff. Like, we're both human beings, right? Both breathe oxygen, red blood, two arms, two legs, one nose each, male, female—whoops! *There's* a little difference—

SPETH: This is really stupid.

ZAC: This is bus fun, come on. Like, counting cars? You do that? One! Two! You're going to have to do better than that, I'm ahead—Three! It's easier in a car; we could have different points for like, imports and domestics? *(Beat.)* Did you bring any cards?

SPETH: I hate cards.

ZAC: Mmm… Twenty questions! Who am I?

SPETH: I'm terrible at these stupid games. OK?

ZAC: What kind of…music do you like…?

SPETH: I don't listen to music.

ZAC: *(Aside.)* My God. I'm fifteen-hundred miles into a road trip with the future love of my life and we have nothing in common.

SPETH: *(Shoving him.)* Here, move over. I just want to sleep...

> *(They're stretched out across the seats, ZAC in a horribly uncomfortable position, but with SPETH's head on his chest, asleep.)*

ZAC: Then again, conversation is a very over-rated form of communication.

> *(Careful not to risk his good fortune, ZAC tries to find a place for his hands, settling them on her shoulders, tenderly cradling her. She jerks her elbow and his hands jump away and stay there. Beat.)*

Ten o'clock at night, the clouds have parted; there's a huge white moon throwing light over the Fraser Valley. It's all incredibly magical and I haven't moved for four hours. The left side of my body is asleep, my spine is screaming with pain. My god, she's beautiful.

> *(ZAC closes his eyes, asleep, SPETH opens hers.)*

SPETH: I tell myself, Zingo's gotta be cool—the guy's a male nurse. I don't have to worry about rent; food—maybe they'll share.

Get real, I've got to get a job—that's OK, I planned on that—what if there's no jobs? There's no jobs in Winnipeg. There's gotta be more jobs in Vancouver, they've got way more people.

It's OK, there's welfare, no problem. They have to give welfare to single mothers, right?

My God, I hope these guys are cool; they will be; I'm going to have a baby; what am I saying, I don't even know if I'm keeping it, I might walk into an abortion clinic tomorrow if I'm in a bad mood.

I can't go mountain climbing if I'm pregnant—what if I meet some guy who's incredible and he's into mountain climbing? Abortion.

I want this baby. I just realized that, I want this baby.

That's crazy, this is self-hypnosis.

Shit.

> *(The bus stops with a bump, jolting them both awake.)*

SPETH: Are we there?

ZAC: *(Peering through the window.)* I can't tell—there's too much rain...

SPETH: *(Pulling her jacket over her head, laughing as they step out.)* Ahh! It's cold! Oh, smell that!

ZAC: Yeah. Diesel fumes.

SPETH: No—wet concrete, earth! Where's downtown? Are we downtown?

ZAC: I don't know...

SPETH: I want to go downtown, let's go to a bar!

ZAC: No! The beach!

SPETH: Yeah!! Let's find the ocean!

(She shrieks and hugs him, stays hugging.)

Ohh, I didn't think we were going to make it.

ZAC: Of course we were.

SPETH: Thank you for making me do this.

ZAC: Well, hey. You're welcome.

SPETH: Call your friends! Now!

ZAC: You're going to love these guys—they've got an old hippy VW van with a mural and everything!

(ZAC turns away to make the call.)

SPETH: *(Aside, fearful and excited.)* Where *are* we? Is this downtown? Like, where's Eaton's and the Bay? How do you get your bearings in this place? And it's raining in February! This is home. I know this is *home.*

(ZAC returns.)

Are they coming?

ZAC: Um. Bad news, kind of...

SPETH: Oh shit. They're not home? That's OK, we can wait, we'll go to a bar...

ZAC: Yeah. Well, kind of. They...don't have room right now.

SPETH: *What.*

ZAC: But maybe in a couple weeks...

SPETH: You didn't call ahead?

ZAC: Hey, life's an adventure...

SPETH: You didn't fucking call?

ZAC: No problem! Zingo gave me the name of a hotel!

(SPETH in a double bed: ZAC in a cot shaped like the letter M.)

SPETH: *(Aside.)* The Roxborough Hotel on Pender. Third floor room, facing the downtown street where traffic never stops all night; a mattress with a sag in the middle, sheets that feel like they're still on somebody else's bed, wallpaper older than my mother. I had to argue with the night clerk to get him to bring in an extra cot. I'm soaking wet, half the clothes in my duffel bag are soaking wet.

(To ZAC.) I've got a 180 dollars left and I am not spending the whole thing on three nights in a hotel, got that? Tomorrow we're looking for apartments and jobs.

ZAC: Absolutely. Tomorrow we work. *(Moving towards her bed.)* Tonight, we have sex.

SPETH: Fuck off.

ZAC: *(Jumping back to his own bed.)* Right!

(Aside.) The next couple of days are kind of tense. I can't believe my mom would cancel her Visa on me. Competition for busking

in this town is unreal. We eat peanut butter sandwiches and stare at CNN for entertainment, 10 hours a day.

SPETH: *(Staring at TV.)* There are no jobs in this town; there are no jobs anywhere in the world. Bachelor suites here go for $550. People are starving on television, I see the same people living out of garbage cans outside the hotel. There's war everywhere, ecological disasters, children and fighting and famine and death.

ZAC: *(Entering with wine.)* Ta Dah!

SPETH: *(Doubtfully.)* You got a job?

ZAC: I made 28 dollars today, busking is *great* in this town—time to order Chinese!

SPETH: Twenty-eight bucks and you're blowing it on wine?

ZAC: Enjoy yourself for a change, tomorrow's another day, lighten up!

(Going to the TV.) Turn this shit off for starters.

SPETH: Would you get real for two seconds! We're out of money, that's it!

ZAC: *(Picking up the phone.)* I found a place where we can stay for free; we're ordering Chinese.

SPETH: Free.

ZAC: Oh you want to know? You want to ask my opinion on something? *(To phone.)* Hi, I wanna order delivery, some kind of chicken—anything with hot peanut sauce.

SPETH: What is this? Are you serious?

ZAC: I met a guy downtown. He invited us to stay. It's a bunch of squatter's houses in the East End. *(To phone.)* Yeah, we're from out of town, give us something really weird.

SPETH: What kind of house?

ZAC: Squatters—all these people have moved in and it's great and it's one big party and it's free. You know what Moo Shoo Pork is?

SPETH: Is it legal? How many people live there?

ZAC: *(To phone.)* OK, and do you have those big fat noodle things?

(To SPETH.) I don't know how many people, lots.

SPETH: No! This sounds ridiculous, this is like your pals Bob and Zingo, I'm not living with all these people I don't know in some old condemned house —

ZAC: *(To phone.)* Tai Chin Conch with Ketchup Sauce! Now you're talkin'!

SPETH: We're not having Chinese! We have to pay 60 bucks for the hotel—we only have 38!

ZAC: We'll sneak out tonight; we've got a place to stay…

SPETH: No!

ZAC: Then I'll go make 50 bucks tomorrow, I want to eat!

SPETH: NO!!

ZAC: *(To phone.)* Forget the delivery, I'll pick it up!

                (ZAC turns away.)

SPETH: *(Aside.)* Tai Chin Conch is actually...pretty good. You ate in the bath tub.

ZAC: *(Aside.)* A hot shower, a glass of wine, an egg roll dipped in Moo Shoo sauce and a Jimmy Stewart movie... Well it works for me.

                (ZAC joins SPETH in front of the TV.)

ZAC: Hi.

SPETH: Hi.

ZAC: Egg roll?

SPETH: Thanks. Sorry about...

ZAC: Yeah, well.

SPETH: Just kind of freaked out I guess. I'm glad you're here. I'm glad we came.

ZAC: Yeah?

SPETH: Yeah.

ZAC: Guess I'm sorta...confused a bit. Not about you and me—I mean, "you" and "me"—I got that straight. Just, you know; that night, a couple months back. I know, we talked about this already. But I've wondered, since I saw you again at the Albert. If that night meant, anything to you. Even just a little.

                (She shakes her head sheepishly.)

        Oh.

SPETH: The old rebound. Sorry.

ZAC: No, no, you're still thinking about Andy. I understand.

SPETH: No. Totally not.

ZAC: Then—I don't know. It's just, you know girls are pretty mysterious. To guys. To most guys. To me.

SPETH: Yeah?

ZAC: Oh yeah. You never really know what's going on inside a girl's head. I mean, anything? *(Into her ear.)* Hello? Are you home?

SPETH: I guess I am pretty mysterious. Lots going on these days; I'm just getting to know you.

ZAC: I'm glad.

                (She reaches around and gives him a hug. The hug ends; they stay next to each other watching TV, inside arms around each other.)

ZAC: How come Jimmy always gets the girl?

SPETH: Well, he's cute...

ZAC: Really? Sexy cute?

SPETH: Noo... Cute cute. Boyish charm.

ZAC: Ah. Charm.

SPETH:	Very charming. And honest; up front; virtuous.
ZAC:	Not real mysterious, is he?
SPETH:	No. Not very mysterious. Sometimes mysterious is good.
	(She kisses him lightly.)
ZAC:	Yeah.
SPETH:	Sometimes straight forward is…perfectly charming.
ZAC:	Oh?
	(He kisses her. A long slow one.)
ZAC:	Now this is mysterious.
SPETH:	*(Beat.)* Yeah. *(She gently untangles herself.)* Sorry.
ZAC:	*(Quickly.)* No need to be sorry…
SPETH:	Look…there's something I want to tell you. I came out here with you because…I'm pregnant.
ZAC:	*(Long, hanging pause.)* …Oh.
SPETH:	I had to get away and think. I haven't told anybody. And I guess, now, I need to talk.
ZAC:	Uh… Wow. Yeah…talk…
SPETH:	I've kind of been, you know, maybe emotional, plus I'm always trying to sneak to the can and puke quietly, and, oh God, you've got no idea how freaky this is—and we're out of money, we're almost completely broke, it's just way too much—have you seen the welfare mothers out there? Can you imagine being poor and no job and have a baby? Just this world—how could you bring a child up in this world?
ZAC:	*(Beat.)* Am I…?
SPETH:	*(Pause.)* What?
ZAC:	The…
SPETH:	The…? *(Suddenly.)* Oh no. Oh *God* no.
ZAC:	You're sure?
SPETH:	I slept with Andy four hundred times, I slept with you once.
ZAC:	But I could be, you can't know—
SPETH:	Zac, that's sweet, but no—*no.* OK?
ZAC:	Oh shit, I gave you wine. *(Reaching for her glass.)* No wine. I know this—
SPETH:	Zac—I'm having an abortion.
ZAC:	*(Beat.)* Are you sure?
SPETH:	I am. Yeah. I am.
ZAC:	You're *sure*-sure? I mean, it wouldn't matter even if we knew it was mine, it's your—wow—it's your body, it's your decision.
SPETH:	You aren't the father.
ZAC:	*(Beat.)* We're going to this squatting place right now. We're

gonna sneak past the night clerk, we'll take a cab...

(As he talks he smoothes her clothes, pats her hair, stands her up.)

You need a real home, and if it isn't perfect we'll make it perfect, I have a great feeling about this. Trust me, it's gonna be—

(They turn and see the Squats in front of them. Pause. They stare.)

ZAC: Well. Those four houses; see, they look totally normal. The ones with the banners.

SPETH: *(Peering in the dark.)* Those are bedsheets!

ZAC: "We finally found a place we could afford!"

SPETH: "Squatting is not criminal—housing left vacant by developers is criminal!"

ZAC: Cool!

(ZAC starts leading her.)

SPETH: Hold it.

ZAC: What?

SPETH: There's a street person sitting on the porch.

ZAC: Yeah...?

SPETH: If there's 20 people in this little house, and they're street people, and street people are fine with me, except hygiene is really important to me right now and I'm not sharing a bedroom with five bag ladies, right?

ZAC: *(Approaching doorway, to SPETH.)* She probably doesn't live here— *(Stepping around bag lady.)* —'Scuse us Ma'am, like your hat— *(Calling in door.)* —Hello?

(SPETH answers the door as SYLVIE.)

ZAC: Willie sent us.

SYLVIE: You came all the way from Winnipeg? *(Long pause of understanding and cosmic warmth.)* Wow. I'm Sylvie, welcome to our home. The furnishings are a bit modest.

ZAC: Look Speth—a statue of the Pope!

SPETH: *(Whispering to ZAC.)* This room is disgusting, I can feel the bugs, I'm not sleeping here.

SYLVIE: I think you're both very brave. To choose a challenging way of living. *(Understanding pause.)* Yay.

(ZAC plays JONATHON.)

JONATHON: New squatters? I'm Jonathon.

ZAC: Hi, Jonathon. Zac.

JONATHON: What's your politics, Zac?

ZAC: Politics?

JONATHON & SYLVIE: "Undecided."

JONATHON: You wash windows, Zac?

ZAC: Uh...

JONATHON: Jan's a window washer. He can teach you the ropes tomorrow. Or you can just go shoot pool.

ZAC: Right on. *(To SPETH.)* I love this place already!

SYLVIE: Are you partners?

SPETH: Partners?

SYLVIE: We have one bed open just now...

SPETH: *One bed?*

JONATHON: Ian and Marylyn just got arrested.

SYLVIE: C'est la Guerre.

JONATHON: Or there's an extra mattress in the men's quarters...

SYLVIE: *(To SPETH.)* ...and you could share a room with Tamara—I think she's out on the porch.

SPETH: With the hat?

SYLVIE: Oh, you've met. Yay.

SPETH: *(Clinging to ZAC, whispering a mantra.)* I want my own bed, I want television, I want white bread and mayonnaise, I want a buttered cucumber sandwich, I want my mother's pork roast and jello and velvet cake...

ZAC: Something smells...weird.

SYLVIE: Are you vegan? Willie's cooking tonight.

WILLIE: *(Played by ZAC, loudly.)* You ain't fuckin' eating, I ain't fuckin' cooking!

    (They reluctantly sit at the communal dinner table.)

SPETH: *(Whispering.)* What *is* it?

    (Weighing a forkful, ZAC shakes his head, baffled. He goes to taste.)

SPETH: *(Stopping him.) They might be a cult!*

    (They stare at JONATHON and SYLVIE.)

JONATHON: Willie's into anarchy.

SYLVIE: He wants to run a health food co-op.

JONATHON: Right after he dynamites B.C. Hydro.

SYLVIE: Erica just left her alcoholic husband—they didn't have room for her and the children at the shelter.

SPETH: *(Timidly.)* Really...?

ZAC: Is this *seaweed*?

SYLVIE: People choose the way they live.

JONATHON: That's a political choice.

SYLVIE: One way of life demands property and self-interest. Another way of life chooses sharing and compassion.

ZAC: *(Whispering to SPETH.)* Are you getting any of this?

SPETH:	Shh!
JONATHON:	In western culture, property and self-interest rule the system.
SYLVIE:	It's a system that denies the value of life.
ZAC:	*(Whispering.)* I gotta eat.
	(SPETH brushes him off with a hand flick; he eats—he likes it.)
JONATHON:	This city has a housing crisis. Reclaiming abandoned homes is an affirmation.
SYLVIE:	It's an affirmation of life within a system of death.
JONATHON:	*(Toasting.)* To life.
SYLVIE:	Yay life.
ZAC:	*(Mouth full, lifting his glass.)* Mm-mm!
SPETH:	*(Elbowing ZAC.)* How much money do we have?
ZAC:	*(Pulling out money.)* Uh...five dollars?
SPETH:	*(Taking it.)* I'm buying some Pine Sol.
	(Announcing.) We'll take the bed.
ZAC:	*Partners!*
SPETH:	*(Age 27, happily nostalgic.)* We were committed to helping the world. Handing out pamphlets for the women's crisis centre, flyers for the food centre, newsletters for the Anarchists for Action...
ZAC:	*(Age 27.)* Jan taught me window washing, Ingmar taught me how to make a dope pipe out of an apple, Nathan and Sara taught me every Bob Dylan and Grateful Dead song ever written...
SPETH:	*(Ignoring him.)* We would sing, every night in the common room; the other houses invited us for dinners; I heard Joni Mitchell songs for the first time in that kitchen. One night it finally stopped raining. We built a fire in the backyard.
	(They join the backyard circle.)
	Thirty-five squatters, eight guitars, congas, a ukulele...hand-holding in a circle, hugs... Singing, talking politics until five in the morning.
JONATHON:	*(Addressing the circle.)* We're losing ground with the media. That's to be expected.
SYLVIE:	The media represent the narrow property interests of the middle class.
JONATHON:	Which unfortunately also describes our neighbours.
SPETH:	*(To the circle:)* The neighbours look at us like we're from another planet.
	(SPETH hesitates, suddenly aware she's the new kid speaking out in front of the veterans, pulls herself up and continues.)
	We've got to show them we're human, like, do something for them. It's been raining for two months, everybody's miserable, let's have a picnic—we can put out tarps or something and play

music and we'll try not to be too weird and scary, and even, like, serve real hamburger meat!

(Aside.) My first political action!

(ZAC lets out a cynical grunt.)

SPETH: What was that?

(ZAC shrugs, gestures "nothing.")

You got something you wanna say?

(Same gesture.)

Fuck you.

(She gets up to leave.)

ZAC: Speth, I'm sorry, I didn't mean anything, come on.

SPETH: You want it all rosy? It isn't. You picked at me for ten years. If something is bugging you, you say it now because it's your last chance.

ZAC: We had…one or two little problems.

SPETH: *Say* it.

ZAC: *(Beat.)* All right. Remember the first time we argued about politics?

(ZAC changes positions, becomes 17, smoking a joint.)

ZAC: So I don't get this. What, political is a state of mind or something?

SPETH: *(Taking the joint.)* No! It's gotta be, I don't know; you have to care about doing something, it has to be important, like the people living in this house. That's political.

ZAC: They're just living in a house.

SPETH: They're rejecting what's false; they're rejecting middle class jobs and homes.

ZAC: Tamara's living here because she's poor. Jan is living here because he happened to ride by the place on his bicycle.

SPETH: But he already rejected the middle class when he became a window washer and started riding a bicycle.

ZAC: He can't afford a car! You think he doesn't want a car? I want a car!

SPETH: That's because you have no political consciousness.

ZAC: Erica is living here because she got beaten up by her husband.

SPETH: And she left him and that's a political action!

ZAC: That's political? Then what isn't political? I'm the only person in this whole squat who isn't capable of political action?

SPETH: Well, *don't you think*?

ZAC: *(Aside.)* Whoa! OK, so I see this is important to you and I better figure it out so I go to Willie the Anarchist who explains everything.

WILLIE: You got violent protest and you got non-violent protest. But

390 /A Map of the Senses

	violent protest isn't legitimate unless you take responsibility for it. That's why when you bomb a power plant you always phone in to say it was you that did it.
ZAC:	*(Aside.)* So we're passing by this restaurant that refused to serve him the day before because they don't like the way he looks, so we go around back and Willie kicks in a basement window.
WILLIE:	Now that's violent protest.
ZAC:	And now we have to go tell them it was us who did it?
WILLIE:	What—and go to jail for a busted window? Run!
ZAC:	*(Aside.)* And OK, I admit it, I never really got the political thing. After Vancouver I just wanted to get away and play music. Anything to get my mind off you. Three years later, I think I'm making serious progress, and then one day I pick up the phone and your voice says:
SPETH:	Hi, I'm in town, I'd love to see you.
ZAC:	Deep inside, Willie the Anarchist is still yelling, "Run!"

(They turn to face each other. Age 20.)

SPETH:	I just felt completely lost in Europe. I didn't have any faith left in anything. I mean, I spent six months on a Greek island and I was depressed!
ZAC:	You needed some time…
SPETH:	I missed you, Zac. I'm sorry about Vancouver, I'm sorry about everything—I just don't want our friendship to stop right there.
ZAC:	OK…
SPETH:	You're my best friend. I think I figured that out somewhere around Brindisi. I love you, Zac.
ZAC:	You…?
SPETH:	I want to do the whole thing again, except this time we'll do it right. We'll set up a house, we'll apply for grants, it'll be a co-op for low-income people. We'll be selective, do interviews, background checks—we've got experience this time, we know what we're doing—
ZAC:	Just… Are you saying you want me back?
SPETH:	Well, platonically, yeah…
ZAC:	Platonically. You mean celibate.
SPETH:	You don't have to be celibate. I mean, with somebody else. *(Beat.)* We *are* lovers, Zac, we're just not *lovers*-lovers. I'm not ready for a relationship with anyone right now…
ZAC:	No! Go away! Stop now! Get out of my life!

(Age 27, to SPETH.) The only politically astute moment in my entire life. But two years later?

(He picks up his guitar, motions her to take her place at the imaginary podium, age 22.)

BOTH:	*Hey, the people say, what about me?* *You took away our jobs and traded 'em free* *We don't want single mothers forced to go on workfare* *Get your grubby hands off our medicare.*
	(ZAC continues to play as SPETH launches into a speech.)
SPETH:	The New Democratic Party is social democracy, and social democracy is Canada! We must remain a party of the Left! Dwindling membership is no excuse for compromise! And that's why the NDP youth wing says *you must vote no! No* drift to the centre! *No* United Alternatives! We will not get in bed with Preston Manning—no matter what it gets us at the polls!
BOTH:	*The left is right for you and me* *We want the NDP!*
	(They join hands, cheer and wave to the crowd. They keep holding hands, stepping away from the podium.)
SPETH:	*(Letting out a whoop.)* YOW!! I feel like a rock star!
ZAC:	We got them, they're still cheering!
SPETH:	I love this! We just swung the whole convention!
ZAC:	That was rockin', thanks for asking me to do it—
SPETH:	We've got an hour till the vote, I got beer in my room, let's go.
ZAC:	Don't you wanna catch the other speeches?
SPETH:	*(Physically advancing on him.)* I said hotel room. One hour. Aren't you listening?
ZAC:	*(Beat. Mystified.)* What happened to this friends thing?
SPETH:	Didn't you ever hear power is the greatest aphrodisiac? Let's go!
ZAC:	*(To SPETH, age 27.)* Great. I fell in love with a New Democrat who only wants to go to bed when her party is doing well. So…
	(It's same day in SPETH's hotel room, an hour-and-a half-later. ZAC begins picking at his guitar, singing, working on a new song, now totally in love.)
ZAC:	*There's a girl I know…* *(He tries a different chord.)* *There's a girl I know…* *(SPETH enters in shock.)*
SPETH:	Ninety-two percent.
ZAC:	*(Delighted.)* Ninety-two? We fucking killed them!
SPETH:	*(Shaking her head.)* The New Democratic Reform Party is born.
ZAC:	Oh my God…
SPETH:	The world has gone mad…
ZAC:	I'm gonna cheer you up—I'm writing a song for you, it'll be ready by breakfast if you can keep your hands off me that long—
SPETH:	I gotta get to the airport.

ZAC: You said you were staying a couple days.

SPETH: This swing-to-the-right bullshit has gone way too far. We aren't sitting around on this, we're starting a new party—think of a catchy name.

ZAC: Us?

SPETH: We've still got eight percent of the old party, we're gonna hit this quick, get people together, talk to the unions—

ZAC: You can do this?

SPETH: I've got personal contacts. I've had conversations with almost half the membership.

ZAC: That's just because you're the receptionist...

SPETH: I'm an unemployed power broker. I'm quitting tomorrow, right after I steal all the fundraising lists.

ZAC: Speth—I had no idea you were so impressive.

SPETH: New blood, new ideas, the old thinking is dead, we're gonna re-invent the left from the bottom up. Gotta plane to catch, wish me luck.

ZAC: What about apartment hunting?

SPETH: We'll start looking the second you get to Ottawa. Bye bye—

ZAC: I can't leave Toronto—

SPETH: You have to leave Toronto.

ZAC: All my contacts are here, I can get gigs here—

SPETH: Zac, I gotta plane...

ZAC: Well wait, don't just leave...

SPETH: *(Leaving.)* We'll figure it out, we'll make it work...

ZAC: *(Age 27.)* Four years back and forth on the 401...membership drives, conventions, protests... The Democracy Party, The Global Consciousness Party, The Third Millenium Party...

           (ZAC, age 26, begins playing the same tune as earlier, now complete. SPETH enters the scene, pumped on adrenaline.)

SPETH: *This* time we got 'em, *this* is the killer issue.

ZAC: *(Sullen, still playing without looking up.)* How long you in town?

SPETH: American dollars—they've just made the big mistake—Canadians will never give up their own money, you wouldn't believe the reaction to this.

ZAC: Nobody cared about UI, nobody cared about medicare, nobody's gonna care what colour the money is.

SPETH: They already do. Announcing... *"The Canada Party!"*

ZAC: *(Totally without interest.)* Uh-huh.

SPETH: You're looking at the new boss in charge of practically everything. We've got huge support, a whole new coalition right across the spectrum—we're launching it next week.

ZAC: No one pays attention to lefties.

SPETH: Get past the left/right thing—that's old paradigm. This is socially responsible fiscal conservatism.

ZAC: You're working with fascists?

SPETH: The Annexationists want our whole country. We'll take allies anywhere we can find them.

ZAC: You seriously think you have a chance?

SPETH: Buddy?

(SPETH advances on him.)

I think tonight even you have a chance.

(ZAC stops playing, looks up for the first time.)

And if you've got time after that, the boss of practically everything is hiring you to write the theme song.

ZAC: You *like* my music?

SPETH: I *love* your music.

ZAC: You never listen to it.

SPETH: I hear it every time I come here.

ZAC: You wanna hear your song?

SPETH: What song?

(ZAC starts playing the tune he's been working at all along.)

ZAC: *There's a girl I know, I'll go wherever she goes...*

SPETH: The one you're always playing?

ZAC: Took a while to get it right.

SPETH: That's *my* song?

ZAC: *I know she loves me but it don't always show...*

SPETH: *(Overwhelmed.)* Oh... Oh... Oh... Oh...

ZAC: Would you rather hear it on the website?

SPETH: My song's on the net?

ZAC: "Zacsongs.ca"— I'm totally web-based and totally mobile.

SPETH: How totally?

ZAC: Say the word, free as a bird.

SPETH: You'd move?

ZAC: You can be living with your very own highly successful indie recording artist, anywhere in the world.

SPETH: We could buy a house? You're making actual money?

ZAC: Well, not actual money yet, it's free, that's the way it works.

SPETH: You just give away the whole album?

ZAC: What album? It's just one song.

SPETH: One song? That's it?

ZAC: *(Slightly defensive.)* It's a good song.

SPETH:	You've been working on *one song* all this time?
ZAC:	(*Very defensive.*) And it's good, and I like it, and it's been downloaded more than 300 times already.
SPETH:	One song in five years that you give away for *free*?
ZAC:	I guess we'll just have to live off the boss of practically everything's paycheque for a while.
SPETH:	What paycheque? I'm practically a volunteer!
ZAC:	Christ, we're fucking made for each other.
SPETH:	We might as well be fucking married.
ZAC:	We might as fucking well.
	(*Beat—they suddenly grab each other by the shoulders.*)
	Seriously?
SPETH:	Yes.
ZAC:	Speth, I don't want to live without you another second.
SPETH:	I am totally nuts about you.
ZAC:	Why are we always fighting?
SPETH:	We're gonna have way more time to fight now.
ZAC:	The new job is smaller?
SPETH:	It's huge.
ZAC:	Then what changes if we're married?
SPETH:	We'll both live in the same apartment.
ZAC:	(*A little edgy.*) While you put in 80 hours a week with the rich people?
SPETH:	That's pretty much it—
ZAC:	(*A lot edgy.*) And this is for what—five years?
SPETH:	As long as it takes.
ZAC:	And with your spare time...?
SPETH:	We aren't suddenly going to raise a family if that's what you mean—
ZAC:	Making a little time for your new husband, *that's* what I mean—
SPETH:	I'm going to try to make this work within our parameters—
ZAC:	You mean *your* parameters, that's what you mean—
SPETH:	Read my lips: no big changes, no big concessions, you will have a monopoly on all my free time, depending on my schedule which is subject to change.
ZAC:	There we go! Lay down the law! Never consulting, always the great leader!
SPETH:	I'm consulting! I'm asking you—
ZAC:	You're not asking, you're telling! Always your terms, Speth, always your terms!
SPETH:	I can't *talk* to you!

ZAC: You never do!

SPETH: Because you are always looking for a way to make it all my fault.

         (Pause, the characters are back to the present.)

ZAC: *(Age 27.)* All in the past. Forgive and forget.

SPETH: *(Age 27.)* You never forgive, Zac. You never do.

ZAC: Speth...

SPETH: Why would it be any different now?

ZAC: The whole political thing—it's over... We have a chance now, we can start over.

SPETH: That isn't it, that was never it.

         (Pause.)

         You don't have a clue what the problem is, do you.

ZAC: *(At a loss.)* Everything I've ever done, I'm sorry.

         (She stares at him blankly.) I'll hoist myself up the flagpole naked. I'll go replant the rainforests for you.

         (He reaches to touch her face; she gently, firmly stops him. Taking a breath, she backs up to make her point through a different tack, a happy memory.)

SPETH: The happiest day of my life. The day I fell in love with you:

         (Pause.) I try to pretend it doesn't matter, that we'll have fun no matter what, but more than anything I want the sun to shine on my picnic.

         But it rains. It *pours*.

         (Standing under the tarp, age 17.) We huddle together under the tarps. Thirty squatters—forty—with children running between our legs, supporters from all over the East End, friends from all over Vancouver, even some of the neighbours show up.

JONATHON: *(Making a speech.)* Today we are proving what most of us have known all along.

SYLVIE: *(Joining in.)* We know today that people working together can create something beautiful.

JONATHON: We all know today that people come before property...

SYLVIE: We know today that the most perfect political act is to create that beautiful thing, no matter what happens next. Let's give ourselves one big cheer. Yay!

SPETH: *(Aside.)* We're alive with love in the rain, hopping from foot to foot to keep warm, we all join hands in a crowded circle that twists back and around under the tarps and we sing...

         All we are saying,
         Is give peace a chance.
         All we are saying,
         Is give peace a chance...

         Zac isn't here! *(To others in the circle:)* Have you seen Zac?

Anyone?

All we are saying,
Is give peace a chance...

(*Aside.*) I want him to share it! Everyone under this tarp in the rain, no matter what the world is doing in this moment, every one of us is in love.

(*To others in the circle:*) Where's Zac?

(*Aside.*) I have to say it—the words are jumping out of my mouth.

ZAC: (*Aside.*) I know what I have to do. I have to take a political action.

   (*ZAC takes his guitar and moves off to the side.*)

SPETH: (*To the crowd.*) I want to say I love you all today. I've just been here since like, Monday, and, I know I love every one of you. I've never felt right before. For the first time in my life I know that what I'm doing is exactly right. You're all my family now. I'm going to have a baby and I want my baby to feel all the love and strength that I'm feeling from all of you in my family right now.

ZAC: (*Aside.*) I'm ready. It's as good as it's ever going to be. Everyone outside is cheering madly. I come out from the basement and suddenly they're all cheering for me. Wow. I'm pumped.

(*To the crowd.*) Hi. Thanks. This is the first song I've ever written. I want to dedicate it to Speth.

   (*To something that sounds an awful lot like something by Bob Dylan.*)

I don't want your bombs. I don't want your acid rain.
I don't want a world of homeless people and corporate criminals and pain.
I only want something real,
And if that's political, political is how I feel.

ZAC: (*Aside.*) Total attention. They like it. I sing about the rain forests and Central America and patriarchal oppression...

I don't want to see your economic muscles flex,
Your American Military Industrial is giving me a complex...

SPETH: (*Aside.*) I'm 17 and it's the most beautiful thing I've ever heard. All 14 verses...

ZAC: *I only want something real,*
And if that's political, political is how I feel.

(*Aside.*) Spontaneous ovation! "Congratulations!" "Way to go you two!"

SPETH: (*Calling across the crowd.*) Zac!

ZAC: (*To himself.*) "Way to go you two?"

(*Grabbing SPETH's hands.*) They're saying we're going to have a baby. Us?

SPETH: (*An invitation.*) ..."Us?"

   (*ZAC kisses her. Big time. It's mutual. Big time.*)

ZAC: (*Age 27.*) The very best kisses are the ones where you can't stop smiling. Where your face is grinning so hard that your teeth keep knocking together.

SPETH: (*Age 27.*) And I fell in love. And so did you. And then—

ZAC: Not yet.

SPETH: You're kidding.

ZAC: (*Age 17. Sitting her down.*) I never had a dad. I want our baby to have one.

SPETH: (*Age 17.*) It might not be "ours".

ZAC: It doesn't matter. I want to be our baby's father. From now on we're doing everything together.

SPETH: Everything!

ZAC: (*His head in her lap.*) April.

SPETH: Basil.

ZAC: Crystal.

SPETH: David.

ZAC: Too boring.

SPETH: Um... Damian!

ZAC: Elspeth.

SPETH: Ohhh...

            (*They kiss.*)

            (*Age 27.*) You were a total goner.

ZAC: (*Age 27.*) Not yet.

            (*He lies her down, bedtime, age 17.*)

SPETH: I say those two abandoned houses over on Fifth Street...

ZAC: So if we start a squat on Fifth in the summer, and then another one in the spring...

SPETH: I want to do the hitchhiking first.

ZAC: Tree planting, then hitchhiking, then baby, then Fifth Street. Do we get married before tree planting, or after?

SPETH: Before. Next week.

            (*They kiss. They remain snuggled. Pause.*)

ZAC: (*Age 27.*) And the offer is officially re-opened.

            (*Pause.*)

            You are seriously considering this, aren't you?

SPETH: (*Age 27, pushing an imaginary mouse button.*) Click.

ZAC: What's that supposed to be.

SPETH: "Zacsongs.ca." Click click. Nothing's happening. Click click.

            (*She hands him his guitar.*)

ZAC: (*Pause, then singing gently.*)

> *There's a girl I know, I'll go wherever she goes,*
> *I know she loves me*
> *But it don't always show—*

SPETH: No, no. That's version one. I want the upgrade.

(Pause.) Click click.

ZAC: *(Pause. Then singing to the same tune.)*

> *Canada's birthright is a continent wide.*
> *We don't need borders*
> *We're on the same side.*
> *We can all be Americans*
> *You and me…*
> *It's our Manifest Destiny.*

SPETH: My song. Zac Halliwell's entry into the American Annexation Party Jingle Contest.

ZAC: I was mad at you, I'm sorry—

SPETH: Sing the chorus.

ZAC: *(Beat.) A greater destiny is ours*
> *Thirteen stripes and fifty-one stars…*

SPETH: You were *always* mad at me. I hurt you, you forgave me, you waited for your chance and then—

ZAC: I just—

SPETH: You sold my song to the enemy!

ZAC: I love you, Speth—

SPETH: *(Cutting him off.)* What difference does it make if you love me? Don't talk to me any more about love. Just give me a single reason to believe there's any hope.

ZAC: *(Beat.)* All I can say is… let me get to the part where I fell in love with you.

SPETH: There's nothing left to tell. The happy part is over.

ZAC: I didn't say it was the happy part.

(Pause.) It's morning. It's about six-thirty in the morning and I'm awake already. I do what I do every morning. I look at you. You're lying on your side facing me.

   (SPETH hesitates, then takes her place asleep.)

My God, you're beautiful.

SPETH: *(Age 17, waking up.)* What's going on?

ZAC: I don't know. Some big deal out on the street.

SPETH: Are people up already?

   (ZAC bangs on the stage or anything else available as WILLIE.)

WILLIE: It's coming, people! The fascists have come to put down the revolution!

SPETH: What's going on?

ZAC:	*(Looking out window.)* Holy shit! There's a school bus full of cops out there—there's two school buses! There's like 60 cops in front of the house!
SPETH:	Those stinking bastards!
ZAC:	There's another school bus! Jesus, they've got riot gear on! It's a SWAT team!
SYLVIE:	This is it, people!
JONATHON:	This is it, people!
SPETH:	What is it?
WILLIE:	Zacko! Give me a hand with these floorboards—we need some fuckin' weapons here!
SPETH:	What?
JONATHON:	*(Peering out the window.)* This is unbelievable! Six cops and a couple of paddy wagons could clear this place! You wanted sixties? You got sixties!
SPETH:	They can't do this! No way are they shutting us down!
ZAC:	*(As a cop with megaphone.)* All right folks, the party is over! We want to do this peacefully!
SPETH:	What's that noise? Is that a helicopter?
WILLIE:	They've got fuckin' choppers! They've got three fuckin' choppers out there! There's probably snipers across the street! I told you we should have made bombs!
SPETH:	Let's link arms around the house or, or chain ourselves to the floor…!
JONATHON:	Good one! We should have thought of chains…
SPETH:	There's reporters out there, I'm going to tie myself to the front porch.
JONATHON:	Perfect! I love this girl!
	(SPETH as SYLVIE settles into a meditation pose.)
SYLVIE:	Passive resistance, people. Link arms. Relax.
	(ZAC links arms with SPETH, cross-legged. They remain in this pose as all the characters.)
SPETH:	We'll all be back, right? They can throw us in jail, but we'll all be back and we'll just keep the squats going!
JONATHON:	Are you kidding? Do you see that bulldozer out there? The squats are finished.
SPETH:	What are you talking about? They can't tear the place down…
JONATHON:	You can't change the world, kid. All you can do is push it until it has to drop the lie that people are more important than property.
SPETH:	Oh my God! Willie!
JONATHON:	Relax! Willie's been smacked in the head a thousand times.
SPETH:	Don't hit me! I'm pregnant!

ZAC: Take it easy, man, we'll go peacefully, we will, just take it easy…

               (In three fast motions their hands are pulled behind their backs, they're pushed into a kneeling position and then straight to the floor, lying on their sides.)

SPETH: I'm scared…

ZAC: It's OK, they can't do anything to us.

SPETH: They smashed Willie's head!

ZAC: He yelled at them, they won't do anything to us, they can't hit us…

SPETH: How do you know? How do you know they can't do that?

ZAC: They can't, we'll be OK…

SPETH: They can throw us in jail, they can kick our heads in, they can rip down our houses, none of it matters!

ZAC: It doesn't matter what else happened, Speth. The world sucks but we did something beautiful. It counts Speth, it matters. Speth?…

SPETH: *(Age 27, getting up off the ground.)* So what? We did something beautiful *once*? And *then* what? Is that supposed to carry us for a whole lifetime?

ZAC: I know. Just…

SPETH: The thing we have never talked about—

ZAC: In the police station.

SPETH: Yes.

ZAC: *(Positioning her.)* You were sitting there just like that…

SPETH: And you were—

               (She stops speaking because ZAC has crouched in front of her, as he was in the police station, age 17.)

ZAC: They said we can go. *(Pause.)* They said everyone can go, they aren't going to press charges.

        Willie was telling me there's some nice beaches just up north a bit. We could probably start hitch hiking and be sleeping on a beach tonight. Maybe we can find a Justice of the Peace tomorrow.

SPETH: *(Not looking at him.)* They let me make a phone call. My mom is sending me airfare home.

ZAC: Oh. I guess I could hitch a ride home within a couple days. I was sort of thinking we could go straight up and start tree planting right away though.

SPETH: I'm having the abortion.

ZAC: *(Pause.)* No.

        (Pause.) I mean it. No. Take a few days to just get things straight in Winnipeg. Just give yourself some time.

SPETH: *(Pause. Age 27.)* And you've never forgiven me.

ZAC:	That's the moment. I fell in love.
SPETH:	*(Beat.) That?*
ZAC:	Everything, exactly, totally, you meant to me, I realized it in that moment.
SPETH:	I took away your baby.
ZAC:	Not the baby. You, Speth. I knew you might never come back. And you never really did.
SPETH:	*(Beat.)* You're saying you haven't hated me all this time?
ZAC:	I hate you every time you walk out the door. And I forgive you every time you come back.
SPETH:	Ten years, all we've ever done is mess it up. How can we have any hope?
ZAC:	The hopeful part for me is, that was the worst day of my life. If I fell in love with you on that day, and I still love you now, I'm in love with you forever.

(She's about to speak another objection, but he stops her.)

ZAC: Why'd you come here tonight?

SPETH: Hope.

ZAC: For...?

(Beat. She kisses him. Sound of fireworks going off.)

ZAC: Happy fourth of July.

SPETH: Welcome to America.

ZAC: Always a second chance. We could give this country a serious shaking up.

(He takes a key out of his pocket, puts it in his padlock.)

SPETH: *(Stopping him.)* Uh-uh.

(She unlocks the padlock, chains herself to him and relocks it, snaps the key off the keyring, puts the ring on ZAC's finger. She tosses the key away.)

I wanna get arrested by an American cop.

(They kiss. Fireworks continue.)

The End

Between Then and Now

HARRY RINTOUL

Production Information

Between Then and Now was first produced by Three Sisters Theatre Company at the Winnipeg Fringe Festival, 1993.
It was also produced at the Gas Station Theatre, Winnipeg (July, 1993), the Edmonton Fringe Festival (August, 1993), and at the Winnipeg Planetarium Auditorium (October, 1993) with the original cast and crew:

LESLIE .... Julia Arkos
BABE .... Michelle Boulet
BOO .... Ardith Boxall
ANDY/BLAINE/RICHARD .... Ross McMillan

Directed by Chris Sigurdson
Dramaturgy by Rick Chafe
Stage Manager: Cheryl Green

Versions of this play were workshopped or read through the Manitoba Association of Playwrights, Playwright Development Program under the direction of Chris Johnson and Kim McCaw and the MAP Playwrights Colony under the direction of Rick McNair.

Staging

The set consists of a love seat USL, a bed Centre, a kitchen table and two chairs SR and a set of steps DSR. The set triples as the apartments of Andy, Babe and Leslie. The approximate running time is 75 minutes with no intermission.

(Lights up. LESLIE enters UC, crosses to the table and begins to read. BABE enters SL, sits on the bed and reads. BOO enters USC, crosses to the love seat with her luggage. ANDY enters USC and crosses to BOO.)

ANDY: OK. This guy's out duck hunting and he shoots this duck, and it falls and bounces off a barn and lands in a farmer's yard. So the duck hunter goes to pick up his duck, when the farmer appears, and this guy's huge, built like a brick shithouse, sorry, and he says to the duck hunter, "What the hell are you doing in my yard?" and the hunter says, "I'm picking up my duck." The farmer says "It's my duck 'cause it landed in my yard." So the hunter and him argue when the farmer says, "We'll settle this the way we settle things in the country." The hunter says, "How's that?" "What we do," the farmer says, "is have a test of endurance. I kick you in the groin, then you kick me in the groin and whoever is left standing at the end gets to keep the duck." Well the hunter's just about to say no way, when the farmer shouts, "My turn!" and hoofs him. The hunter screams in pain cause it hurts, every bone in his body, and I mean every bone in his body. Finally, after the pain stops, he's standing in front of the farmer, and he hoists up his pants, throws his shoulders back, looks the farmer right in the eye and says, "Now it's my turn." And the farmer says... *(Beat.)* "Forget it, you can keep the duck!"

(BOO laughs. ANDY watches her. She finishes laughing and looks expectantly at ANDY.)

BOO: Well here we are.

ANDY: Here we are.

BOO: It's good to see you, Andy.

ANDY: It's good to see you, Boo.

(BOO walks towards ANDY. ANDY starts to back up.)

BOO: I was wondering when we'd see each other again.

ANDY: So was I.

BOO: Then, I find out I have two weeks of holidays left and I have to take them and...so here I am.

ANDY: Yeah.

BOO: Yeah.

ANDY:	Uh, sorry the place is such a mess. It's furnished in early Sally Ann.
BOO:	It's OK, Andy.
ANDY:	It could be better.
BOO:	Then why isn't it?
ANDY:	You've got the spare room, your bags can go in there. Everyone needs a place for their stuff. Want to do it now?
BOO:	What do you want to do?
ANDY:	What do you want to do? I'll do whatever you want to do. What do you want to do?
BOO:	I asked you.
ANDY:	Want a cup of tea?
BOO:	That would be nice.

(ANDY crosses to the kitchen. BOO steps in front of him.)

	It's been a long time.
ANDY:	Four months.
BOO:	Four months, 13 days, 11 hours and 17 minutes since I saw you last.
ANDY:	You kept track?
BOO:	Yeah.
ANDY:	It's not like we haven't talked.
BOO:	It's better.
ANDY:	Better? Than what?
BOO:	Than letters and phonecalls.
ANDY:	You didn't like the letters?
BOO:	I liked…I loved the letters. Three letters a week for four months, that's a lot of letters.
ANDY:	I had a lot I wanted to say to you.
BOO:	I read and reread them.
ANDY:	You do?
BOO:	Uh huh. There's some very special things in them.
ANDY:	Well you know I'm a deep guy.
BOO:	Are you?
ANDY:	Sure am. I've got thoughts I haven't even thunk yet.
BOO:	Now you're being silly.
ANDY:	Yeah.
BOO:	Sit here beside me.
ANDY:	I could show you around the apartment. Do you wanna see the apartment?
BOO:	Andy…what's the matter?

ANDY: The matter? Nothing's the matter. Why would anything be the matter?

BOO: Well first off, you met me at the bus and you shook my hand. And we've been standing here in your apartment for the last twenty minutes and all you've done is tell me duck jokes.

ANDY: You don't like my jokes?

BOO: I like your jokes, I love your jokes. But everytime I get close to you, you walk away from me. Aren't you glad to see me?

ANDY: Yes.

BOO: Then show me.

(ANDY looks at BOO. BOO closes her eyes, leans in as if ANDY is going to kiss her. ANDY exits SL. BOO opens her eyes.)

Andy?

(ANDY returns with his play.)

ANDY: Here.

BOO: What's this?

ANDY: My first play. I just finished it before I went to meet you at the bus.

BOO: *(She sits.)* "The Light In The Dark. For Boo, because…" You dedicated it to me.

ANDY: You were very important to the writing. I can give it to you to read because I trust your opinion.

BOO: Thank you, Andy.

ANDY: Hey, I promised you tea, didn't I? *(ANDY begins crossing to the kitchen.)*

BOO: Yes, but Andy…

ANDY: I got regular tea but I've also got some chamomile, black cherry, wild raspberry, lemon, rose hip…

BOO: Andy!

ANDY: Yes, Boo?

BOO: Andy sit down for a minute. Please? I want to talk to you.

ANDY: *(ANDY sits down.)* What do you want to talk about?

BOO: I want to talk about us. You and me. And why I'm here. I wanna talk about your letters.

ANDY: What about my letters?

BOO: You say so much in those letters, so much of what you've written has touched me in a very beautiful way.

ANDY: I meant it.

BOO: I've grown very fond of you.

ANDY: Uh huh.

BOO: I feel very close to you.

ANDY: Yeah?

BOO: I like you and you like me, right? What do you want to do right now?

ANDY: That's a loaded question.

(BOO grabs him and kisses him.)

BOO: That was nice.

ANDY: Not 'nice'. It was better than nice...it's just that nice is such a nowhere word.

BOO: We're good friends, right?

ANDY: Right.

BOO: So good friends should feel comfortable with each other should be able to touch each other, right? I like you Andy, I like you a lot. *(He kisses her.)* That was nice—that was very good.

ANDY: It was?

BOO: Yes, it was.

ANDY: I never had much luck with girls.

BOO: *(She leans in to kiss him.)* I think your luck's changing.

(They embrace. They become heavily involved, squirming and shifting as they try to lie together on the love seat. ANDY's hand proceeds under BOO's blouse and rests on her breast, when they start to slide off the couch onto the floor.)

Andy?

ANDY: Uh huh.

BOO: Andy!

(ANDY disengages himself, gets up and walks across the room.)

ANDY: I'm sorry I'll never do it again. You must think I'm awful. We haven't seen each other in over four months, we've talked on the phone and written letters, but we never even kissed before today and the first thing I do is slip my hand under your blouse and I didn't even ask you if I could but I thought, see I thought...

BOO: What?

ANDY: I thought you'd like it...that it would make you feel good.

BOO: I only stopped you because we were sliding off the couch.

ANDY: Oh.

BOO: And if I didn't like it, I would have said so. No means no. Yes means yes.

ANDY: An' it's OK?

BOO: It is now.

ANDY: I understand. I'm glad you told me.

(He kisses her, they embrace and become involved. Again.)

BOO: Hey whoa. Let's slow down.

ANDY: We got lots of time to slow down.

BOO:	Andy…
ANDY:	Boo.
BOO:	Andy please.
ANDY:	That's my name don't wear it out.
BOO:	Andy stop it.
	(She pushes him away. They sit up.)
ANDY:	Sorry.
BOO:	Andy you're so intense.
ANDY:	Am I scaring you?
BOO:	You're not, I'd just like it if we took things a little slower. I had this boyfriend, Joseph. We'd be on the couch and he'd get going like you did and I'd ask him to stop. He wouldn't. I hated that feeling.
ANDY:	I'm sorry.
BOO:	He'd always say he was sorry…
ANDY:	I understand Boo.
BOO:	I just don't want that to happen again.
ANDY:	It won't. Last thing I wanna do is remind you of someone else.
BOO:	You're not anything like Joseph. You're very special to me.
ANDY:	And you're very special to me, too. *(BOO holds ANDY's hand.)*
BOO:	I'm glad you understand, Andy. It's important. So let's not keep things from each other. Let's tell each other what's wrong. Then we don't have to guess. That way we'll always know what each other is thinking. There won't be any surprises then, OK?
ANDY:	OK. *(ANDY stands up.)* How about some tea?
BOO:	That would be nice. I didn't mean that…
ANDY:	Fantasmagorical.
BOO:	Fantasmagorical?
ANDY:	It's your word. I just made it up. For you. It's better than nice.
BOO:	Some tea would be fantasmagorical. *(BOO exits DSL.)*
	(ANDY watches her leave. BLAINE enters.)
BABE:	*(Looking up and smiling.)* Fantasmagorical.
BLAINE:	*(Lights dim SL. BLAINE turns towards the bed.)* What?
BABE:	Nothing.
BLAINE:	I didn't hear you.
BABE:	I didn't say anything. Oh Blaine, did you lock up?
BLAINE:	No.
BABE:	Pardon?
BLAINE:	*(Sitting on the foot of the bed.)* I left a sign on the front porch that says we're heavy sleepers, come on in, rob us blind.

BABE: Who peed in your cornflakes?

BLAINE: I locked up. You ask me the same thing every night.

BABE: Then I won't ask anymore. Sorry.

BLAINE: Fine.

BABE: Blaine, what's the matter? Why are you in such a rotten mood?

BLAINE: I'm not.

BABE: You are.

> *(Pause.)*

So it starts out neat.

BLAINE: What?

BABE: The play.

BLAINE: I'm glad you think so.

BABE: It's not your usual 'art' stuff, there's no eviscerated chickens being thrown around or people in black sheets chanting Wittgenstein and all that other stuff I never understood.

BLAINE: I'm trying something different. That's all.

BABE: I thinks it's very good. So far. And I caught fantasmagorical.

BLAINE: It's your word. You made it up.

BABE: It was neat to see it.

BLAINE: You've said.

BABE: Who's Joseph?

BLAINE: A character.

BABE: He reminds me a little of Ralph.

BLAINE: I never met Ralph.

BABE: I told you about him.

BLAINE: You told me about all your boyfriends that doesn't mean fucking Joseph is Ralph.

BABE: Don't swear.

> *(BABE sets the binder on the floor next to the bed.)*

You could have met Ralph if you wanted to.

BLAINE: I don't want to meet your old boyfriends. I'm insecure enough without trying to live up to his good points, though he never has any unless I say something about him then I'm being paranoid and besides who gets involved with anyone named Ralph unless Ralph is a Bassett Hound.

BABE: Quit trying to change the subject.

BLAINE: I'm not.

BABE: The easiest thing for you to do when you don't want to talk about what I want to talk about is to wander off the topic with one of your goofy ideas about what you wanna talk about.

BLAINE: So what I say about my play isn't important then?

BABE: All I asked was...

BLAINE: I don't have to use your old boyfriends to create a character.

BABE: Fine. Let's just drop it.

BLAINE: Lots of women have had boyfriends they've loved who have left them emotionally scarred.

BABE: Joseph left Boo scarred? Sounds like Ralph to me.

BLAINE: It's never discussed.

BABE: Is Joseph Ralph?

BLAINE: I never said that.

BABE: Is he? That's all I want to know. Yes or no.

BLAINE: Yes. Joseph is loosely based on Ralph.

BABE: "Loosely?" Loosely? How loosely?

BLAINE: Very loosely.

BABE: *(BABE slams the script down on the bed and stand up.)* How dare you! How dare you take something I told you in confidence and trust, something that was meant for just you, something that really hurt me and was hard for me to tell you and put it in your play!

BLAINE: Nobody's gonna know it's you.

BABE: I'll know. You gonna throw my mother's miscarriages in?

BLAINE: No.

BABE: How about Minnn-ddy?

BLAINE: No!

BABE: Why not? Mindy broke your heart and tore you apart when she left you. That's tragic. Lotsa conflict there.

BLAINE: Babe...

BABE: If you're gonna throw Ralph in then throw Mindy in. Every play needs a tramp doesn't it?

BLAINE: Babe...

BABE: *(BABE takes off her robe and gets into bed.)* Create out of your own life. Don't use mine!

(Pause. BABE pulls the blankets up around her and rolls over.)

BLAINE: Babe I'm sorry. I'm sorry about putting Ralph in the play. I'll never do it again. You're right. I have no right to co-opt your life. Look Babe, I don't want to fight. *(BLAINE removes his clothes and gets into bed.)*

BABE: Then don't.

BLAINE: Babe...

BABE: I'm trying to sleep.

BLAINE: BAAAAABBBE?

BABE: Blaine go to sleep.

BLAINE: I'll cut Joseph out, I'll change it.

BABE: It's not *my* play. Do whatever you want. I'm going to sleep.
            (Pause.)

BLAINE: You really tired?

BABE: Yes I am.

BLAINE: Real tired?

BABE: Whatever you're taking so long to say, say it.

BLAINE: You wanna make love?

BABE: No.

BLAINE: It might make you feel better.

BABE: I don't think so. Blaine, let me sleep.

BLAINE: Kiss and make up?
            (She kisses him quickly, lightly and rolls over.)

BABE: Now go to sleep.

BLAINE: *(BLAINE snuggles up next to her.)* I'm sorry if I upset you…

BABE: Blaine, forget about it.

BLAINE: OK it's just…wanna play a fast game of tickle?

BABE: Blaine I'm tired! I don't want to make love.

BLAINE: Could we cuddle? *(She doesn't respond.)* I mean if you're tired and
            you don't want to make love, you can just lie there I'll take care of
            everything.

BABE: Listen to yourself!

BLAINE: I didn't mean that the way it sounded. I must sound like Ralph.
            (BABE rolls over and looks at him.)

BABE: You never met Ralph. You don't know what he was like so
            you've got no right to compare yourself to him.

BLAINE: I don't.
            (BABE gets out of bed and rips the blanket off BLAINE.)
            Where are you going?

BABE: Downstairs. I'll sleep on the couch.

BLAINE: Why?

BABE: I want to get some sleep.

BLAINE: What about me?

BABE: You can sleep up here.

BLAINE: Fine then. Sleep downstairs if that's what you wanna do.

BABE: That's what I'm gonna do.

BLAINE: Fine. You're gonna do what you wanna do anyways. It doesn't
            matter what I want.
            (BABE picks up the binder.)
            Why are you taking that?

BABE:	Because I might want to read it.
BLAINE:	What would you want to do that for?

(BABE starts to exit.)

BABE:	Because I want to know what happens next and now I'm too awake to sleep!
BLAINE:	Whoever said the first time was the best wasn't whistling into the wind.
BABE:	Blaine…it was the first time is the most memorable.
BLAINE:	Used to be you couldn't wait to get into bed.
BABE:	I've asked you what's wrong a dozen times, you wouldn't tell so now I'm going to bed.
BLAINE:	You'd rather sleep alone, is that it?
BABE:	Goodnight Blaine.

(BABE crosses behind the bed and enters the living room, lies on the love seat, opens the binder. BOO enters the bedroom, wearing a very sexy nightie.)

BOO:	Do you like it?
ANDY:	Yeah.
BOO:	I bought it special for the trip out here. For you.
ANDY:	That's great.
BOO:	So is there room in there for me?
ANDY:	Uh yeah…sure.
BOO:	Hi.
ANDY:	Hi.
BOO:	Andy?
ANDY:	Yeah.
BOO:	Something wrong?
ANDY:	No uh it's just that…
BOO:	What?
ANDY:	What about you know…
BOO:	What?
ANDY:	Are you on the pill?
BOO:	No.
ANDY:	I don't have any condoms.
BOO:	It's OK. I do.
ANDY:	Boo…
BOO:	Andy, I've missed you. This is the first night we've had the chance to be together. I want to make love.
ANDY:	I know you do, so do I, it's just… See I've thought about making love with you, fantasized about it, woke myself up in the middle of night dreaming about you, don't get me wrong, I do want to

	make love to you, it's just, sometimes when you think about something long enough and you anticipate it...when it does happen it isn't what you thought it would be. I don't want it to be like that.
BOO:	Neither do I, Andy.
ANDY:	And like I said I'm nervous and well, it might take a while. So if we just take things nice and easy, is that OK with you?
BOO:	Uh huh. *(BOO kisses him. They embrace and kiss, become heavily involved. After a moment ANDY sits up.)*
ANDY:	You asked me why the place wasn't better, I said it was furnished in early Sally Ann, it could be better and you said why isn't it better, well I'm doing the best I... Trust me. It will get better. I'll get better. I promise you.
BOO:	I know. I know that someday you're gonna be everything you wanna be.
ANDY:	I knew you'd understand Boo. I knew it. I love you, Boo.
	(BOO removes ANDY's glasses, they embrace and lie back down.)
BABE:	You know Blaine I wonder what it would it be like to be involved with someone who was well-adjusted. I wish you'd tell me what's going on!
	(BABE puts the binder down, pulls a blanket around her. Lights fade on BABE, BOO and ANDY but remain up on LESLIE. LESLIE looks up from the script, takes a sip from her coffee cup, holds up the page she has finished reading, sets it down and continues reading. Lights rise slowly on the rest of the stage. It is the next morning. ANDY gets out of bed, looks fondly at BOO as he gets dressed. BABE gets up, folds the blanket she used the night before. BOO wakes up and notices ANDY.)
BOO:	Morning, Andy.
BABE:	Morning, Blaine.
	(BLAINE looks at BABE. ANDY smiles at BOO.)
ANDY:	Good morning yourself.
BOO:	Good morning yourself. Sleep OK?
ANDY:	When I slept. You?
BOO:	About the same.
BABE:	*(BABE places the script on the bed.)* Morning, Blaine.
	(BLAINE looks at her. ANDY smiles at BOO again.)
BOO:	I'll make us a good breakfast and we can think about what we're going to do today.
ANDY:	*(ANDY puts his arms around BOO.)* I know what we can do.
BOO:	I'm sure you do. You keep your hands to yourself. I'll make breakfast, then we can plan the day.
BABE:	*(Throwing the blanket on the bed.)* Good morning, Blaine.
	(BLAINE ignores her.)

ANDY:	I should write. I always write at least an hour a day.
BOO:	You can write. Then we can do something.
BABE:	Would you like some breakfast, Blaine?
BLAINE:	I'm not hungry.
BABE:	Suit yourself.

(BABE exits to the kitchen, picks up LESLIE's cup and leans against a chair.)

BOO:	So what would you like for breakfast?
ANDY:	I don't usually eat breakfast.
BOO:	You should. Breakfast is the most important meal of the day.
ANDY:	It's too much hassle.
BOO:	I'll make it.
ANDY:	You will?
BOO:	Even writers have to eat, don't they?
ANDY:	Yes they do. Particularly when they've worked up a big appetite.
BOO:	So what can I fix you?
ANDY:	Whatever you're making for yourself is fine. I'm just gonna go outside and have a smoke.
BOO:	First thing in the morning?

(BABE enters with a coffee.)

BLAINE:	*(To BABE.)* You sleep OK?

(BABE ignores BLAINE.)

BOO:	Have you thought about quitting? I mean it must cost you a lot.
ANDY:	I like smoking.
BOO:	Really?
ANDY:	*(To BOO.)* Really. Look, first thing I do in the morning is have a cigarette. I always do that. It's my routine.
BOO:	Oh.
BLAINE:	You sleep OK?
BABE:	I slept fine.
BLAINE:	Oh. Did you make any toast?
BOO:	Do you want a cup of coffee or tea with your cigarette? I mean you don't just have a cigarette all by itself, do you?
ANDY:	Yes I do.
BABE:	You told me you weren't hungry.
BLAINE:	I am kind of.
BOO:	Oh. So should I wait for you to come in or what? Before I start breakfast?
ANDY:	Whatever. I won't be long.
BABE:	Why didn't you say you were hungry when I asked you?

BLAINE:	I don't know.
BOO:	We could cook breakfast together. I could show you how easy it is to make a good breakfast.
ANDY:	Boo. First thing I do every morning, is go out and have my cigarette. OK? I sit and think. It's how I start my day.
BOO:	Oh. OK.
BLAINE:	So what's for breakfast?
BABE:	Ground glass! You know where the kitchen is, make whatever you'd like, do whatever you want.
BLAINE:	Where you going?
BABE:	I'm going to shower, get dressed then I don't know. I don't know what I'm going to do. Why don't you go have a cigarette?
	(BLAINE exits to the steps has a cigarette. BABE and BOO sit. They notice each other.)
	I ask him what's wrong and he sits there. Won't say a word.
BOO:	This is so frustrating.
BABE:	Sometimes he's such a child.
BOO:	He has his way of doing things.
BABE:	Trying to get him to say something, to tell you something that means anything is like pulling teeth.
BOO:	He's got his routines.
BABE:	You can get him to talk to you when you force him, when you threaten him but why should you have to do that?
BOO:	But I thought he'd want to be with me, spend time with me. Why couldn't we make breakfast together?
BABE:	He used to be funny, he used to make me laugh, he had all these weird little routines he used to do and it doesn't happen anymore, he's so...different. He's so serious.
BOO:	He needs to have some time to himself. You have to listen to what he's really trying to say.
BABE:	And listening's important.
BOO:	Listening is very important. Very important. *(BOO crosses and sits on the steps next to ANDY.)*
BOO:	Andy, you OK? What's the matter?
ANDY:	Just thinking.
BOO:	Is something wrong?
ANDY:	I'm sorry if I barked at you Boo, about coming out for a smoke. I'm used to being alone when I get up and I'm not really a morning person.
BOO:	You were this morning. And earlier this morning. And late last night.
ANDY:	Thanks for listening to me last night.

BOO: Thanks for telling me.

ANDY: You wanna take a walk with me to the post office?

BOO: Sure. You gotta pick something up?

              (They kiss.)

ANDY: I think this is a very special day. Know why? Because of you. Before I met you I didn't, didn't know what was gonna happen.

BOO: I thought we were talking about a trip to the post office?

ANDY: Boo, I want to submit my play. I've thought about sending it out, thought I could be a writer, I've even written the covering letters, but I never believed it until last night, until you said you knew I could be everything I want to be.

              (BOO exits SL. BABE watches her go. BLAINE crosses to the bed. They notice each other.)

BABE: Oh you're in here.

BLAINE: I can go downstairs.

BABE: No, it's OK. Stay here.

BLAINE: You sure?

BABE: I'm sure.

              (BABE and BLAINE stand awkwardly, trying not to look at each other. BOO enters in her dress, reading one of ANDY's letters and sits on the love seat. BLAINE starts to make the bed, BABE watches.)

BOO: Well my baboo, again our refrain sounds and echoes through my soul. Anyone could say that it'll never work out, you live a thousand miles from me and the distance alone, I wish you were here so I could hold you and hug you, tell you that I care for you. I've got the separation blues and I know it's not for a long time but the miles are the difference. *(BOO pulls another letter from the bundle and reads silently.)*

BLAINE: Look I'll go downstairs...

BABE: You don't have to do

BLAINE: It's your room.

BABE: It's OK. I can go downstairs.

BLAINE: I can go.

BABE: Stay. Do whatever you're doing. I'll go downstairs. *(BABE grabs her pants and exits to the living-room where she changes. After a moment, BLAINE follows.)*

BOO: It might sound silly, but I ask myself why I care about you, and I don't come up with a concrete answer, just, it's nature of man to care about causes and things, but also to know when to care about another human being. Besides, you laugh at all my jokes, what else could a man ask for?

              (BLAINE enters the living room. BOO lies down on the love seat and goes to sleep.)

BLAINE:	You mad at me about last night?
BABE:	Blaine, why do you wait until you feel like you have to talk about something, until your stomach aches and you're all tied up in knots?
BLAINE:	I don't.
BABE:	You came downstairs this morning and you're still mad about last night. Why didn't you talk about it last night?
BLAINE:	I thought I did.
BABE:	You thought. Blaine I can't read your mind. *(BABE sits on the love seat in front of the sleeping BOO.)*
BLAINE:	Did you sleep downstairs because of what I said?
BABE:	I slept down here because you kept talking and I wanted to sleep.
BLAINE:	Oh.
BABE:	Did you act like this with Mindy?
BLAINE:	Never talked much with Mindy.
BABE:	Why not?
BLAINE:	I should work.
BABE:	I didn't think you were working on anything. Why don't you take it easy for awhile?
BLAINE:	I work everyday. I work hard. I practice my craft.
BABE:	OK, what happened?
BLAINE:	Nothing happened.
BABE:	Something happened! When you start mentioning the word craft, something's happened.
BLAINE:	*(Pulls letter from pocket.)* Blah blah blah "...we thank you for your script however upon careful thought we feel your story is too linear, which means it tells a story in a straightforward manner, and does not address the current trends in Canadian theatre." Trends? What trends? "While it is clear that you can write well, we feel further training..." blah blah blah. Asshole. *(He hands her the letter.)*
BABE:	I don't believe this. When did you get this?
BLAINE:	Yesterday.
BABE:	Great! This explains why you were in an absolutely lousy mood all day yesterday and last night. Well that's too bad. I'm sorry this goof doesn't like your play but I don't like having to deal with your self-pity. At least he said you could write. If you can't stand the rejection maybe you should think about doing something else.
BLAINE:	That's very supportive. Thank you very much.
BABE:	You make me crazy! Blaine I don't care if you're a writer, I could care less if you worked at McDonald's or pumped gas. I care about you, not what you do. You wanna write, be a writer, fine,

but I care about the man. *(Pause.)* Blaine…aw you're wearing me out. Have you listened to one word of what I said?

BLAINE: I heard you.

BABE: But did you listen?

BLAINE: I heard you.

BABE: Fine. I'm gonna get a coffee. You want one?

BLAINE: I can get it.

BABE: I'm already up.

BLAINE: I don't need your pity.

BABE: Pardon me?

BLAINE: I've got two legs. I'm not helpless.

BABE: I never said…

BLAINE: Then let me get my own coffee.

BABE: Fine. Do anything you want to.

BLAINE: That's your answer for everything isn't it?

(BABE picks up BLAINE's script and crosses to the steps and begins reading. ANDY kneels down next to the sleeping BOO.)

ANDY: Hi.

BOO: Hi. You're back.

ANDY: Listen, I got a joke for you.

BOO: Andy…

ANDY: There's this guy driving down this country road when he hits this rabbit, and he stops the car and he gets out and kneels next to the rabbit and the rabbit is in pain, did you know rabbits cry, sound like a baby crying. Anyways he's trying to make the rabbit comfortable when this car stops and the guy gets out and asks what the matter is. He tells the guy and guy looks at the rabbit and says he's got something that'll fix the rabbit up. He goes to the car and comes back with a bottle and gives the rabbit a sip. So they wait and nothin' happens when all of a sudden the rabbit twitches his little rabbit nose, gets up hops aways, stops and waves, then it hops some more, stops, turns and waves and it keeps doing this till it's out of sight and the guy asks the other guy what he gave the rabbit to drink and the guy tells him, he says are you ready for this, oh it was just a little hare restorer with permanent wave. Get it? *(He waves.)* Permanent wave? Get it? You're not laughing. *(Beat.)* I know what you need. *(ANDY wraps his arms around her and starts to kiss her. BOO pushes him away, sits up.)*

BOO: Andy don't. We should get going.

ANDY: Going?

BOO: We have to go grocery shopping, there's almost nothing in the fridge.

ANDY: We can do that later.

BOO: We can't do it later; I've made up a schedule for the rest of the day.

ANDY: A schedule. Really.

BOO: We can go grocery shopping, allow an hour for that there and back. Then a tour through the museum, say an hour and a half. After the museum we can go to the art gallery. We can have lunch at the art gallery. Then I thought a walk would be a nice change of pace, maybe do a little window shopping. After which we could go out for dinner and then to a movie and then home. How's that sound?

ANDY: Like a lot.

BOO: It's not really. I was thinking we should also think about a long-range schedule. Try and work out when you'll be coming out to see me, what times are good for me, what's good for you, best time to travel. If we plan far enough ahead we won't have any surprises.

ANDY: None at all.

BOO: If we throw a load of laundry in now we can put it in the dryer after we come back from the store. After we get back tonight, we can fold laundry and make love. Everything works out if you keep to a schedule.

ANDY: I wouldn't know. *(ANDY gets up.)*

BOO: Andy?

ANDY: I don't believe this. It's happening. *(ANDY crosses in front of the bed.)*

BABE: *(Crossing to BLAINE in front of the bed.)* I want to talk to you about this mister. *(She waves the script.)*

BLAINE: I'm sorry Babe. I know what I did. You don't have to tell me.

BABE: It's not what you did

BLAINE: I know what I did.

BABE: It's what you won't do. Or can't seem to do.

BOO: *(Stands.)* What's happening?

BABE: Why do you fight me all the time?

BLAINE: I don't want to. I try not to.

BABE: You don't try hard enough.

ANDY: I thought we were different.

BOO: *(Crossing to ANDY.)* From what? Who?

BABE: Why won't you let go of things once they're over? All I wanted to do was get you a cup of coffee.

BLAINE: You're right. You're right. I know you are.

BOO: Different from what?

ANDY: From before. It's happening again.

BOO: We said we'd always talk to each other. I want to know what's wrong?

BOO/BABE:	What's so hard about talking to me?
BLAINE:	This has nothing to do with you, with now, with us…
BOO/BABE:	Don't you know I care about you?
ANDY:	You've got everything scheduled out, no surprises. You know exactly what you want.
BOO:	I want you.
BABE:	Blaine what's going on?
BLAINE:	All I did was write a play.
BABE:	Blaine?
BLAINE:	And you start tearing me apart.
BOO:	All I'm asking is…
ANDY:	Everything changes. It always does.
BABE:	What are you talking about?
ANDY:	I've heard about this happening.
BOO:	Heard about what? What?
BLAINE:	There's nothing left.
BABE:	That's not true.
BOO:	What are you talking about?
ANDY:	It's only been three days and you're already trying to change me. So I'll go now. *(ANDY/BLAINE start to exit.)*
BABE:	Where are you going?
ANDY & BLAINE:	We're finished.
BOO:	We haven't started anything.
ANDY:	I didn't think it would happen to us.
BABE:	WHERE ARE YOU GOING? WHAT DO YOU MEAN 'WE'RE FINISHED?'
BLAINE:	I don't know how to do this.
ANDY:	After you make love there's nothing left.
BABE:	What do you mean we're finished?
BOO:	I don't understand what's happening.
BABE:	Don't you go, don't you run away from me… Blaine you hear me? Blaine!
BOO:	Andy!
	(ANDY/BLAINE exit.)
	I don't understand.
BABE:	What's it mean there's nothing left?
BOO:	I thought if I just asked him…
BABE:	*(Crossing to love seat.)* He might open up to you…
BOO:	Let me inside.

BABE: Enough to let you be there…then it doesn't happen

BOO: And you wonder…

BABE: Is it ever going to?

BOO: What did I do wrong? *(BOO sits beside BABE.)* I think I'm gonna cry.

BABE: Don't. If you start crying I'll start crying.

       (BABE and BOO look at each other and start to cry.)

LESLIE: Babe and Boo start to cry. *(BABE and BOO hug.)* Babe and Boo hug. Lights dim. *(Lights dim on BABE and BOO but do not go out.)* Well. *(She smiles, pushes the paper away from her.)* Well, well, well. *(She looks at the script, happy as she fidgets with the pages. RICHARD enters. He's a little nervous.)*

RICHARD: Hi! I'm back.

LESLIE: Good. Because I've got something to tell you.

RICHARD: You've got something to tell me? Really? Is it something I'm going to want to hear?

LESLIE: I think so.

RICHARD: So? What is it? Yes or no?

LESLIE: Yes.

RICHARD: *(Excited.)* Yes? Yes what?

LESLIE: Yes, I like the play.

RICHARD: Oh. You like the play. That's good. *(Beat.)* Did you read the whole thing?

LESLIE: Not yet.

RICHARD: Oh, OK.

LESLIE: It's exciting. I can't believe you would do this for me.

RICHARD: I wanted to write something that would let you know how much I care about you, so I did. It's a gift. To you from me.

LESLIE: There's just one little thing.

RICHARD: OK. If it's just one little thing it won't take much to fix it. What is it?

LESLIE: Fantasmagorical. *(BABE and BOO perk up at the mention of the word.)*

RICHARD: Fantasmagorical? What about it?

LESLIE: I hate that word!

RICHARD: You do?

LESLIE: It's a stupid, immature, teenage word I find really irritating.

RICHARD: You hate it?

LESLIE: I've told you that a hundred times.

RICHARD: Really? Oh. Well I can cut it.

BOO: He wants to cut my word.

BABE:	It's not your word. It's mine!
BOO:	He can't cut our word. Can he?
RICHARD:	OK so I'll cut fantasmagorical. *(RICHARD takes a pen and crosses out the word.)*
BABE:	There it goes.
LESLIE:	Thank you.
RICHARD:	So I'll let you read the second act…
LESLIE:	Uhhm, there's something else that bothers me.
RICHARD:	Something else?
LESLIE:	Just a couple of small discrepancies.
RICHARD:	Discrepancies?
LESLIE:	Inaccuracies. For example…
RICHARD:	You've got examples?
LESLIE:	The scene where Boo goes into Andy's bedroom, Boo's practically throwing herself at Andy. *(BOO stands at the mention of her name and tentatively crosses towards LESLIE and RICHARD.)*
RICHARD:	Yeah, so?
LESLIE:	Our first night together I admit I did want to make love but I didn't attack you like that.
RICHARD:	I took a little dramatic license with that.
LESLIE:	I look like a tramp.
BOO:	Hey!
RICHARD:	Boo's not a tramp, she wants to make to love.
LESLIE:	I look like a cat in heat.
RICHARD:	OK. Fine. I made a mistake. I'll fix it. *(RICHARD sits at the table. BOO watches over his shoulder.)*
LESLIE:	I just think if you're going to depict us then do it accurately. All that talk about taking it slow and not rushing, that wasn't you, it was me.
RICHARD:	It's just a play.
LESLIE:	When you revise and change what happened to make yourself look better, I think that's going too far.
RICHARD:	Where did I do that?
LESLIE:	The bedroom scene where Blaine wants to make love and Babe is tired and goes to sleep downstairs…
RICHARD:	Yeah?
LESLIE:	…wasn't like that. If you remember correctly, and obviously you don't, I was tired, I didn't want to make love, you did…
RICHARD:	Yeah.
LESLIE:	I let you! I didn't want to! I didn't feel like it! But I let you!
RICHARD:	OK, yes, you're right. You did. You're right. It was terrible of me to include that. I was wrong.

LESLIE:	*(Sitting on the foot of the bed.)* You know what it's like to have someone on top of you grunting and groaning?
RICHARD:	No I don't.
LESLIE:	It's not a lotta fun let me tell you.
BABE:	She's right about that. The things we do.
BOO:	I think any time you make love is wonderful. *(BABE looks at BOO like she's from another planet.)*
RICHARD:	OK, you've made your point. But you do like it, don't you?
LESLIE:	I'm finding it really interesting.
RICHARD:	You don't like it.
LESLIE:	I do.
RICHARD:	Interesting's what people say when they don't like something. The only thing worse is 'It's nice.'
LESLIE:	Richard I love you. I love the fact that you wrote a play for me.
RICHARD:	I love you, too.
LESLIE:	I'd like to think you trust me.
RICHARD:	I do. What have I done that says I don't trust you?
LESLIE:	What have you done? How about co-opting my life? How about changing the focus of some events and totally rewriting others?
RICHARD:	OK, Babe you've made your point...
LESLIE:	Don't call me Babe, I hate that.
RICHARD:	You don't have to get upset...
LESLIE:	I'm not upset.
RICHARD:	I know when my baboo's upset. *(RICHARD sits next to LESLIE.)*
LESLIE:	I am not your bloody baboo!
RICHARD:	Hey, know what? I finally remembered where my sweet baboo comes from. From *Peanuts*. *(LESLIE looks at RICHARD. Beat.)* I'm sorry, OK? Why are you so angry?
LESLIE:	You mention my mother's miscarriages.
RICHARD:	Well...
LESLIE:	No one wants to hear about my mother's miscarriages. I don't want to hear about them. My mother won't want to hear about them. How could you put that in the play?
RICHARD:	I can change it. I've got a pen, we'll take care of this right now. Now the line is... *(He crosses to the table, flips through the script. Finds it.)*
BABE:	*(Stands.)* You gonna throw my mother's miscarriages in?
	(RICHARD scribbles on the page.)
RICHARD:	There ya go, nothing's carved in stone.
BABE:	You gonna throw my mother's alcoholism in?
LESLIE:	*(Watching BABE.)* My mother doesn't drink. *(He rewrites it.)*

BABE: You gonna throw my mother's five divorces in?

LESLIE: Richard!

RICHARD: OK, OK I'm thinking.

BABE: My mother's body odour?

LESLIE: No.

BABE: Her Valium addiction!

LESLIE: That's awful!

BABE: My mother's warts!

LESLIE: It's a skin condition!

BABE: Body odour. Big feet. Smokes too much. Likes younger men.

LESLIE: You're not being serious.

RICHARD: *(He crosses out the line.)* Forget it.

BABE: What?

RICHARD: I cut the line. She's an orphan.

BABE: *(To BOO.)* He killed my mother!

LESLIE: Thanks. I wouldn't want my mother to see that.

RICHARD: You're welcome. If there's nothing else, I'll let you finish reading. I'm glad you like the play.

LESLIE: *(Walking towards RICHARD.)* Why'd you write this?

RICHARD: I told you.

LESLIE: You did. A gift. What's the real reason?

RICHARD: I was in the store the other day, getting cigarettes and some things you asked me to pick up for you and I got your money and mine mixed up. I was worrying about whose change was whose. And I thought it really doesn't matter, it shouldn't matter but then you never know what's going to matter and I started worrying about it and it really had the potential to become one those things that could become something and I thought and then I figured well what the hell why do I have to worry about whose change is whose.

LESLIE: What you're saying is that I've turned into Babe.

BABE: Don't drag me into this!

RICHARD: What's wrong with Babe?

LESLIE: Babe's a bitch.

BABE: Hey!

LESLIE: And Boo's a bimbo.

BOO: I really think you should just lighten up!

RICHARD: Babe's a very understanding woman.

LESLIE: Blaine comes off as this poor misunderstood male who can't get what he wants and Babe looks like a bitch.

BABE: She said it again.

BOO:	He wrote you a play! Why don't you read it?
LESLIE:	*(To BOO.)* Why don't you shut up?
BABE:	What did you say? *(BABE walks towards her.)*
LESLIE:	What's going on?
BABE:	*(To BOO.)* This puts her in an interesting position, considering her boyfriend wrote the play...
LESLIE:	I beg your pardon?
BABE:	*(Closing in on LESLIE.)* In the eyes of the audience, am I you? And are you, God forbid, me?
BOO:	*(Picking up on what BABE means.)* Were you once me?
BABE:	And did you become me? And more importantly, how are you going to feel when people see the play and believe we, are really you?
LESLIE:	*(LESLIE looks at both BABE and BOO and quickly crosses to RICHARD.)* You don't show this to anybody before you make changes! You hear me?
RICHARD:	I'll change it when we're in rehearsals.
LESLIE:	What do you mean 'when'?
RICHARD:	What?
LESLIE:	Is this being produced?
RICHARD:	Uhmm, I was going to tell you.
LESLIE:	When do you start rehearsal?
RICHARD:	Tuesday. Surprise. Happy anniversary.
LESLIE:	Call it off!
RICHARD:	I can't.
LESLIE:	Get out!
BOO:	She can't do that.
BABE:	She can do what she feels she has to.
RICHARD:	Leslie...
BOO:	*(To LESLIE.)* You can't do that.
RICHARD:	Leslie...Leslie I'll change it! I've got two days.
LESLIE:	You've had three years. And now I find out this is what you think about our relationship.
RICHARD:	If you'd listen, Leslie, we can work this out, we can talk.
LESLIE:	Talk? Instead of talking to me you write about it. You talk to your computer more than you talk to me.
RICHARD:	I am not leaving until we talk about this.
LESLIE:	You want to know what I think of your play? You know what I think of your play, Richard? It's... *(Softly.)* nice. It's very, very nice.

(RICHARD looks at her, very hurt, then exits offstage.)

BABE: Now who's a bitch?

BOO: You didn't have to say that.

LESLIE: Do you think I wanted to?

BOO & BABE: YES!

     (RICHARD rushes onstage.)

RICHARD: For someone who says they know me, you don't know anything at all, you know that, Leslie? You really don't. You don't have any idea about me at all. So read the second act. Read the second act, maybe you'll see what I had in mind.

     (RICHARD exits. BOO crosses to the table, sits down and starts flipping through the script.)

LESLIE: What are you doing?

BABE: Boo stay out of her way. Leave that alone.

BOO: I'm just looking.

BABE: Don't be fooling around with that...

BOO: I'm not 'fooling around' with anything.

LESLIE: Leave that alone, it's not yours.

BABE: Boo come on...

BOO: She never finished.

LESLIE: Give me that!

BOO: No.

LESLIE: You're not supposed to have that.

BABE: Boo give it to her.

BOO: No. Why should I? She doesn't care.

LESLIE: Give me that.

     (BOO and LESLIE chase each other around the table. To avoid BABE and LESLIE she jumps up onto the love seat. LESLIE and BABE try to pry the script out of BOO's hands. As they struggle, they all loose their grip and the script explodes and pages rain down upon the stage.)

LESLIE: Great. Are you happy now?

BOO: She can't read parts of it, it's not fair.

LESLIE: There's more to it than that.

BOO: So says the dragon lady.

LESLIE: I resent that.

BABE: Face it. You were a bitch.

LESLIE: I don't have to talk to you.

BABE: Try avoiding me.

BOO: *(Stepping down from the love seat and sitting down amongst the scattered pages.)* I care about him even if you don't. You were cruel saying his play was nice. You might as well've stabbed him in the heart.

LESLIE:	I wanted him to leave; he wouldn't. I shouldn't have said that but I felt I didn't have any choice.
BABE:	He's such a pain. I don't know why I put up with him.
BOO:	Isn't that what being in love is?
LESLIE:	It's more than that.
BOO:	More than what?
BABE:	Go ahead. Tell her.
LESLIE:	She'll find out for herself.
BOO:	You just can't forget everything that's happened.
LESLIE:	It's easy to forget what you can't remember.
BABE:	And there's no future in the past.
BOO:	But he cares and he's kind…
BABE:	Boo, you don't have to worry.
BOO:	I do.
BABE:	Andy's coming back.
BOO:	I knew it.
LESLIE:	How do you know what's going to happen?
BOO:	If she says she knows, then she knows.
BABE:	Richard's play is finished. Our world is set.
LESLIE:	So?
BOO:	And if Andy comes back, then Blaine comes back?
BABE:	Whatever is going to happen is going to happen, we will have a resolution. The only person who really has to worry about anything is *(BABE and BOO look at LESLIE.)* you.
LESLIE:	And I'm not worrying about anything because I'm not going to read it.
BOO:	You've got to.
LESLIE:	I wouldn't hold your breath.
BABE:	Think about the possibilities. He already attacked your mother. Lied about your sex life. Made you out to be a sleazy bimbo. He's got the whole second act, he might get it right. Aren't you just the least bit curious?
BOO:	Just the littlest tiniest bit?
	Maybe he examines something loving and tender. *(BABE and LESLIE look at BOO.)* He could. *(Beat.)* You can't let it end like this. How good would you feel if you didn't give yourself every chance.
BABE:	Can you just throw three years away? Just like that?
	(LESLIE looks at them, looking at her, she feels uncomfortable. LESLIE picks up pages of RICHARD's script.)
LESLIE:	Babe picks up the script, crosses and sits on the steps. Andy enters.

(BABE does so, grabbing BLAINE's script from the bedroom. LESLIE sits on the love seat.)

BOO: Thank you. And on behalf of Andy. Thank you.

LESLIE: *(Forceful.)* Babe picks up the script, crosses and sits on the steps. Andy enters.

(BABE crosses and sits on the foot of the bed. ANDY enters. He stands, shifting from foot to foot, staring at the ground.)

BOO: Hi, Andy.

ANDY: Hi, Boo.

BOO: *(Smiling, looking at BABE and LESLIE.)* You came back.

ANDY: I'll just throw a few things into a bag.

BOO: *(Stands.)* Are you leaving?

ANDY: I'm gonna stay with a friend. You can stay here.

BOO: Why? What's going on?

ANDY: No point in ruining your whole two weeks. It'll be like a vacation.

BOO: It is a vacation. I came to see you. What are you doing this for?

ANDY: It'll be better this way.

BOO: What will be better? I don't know what you're talking about. You ran out of here this morning. And now you come back and say you're moving in with a friend. I don't wanna stay here if you're not here. What did you mean when you said after you make love there's nothing left?

ANDY: Uhh well… It's only been three days.

BOO: Would you explain to me what that means.

ANDY: Whenever you start going out with someone all you do is laugh and make love, sleep late and have fun. Then one of the parties starts laying down the rules.

BOO: And that's what was happening?

ANDY: You started making schedules. You had the whole day scheduled out and then you wanted to schedule out the rest of the year. You were hassling me about my smoking.

BOO: And you were gonna leave me because of that?

ANDY: You said you didn't want to make love. You'd rather go shopping and do laundry.

BOO: Andy, what did we do last night, after I came into your room?

ANDY: We made love.

BOO: And an hour after that?

ANDY: Made love. Again.

BOO: And before breakfast?

ANDY: Made love.

BOO: And after you told me you wanted to submit your play, and

	before you went to the post office and after lunch, what did we do?
ANDY:	Made love.
BOO:	*(Beat.)* You're wearing me out!
ANDY:	We do fit together pretty good, don't we?
BOO:	Yes we do, but I needed a rest. When I said I didn't want to make love, I meant I didn't want to make love, then.
ANDY:	Oh. I thought...
BOO:	I know what you thought.
ANDY:	I don't like having everything scheduled out.
BOO:	I'm sorry. I didn't mean for you to think I was trying to run your life.
ANDY:	That's what it felt like.
BOO:	I'm sorry. I won't do it again. I won't schedule anything. I won't hassle you about your smoking or doing the laundry. If I'd known you were gonna get so upset, I wouldn't have said a word. So is there something I can do for you? *(BOO very seductively crosses to ANDY.)* Something you'd like me to do?
ANDY:	*(ANDY looks over his shoulder, then back to BOO.)* Would you hem my jeans? I've got a drawer full of jeans that need to be hemmed and I hate sewing.
BOO:	I love to sew!
BABE:	*(Getting up from the steps.)* OK, whoa! Just hold it a minute.
BOO:	Babe what are you doing?
BABE:	*(Walking into the scene.)* What are you doing?
ANDY:	We're working things out.
BABE:	You take a walk. When we wanna hear from you we'll pull your chain, OK? *(BABE walks ANDY over to the steps and sits him down.)*
BOO:	That was rude. *(BOO crosses over to BABE. They talk behind ANDY's back.)*
BABE:	Rude? Boo, do you know what you just did?
BOO:	We came to an agreement, worked things out.
BABE:	You didn't work anything out, you surrendered. You gave in. You gave him everything he wanted.
BOO:	And what was I was supposed to do? Let him leave?
BABE:	Listen to me. Never, EVER, give him everything he wants.
BOO:	So I was supposed to let him leave?
BABE:	No, but you get him to give you as much as you gave him.
BOO:	Like you and Blaine?
BABE:	If you give him everything then he'll end up taking you for granted.
BOO:	My way may not be the right way, but it's a beginning.

BABE: You're being manipulated. You're making a mistake.

BOO: I don't think so.

BABE: Then do it your way.

BOO: You know you do tend to have a very cut-and-dried attitude about things that, possibly, could be interpreted as being a bit of a bitch.

BABE: Or it could be seen as being firm, could it not?

BOO: I guess it could.

BABE: *(Walking out of the scene.)* Just remember what I told you.

BOO: Is it OK if we continue?

BABE: Fine. Go ahead.

BOO: *(Marching back into place.)* Andy? *(ANDY walks over. BOO looks at BABE and then to ANDY.)* Where's those jeans you want hemmed?

ANDY: I'll go get them. *(ANDY exits.)*

BOO: *(To LESLIE.)* How was it? Truthful? Honest?

BABE: Oh we're off to a real good start. I can hardly wait to see what happens next.

LESLIE: He did get one thing right.

BOO: What?

LESLIE: We do fit together pretty good.

BABE: Let's keep going.

LESLIE: *(Sorting through pieces of the script.)* Andy, Boo. Andy Boo kiss, Andy Boo make love, Andy Boo stop making love, Andy Boo make love again

BOO: Hey, that's my life you're passing by.

BABE: It's not like we don't know what happens.

LESLIE: Andy Boo make love.

         (BOO walks over and slams her foot down on a page of the script.)

BOO: Read it. Please.

LESLIE: Fine whatever.

ANDY: Boo! *(ANDY runs onstage.)*

BOO: Andy. *(She runs to where she should be in the scene.)*

ANDY: Boo! You can't leave!

BOO: Andy what are you saying?

ANDY: I don't want you to leave.

BOO: I have to go back to work.

ANDY: Work? What's work? It's just a job.

BOO: It's my job.

ANDY: This is more important.

BOO:	What's more important?
ANDY:	I've had a revelation.
BOO:	A what?
ANDY:	*(Crossing towards the steps.)* It's all so simple. The answer was right in front of me.
BOO:	What answer?
ANDY:	I've got something to ask you.
	(LESLIE turns the page.)
BLAINE:	*(ANDY turns away from BOO. BLAINE addresses BABE.)* I've tried to explain it you. You heard what I said.
BABE:	I heard you. *(BABE sits, very upset. BLAINE watches her.)*
BLAINE:	I knew I shouldn't have told you.
BOO:	What's going on?
BABE:	But you did.
BLAINE:	Babe. Babe, you crying?
BABE:	I am not crying.
BOO:	*(To LESLIE.)* This is my scene! What's he going to ask me?
LESLIE:	Hang on the pages are out of order.
BOO:	Then hurry up and sort the pages.
BABE:	Don't touch the pages. He's just told me something to make me cry. We're playing this scene.
BOO:	It's my scene! He's got something to ask me.
LESLIE:	And it's my life!
BOO:	Leslie!
BABE:	Leslie!
	(LESLIE reads. BOO tries, unsuccessfully, to remain patient while BABE and BLAINE play their scene.)
BLAINE:	Babe. Babe, you crying?
BABE:	I am not crying.
BLAINE:	You are. *(He stands next to her.)* Babe... *(He puts his arm around her.)* Come on...
BABE:	*(She pushes his arm away.)* Don't touch me. I would prefer that you not touch me. *(Pause.)* At least I know how you feel. *(Pause.)* I believed you. Know that? I believed you when you said you'd always tell me the truth.
BLAINE:	I know what I said.
BABE:	I believed you!
BLAINE:	I know.
	(LESLIE turns the page.)
ANDY:	Boo! I want you to move in with me!
BOO:	Andy that's asking a lot.

(LESLIE looks for the rest of BABE's scene.)

LESLIE: What's going on now?

BABE: How am I supposed to know? Where's the rest of the scene?

LESLIE: *(Sorting through the script.)* I don't know.

BOO: Why aren't you reading! This is my scene. Not hers! Mine! Leslie, what's my next line?

BABE: Leslie, find my scene. He's told me something. It makes me cry. It's a lot more important than whatever Dopey has to say to you.

BOO: Don't call him Dopey! His name's Andy! Leslie read my scene!

BABE: She's looking for my scene, Boo.

BOO: I want my scene! I want my scene! I want it want it want it! Read my scene! Read my scene!

BABE: Leslie, where's the rest of my scene!

LESLIE: I can't find it. It's not here.

BABE: Whaddya mean it's not there. It has to be there! It has to be!

BOO: I'm not listening to this. I want my scene! I want my scene! I want my scene! I want my scene! Leslie read my scene!

BABE: Leslie! Find my scene.

LESLIE: I've looked, it's not here.

BOO: *(Collapsing onto the floor and stomping her feet.)* Read my scene! Read my scene!

(LESLIE turns the page.)

ANDY: I want you to move in here with me.

BOO: *(Jumping into place. Sweetly.)* Andy that's asking a lot.

ANDY: But if it's what we want...is it what you want?

BOO: I want to be with you, Andy.

ANDY: I know there's all the stuff about routines, we just worked out the thing about schedules and all the little things we do that might irritate each other, our habits, those can be overcome, we know they're there and we can deal with them.

BOO: Andy, I don't know.

ANDY: Say you'll think about it.

BOO: I'll think about it.

ANDY: You'll think about it?

BOO: I'll think about it.

ANDY: Good. *(ANDY goes to leave.)*

BOO: *(Taking his hand.)* Where you rushing off to? Don't I even get a kiss?

ANDY: I thought I'd let your lips cool off.

BOO: Well sit, I've got something to tell you. *(She sits him at the table.)* OK. There's these three couples and they all got married on the same day and they all decided...they're all best friends, did I tell you they were all friends, well they're all friends, and they decide to go to the same place for the honeymoon. So it's the morning after the night before, their wedding night, and they all come down for breakfast and they're sitting there and one husband says to his wife pass the sugar, sugar. And she does and they kiss and it's all very lovey dovey. Now, the second husband, not wanting to look bad, says pass the honey, honey and she does and they're all smiles and they kiss each other when the third wife wanting to show everyone else that her husband isn't a slob kicks him under the table and he says, ...I forget, I can't remember what she says. Oh damn it! I wanted to tell you a joke.

ANDY: It's OK. You'll remember the punch line.

BOO: But I wanted to get it right.

ANDY: *(He gives her a nudge.)* So, what you wanna do?

BOO: I'm gonna go for a walk. Think about what we've talked about. You?

ANDY: I'll go for cigarettes. Do sorta the same thing.

BOO: OK, see you in awhile. *(BOO crosses to the steps.)*

BABE: Keep reading!

(LESLIE picks up part of the script. BLAINE crosses to BABE. BABE and BLAINE play this scene standing on either side of LESLIE who is sitting on the love seat.)

BABE: You're back.

BLAINE: Looks that way.

BABE: Blaine, what's the problem?

BLAINE: If I could explain it I would.

BABE: You wanna talk about this morning?

BLAINE: No. Not now. I wouldn't know where to start.

BABE: OK. We could talk about this. *(She holds up the script.)*

BLAINE: Something else you don't like?

BABE: No, I'm not trying to be critical. I'd just, I'd like to know what you're trying to tell me?

BLAINE: I'm not trying to tell you anything.

BABE: Do you want me to be like Boo?

BLAINE: I've never said that.

BABE: But is that what you want?

BLAINE: This play has nothing to do with us.

BABE: Blaine, I'm not an idiot. If this is what you want—a fantasized, romanticized version of our life—

BLAINE: It's not us. It's just a play. It's fiction.

BABE: Maybe when we first met we were like Andy and Boo. For two minutes or two day or a month, whatever. I'm not Boo. I'm Babe.

	You have to talk to me about this. If you can't talk to me then what's gonna happen?
BLAINE:	Something is always going to happen Babe. There are no guarantees. *(BLAINE exits.)*
LESLIE:	Who's asking for guarantees, Richard? All I want you to do is what you said you were going to do. *(LESLIE reads. ANDY enters, crosses to the steps.)*
ANDY:	Hi. Good walk?
BOO:	Yes.
ANDY:	So did you think about what I said, what we talked about?
BOO:	Yes.
ANDY:	And what do you think?
BOO:	Yes.
ANDY:	You mean it?
BOO:	Yes.
ANDY:	God Boo, I don't know what to say, oh great, oh wow!
BOO:	Yes.
ANDY:	*(He hugs her.)* Yes. *(He picks her up and swings her around the room.)* Yes, yes, yes, yes, yes!
BOO:	I oughtta have my head examined. But…
ANDY:	Yes! Yes! Yes!
BOO:	My mother's gonna think I'm totally crazy but if we're ever gonna know if we have any kind of a chance, we better find out now. Before we waste hundreds and hundreds of dollars travelling back and forth. Now I have to go pee.
ANDY:	I'll carry you to the bathroom. *(They exit.)*
BABE:	So that's it!
LESLIE:	What's 'it'?
BABE:	That's what he wants me to do.
LESLIE:	Think so?
BABE:	Yes I do. Well watch this. Keep reading, Leslie.
	(LESLIE starts to read. BLAINE enters.)
BABE:	Blaine listen, there's something I have to tell you…
BLAINE:	No you have to listen, OK Babe?
BABE:	But I have to tell you…
BLAINE:	No! I have something to say. So just sit and listen.
BABE:	OK.
BLAINE:	I know I've made things hard for you, you're confused, you don't trust me. That's fair, you've got every reason not to, but it's just, Babe it's just…
BABE:	Blaine…

BLAINE: Just listen. Please?

    (BABE sits on the bed.)

BLAINE: I tell you in the letters, I tell you on the phone, I promise you we're gonna be together and I promise you I'm not gonna run away but then, we get into an argument or we have a fight and I think that's it, we can't go on like this.

BABE: What are you saying?

BLAINE: I'm saying I want to move in here with you.

BABE: *(Glances at LESLIE.)* You wanna move in here with me?

BLAINE: No more planes or buses. And we start working out all the things that are problems.

BABE: Do you really mean this?

BLAINE: *(Sitting beside BABE.)* When I first met you, here was this weird kinda funky lady staying up all night talking to this guy, listening to this guy and I was a mess when I met you and we sat in front of the fireplace with the TV on and we laughed and talked and talked and laughed and at six o'clock we were lying there in each other's arms, watching *Wild Kingdom* and you said—

BABE: I better go to bed I have to be up in three hours.

BLAINE: And then before you went up, you kissed me.

BABE: I thought, he's going home the next day, I'll never see him again.

BLAINE: You're always telling me that I don't trust you. But it's not you I don't trust.

BABE: Blaine...

BLAINE: You were right. I wanted you to be, Boo. All the other relationships never lasted because I didn't want them to. The only thing I know right now is... I don't want to leave you. For some people they know that in three days or six months or four weeks but it's taken me this long. *(BLAINE kneels in front of her.)* Will you marry me?

LESLIE: *(Looking up from the script.)* Oh, Richard.

BABE: He asked me to marry him.

LESLIE: I know.

    (BOO enters. BLAINE exits.)

BOO: What's going on?

BABE: Blaine asked me to marry him.

BOO: That's wonderful! See and you were convinced that there had to be something bad happen. That's great. Isn't that great?

LESLIE: *(Flat.)* Great. Congratulations.

BABE: Thanks.

BOO: Oh Babe, I'm so happy for you. Aren't you happy for her, Leslie?

LESLIE: I'm delighted Boo.

BABE: What's the matter?

LESLIE: He made you cry.

BABE: Leslie it doesn't matter. OK? It doesn't matter.

LESLIE: You're not acting like yourself. Up until three pages ago you wanted to know what Blaine said that made you cry and now he asks you to marry him and everything's forgotten.

BABE: What he said to make me cry doesn't matter.

LESLIE: You're not being true to your character because your character has been distorted by Richard. Can you do that?

BABE: Leslie, I do what ever the script says I do.

LESLIE: Fine.

BOO: Can't you just be happy for her?

LESLIE: Boo, oh never mind. (LESLIE collects the rest of the scattered pages, sits on the love seat and reads.)

BOO: You've got so much to think about. There's dresses to order and you'll have to get registered, halls to rent and oh, invitations to be sent out, I can help you with those. We better get started. What are your colours? Have you had your colours done?

           (BABE and BOO start to exit to the bedroom. ANDY enters and crosses to the steps. BOO watches ANDY.)

BABE: Not lately. Years ago I was a spring but I don't know if that changes. Boo, Boo what's the matter? (BABE notices ANDY.)

BOO: You go on, I'll be back. (She crosses to the steps.)

BOO: Hi.

ANDY: Oh hi.

BOO: What you doing?

ANDY: Thinking.

BOO: You're having second thoughts, aren't you?

ANDY: I guess so. Yeah.

BOO: It'll all work out if we want it to.

ANDY: Think so?

BOO: You're a good person. I'm a good person. I'll find a job, they're always looking for legal secretaries, at least I've got a couple years of experience. You've got your job.

ANDY: There is talk of making me an assistant manager, or so Jerry says.

BOO: That's good. But I...I wouldn't pin all my hopes for the future on being an assistant manager at Bunny Burger, I mean I just don't think, contrary to what Jerry says, that rabbit burgers are going to replace McDonald's.

ANDY: Sales aren't what they thought they would be.

BOO: That should tell you something.

ANDY: I can look around.

BOO:	It could be part time. That would give you time to write.
ANDY:	Working full time and writing, it's not that easy. Boo?
BOO:	Andy?
ANDY:	What's gonna happen to us?
BOO:	What we want to, Andy. What we want to.
ANDY:	What if I'm no good, I mean what if I can't do it. Be a writer.
BOO:	I think you can.
ANDY:	But what if... *(She puts her fingers against his lips.)*
BOO:	No more what-ifs, OK? There's only one thing we can know. I'll be there for you.
ANDY:	And I'll be there for you.
BOO:	Wherever.
ANDY:	Whatever.
BOO:	You and me—
ANDY:	Andy and Boo. *(They kiss, then exit arm in arm. LESLIE stares at the script.)*
LESLIE:	My God Richard!
	(RICHARD enters.)
	I wanna talk to you.
RICHARD:	OK, but I gotta tell you this. Hnason's pit bull comes in with Kelly Peters' pet rabbit in its mouth—
LESLIE:	Is this a proposal?
RICHARD:	*(Beat.)* Well Hnason freaks out...
LESLIE:	Is this a proposal?
RICHARD:	It was. But you said you wanted me to depict things accurately, so I've written a new ending. Read this. *(He hands her some pages.)*
LESLIE:	Richard!
	(RICHARD exits. LESLIE places RICHARD's old script on the table, takes the new pages, sits on the love seat and starts to read as BABE and BLAINE enter the living room. As BABE and BLAINE act out the scene, LESLIE will eventually look up from the script and watch the scene.)
BABE:	You're back.
BLAINE:	Looks that way.
BABE:	Blaine, what's the problem?
BLAINE:	If I could explain it I would.
BABE:	OK. We could talk about this. *(She holds up the script.)*
BLAINE:	Something else you don't like?
BABE:	If you can't tell me what's wrong, tell me what's right. Something has to be right.
BLAINE:	What's right? I got a career, two productions next season, a radio

	treatment that looks like it might sell. The warranty on my computer just expired and it hasn't crapped out. Yet.
BABE:	What about us?
BLAINE:	I don't know what to think.
BABE:	*(Crosses and sits on the foot of the bed.)* What did you mean when you said "I don't know how to do this?" What is it you don't know how to do?
BLAINE:	I don't know. We don't get along very well any more, do we?
BABE:	No. Not really.
BLAINE:	*(Sits next to BABE.)* We used to. You'd meet me at the airport, we'd get back here and we'd be making love in the hallway as soon as the door was closed.
BABE:	People get to know one another, that part of a relationship always changes.
BLAINE:	When was the last time we made love?
BABE:	The other night. Thursday.
BLAINE:	Thursday.
BABE:	We always make love on Thursday.
BLAINE:	Once we couldn't keep our hands off each other. It's not a lot of fun anymore.
BABE:	I beg your pardon?
BLAINE:	I used to get excited thinking about being with you.
BABE:	You used to undress me. You don't do that anymore.
BLAINE:	You don't meet me at the bus or the plane anymore.
BABE:	So what if this time we drive back together and look for an apartment?
BLAINE:	Moving in together now wouldn't change anything.
BABE:	Blaine. You used to scream how unfair and how unreasonable it was that I wouldn't move. I had my reasons. Now I'm saying I will move. And now you're saying no?
BLAINE:	I like the arrangement we have. What I don't like is who we've become.
BABE:	You don't like us? But you enjoy travelling back and forth, three weeks here and three weeks at home? You, you...you like that? Would you mind explaining that to me!
BLAINE:	It gives me time at home to work...
BABE:	You can work here.
BLAINE:	I come out here to spend time with you. I get to see you. Then I go home, have some time to myself and I get to work and take care of business. It works.
BABE:	I'm a convenience. Come out here, get me to do your sewing, go to a movie or two, spend some time together, get laid a couple of times and then go back home. Don't do me any favours.

BLAINE: You don't understand.

BABE: I come third after your work and "time to yourself".

BLAINE: You don't understand what I'm trying to say.

BABE: Are you seeing someone else?

BLAINE: No, of course not.

BABE: When I'm 800 miles away, it's OK. But take me back home and it's what? Afraid of what your friends will think? Afraid I'll embarrass you?

BLAINE: No.

BABE: Am I too fat?

BLAINE: Don't do this Babe.

BABE: Why did you bother coming back?

BLAINE: I like what we have, I just think we have to work at it. The last few trips, the minute I'm on the plane I'm so damned glad to be leaving. You've felt like that too.

BABE: You don't know anything about how I feel.

BLAINE: That's not fair.

BABE: I have men asking me out, Blaine. I tell them I'm involved. Women I work with say it must be hard but I say no, not at all, it's not like he's next door and you have to work harder but it's worth it because we love each other! Maybe I'm not being as romantic as I was, I don't pamper you the way I did or wanna make love on the kitchen table. But if you think I don't care—if I didn't think there was something about us worth saving—do you think I'd have put up with you for as long as I have? Do you?

BLAINE: I understand how you might feel like...

BABE: Don't be so fucking understanding. It's not the way I might feel. I feel it. I don't want to see you anymore. So just leave. Go home. *(She crosses to the steps. BLAINE follows her.)*

BLAINE: Will you listen to me?

BABE: Listen? *(She laughs.)* Listen? I've spent 90 percent of my time trying to get you to talk to me and now I have to listen.

BLAINE: I knew I shouldn't have told you.

BABE: But you did.

BLAINE: Babe. Babe, you crying?

BABE: I am not crying.

BLAINE: You are. *(He stands next to her.)* Babe... *(He puts his arm around her.)* Come on...

BABE: *(She pushes his arm away.)* Don't touch me. I would prefer that you not touch me. I believed you. Know that? I believed you when you said you'd always tell me the truth. I believed you!

        (BABE gets up, exits SL and returns carrying a suitcase and a pair of jeans.)

	Here's your suitcase. And your jeans. I didn't hem them.
BLAINE:	We don't have to do this. We can work this out.
BABE:	Like Andy and Boo? Like your play? You didn't ever sit down three months ago and say to me listen there's something we should talk about.
BLAINE:	I do love you.
BABE:	Here. (*She picks up the ANDY/BOO script, offers it to BLAINE.*) I'm finished with Andy and Boo. (*BLAINE reaches for his suitcase.*) My keys. Give me my keys.

(*BLAINE gives her his set of her house keys.*)

BLAINE:	Babe!
BABE:	Goodbye, Blaine.

(*BLAINE stands looking at her waiting for her to say something. He picks up his stuff and starts to exit. After a few steps, he stops and turns.*)

BLAINE:	Babe? (*BABE doesn't respond. BLAINE looks at her and exits. BABE looks at LESLIE.*)
BABE:	Thanks a lot, Leslie!
LESLIE:	I didn't want him to break up with me.
BABE:	But he didn't break up with you, did he?
LESLIE:	I'm sorry Babe, but I've got problems of my own right now! (*LESLIE crosses to the table. BABE follows.*)
BABE:	You know sometimes you're a cold-blooded bitch.
LESLIE:	Two can play this game, Richard. (*LESLIE sits at the table and writes. BABE reads RICHARD's script. BOO and ANDY enter.*)
BOO:	Guess what?
ANDY:	What?
BOO:	I remembered the end of the joke. OK so the two husbands had said pass the sugar, sugar, pass the honey, honey and the third wife wanting to show everyone else that her husband isn't a slob kicks him under the table and he says, pass the bacon, pig. He's trying to be suave like the other husbands but he blows it. I guess it's funnier if you hear the whole joke.
ANDY:	You know that's one of the things that attracted me to you.
BOO:	What? That I can't tell a joke?
ANDY:	You don't give up and you're intelligent and you've got a good sense of humour. You always listen and even when I don't know what I'm gonna say, you wait.
BOO:	You always know what you're gonna say, just have a problem getting it out sometimes.
ANDY:	And you're attractive.
BOO:	So are you.
ANDY:	Aw, so you just want me for my body?

BOO:	Amongst other things. *(BOO exits. ANDY crosses to the steps. BABE watches BOO and ANDY part.)*
BABE:	It's not fair. Andy and Boo get to live happily ever after and they don't even know what they're doing and Blaine and I, who do try, break up and everything goes down the drain. It's not fair. *(To LESLIE.)* I don't want to be alone. This is all your fault. Everything would have been fine, we were gonna have a life together and you made him go and change it.
LESLIE:	Babe…
BABE:	I'm a character, Leslie. I'm only real in my world. Get him to write a new ending.
LESLIE:	I'm sorry, Babe.
BABE:	Get him to write a new ending!
	(LESLIE crosses to RICHARD who sits on the steps.)
RICHARD:	So have you finished… *(LESLIE hands RICHARD her rewrite. He reads, smirks and hands it back. LESLIE refuses. RICHARD puts out his cigarette, stands up and squares off to LESLIE. They lift the manuscript up simultaneously and read aloud.)*
LESLIE:	Leslie!
RICHARD:	Hello, Richard.
LESLIE:	Leslie, Leslie, Leslie.
BABE:	*(Catching on.)* Leslie.
RICHARD:	*(To BABE.)* Richard.
BABE:	*(To RICHARD.)* You look like you weren't expecting me.
RICHARD:	I don't know what to expect Richard. You're so damned inconsistent.
BABE:	Not all the time Leslie.
LESLIE:	Leslie the time has come for us to discuss many things.
BABE:	It's time Leslie.
RICHARD:	It's good, I know it's good, talking is good.
LESLIE:	Leslie, I have plans for us. The future is more than just the dreams of the present. It's what's going to happen to us.
BABE:	I think about what it's like when you're not here. What I'd miss. What I'd want. I'd miss you if you weren't here.
LESLIE:	You and me together. That's what I want. It's what you want too, isn't it?
BABE:	You do want the same things I want don't you?
RICHARD:	Yes.
LESLIE:	I see it like this. We get to know each other. We know what we want.
BABE:	We communicate to each other, our dreams, the hopes we share.
RICHARD:	Oh Richard, you don't know how long I've waited for you to say

	this. I've wanted to talk to you about this, but I wasn't sure.
LESLIE:	Be sure. *(She kisses RICHARD.)*
BABE:	I'm sure. *(She kisses RICHARD.)*
RICHARD:	Now that we can, let's start…
LESLIE:	*(Moving away from RICHARD.)* Well. We can't do it right now.
BABE:	*(Joining LESLIE.)* No, no, no. Not right now.
LESLIE:	Our time together is precious.
BABE:	Besides we've both been thinking along the same lines anyways, we don't have to talk about it. Really.
LESLIE:	Least not now.
RICHARD:	*(Beat.)* If we don't talk about it now when we will talk about it?
LESLIE:	Soon. Very, very soon.
BABE:	When the time's right.
RICHARD:	But the time's right now. If it's important we should talk about it.
LESLIE:	And we will.
BABE:	Of course we will.
RICHARD:	But we will talk about it? Won't we? *(He sits on the foot of the bed.)*
LESLIE:	I want to spend the rest of my life with you. *(BABE and LESLIE sit on either side of RICHARD.)*
BABE:	I wish we could be together. Always.
RICHARD:	So do I, Richard. So do I.
LESLIE:	I love you, Leslie.
BABE:	I love you, Leslie.
RICHARD:	But Richard, there's so much we don't know, so much I'm unsure of.
LESLIE:	I'll take care of you. I'll be here. You have nothing to worry about. Leave it to me.
BABE:	I've never met anyone like you. Ever.
RICHARD:	Are you sure? Do you really mean it? You're not rushing into this, are you?
LESLIE:	I never rush into things. I know what I want and what I'm doing.
RICHARD:	Then we're more than just dating? We're talking about a real commitment then? You mean it?
LESLIE:	Of course.
BABE:	I'm not gonna let you down. I give you my word.
LESLIE:	Everything's gonna be alright. Trust me.
BABE:	I promise you. It's not just words. It means something.
	(BABE and LESLIE ease RICHARD down onto the bed.)
RICHARD:	*(Sitting up.)* But what is it? If it does mean something, tell me what it is.

LESLIE: Why do we have to define it?

BABE: Who needs labels or pigeon holes?

RICHARD: We have to be something. I need something more than just words, promises.

                (LESLIE and BABE flop back on bed.)

BABE: *(Running their feet up RICHARD's legs.)* I think about the things I miss when I'm not here. Your hands…

RICHARD: *(Standing.)* You keep saying we're going to talk. You keep telling me what's going to happen, but it never does happen. I don't know what to believe.

LESLIE: *(She stands behind RICHARD and undoes the first few buttons on his shirt.)* You're confused. Don't be. Don't worry. I won't let you down.

BABE: *(Joining LESLIE.)* At the very least…

RICHARD: *(Clutching his shirt closed.)* Don't you worry that maybe this is all we've got.

BABE: A good sexual relationship is healthy.

LESLIE: Sex is a healthy part of any relationship.

BABE: Fingertips on bare flesh.

LESLIE: Tongues entwined.

BABE: Sweating bodies.

RICHARD: The way you melt inside me.

LESLIE: Hold me in your hand.

BABE: Your little love bites.

RICHARD: Your tongue between my legs.

LESLIE: Fingernails raking my spine.

BABE: I want you. I wanna be in you, on top of you.

LESLIE: I wanna become you.

RICHARD: Richard…Richard… *(He removes his shirt.)*

LESLIE: It'll be alright. Just leave it to Richard.

BABE: I'll take care of you Richard.

LESLIE: Don't worry Leslie. You don't have to worry about anything.

                (LESLIE unbuttons RICHARD's pants. BABE and LESLIE slowly pull them down.)

RICHARD: Richard. Richard, I believe you. I trust you. I love you. I put my faith in you. I put my faith in us. Everything's gonna be alright. Hold me. Touch me. Love me. I want to spend the rest of my life with you.

LESLIE: *(Stopping abruptly.)* The rest of your life? Hey! We have to talk about this.

BABE: What's wrong with what we've got?

LESLIE: We're talking about taking a big step here. (*Crosses to the love seat and sits.*)

BABE: A very, very big step. I think someone's a little confused. (*Crosses to the kitchen table and sits.*)

RICHARD: What's going on? You said, you told me...you promised. What the hell was I supposed to believe? (*Beat. RICHARD looks from BABE to LESLIE, then at his pants around his ankles.*)

Leslie? Leslie...

LESLIE: Yes, Richard.

RICHARD: Uh uh I uh...

LESLIE: Something the matter?

RICHARD: No. I...uh...I get it.

LESLIE: Do you? Really?

RICHARD: Yes.

LESLIE: How do you think it would feel to be like that for three years?

RICHARD: Well, I ...uhhmmm...I... (*LESLIE starts to leave.*) Humiliating! (*He pulls up his pants and puts on his shirt.*) Can we talk about this? Please.

LESLIE: Is that what you want?

RICHARD: Yes.

LESLIE: OK.

RICHARD: (*Pause.*) I don't know how.

LESLIE: Now, you get it. (*They exit.*)

BABE: Well that looks promising. Good luck. Maybe they'll work it out. I hope so. Boo? (*She pulls a page from RICHARD's script.*) Boo where are you when I could use cheering up?

(*BOO chases ANDY onstage.*)

BOO: "...and the rabbit says, that wasn't a missing hare it was a cottontail.'

(*BOO laughs and chases ANDY off and the lights fade except for the lights on BABE.*)

BABE: Live long and prosper, Boo. Have fun.

(*LESLIE enters with some pages. She crosses to BABE who turns away from LESLIE.*)

LESLIE: Babe...

BABE: All's well that ends well. At least for you anyways.

(*LESLIE hands BABE the new pages and exits. BLAINE enters and kneels by the bed.*)

BLAINE: Babe?

BABE: Richard? Andy?...Blaine...

BLAINE: (*BLAINE crosses to BABE.*) You never answered my question.

BABE: What, what did you say? *(BABE looks at BLAINE, then reads the bottom of the new pages. She smiles.)* Well. Well, well, well.

                 (She looks up at BLAINE. Lights fade.)

                 The End

Heart of a Distant Tribe

IAN ROSS

Production Information

Heart of a Distant Tribe was originally produced by Red Roots Theatre and premiered at the Aboriginal Centre, Winnipeg, in June, 1996, with the following cast:

ROBIN .... Tracey McCorrister
MOSES .... Jack Clarke
PAUL .... Michael Lawrenchuk
YOGI.. Bossy Ducharme
ELLIE.. Susan Olson
BELLA .... Sharon Pasula

Directed by Ian Ross
Co-directed by Tina Keeper
Set and Costume Design by Louis Ogemah
Stage Manager: Marlene Meaden

Characters

ROBIN Chartrand: Young, mature woman. Unemployed. Possesses a serene beauty. Lived in the city all her life. A sculptor. In love with Moses.

MOSES Blood: Angry young man. Edgy but thoughtful. Moved around all his life. Does whatever he can to get by. In love with Robin.

PAUL Houle: Savvy businessman. Dresses smartly. Willing to take risks. "Tolerates" his family.

Eugene Spence (YOGI): Moses' friend and Paul's cousin. Recently moved to the city from the Reserve. Younger family man.

ELLIE Houle: A free spirit, unfettered by possessions or people, except perhaps a small flute. Paul's sister. A survivor.

BELLA Matwayashing: Paul, Yogi and Ellie's aunt. Full of wisdom and ways which can be soon forgotten. Loves bingo.

Setting

Winnipeg, the present

(Lights up on ROBIN and MOSES, at the Winnipeg Forks. MOSES is eating a tomato.)

ROBIN: Listen.

MOSES: What?

ROBIN: You hear that?

MOSES: What is it?

ROBIN: Don't know. Nothing I guess.

MOSES: What did it sound like?

ROBIN: Don't know.

MOSES: Then how do you know you heard it?

ROBIN: Didn't you hear anything?

MOSES: No.

ROBIN: I think it was far away.

(MOSES offers ROBIN a tomato.)

No thanks. Where'd you get that anyways?

MOSES: Took them from Yogi's garden.

ROBIN: Why?

MOSES: I was hungry.

ROBIN: How do you pronounce that?

MOSES: What?

ROBIN: That.

MOSES: Tomato.

ROBIN: Good. Me too.

MOSES: Sometimes you're weird, Robin.

ROBIN: Takes one to know one. So why'd we come here?

MOSES: I have to ask you something.

ROBIN: Go ahead.

MOSES: You know how I feel about you, right?

ROBIN: No. Just kidding. How do you feel about me?

MOSES: I think you're…pleasant.

ROBIN: Pleasant? You make me sound like an air freshener.

MOSES:	Quiet first, OK? I've been thinking a lot about what you said about us being together and that, and since I'm starting this new job and you're getting sponsored for school. I want to ask you something.
	(MOSES gets down on one knee.)
	I wanted to ask you…if….
	(ROBIN starts to react. MOSES gets up.)
	That's not what I'm gonna ask you.
ROBIN:	What?
MOSES:	I'm scared enough as it is. That's not the question I was gonna ask you.
ROBIN:	Well what else does a man ask a woman for on his knees?
MOSES:	Forgiveness? I just wanted to ask…if we could find a place together. You and me. Together.
	(ROBIN thinks.)
	Well?
ROBIN:	Are you sure you want to do this?
MOSES:	Yes.
ROBIN:	You won't chicken out?
MOSES:	No. I want to be with you. All the time. OK?
ROBIN:	OK then. But we can't have no place with a funny coloured bathtub and toilet, like pink or green. It's got to be white.
MOSES:	You got it.
ROBIN:	And it's got to have a big window. Or else a balcony.
MOSES:	What if it's a house?
ROBIN:	We can't afford a house. And it has to be close to a bus stop.
MOSES:	And a 7-Eleven.
ROBIN:	And it can't be a building where you can smell what everyone's cooking.
MOSES:	I don't think you should expect too much.
ROBIN:	I don't. I go out with you don't I?
	(The sound of a far-off flute can be heard.)
MOSES:	Listen. Is that what you heard?
ROBIN:	Don't know.
	(The flute gets closer.)
	Hey is that…
MOSES:	Shhh.
	(ELLIE enters playing her flute. They all exchange smiles and greetings. MOSES gives ELLIE some tomatoes. ELLIE gives MOSES a toonie.)
MOSES:	I can't.

(ELLIE insists and tells a story with her hands and body about how he needs the money more than she does, and how much she needs the tomatoes. And how grateful she is for the flute and [To ROBIN] how MOSES gave her the flute.)

ROBIN: OK. I'll see you at Bella's maybe.

(ELLIE leaves.)

Why didn't you tell me?

MOSES: Tell you what?

ROBIN: That you gave her that flute.

MOSES: I don't know. What's the big deal?

ROBIN: It's nice. That's all.

MOSES: I can't play the flute anyhow. Just guitar.

ROBIN: What? I've never seen you with a guitar.

MOSES: I had a nice one, but I had to pawn it.

ROBIN: Can you get it out?

MOSES: None of this stuff.

(MOSES shakes the two-dollar bill and looks at it more closely.)

I never noticed that before.

ROBIN: What?

MOSES: Is the queen ever ugly. I'm kidding. Look what bird's on the back.

ROBIN: Robins. So?

MOSES: So that's your name. And there's two of them. Like us.

ROBIN: Let's see. Oh yeah. This one looks like you. Kind of stupid. Actually they both look the same.

MOSES: One day we'll have more of these than we need.

ROBIN: Robins?

MOSES: Bills.

ROBIN: Thanks a lot.

MOSES: I mean dollar bills. Money. Then we'll be happy.

ROBIN: You're not happy now?

MOSES: Not all the time, only when I'm with you.

(MOSES walks to what's become The Homestyle Laundry, his new job, where EUGENE [YOGI] has been waiting. YOGI is dressed in jeans and a T-shirt. He has a tool belt around his waist.)

YOGI: There you are. I was just about to go grab some guy from casual. Just kidding. How's it going?

MOSES: OK. Boss here yet?

YOGI: You're lookin' at him.

MOSES: I mean your cousin.

YOGI: Not yet. Hey, you know what happened to me last night?

MOSES:	Hmmm?
YOGI:	Some stupid guy stole my tomatoes.
MOSES:	Really?
YOGI:	Yeah. I was growing them in the back yard and someone stole them. Man that pissed me off. I was gonna make B.L.T's with those.
MOSES:	Maybe they were hungry.
YOGI:	Well they should just go to the store and buy them.
MOSES:	So what's this Paul guy like?
YOGI:	I don't know. Weird. If it wasn't for his looks I'd forget he was Indian. Hey you ever hear of the five 'B's?
MOSES:	Of what?
YOGI:	Indians.
MOSES:	No.
YOGI:	My kid was telling me there's these five 'B's, that if you've got them you're an Indian.
MOSES:	What are they?
YOGI:	Bannock. Braces. I mean, braids. Uhh...bingo, beer...and... I forget.
MOSES:	That's racist.
YOGI:	Really? But my kid learned that at school.
MOSES:	So?
YOGI:	What if it's true though?
MOSES:	Prejudice don't care about the truth.
YOGI:	I wonder what that fifth 'B' was? Maybe baloney or broke. I'm always broke.
MOSES:	Or bullshit.
	(PAUL HOULE enters, dressed in business attire. He wears sunglasses and his hair is braided. He overhears the last two lines.)
PAUL:	Perhaps it's business.
YOGI:	Hey, Paul.
PAUL:	Eugene.
YOGI:	Yogi.
PAUL:	Right. Hey, Boo Boo. I'm Paul. You can call me Paul. Is this the guy from casual?
MOSES:	Moses.
PAUL:	That's pretty biblical.
MOSES:	You should talk.
PAUL:	Yeah, but mine's new testament. So what were you guys talking about?
MOSES:	Nothing.

YOGI: Just some racist stuff about Indians.

PAUL: You guys don't strike me as the types to be racist.

YOGI: We're not.

MOSES: Everybody is.

YOGI: It was just some thing about five 'B's that make you an Indian.

PAUL: That's easy. Brave. Brains. Brawn. Best...and belong.

MOSES: Belong to who?

(PAUL, MOSES and YOGI enter the store.)

PAUL: The system. Hey if you can't beat 'em join 'em. And you can see we sure as hell aren't gonna beat 'em so we may as well join 'em. Belong.

(MOSES shakes his head.)

PAUL: That way you fit in. Gain respect. Look at me. I've adapted and I'm accepted. So what do you think about my laundromat?

MOSES: I thought this was gonna be a drop-in centre?

PAUL: *(Laughs.)* Who told you that? I'm a businessman, not a charity. The North End needs a laundromat. Find a need and fill it. Right?

YOGI: Auntie Bella's askin' about you. She wants you to come visit.

PAUL: Great. But I'm pretty busy. Tell her I'll call her. So you guys ready to start?

YOGI: I guess so.

PAUL: Great. Here's the keys. Make sure this guy works. *(He throws YOGI the keys.)* The bin's in back. I'll see you later.

YOGI: What about auntie?

PAUL: I'll call her.

YOGI: Fuckin' guy.

MOSES: What's that supposed to mean, "make sure this guy works." What would he know about working?

YOGI: Prob'ly a lot. He says he's always doing it. At least that's his excuse for never having nothing to do with our family. Only if he needs something.

MOSES: I thought he got you this job?

YOGI: Only 'cause of Section 25. That's the first time I talked to him in about ten years. He may as well be a white guy. Ahh well.

(YOGI opens the front door.)

MOSES: What'd this used to be? Pawn shop maybe.

YOGI: No. I think it was a spice store.

MOSES: So what do we have to do?

(YOGI walks over and starts working.)

YOGI: Just tear it apart. We have to tear all this stuff down. And remember it's not your granny's head. Pretend it's something you hate.

MOSES: How 'bout Paul?

YOGI: You just met him.

MOSES: There's such a thing as hate at first sight.

YOGI: Pretend it's something else. Or else nothing.

MOSES: OK then. How 'bout this city. Or else any city. Do you know we helped build them? So we may as well help tear them apart.

YOGI: We didn't help build anything.

MOSES: Sure we did. You ever see those skyscrapers, like in Toronto?

YOGI: Yeah.

MOSES: It was us Indians who made those.

YOGI: Why would they use us?

MOSES: 'Cause we weren't afraid of heights. We weren't afraid of anything.

YOGI: Who told you that stuff?

MOSES: Robin.

YOGI: I like her. She's a good woman.

MOSES: Yeah. We're gonna find a place together.

YOGI: That's good. So I guess you guys have been carmel then.

MOSES: What?

YOGI: Carmel. You know. (*He makes a thrusting motion with one of his fingers through an "o" with his other fingers.*)

MOSES: Carnal. None of your business.

YOGI: I'm just kidding. I'm happy for you. Native girls are the best women to go out with.

MOSES: Why's that?

YOGI: Don't know. Lots of pain makes you love better I guess. Hey. You wanna meet my sister?

MOSES: Does she look like you?

YOGI: Only her build. But she's got a nice personality.

MOSES: No thanks.

YOGI: You know what women are really good too?

MOSES: Who?

YOGI: Ornamentals.

(*Light shift. PAUL on the street. He bumps into ELLIE, who spots PAUL and moves towards him. PAUL, tries to avoid her.*)

PAUL: Go on.

(*He tries to shoo ELLIE away. He offers her some money.*)

Here. Take it. Take it.

(*ELLIE touches it. PAUL lets go and the money falls to the ground.*)

Well I don't know what you want.

(ELLIE moves towards him. PAUL leaves. ELLIE watches him leave, looks down and wanders off.

Cross-fade to ROBIN and MOSES looking at places to live. All are suggestive and in succession, one after another.)

ROBIN: What colour's the toilet?

LANDLORD: Toilet?

(A different apartment.)

MOSES: This place seems perfect. Can we check the can?

LANDLORD: Sure.

MOSES: Shit.

ROBIN: No green I said.

(They're whisked into a dingy little apartment. With a landlord who fits right in.)

It says in the paper, "One bedroom."

LANDLORD: That's right. One bedroom.

ROBIN: Well where is it?

LANDLORD: You're standing in it. One bedroom.

ROBIN: So one bedroom means one room.

LANDLORD: One bedroom.

MOSES: Let's go.

(They enter a nicer apartment. With a landlord who fits right in.)

ROBIN: Oak floors.

LANDLORD: That's right yeah.

ROBIN: Two bedrooms?

LANDLORD: Yeah that's right.

MOSES: Two seventy-five a month?

LANDLORD: Right. Yeah.

ROBIN: I think we should take it.

LANDLORD: Sorry. Can't. It's already been let.

MOSES: Then why the hell...forget it.

(Another apartment.)

LANDLORD: No cats.

ROBIN: OK.

LANDLORD: No dogs neither.

MOSES: What about fish?

LANDLORD: Only for dinner.

ROBIN: No pets?

LANDLORD: No cats.

MOSES: You must hate cats, hunh?

LANDLORD: No dogs neither.

ROBIN: What about people? Any people allowed?

            (*A place with a little old lady landlord.*)

LANDLORD: Are you married?

ROBIN: We hope to be.

LANDLORD: Have you been carnal yet?

ROBIN: Excuse me?

MOSES: Come on.

            (*Another apartment.*)

LANDLORD: Sorry it's taken.

            (*And another.*)

            Sure no problem.

ROBIN: Great.

LANDLORD: Sorry someone just took it.

            (*And another one.*)

            Sorry.

            (*And another.*)

            Hi.

MOSES: Do you take Indians here?

ROBIN: Moses.

LANDLORD: Pardon me?

MOSES: For tenants.

LANDLORD: Well we—

MOSES: Forget it.

            (*At the entrance of one more place. ROBIN knocks.*)

            No, let's go.

ROBIN: This'll be it. OK?

MOSES: No. Look at it. It's too nice. We can't afford this. I want to go.

ROBIN: Please. Just one more.

MOSES: I don't want to do this anymore

ROBIN: What?

MOSES: I'm thinking this wasn't a good idea.

ROBIN: Don't be like that. Come on.

MOSES: No. Really…

            (*The best LANDLORD in the city opens the door.*)

LANDLORD: Mr. Blood? Ms. Chartrand?

ROBIN: Yes.

LANDLORD: I've been expecting you. Sorry it took so long to answer the door,
            I was making you some tea. Come in.

MOSES: Can I see the bathroom?

LANDLORD: By all means.

MOSES: Oh it's brown. Oh well.

LANDLORD: Actually the colour is more of a taupe.

MOSES: A what?

LANDLORD: It's called "space".

ROBIN: Are you near a bus stop?

LANDLORD: Right out front. And you're near a school, church and a hospital.

MOSES: What about a 7-Eleven?

LANDLORD: We have one in the building.

ROBIN: The cost.

LANDLORD: Very affordable. And as you can see we have a large window with a lovely balcony. And all the units are climate contained, so you can't smell what everyone else on the floor is cooking. And best of all. Best of all.

MOSES: Yeah?

LANDLORD: We love Indians.

ROBIN: I think we should take it.

MOSES: I don't know.

ROBIN: Why not?

MOSES: It's…I don't know…let's look some more.

ROBIN: You said you didn't want to.

MOSES: I know.

ROBIN: Do you want to find a home together?

MOSES: Yeah. Sure. Of course.

ROBIN: Then what's the problem?

MOSES: Nothing. Let's do it.

ROBIN: You're sure?

MOSES: Yeah.

ROBIN: We'll take it.

(Lights up on BELLA and ELLIE collecting wood.)

BELLA: Here. *(She gives ELLIE some wood to carry.)* So you saw him, eh?

(ELLIE nods.)

Were you following him?

(ELLIE nods.)

What'd he say to you?

(ELLIE signs what happened between her and PAUL.)

That boy. That poor boy.

(Lights up on YOGI and MOSES building the laundromat.)

YOGI: Paul said you're supposed to make sure there's no dead bugs and stuff where the washing machines are gonna go.

MOSES: How am I supposed to check that?

YOGI: With your hand I guess.

MOSES: I'm not doing that.

YOGI: OK then. So how's you and Robin?

MOSES: Almost got in a fight.

YOGI: Oh man. I got to teach you how to lie. What'd you do?

MOSES: I'm starting to think this moving in together's a bad idea.

YOGI: Why? She got habits? This one girlfriend I had man, she loved to whistle all the time, eh? Like a bird or something. We had to break up 'cause she was afraid of commitment.

MOSES: I want to leave this city.

YOGI: And go where?

MOSES: I don't know. Maybe back to the reserve.

YOGI: You don't want to do that yet. You're young. Take some time. Anyways if you went back to the reserve do you have a place to stay?

MOSES: Not really. What about where you're from? Do you know any houses we could rent?

YOGI: I would've rent you mine, but...

MOSES: What?

YOGI: Didn't I ever tell you 'bout my house?

MOSES: No.

YOGI: That's a sad story. To this day I wish I never tried cooking those french fries. That's the reason why I don't cook no more. I tried to cook a new recipe for french fries and the drapes catch fire and my house burns down.

MOSES: Well what the hell were you doing trying to cook the drapes for anyways?

YOGI: Aweenuk. That whole pot just caught fire. My eyebrows even got burnt off. You know how stupid people look when they got no eyebrows? My own dog was growling at me. Stupid bastard. (YOGI starts to laugh.) Fred kept growling at me, and I felt like he was making fun of me, eh? So I shaved off some of his hair. Gave him a Mr. T haircut.

MOSES: What for?

YOGI: I thought Mr. T was tough.

MOSES: I mean why'd you shave his hair.

YOGI: So he'd know what it felt like.

MOSES: He was a dog.

YOGI: Well he never growled at me after that.

MOSES:	I need money. I gotta get out of here.
YOGI:	I'm broke.
MOSES:	I wasn't asking. When we're done this I want to leave.
YOGI:	To where?
MOSES:	Don't know.

(YOGI stops working.)

YOGI:	Lunch time.
MOSES:	We got ten minutes yet.
YOGI:	I know. But since I was gonna go take a leak and that would've taken me five minutes and then another five to get ready for work again I may as well take my lunch now.
MOSES:	You're gonna get us fired.
YOGI:	You can't fire a section 25-er. It's illegal. Besides, Paul wouldn't fire me. Maybe he would.
MOSES:	Sure he would. All that type of guy cares about is money. He only cares about himself. Fitting in. Selling out is more like it. He sure doesn't look Indian to me. East Indian maybe, or Portuguese.
YOGI:	Some of that's not his fault. He was adopted out.
MOSES:	So?
YOGI:	Nothing. Hey you want to come to my bingo tonight?
MOSES:	You got a bingo?
YOGI:	No. I'm just a caller. You wanna come?
MOSES:	Can't. I got to go see Robin.

(YOGI opens his lunch.)

YOGI:	I wish I had a subway for lunch. You know who makes the best subways?
MOSES:	Who?
YOGI:	Subway.
MOSES:	What?
YOGI:	Subway makes the best subways.
MOSES:	You mean subs.
YOGI:	That's what I said. If I had money I'd invest in one of those. Call it Yogi's Way.
MOSES:	Sounds like one of those books Robin reads.
YOGI:	Son of a bitch anyways.
MOSES:	What?
YOGI:	She's been making me baloney again. Every time I tell her don't put baloney in my lunch, and what does she do? Puts baloney in my lunch. A man can only eat so much Pungassee steak, you know what I mean? You ever eat that kind that's got macaroni in it?

MOSES:	What's that?
YOGI:	Baloney.
MOSES:	And macaroni?
YOGI:	Yeah.
MOSES:	No.
YOGI:	Oh. Hey you want some baloney?
MOSES:	No thanks.
YOGI:	No I mean, like a box full. I got a whole bunch at home. I found it in that pizza place that blew up. I just missed it too. If I was walking by there two hours earlier I would've been dead. I was hoping I'd find lots of cheese or else drinks, but all I could find was a whole bunch of baloney. They must've been using that for pepperoni.
MOSES:	Too bad it wasn't a McDonald's or something.
YOGI:	Yeah, eh? I wouldn't mind this stuff so bad if they had big chunks of bacon or else cheese in there. What the hell you think that means anyways, baloney?
MOSES:	I think that's the place where it's from.
YOGI:	There's a place called baloney?
MOSES:	I think so.
YOGI:	Holy shit. There must be a salami too then, eh?
MOSES:	Probly. I think all those meats come from places.
YOGI:	Poor bastards. Imagine having to be from salami? It's bad enough I gotta tell people I'm from Dog Creek. Hey where are you from anyways?
MOSES:	What do you mean?
YOGI:	Your home. Where's your home?

> (MOSES shrugs.
>
> Cross-fade to ROBIN and MOSES. She's on a phone.)

ROBIN:	I already spoke to the education officer. No. I know. Yes, my band belongs to the tribal council. No, I've never lived on the reserve. They already said I was funded. To go to school. University, yes. Of course I have a treaty number. No I'm not Bill C-31, even if I was what does that have to do with it? You can't do this. Who made the mistake then? Hunh? How come I'm going to school one minute and now I'm not? I don't care. I'm fighting this. So since I don't live on the reservation my needs are deemed less than those of band members living on the reserve. Well tell me then. Oh and yet when it comes time for government funding I'm suddenly counted as a band member again. You can't do this. No. You can't do this.

> (She hangs up. MOSES storms in.)

MOSES:	I'm quitting my job. I hate it. My boss is an asshole. I was

supposed to be looking for dead bugs today. What the hell kind of job is that? And I hate this city.

ROBIN: You're quitting?

MOSES: I have to. I can't work for that guy. Besides, I don't want to build some stupid laundromat.

ROBIN: So that's it then? You're just quitting.

MOSES: Didn't I say that? What's wrong?

ROBIN: They took my funding away.

MOSES: Who?

ROBIN: The band.

MOSES: When?

ROBIN: Just now.

MOSES: They can't do that.

ROBIN: Tell them that.

MOSES: So now what are you supposed to do?

ROBIN: I don't know. What are we supposed to do?

MOSES: Fight it.

ROBIN: I mean about our place. How are we supposed to afford it?

MOSES: We'll just hold off a bit. Move in later or something.

ROBIN: I'll lose the deposit.

MOSES: I'll pay you back.

ROBIN: How, if you're quitting?

MOSES: Well I guess I can't quit now then, eh?

ROBIN: You can do whatever you want.

MOSES: Come here.

ROBIN: No.

MOSES: Don't worry. I won't quit.

ROBIN: Sssh. Quiet OK? I just want quiet.

(*Lights up on BELLA, ELLIE and YOGI outside the bingo hall.*)

BELLA: I shoulda bought that special. On the letter "H". I bet I would've won. Why didn't you call me a winner, Yogi?

YOGI: You're a winner.

BELLA: Aaeenh. I don't think those Nevada sellers should be allowed to play. One of them always wins.

YOGI: Are you OK getting home?

BELLA: Yeah. Ellie's with me.

YOGI: OK. I got to get home before the old lady starts playing Patsy Cline. Goodnight.

(*ELLIE signs "goodbye".*)

BELLA: Goodnight.

(*BELLA and ELLIE walk.*)

Lots of good sweats tonight though.

(*ELLIE signs.*)

BELLA: Maybe next time my girl.

(*They walk a bit more. PAUL stumbles on. He's been in a fight.*)

PAUL: Son of a bitch. You don't know me. (*Noticing BELLA and ELLIE, who doesn't look at him.*) Auntie Bella. I was gonna call you. Do you know what they did? To me. Those bastards grabbing me like I'm some vagrant.

BELLA: What happened?

PAUL: I was in the bar. Minding my own business. And this guy comes up and WHAM (*He throws his head back.*) right in the fuckin' head. Then BAM WHAM he just starts hitting me. And they take me outside. Six of them. Six of them. And start WHAM WHAM BAM. All over. All over. "Go back to the reservation you welfare case ya." Me? Me. WHAM. Right in the fuckin' head. And they're hitting me. "Wagon burner. Chug. Fuckin'..." everything. They called me everything. They don't know me. But they never got me down. BAM WHAM, kept hitting me. And then they let go and, "Come on. Come on you fuckers." WHAM. And then POW POW two shots he goes down. Next guy. POW POW FOO three shots. Down he goes. "Go back to the reservation." "Come on. COME ON you fuckers. I'll take all of you on." And they left. And my jacket. Took my jacket.

BELLA: My poor boy.

(*BELLA embraces PAUL. ELLIE moves toward them.*)

PAUL: They don't know me. They don't...

(*PAUL pushes BELLA away.*)

PAUL: No. Don't. I don't...can't. I'll call you. (*He exits.*)

(*MOSES and YOGI in the laundromat.*)

YOGI: I ever tell you about Waylan Shorting? This skinny little guy from Norway House who kept going on compensation?

MOSES: No.

YOGI: One time he was with Sheldon and me building some of those new houses in Linden Woods. He was using this nail gun.

MOSES: Yeah.

YOGI: And he's holding this board like this and he's shooting nails into this "took", "took" and I'm watching him and I'm thinking oh shit. And sure enough "took", "took", "took", and then he stops. He looks up at me and shows me his hand. Big fuckin' nail sticking right through it.

MOSES: Was it bleeding?

YOGI: No. He just makes this funny little noise like he just pissed his pants. I think he did. And I say, "What the hell are you doing?"

And he says "I don't know." So, I grab him and there was this other guy there. From Gyp. Charlie Flett. And I tell Charlie to hold Waylan's arm.

MOSES: Why?

YOGI: 'Cause I gotta pull this nail out.

MOSES: Why didn't you take him to the hospital?

YOGI: He had no I.D. or nothing. They wouldn't've taken him.

MOSES: Sure they would.

YOGI: No they wouldn't. So I grab my pliers and I tell Waylan, "I'm gonna pull this out. I'm gonna count to three, OK?" And he says "Yeah." So I get Charlie to hold his arm with all his weight. And Charlie's a big guy. And I look at this nail and it's right in there. I could barely get the pliers in under the head of the nail. Holy shit. That skinny little guy just lifted up Charlie like nothing. And scream. It sounded like I was pulling off his balls instead of a nail through his hand.

MOSES: Moses.

YOGI: But I'll never forget what he said after that. Just like a little kid.

MOSES: What's that?

YOGI: I wanna go home. I wanna go home.

(PAUL enters.)

PAUL: You can both go home if you're not going to work. I don't pay you guys to tell stories.

YOGI: What happened to your mouth?

PAUL: Nothing. Did Boo Boo here finish all the painting?

YOGI: We haven't got that far yet.

PAUL: We open in a few days, what the hell's taking so long? You're not doing that right, Boo Boo.

MOSES: Moses.

PAUL: Moses.

MOSES: What is your problem?

PAUL: Sounds like it could be you.

MOSES: Fair enough. You're mine.

PAUL: I shoulda known better than to hire friends and family.

MOSES: I'm not your friend.

YOGI: Hey come on you guys.

PAUL: And you're lucky you're not family.

MOSES: Why? You'd just ignore me like you do everyone else who's related to you.

PAUL: Don't talk about my family.

YOGI: OK shut up now.

PAUL:	Get back to work.
MOSES:	Forget it.
YOGI:	Moses.

(MOSES walks out.)

	Come on, don't be like that. What about you and Robin's place? Don't quit. Son of a bitch anyways. Why'd you do that?
PAUL:	I didn't do anything.
YOGI:	Sure you did. Both of yous.
PAUL:	It's done.
YOGI:	So now who's gonna help me?
PAUL:	I will.

(Lights up on BELLA and ROBIN.)

ROBIN:	I was really counting on that funding. I wanted to go to school so bad. How can they promise something like that and then just take it away?
BELLA:	Happens all the time.
ROBIN:	About the only good thing right now is the place we're moving into.
BELLA:	It's nice?
ROBIN:	It's kind of scary. This place Moses and me are getting, there's almost nothing wrong with it.
BELLA:	Except?
ROBIN:	Except we're not living there yet. And I think Moses is having second thoughts.
BELLA:	What's he afraid for?
ROBIN:	I wish I knew.
BELLA:	You love this man?
ROBIN:	Yes.
BELLA:	That's good.
ROBIN:	What should I do?
BELLA:	Sounds like this Moses is scared too. It's funny how we always get scared when we get close to something we want.
ROBIN:	What does he want?
BELLA:	A home. Would you do me a favour?
ROBIN:	Anything.
BELLA:	Take me to bingo tomorrow.
ROBIN:	OK.

(Lights up on ROBIN. MOSES enters.)

ROBIN:	What're you doing here?
MOSES:	I have to tell you something.

ROBIN: Oh no, Moses.

MOSES: I had to quit. That Paul guy's an asshole.

ROBIN: He's a boss. He's supposed to be an asshole.

MOSES: I'll get another job.

ROBIN: Where? Look how long it took you to get that one. Which you wouldn't have even got if it wasn't for Yogi.

MOSES: I'll go back to casual.

ROBIN: I don't want that.

MOSES: This is what I want.

ROBIN: I thought it was about what we want. How are we gonna get our place now? Hunh?

MOSES: It'll have to wait.

ROBIN: Just like that, eh? It'll have to wait. And what about my deposit? How do we get that back?

MOSES: Oh now it's "your" deposit. What happened to "us"?

ROBIN: You tell me.

            (ROBIN stares at MOSES.)

MOSES: What?

ROBIN: Why don't you want to live with me?

MOSES: It's not that.

ROBIN: What then?

MOSES: I do want to live with you. I just don't want to live here.

ROBIN: Where then?

MOSES: I don't know. Maybe Toronto. Or Vancouver.

ROBIN: What? Are we even on the same planet? What the hell are you talking about?

MOSES: I have to leave this place. I thought it'd be different, but this thing inside me isn't going away. It feels like it's getting bigger. I need to go home.

ROBIN: To the reserve?

MOSES: No.

ROBIN: Where then?

MOSES: Home.

ROBIN: Where is that?

MOSES: I don't know.

ROBIN: You're not making any sense, Moses. Why are you doing this?

MOSES: I'm not doing anything.

ROBIN: Yes you are. You're screwing everything up. And you were the one who wanted this. You were the one who wanted to move in together. Remember?

MOSES: Yeah but—

ROBIN: And I trusted you. That deposit was next month's rent. Did you know that?

MOSES: I'll pay you back your money if you care so much about it. Here.

                (MOSES gives ROBIN the toonie from the first scene. She throws it away.)

ROBIN: Don't you dare. Don't you dare say that to me. I don't care about the money. Do you get it? No. You don't. It's obvious you don't.

MOSES: Get what?

ROBIN: What this is all about. Why I'm upset. No, fuck that. Angry. Really fuckin' angry.

MOSES: You're mad 'cause we're not moving in together.

ROBIN: Why?

MOSES: That's it.

ROBIN: No that's not it. "It" is about commitment.

MOSES: To what?

ROBIN: Us. Our future.

MOSES: So why can't we make a future someplace else?

ROBIN: I don't want to go someplace else. This is my home. I love it here.

MOSES: Well I'm sorry. I don't. I need to find where I belong.

ROBIN: Well good luck, because you'll never find it running away.

MOSES: I'm not running away. I'm seeking.

ROBIN: Go.

MOSES: No. I'm not finished yet.

ROBIN: Oh yeah. We are.

                (Lights on PAUL in BELLA's backyard. BELLA's sitting, plucking a goose over a fire, throwing in the feathers.)

PAUL: Hello.

BELLA: Hi. Come sit down.

PAUL: What're you doing?

BELLA: Plucking a goose.

PAUL: Wouldn't it be quicker if you just held it in the fire and burnt them all off at once?

BELLA: Maybe. But why does it have to be quicker?

PAUL: To save time.

BELLA: How is your head?

PAUL: My jaw's pretty sore. I thought it was broken.

BELLA: We were worried for you.

PAUL: I do OK.

BELLA: Do you?

(*PAUL smiles.*)

PAUL: I came to...visit.

BELLA: Here. (*She gives PAUL the goose.*) Pull like that. Get all of it.

PAUL: Soft.

BELLA: You hungry?

PAUL: No. I already ate.

BELLA: We'll eat this one later.

PAUL: We'll make a paté out of him.

BELLA: Gooses don't make good pets. Besides he's dead.

PAUL: Right.

BELLA: You see your sister lately?

PAUL: Uhh...yeah. She looked OK.

BELLA: She looks like your mom. Almost the same. I even think that's her sometimes. It's good Ellie reminds me, I miss her. And she missed you very much.

PAUL: Then she shouldn't have let them take me.

BELLA: Your life that bad?

PAUL: It was.

BELLA: Hers too.

PAUL: I don't care. What's done is done, right? I just figured I'd come to say...apologize.

BELLA: Don't have to.

PAUL: And to thank you for your concern.

BELLA: You wanna come with me?

PAUL: Where?

BELLA: Bingo.

PAUL: I've never been.

BELLA: Oh that's OK, I've been lots. And lots. And lots.

(*Lights up on YOGI and MOSES at the laundromat. YOGI's working. MOSES is not working.*)

YOGI: Why did you quit, man?

MOSES: Paul pissed me off.

YOGI: It's boring here now. I'm sick of talking to myself.

MOSES: Could I get a couple bucks off you?

YOGI: I'm broke.

MOSES: Me too.

YOGI: How's Robin?

MOSES: We broke up.

YOGI: Why?

MOSES: 'Cause I quit.

YOGI:	Smart woman.
MOSES:	Don't pick sides.
YOGI:	Can you work it out?
MOSES:	No.
YOGI:	Maybe you just need to spend some time apart. That's what me and my first girlfriend did. Couple years oughta do it.
MOSES:	Thing is I can't be away from her. I need her.
YOGI:	Tell her that.
MOSES:	She doesn't want to talk to me
YOGI:	Wait a little bit.
MOSES:	I need money. I guess I'll go to McPhillips.
YOGI:	Come to my bingo at St. Peter, Paul and Mary's. The loonie jackpot's over a thousand bucks.
MOSES:	What time?
YOGI:	Earlybird's at seven. We got a 50-50 split on two lines anyway, four corners and I forget. But there's about five games there, then the other ones start at 7:30. You'll see Robin there.

(MOSES enters the bingo hall. ELLIE's selling cards. YOGI's the caller.)

YOGI:	Hey, you made it, how's it going?
MOSES:	She here yet?
YOGI:	Not yet. How many cards you guys want?
MOSES:	Six.
YOGI:	You should buy nine or else you can't win the loonie jackpot.
MOSES:	OK then, gimme nine.
YOGI:	Do you want any specials? Here. Take some. Just take some.
MOSES:	Thanks.
YOGI:	You need a dabber?
ROBIN:	Got one already. Thirty-nine cents at Superstore.
YOGI:	Those guys are gonna put us out of business.

(PAUL, BELLA and ROBIN enter. MOSES sees ROBIN. She looks away.)

YOGI:	Well holy hell, what're you doin' here?
BELLA:	He's with me.
YOGI:	Good to see you.
PAUL:	Good to see you.
YOGI:	Hi, Robin.
ROBIN:	Hi.
YOGI:	Nine?
BELLA:	Thirty.

YOGI: Alright. Robin?

ROBIN: Nine.

YOGI: Paul?

BELLA: Give him nine too.

     (BELLA pays for the cards.)

PAUL: That's OK, I can get this.

BELLA: No. No. No. That's OK. You calling tonight Yogi?

YOGI: Yeah. Cutbacks, eh?

     (MOSES calls over YOGI.)

MOSES: What's going on?

YOGI: With what?

MOSES: Them.

YOGI: Nothing.

MOSES: Did she say anything about me?

YOGI: No.

MOSES: What's he doing here?

YOGI: Who?

MOSES: Paul. He doesn't need any more money.

     (YOGI and ELLIE spring into action. MOSES and ROBIN spend a lot of time trying to look at each other without looking at each other.)

YOGI: Thanks for coming everyone. Your support's very much appreciated, 'cause those kids in Charleswood really need that new playground. Our number for the loonie jackpot tonight is B 5. That's B 5. Anyone who bingos on that number wins our loonie jackpot of over a thousand bucks.

PAUL: I didn't know bingo was a verb.

BELLA: It's a way of life.

YOGI: Anyways. Let's get the balls rolling or bouncing or whatever. First game. Pink. Any line or four corners. That's any line or four corners.

BELLA: This stupid Yogi talks too much.

PAUL: Four corners. What's that?

YOGI: Alright then.

     (A bingo ball drops from the sky. ELLIE catches it or picks it up and hands it to YOGI.)

Under… the B…14.

(Some more balls drop in rapid succession.)

N 40. Under the N 40. O 75. G 63. G 63. Our loonie number, under the B…5. …No bingos? Under the I…

(There's a gasp of expectation. No one wins. Light shift.)

That was wee house. Hold your cards for the next game. Empty house. That's the four outside lines on your card. Here we go.

(*More balls. YOGI calls them off in rapid succession. Until:*)

MOSES: (*To ELLIE.*) I got a sweat. Just need B 4.

BELLA: Look—you got a sweat there.

PAUL: A what?

BELLA: You need that B 5. If you get that you got a bingo. That's a sweat.

PAUL: Not a bingo?

BELLA: It'll be a bingo if you get it.

PAUL: What's a sweat then?

BELLA: Just hope for that number.

YOGI: Under the "A". Just kidding, I thought we were in Jackhead. You get to add an "A" 'cause they play bingo, eh?

MOSES: Yogi.

BELLA: I can't hear the numbers.

PAUL: I can't believe this. I'm getting a rush.

YOGI: Under the "I", just want everyone here at the St. Peter, Paul and Mary's Divinity Evangelical Holy Mother's Catholic Church basement bingo—

MOSES: Call the number Yogi.

YOGI: —to know that it's been a pleasure being your caller tonight. I know Chico's in the hospital with that female problem and I just want to thank you for letting me live my dream.

PAUL: Call the number.

ROBIN: Call it.

YOGI: Those little kids in Charleswood are gonna love you. Alright. Here we go... drumroll please... under the "O" ...my God, did I tell you that this loonie jackpot is over a thousand bucks...

BELLA: YOGI.

YOGI: Under...the Boardwalk, just kidding...

BELLA: Where's this guy from?

MOSES: Dog Creek.

(*A ball drops, ELLIE picks it up and hands it to YOGI.*)

YOGI: Under the B...

MOSES: Four.

PAUL: Five.

MOSES: Four.

PAUL: Five.

YOGI: Under the before I—

MOSES: BINGO!

YOGI: Did I hear a bingo?

MOSES: Bingo. Right here.

YOGI: But I didn't call the number yet.

PAUL: Oh well...

BELLA: Hold it. Just wait.

YOGI: OK. Bingo called.

        (ELLIE checks the number and signs "10971".)

YOGI: No. I'm sorry that is an incorrect bingo.

MOSES: No. You called B 4.

YOGI: I said "before".

MOSES: If you weren't screwing around..

YOGI: Sorry.

MOSES: No. This is bullshit. I won.

YOGI: OK. Our next number is...

MOSES: I won, Yogi. I won.

YOGI: B 5.

BELLA: Say bingo.

PAUL: What's going on?

BELLA: You won.

PAUL: I won. I bingoed?

MOSES: NO...

BELLA: You got the loonie jackpot.

PAUL: I got the loonie jackpot. Bingo. Bingo.

YOGI: Do I hear a bingo?

MOSES: He doesn't need any more money.

        (ELLIE runs over to PAUL. He turns away.)

YOGI: Yup that is a correct bingo.

MOSES: This is bullshit. You don't need any more money.

PAUL: Boo boo. Lost again, eh?

ROBIN: Moses, sit down.

MOSES: Oh now you talk to me. What's going on?

ROBIN: Nothing.

MOSES: Why are you with this guy?

ROBIN: I'm not with this guy. I'm with Bella.

MOSES: It's 'cause he's rich right? And I'm not.

PAUL: Why don't you leave?

MOSES: Why don't you shut up?

ROBIN: Moses. He hasn't done anything to you.

MOSES: Don't stick up for him. He's an asshole. He's some wannabe Indian who only uses it when he can get something out of it.

	Getting to pick when he's an Indian, not like us who have to be one all the time.
PAUL:	You don't know me.
MOSES:	Sure I do. Belong my ass. You belong nowhere.
BELLA:	Moses.
MOSES:	What?
ROBIN:	Stop it.

     (Lights up on PAUL, BELLA and ELLIE.)

PAUL:	He was right about me.
BELLA:	Don't say that.
PAUL:	It's true. I can feel it.
BELLA:	He doesn't know you.
PAUL:	I don't know me.
BELLA:	You just forget.

     (PAUL's looks at the ten $100 bills.)

PAUL:	That's a lot of geese, eh?
BELLA:	I knew you were gonna win.
PAUL:	How?
BELLA:	It was your first time.
PAUL:	Let's go somewhere. Let me buy you something.
BELLA:	That's OK.
PAUL:	Here. You take the money, you need it. I don't.
BELLA:	No, I don't.
PAUL:	Then why do you play bingo?
BELLA:	For the sweats. Makes me shiver.
PAUL:	I want to do something for you.
BELLA:	OK then. Talk to your sister.

     (PAUL stops and looks at ELLIE.)

PAUL:	I can't.
BELLA:	Why?
PAUL:	She...
BELLA:	What?
PAUL:	She reminds me.
BELLA:	Reminds you what?
PAUL:	Who I was supposed to be.
BELLA:	That's not a bad thing.
PAUL:	It is for me.
BELLA:	You're both alike. You talk more without words.
PAUL:	I'm not like her.

BELLA:	Yes, you are.
PAUL:	No. I'm not.
BELLA:	My poor boy. You're like these geese.

(She shows him the money.)

PAUL:	What?
BELLA:	When baby gooses are born from the egg. The first thing they see. That's what they grow up thinking they are. So if they see a dog. They think they're a dog. But they're still a goose. You can't change that. And you can't change who you are. Or who you're related to.

(PAUL moves towards ELLIE. They look at each other. PAUL hands ELLIE the money. She looks down sadly and takes it. She leaves.)

(Lights up on MOSES sitting lost. ELLIE enters. She sits beside MOSES.)

MOSES:	Hey, Ellie.

(ELLIE sits and starts to rip some of the money.)

Hey don't. Come on.

(ELLIE explains how she doesn't want the money. MOSES doesn't understand. ELLIE leaves. MOSES picks up the money.)

(YOGI is putting the finishing touches on the laundromat, including some ribbons and possibly a balloon or two. MOSES enters.)

MOSES:	Hey, Yogi.
YOGI:	What're you doing here? I thought you took off.
MOSES:	I got nowhere to go.
YOGI:	Sure you do.
MOSES:	She wouldn't take me back. If I were her I wouldn't.
YOGI:	How do you know? People do crazy things when they're in love. You should go to her.
MOSES:	I don't know what to say.
YOGI:	Don't plan it. Do what's in your heart.

(Lights down and up on ROBIN. MOSES enters.)

ROBIN:	So what do you want?

(MOSES gets on a knee.)

MOSES:	To say I'm sorry.
ROBIN:	OK, fine.
MOSES:	Robin...I'm sorry.

ROBIN: You already said that.

MOSES: I know. I want to come back to you.

ROBIN: Oh yeah?

MOSES: Yeah.

ROBIN: You're sure about that?

MOSES: Yes.

ROBIN: I don't believe you. Why should I?

MOSES: Because.

ROBIN: Oh. That's a good reason. Because.

MOSES: I know you're smarter than me. So don't do that, OK?

ROBIN: No. I'm not smarter than you. If I was I wouldn't be in this mess.

MOSES: I want to make it better for us.

ROBIN: Look. I have to go. Is there anything else?

MOSES: I'm sorry I hurt you. But when your heart is far away, like mine, it's easy to hurt people, and it shouldn't be like that. I never had a home. Ever. Some place I could feel was...mine. This place is your home. It feels like that right?

ROBIN: Yes.

MOSES: Why?

ROBIN: Because. I've lived here all my life.

MOSES: And?

ROBIN: And when I walk down the street I know I'll see another native person. And that makes me feel...safe.

MOSES: See. I always thought home was supposed to be a place. Like a building. Or a city or town. But it's not always a place. Sometimes it's someone else. You're my home, Robin. Not this city. You.

            (MOSES holds out a key.)

ROBIN: What's this?

MOSES: A key.

ROBIN: To what?

MOSES: A place. Listen. Did you hear that?

ROBIN: Sometimes you can hear the spirits of our people.

MOSES: What're they saying?

ROBIN: Listen harder.

MOSES: Help me.

            (MOSES holds out the key. Lights out.)

            The End

Better Looking Boys

DENNIS TROCHIM

Production Information

Better Looking Boys premiered at the Winnipeg Fringe Festival in July, 1997, with the following cast:

ALEX .... Leith Clark
STEVE .... Gary Jarvis
MARK .... Bradley Sawatzky
TROY .... Jason Neufeld

Directed by Ross McMillan
Stage Manager: Marlene Meaden

Better Looking Boys subsequently received a professional reading by Manitoba Theatre Projects in October, 1997, at the Colin Jackson Theatre, Prairie Theatre Exchange, Winnipeg, with the following cast:

ALEX: .... Brian Drader
STEVE: .... Arne McPherson
MARK: .... Graham Ashmore
TROY: .... James Durham

Directed by Ross McMillan

Characters

ALEX
STEVE
TROY
MARK
(all mid-to late 20s)

The set serves various locations.

Scene One

(Inside fashionable store. ALEX and STEVE.)

ALEX: What about leather?

STEVE: Not in our apartment.

ALEX: It has a certain look.

STEVE: A tacky look.

ALEX: Four-thousand-dollar sofas from Design Village are not tacky. They're chic.

STEVE: Four thousand? What were they? Sacred cows?

ALEX: I wonder if it's available in green.

STEVE: At the bar you turn up your nose at leathermen, but it's OK to throw around the apartment.

ALEX: There's a big difference between sitting in it and sitting on it. I'm not crazy about this matching chair.

STEVE: You never listen to what I say.

ALEX: What's that, sweetie?

STEVE: Why do I bother?

ALEX: A deal is a deal. You get the kitchen and bathroom, but the living room and bedroom are mine mine mine.

STEVE: I liked our original idea.

ALEX: Separate apartments?

STEVE: Sharing responsibilities equally.

ALEX: That wasn't an idea, that was a drunk fantasy after too much white wine.

STEVE: It worked for my parents.

ALEX: Your parents are divorced.

STEVE: You loved the house.

ALEX: Of course. It was fabulous. For Lindenwoods. But we're upscale Osborne Village homosexuals. We have reputations to maintain. Oh, here comes the salesman. Get ready to dicker.

STEVE: Dicker? Oh fuck.

Scene Two

(MARK's apartment. TROY is asleep in bed. Enter MARK.)

MARK: Good morning.

TROY: *(Awake.)* Is it?

MARK: The sun is shining, the birds are singing.

TROY: Is it morning?

MARK: For a few minutes.

TROY: Almost noon?

MARK: My alarm was set for twelve in case we slept in.

TROY: *(Getting up.)* Shit.

MARK: I have to work soon, but we have time for coffee.

TROY: *(Dressing.)* No thanks.

MARK: Or orange juice.

TROY: I have to go.

MARK: What's the rush?

TROY: I shouldn't have stayed.

MARK: Back to the wife?

TROY: No.

MARK: Or girlfriend?

TROY: You know where my socks are?

MARK: So you're single.

TROY: I'm running late. *(Finds one sock.)*

MARK: For work maybe?

TROY: Work, right, is that my T-shirt?

MARK: I hope you're not rushing off because of me.

TROY: No.

MARK: Or because you're embarrassed.

TROY: I'd rather not—

MARK: —Answer any questions?

TROY: —Waste any time. I had two socks.

MARK: No kidding.

TROY: Can you help me look?

MARK: I don't do this often.

TROY: Can you help me look, please?

MARK: *(Helps.)* I was coming from a friend's party—

TROY: You don't owe me any explanations.

MARK: A few drinks, a cute guy in a car drives by, you know how it is.

TROY: Were we only in this room?

MARK: Actually, there is one thing I need to know.

TROY: Oh well, it's just a sock.

MARK: If I don't ask it's going to nag at me.

TROY: If you find it, well, throw it out.

MARK: Were we safe?

TROY: Aren't you usually?

MARK: Always.

TROY: Then if it's always, why don't you remember?

MARK: I rarely drink, but my head was spinning, and your kisses were so incredibly deep and powerful—

TROY: We were safe. The condom was flushed down the toilet.

MARK: Good. Uhm, I'm sorry I can't remember getting fucked. I guess you should. Don't get the wrong idea about me.

TROY: Relax. It was just sex.

MARK: Just sex.

TROY: Exactly.

MARK: Did you enjoy it?

TROY: I'm going now.

MARK: Did you?

TROY: It was OK.

MARK: OK? That's reassuring.

TROY: See ya.

MARK: Will you?

TROY: Probably not. Oh, and for the record, you fucked me.

MARK: Really?

TROY: Really. Really aggressively, in fact. Bye.

             (MARK sits on bed. His alarm clock rings. As he turns it off, he finds the sock in the sheets.)

MARK: I'm in a gay version of *Cinderella*.

Scene Three

             (ALEX and STEVE on street.)

STEVE: Nice dickering.

ALEX: I talked him down to 36.

STEVE: By agreeing to spend 800 on end tables.

ALEX: We need end tables.

STEVE: It's no saving when you end up spending more.

ALEX: On my credit card. Technically I bought it.

STEVE: Technically we agreed to do everything fifty/fifty.

ALEX: You were standing next to me, weren't you?

STEVE: It doesn't feel like my home, too.

ALEX: Your name is at the top of the lease.

STEVE: Everything is your decision. The drapes, the carpet, the china.

ALEX: We made a deal—

STEVE: You made a deal to choose the rooms you wanted. Even with what you gave me, you're saying do this and that.

ALEX: You hate decorating.

STEVE: I don't hate it. But I don't do it well. I don't know about fabrics or furniture or what's fashionable. I don't care if a room has good sight lines. It's a bathroom. Can you see the toilet, can you see the sink, you have good sight lines. And those ridiculous colours— mauve, taupe, paisley—

ALEX: Paisley's not a colour.

STEVE: I want a say in the things I know. Is it comfortable? Does it fit? Am I spending a fortune on something I'm not even allowed to put my feet on? Alex, you could decorate the whole place for all I care, so long as you include the things that matter to me.

ALEX: And if they're incompatible to the things that matter to me?

STEVE: Then we have a problem.

ALEX: Do you want to cancel the couch?

STEVE: It's bigger than a couch.

ALEX: I suppose you could put your feet on it as long as you take off your shoes. And if the tables don't look good, we'll return them. I promise. ...That's called a compromise, Steven.

STEVE: OK, I'm off to aerobics. Meet you where?

ALEX: We can pick up some dessert at Baked.
    (STEVE exits.)

ALEX: Good. I kept the couch.
    (ALEX exits.)

Scene Four

(STEVE is at the gym. TROY enters, rushing, wearing only one sock.)

STEVE: The class is running over time.

TROY: Yeah?

STEVE: Save your energy, it's a killer.

TROY: It's a beginners' class.

STEVE: There was a schedule change posted all week.

TROY:	Change to what?
STEVE:	Advanced muscle-builder program. Ninety minutes of step combinations with weights and 10 minute high-impact intervals.
TROY:	Okaaay.
STEVE:	Take it at your own pace, you'll be fine.
TROY:	My own pace is a pacemaker pace. I've only been at this a week.
STEVE:	This should be fun.
TROY:	Right.
STEVE:	I meant for the rest of us.
TROY:	Maybe I should just go—
STEVE:	Wait. It only sounds gruelling. You'll love it.
TROY:	Promise?
STEVE:	No. But I will promise to call 911 if you collapse.
TROY:	Fair enough. Watch out for me. *(Exits.)*
STEVE:	My pleasure.

Scene Five

(Lights rise on table in cafe where MARK is a waiter.)

ALEX:	Excuse me, but can I get some service?
MARK:	I'm sorry, but we don't serve snotty fags.
ALEX:	You certainly hire them.
MARK:	Buy anything?
ALEX:	Sofa and tables. Only four thousand.
MARK:	Only, he says.
ALEX:	It was leather and the tables are hand crafted.
MARK:	By who, Michaelangelo?
ALEX:	That's not much for Design Village.
MARK:	Geez, last week I went to Value Village and spent $30 for a chair. And I was complaining then, too. *(Turns.)* Beth, I'm taking a quick five, watch my table? *(Sits.)*
ALEX:	You look like shit.
MARK:	Tossed and turned all night. I was dreaming about a guy in a red Mazda.
ALEX:	Front seat or back?
MARK:	Front. Only I can't remember his name. Five-eleven. Brown hair. Very boy-next-door.
ALEX:	What part of town do you consider next door? A parking lot at the Hill where you gave him a blowjob?
MARK:	I am so offended by that insinuation.

ALEX:	You did!
MARK:	We met in the parking lot and went back to my place.
ALEX:	Why can't you remember his name?
MARK:	I had a few drinks.
ALEX:	What does he do? What did you talk about?
MARK:	I can't remember that either.
ALEX:	What do you remember?
MARK:	He wears black socks.
ALEX:	Were you only drinking?
MARK:	Yes.
ALEX:	Look me in the eye.
MARK:	Why?
ALEX:	Do it.
MARK:	They're not bloodshot or anything.
ALEX:	Open wide.
MARK:	And if they are, it's because I didn't get much sleep.
ALEX:	Hmm.
MARK:	What do you expect to see?
ALEX:	The truth.
MARK:	I have to get that couple some coffee. Do you want anything?
ALEX:	Coke.
MARK:	A glass of coke?
ALEX:	Were you?
MARK:	No. Honest. I don't do that shit anymore.
ALEX:	OK. A small latte.
MARK:	Be back in a sec. Oh, and I tried Ecstasy.
ALEX:	What?
MARK:	(Across cafe.) I'll be right there with a refill. (MARK walks away.)

Scene Six

(The gym. STEVE and TROY enter.)

TROY:	Oh. My. God.
STEVE:	Wasn't that great?
TROY:	No.
STEVE:	Don't you feel exhilarated!?
TROY:	Exhausted.
STEVE:	But incredible!

TROY:	Incredibly exhausted.
STEVE:	You lasted the class.
TROY:	Barely. My heart. Won't stop pounding. Will explode.
STEVE:	I warned you. Keep it at your pace.
TROY:	I had the slowest pace. Any slower, I'd have gone back in time.
STEVE:	Next week will be easier.
TROY:	Not next week, oh no.
STEVE:	You can't give up.
TROY:	I just did.
STEVE:	My first time, I was so out of shape.
TROY:	You? Right.
STEVE:	But I kept at it, and look at me now.
TROY:	How long ago was this?
STEVE:	Five years.
TROY:	That sounds like a manageable time frame.
STEVE:	Good, have a sense of humor about it. That's the key.
TROY:	Are you always so happy?
STEVE:	I just like working out.
TROY:	My stomach is doing somersaults.
STEVE:	You OK? I mean, seriously.
TROY:	Yeah. I wasn't prepared, that's all.
STEVE:	The weekday classes are better. Mondays, Wednesdays, and Fridays at five thirty.
TROY:	I work until six. I'll be at the seven o'clock class.
STEVE:	Explains why I haven't seen you before. My name's Steve.
TROY:	Troy. And thanks for the encouragement. I appreciate it.
STEVE:	Anytime.
TROY:	I better hit the showers. Keep an eye out for me. *(Exits.)*
STEVE:	You have got to be kidding.

Scene Seven

(The cafe.)

MARK:	Refill?
ALEX:	*(Dragging him into chair.)* I am so disappointed in you.
MARK:	Gee, Mom, sorry I can't be the son you always wanted.
ALEX:	Need I remind you how drugs and alcohol cloud your judgment about sex?
MARK:	No they don't. I enjoy it just as much.

ALEX:	You're too old to be experimenting. And you're too old for Ecstasy. You're not some 19 year old off to a rave.
MARK:	Well it wasn't worth it since I can't remember what happened. But I'm going to find him again.
ALEX:	Maybe this was your one chance at happiness. Maybe he was the man of your dreams, and you let him get away because you were too high to remember his name.
MARK:	I can always depend on you for a pep talk.
ALEX:	I'm not peppy. I'm bitchy and jaded. And your conscience since you don't have one.
MARK:	I want a boyfriend.
ALEX:	Whose?
MARK:	I dunno. How about yours? Is he still happy with you?
ALEX:	Deliriously.
MARK:	Explains why he puts up with you.
STEVE:	(Entering.) What did I tell you about hanging around dives like this?
ALEX:	Every once in awhile I like to slum it.
STEVE:	Busy, Mark?
MARK:	Why no, Steve, why do you ask?
STEVE:	(To ALEX.) We staying for coffee?
ALEX:	I want to drop by Safeway and pick up a few things.
MARK:	Produce sections. Lots of pick-ups on a Saturday afternoon. Will you guys be at the bar later?
STEVE:	(Same time as ALEX.) Maybe.
ALEX:	(Simultaneously.) No.
MARK:	OK. Better get back to work. Beth has that "fire him" look in her eyes again. Later. (MARK walks off.)
ALEX:	Don't you want to rent a movie?
STEVE:	You're the one who says we don't socialize anymore.
ALEX:	You say we go out too much.
STEVE:	I'm feeling restless.
ALEX:	Let's talk about it after dinner.
STEVE:	I know what that means.
ALEX:	Steve—

(ALEX exits, followed by STEVE.)

Scene Eight

(The gym, two weeks later. STEVE and TROY are stretching.)

STEVE:	*(Easy stretch.)* Hey.
TROY:	*(Not so easy.)* Heyyy.
STEVE:	I think you're beginning to like this Saturday morning class.
TROY:	Last week I only had one collapsed lung. I'm getting the hang of this. *(More stretching.)*
STEVE:	Uhm, Troy. I was wondering. Usually after class, I do lunch with this friend, but she's not around today, she had this appointment, and I was wondering, I dunno, if maybe you'd like to—
TROY:	Do lunch?
STEVE:	Nothing fancy. Someplace quick, or nearby.
TROY:	Why not?
STEVE:	Great.
TROY:	Better hurry up. The dominatrix is waiting.

Scene Nine

(MARK's apartment. MARK is in bed, ALEX is kicking the bed.)

MARK:	I'm not going.
ALEX:	Yes you are.
MARK:	You can't make me.
ALEX:	Watch me.
MARK:	I'm not 12 years old.
ALEX:	Then stop acting like it. Get out of bed now.
MARK:	I really must protest this inhumane treatment—
ALEX:	Before I throw cold water on you.
MARK:	I don't need drug counseling.
ALEX:	Then why can't you go a week without Ecstasy?
MARK:	It's not that I can't.
ALEX:	It's a choice—
MARK:	That I can control.
ALEX:	And when you don't feel like doing it anymore—
MARK:	I'll stop.
ALEX:	Just like that.
MARK:	Exactly.
ALEX:	And that's exactly what the clinic said you'd say. Let's go. You promised me and Steven.
MARK:	Of course I did. I was high. I'll promise anything.
ALEX:	Friends don't abandon friends. Friends help each other out.

MARK:	You've been watching too many American sit-coms.
ALEX:	Listen, you drug-infested pathetic little faggot. Get your feeling sorry-for-yourself lazy ass out of that bed and into your cheap retro Value Village wardrobe and keep this appointment because I am missing a valuable Saturday that I could spend shopping, doing lunch, or any number of things more interesting than watching you dry out!!
MARK:	I don't appreciate that tone.
ALEX:	You wanted my help.
MARK:	Help, yes, not enlist me in boot camp.
ALEX:	Why do you do it?
MARK:	I get bored.
ALEX:	Of what?
MARK:	Everything.
ALEX:	Get over it. Deal with it.
MARK:	Easy for you to say. Nice boyfriend, nice apartment, money coming out of your ass.
ALEX:	Time to bring out the big guns.
MARK:	I'm scared.
ALEX:	You will be when I tell your mother.
MARK:	You wouldn't.
ALEX:	"Hello, Mrs. Remillard? It's Alex. Remember me? The stylish gay friend of your son's?"
MARK:	*(Getting out of bed.)* "Oh, yes, the queeny one."
ALEX:	"He's doing drugs again!"
	(They exit.)

Scene Ten

(The cafe. STEVE and TROY are sitting.)

TROY:	And after I finished my apprenticeship I've been working steady since.
STEVE:	You don't look like any plumber I've ever met.
TROY:	Talk to me in twenty years, I'll have it all down pat. Tight work slacks, belly spilling out.
STEVE:	Whoa, plumber's crack.
TROY:	One day.
STEVE:	Not while you're in aerobics, I'll make sure of that.
TROY:	Well, Steve, I have to admit. You're not like any loans officer I've ever met. You're not a completely insensitive asshole.
STEVE:	Industry stereotype. We're really quite sweet.

TROY:	Yeah, he was real sweet for my car loan. I'll be in debt for years.
STEVE:	How is your credit rating?
TROY:	I take that back. You are like other loans officers. I just wish there was some value in trust. Faith in your fellow man… So this girl you do lunch with. Somebody special?
STEVE:	Sort of. You serious about that trust stuff?
TROY:	Sure.
STEVE:	She's not a girl.
TROY:	Oh yeah?
STEVE:	I don't want you to freak. I mean, a guy asking another guy out. Not that there's anything wrong with it. Happens all the time. Lunch. Two guys. A guy thing. A friendly guy thing. Friends. And if one of those friends happens to be gay, so what. Right?
TROY:	Right.
STEVE:	You're OK with that?
TROY:	Shouldn't I be?
STEVE:	You must have gay friends.
TROY:	Nope. Not one. No reason, just don't. And now I sort of do! Cool.
STEVE:	But aren't you the least bit shocked that I'm gay?
TROY:	Nope.
STEVE:	It's not like I'm gay at first sight.
TROY:	Not until I talked to you.
STEVE:	Hey, I'm not obvious.
TROY:	Obviously.
STEVE:	I blend in at work, at the grocery store—
TROY:	At the gay bar.
STEVE:	Hey, being butch and gay, these are important things.
TROY:	Yeah? Why?
STEVE:	It's part of the gay ideal. Very hard to explain.
TROY:	Gee, try to speak slowly, I'm just the dumb straight guy.
STEVE:	There's this stereotype of gay men. Queeny. Bitchy. Always trying to seduce straight men. Not that you have to be queeny to do it. Not that you have to do it at all. But this stereotype. It's not sexy. And we don't always talk about sex or think with our dicks. Penises, I mean. Uhm, I'm not the most qualified person to talk about this.
TROY:	Do you sometimes think with your dick?
STEVE:	Only sometimes.
TROY:	I do all the time.
STEVE:	You're straight. You're allowed to.
TROY:	And this special someone you were talking about. He's like you?

STEVE: No. He's...got quite the sense of humor. He's a graphic artist. Very artistic. Artistic, and funny, and...well, he makes good money.

TROY: You both must make a bundle.

STEVE: Picture perfect guppy dinks.

TROY: What?

STEVE: Gay urban professional, double income, no kids. New condo, two cars, four weeks vacation a year.

TROY: Enough to make a guy switch. Almost. I'll have to think about this gay ideal stuff. Always willing to learn something new.

STEVE: ...So. Dessert?

(Crossfade to ALEX and STEVE's apartment. MARK and ALEX. ALEX has a bottle of gin and glass.)

MARK: And as part of the 12-step program, there's therapy.

ALEX: Not so terrible. A couch to lie on, a psychiatrist to tell all your troubles.

MARK: Group therapy.

ALEX: God, straight people and their problems. Stay for dinner?

MARK: You should be spending a quiet evening with Steve. Make him dinner.

ALEX: Why do I always have to wear the apron? He can cook.

MARK: I'd kill to have what you have.

ALEX: You know the saying, sweetie. You don't know how it feels till you've walked in my heels.

MARK: I better go.

ALEX: Straight home and read a good book.

MARK: Right after the bar.

ALEX: Good. Start a 12-step program by taking two back.

MARK: There are some people I haven't seen in awhile.

ALEX: Drug dealers? Fellow addicts?

MARK: Only water and dancing, no E.

ALEX: That goes for all the other vowels, sometimes Y too.

MARK: Enough, Alex. Have a wonderful night. *(Exits.)*

ALEX: Wonderful. Make him dinner. Make him a drink. Make him fall in love with you all over again. No problem. Just make him a good stiff drink, that ought to do it.

STEVE: *(Off stage.)* Alex?

ALEX: In here.

STEVE: *(Entering.)* Smells like—

ALEX: Teriyaki chicken?

STEVE: Marinated with booze.

ALEX:	Did you see Mark in the elevator?
STEVE:	We took the stairs.
ALEX:	We?
STEVE:	A friend from the gym. He's in the hallway. He's straight.
ALEX:	I made dinner.
STEVE:	We had a huge lunch. Pigged out all afternoon. I hope you don't mind if we go to a hockey game.
ALEX:	A what?
STEVE:	Something to do.
ALEX:	What do you know about hockey?
STEVE:	I used to play.
ALEX:	When you were eight.
STEVE:	I'll be home around ten.
ALEX:	Well, then, let's meet him.
STEVE:	Remember, he's straight.
ALEX:	Like I spontaneously kiss everyone I meet.
STEVE:	Troy! In here! *(To ALEX.)* You've been drinking?
ALEX:	A little.
STEVE:	What's a little?
ALEX:	Watch.
	(TROY enters.)
STEVE:	Alex, Troy. Troy, Alex.
TROY:	*(Extends hand.)* Hey.
ALEX:	*(Very deep, macho.)* Hi there.
TROY:	Nice place.
ALEX:	We're still decorating.
STEVE:	Buying furniture, laying down carpet, you know how it is.
TROY:	Oh yeah. This condo must have set you guys back.
STEVE:	Couldn't have done it alone. That's one advantage of being together.
ALEX:	Only one?
STEVE:	Of many.
ALEX:	So, Troy. That's very Greek.
TROY:	What?
ALEX:	City of Troy. The Trojan Horse. Achilles heel.
TROY:	Never saw that movie.
STEVE:	Troy's a plumber.
ALEX:	We should get him to look at the shower sometime. It leaks.
TROY:	I'll give Steve my card.

STEVE:	We should go. Troy has season tickets.
TROY:	The Moose are on a streak and host Vegas.
ALEX:	Those wild streaking moose. Hosting Vegas. Regular party animals.
STEVE:	We should go now.
TROY:	Nice meeting you.
ALEX:	Steve. Can I speak to you for a moment?
STEVE:	Now?
TROY:	I'll wait in the car. *(Exit TROY.)*
STEVE:	What?
ALEX:	He's a young plumber.
STEVE:	He's straight.
ALEX:	As long as you remember.
STEVE:	Give me a break. I made a new friend. I don't have that many left. They've either moved or drifted away or died.
ALEX:	It's no big deal. I only want you to hurry home so we can spend time together.
STEVE:	Sure.
ALEX:	Quality time.
STEVE:	OK. Troy's waiting. *(STEVE exits.)*
ALEX:	Me, too.
	(Lights fade over ALEX.)

Scene Eleven

(MARK's apartment. MARK and TROY enter.)

MARK:	You shouldn't have been driving around the Hill. You nearly crashed into that fence.
TROY:	Hey, if I wanted to crash into that fence I would have.
MARK:	Where you coming from?
TROY:	A hockey game.
MARK:	Some hockey game.
TROY:	They serve beer at hockey games.
MARK:	No kidding. Who'd you go with?
TROY:	A buddy.
MARK:	A close buddy?
TROY:	A new buddy. A special buddy.
MARK:	How special.
TROY:	I dunno. A nice guy. Cool. Fit. Good looking. He wants to suck my cock.

MARK:	Why don't you let him?
TROY:	Maybe I will. Hey, you're not drunk this time.
MARK:	Or high.
TROY:	You mean drugs?
MARK:	Yes.
TROY:	You do drugs?
MARK:	Sporadically.
TROY:	Don't know that one. Is it like pot?
MARK:	You are pickled.
TROY:	You want to see my pickle?
MARK:	Do you want to show me your pickle?
TROY:	Show me yours.
MARK:	Waste no time. *(Moving close.)* I have an idea. We climb into bed.
TROY:	*(Doing so.)* Yeah.
MARK:	Strip naked.
TROY:	Yeah.
MARK:	Watch an old movie.
TROY:	What.
MARK:	Hold each other. Get to know each other. Cuddle.
TROY:	When are you going to fuck me?
MARK:	I don't have to.
TROY:	Yes, you do.
MARK:	It's not important.
TROY:	Says you.
MARK:	What's the big deal?
TROY:	Fucking? It's everything, fuck. It makes it happen.
MARK:	What happen?
TROY:	The whole thing. When you fuck me, all your energy from wanting and needing, I can feel it going into me. Out of your dick and into me, recharging me, I swear, it makes me stronger. And you, like every other fuck, you shoot, you're nothing after that. And I'm everything. I want it.
MARK:	Listen to you. And I thought you weren't gay.
TROY:	I'm not gay.
MARK:	Right.
TROY:	I'm not.
MARK:	What's that about fucking?
TROY:	It's just fucking.
MARK:	Making love?
TROY:	Love? Fuck, you gay guys and your labels.

MARK:	I dunno, I think a label would look good on you.
TROY:	Are we gonna do it or not?
MARK:	Let's take this slowly. Get to know each other. See what happens.
TROY:	Some other night. *(At door.)* And next time, we got to get you some fucking drugs. You're bringing me down.
	(TROY exits.)

Scene Twelve

	(Four weeks later. ALEX and STEVE's apartment. ALEX is sitting in chair upstage, at imaginary mirror. STEVE is getting ready to leave.)
STEVE:	Will you have time to look for wallpaper today?
ALEX:	Maybe next week.
STEVE:	What happened to all your creative energy?
ALEX:	I'm in a decorative slump. Don't worry, the apartment will be fine.
STEVE:	*(Stepping closer.)* What are you doing?
ALEX:	Nothing.
STEVE:	What's that on your face?
ALEX:	There's nothing on my face.
STEVE:	That spot.
ALEX:	A little smudge.
STEVE:	Of what?
ALEX:	Dirt or dust.
STEVE:	Or…make-up?
ALEX:	It's not make-up. It's cover up for men.
STEVE:	What are you covering up?
ALEX:	Three years of fighting with you, sweetie.
STEVE:	How long have you been wearing that?
ALEX:	A few minutes.
STEVE:	How many days?
ALEX:	Days?
STEVE:	Weeks? Months? Oh, God, you've been wearing it for years and I've only found out now?
ALEX:	A few weeks. It's no big deal.
STEVE:	My partner wears make-up.
ALEX:	I want to look good. So do you. That's why you're at the gym so much, isn't it?
STEVE:	Yeah, but I look good naturally… Wear what you like. I don't mind.

(STEVE exits, passing MARK.)

MARK: Hey, Steve, how's it...going.

(MARK enters.)

MARK: OK, I've psyched myself up for the trip to the clinic. Ready to go? Alex? Things OK?

ALEX: Steve doesn't think I'm attractive.

MARK: Neither do I. *(Pause.)* Oh, you're serious. Did he say so?

ALEX: He didn't have to. Sometimes I only think he stays in this relationship because he has no better place to go.

MARK: Don't create problems if they don't exist.

ALEX: You couldn't understand. It's been awhile since you've been in a relationship.

MARK: I'm looking.

ALEX: In all the wrong places.

MARK: I've met a few nice guys.

ALEX: Like that clueless closet case you've been mooning over?

MARK: He's sexy and secretive.

ALEX: And a serial killer.

MARK: You're the one who said that maybe it was my one chance at happiness. Well, maybe I'll get another chance. Even if it does end in heartbreak, it's nice to know there's still a heart to break.

ALEX: The more I think about love, the more I wonder if it's worth it.

MARK: How did it happen? I'm a slop pail with more pick ups than Purolator. You've been in a steady relationship with a pretty decent guy. Yet somehow I end up more of a romantic than you.

ALEX: OK, Mr. Romantic, let's go get the results of your HIV test. How do I look?

MARK: Divine.

ALEX: Thank-you.

MARK: Of course he's dead now.

ALEX: You're riding in the trunk again.

Scene Thirteen

(The gym. STEVE and TROY.)

STEVE: How about that new Thai place? We can get stir-fry.

TROY: Or how about a sauna?

STEVE: A what?

TROY: Grab a towel.

STEVE: But I don't... *(TROY is off-stage.)* like saunas.

(Crossfade to clinic. ALEX is reading a pamphlet. MARK enters.)

ALEX: Took long enough.

MARK: I was talking to the doctor about safe sex practices.

ALEX: Like you need practice. Are you going to live?

MARK: Uh huh.

ALEX: I'm taking these pamphlets with me. I thought I knew enough about this damn virus. Seems I know very little. Are you coming?

        (They exchange a look.)

        No.

MARK: Oh, no. I tested negative. But I have hepatitis A.

ALEX: Hepatitis? Weren't there symptoms?

MARK: Sure. Sore throat, tired all the time. I figured, hey, last of the party boys. It was all par for the course. I've got these prescriptions for...something.

ALEX: I'm sorry.

MARK: Me too.

ALEX: You can pick where we go for lunch.

MARK: I'm not hungry.

ALEX: Or a drink maybe.

MARK: This is serious.

ALEX: If it were serious, you'd be hospitalized.

MARK: But it shouldn't have happened. I was careful. I'm always careful. Guess not careful enough. Shit, if I got this, I could have got something else. I could have got it.

ALEX: They're not the same.

MARK: I have to start changing my life.

ALEX: Fine. But let's do it like any civilized person would.

        Over salads and white wine.

MARK: I need something stronger.

ALEX: That's why you have me. Come on. I have pamphlets.

        (They exit. Lights rise over the sauna. STEVE and TROY are sitting in towels. TROY is relaxed. STEVE is not.)

TROY: Great, huh?

STEVE: Yeah.

TROY: You can feel the pores opening.

STEVE: Wide open.

TROY: Relaxes you.

STEVE: Uh huh.

TROY: You don't look relaxed.

STEVE: No, no. I love it. It's just so...goddamn hot.

TROY:	Ten more minutes.
STEVE:	We've been here over twenty. The sign says long enough.
TROY:	I don't pay attention to signs. Not all of them anyway.
STEVE:	What?
TROY:	If you want to wait for me in the change room, I'll be there in a bit.
STEVE:	I'm enjoying this.
TROY:	Not feeling dizzy or anything?
STEVE:	Nah. I'll keep you company. OK?
TROY:	If you want to.
STEVE:	If you want me to.
TROY:	If I want you to?
STEVE:	Yeah.
TROY:	OK. Keep me company then. *(Leans back, spreads legs apart.)* Think you can handle it?
STEVE:	*(Looking while not looking.)* Uhm, yeah.
TROY:	Good… Sitting here like this. It's kind of hard, huh?
STEVE:	Oh, more than kind of.
TROY:	Yeah.
STEVE:	This heat is, uhm, maybe, kind of, making me, uhm—
TROY:	Steve.
STEVE:	What?
TROY:	If you're that hot and bothered, maybe you should do something about it.
STEVE:	*(Standing.)* I think I better uh…
	(STEVE starts to walk past TROY. Stops. Puts his hand on TROY's chest.)
TROY:	Steve.
STEVE:	*(Removing hand.)* Sorry, I, uh—
TROY:	Not here. Someplace else.
	(Lights fade out on sauna. Lights rise on MARK and ALEX, sitting at a table.)
MARK:	Getting drunk in the middle of the afternoon. Isn't it terrible.
TROY:	Only if you can't afford it. Otherwise it's decadent.
MARK:	I can't afford it.
ALEX:	I can.
MARK:	You're always paying for lunch.
ALEX:	It gives me pleasure. Would you deny me that? Let's get another round.
	(ALEX gestures for a waiter.)
MARK:	If we were straight, you'd be married with two kids. I'd be going

	through a divorce, chasing younger and younger women. This would be a bad thing.
ALEX:	Drinking is still a bad thing. Don't spoil it.
MARK:	But it seems less bad because we're gay.
ALEX:	Socially unacceptable behavior in socially unacceptable people. I guess two wrongs can make a right.
MARK:	Think about it. It's because we have less responsibilities.
ALEX:	Please. There are plenty of gay people with responsibilities. And look at lesbians. They're the most responsible people I know.
MARK:	But it seems we have lesser expectations of ourselves. Is that because we're gay men, or in spite of it?
ALEX:	What have you been drinking?
MARK:	Scotch.
ALEX:	No wonder you're so earnest. Switch to martinis.
MARK:	We have no sense of purpose. No families to raise, no status quo to protect. And now that we're out to everyone around us, we don't know what to do with the rest of our lives.
ALEX:	*(To imaginary waiter.)* One more please. And you?
MARK:	What am I supposed to do with my life?
ALEX:	I don't know. Get a real job for starters. You can't be a waiter forever. *(To waiter.)* Oh, no offence! But he's twenty eight! Just the margarita! We'll get him later! *(To MARK.)* Great. I have to tip him big time now.
MARK:	Find a job. Find a relationship. Settle down. That's the solution.
ALEX:	Maybe get a cat.
MARK:	Gay, straight, it doesn't matter.
ALEX:	Revolutionary, isn't it?
MARK:	But it doesn't work for everyone. Not me. Not you.
ALEX:	Yes it does. I have a wonderful man. A wonderful home. Our combined income is greater than that of our parents. They can't look at me and say, what are you doing with your life, son, because I can look back and say, living better than you ever did, Dad. You should have seen the look on his face.
MARK:	Are you happy?
ALEX:	It's happy hour. How can I be otherwise?
MARK:	Bullshit.
ALEX:	What?
MARK:	Bullshit bullshit bullshit.
ALEX:	Fuck off.
MARK:	Liar.
ALEX:	I may not seem happy, but that's because I'm a naturally bitchy person.

MARK:	You're scared, just as much as me.
ALEX:	Of what.
MARK:	Of not knowing what comes next. Alex, when we came out, being gay was so exciting. Every gay book or movie was about being young and in love and coming out. And we did it all. First sex, first love, first heart-break, we've had hundreds of first times. Now we're older. With nobody to tell us anything new. So you bitch and drink and I do drugs because our lives really are boring. No angels crashing down in our bedrooms. Nothing.
ALEX:	Such philosophical pondering. And it's not even five!
MARK:	At least I've got the guts to ask them.
ALEX:	Yes, darling. This brand new look at your life. Tell me. Is it a result of your extensive soul searching from rehabilitation program or is a delusional after-effect from your newly-acquired STD.
MARK:	...I know you always pay for me, Alex, so you can feel better than me. Not anymore. After I'm gone, take a look at your own life, sweetie, and then see how sweet it is. *(MARK exits.)*
	(Lights fade and rise over STEVE and ALEX's apartment. ALEX crosses stage, where STEVE is standing.)
ALEX:	Driving around where?
STEVE:	Nowhere. Just listening to music. You been drinking?
ALEX:	What was your first clue, Nancy Drew.
STEVE:	You're ugly when you drink.
ALEX:	Why stop there? What about when I'm sober.
STEVE:	I'm going to bed.
ALEX:	So early?
STEVE:	I'm tired.
ALEX:	From what?
STEVE:	This conversation.
ALEX:	Steve? Why don't we make love anymore?
STEVE:	What was Sunday?
ALEX:	You getting off on the sheets, with me caught between.
STEVE:	Good night.
ALEX:	Do you love me?
STEVE:	Yes, I love you. Alex, we have everything. I have everything. I'm satisfied.
ALEX:	You avoid me. You avoid fighting with me. You avoid being honest with me. You avoid everything. A nuclear bomb could fall on this city, you'd avoid getting hit, you're so good at it.
STEVE:	Do you want the truth?
ALEX:	Yes. I've had enough alcohol to sedate an elephant. Hit me.

| STEVE: | Sometimes you bitch and annoy and it gets under my skin. But I'd rather be here living with you than anywhere else. I want to go to bed now. OK? |
| ALEX: | OK. |

(STEVE walks off.)

For now.

(ALEX exits.

Sound cue; dance music, very distorted, perhaps a different sort of lighting. Lights rise on MARK in a bar—he is "on" something.)

| MARK: | Hey! Great! …Yeah, well you look like shit too! …This song, I love this song… Diii-aaannaa Roosss, III wiiilll suuurviiive—oh, God, no you won't girl… Hey! You! I love you! Call me? Asshole! *(Starts laughing.)* Hey, how are you! No, I quit! I don't do that shit anymore. This is a different kind of shit. Yeah? What's a good price? No shit. |

(Music and lights fade to blackout.)

Scene Fourteen

(Spotlight on ALEX.)

| ALEX: | Hello. I'm with the Clinic Meals On Wheels program. How are you today? …Oh, that's too bad. I bet I know what would make you feel better. A warm, delicious chicken dinner with mashed potatoes and vegetables and… No, I don't think it's crap… Of course, I'd eat it…I would… Then I'll leave it here and you can finish it later. Anything else I can get for you or do for you or.. *(Not so nice.)* Listen. Throw it out, spit on it, sit on it, I really don't care. But it's good hot food and you'd have to be stupider than you already look to not appreciate it. *(Nice again.)* I have to go now. We'll see you again. |

(ALEX exits.

Lights rise over STEVE and ALEX's apartment on STEVE and TROY.)

TROY:	It's not right.
STEVE:	It'll be exciting in our bedroom.
TROY:	Pig.
STEVE:	I know. Something's awakened inside me. Like I forgot how wonderful it is to be so horny. I think about you at work. I think about sex at work. I see guys all day and I think, my God, all these good looking guys I'll never do. It's not fair. I want to kiss them. I want to grab their bums at bus stops. I want to pull them to the ground in the aisles of department stores-
TROY:	You want it that bad?
STEVE:	Yes.

TROY:	Prove it.
STEVE:	What?
TROY:	Get down on your hands and knees and beg for it.
STEVE:	Oh come on—
TROY:	Do it.
STEVE:	No.
TROY:	If you're going to be a pig, then let's go all the way. Show me how far you'll go.
STEVE:	This is ridiculous—
TROY:	Now.
STEVE:	*(Half-joking.)* Okaaay. *(Then, on knees.)* OK.
TROY:	What do you say?
STEVE:	Please.
TROY:	What.
STEVE:	Please will you let me—
TROY:	I can't hear you—
STEVE:	This is so stupid—
TROY:	Show me the extreme, man, or I'm outta here, I swear I will—
STEVE:	Please will you just let me fuck you!
TROY:	Better. Why didn't you say so?

(Lights out. Spotlight on ALEX.)

ALEX: —with chicken and vegetables and potatoes and...gravy, I think... You're welcome... Oh, this is my second week now... Yes, yes, lots of fun... No, sick people don't bother me. It's the ones who never get sick, I mean what's their story? ...I'd love to stay for a game of cribbage, really, but I have three more dinners to drop off *(Looking at list.)* on Portage, and Donald Street, and...oh no.. Excuse me. I have to...get out of something. Bon appetit.

(ALEX exits. Sound cue—answering machine switching on:)

ALEX: *(On machine.)* Steve? Are you screening calls again, sweetie? Listen, remember when we went skiing to Banff and you bought that dark ski mask, do we still have it in the closet? I'm calling from the car phone about a block or two away. Do you know where it is? Sweetie? Never mind.

(Answering machine clicks off as STEVE runs in half-dressed.)

STEVE:	Troy!
TROY:	*(Entering in jeans, carrying shoes, no shirt.)* I heard.
STEVE:	Get dressed—
TROY:	I thought he was gone all afternoon—
STEVE:	I thought so too—

TROY:	Did he say a block—
STEVE:	*(Throwing shirt.)* Here—
TROY:	Does he know?
STEVE:	I don't think so.
TROY:	What'll we do?
STEVE:	Nothing.
TROY:	Nothing?
STEVE:	You're looking at the plumbing.
TROY:	Where?
STEVE:	You're the plumber.
TROY:	The bathroom.
STEVE:	Good, the bathroom.
TROY:	My sock, where's my other sock?
STEVE:	Hurry up.
TROY:	Why do these things always happen to me?
STEVE:	*(At window.)* He's getting out of the car.
TROY:	I only have one sock.
STEVE:	Put on your shoes, he'll be up in a minute.
TROY:	My shoes.
STEVE:	Faster.
TROY:	There's a fucking knot—
STEVE:	Come on.
TROY:	I'm trying. What's the fucking point.
STEVE:	The point is if he finds out, we're dead meat. In the bathroom—
TROY:	Right, hide in the bathroom.
STEVE:	You're not hiding. You're looking at something. And you're straight. Nothing is happening. The idea makes you sick. Got it?
TROY:	Got it.
ALEX:	*(Off-stage.)* Steve?
	(STEVE gives TROY a quick kiss and pushes him out. Enter ALEX.)
STEVE:	Alex? Did you just call?
ALEX:	Why didn't you pick up?
STEVE:	I was in the bathroom. What were you saying about a ski mask?
ALEX:	I need it.
STEVE:	Probably at the back of the closet with the winter things. Uhm, remember Troy? He's looking at our bathroom.
ALEX:	Oh. OK.
STEVE:	Troy! Alex is home! *(To ALEX.)* He'll give us an estimate.

ALEX: I hope he's not too expensive.

STEVE: Oh, no, fairly cheap.

          (TROY enters, two shoes, one sock, can't tell under jeans.)

TROY: Hey.

ALEX: How's the bathroom.

TROY: Oh, gee, wonderful. A plumber's wet dream. Get it? Plumbers, wet—never mind. Uhm, I was checking out the taps.

ALEX: *(To STEVE.)* What about the head.

TROY   Excuse me?

ALEX: The shower head was leaky, not the taps.

STEVE: Shit, I got it wrong.

TROY: No wonder I couldn't find anything.

ALEX: *(To STEVE.)* In the closet you said?

TROY: Hey, no way, man. I'm straight. God, the very idea.

ALEX: I was talking about our winter clothes.

STEVE: A box at the back.

ALEX: Thank-you.

          (ALEX exits. TROY gives a questioning look. STEVE shrugs his shoulders. TROY begins to touch STEVE playfully, who has to shoo TROY away.)

STEVE: Are you finished for the day?

ALEX: *(Off stage.)* A few more visits!

STEVE: Uhm, there were no phone calls. Not that we were here all afternoon. We were lifting weights.

ALEX: Which box?

STEVE: On top with the scarves.

ALEX: See it!

TROY: *(Whisper.)* Does he suspect?

          (STEVE shrugs, slaps TROY's hands away.)

STEVE: Alex, honey?

ALEX: What?

STEVE: Are you going out again?

ALEX: In a minute.

          (Enter ALEX, with a ski mask and a sock.)

ALEX: Steve? Whose sock?

STEVE: Gee, I must have left that in…

ALEX: The hallway.

STEVE: Uhm, it must have fallen from, uhm..

ALEX: What? Your leg?

STEVE: My gym bag, around here somewhere—

ALEX: You wore white socks this morning.

TROY: You know, I think it's mine.

STEVE: Yours?

TROY: At the gym, it must have gotten in your bag by mistake.

STEVE: Right. Because you lost it—

TROY: At the gym—

STEVE: Of course.

TROY: I was wondering what happened to it. Thanks.

       (TROY is about to retrieve it. ALEX lets go of it and it drops on the floor. TROY carefully picks it up and slinks away.)

ALEX: I have food in the car. *(About to walk off, stops.)* It's a beautiful day in the middle of May. Don't you want to know why I want a ski mask?

STEVE: Why do you want a ski mask?

ALEX: I'm going to rob your bank.

STEVE: Right, ha ha.

ALEX: Just kidding. I don't want to get you in trouble. Nice seeing you again, Troy. And nice shirt. Too bad it's inside out. Steve?

STEVE: Yes?

ALEX: I'm going to be back here in about an hour. If what I think is true, you shouldn't be here. Got that, sweetie?

STEVE: Oh yeah.

       (ALEX exits. STEVE collapses. TROY goes to window.)

TROY: He's leaving.

STEVE: He knows.

TROY: Seems that way, huh?

STEVE: I'm in big trouble.

TROY: Now what?

STEVE: I'm thinking.

TROY: Do you want to finish?

STEVE: Are you joking?

TROY: I dunno. Steve? Hey, I'm sorry. I mean, I tried my best to lie.

STEVE: I know.

TROY: But man, he's quick. I'm impressed.

STEVE: I have to go somewhere.

TROY: Where?

STEVE: What about your place?

TROY: My place?

STEVE: So we can work this out.

TROY: Work what out?

STEVE:	What's going to happen.
TROY:	Not much. We were caught.
STEVE:	It doesn't have to end.
TROY:	Yes, it does. Game over.
STEVE:	Who said it was a game?
TROY:	Who said it wasn't?
STEVE:	Troy, I think I have these feelings—
TROY:	No way—
STEVE:	Don't you feel the same way?
TROY:	No.
STEVE:	Why not?
TROY:	It's not about feelings. It's about sex.
STEVE:	Sex?
TROY:	It always was.
STEVE:	And no feelings whatsoever?
TROY:	Why would I? You cheat on your boyfriend, man. Hey, I'm sorry. See? I do feel sorry. See ya at aerobics.

(TROY exits.)

STEVE:	Sex. Feelings. Fuck.

(Lights fade on STEVE. Lights rise on MARK in a bathrobe at his door.)

MARK:	Who is it?
ALEX:	*(Deep voice, off stage.)* Meals on Wheels.

(MARK lets him in. Enter: ALEX, in a ski mask with meal.)

MARK:	Is this some joke?
ALEX:	My face was burned in an accident. I might scare people.
MARK:	And this won't.
ALEX:	Here's your meal.
MARK:	You're not going to catch anything.
ALEX:	Anything else you need? Groceries? Household items? Refill a prescription for AZT?
MARK:	AZT?
ALEX:	Or whatever they give these days.
MARK:	Do I know you?
ALEX:	Nope.
MARK:	Did we sleep together and you're embarrassed or something?
ALEX:	Oh no no no.
MARK:	Those eyes.
ALEX:	I better go.

MARK:	They let you deliver food like this?
ALEX:	Yep.
MARK:	I should check.
ALEX:	Wait. *(Pulls off mask.)* Surprise...I'm sorry, but you wouldn't have let me in.
MARK:	Out.
ALEX:	In, out, out, in, it's so terribly confusing. When I saw your address on the delivery sheet, I panicked. There was nobody else to take over the food, and then I began to worry, oh God, is everything OK? I knew you wouldn't talk to me, so I brought your dinner.
MARK:	What is it, chicken a la cyanide?
ALEX:	I'm concerned.
MARK:	Captain's log. Alex is concerned. Noted. Good-bye.
ALEX:	Are you OK?
MARK:	You asked about AZT.
ALEX:	Are you?
MARK:	No.
ALEX:	Good.
MARK:	It's the hepatitis.
ALEX:	There was medication.
MARK:	Which isn't always effective.
ALEX:	Did you take it?
MARK:	Yes.
ALEX:	As prescribed?
MARK:	Thanks for the food. Bye-bye.
ALEX:	I'm here if you need me.
MARK:	No. I may be sick and poor and not able to work and on social assistance until I'm back on my feet. But I don't need you.
ALEX:	Obviously.
MARK:	Yes. Because I have been without your bitching. Your sniping. Your constant put downs. Everything you do to make me feel like a piece of shit—
ALEX:	I don't—
MARK:	You do. Like I don't feel like a piece of shit enough, like I really need you on top of everything.
ALEX:	I'm sorry.
MARK:	Like hell.
ALEX:	Please let me—
MARK:	No. Never. You're an asshole.
ALEX:	Yes.

MARK:	A fucking goddam asshole.
ALEX:	I know.
MARK:	I hate you, you fucking, bitter, miserable asshole.
ALEX:	I know. And all the more miserable without my best friend.
MARK:	Alex.
ALEX:	Please.
MARK:	I can't do this.
ALEX:	Then let's not and say we did, OK? Mark? I miss you.
MARK:	Oh, God, Alex. What do I do? I'm here. And you're...Meals on Wheels. You're a shitty waiter.
ALEX:	I just watched you.
MARK:	No wonder.
ALEX:	You made me think. Maybe I am shallow. So I wanted to do some good for a change. At first I wanted to do phone counseling. But the volunteer coordinator said something about my lack of experience in dealing with people, not to mention my quick abrupt nature. Bitch. I was going to see you when the transformation to saint was complete. But the chrysalis is cracked open.
MARK:	How's Steve?
ALEX:	Fine. And having an affair with the plumber, I think.
MARK:	You've devised a devious plan, no doubt.
ALEX:	I haven't the energy. I don't know. Maybe it's over. It was a wonderful experiment. A fabulous time held by all. Not to mention a spectacular divorce. I'll demand everything of course.
MARK:	Really.
ALEX:	Maybe. Don't make me do it alone.
MARK:	I don't know if I'm up to this.
ALEX:	Then by the powers vested in me, I'm upgrading you to the executive program. Amici's.
MARK:	Some transformation.
ALEX:	Fine. You pick.
MARK:	Make me dinner.
ALEX:	Right.
MARK:	Steak and potatoes.
ALEX:	Hand you the world on a plate already.
MARK:	An understanding, Alex. That's enough.
ALEX:	You're the world to me, sweetie.
MARK:	The perfect gay life. What's the secret?
ALEX:	Three years ago, I would have said good sex. Two years ago, a good man. One year ago, good food and a good, stiff drink. Now

I just say, good God, I don't know. "Tomorrow is another day" and "the kindness of strangers." Just try to fuck us over.

(There is a knock at the door.)

MARK: Can you get that?

(ALEX opens door. TROY enters.)

TROY: Whoa—

MARK: Troy?

ALEX: Are you following me?!?

TROY: No, I'm here to see Mark.

ALEX: Mark?

MARK: You know Alex?

TROY: *(To ALEX.)* You're having an affair too?

ALEX: Us?

MARK: An affair?

ALEX: Of course not.

MARK: We're friends.

ALEX: Best friends.

TROY: Really?

ALEX: What do you mean, affair too?

MARK: What affair?

ALEX: With Steve.

MARK: You're having an affair with Steve?

TROY: Uhm, well—

ALEX: Are you gay?

TROY: That's sort of a difficult question to answer—

MARK: Troy.

TROY: I'm gay.

ALEX: Uh huh.

TROY: I'm here to see Mark.

MARK: Remember the guy in the red car?

ALEX: Him?

MARK: And you're a plumber?!?

TROY: Yes! And hey, about Steve. We're friends. Now.

MARK: What are you doing here?

TROY: I wanted to see you, talk to you. I'm confused. Well, now I'm more confused than ever. You guys are just friends?

MARK: Yes.

ALEX: Please.

TROY: You've never—

ALEX:	Never.
MARK:	Ever.
ALEX:	It wouldn't last.
MARK:	At all.
ALEX:	A week.
MARK:	A day.
ALEX:	I'd kill him.
MARK:	I'd let him.
TROY:	Sorry. Geez. *(To ALEX.)* I'm sorry. You seem so nice.
MARK:	Nice?!? This *is* confusing.
TROY:	But I want to talk to Mark. I want to come clean. I'm not going to see Steve again. I just left. Talk to him if you don't believe me. Mark, I just gotta talk to you.
ALEX:	What about?
TROY:	Stuff.
ALEX:	I don't know.
MARK:	OK already.
ALEX:	We don't know what he wants.
TROY:	I wouldn't hurt Mark.
ALEX:	Any more than you already have.
TROY:	Mark, can I please talk to you?
MARK:	Yes.
ALEX:	Oh come on!
	(MARK gives ALEX a look.)
ALEX:	OK. *(Steps back.)*
TROY:	Alone.
MARK:	Whatever it is, you can say in front of him. He won't interrupt.
	(ALEX mimes zipping his mouth shut.)
TROY:	I dropped by your work. They said you were sick.
MARK:	Hepatitis.
TROY:	No shit.
MARK:	You should get checked.
TROY:	I took the vaccination months ago.
MARK:	You did?
TROY:	Hey, I'm closeted. Not completely in the dark.
	(TROY looks to ALEX who gives a small "hmmph.")
MARK:	What do you want?
TROY:	To see you again.
MARK:	In what way?

TROY: You know.

MARK: Tell me.

TROY: When we, you know, together. Alone.

MARK: What about Steve?

TROY: It is over. Mark, I was hoping we could pick up where we left off.

MARK: You mean it?

TROY: Yes.

MARK: OK. Where we left off. Troy? You lying, cheating, son of a bitch.

TROY: Huh?

MARK: Are your fingers broken that you can't pick up a phone? Did you get amnesia and forget where I lived?

TROY: I was busy.

MARK: With my best friend's boyfriend. What were you thinking?

TROY: Uhm, I wasn't?

MARK: No. You weren't.

TROY: So, what, you're like...rejecting me?!? Hey, that's cool. I mean, it was just sex, right?

MARK: Right.

TROY: Good while it lasted.

MARK: Yep.

TROY: Great in fact.

MARK: Don't push it.

TROY: Yeah, I better go—

MARK: Wait. Before you do.

          (MARK takes a black sock out from the bed.)

MARK: I washed it.

TROY: Thanks. Uhm, if you want to like, keep it—

MARK: No, I really *really* don't need it.

          (TROY takes the sock. Moves to kiss MARK, who turns his cheek. TROY awkwardly stops short, retreats.)

ALEX: (At doorway.) I knew you weren't straight.

TROY: You know. (Sizes him up.) You're kind of cute when you're bitchy. (Gives ALEX a big slap on the bum.) See ya.

          (TROY exits, and for a moment, ALEX is speechless.)

ALEX: (To MARK.) Well, that was quite the performance.

MARK: I just watched you.

ALEX: You ain't seen nothing yet. Later?

MARK: What do you think?

ALEX: I think I've found the energy to devise devious plans. I love you, sweetie.

MARK:	Me too. *(They hug as lights fade. MARK walks off.)*
	(Crossfade to ALEX and STEVE's apartment. STEVE enters and sits. ALEX is staring him down.)
STEVE:	How do you want to end this?
ALEX:	Well, at first I thought about garden clippers. But I'd never get the blood out of the carpet.
STEVE:	We each keep our car.
ALEX:	Oh no, I paid half of yours.
STEVE:	I paid for the vacations.
ALEX:	Did you keep the receipts?
STEVE:	I'm staying in the apartment.
ALEX:	Cremated in an urn when I kill you for it.
STEVE:	I found it.
ALEX:	I decorated it.
STEVE:	Which you still haven't finished.
ALEX:	Which you hate.
STEVE:	I don't hate it.
ALEX:	You complained enough.
STEVE:	I complained because you wouldn't listen to my ideas.
ALEX:	Of course not. They were bad.
STEVE:	They weren't bad.
ALEX:	You wanted wicker!
STEVE:	Yeah, well. I only fought with you because—
ALEX:	Because you don't like me getting my way.
STEVE:	You always got your way.
ALEX:	Then why bother fighting me on it.
STEVE:	Because if I didn't, you wouldn't appreciate me, Alex.
ALEX:	What?
STEVE:	You enjoy a good scrap. And for some strange reason, so do I. Maybe that's why I rebelled. So you'd pay attention to me.
ALEX:	Excuse me. What sort of weird psycho-babble bullshit are you trying to pull? If this has anything to do with Jenny Jones, you're not getting a goddamn thing.
STEVE:	There are so many things about our relationship I like. And only a few I don't.
ALEX:	Like what?
STEVE:	Monogamy.
ALEX:	And honesty, and trust. Nothing important.
STEVE:	Listen. Please. I like our life together. I like our home together. Even the sex is sometimes good. I don't want to change anything.

Except I've come to realize I want, and I mean occasionally, I want to try seeing other people. Just let me finish. Cheating was wrong. I know. But I can't change that. And I can't change feeling this way either. I'll never find a better relationship. I just want to...try something different with ours.

ALEX: I felt so humiliated.

STEVE: I'm sorry.

ALEX: I hate being the last to know a horrible secret. Especially when it's about me.

STEVE: Nobody knew, I swear.

ALEX: Gallivanting around town.

STEVE: We weren't.

ALEX: When I felt so inadequate.

STEVE: You're not. You're funny, you're brilliant, you're—

ALEX: I'm not a jealous boyfriend.

STEVE: Alex? Those four weeks of vacation we take? What if we took them separately? Sort of like an open relationship, but not really. Not in this city. Not under each other's noses. No so anyone can know or care. Only in other cities. Spring, summer, winter, fall, one week at a time. And when it's over, it's over. The other person never has to know. Four weeks out of 52. That's called a compromise, sweetie.

ALEX: You really do care about me?

STEVE: I swear.

ALEX: Then I want to see it. Those 48 weeks of the year? They better count. And most importantly, I want everyone else to know that they count. I want to be taken out, showed off, put on a pedestal. Sing my praises. Let everyone know how lucky you are to have me. And make me believe it.

STEVE: No problem.

ALEX: And Mark is going to stay with us for a few weeks until he's back on his feet.

STEVE: Alex.

ALEX: Make him believe it, too.

STEVE: OK. We'll do this right. It won't be easy, but we'll work on it. I'll work on it. Safely, discreetly, honestly.

ALEX: Honestly?

STEVE: I love you. Really.

ALEX: Good. But next time, try it with feeling.

            (ALEX takes hold of STEVE's face, as STEVE tries to say something next. The lights dim. Blackout.)

            The End

Biographies

Rick Chafe has had more than a dozen plays produced in a dozen years including *The Last Man and Woman on Earth, Six Times a Day* and is currently adapting *The Odyssey* for a large-scale outdoor production. He freelances as a documentary and educational video producer and has taught playwrighting throughout Manitoba through the Artists in the School program for the past ten years, including half a dozen cross-cultural exchanges between northern and southern high schools.

Bill Harrar lives in Birtle, Manitoba and has been a member of the Manitoba Association of Playwrights since 1982. He has written several radio plays produced by CBC, as well as the stage plays *Bolshie Bash* and *Bear With Me*. He is currently working on *The Way You Look Tonight*, a play exploring the falsehoods inherent in autobiographical occasions.

Maureen Hunter is a Winnipeg playwright whose work has attracted international attention. She is the author of six full-length plays, including *Transit of Venus*, which premiered at Manitoba Theatre Centre in November 1992 and has since been produced across Canada, and in Britain by the Royal Shakespeare Company and by BBC Radio. Following its Toronto production in 1995, *Transit* was nominated for a Dora Mavor Moore Award for Outstanding New Play. Other plays include *The Queen of Queen Street, Beautiful Lake Winnipeg* and *Atlantis*, which was nominated for the 1997 Governor General's Award for Drama. *Footprints on the Moon* received the same honour in 1988.

Bruce McManus is the author of sixteen plays including *The Chinese Man Said Goodbye, Ordinary Days, Schedules, Calenture* and *Selkirk Avenue*, which was nominated for the Governor General's Award for Drama in 1998. Prairie Theatre Exchange produced his adaptation of *A Doll's House* in 1998. He is the Artistic Director of Theatre Projects Manitoba, a professional theatre that produces new plays by established and emerging playwrights.

Ross McMillan is a Winnipeg playwright and actor. His plays include *Legion* (1990), *Washing Spider Out* (1994), *Toby's Made Up Mind* (1997), and *The History of Manitoba From the Beginning of Time to the Present in 45 Minutes* (2000).

Elise Moore hails from Winnipeg and currently lives in Regina. Her plays include *Live With It, Non Sequitur* (performed at the 1999 Toronto Fringe), *Uncle*, and *Beverly Hills Waiting for Godot*, originally produced for Short Shots. She wants to be Oscar Wilde, or Camille Paglia.

Yvette Nolan is a playwright, director and educator whose plays include *BLADE*, *Job's Wife*, *Video* and *A Marginal Man*. *Shakedown Shakespeare*, her co-creation with Philip Adams, toured Yukon communities in the spring of 1997. Other credits include Miche Genest's *The Fasting Girl*, Drew Hayden Taylor's *Someday*, Philip Adams' *Free's Point* (director), Nakai Theatre's *New Theatre North* (producer), Beth Mulloy's *The Stikene Gamble* (dramaturg). Her most recent play, *Annie Mae's Movement*, was produced in Whitehorse and Winnipeg the fall of 1998, and in Nova Scotia in May, 1999. Yvette is the President of the Playwrights Union of Canada.

Deborah O'Neil lives in St. Boniface, Manitoba and teaches at an inner-city Winnipeg school. Her other plays include *#1 Gem*, *Magnetic North*, *Nobody Waltzes Carrying a 30lb Underwood*, *Virgins Don't Eavesdrop*, *Bivouac*, and *Fill in the Blanks*.

Harry Rintoul is a playwright, freelance writer, and dramaturge. He was the founding Artistic Director of Theatre Projects Manitoba. He has written twelve plays, has had thirty productions across Canada and the United States, and has had two plays and several short stories published. He was nominated for a Dora Mavor Moore Award for his play *Brave Hearts*. He has worked as a dramaturge with emerging playwrights in Manitoba and Saskatchewan. Harry was the Writer-in-Residence at the Saskatoon Public Library in 1997-98, and at the Southwest Art Gallery in Brandon in 1997. He writes book reviews for the *Winnipeg Free Press* and *NeWest Review*.

Ian Ross was born in McCreary, Manitoba, and calls the communities of Fairford, Kinosota and Winnipeg home. He has been writing plays for several years, and *fareWel* marked his first professional mainstage production. That play was also the winner of the 1997 Governor General's Award. His first children's play, *Baloney!*, about child poverty in Canada, was produced in the spring of 1998 by Manitoba Theatre for Young People. In addition to writing for the stage, Ian has weekly CBC Radio and television shows that follow the exploits of his fictional chraracter, "Joe from Winnipeg."

Alfred Silver was a high school dropout (not a course he recommends) and spent the next 10 years waorking as a day labourer, short-order cook, nude model, cab driver, bar band bass player, etc. until his first novel was published in 1978. Since then he's had six more novels published, including the award-winners *Acadia* and *Lord of The Plains*, eight plays produced in venues ranging from the Manitoba Theatre Centre to Mermaid Theatre of Nova Scotia, several dozen scripts produced on CBC Radio, including the mystery series *Clean Sweep*, and has released two albums of his oown songs—*Shadows* on vinyl in 1980 and *They Don't Make 'Em Anymore* on CD in 1999. After a childhood in Winnipeg, Calgary, Vancouver, Toronto—before realizing he was a country boy at heart—he now lives in an old farmhouse in Nova Scotia with his wife, Jane Buss.

Dennis Trochim's other playwriting credits include *Unlovable You*, *Long Johns and Silver*, a play for young audiences for Prairie Theatre Exchange, and *I Do, Do You*, for Theatre Projects. He has been a member of MAP since 1988.

Notes Toward an Archive

What follows is a directory of the activity of the play development programs supported by the Manitoba Association of Playwrights from 1982 to 2000. This could be considered an archive in progress.

I have tried to be as complete and consistent in reporting as possible, but there are certainly readings that will have been overlooked. I must also apologize for any errors or oversights in listing the productions outside Manitoba. As you will note, the work increased greatly as the years wore on, as did the type, scope, and meaning of "workshop."

My listing of a play's first production comes usually after the last major work done with MAP on it, but not always. This is true more of later years, when there was less formal "blocks" of workshop, and more flexibility. I have also included almost everything under Playwrights Development (the catch-all PDP), including our Open Door program (where a lot of Fringe plays developed from the mid-nineties), but have noted the two years of the Playwrights' Unit in the eighties, with PTE because it was formally apart from the PDP.

Playwrights Development Program, 1982
Climate of the Times by Alf Silver (Manitoba Theatre Centre, 1983)
Fields of Sorrow by Rosemary De Graff (Agassiz Theatre, 1985)
St. Peter's Asylum by William Horrocks (Prairie Theatre Exchange, 1983)
House by Nick Mitchell (Agassiz, 1983)
221B Baker Street by Martin Reed

Playwrights Development Program, 1982-83
The Salvation of Crazy Charlie by Arnold Mickelson (Agassiz, 1984; reading Minneapolis Playwrights' Center, 1986)
Why the Dishes Can't Wait for Tomorrow by David Demchuk (Theatre Projects, 1991)
Dogs With No Tails by Bruce McManus (Manitoba Independent Productions, Gas Station Theatre, July, 1987)
On The Line by Wendy Lill (Agassiz, 1982)

Playwrights Development Program, 1983-84-85
The Garbageman's Daughter by Arnold Mickelson
Mary and the Bears by Polly Woodward

Something You Should Know by David Demchuk
Departures and Arrivals by Carol Shields (Black Hole Theatre, University of Manitoba, etc.)
Bolshie Bash by William Harrar (Agassiz, 1985; Winnipeg Fringe, 1990)
The Coast (further workshop and public reading Writers Theatre, New York; Playwrights' Center, Minneapolis, 1986)
Not Another Anniversary by Carol Shields and David Williamson (as *Anniversary*, Solar Stage, Toronto, 1986; Gas Station Theatre, 1996)
Connor and Grove by Nick Mitchell
Life and Times by Harry Rintoul

Playwrights Development Program, 1985-86
refugees by Harry Rintoul (KAM Theatre, Thunder Bay, 1987; Winnipeg Fringe, 1988; etc.)
Franklin by James Durham (Agassiz Festival One, 1987; Edmonton Fringe Festival, 1990)
The Courier by Vern Thiessen (reading)
Footprints on the Moon by Maureen Hunter (first version)
Persona Non Grata by Tannis Zboroluk
The Grave Will Decide by George Seremba

Manitoba Playwrights Colony, 1986
Footprints on the Moon by Maureen Hunter (Agassiz, 1987; etc.)
Schedules by Bruce McManus (PTE, 1986, etc.)
The Revival by Sandra Birdsell (PTE, 1986)
I Met A Bully on the Hill by Maureen Hunter (PTE, 1986; etc.)
Mum by Nick Mitchell (Agassiz, 1987)

Playwrights Development Program, 1986-87
Player Pool by Rick Chafe (Winnipeg Fringe, 1988)
The Courier by Vern Thiessen (reading, dramaturgy) (Agassiz Festival One, 1987; Theatre Centre, Toronto, 1988; Edmonton Fringe, 1988)
The Bad Life by David Williamson (MTC commission)

Playwrights Unit, 1986-87
Beautiful Lake Winnipeg by Maureen Hunter (MTC, 1990)
Rick Chafe worked on *Player Pool*

Playwrights Development Program, 1987-88
Bear With Me by William Harrar (Winnipeg Fringe, 1989, commissioned by MTC for 1990)
Magnetic North by Deborah O'Neil
House Mouse by Edwin Schaan

Playwrights Unit, 1987-88
montana by Harry Rintoul (Winnipeg Fringe, 1989; Play Works Festival, Saskatoon, August, 1989)
The Resurrection of John Frum by Vern Thiessen went from the Unit to the Colony

Playwrights Colony, 1988
The Chinese Man Said Goodbye by Bruce McManus (PTE, 1989)

The Resurrection of John Frum by Vern Thiessen (National Arts Centre, Ottawa, 1990)
Andrew's Tree by Martha Brooks (PTE, 1988, Young People's Company)

Playwrights Development Program, 1988-89
No.1 Gem by Deborah O'Neil (Women's Playwright Project, November, 1989)
Right For It by Michael Nathanson (Winnipeg Fringe, 1989; Play Works Festival, Saskatoon, August, 1989)
Lisa by Carol Matas and Per Brask (PTE commission and production, and tour 1991-92)
Becoming by Jake Macdonald

Playwrights Development Program, 1989-90
Brave Hearts by Harry Rintoul (produced by Buddies in Bad Times, Toronto, April, 1991)
Coleen Rue by Brian Richardson (independent production, fall, 1991, West End Cultural Centre)
Rats by Graham Ashmore and Melanie Wight (commissioned by Manitoba Theatre For Young People)
Selkirk Avenue by Bruce McManus (Popular Theatre Alliance Manitoba, 1990; PTE, 1991; etc.)
Birth of a Dancing Star by Valorie Bunce and *The Sideshow* by Allana Lindgren (Women's Playwright Project, PTAM/MAP/Les Dolles, 1989)

Manitoba Playwrights Colony, 1990
The Laws of Modesty by Michael Nathanson (commissioned by MTC)
Between Then and Now and *1919* by Harry Rintoul
Tuk Tuk by Brian Drader (further workshop by PTE; ATP, 1992)

Playwrights Development Program and Workshop, 1990-91
To Kill the Weatherman by Michael Nathanson (Theatre Projects, September, 1991)
Two Shot by Rick Chafe (Winnipeg Fringe, 1991)
All or Nothing by Dennis Trochim (independent production, June, 1992)
The Womb Demon by Ross McMillan (produced at Winnipeg Fringe, 1991)
Thirteen Hands by Carol Shields (PTE, 1993)
Questions About Cleopatra by Valorie Bunce (Winnipeg Fringe, 1991)
Columbia Ice Fields Tour by Deborah O'Neil (Winnipeg Fringe, 1991)

Playwrights Development Program, 1991-92
Hedda Gabler, new translation by Per Brask (MTC, 1991)
Shooting .J.J. by Bill Harrar
Thirteen Hands by Carol Shields (initial workshop MTC, *Thirteen Hands*, as noted, later produced PTE; etc.)
The Grimm Sisters (later called *Journey of the Dragon Boy*) by Lora Schroeder/ Tannis Kowalchuk (PTE, 1992; Young People's Theatre, Toronto, 1994)
Story of My Life by Harry Rintoul
The Escape by Carol Matas (Winnipeg Jewish Theatre, 1993)
CDED by Ian Ross (Winnipeg Fringe, 1992)
Calenture (called *Make Up Bet*) by Bruce McManus (PTAM, 1993)
Slender Acquaintances by Dennis Trochim and John Dobson (Winnipeg Fringe, 1992)

Between Then and Now byHarry Rintoul (Winnipeg/Edmonton Fringe, 1993)
Live with It by Elise Moore (first workshop)
We Promised Not to Tell by Kelly Daniels
Zac and Speth by Rick Chafe (Winnipeg Fringe, 1992)
Job's Wife by Yvette Nolan (Theatre Projects, 1992)

Manitoba Playwrights Colony, 1992
The Missing Person by Ross McMillan (this became *Washing Spider Out*, 1995)
Tin Can Cathedral by Nick Mitchell (PTE 1993, also assisted Mitchell trip to work at Theatre Direct, Toronto)
Fireweed by Billy Merasty

Playwrights Development Program, 1992-93
Assisted Maureen Hunter trip to Toronto for work on *Transit of Venus*
Tangled Souls. A cross-cultural exchange play (students from Norway House/ Winnipeg (coordinated by Rick Chafe and Kayla Gordon)
Inquest by Bill Harrar (formerly *Shooting J.J.*, PTE, 1994)
A Marginal Man by Nolan (first workshop for PTAM)
The Missing Person by Ross McMillan (final public workshop, became *Washing Spider Out*, Adhere and Deny/PTE Studio Series, 1995)
Power by Robert Johannson. (PTE Studio Series reading, 1994)
The Blue Egg by Dale Lakevold

Playwrights Development Program, 1993-94
Etienne by Steve McIntyre (Theatre Projects, 1993)
My Old Man by James Durham (Theatre Projects, 1993)
A Marginal Man by Yvette Nolan (final workshop, PTAM, 1994)
Photogenic by Grant Guy (Adhere and Deny)
Sophie and the Wiener Man by Carolyn Gray (Theatre Projects, 1995)
Six Times a Day by Rick Chafe (Lunchtime Theatre, 1994)
1919 by Harry Rintoul (PTE Reading Series, 1994)
The Always Prayer Shawl by Sheldon Oberman (WJT, 1995)
The Thirteenth Beer by Peter Schultz (Winnipeg Fringe, 1994)
The Blue Egg by Dale Lakevold (public presentation part of playwrights exchange; Playwrights Workshop, Montreal, Saskatchewan Playwrights Centre)
Land of Milk and Honey by Garth Buchholz (major public workshop)
Till Death Do Us Part by Michael Bell (Winnipeg Fringe,1994)

Manitoba Playwrights Colony, 1994
Jack of Hearts by Harry Rintoul
Cinderella Stories by Lora Schroeder (PTE, 1994-95)

Playwrights Development Program, 1994-95
The Tomato King by Laurie Block (Theatre Projects, 1997)
Never Never Mind Kurt Kurt Cobain by Dale Lakevold (Theatre Projects, 1998)
Getting Out by Margaret Pople
Jazz Is by Ron Paley

Playwrights Development Program, 1995-96
Elise Moore Non Sequitur by Elise Moore (major workshop, 1996; Toronto Fringe, 1998)

Heart of a Distant Tribe by Ian Ross (Red Roots, 1996)
Ma Cousin Josephine by Germaine Jacob
Jack of Hearts by Harry Rintoul (Theatre Projects, 1996)
Bubba and the Peter Eater by Brian Drader
The Gypsy Diaries by Tannis Kowalchuk (Nightwood Theatre, Toronto, 1998)

Manitoba Playwrights Colony, 1996
Uncle by Elise Moore
Toby's Made Up Mind by Ross McMillan
Will by Bruce McManus
Key of Cranes by Nick Mitchell

Playwrights Development Program, 1996-97
Translation workshop of *Lonely Planet* (Steven Dietz) by Claude Dorge, Le Cercle Moliere
Dramaturgical assistance on *10 x 10 short plays by Women* (WJT, 1997)
Never Never Mind Kurt Kurt Cobain by Dale Lakevold (Theatre Projects,1998)
Uncle by Elise Moore
The Tomato King by Laurie Block, final workshop (Theatre Projects, 1997)
Toby's Made Up Mind by Ross McMillan (independent production, Gas Station Theatre, 1998)
Wild Geese by Dale Lakevold (workshop, PTE)
The Convergence of Luke by Harry Rintoul (workshop, PTE)
Bubba and the Peter Eater by Brian Drader (workshop, produced at Queer Stages Festival, 1997)

Playwrights Development Program, 1997-98
The Wave by Olaf Pyttlik (music and lyrics)
Hectic by Margaret Sweatman (PTAM, 1998)
Last Man and Woman on Earth by Rick Chafe
Looking Glass by Jarvis (Playwrights Theatre Centre, Vancouver, 2000)
A Doll's House by Bruce McManus (PTE, 1998)
The Mother Load by Sharon Bajer (first version)
Baloney by Ian Ross (MTYP, 1998)
The Norbals by Brian Drader (PTE, 1998)
Doing Dates by Bill Harrar
Tumblin' Dice by Bob Hume (Winnipeg Fringe, 1998)
The Tower by Holly Harris (book and lyrics), Syd Rabinovitch (music) (WJT, in preparation)

Manitoba Playwrights Colony, 1998
The MotherLoad by Sharon Bajer (Winnipeg Fringe, 1999)
Living Room by James Durham (now called *Cruel and Unusual Punishment*)
Viriditas by Muriel Hogue (Red Hen Productions,1999)
Wild Geese by Dale Lakevold (University of Winnipeg Theatre, 1999)
The Last Man and Woman on Earth by Rick Chafe

Playwrights Development Program, 1998-99
Assisted Rick Chafe to attend workshop of his adaptation of *The Odyssey* (Shakespeare in the Ruins Theatre, 2000)
Assisted Dennis Trochim to attend workshop of *Long John's and Silver* (PTE/

Playwrights Workshop, Montreal, produced PTE, 1999)
The Last Man and Woman on Earth by Rick Chafe, pre-rehearsal (Theatre Projects, 1999)
Trojan Women by Ted Wynne (adaptation)
The Pathetic Longing Workshop by Nancy Jackubic (Winnipeg Fringe, 1999)
I Do, Do You by Dennis Trochim (Theatre Projects, 1999)
Misty Lake by Dale Lakevold (Winnipeg Fringe, 1999)
Black and White Pictures by Bob Hume (Winnipeg Fringe, 1999)

Playwrights Development Program, 1999-2000
Conference on Canadian Play Dramaturgy, plays in workshop
Cruel and Unusual Punishment by James Durham (major public workshop, March, 2000; scheduled by Theatre Projects, 2001)
Lake Nowhere by Harry Rintoul
Step 9 by Michael Bell (scheduled for production 2001)
Uncle by Elise Moore

Selkirk Avenue by Bruce McManus (book and lyrics), Danny Koulack (music) first workshop, PTE (scheduled fall, 2001)
The Seal Woman by Ross McMillan (workshop, August, 1999)
faust flying by Margaret Sweatman/Glen Buhr (August, 1999)
The Indecent End of Dr. Shadie's Revolution by deco dawson (public workshop, 2000)

Also to be mentioned is the work done with Rural Dramaturgy Project especially spring workshopping since 1994 at various venues, i.e. Prairie Theatre Exchange, University of Winnipeg, and in Brandon with Nancy Drake's New West Theatre and the Westman Playwrights' Group, and James Forsythe, University of Brandon. Dramaturges have been Harry Rintoul, Rick Chafe, Nancy Drake. I am leaving out some names, I know, but will mention the work of James Kostuchuk, Terry Tully, Erin Bowie, Margaret Pople, among many others.

Short Shots (and its variants)
In 1991 we started producing workshop-style productions of short plays by Manitoba playwrights as a lunch time theatre. It changed over the years to somewhat longer plays, and presented by Theatre Projects (from 1996) as part of its season, in the evenings. Many of the plays have been published, been the basis of full length plays, or short films, or even radio plays. MAP continues to commission the playwrights, aiming for a mix of experienced and emerging writers. Here are their names in the story so far:

1991
Ruth Andrishak, Valorie Bunce, Brian Drader, David Gillies, William Harrar, Tannis Kowalchuk, Steven McIntyre, Alison McLean, Bruce McManus, Michael Nathanson, Deborah O'Neil, Harry Rintoul, Lora Schroeder, Carol Shields, Melanie Wight

1992
Per Brask, Garth Buchholz, Rosemary De Graff, Claude Dorge, James Durham, Maureen Hunter, Ron Jenkins, Ross McMillan, Arnold Mickelson, Dennis Noble,

Yvette Nolan, Ellen Peterson, Wanda Ryder, Dennis Trochim, VeraLyn Warkentin

1993
Sharon Bajer, Marie Baker, Laurie Block, Patrick Friesen, Carolyn Gray, Grant Guy, Kevin Longfield, Phil McBurney, Rick McNair, Doug Melnyk, Nick Mitchell, Elise Moore, John Philbin, Brian Richardson, Ian Ross

1994
Michael Bell, Linda Fletcher, Martine Friesen, Robert Johannson, Angus Kohm, Dale Lakevold, Donna Lewis, Arne MacPherson, Kris Peterson, Valerie Wynne

1995
Scott Douglas, Catherine Johannson, Maggie Nagle, Sheldon Oberman, Deborah Patterson, Margaret Pople, Armin Wiebe

1996
Rick Chafe, Leanne Foley, Muriel Hogue, Laurie Lam, Ross McMillan, Elise Moore, Harry Rintoul, Ian Ross, Margaret Sweatman, Dennis Trochim, Duncan Thornton

1997
Erin Bowie, deco dawson, Gary Jarvis, James Kostuchuk, Rick McNair, Deborah O'Neil, Ellen Peterson

1998
Laurie Block, Angus Kohm, Margaret Pople, Ian Ross

2000
Leigh Anne Kehler, Bob Hume, Harry Rintoul, Bill Harrar